PLEASE TO THE TABLE

THE RUSSIAN COOKBOOK

PLEASE TO THE TABLE

THE RUSSIAN COOKBOOK

by Anya von Bremzen and John Welchman

Workman Publishing • New York

Library of Congress Cataloging-in-Publication Data

Von Bremzen, Anya.
Please to the table : the Russian cookbook / by Anya von Bremzen and John Welchman.
p.   cm.
Includes index.
ISBN 0-89480-845-1   ISBN 0-89480-753-6 (pbk.)
1. Cookery, Russian.   I. Title.
TX723.3.V66   1990
641.5947—dc20
90-50360
CIP

Front and back cover illustrations: Patty Dryden
Book illustrations: Randy Harelson

Workman Publishing Company, Inc.
708 Broadway
New York, NY 10003

Manufactured in the United States of America

First printing November 1990
10 9 8 7 6 5 4 3 2 1

FOR LARISA

◆◆

Acknowledgments

We seem to have traveled halfway around the world (and back), gathering recipes and listening to a thousand stories about the food and the culture of the many nations that lie along (and within) the vast borderlands of Russia. We've roamed from Los Angeles and London to Leningrad and Latvia; we've spent countless wonderful hours with emigrés in New York, San Diego, and Vermont. We've visited elderly White Russians in Paris and Istanbul. We've toured the country markets of Georgia and compared the Armenian dishes of Yerevan and Santa Monica.

Sometimes, however, it seems that we've learned our most eloquent preparations and many of our most useful tips in railroad sleeping cars, at unplanned street corner meetings, and in innumerable other chance encounters. So first we must say a loud and heartfelt "thank you" to all the people, places, and institutions that have so generously hosted and helped us. We apologize for not being able to record every name here.

Our greatest debt of gratitude is to Anya's mother, Larisa Frumkin, and to her father, Sergei Bremzen. Larisa taught us that cooking is first and foremost a pleasure, and that it is a pleasure to be shared. Larisa kept virtual "open house" for the two years or more that we were working on our book. *Please to the Table* would have been half as long and less than half as happy without her, for in many ways it is her table to which we pay tribute here. Sergei first introduced Anya to the joys of ethnic cooking in her Muscovite days, and made our visits to Russia and the republics run so smoothly.

At Workman Publishing, special thanks to Peter Workman for his vision and adventurousness in signing up such an original (though potentially difficult!) idea and to our editor Suzanne Rafer, who made perfect cooking and literary sense from the kaleidoscope of strange ingredients and dictionary-defying foreign names and places that we unfurled before her month after month. She was our lifeline in the labyrinth of one of the world's most diverse yet little known culinary regions. Our copy editor, Margery Tippie, put the final touches to the text and the book was rendered into the elegant and joyous volume you have before you by Workman's designers,

Lisa Hollander and Charles Kreloff, with the aid of illustrator Randy Harelson. Also at Workman, a big thanks to Andrea Bass Glickson, Carolan Workman, Cathy Dorsey, Mary Wilkinson, and Shannon Ryan. Thanks, too, to Laura and Joe Peary for their help with the book.

Every table, of course, needs to be not only piled with tempting foods but also surrounded by friends and good company. Thanks, then, to our dear friends and relatives for all their help and support. In New York: Mark Cohen, Adam Cvijanovic, Orshi Drozdik, Artiom and Marina Englin, Sonia Gropman, Joseph Kosuth, Cornelia Lauf, Patrick McGrath, Adele Nikolsky, Ida Panicelli, Yvonne Shafir, and Natasha and (the late) Boris Shragin. In California: Suzanne, David, and Erin Booth; Steve Fagin, Diana and Jerome Rothenberg (for their books and advice); Jahanne Teillhet-Fisk, Zack, and Samantha (for their friendship and their table); and Lilyan, Doug, and Scott White, and all our friends from the University of California. In London: Barbara, John, and Alistair Welchman, (the late) Reverend W.E.B. Taylor and Gretta; Victor and Dorothy Welchman, and everyone at 85 Gloucester Place; and Lawrence Carolina and Tadeucz Osborne. In Istanbul: John and Birin Scott. In Melbourne: Ian Friend and Robin Daw. In Seoul: Young-Oak Kim (for his after-dinner acrobatics).

And thanks to Anya's relatives and friends (and all those perfect strangers) who opened their hearts and homes, shared their meals, and let us pry into their refrigerators and peek into their pots. In Moscow: *babushka i dedushka*; Yulia, Sasha, Masha, Dasha; (both Seriozhas; Naziushka Bremzen and family and Elena Skulkova for taking such wonderful care of us; Rozetta and Max Nemchinsky; Margarita Eskina and her family; Zoya Boguslazskaya; and the Kokovkin family both in Moscow and Leningrad for their help and hospitality. In Georgia: Osik Shapiro; Nino Chachkhiani and Vaja; and Davi, Zaza, and Goghi. In Armenia: Suzy and Aram Karapetian and George Isaakian.

Among the ethnic communities outside the Soviet Union we have greatly benefited from recipes, assistance with ingredients, and timely morale boosts freely given by Christina Nawrocky, Tamara Khanukashvili, Venera Batashvili, Raisa Amiranova, Mahnaz Salmassi, Samira Ram, Julia Mississian, Vartouhi Papazian, Rufa Azizova, Nana Mukhadze, Mara Soudakoff, Tatiana Ziritskaya, Grigori Furmanov of Catering à la Russe, Roman Kaplan of Russian Samovar, and Sam Martirossian of Ararat Dardanelles.

A toast to our friend Jonathan Nossiter, who made the menus in this book sparkle by suggesting the perfect wines.

Special thanks to Lynn Visson for sharing her knowledge, recipes, dinnertimes, and her precious cookbook collection; and to Lev Losev for pointing out fascinating historical sources and literary references.

Our gratitude goes to our agent, Alice Martell, who took the book on with such enthusiasm and energy. And thanks to Lauri Alberts, Mary Lee Grisanti, and Gary Muller for their advice and support at the early stages of this project; and to Francine du Plessix Gray for her kindness and help.

Contents

LAMB DISHES Baranina

Enticing ways with lamb. Choice cuts combine with exotic spices and fresh herbs to create grilled kebabs from Uzbekistan, a warming lamb casserole from Georgia, and a yogurt-enriched Armenian stir-fry

PORK DISHES Svinina

"Pork is the real hero of the feast," or so thought Nikita Vsevoldovich Vselolzhsky, a nineteenth-century gourmet. Garlicky sausages with pomegranate seeds from Georgia. Richly satisfying pork and sauerkraut from the Ukraine. Luscious roast suckling pig. Exquisite aromas fill your house as you feast

POULTRY AND GAME DISHES Ptitsa i Dich

Crispy Chicken Kiev; Grilled Chicken with Garlic and Walnut Sauce; and the classic Chicken Pozharsky, a dish immortalized by Alexander Pushkin. In Russia, when company is expected, a hostess turns to her extensive collection of poultry recipes

FISH DISHES Riba

". . . there's nothing I'd rather do than fish," reflected Anton Chekhov. Sturgeon and smelts, carp, haddock, and the sweetest, most delicate-tasting trout; Baked Fish with Eggplant and Pomegranate Sauce; and an elegant Steamed Salmon with Sorrel and Spinach Sauce

VEGETABLE DISHES Ovoshchi

In the Soviet Union there is a simple reverence for an unblemished potato or a splendid, crunchy carrot. Unpretentious dishes are prepared from cabbage and beets. But there are also savory wild mushrooms, eggplant ragout, the quintessential fried potatoes. And a host of irresistible stuffed vegetables

Introduction

Culinary Routes

Please to the Table is woven from a hundred strands that we've researched and stumbled upon, sorted, and assembled during half a decade of exhilarating travel in the largest culinary landscape on earth, the Soviet Union. Anya is a Soviet emigré pianist and food historian, writer, and consultant, and John is an English art historian and writer who has written extensively on world travel. Together we have prepared this book while living and researching in Moscow, Leningrad, Armenia, Georgia, and Turkey, as well as in New York, London, Paris, and California. But like every major project and every recurring dream, ours has a simple and heartfelt point of origin.

For us the book was born out of Anya's poignant childhood memories of the wondrous central market in Moscow. Accompanied by her grandmother, an architect and planner who had traveled to almost every corner of the USSR, Anya would sometimes spend whole days in the market, transfixed by a veritable babble of ethnic languages and barter of exotic fruits and vegetables.

Imagine round-faced Uzbek women in traditional striped dresses, wearing a myriad of long, black braids, selling a riot of melons and translucent jade-green radishes tasting of wild honey. Picture

> Go along, go along quickly, and set all you have on the table for us. We don't want doughnuts, honey buns, poppy cakes, and other dainties; bring us a whole sheep, serve a goat and forty-year-old mead! And plenty of vodka, not vodka with all sorts of fancies, not with raisins and flavorings, but pure foaming vodka, that hisses and bubbles like mad.
>
> — Nikolai Gogol
> *Taras Bulba*

mustached Georgians in tall black hats waving unbearably aromatic spice mixes (*khmeli-suneli*); or pickle sellers from rugged Dagestan, whose necks and fingers were adorned with the miraculous products of their native silversmiths; or Koreans from the Far East showing off their famous watermelons; or Kazakh farmers selling enormous red apples. Nearby were hay-blond Latvians, dexterously apportioning tiny, fragrant wild strawberries into makeshift paper cones fashioned from the morning's *Pravda.* Under her grandmother's careful tutelage, Anya collected all the information she could about the fifteen Soviet republics, and prided herself on being able to identify each and every item of the various national costumes and to sing ethnic songs in a dozen national languages.

The market scene continued to haunt Anya until she conceived the idea to render the astonishing spectacle in recipes and descriptive travelogs. Not surprisingly, when regaled with these enchanting memories, John was easily persuaded to lay down his art books and take off with Anya on a strange recipe-collecting odyssey across several continents, a dozen capital cities, and a vivid flourish of regional villages and ethnic suburbs; through teeming markets, upscale restaurants, street corner dives, and cosy family homes — we even got recipes from fellow-travelers in subway trains and railroad waiting rooms.

A Joyous Cacophony of Foods

Although this is perhaps the first book to concentrate so intensively on the *regional* cuisines of the USSR, we are the first to admit that what we are offering is a mere drop (though a tempting and representative drop) in the ocean of recipes, feasts, and flavors that make up the world's last great uncharted culinary zone. We hope it will be an invitation for closer scrutiny of lesser known regional cuisines that so richly deserve a comprehensive description.

What we have set out to do is to convey some real sense of the almost giddying diversity of Soviet cooking, and to dispel the prevailing myth that there is little more to Russian (or Soviet) food than *blini* and borscht. We are also setting out to redeem the sad reputation of the cuisines of the USSR, the result of more than fifty years of constant food shortages and the substandard restaurant cooking and service that visitors have had to endure in Moscow and Leningrad. There is some quite marvelous and adventurous food to be had outside the republic of Russia and the essence of Soviet food will never be found in an uneven struggle with a greasy plate of chicken Kiev or an order of tough Stroganoff.

Representative ethnic dishes are now a fact of everyday life in Moscow, just as Russian food is, in turn, eagerly served up in the other republics. When we eat out with friends and family in Moscow, we go to the Aragvi (a Georgian restaurant), Uzbekistan, Minsk (Byelorussian), or Baku (Azerbaijani). Within the last few years, new economic reforms allowed a significant number of quality ethnic "cooperative" (private) restaurants to flourish. These establishments get their supplies, their chefs, and their service staff straight from the republics. The cuisine and decor are of a refinement and sophistication that have not been seen in Russian cities for most of the twentieth century. There are also stores that stock produce, spices, and kitchen whatnots from almost all the republics.

On the tray were a bottle of herb-brandy, different kinds of vodka, pickled mushrooms, rye-cakes made with buttermilk, honey in the comb, still mead and sparkling mead, apples, plain nuts and roasted nuts, and nuts in honey . . . preserves made with honey and with sugar, a ham and a fowl that had just been roasted to a turn.

— Leo Tolstoy
War and Peace

Tea in Russia and tea in England are as different as peppermint-water and senna. With us it is a dull, flavorless dose; in Russia it is a fresh invigorating draught.

— Robert Brenner
Excursions into the Interior of Russia

We embrace a vast confection of styles, tastes, and ingredients, from the robust fare of the Ukraine to the delicate fruit pilafs of Azerbaijan. But we have a special fondness for those dishes from the Caucasus and Central Asia that are related to the great cooking traditions of the Mediterranean and the Middle East. These cuisines share a healthful emphasis on all kinds of tempting vegetables and legumes; rice in a thousand disguises; bulgur; refreshing yogurts; tart, piquant flavorings; freshly grilled meats and fish; prodigious sheep's cheeses; and preparations that work magic with fruit and nuts.

Few of the dishes in our sphere are wholly unrelated to one or another of the great cuisines of the world — Middle Eastern, French, Chinese, Scandinavian, or the simple fare of the Eastern European plainlands. You will find a profound French influence on classic Russian cuisine; Chinese and Indian influences in Uzbekistan; Turkish and Persian in the Caucasus; and Scandinavian in the Baltic republics. Ukrainian, Byelorussian, and Moldavian food has much in common with the cuisines of Poland, Hungary, and Romania. In Uzbekistan, alone, for example, you can find people from Afghanistan, Turkey, Iran, China, Korea, Mongolia, Russian, and the Ukraine; and there are also sizable communities of Jews and Gypsies. Here you might sit down to a dinner that includes a dish of stuffed vegetables imported from Turkey; Uzbek filled fritters (*samsa*, from the Indian *samosa*); steamed dumplings of Chinese origin; and a beloved Russian herring dish, dressed Scandinavian style.

This dizzying array of hybrids and borrowings makes for a complex barter economy between the republics and their neighbors, a delightfully flexible culinary give-and-take, that ranges from the subtle shadings achieved by a fine local ingredient all the way to a level of independent thinking and creative flair maintained by the Georgians that can rival the most lavish ambitions of the more established national cuisines.

Making good-cooking sense out of the vastness of the USSR was an overwhelming prospect, and one that often found us counting teaspoons in twenty different dialects. We decided to organize the book not by region or republics (Russia, the Caucasus, the Baltic republics), but by food type (appetizers, soups, entrées, and so on) in the customary western way. This makes the book simple to use for the preparation of either a full-fledged dinner or a quick snack. To prevent such generic organization from homogenizing the terrific diversity of foods in the USSR, we have inserted maps, drawings, and details of local cultures throughout the book and offer essays and sundry observations on regions and republics whose foods are featured most prominently in the book.

A Quick Look at the Geography of the USSR

There are over one hundred nationalities and languages in the USSR making it the most ethnically diverse "empire" on earth. The USSR occupies no less than a sixth of the globe, stretching from the eastern edge of Poland all the way to the tip of Japan. Siberia alone is a third larger than the entire United States. Both China and the United

States could easily fit inside the borders of the Soviet Union and *still* leave room for all the nations of Western Europe.

The USSR is divided into fifteen major republics, of which Russia is the largest and most populous, and subdivided further into numerous "autonomous" republics. The climate ranges from endless zones of arctic permafrost to the subtropical balm of the Southern Caucasus.

As we go to press, the political map of the Soviet Union is being rewritten by momentous changes in the structure of the Socialist world set in motion by Mikhail Gorbachev's policy of *glasnost*. More and more, these changes are focusing on ethnic differences and national identities as citizens find outlets in social protests and demonstrations against the century-long domination of the disparate Soviet regions by the Slavic bureaucratic center in Moscow. If a peaceful transition to some form of shared or autonomous government can be achieved, then the richness of culture and cuisine suggested in our book will be multiplied a thousand fold as the republics begin a new life of freedom and international exchange.

Where Have We Found Our Recipes?

Our raw material is drawn from research, wanderings, and dining experiences in the Soviet Union; from friends and food writers from San Diego to Samarkand; from dozens of homes and restaurants in the ethnic communities of New York, Los Angeles, London, Paris, and Istanbul; from a library of books ancient, old, and new. We should say a word about each of these invaluable sources, as they have contributed profoundly both to the overall design and to the nuances, nooks and crannies of our project.

Pride of place must go to family recipes and family lore. Almost everyone in Anya's family cooks beautifully. Her mother, Larisa, has a wand-like hand in the kitchen, transforming workaday Russian staples into virtuoso feats of elegance in seemingly no time at all. Her father, Sergei, on the other hand, has always been a meticulous gourmet with a special feeling for Georgian cuisine. Going back a generation, Sergei's mother was raised in Uzbekistan and had at her disposal an astonishing repertoire of exotic pilafs and spicy stews; and Anya's maternal grandmother would always delight us with wonderful Jewish dishes from her native Odessa, on the Black Sea.

Outstanding, indeed inspirational, for us among Russian-language cookbooks is Vilyam Pokhlyobkin's *The Ethnic Cuisines of the USSR*. Its author is probably the closest the Soviet Union has ever come to a culinary cult figure. Particularly active during the 1970s, when he wrote a lionized food column for *Nedelya*, Pokhlyobkin brought a rare rhetorical and historical edge to the art of Russian food writing. But still, his was a cuisine of words and not of tastes; and we have, accordingly, found his digressions much more appealing than this dishes.

Other useful sources include Elena Molokhovets's *A Gift to Young Housewives*, a hefty tome, first published in the 1870s, which successfully codified the Russo-French and traditional Russian recipes of nineteenth-century *cuisine bourgeoise*. This precious text, as well as sumptuous

After the snacks came the dinner. Here the good-natured host let himself go. As soon as he noticed that a guest had only one piece of anything left, he immediately helped him to another, saying as he did so 'Neither men nor birds can survive without pairing'. If anyone had two morsels left, he added a third, saying: 'Two doesn't go far. God favors the Trinity'. If a guest had three morsels, the host would say to him: 'Where have you seen a cart on three wheels? Or a house with three corners?' He had an apt phrase for four morsels, and for five also."

—Nikolai Gogol
Dead Souls

descriptions of food and eating from the writings of Chekhov, Tolstoy, Gogol, and others, has become a venerated anthropological document testifying to a way of life that has been all but lost since the Revolution. Never republished by the Soviets (it was printed in Russian in the United States), *A Gift to Young Housewives* became a kind of underground culinary classic. True to the native sense of irony, the most quoted passage offered instructions concerning the correct behavior should guests turn up unexpectedly (which they do as much today as they did in Tolstoy's time): One should dispatch the maid to the cellar, bidding her fetch a leftover leg of veal, a few dozen eggs, a jar of caviar . . . and so on. The niceties of nineteenth-century propriety would be rehearsed around a cramped Soviet dining table, against a background of bellowing laughs and elaborate mock preparations.

The Soviet response to Molokhovets was the *Book of Healthy and Nutritious Food*, a kind of Russian *Joy of Cooking*. This was first published under Stalin, and was reissued every few years. Actually it furnishes quite a serviceable account of the traditional Russian staples, and also includes a few ethnic recipes. Playing their part in the mid-century Soviet appeal to the ultra-rational and fact-driven citizen, the sidelines of the book are teeming with pseudo-scientific statistics on the preparation and consumption of food. And the text gravely admonishes its readers against the evil of overindulgence in both food and drink.

The most useful English-language books include the beautiful *Time-Life* book on Russian food by Helen and George Papashvily, Anne Volokh's *The Art of Russian Cuisine*, Darra Goldstein's *A la Russe*, and our good friend Lynn Visson's *Russian*

They brought the guests spiced vodka with raisins and plums in it and wedding bread on a big dish. The musicians began on the bottom crust, in which coins had been baked, and put their fiddles, cymbals, and tambourines down for a brief rest.

— Nikolai Gogol
Evenings on a Farm near Dikanka

Cookbook (in which she skillfully selects recipes from the Russian emigré communities in the United States), as well as a number of older Russian cookbooks published a while back.

The problems of poorly written records and deplorable recipe testing standards haunted us time and again during our visits to the USSR. Everywhere there were recipes calling for "exotic" ingredients that haven't been available in Moscow since the time of the Czars. These recipes also describe elaborate preparations that are so time-consuming, they are impossible for the mother-cook, who might stand in line for half a day for a scrawny chicken. Yet such is the resilience of the Soviet housewife that almost anything can be redeemed by recourse to her armory of stunning technical improvisations and breathtaking compromises with the food supply.

The difficulties in Russia were further compounded by the habits of measuring "by the eye," seasoning "to taste," and pouring out liquids "by the knuckle." And they were underscored by the carefree culinary trial-and-error that we found in so many emigré households, whose designated master-chefs would often produce the strangest hybrids of American ingredients and ethnic ideas. We have peered over a hundred shoulders at hundreds of stoves and ovens and worn a thousand expressions of fascination and astonishment.

Symbolic for us of both the treats and the trials of our research were Anya's summer days spent in the bowels of the imposing Lenin Library in Moscow—the Soviet equivalent of the Library of Congress. As an American citizen she was given a special pass usually reserved for distinguished academics. And there she sat, amid piles of dusty volumes on military history, a young woman surrounded by ranks of bemedaled war veterans and decrepit Socialist heros, waiting endlessly for (of all things) a stack of pre-Revolutionary cookbooks. Often more was gleaned from lunchtime chats in the Tatar and Uzbek cooperative cafés across the Moscow River than was ever learned in the library.

Yet, when all is said and done, we enjoyed to the full our grand tour of Soviet ethnic restaurants from the *faux* glamour of Brighton Beach in Brooklyn to the festive glitz of the Rasputin in Paris. Most of these establishments, at all levels of service and sophistication, offer an attractive mélange of Russian and ethnic staples. In this they resemble the English-language cookbooks on Russian and Soviet cuisine, which similarly combine celebrated Slavic dishes such as beef Stroganoff or borscht with a good selection of dishes such as *shashlik* and pilafs from the Caucasus and Central Asia. Some books and some restaurants, such as the flamboyant Russian cafés of Paris with their gypsy music and lavish decors, obviously appeal more to the eye and the ear than to the palate. We have tried not to lose sight of the celebrated central traditions in Soviet cuisine, but at the same time we have sought to give a special emphasis and depth to outstanding regional preparations that are less well known but profoundly worth their due.

A Few Notes on Preparation

The most significant fact to report about the ingredients featured in this book is that the miniboom in quality delis and other specialty food stores makes it possible for today's kitchen enthusiast to be

pretty ambitious without actually venturing any further than the bookshelf and main street. Many herbs, spices, fruits, and vegetables that were extremely difficult to locate as recently as a decade ago are now quite commonplace, especially in the major urban areas of the United States. Ingredients such as bulgur, phyllo dough, sumakh, pomegranate juice, fenugreek, and some of the once unusual fresh herbs used in many of the dishes in this book are now available in most quality food stores and health-food shops. Wild mushrooms (so important for our Slavic recipes) have also firmly established themselves in the American gourmet market. And if not readily available in your local stores, most of the ingredients we recommend can be ordered from reliable mail-order sources (see the Contents).

However, there are other ingredients for which you will have to make substitutions. One of these is the superbly flavorful fat of the fat-tailed sheep (*kurdiuk*) used extensively in Central Asia or the Caucasus. Depending on the recipe, this can usually be substituted for by butter or a light vegetable oil. More unusual still are two of the principal ingredients of Central Asian cuisine — the camel and the horse. Suffice it to say that we will not be proposing dishes that feature horse steak or camel's leg; and such delicacies as the excellent dried horse-meat sausage (*kazi*) and the refreshing fermented mare's milk drink (*kumiss*) we will leave for you to enjoy through our words alone.

As far as fruit and vegetables are concerned, it is sad to report that while you can buy first-class plantains and kiwis in almost every corner store, fresh sour cherries, fresh currants (red and black), lingonberries, wild strawberries, and tart gooseberries — all so familiar to most northern Europeans —

Day faded; on the table, glowing, the samovar of evening boiled, and warmed the Chinese teapot; flowing beneath it, vapour wreathed and coiled. Already Olga's hand was gripping the urn of perfumed tea, and tipping into the cups its darkling stream — meanwhile a hallboy handed cream.

— Alexander Pushkin
Eugene Onegin

are not readily available here. From the Caucasus, the exquisitely tart *tkemali* plum, used to make a splendid sauce to flavor meats and poultry in Georgia, is a big loss. Yet so greatly is it mourned in the emigré communities that those with a backyard often grow them at home, and those who are not so lucky have come up with an ingenious substitute in tamarind concentrate imported from India. *Kizil* (a kind of Cornelian cherry) is another fine tart fruit, used for similar purposes as *tkemali*. If you cannot find the tamarind concentrate, these plums can be approximated in some cases by lemon juice, and in others by using slightly unripe fresh prunes.

Differences in the type and quality of fish are also quite profound. Many of the freshwater fish that have earned such a reputation in the Russian waterways are hard to find or simply not popular in the United States; Black Sea fish such as grey mullet and Caspian whitefish (*kutum*) are also hard to duplicate or substitute. Nevertheless, appropriate fish have been suggested for individual recipes, and you are invited to experiment further.

A Panoramic Offering

Most people think of Russian food as heavy and fattening. While some Slavic dishes are indeed rich in dairy products and fats, many others are based on fish and grains (including buckwheat and millet), and others feature brined and pickled foods. And as for the Caucasus — whose dishes are the backbone of our book — nowhere is the dietary value of a cuisine so obviously healthful. It's no accident that this region has seen more centenarians per

---

In Russia, the use of [mushrooms] is universal, from the emperor to the beggar; and those who know what a delectable dish they make — the salted ones excepted — need not be told that they are always welcome, whether dressed with a rich sauce, as at the tables of St. Petersburg, or with the plainer art of a hut by the wayside. Many peasants live almost entirely upon them, at some seasons of the year. In the summer afternoons, bands of village children may be seen searching for them in the woods, with little baskets on their arms . . .

— Robert Brenner
Excursions into the Interior of Russia

capita than any other on earth. Simple vegetable preparations, an abundance of fruit and nut-based sauces, bulgur and rice dishes, fresh herbs munched on their own or eaten with thin *lavash* bread, yogurt, and legumes — all these have allowed many Georgians to eat, drink, and be merry long into their nineties and even well into their hundreds.

And so, we are delighted to offer you a whole panorama of tastes, textures, and flavors from around the Soviet Union. Some of our dishes are spicy and exotic; some are heartwarming and home-style; some are versions of the best-loved classics. The collection is an adventure for the taste buds that will add flare and drama to your culinary repertoire, and take you, in the process, half way around the globe. Accompanying this rich collection of recipes, are six descriptive essays describing the diverse ethnic cuisines that make up the Soviet's vast multi-national state.

But diversity aside, our final message is the same in any language: Let's eat! or as they say in Russia, *prosim k stolu* — Please to the table.

Anya von Bremzen
John Welchman

The Soviet Republics at a Glance

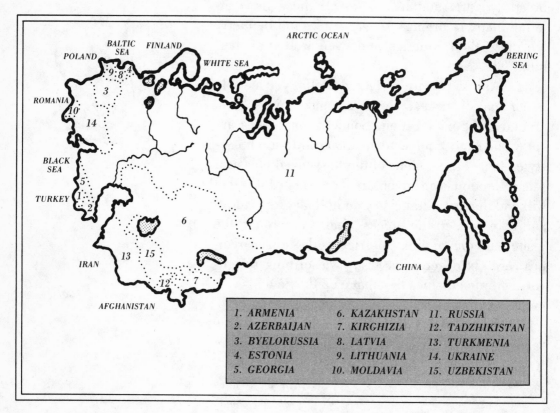

1. ARMENIA	6. KAZAKHSTAN	11. RUSSIA
2. AZERBAIJAN	7. KIRGHIZIA	12. TADZHIKISTAN
3. BYELORUSSIA	8. LATVIA	13. TURKMENIA
4. ESTONIA	9. LITHUANIA	14. UKRAINE
5. GEORGIA	10. MOLDAVIA	15. UZBEKISTAN

Armenia

A little larger than the state of Maryland, Armenia is the smallest of the Soviet republics, and a fraction of the size of the ancient kingdom of Armenia, whose lands are today divided between Turkey, Iran, and the USSR. It is a wild, mountainous republic, whose capital, Yerevan, stands on the site of a fortification built in the eighth century B.C.

Azerbaijan

To the east of the Caucasus and to the west of the Caspian Sea, Azerbaijan shares its southern border with Iran. The republic is rich in oil and actually derives its name, which means "Land of Flames," from a continuous history of oil production that dates back more than a thousand years. The capital, Baku, is located at the end of a large spur that juts into the Caspian.

Byelorussia

Literally "White Russia." Located on a forested plain at the western edge of the Soviet Union, and bordering on Poland, Byelorussia's capital city, Minsk, was founded in the eleventh century.

Estonia

Northernmost and smallest of the three Soviet Baltic Republics (slightly larger in area than Switzerland), the Estonian people have the highest standard of living in the Soviet Union. The Estonian language is related to the Hungarian/Finnish group of languages. Its capital, Tallinn, features a thirteenth-century cathedral and is ringed by medieval walls.

Georgia

Georgia takes up an area in the Caucasus to the east of the Black Sea that is rather less than half the size of its namesake American State. It is, nevertheless, the largest republic in the Caucasus. Extremely rich in fruits and vegetables, it also has a strong cultural tradition with its own language and alphabet. Today Georgia has two main claims to fame: as the birthplace of Joseph Stalin, the Soviet Union's most notorious son; and as a producer of centenarians, 1 person in every 2,500, it is said, lives to over 100 years old. The capital, Tblisi, is one of the oldest continuously inhabited cities in the world.

Kazakhstan

This republic is surprisingly large, approaching the size of India. Like the giant Russian republic, it contains over a hundred different nationalities, including its native Muslim Kazhaks. Its plains and plateaus are the main livestock areas of the Soviet Union. The capital, Alma-Ata, is located near the Chinese border, and is named for the famous apples of the region.

Kirghizia

Kirghizia is a mountainous republic lying to the northwest of the Chinese border. The people are of Mongol descent, and the capital, Frunze, is a modern industrial city.

Latvia

Like its neighbors Estonia and Lithuania, Latvia has had almost a continuous history of occupations — by the Danes, the Vikings, Germans, Poles, and Russians, and only a brief twenty years of independence (1920 to 1940) in recent times. Over half the population are Letts, native Latvians. The capital, Riga, is a bustling historic port town.

Lithuania

Southernmost of the three Baltic republics, Lithuania was once (in the thirteenth and fourteenth centuries) at the center of a Catholic empire that included much of the Ukraine and Poland. The Roman Catholic religion and culture are still powerful influences today in the republic, as reflected in the architecture of the capital, Vilnius.

Moldavia

Rather smaller than Switzerland in area, Moldavia has the distinction of being both the most rural and the most densely populated of the Soviet republics. It has a history stretching back to the Romans, and a temperate climate that can sustain grapes, walnuts, wheat, and tobacco.

Russia

Properly (if rather bureaucratically) called the "Russian Soviet Federated Socialist Republic," Russia is over 6,500,000 square miles, and thus almost as large as the USA and Canada combined. It contains over a hundred nationalities and languages (with Russian the large majority) and is sub-divided into sixteen "autonomous republics" as well as other designated regions. The capital, Moscow, is the great nerve center of the Soviet empire.

Tadzhikistan

Situated on the Afghan and Chinese borders, the Tadzhik Republic, slightly larger in area than Greece, is the most mountain-ous in the Soviet Union. Cotton and mulberry trees (for silk) are cultivated in the irrigated valleys and processed in the modern capital of Dushanbe.

Turkmenia

The formidible Kara Kum desert (taking up an area the size of California) occupies over three-quarters of this, the driest of the Soviet republics. Its capital, Ashkhabad, near the Iranian border east of the Caspian Sea, is the southernmost Soviet city.

Ukraine

The third largest republic, though second only to Russia in population, the Ukraine is a fertile agricultural and industrial region with strong Slavic cultural traditions. The capital, Kiev, on the Dnieper River, dates back to the sixth century and is still called the "mother of cities" in the Soviet Union.

Uzbekistan

Named for Khan Uzbek, one of the thirteenth-century Mongol warlords, Uzbekistan is made up of vast deserts and plains that fan out from the Aral Sea. Its chief cultural glory is the city of Samarkand, one of the most venerable cities in Central Asia. The capital, Tashkent, has been rebuilt following a devastating earthquake in 1966.

Appetizers

ZAKUSKI

Before dinner, even in the house of persons of the first distinction, a small table is spread in the corner of the drawing room, covered with plates of caviare, dried and pickled herrings, smoked ham or tongue, bread, butter and cheeses, together with bottles of different liqueurs; *and few of the company of either sex omitted a prelude of this kind to the main entertainment.*

— *William Coxe, 1778/79*

A *zakuska* is literally a "little bite," and the assortment of bite-sized morsels (*zakuski*) that accompany the mandatory predinner shots of vodka at a Russian gathering are for many Russians, myself among them, really the heart of the meal.

The origin of the *zakuska* table is said to be found in the Scandinavian smorgasbord — an hypothesis made more plausible by the fact that the great pre-Christian Russian rulers, such as Rurik, were of Scandinavian stock. Others claim, though, that the preparation of *zakuski* really derives from a long peasant tradition. Perhaps the second origin is more convincing, if only because I can't quite imagine those six-foot-tall pagan warriors savoring such diminutive offerings as the *zakuski*. But it's a pretty story all the same.

Once Upon a Time

T he popularity of the *zakuska* table increased in the nineteenth century among the gentry of the great Russian estates as the perfect answer to the unexpected arrival of guests from out of the cold. The guests, of course, would be supplied with a hearty shot of vodka (which the Russians swear by as the best remedy for colds) and a tempting small accompaniment to quiet it down. As a rule of thumb, by the way, you should never drink a shot of vodka without eating something immediately. That way the vodka will behave like a well-mannered Dr. Jekyll, and give you a pleasant, warming glow; the alternative risks an encounter with Mr. Hyde and a sledgehammer aftereffect!

At more elaborate occasions in the nineteenth century, the *zakuska* table would be adorned with a glittering array of beautifully prepared and presented little dishes: several shining caviars heaped in silver bowls; perfect slices of hot and cold smoked fish; sparkling aspics; richly decorated pâtés; a variety of filled pastries; galantines; hams; artfully composed salads; and crunchy pickles of all kinds.

These would be carefully arranged on a round table in a separate ante-dining room, and accompanied by cut-crystal decanters of ice-cold vodka, the best Sèvres chinaware, and a lavish display of the family's finest silver. Most of the dishes were decorated with elaborate butter rosettes, carved vegetable flowers, and ornate curly greens. The food would be eaten with the guests standing up to drink and socialize before the formal dinner.

A More Frugal Table Today

In Russia today, of course, there isn't the splendor and opulence of the Czarist past, when a whole hundred-pound sturgeon might preside proudly at the table, surrounded by rare and costly golden caviars, and by such immensely time-consuming efforts as entire dishes made just from the cheeks of the herring. But you can still sample some excellent light dishes. There's always smoked fish, especially salmon and sturgeon; various vegetable caviars; flaky filled pastries; assorted cold meats; canapés; stuffed eggs; pickles (my favorite are brined apples); and a selection of delicious flavored vodkas.

It's recently become popular to serve fish and meat assortments called, appropriately enough, *assorti*. They can make a striking and effective platter of tidbits. Fish *assorti* might include eggs

Chekhov's *Siren*

Anton Chekhov's short story *The Siren* is a true homage to the Russian passion for food. The judges from a provincial court have just come out of their local sessions. They are tired, hungry, and thirsty. As they are finishing up the day's work and gathering their strength to go home, the clerk of the court regales them with one of the greatest reveries on food in world's literature.

"Suppose you are coming home after a day's shooting," says the clerk, "and want to bring an appetite to your dinner. Then you mustn't let your mind dwell on anything intellectal. Intellectual things, learned things, ruin the appetite. You know yourself that thinkers and scholars are just nowhere when it comes to eating. . . . As I was saying, you are on your way home, and you must make sure that your mind dwells on nothing but the wineglass and the appetizer. Once I was traveling; I closed my eyes and pictured to myself a suckling pig with horseradish. Well sir, I became virtually hysterical with sheer appetite! Now this is important: when you drive into your own courtyard, you should be aware of a smell from the kitchen, a smell of something you know . . ."

"Roast goose is a prime smeller," observed the Honorary Justice, breathing heavily.

stuffed with caviar, smoked fish topped with lemon slices, and various fish canapés with, perhaps, a mound of crab salad at the center of the plate. Meat *assorti* would include sliced cold cuts — such as Hungarian salami, Westphalian ham, and smoked turkey breast — and squares of jellied veal or veal meat loaf, all served with a selection of mustards and horseradish.

The Russian way with vodka and *zakuski* has been exported throughout the whole Soviet Union and adopted, often with mouthwatering regional additions and flourishes, in homes and hotels everywhere except in the Caucasus, which has its own distinctive traditions and recipes. When serving these appetizers, remember to consult Chapter 14 for various pickles, cucumbers, tomatoes, and brined apples; and Chapter 12 for the tiny filled pastries that are a must for any *zakuska* table. Many of the salads described in Chapter 3 also make a tasty contribution. Remember, as well, that these appetizers can be served equally before a formal or informal sit-down dinner, or at a buffet. Many of them will also make excellent lunch or light supper entrées.

Tahini and Hazelnut Dip

Fundukli Tahin

This recipe was given to me by a friend and connoisseur of Russian cuisine, who received it in turn from the chef of a fine restaurant in Baku, the capital of Azerbaijan. The dip is perfect with crisp crudités, with pita triangles, or as a sauce for any cold, poached white-fleshed fish. Sumakh is a tangy-flavored powder that is made from tiny tart berries. It is available in most Middle Eastern stores.

1 cup shelled hazelnuts
2 medium cloves garlic, minced
¾ cup tahini
¼ cup fresh lemon juice

½ cup water, or as needed
Salt, to taste
Sumakh for garnish (optional)

1 Reserving a few hazelnuts for garnish, pan-roast the remaining nuts in a large skillet over medium heat until golden, about 5 minutes. You can also toast them in a preheated oven at 350°F on a baking sheet for 5 to 7 minutes, but pan-roasting will fill your kitchen with the wonderful aroma of hazelnuts.

2 Rub the hazelnuts in a kitchen towel to remove the skins. Grind in a food processor.

3 In a deep bowl, combine the garlic with the tahini. Drizzle in the lemon juice, beating with a fork. Slowly drizzle in the water, continuing to beat with the fork until the mixture is a little thicker than heavy cream. You might need to add a little more than ½ cup water.

4 Combine the hazelnuts with the tahini. Add salt and stir until blended. Cover and refrigerate for several hours.

5 Serve garnished with the reserved hazelnuts and sprinkled with sumakh, if available.

Makes about 3 cups

Cucumber and Yogurt Dip

Jajik

This refreshing dip—called *tzaziki* in Greek, *cacik* in Turkish, and *jajik* in Armenian—is a great favorite throughout the Caucasus, Turkey, and the Middle East. Serve it as part of an Armenian or Middle Eastern buffet, or as an accompaniment to savory pilafs and lamb or chicken dishes. It is also a marvelously cool and soothing remedy for overeating!

1½ cups plain low-fat yogurt
⅓ cup sour cream
2 large cloves garlic, minced
2 medium-size cucumbers, peeled, grated, and squeezed dry with paper towels
2 tablespoons chopped fresh mint

1 tablespoon chopped fresh cilantro
1½ tablespoons olive oil
Whole mint leaves for garnish
Sumakh for garnish (optional)
Toasted pita triangles

1 In a serving bowl, combine the yogurt, sour cream, garlic, cucumbers, mint, cilantro, and oil. Cover and refrigerate for 6 to 8 hours, to allow the flavors to settle.

2 Before serving, garnish with mint leaves and sprinkle with sumakh, if available. Accompany this dip with toasted pita triangles.

Makes about 2½ cups

Zesty Eggplant Slices

Skhtorats

Meza

In Armenia *zakuski* are called *meza* and a *meza* table would be loaded with such exciting and unusual dishes as the special spicy, dried meat, *basturma*; home-cured green olives; cold stuffed vegetables in olive oil; a distinctive brined string cheese; stuffed mussels or clams; spicy sausage (*sudjuk*); piquant meat balls; wonderful, fluffy *bourek* (pastries filled with meat, spinach, or cheese); various pickled vegetables; and toasted almonds and pumpkin seeds, along with the mandatory *jajik*, a cooling yogurt and cucumber dip. These are washed down with *raki*, an anise-flavored drink, and served with *lavash*, the Armenian flatbread.

In this recipe, which is one of my favorite Armenian eggplant preparations, fried eggplants are gently marinated in a mixture of vinegar, cilantro, and lots of garlic.

> *1¾ pounds long, narrow eggplants, cut into ½-inch slices*
> *1 tablespoon coarse (kosher) salt*
> *4 large cloves garlic, crushed in a garlic press*
> *3 tablespoons red wine vinegar*
> *½ cup olive oil, or as needed*
> *¼ cup chopped fresh cilantro*
> *Freshly ground black pepper and salt, to taste*

1 Place the eggplant slices in a colander and toss with the salt. Let stand for 30 minutes. Rinse the eggplant well under cold running water and pat completely dry with a kitchen towel.

2 In a small bowl, combine the garlic and vinegar and let stand while you cook the eggplant.

3 Divide the oil between 2 large skillets and heat until it begins to sizzle. Add eggplant slices to both skillets, without overcrowding, and fry until deep golden on both sides, 12 to 15 minutes. Repeat with any remaining eggplant slices.

4 Transfer the fried slices to a large bowl, without draining. Let cool.

5 Place the cooled eggplant slices in a serving dish in layers, sprinkling each layer with the vinegar-garlic mixture, pepper, salt (if needed), and fresh cilantro. Cover and refrigerate for at least 2 hours before serving.

Serves 4 to 6

Moldavian Marinated Peppers

Ardei à la Moldova

Together with squash, eggplants, and beans, sweet juicy peppers are among the most prized foods in Moldavia, whose culinary heritage is a blend of Greek, Romanian, Middle Eastern, and Slavic. These marinated peppers taste so good that I must confess that in my house most of them get consumed before they ever find their way to the table. Remember that 3 pounds of peppers will "shrink" considerably during cooking and marinating — so don't be fooled by the big bag of peppers that you'll buy at the greengrocer's. Serve as part of a summer appetizer buffet with black bread.

3 pounds Italian (pale green frying)
*   peppers, cored and seeded*
1 large onion, thinly sliced
6 tablespoons olive oil
3 tablespoons red wine vinegar

Small pinch of sugar
4 cloves garlic, thinly sliced
Salt and freshly ground black
*   pepper, to taste*

1 Preheat the oven to 400°F.

2 Place the peppers on a baking sheet and bake, turning halfway through, until soft, about 25 to 30 minutes. Remove from the oven and cover with a kitchen towel.

3 After the peppers have cooled off, remove and discard the skins and place the peppers with the onion in a large, deep dish.

4 In a small bowl, whisk together the oil, vinegar, and sugar. Stir in the garlic. Pour over the peppers and onion and season with salt and pepper. Cover and refrigerate overnight.

5 Serve in a colorful rustic bowl.

Serves 6 to 8

In Moldavia

Moldavia boasts a range of skillfully prepared vegetable appetizers similar in style, taste, and presentation to those of Turkey, Greece, and the Balkans. Beans, eggplants, peppers, and simple vegetable salads are brought to life with a dressing of fragrant sunflower oil. Feta cheese is abundant and innovatively used in many dishes. Instead of bread, the Moldavians prefer to serve their own *mamaliga*, a cornmeal pudding similar to Italian polenta.

Spiced Feta

Brinza

This appetizer is one of the most beloved in the Caucasus. It consists of slices of local salty cheese spiced with dried herbs and sumakh and accompanied by sprigs of fresh herbs — cilantro, basil (preferably opal), tarragon, mint, and chives — which are eaten together, wrapped in pieces of flatbread. Cheese with herbs is the mandatory nucleus of the appetizer table, around which other appetizers grow and multiply, according to the occasion.

¾ pound feta cheese, preferably
   Bulgarian, sliced medium thick
2 teaspoons tarragon vinegar
3 tablespoons extra-virgin olive oil
¼ teaspoon hot Hungarian paprika

½ teaspoon dried tarragon
½ teaspoon dried oregano
Generous pinch of sumakh
6 to 8 sprigs each fresh cilantro,
   basil, tarragon, mint, and chives

1 Arrange the feta slices in a shallow serving dish.

2 In a small bowl, whisk the vinegar with the olive oil, paprika, and dried herbs. Drizzle this mixture over the feta slices.

Sprinkle with sumakh and let stand at room temperature for 1 hour. Serve accompanied by the herbs.

Serves 6

Feta Cheese Spread

Pashtet iz Brinzi

A personal favorite of mine from southern Russia. Serve with pita bread or on slices of French bread that have been sautéed gently in olive oil. If you find your feta cheese to be too salty, soak it in cold water for several hours beforehand.

½ pound feta cheese, preferably
   Bulgarian
1 large clove garlic, minced
1 hard-cooked egg, chopped
3 tablespoons chopped fresh dill

2 tablespoons sour cream
Freshly ground black pepper,
   to taste
Black olives for garnish

1 Place the feta cheese in a food processor and mince.

2 Transfer the cheese to a bowl. Stir in the garlic, chopped egg, dill, and sour cream until well blended. Season with pepper, cover, and refrigerate for 4 to 6 hours. Transfer to a serving bowl and garnish with olives.

Makes about 2 cups

Garlicky Farmer's Cheese with Walnuts

Achot

T his recipe comes from Ararat Dardenelles, a fine Armenian restaurant in Manhattan. The owner and chef, Sam Martirossian, invented the dish, naming it for a friend. Serve with toasted pita triangles.

1 cup farmer's cheese
3 tablespoons finely chopped walnuts
¼ cup plain low-fat yogurt
1 tablespoon finely chopped fresh dill
1 tablespoon finely chopped fresh parsley
1 medium-size clove garlic, minced
Salt, to taste
Boston lettuce leaves for garnish
¼ cup coarsely chopped walnuts
Toasted pita triangles

1 Process the farmer's cheese, finely chopped walnuts, and yogurt in a food processor until smooth.

2 Transfer the cheese to a bowl and mix with the herbs, garlic, and salt. Shape into a ball, cover, and refrigerate for 4 hours.

3 Line a small serving platter with several lettuce leaves and carefully transfer the cheese ball to the platter. Press the coarsely chopped walnuts into the ball so they more or less cover it. Serve with the toasted pita triangles.

Serves 4 to 6

Caviar and Cheese Ball

Zakuska iz Tvoroga i Ikri

This improvised spread is pretty to look at and easy to make. Serve on a platter surrounded by rye bread triangles. It will add an attractive splash of color to your *zakuska* table.

8 ounces whipped cream cheese, at
    room temperature
¼ cup farmer's cheese

2 tablespoons sour cream
4 ounces salmon caviar

1 Process the cheeses in a food processor until smooth.

2 Transfer the cheese mixture to a bowl and refrigerate until firm, 2 to 3 hours.

3 Form the cheese into a ball. Place on a serving platter with a rim. Coat the cheese with sour cream, then gently press the caviar into the surface, taking care not to break the eggs.

Makes 6 to 8 servings

Eggs Stuffed with Mushrooms

Yaitsa Farshirovanniye Gribami

You can serve these cold, as part of an appetizer spread, or slightly warm for breakfast or lunch. Pass some homemade mayonnaise on the side, if you wish.

3 tablespoons unsalted butter

1 medium-size onion, finely chopped

½ pound fresh white mushrooms, wiped clean and thinly sliced

5 tablespoons heavy or whipping cream

¾ teaspoon Dijon mustard

6 hard-cooked eggs, peeled and halved lengthwise

2 tablespoons chopped fresh parsley

2 tablespoons chopped fresh dill

1 tablespoon mayonnaise, preferably Hellmann's

Salt and freshly ground black pepper, to taste

Romaine or Boston lettuce leaves for garnish

1 Melt the butter in a heavy skillet over medium heat. Add the onion and mushrooms and sauté, stirring occasionally with a wooden spoon, until nicely browned, about 15 minutes. Stir in the cream and mustard, raise the heat to high, and cook, stirring frequently, for 3 minutes. Remove from the heat and cool completely or until just warm.

2 Remove the yolks from the eggs and place them in a bowl. Mash the yolks with a fork. Mix the yolks with the cooled mushroom mixture. Add the parsley, dill, and mayonnaise. Mix thoroughly and add salt and pepper.

3 Spoon the yolk mixture back into the whites, arrange the eggs on the lettuce leaves, and serve either slightly warm or at room temperature.

Serves 4 to 6

Stuffed Eggs
Farshirovanniye Yaitsa

Stuffed Eggs is an appetizer widely enjoyed in western Russia and in the Baltic republics. The filling might be mushrooms in Byelorussia, sardines or anchovies in the Baltic, or caviar in the republic of Russia. Experiment with various fillings. You can mix the egg yolks with chicken livers, chopped ham, leftover veal or chicken, or Parmesan cheese. As a general rule, use 1 tablespoon of softened butter or mayonnaise for every 2 egg yolks and season with mustard, horseradish, chopped chives, parsley, or dill, depending on the filling.

Eggs Stuffed with Caviar

Yaitsa Farshirovanniye Krasnoy Ikroy

This pretty and delicious dish is one of the most popular Russian hors d'oevres. Salmon caviar is relatively inexpensive, but still a treat. I always keep a jar in my refrigerator, as it makes a lovely garnish.

6 hard-cooked eggs, peeled and
  halved lengthwise
¼ cup Crème Fraîche (see Index) or
  or sour cream
3 tablespoons snipped fresh chives

2 tablespoons fresh lemon juice
Small pinch of salt
4 ounces salmon caviar
Lettuce leaves for garnish
Small parsley sprigs for garnish

1 Remove the yolks from the eggs and place them in a bowl. Mash the yolks with a fork. Add the crème fraîche, chives, and lemon juice to the yolks, season very lightly with salt, and mix until the ingredients are well blended.

2 Spoon the yolk mixture back into the

whites and top with a teaspoon of caviar. Refrigerate for 1 hour.

3 Arrange on lettuce leaves, garnish each egg with a small parsley sprig, and serve.

Serves 4 to 6

Calf's Liver Pâté

Pechionochniy Pashtet

This recipe comes from my mother, who, schooled in adversity like all Russian women of her generation (eight hours work, three hours on line, and whatever time was leftover in the kitchen), still rarely spends more than half an hour on a recipe. Her experience has certainly come into its own again in unexpected ways since we moved to New York City, where it's still the same story in the kitchen, though the excuses from outside are thankfully a lot more interesting!

The addition of raw onion and carrot lend the pâté a crisper texture and a livelier flavor. For a more formal presentation, you can pipe the pâté onto buttered white toast squares, using a pastry bag fitted with a decorative tip. Otherwise, serve in a colorful rustic bowl accompanied by crackers; or spread on white toast triangles or squares of rye bread.

4 tablespoons (½ stick) unsalted
butter
1 pound calf's liver, sliced into
¼-inch strips
1 medium-size onion, finely chopped
1 medium-size carrot, peeled and
diced
1 small onion, quartered
5 tablespoons unsalted butter,
softened

2½ tablespoons mayonnaise,
preferably Hellmann's
2 tablespoons dry vermouth
Salt and freshly ground black
pepper, to taste
1 hard-cooked egg, finely chopped,
for garnish (optional)
1½ teaspoons finely chopped scallion
(green onion) for garnish
(optional)

1 Melt 2 tablespoons of the butter in a skillet large enough to accommodate all the liver. Add the liver and sauté for 2 to 3 minutes on each side over medium heat until it just loses its pinkness inside. Be careful not to overcook, though, because the liver will become too tough. Drain on paper towels.

2 Melt the remaining 2 tablespoons butter in the cleaned-out skillet and sauté the chopped onion over medium heat until golden, about 15 minutes.

3 Process the liver in a food processor with the cooked onion, carrot, quartered raw onion, and softened butter. To get a smoother mixture, you will probably have to do it in batches. As you process, keep dribbling in the mayonnaise and vermouth.

4 Transfer the mixture to a bowl. Season to taste with salt and pepper. Cover and refrigerate for 2 to 3 hours.

5 Transfer to a serving bowl and sprinkle with egg and scallions, or spread on white toast or rye bread.

Makes about 3 cups

Wild Mushrooms on Toast

Tost s Gribami

2 ounces imported dried wild mushrooms, preferably porcini, well
  rinsed
2 tablespoons unsalted butter
1 small onion, finely chopped
1 teaspoon all-purpose flour
1½ tablespoons Crème Fraîche (see
  Index) or sour cream
2 cloves garlic, minced
Pinch of sweet Hungarian
  paprika
Salt and freshly ground black
  pepper, to taste
3 tablespoons olive oil
12 slices French bread
3 tablespoons freshly grated
  Parmesan cheese
Finely chopped fresh parsley for
  garnish

1 In a small saucepan, simmer the mushrooms in 2 cups of water until soft, about
40 minutes. Remove the mushrooms with
a slotted spoon. Strain the cooking liquid
through a coffee filter and set aside. Pat
the mushrooms dry with paper towels and
finely chop.

2 Melt the butter in a small skillet over
medium heat. Add the mushrooms and
onion and sauté, stirring, for 15 minutes.

Russian Roots

People have a dif-
ficult time con-
vincing me that mush-
rooms on toast is an
English dish. And I'm
happy to announce
that after months of
working with me on this cookbook, even John
has officially given up his country's exclusive claims. My story of the Russian diplomats who worked in England finally did the
trick, I think.

These fellows went into the countryside
on a mushroom-picking expedition (a must
for every homesick Russian) and were
promptly arrested for trespassing. When the
country policeman actually realized what
they were doing, however, he became so
concerned for their health (certainly no con-
stable wants two dying Soviet embassy per-
sonnel on his hands six miles from the
nearest Wiltshire hamlet) that he dropped
all charges and insisted that they call an
emergency number in case of poisoning.
The diplomats had a
good laugh with their
friends later that even-
ing over an exquisite
mushroom dinner back
in London.

3 Sprinkle with the flour, stir, and cook for 1 minute. Stir in ¼ cup of the reserved mushroom cooking liquid and simmer for 2 to 3 minutes more.

4 Stir in the crème fraîche and simmer over medium heat for 5 minutes. Add the garlic and season with paprika, salt, and pepper. Simmer for 2 more minutes and remove from the heat.

5 Preheat the oven to 350°F.

6 Heat the olive oil in a large ovenproof skillet over medium heat. Add the bread slices and lightly brown, about 1 minute on each side.

7 Heap some of the mushroom mixture on each bread slice. Sprinkle with Parmesan cheese and bake for 10 minutes.

8 Sprinkle with parsley and serve immediately.

Serves 4 to 6

Beet Caviar with Walnuts and Prunes

Svyokla s Orekhami i Chernoslivom

This dish from the western part of the Soviet Union is unfailingly present on every Russian table today. Familiarity, for me, has bred only a great personal fondness for beet caviar, but I am aware that many Americans are not as enamored with beets as the Russians or the Ukrainians. John is a case in point — although he still doesn't get excited over simple cooked beets, served hot or cold on their own, he has been a wonderfully enthusiastic convert to my borscht, my beet salads, and my beet caviar.

This caviar can also function very successfully as a salad to accompany roast duckling or goose, or Boiled Beef à la Russe. Its flavor, which is enriched appealingly by the walnuts and prunes, is much enhanced by being made a day in advance.

3 large beets, with their skins, but
   stemmed, washed, and dried
⅓ cup brandy
7 pitted prunes
3 medium-size cloves garlic, cut
   in half
2 tablespoons fresh lemon juice
¾ cup walnut pieces, finely
   chopped
3 tablespoons mayonnaise, preferably Hellmann's
Salt and freshly ground black
   pepper, to taste

1 Preheat the oven to 375°F.

2 Wrap the beets in aluminum foil and bake until tender, about 1¼ hours.

3 Meanwhile, bring the brandy to a boil in a small saucepan. Pour over the prunes in a bowl and let soak for 30 minutes. Remove the prunes from the brandy, reserving the brandy. Finely chop the prunes and set aside.

4 When the beets are cool enough to handle, peel them and chop coarsely. Process the beets and garlic in a food processor until finely minced but not puréed.

5 Transfer the beets to a bowl and add the lemon juice, 2 tablespoons of the reserved brandy, the chopped prunes, and walnuts. Toss thoroughly with the mayonnaise and season with salt and pepper. Cover and refrigerate for 6 hours or overnight.

Makes about 2½ cups

A Vodka Chasing Party

Miniature Salmon Croquettes with Dill Mayonnaise

Herring in Mustard Sauce

Calf's Liver Pâté

Eggplant Astrakhan Style

Beet Caviar with Walnuts and Prunes

Pirozhki

My Mother's Marinated Mushrooms

Assorted Smoked Fish

Horseradish and Assorted Mustards

White, rye, and pumpernickel breads

•

Flavored Vodkas

•

Rum Baba

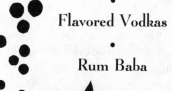

Wild Mushroom Caviar

Gribnaya Ikra

The Russians commonly make this caviar with pickled wild mushrooms. This version, made with fresh wild mushrooms, comes from my dear friend Nina Beilina, a great violinist and a virtuoso in the kitchen. Serve toast points or black bread squares alongside.

1½ pounds fresh porcini (cèpes),
portobello, or cremini
mushrooms
4 tablespoons light olive oil
1 medium-size onion,
chopped
3 cloves garlic, chopped
3 tablespoons mayonnaise, prefer-
ably Hellmann's

2 teaspoons fresh lemon juice,
or more to taste
2 tablespoons chopped fresh dill
(optional)
Salt and freshly ground black
pepper, to taste

1 Wipe the mushrooms with a damp cloth. Separate the stems from the caps and coarsely chop both.

2 Heat 3 tablespoons of the oil in a large skillet over medium heat. Add the mushrooms and cook, stirring until they begin to throw off their liquid. Turn the heat up to high and continue to cook and stir until the mushrooms reabsorb most of the liquid and are lightly browned, 10 to 12 minutes. Remove from the heat and set aside.

3 Heat the remaining tablespoon of oil in the same skillet and sauté the onion until deep golden, about 15 minutes.

4 Combine the mushrooms, onion, and garlic in a food processor and process until minced but not puréed.

5 In a large bowl, combine the mushroom mixture, mayonnaise, 2 teaspoons each lemon each juice, dill, and salt and pepper. Mix well, cover, and let stand at room temperature for 1 hour to allow the flavors to settle. Taste and add more lemon juice if desired.

Makes about 1¼ cups

Ah, Odessa

Odessa — or Odessa-Mama as its sons and daughters affectionately call it — is a bustling port on the Black Sea. Elegant and vulgar, provincial and cosmopolitan by turns, the city is something of a cross between Marseilles (it was actually occupied by the French in the early 1800s) and Babylon.

> Ah, Odessa, a gem by
>   the sea
> Ah, Odessa, you have
>   known much grief . . .

So goes a popular song from the 1920s, a time when the underworld flourished and gangsters wined and dined in style, taking advantage of the momentary decadence of the NEP — the New Economic Policy, instituted by Lenin in an attempt to salvage the nation's sinking

economy through a renewal of private enterprise. Strangely enough, even today when the NEP itself has all but faded from living memory, many American immigrants from Odessa still attempt to recreate the nostalgic gilded decor and mirrored spaces of those 1920s establishments in the restaurants they've opened in Brooklyn's Brighton Beach. The food they serve, though, is more like the typical Soviet mélange of Russian, Georgian, and Ukrainian staples than the delicious fish and vegetable dishes of their own native city.

Eggplant Caviar, Odessa Style

Baklazhannaya Ikra

Eggplant is so familiar to the Odessians that they call it simply by its color — *siniy* (blue). As in most Mediterranean and Middle Eastern countries, it is prepared in a huge variety of ways, and often with great skill and finesse. Spread this caviar on pita triangles or cocktail rye bread.

1 large eggplant, 1½ to 1¾ pounds
1 medium-size onion, finely chopped
1 medium-size meaty tomato, peeled
   and finely chopped
2 cloves garlic, minced

1 tablespoon olive oil
2 tablespoons red wine vinegar
Salt and freshly ground black
   pepper, to taste
Chopped fresh parsley for garnish

1 Preheat the oven to 375°F.

2 Pierce the eggplant in several places with a knife and bake on a baking sheet until soft, about 50 minutes, turning midway through. Remove from the oven and cool.

3 Cut the eggplant lengthwise in half. Scoop out the pulp and finely chop.

4 In a large bowl, combine the pulp with the onion, tomato, garlic, oil, and vinegar. Mix thoroughly and season with salt and pepper. Cover and refrigerate for several hours.

5 Place in a serving dish and garnish with parsley.

Serves 6 to 8

Vegetable Caviars
Ikra iz Raznikh Ovoshey

The Russians adore caviar, and they love vegetables. So, *voilà!* the perfect culinary hybrid.

These vegetable caviars have a terrific reputation. A famous Russian concert violinist was recently heard to swear that her mushroom caviar dis-appears at musical gatherings well before the "real thing." And I've often noticed myself how eagerly my Western friends enjoy these piquant vegetable spreads, which can be made from eggplant, squash, beans, mushrooms, or beets.

In Russia vegetable cavi-ars are served in colorful rustic bowls and eaten spread on squares of black bread. But they can be more formally presented, scooped into hollowed-out vegetables like cucumbers, zucchini, eggplant, or yellow squash, or spooned into endive or radicchio leaves.

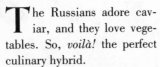

Mixed Vegetable Caviar

Givech

By now *givech* has become almost a generic name for any Balkan vegetable ragout dish. This version is a Moldavian-style ratatouille, usually put together from whatever fresh vegetables are at hand — eggplants, peppers, squash, green beans, potatoes, for example. This particular recipe, however, makes an especially tasty appetizer. Serve with rye or black bread, or pita triangles.

1 medium-size eggplant, about 1¼ to
    1½ pounds
¼ cup olive oil
2 carrots, peeled and cut into fine
    dice
1 medium-size red bell pepper,
    cored, seeded, and cut into
    fine dice
2 large green bell peppers, cored,
    seeded, and cut into fine dice
2 small zucchini, peeled and diced

1 small tart apple, cored, peeled,
    and chopped
4 large cloves garlic, finely minced
¾ cup drained canned tomatoes,
    seeded and chopped
¼ cup fresh lemon juice, or to taste
½ teaspoon sugar
Salt and freshly ground black
    pepper, to taste

1 Preheat the oven to 375°F.

2 Pierce the eggplant in several places with a knife and bake on a bakery sheet until soft, about 50 minutes, turning midway through. Remove from the oven and cool.

3 Cut the eggplant lengthwise in half. Scoop out as much pulp as possible and coarsely chop.

4 In a large Dutch oven, heat the oil over medium-high heat. Add the carrots and sauté, stirring, for 5 minutes. Continue adding ingredients — red pepper, green pepper, zucchini, and apple — spacing 3 to 4 minutes apart.

5 Stir in the eggplant pulp and half of the garlic, cover, and simmer over low heat for 40 minutes.

6 Add the tomatoes and continue simmering for another hour, stirring from time to time.

7 Off the heat, add the remaining garlic, lemon juice and sugar. Season with salt and pepper. Transfer the mixture to a bowl, cover, and refrigerate for several hours before serving.

Makes about 3½ cups

Chopped Eggplant with Mayonnaise

Baklazhan

Here is a variation of the Eggplant Caviar, Odessa Style on page 20. This time the caviar is made with mayonnaise instead of tomatoes, giving it a smoother, more luxurious texture.

1 large eggplant, 1½ to 1¾ pounds
1 small onion, finely chopped
1 clove garlic, minced
1½ tablespoons mayonnaise, preferably Hellmann's

1 tablespoon fresh lemon juice
Salt and freshly ground black pepper, to taste
Black olives for garnish
Parsley sprigs for garnish

1 Prepare the eggplant as directed in Steps 1 to 3, page 20.

2 In a large bowl, combine the eggplant with the onions, garlic, mayonnaise, and lemon juice. Mix thoroughly and season with salt and pepper. Cover and refrigerate for several hours.

3 Place in a serving dish and garnish with black olives and parsley sprigs. Spoon out or serve as a dip.

Serves 6 to 8

Red Beans with Walnut Sauce

Lobio

Beans are called *lobio* in Georgian, and they are one of the most popular and abundant vegetables in the republic. In Russia the most common *lobio* is made from red kidney beans in a sauce similar to *pkhali* (page 25). Georgians prefer their *lobio* more spicy, and the amount of red pepper should be adjusted for individual tastes. Serve accompanied by *lavash* or pita triangles or eat as a salad.

1 cup dried kidney beans
1 medium-size red onion, finely
    chopped
1 cup ground walnuts
4 cloves garlic, minced
1/2 cup finely chopped fresh cilantro
1/2 teaspoon coriander seeds, crushed
3 tablespoons red wine vinegar

1 tablespoon water
2 tablespoons olive oil
1/4 teaspoon cayenne pepper, or more
    to taste
Salt, to taste
Cilantro sprigs for garnish
1/2 small red onion, halved and
    thinly sliced, for garnish

1 Soak the beans overnight in water to cover.

2 Drain and rinse the beans, then cook, covered, in 2 quarts salted water until tender but not mushy, 45 minutes to 1 hour, adding more water if necessary.

3 Drain the beans thoroughly, transfer into a large bowl, and cool.

4 Mash the cooked beans lightly with a wooden spoon, so that about half of the beans are crushed. Add the onion, walnuts, garlic, chopped cilantro, coriander seeds, vinegar, water, and oil. Mix well and season with cayenne and salt. Cover and refrigerate for 6 to 8 hours.

5 Serve garnished with cilantro sprigs and sliced onion, accompanied by *lavash* or toasted pita triangles.

Serves 6 to 8

Open-Face Sandwiches
Buterbrodi

The name *Buterbrodi* means "butter and bread" in German. The idea of open-face sandwiches was imported to Russia, like so much else, by Peter the Great. Even though I haven't lived in Moscow for well over a decade now, I can still sometimes be caught peeling off the top piece of bread from a store-bought sandwich and quietly discarding it. John lectures me on the refined glories of crustless, double-ply cucumber sandwiches, and reckons that my one-slice habit is probably the best way to spot an unassimilated Russian across a crowded room, but I won't give in. I still think one piece of bread is better than two.

In Russia *buterbrodi* are even more popular for breakfast or lunch than sandwiches are in the United States. And when cut into neat two-bite-size pieces, they are called *buterbrodik* (the diminutive) or *canapé* (from the French). These popular smaller relatives make great accompaniments for cocktails and often feature in the elaborate *zakuska* buffet. If you arrive unexpectedly at a Russian home, you will almost certainly be treated to *buterbrodi* in some form or another, often ingeniously concocted from scraps and leftovers, but always delicious and attractive. As the name suggests, bread and butter are the only prerequisites. In Russia pride of place in the hierarchy of sandwiches is of course accorded to a slice of freshly baked white bread, buttered then liberally piled with the best available black caviar. Even as recently as a decade ago, quality caviar was still not impossible to find for a normal family in Russia; though it has become more difficult and more expensive since then. I usually serve at least three or four different kinds of *buterbrodi*, arranged in an imaginative mosaic of colors and flavors. Favorite quick combinations include:

- Cocktail rye with dill and lemon butter, topped with smoked salmon, capers, and a small dill sprig
- White bread triangles with horseradish butter, topped with smoked sturgeon or whitefish, a thin slice of lemon, and a small dill sprig
- Buttered pumpernickel rounds topped with a slice of hard-cooked egg and an anchovy fillet
- Buttered black bread, topped with a piece of herring fillet, chopped egg, and a cornichon
- Buttered toast triangles topped with crab meat, shredded lettuce, and a dab of mayonnaise
- Buttered cocktail rye topped with thinly sliced cucumbers and sprats
- Buttered pumpernickel topped with chopped liver, chopped egg, and scallions
- Buttered cocktail rye topped with chopped herring and a thin slice of apple
- White bread with horseradish butter, topped with poached tongue and pickle slices
- Cocktail rye bread with mustard butter, topped with ham and chopped parsley
- Pumpernickel rounds with anchovy butter, topped with thinly sliced red radishes

Vegetables with Walnut and Garlic Sauce

Pkhali

A kind of salad or dip, *pkhali* is made from a finely chopped cooked vegetable (spinach, cabbage, beans, eggplant, or red beets) with a dressing of ground walnuts, garlic, vinegar, spices, and herbs (sometimes onions are used as well). At a good Georgian party you will probably sample at least two or three different kinds of *pkhali*. The same dressing produces a distinctive flavor in combination with each vegetable, so the effect can be one of great variety with a minimum of effort. But remember, *pkhali* has to be made at least 6 to 8 hours ahead for the flavor of the garlic to settle properly. Following are just three of the better known types of *pkhali*.

Spinach *Pkhali*

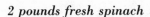

2 pounds fresh spinach

WALNUT SAUCE AND GARNISH

¾ cup ground walnuts	Pinch of cayenne pepper
4 cloves garlic, minced	¼ teaspoon ground fenugreek
1 small onion, minced	1½ tablespoons tarragon vinegar
3 tablespoons finely chopped fresh cilantro	3 tablespoons water
	Salt, to taste
½ teaspoon crushed coriander seeds or ¼ teaspoon ground coriander	Pomegranate seeds or walnut pieces for garnish

1 Rinse the spinach thoroughly and discard the stems. Cook in salted water until tender, about 5 minutes.

2 Drain the spinach and cool until manageable. Squeeze out as much liquid as possible.

3 Chop the spinach as fine as you can, or mince in a food processor, being careful not to overpurée. (The Georgians insist that it is best to put it through an old-fashioned meat grinder.)

4 To make the sauce, mix the ground walnuts with the garlic, onion, cilantro, coriander seeds, cayenne, fenugreek, vinegar, and water in a bowl.

5 Add this mixture to the spinach and stir until thoroughly blended and smooth. Season with salt. Cover and refrigerate for 6 to 8 hours.

6 To serve, spread the *pkhali* on a plate and smooth the top with a spatula. With a knife, make a pattern of diamonds in the top and sprinkle with pomegranate seeds, if available, or with walnut pieces.

Serves 4 to 6

Eggplant *Pkhali*

1 large eggplant, about 1½ to 1¾ pounds
Walnut Sauce, made as directed for Spinach Pkhali (see above)

Chopped fresh cilantro for garnish

1 Preheat the oven to 375°F.

2 Pierce the eggplant in several places with a knife and bake on a baking sheet until soft, 50 minutes to 1 hour, turning midway through. Remove from the oven and cool.

3 Cut the eggplant lengthwise in half. Scoop out the pulp, removing some but not all of the seeds, then coarsely chop.

4 Combine the eggplant with the walnut sauce in a bowl. Cover and refrigerate for 6 to 8 hours.

5 Place in a serving dish and serve at room temperature, garnished with the cilantro.

Serves 6

Beet *Pkhali*

3 large beets, with their skins, but stemmed, washed, and dried
Walnut Sauce, made as directed for Spinach Pkhali (see page 25)

2 tablespoons chopped fresh parsley
1 tablespoon tarragon vinegar, or more to taste
Salt, to taste

1 Preheat the oven to 375°F.

2 Wrap the beets in aluminum foil and bake until tender, about 1¼ hours. Cool completely.

3 Peel the beets and cut into pieces. Mince in a food processor.

4 Combine the beets with the walnut sauce in a bowl. Add the parsley and 1 tablespoon vinegar. Mix thoroughly and season with salt. Taste and add more vinegar, if desired. Cover and refrigerate for at least 4 hours.

5 To serve, spread the *pkhali* on a plate and smooth the top with a spatula. With a knife, make a pattern of diamonds in the top.

Serves 4 to 6

Marinated Herring Rolls

Rollmops

No Baltic appetizer spread is imaginable without *rollmops* — herring rolls that are stuffed with pickles and capers and marinated for several days. When I feel lazy, I forgo the stuffing, and marinate pieces of herring fillets to be eaten with buttered black bread, and washed down with chilled aquavit or flavored vodka.

MARINADE AND HERRING

¾ cup white wine vinegar

½ cup water

10 black peppercorns

2 bay leaves

4 allspice berries

½ teaspoon mustard seeds

2 cloves

1 teaspoon sugar

1 small onion, thinly sliced

1 small carrot, peeled and diced

1½ pounds matjes herring fillets
    (don't substitute salt herring)

⅓ cup whole-grain mustard

¼ cup minced red onions

¼ cup chopped dill pickles

3 tablespoons small capers, drained

GARNISHES

Boston lettuce leaves

Diced cooked beets

Diced cooked potatoes

Dill sprigs

1 Place all the ingredients through the carrot in a small enameled saucepan and bring to a boil. Boil for 1 minute, then remove from the heat and cool to room temperature. Remove the carrots from the marinade and set aside.

2 Rinse the herring fillets under cold running water and pat dry with a paper towel.

3 Spread the skinless side of each fillet with some of the mustard. Place some of the red onions, chopped pickles, capers, and reserved carrots on each piece. Roll up and secure with a toothpick.

4 Place the rolls upright in a glass jar with a tight fitting lid and pour the marinade over them. Cover and refrigerate for 7 to 9 days. If the marinade doesn't cover the rolls, turn the jar once a day.

5 To serve, line a platter with the lettuce leaves and arrange the rollmops on top.

Garnish them with the beets, potatoes, and dill sprigs.

Makes 4 to 6 servings

"The man in the wilderness

asked me,

How many strawberries grew

in the sea?

I answered him, as I thought

good,

As many as red herrings grew

in the wood."

Traditional nursery rhyme

"The Best Appetizer Is Herring"

So wrote Anton Chekhov in *The Siren*, and I think most Russians would concur with the food-besotted character in this marvelous short story. A popular Russian song goes on to match herring with just the right partner: "If there only was vodka/And with it *seliodka*/ Then everything would be okay." Suffice it to say that no Russian get-together would be complete without the appearance of this much-beloved fish.

Although the common practice in Russia is to buy the  herring whole and fillet it yourself, it's much easier to bring home salt (schmaltz) herring fillets from a good delicatessen. They should be served in a long oval dish, accompanied by black bread, freshly boiled new potatoes with butter and dill, and, of course, plenty of chilled vodka, still viscous from the freezer.

Chopped Herring

Seliodochny Pashtet

I always find chopped herring most delicious when served on a square of buttered rye bread, topped with a slice of apple or cucumber to balance the salty flavor of the fish.

2 salt (schmaltz) herring fillets
1 cup milk
2 tablespoons water
2 tablespoons red wine vinegar
1½ slices white bread, crusts
    removed
1 small green apple, peeled, cored,
    and quartered

1 small onion, quartered
1 hard-cooked egg, quartered
1 tablespoon sour cream
1 tablespoon fresh lemon
    juice
¼ teaspoon sugar, or more
    to taste

1 Soak the herring in milk covered, in the refrigerator for 6 to 8 hours.

2 Pour the water and vinegar over the bread and let it stand for 10 minutes. Squeeze the bread to remove the excess liquid.

3 Rinse the herring, pat dry with paper towels, and cut into 1-inch pieces. Place the herring, bread, apple, onion, and egg in a food processor and process until the mixture is smooth but not overpuréed.

4 Transfer the mixture to a bowl and stir in the sour cream, lemon juice, and sugar. Taste and add more sugar, if desired. Cover and refrigerate for several hours.

Makes about 2 cups

Herring with Sour Cream Sauce

Seliodka pod Smetannim Sousom

An old world herring dish that is even more popular in the United States than it is in the Soviet Union. If you prefer your herring less salty, use matjes fillets instead of schmaltz.

2 salt (schmaltz) herring fillets
1 cup milk
1 small red onion, cut into thin rings
½ cup sour cream
3 tablespoons heavy or whipping cream

1 tablespoon white vinegar
½ teaspoon sugar
2 tablespoons chopped fresh dill for garnish

1 Soak the herring in milk, covered, in the refrigerator for 2 hours.

2 Rinse then pat dry with paper towels, and cut into 1-inch pieces. Place, along with the onion rings, in a glass or plastic jar with a lid.

3 In a small bowl, whisk together the sour cream, heavy cream, vinegar, and sugar. Combine with the herring and onion rings. Cover and refrigerate for several hours.

4 Arrange in a serving dish and serve sprinkled with dill.

Serves 8

Herring in Mustard Sauce

Seliodka pod Gorchichnim Sousom

Serve this herring, which has been gently marinated in a mustard vinaigrette, in a pretty oval dish or on pumpernickel squares, accompanied by icy cold vodka.

2 salt (schmaltz) herring fillets
1 cup milk
2 tablespoons cider vinegar
1 tablespoon Dijon mustard
¼ cup olive oil

¼ teaspoon sugar, or more to taste
⅛ teaspoon freshly ground black pepper
1 hard-cooked egg, finely chopped
2 tablespoons finely chopped scallions
   (green onions)

1 Soak the herrings in milk, covered, in the refrigerator for 6 to 8 hours.

2 Rinse and pat dry with paper towels. Cut the fillets into 1-inch pieces. Arrange the pieces on an oval dish side by side, skin side up.

3 In a small bowl, whisk together the vinegar and mustard. Gradually add the oil, whisking to incorporate completely. Whisk in the ¼ teaspoon sugar and the pepper. Taste and add more sugar, if desired.

4 Sprinkle the herring with the sauce, cover, and refrigerate for several hours.

5 Before serving, sprinkle with chopped egg and scallions.

Serves 8

Zakuski

". . . when you come in the table must be set, and when you sit down you tuck the napkin into your collar and you take your time about reaching for the vodka decanter. And mind you, you don't pour it into an ordinary wine glass, you don't treat a sweetheart that way! No. You pour it into something antique, made of silver, an heirloom, or into a quaint pot-bellied little glass with an inscription on it, something like this: 'As you clink, you may think, monks also thus do drink.' And you don't gulp it straight off, but you first sigh, you rub your hands together, you gaze nonchalantly at the ceiling, and only then, slowly, you raise it up to your lips, and at once sparks from your stomach flash through your whole body."

— Anton Chekhov, *The Siren*

Swordfish with Zesty Tomato Sauce

Riba pod Marinadom

In the Soviet Union this dish is usually made from cod, which at one time was particularly cheap and abundant. In New York, I once tried the recipe with some very good-looking swordfish steaks, and to my slight surprise, it turned out wonderfully. Although swordfish is not at all a Russian fish, its firm texture goes particularly well with this robust and flavorful sauce. This dish is better when made a day ahead.

2 pounds swordfish steaks not more than ¾ inch thick (you can also use cod or halibut)
½ cup olive oil

Juice of 1 lemon
Salt and freshly ground black pepper, to taste

SAUCE

3 tablespoons unsalted butter
2 large carrots, peeled and cut into julienne
1 parsnip, peeled and cut into julienne
2 large onions, chopped
1 large leek, white part only, well rinsed, patted dry, and chopped
1 can (6 ounce) tomato paste
1¾ cups Fish Stock (see Index)
Bouquet garni (2 bay leaves, 6 peppercorns, small piece of cinnamon stick, and 2 cloves tied in a cheesecloth bag)

3 tablespoons fresh lemon juice
1 teaspoon sugar
Salt and freshly ground black pepper, to taste
¼ cup chopped fresh dill
1½ tablespoons small capers, drained
Finely chopped fresh scallions (green onions) for garnish

1 Rub the fish steaks on both sides with olive oil, lemon juice, salt, and pepper. Let stand in a glass dish at room temperature for 1 to 2 hours. Remove the fish and save the marinade.

2 Preheat the broiler.

3 Cut the fish into 2-inch pieces. Broil the fish on both sides, 4 inches away from the heat, until done (approximately 4 minutes on each side), basting with the reserved juices. Place on a serving dish and set aside to cool.

4 To make the sauce, melt the butter in a large deep skillet over medium heat. Add the carrots, parsnip, onions, and leek, and sauté until the vegetables are soft and lightly colored, about 10 minutes.

5 In a bowl, dilute the tomato paste with the fish stock and stir until smooth. Add this to the vegetables and bring to a boil. Add the bouquet garni, reduce heat to low, cover, and simmer the mixture for 15 minutes.

6 Remove the bouquet garni and add the lemon juice and sugar. Season with salt and pepper and simmer for 2 minutes more. Remove from the heat and stir in the dill and capers.

7 Pour the sauce evenly over the fish, cool, and refrigerate for several hours. Serve sprinkled with scallions.

Serves 8 as an appetizer, 6 as a supper entrée

Stuffed Mussels

Midia Dolma

Dolma means "stuffed" in Turkish, and it's from Turkey that stuffed dishes are said to originate. The rice stuffing in this recipe is common in Armenia and Turkey and can be used to stuff chicken, fish, vegetables, or even such fruits as apples or quinces. This is a somewhat simplified version of the original recipe, in which raw mussels are stuffed with rice and then cooked. Cook the mussels and rice separately and just spoon the stuffing into the mussels. This saves a lot of time, and in my opinion the results taste just as good as the original.

30 large mussels (about 2 pounds),
    well scrubbed
2 cups water
3 sprigs parsley, tied together
Salt
⅓ cup olive oil
1 cup finely chopped onions
½ cup long-grain rice
3 tablespoons dried currants
4 canned tomatoes, drained and
    chopped
3 tablespoons fresh lemon juice
¼ cup pine nuts (pignoli)
½ teaspoon sugar
¼ teaspoon ground allspice
Large pinch of ground cinnamon
3 tablespoons chopped
    fresh parsley
Boston lettuce leaves for garnish
2 lemons cut into wedges
    for garnish

1 Rinse the mussels well under cold running water. Place in a bowl, add enough cold water to cover, and soak the mussels for 10 minutes. Place in a colander and rinse again. Beard the mussels right before cooking them.

2 Place the mussels in a pot with the water, parsley sprigs, and ½ teaspoon salt. Bring to a boil and steam the mussels until they open. Transfer the mussels in their shells to a large bowl, discarding the unopened ones. Strain the mussel broth through a sieve lined with a double thickness of cheesecloth. Reserve 1 cup of the broth.

Armenian Meza Buffet

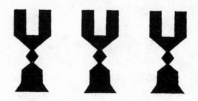

Spiced Feta

Zesty Eggplant Slices

Stuffed Mussels

Tiny Meatballs with Pine Nuts
and Raisins

White Bean Plaki

Armenian Pizza

Armenian Mixed Pickles

Salted Pistachio Nuts

Pita triangles

•

Raki or Ouzo

•

Butter Cookies

Farina Halvah

• • •

3 In a kettle, heat the oil over medium heat. Add the onions and sauté until softened, about 5 minutes. Add the rice and the currants and stir for 5 more minutes. Add the tomatoes, lemon juice, and the reserved mussel broth and bring to a boil. Reduce the heat to low, cover tightly, and simmer until the rice is tender and has absorbed all the liquid, about 15 minutes.

4 Off the heat, stir in the pine nuts, sugar, allspice, cinnamon, parsley, and season with salt. Let the mixture cool to room temperature.

5 Spoon some of the stuffing mixture into each mussel shell and arrange the mussels in a single layer on a serving platter lined with lettuce leaves. Scatter the lemon wedges among the mussels and serve.

Makes 6 to 8 servings

Caviar Tartlets

Tartaletki s Ikroy

These precious little puff pastry tartlets, filled with two or three kinds of caviar, will make an hors d'oeuvre fit for a Czar. The crème fraîche is actually optional. A true Russian will insist on pure caviar, of course. The decision is yours.

All-purpose flour for rolling out the
   pastry
1 sheet commercial puff pastry, preferably Pepperidge Farm
¼ to ⅓ cup Crème Fraîche (see Index)

2 teaspoons fresh lemon juice
1 tablespoon finely chopped fresh dill
3 to 4 ounces assorted caviars (black, salmon, and golden)
Tiny dill sprigs for garnish

1 Preheat the oven to 375°F.

2 On a lightly floured surface, roll out the pastry with a floured rolling pin to ⅛ inch thick. Use a 2-inch cookie cutter or a drinking glass to cut out 24 circles from the pastry. You may have to gather up the scraps and roll out the pastry again.

3 Press each circle into a cup of a small-cup (1½-inch size) muffin tin. Prick the bottoms of the tartlet shells with a fork, line each with aluminum foil, and fill with dried beans, pie weights, or rice. Bake until the edges are golden and the shells are baked through, about 15 minutes. (If they are not baked properly, remove the foil and pie weights, and bake for 5 minutes more. Cool completely and remove from the tins.

4 In a small bowl, mix together the crème fraîche, lemon juice, and dill. Spoon about ½ teaspoon of the crème fraîche mixture into each tartlet. Top with some caviar and garnish with a dill sprig.

Makes 24 tartlets

Smoked Salmon Vinaigrette

Vinegret iz Syomgi

This recipe is adapted from a wonderful cookbook published by Princess Kroptkina, one of the last hostesses in the grand Russo-French tradition. It makes a simple and elegant appetizer or first course.

6 ounces smoked salmon, sliced approximately ⅛ inch thick
3 medium-size red potatoes, boiled, cooled, and cut into ¼-inch dice
1 tablespoon minced red onion
1 tablespoon small capers
¼ cup sliced, pitted black olives

1½ tablespoons minced fresh dill
1 tablespoon tarragon vinegar
1 teaspoon Dijon mustard
3 tablespoons olive oil
Salt and freshly ground black pepper, to taste
Boston lettuce leaves for garnish

1 Cut the salmon into ¼-inch dice.

2 In a glass salad bowl, combine the salmon, potatoes, onion, capers, olives, and dill, mixing carefully with two salad

spoons so the potatoes don't crumble.

3 In a small bowl, whisk together the vinegar and mustard. Slowly dribble in the oil, whisking constantly until the dressing is creamy-thick. Season with salt and pepper.

4 Toss the dressing into the salad to coat it evenly, but avoid extra mixing. Cover and refrigerate for 2 hours.

5 Serve arranged on individual plates on the lettuce leaves.

Serves 2 to 3

Miniature Salmon Croquettes with Dill Mayonnaise

Pozharskie Kotletki iz Lososini

This is an appetizer version of a classic Russian entrée of crispy croquettes, which were once made from ground partridge meat with a sauce of wild mushrooms. Today the croquettes are prepared from a combination of chicken and veal, or occasionally, fresh salmon. So while my recipe here is but a distant cousin of the main course version — Chicken Cutlets Pozharsky — it's unquestionably an original in its own right.

You can make this dish into a light entrée (serving three to four) by shaping the mixture into regular 3-inch croquettes. Otherwise, serve as you would cocktail meatballs, with Dill Mayonnaise on the side. All they need for company is a light, dry white wine or a glass of Champagne.

⅓ cup heavy or whipping cream

2 slices white bread, crusts removed

1 pound skinless salmon fillets

3 tablespoons unsalted butter, softened

1 large egg yolk, lightly beaten

1 small onion, grated

¼ cup finely chopped fresh dill

Juice of ½ lemon

Salt and freshly ground black pepper, to taste

2 tablespoons unsalted butter

1 tablespoon vegetable oil

2 tablespoons all-purpose flour

Dill Mayonnaise (recipe follows)

1   Pour the cream over the bread and let stand for 5 minutes. Squeeze out any excess cream from the bread and tear the bread into small pieces.

2   Place the salmon in a bowl of a food processor and process at high speed just until the salmon flesh is finely minced but not puréed. Add the softened butter and process at low speed for 3 seconds.

A Seaside Zakuski Party

Caviar Tartlets

Miniature Salmon Croquettes with Dill Mayonnaise

Herring with Sour Cream Sauce

Smoked Sturgeon *Buterbrodi*

Sprat *Buterbrodi*

•

Lemon Vodka

Champagne

---

3   Transfer the salmon mixture to a bowl and stir in the bread, egg yolk, onion, dill, and lemon juice, and salt and pepper to taste. Knead into a smooth mixture and refrigerate, covered, for at least 1 hour.

4   Preheat the oven to 375°F.

5   Form the salmon mixture into balls the size of walnuts.

6   Heat the butter and oil in an ovenproof skillet over medium heat. Roll the balls lightly in flour and add them to the skillet. Sauté until lightly browned all over, about 5 minutes. Drain on paper towels. Wipe out the skillet.

7   Place the croquettes back in the skillet and bake until cooked through, about 10 minutes. Serve warm or at room temperature, accompanied by Dill Mayonnaise.

Makes 6 servings

Dill Mayonnaise

Maionez s Ukropom

1½ cups Homemade Mayonnaise
    (see Index)
1 cup chopped fresh dill
1 large clove garlic, finely minced
1 tablespoon capers, drained
2 tablespoons fresh lemon juice
2 tablespoons sour cream

Place all the ingredients in a food processor. Process until well blended, about 3 to 4 seconds.

Makes about 2 cups

Byelorussian Mushroom Croquettes

Gribniye Sicheniki

M ushroom picking is truly a national sport in the gorgeously wooded western republic of Byelorussia. One of the many fine Byelorussian dishes, these savory croquettes don't have to be made with wild mushrooms — commerically grown white mushrooms make a fair substitute. But if you're an ardent mushroom gatherer and live in New England, upstate New York, or Canada, try to make the effort to prepare these crispy croquettes from your pick of the day.

4 slices bacon

1 medium-size onion, chopped

3 slices white bread, crusts removed

⅓ cup milk

5 tablespoons unsalted butter

10 ounces fresh porcini (cèpes), chanterelle, or fresh white mushrooms

1 large clove garlic, minced

3 tablespoons finely chopped fresh parsley

1 large egg yolk, lightly beaten

1½ tablespoons mayonnaise, preferably Hellmann's

Salt and freshly ground black pepper, to taste

⅓ cup unflavored fine, dry bread crumbs

3 tablespoons vegetable oil

Lemon wedges for garnish

1 In a large skillet, fry the bacon over medium heat until crisp. Drain on paper towels, then crumble and set aside. Add the onion to the bacon fat and sauté over medium heat until golden, about 15 minutes. Set aside. Wipe out the skillet.

2 Meanwhile, soak the bread in the milk for 10 minutes. Squeeze the bread to remove any excess liquid and set aside.

3 In the same large skillet, melt 3 tablespoons of the butter over medium heat. Add the mushrooms and cook, stirring until they begin to throw off their liquid. Turn the heat up to high and continue to cook and stir until the mushrooms reabsorb all the liquid and are nicely browned, 12 to 15 minutes.

4 Place the mushrooms and onion on a cutting board, allow them to cool slightly, then finely mince them.

5 In a bowl, combine the mushrooms and onion with the bacon, bread, garlic, parsley, egg yolk, mayonnaise, and salt and pepper to taste. Mix thoroughly and form into 8 oval croquettes. Roll the croquettes in the bread crumbs.

6 Heat the oil and the remaining 2 tablespoons of butter in a large skillet over medium-high heat until they sizzle.

7 Fry until golden brown on all sides, 5 to 7 minutes. Serve warm, accompanied by lemon wedges.

Makes 4 servings

Lamb Liver and Red Pepper Salad

Arnavut Giger

I first tasted this dish in Turkey, where it is a mandatory feature on the *meza*, or appetizer table. But I was not surprised to learn that the Armenians also love it, and, as is common in this region of great culinary overlaps, have enthusiastically adopted it as their own. Although it's not particularly Turkish or Armenian to do so, the addition of half a diced yellow pepper will make the presentation of this dish more exciting.

2 tablespoons olive oil

1 pound lamb's liver, trimmed and
cut into ½-inch dice

¼ cup all-purpose flour, or as
needed

Salt, to taste

1 red bell pepper, cored, seeded,
and cut into ½-inch dice

½ yellow bell pepper, cored, seeded,
and cut into ½-inch dice

¼ cup finely chopped Italian (flat-
leaf) parsley, plus 1 tablespoon
for garnish

2 tablespoons fresh lemon juice

Freshly ground black pepper, to
taste

½ medium-size red onion, sliced into
thin rings

1 teaspoon sumakh or additional 1
tablespoon fresh lemon juice

1 In a heavy skillet, heat the olive oil.

2 Dust the liver pieces lightly with flour and sauté over medium-high heat until light brown but not overcooked, 2 to 3 minutes. Season with salt. With a slotted spoon, transfer the liver to paper towels to drain. Cool completely.

3 In a serving bowl, combine the liver with the bell peppers, ¼ cup parsley, and the lemon juice. Season with salt and pepper.

4 Arrange the onion on top of the salad, then sprinkle with sumakh or lemon juice and 1 tablespoon parsley. Serve at room temperature.

Makes 6 servings

Please Be Seated

I n the past, *zakuski* were served buffet style, but today's Russians wouldn't dream of standing to eat. In fact, they're the most dedicated table-huggers I know. When I invite Russian friends for dinner, we all squeeze around the table—no matter how many extra friends and relatives they've brought along as well. This simulates an intimacy to which most of us have long grown accustomed growing up as we did in the cramped confines of our Soviet apartments. The variety of *zakuski*, the ceaseless to-and-fro of col-orful plates and bowls, and the friendly competition for elbow and air space, all remind us of the spirited conviviality of a Moscow supper.

Salad Olivier in Tartlets

Salat Oliviye v Tartaletkakh

This classic Russian salad is known as Olivier in the Soviet Union, but simply as Russian salad everywhere else. It's one of the handful of Russian dishes to have joined that group of supposedly representative platters that make up "international cuisine." I'm always surprised when the salad crops up well prepared, since it seems to be on every hotel menu in both eastern and western Europe.

The salad is named for a French chef, once a chef to Czar Nicholas II, who became the proprietor of L'Ermitage, a Moscow nightclub fashionable in the 1860s and famous for its sumptuous gilded decor and immaculate French service. Because I have grown slightly weary of encountering the usual salad Olivier at almost every Russian gathering, I prefer to serve it in puff pastry shells or tartlets, which look beautiful and are easier to present and consume at a buffet. However, if you and your friends are not confronted with it three times a week, it will always be a hit on its own; and like most of the routinely overadvertised, underprepared, and standardized international dishes, you will soon find out exactly why it became so popular in the culinary world at large if you give it the careful preparation and presentation it warrants, though seldom receives. The salad recipe on its own will serve four to six.

All-purpose flour for rolling out the
    pastry
½ recipe Sour Cream Pastry (see Index)
2 tablespoons unsalted butter, melted
1 cup diced, cooked chicken breast
1 large potato, peeled, boiled, and
    cut into ½-dice
1 medium-size carrot, peeled,
    cooked, and cut into ½-inch dice

⅔ cup cooked green peas
1 medium-size red apple, cored and
    cut into ½-inch dice
1 large dill pickle, diced
2 hard-cooked eggs, chopped
2 tablespoons chopped fresh dill
Salt and freshly ground white
    pepper, to taste

DRESSING

½ cup Homemade Mayonnaise (see
    Index)
⅓ cup sour cream
1½ teaspoons Dijon mustard

1 tablespoon fresh lemon juice
½ teaspoon sugar
Grated zest of ½ lemon

Cherry tomatoes for garnish

1 Preheat the oven to 350°F.

2 On a floured surface, roll out the dough ⅛ inch thick. Cut into eight 4-inch rounds, using a cookie cutter.

3 Grease eight 3-inch tartlet pans with melted butter. Line the pans with the dough rounds. Trim and crimp the edges. Prick the bottom of the tartlet shells all over with a fork to prevent puffing. Line the shells with aluminum foil and fill with dried beans, pie weights, or rice. Bake until golden, 15 minutes. Remove the tartlet shells from the pans and cool on cake racks.

4 In a large bowl, combine the chicken, potato, carrot, peas, apple, pickle, eggs, and dill. Mix thoroughly and season with salt and pepper.

5 To prepare the dressing, combine all the ingredients in a small bowl, and mix thoroughly. Add the dressing to the salad and toss gently, being careful not to mash the ingredients.

6 Fill the cooled tartlet shells with the salad. Garnish with cherry tomatoes. Serve at once.

Makes 8 tartlets

Chicken with Walnut Sauce

Satsivi

No Georgian party is complete without this enormously popular cold dish, which is named for the *satsivi* (meaning "eaten cold") sauce which can also be served with poached chicken, turkey, fish, or eggplant. *Satsivi* is usually made in huge quantities, and I remember going to visit my Georgian friends two or three days after one of their notorious get-togethers just to dip hot flatbread into this exquisite sauce — the meat itself had long since disappeared. We reminisced about our grandmothers' "famous" *satsivis,* and argued long and hard over whether watercress makes an acceptable substitute for the local *tsistmat* and what the best herbs are to use for the *khmeli-suneli,* the particular blend of dried herbs for which all Georgians have their own "magic" combination. I recently traveled all the way across Georgia in search of the perfect *satsivi,* only to return to Moscow, where I sampled my father's version and had to admit that it tasted best. A case of the disciple outdoing the tradition.

As *satsivi* is really a party dish par excellence, the following recipe serves up to ten people. For a more elegant presentation, use about 2½ pounds poached chicken breasts, cut into medium-size pieces, and half the amount of sauce given in the recipe. The dish should be made a day ahead to allow the flavors to settle.

2 pounds chicken breasts with bone, well rinsed and patted dry
2 pounds chicken thighs, well rinsed and patted dry

2 quarts Chicken Stock (see Index) or canned broth

SAUCE

3½ cups walnut pieces
10 large cloves garlic, coarsely chopped
1 large bunch fresh cilantro, stems removed
1 small dried red chili pepper, chopped
½ teaspoon coarse (kosher) salt
3 tablespoons unsalted butter
3 large onions, finely chopped
1 tablespoon all-purpose flour
6 cups hot stock from cooking the chicken
3 large egg yolks

¾ teaspoon sweet Hungarian paprika
¼ teaspoon cayenne pepper, or more to taste
½ teaspoon ground fenugreek
¾ teaspoon ground coriander
Small pinch of ground cinnamon
¾ teaspoon ground tumeric
½ teaspoon dried tarragon
Salt to taste (optional)
3 tablespoons white vinegar
Walnut pieces for garnish
Cilantro sprigs for garnish

1 Combine the chicken and the stock in a large soup pot. Bring to a boil and skim off the foam as it rises to the top. Reduce the heat to low and simmer, covered, until the chicken is cooked, about 45 minutes. Strain out the chicken, reserving 6 cups of the stock for the sauce.

2 Cool the chicken until manageable, then remove and discard the skin. Remove all the meat from the bones and shred the meat into medium-size pieces. Set aside.

3 To make the sauce, finely grind the walnuts, garlic, cilantro, and chili pepper with the coarse salt in a food processor. You will probably have to do this in batches. Set aside.

4 Melt the butter in a large Dutch oven over medium heat. Add the onions and sauté until they just begin to color, about 8 to 10 minutes. Stir in the flour and cook, stirring for 1 minute more. Gradually stir in the chicken stock. Let simmer for 5 minutes without boiling.

5 Turn the heat down to low and gradually add the ground walnut mixture, stirring with a wooden spoon. Let simmer for 3 to 4 minutes.

6 Whisk the egg yolks in a small bowl, then stir in about a ladleful of the simmering mixture. Whisk the yolks into the sauce.

7 Add all of the spices, the tarragon, and salt, and let simmer without ever allowing the sauce to boil, about 10 minutes. Off the heat, stir in the vinegar.

8 Add the reserved chicken to the sauce and stir to coat. Cool to room temperature, cover, and refrigerate overnight.

9 To serve, remove from the refrigerator about 20 minutes before serving and carefully stir. Place the *satsivi* in a large serving bowl and garnish with walnut pieces and cilantro sprigs.

Serves 8 to 10

Georgian Extravaganzas

For the Georgians, a family get-together, a wedding, or a gathering of friends is the most important thing in the world. A simple everyday meal might consist only of fresh herbs wrapped in flatbread; but when a guest arrives, the Georgian table will suddenly be groaning with unimaginable bounty. Because a Georgian meal-for-guests will invariably stretch into the small hours of the morning, the vast majority of the dishes tend to be cold appetizers. These are accompanied by hot flatbreads, or *lavash*, platters of fresh herbs such as cilantro, parsley, and opal basil, as well as watercress, scallions, and beautiful fruit and vegetables, usually from the garden. The one hot dish might be a simple cheese bread or grilled chicken or lamb. The meal is washed down by some of the superb Georgian red wines, which are, again, often homemade.

Tiny Meatballs with Pine Nuts and Raisins

Kololik

Just when I thought I had tasted every conceivable kind of meatball, I came across this wonderful preparation in an old Armenian cookbook. And now, after a bit of updating and adapting, it's my favorite way to make meatballs. The combination of pine nuts, plump raisins, and aromatic herbs is emphatically Armenian, and will win over any palate. I prefer to use a combination of lamb and beef; beef alone can be somewhat bland, and lamb by itself doesn't sufficiently enliven the subtlety of the other ingredients.

Serve as part of a colorful Armenian *meza* buffet, with a yogurt and cucumber dip and Armenian flatbread or pita. Though I like them best with just a sprinkle of fresh lemon juice, these meatballs are also delicious with Sour Plum Sauce or with a tomato sauce, such as Quick Tomato Sauce (see the Index for the recipe page numbers).

2 tablespoons unsalted butter, or
  more if needed
2/3 cup chopped onion
2 cloves garlic, minced
1/3 cup golden raisins
1/3 cup pine nuts (pignoli)
10 ounces lean ground beef
8 ounces lean ground lamb
  shoulder
1 large egg, lightly beaten
2 tablespoons unflavored fine, dry
  bread crumbs
3 tablespoons ice water
1/4 teaspoon hot Hungarian paprika

1/8 teaspoon ground cinnamon
1/8 teaspoon ground allspice
1/4 cup finely chopped fresh
  cilantro
1/4 cup finely chopped fresh
  mint
Salt, to taste
1 tablespoon olive oil, or more if
  needed
3 tablespoons all-purpose flour,
  or more if needed
Lemon wedges for garnish
Mint sprigs for garnish

1 Melt 1 tablespoon of the butter in a medium-size skillet over medium heat. Add the onion and cook for 5 minutes. Stir in the garlic, raisins, and pine nuts and continue to cook, stirring, until the onion and pine nuts are lightly colored, 8 to 10 minutes. Set aside.

2 In a large bowl, combine the beef and lamb. Add the pine nut mixture, egg, bread crumbs, water, spices, herbs, and salt. (If you are not sure about the amount of salt, sauté a small piece of the mixture to taste for seasoning.) Mix thoroughly.

3 Have a bowl of cold water ready. Dipping your hands in the cold water to prevent the meat from sticking to your hands, form into meatballs the size of small walnuts.

4 Heat the oil and remaining 1 tablespoon butter over high heat until they begin to sizzle. Roll the meatballs lightly in flour. Sauté for 3 minutes, turning the meatballs to brown on all sides. Reduce the heat to low, cover, and cook for another 10 minutes, turning occasionally. If the meatballs don't all fit in your skillet you can fry them in batches, or in two skillets as appropriate. Adjust the amount of oil and butter as necessary.

5 Drain the meatballs on paper towels and arrange on a large platter. Garnish with lemon wedges and mint sprigs. Serve either hot or at room temperature.

Serves 8

Veal Kidneys in Madeira Sauce

Pochki s Maderoi

This sophisticated dish, so much sought after by the nineteenth-century St. Petersburg aristocracy, is, sadly, just a fond memory in present-day Russia, although in a pinch you can sometimes find it on the menu of one of the elegant Russian restaurants in Paris, or at the table of one of the widely scattered white Russian emigré families. Fortunately the recipe has survived, and we can now enjoy it at home as a fine appetizer or light supper entrée. A vintage Sercial Madeira makes an excellent accompaniment.

2 veal kidneys, about 1½ pounds

4 tablespoons (½ stick) unsalted butter

½ pound sliced fresh white mush-
*   rooms, thinly sliced*

3 scant tablespoons all-purpose flour

1 cup best-quality imported Madeira

⅔ cup Chicken Stock (see Index) or
*   canned broth*

½ cup Crème Fraîche (see Index) or
*   sour cream*

Generous pinch of freshly grated
*   nutmeg*

Salt and freshly ground black
*   pepper, to taste*

Chopped fresh parsley for
*   garnish*

1 Remove all membranes and fat from the kidneys with a small sharp knife, then soak the kidneys in cold water to cover for 45 minutes. Thoroughly pat dry and cut crosswise into ¼-inch strips.

2 Melt 2 tablespoons of the butter in a heavy skillet over medium heat. Add the mushrooms and sauté, stirring occasionally, until softened, 12 minutes. Remove from the skillet and place on a heated platter.

3 In the same skillet, melt the remaining butter over medium-low heat. Roll the kidneys in flour and turning to brown on all sides sauté gently until softened, 5 minutes. Place on the same platter as the mushrooms.

4 Pour the Madeira into the skillet and scrape the bottom with a wooden spoon. Raise the heat to high and let the Madeira boil until it reduces by half. Lower the heat and stir in the stock. Cook for 5 minutes. Add the crème fraîche and stir to blend.

5 Return the kidneys and mushrooms to the skillet. Stir to ensure that they are evenly coated with the sauce. Season with nutmeg, salt, and pepper and simmer, without boiling, 5 minutes.

6 Transfer the kidneys and the sauce to a decorative serving dish. Sprinkle with parsley and serve immediately.

Serves 6 as an appetizer

I n the Baltic republics, whose fisheries are world famous, the appetizer spread naturally includes a fabulous selection of fish dishes — smoked eel, anchovies, sprats, and many different herring combinations — as well as pickled mushrooms, cucumber and dill salad, the flavorful *Rassolye* (Potato and Herring Salad), and Estonian Jellied Veal *(Sult)* wonderfully suffused with garlic. These dishes are served with appetizing dark and rye breads, and with chilled vodka infused with caraway seeds — a flavoring that is also used in Scandinavian aquavit.

Cold Veal Meat Loaf with Horseradish Sauce

Veršienos Vyniotinis su Krienų Padažas

This is a Lithuanian dish that is tasty, elegant, and simple to make. Place a sauce dish in the middle of a large serving plate to hold the creamy horseradish accompaniment, and arrange the meat loaf slices on Boston lettuce leaves in an overlapping wheel around it.

2 slices white bread, crusts removed
¼ cup milk
1½ pounds ground veal, preferably shoulder
1 medium-size onion, grated
2 cloves garlic, minced
1 large egg, lightly beaten
¼ cup canned chicken broth
2 tablespoons finely chopped fresh parsley
Salt and freshly ground black pepper, to taste

3 hard-cooked eggs, peeled
2 medium-size dill pickles, quartered lengthwise
1 tablespoon mayonnaise, preferably Hellmann's
1½ tablespoons unflavored fine, dry bread crumbs
Generous pinch of sweet Hungarian paprika
Boston lettuce leaves for garnish
Horseradish Sauce (recipe follows)

1 Preheat the oven to 375° F.

2 Soak the bread in the milk for 5 minutes. Squeeze the bread to remove any excess milk.

3 In a large bowl, combine the bread with the veal, onion, garlic, lightly beaten egg, stock, and parsley. Mix thoroughly and season with salt and pepper.

4 On a baking sheet, spread out half of the meat mixture to form a rectangle 11 × 6 inches.

5 Place the hard-cooked eggs in a lengthwise row down the middle of the rectangle. Place the pickle quarters

Beyond a Condiment

The Slavs use horseradish so prodigously that it maintains a metaphoric presence in the Russian language. *Stariy khren,* "old horseradish," denotes a mean old man, while *khrenovo,* feeling "horseradishy," means that things could be going much better.

lengthwise in two neat rows 2 inches from the sides.

6 Spread the second half of the mixture on waxed paper or aluminum foil, to form a slightly larger rectangle than the first. Invert the paper or foil over the first half of the meat to cover it. Peel off the paper or foil and seal the edges of the meat securely.

7 Brush the meat loaf with the mayonnaise and sprinkle with bread crumbs and paprika. Bake until a toothpick comes out clean and the top is well browned, about 45 to 50 minutes.

8 Transfer the meat loaf to a serving platter, cool, then refrigerate for several hours.

9 Cut into fairly thin slices, arrange on a serving platter lined with lettuce leaves, and serve with Horseradish Sauce.

Makes 6 to 8 servings.

Horseradish Sauce
Krienų Padažas

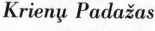

Horseradish is truly a favorite Slavic condiment, much preferred over mustard or tomato-based sauces. This sauce of mayonnaise, horseradish, mustard, and sour cream is a perfect accompaniment to cold ham, boiled beef, or tongue.

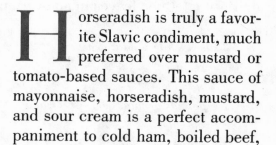

1 cup Homemade Mayonnaise (see Index)
⅓ cup sour cream
3 tablespoons prepared white horseradish, drained
1½ teaspoons whole-grain mustard
2 teaspoons cider vinegar
½ teaspoon sugar, or more to taste

Place all of the ingredients in a bowl and whisk until well blended. Taste and add more sugar, if desired. Cover and refrigerate for 1 hour before serving.

Makes about 1½ cups

Jellied Veal

Sult

Glistening aspics and jellied meats and fish are great favorites of the Baltic peoples. I like to serve this Estonian dish as the first course of an informal winter supper, along with marinated mushrooms, Sweet and Sour Beet Salad, rich, dark bread and plenty of iced vodka.

2 pounds boneless shoulder of veal, cut into 2-inch pieces

3 pounds calf's knuckles, cracked with a cleaver

3 quarts water

1 large onion, peeled

2 large carrots, peeled

1 large leek, white part only, well rinsed

1 rib celery with leaves

4 cloves garlic, sliced

Bouquet garni (6 parsley sprigs, 6 dill sprigs, 2 bay leaves and 8 black peppercorns tied in a cheesecloth bag)

Salt and freshly ground black pepper, to taste

2 large egg whites, lightly beaten

2 eggshells, crushed

1 packaged unflavored gelatin

2 cloves garlic, crushed in a garlic press

5 hard-cooked eggs, sliced lengthwise

Parsley sprigs for garnish

Horseradish Sauce (see facing page)

A selection of mustards (such as Dijon and whole-grain)

1 In a deep kettle, combine the veal, knuckles, and water and bring slowly to a boil. Cook, skimming the foam as it rises to the top, for 15 minutes.

2 Add the onion, 1 carrot, the leek, celery, sliced garlic, bouquet garni, and salt and pepper. Simmer over low heat, partially covered, for 2 hours.

3 Remove and discard the cooked carrot, and add the other carrot. Continue to simmer for 25 minutes or more.

4 With a slotted spoon, remove the veal shoulder and the second carrot from the stock and set aside to cool. Strain the stock into a clean pot and discard all the remaining solids.

5 When the veal is cool enough to manage, tear into shreds. Slice the carrot thin and reserve.

6 Reduce the stock by boiling it down over high heat to 6 cups. It will take about 20 minutes. Reduce the heat to medium low. Add the egg whites, eggshells, and gelatin and bring to a boil, whisking constantly. Reduce the heat to low and simmer until a foam forms on the surface. Slowly strain the stock through a colander lined with several thicknesses of dampened cheesecloth.

7 Season the stock with additional salt and pepper. Add the crushed garlic and the shredded veal. Let the mixture cool to room temperature, then cover and refrigerate until the mixture thickens to the consistency of unbeaten egg white, about 30 to 45 minutes.

8 Select a 2-quart rectangular mold at least 3 inches deep. Arrange the reserved carrot slices on the bottom of the mold. With a tablespoon, gradually add one-third of the veal and stock mixture, distributing it evenly throughout the mold. Arrange half of the sliced eggs lengthwise on the mixture. Add half the remaining veal and stock mixture and the rest of the eggs in the same fashion. Top with a layer of the remaining veal and stock and smooth the top with a rubber spatula. Cover with plastic wrap and refrigerate until the stock is set, 4 to 6 hours or overnight.

9 To unmold, run the tip of a knife or a metal spatula around the edge of the mold. Place the mold in hot water for 5 to 10 seconds. Tap to loosen. Place a rectangular serving platter over the mold and invert quickly to unmold.

10 Garnish with parsley sprigs and serve with Horseradish Sauce and the mustards.

Serves 8

Vol-au-Vents with Mushrooms and Sweetbreads

Volovani s Gribami

These *vol-au-vents* derive from a French recipe, which, like many others, was imported into Russia sometime in the eighteenth or nineteenth centuries — along with good doses of French culture and couture and the French language itself, all of which were much prized at the courts and in the wealthier Russian households. The Russians fill their *vol-au-vents* with brains instead of sweetbreads; but I prefer the French version — even though they don't usually use the fragrant wild mushrooms. When it comes to mushrooms, of course, I am wholeheartedly with the Russians.

Serve as part of an appetizer buffet, or as a starter for supper or lunch, followed by a veal or fish entrée.

2 pairs veal sweetbreads

1 ounce imported dried wild mush-
rooms, preferably porcini, well
rinsed

2 tablespoons fresh lemon juice

1 tablespoon unsalted butter

1 small onion, finely chopped

1 cup diced, cooked chicken
breast

3 tablespoons Chicken Stock (see
Index) or canned broth

Salt and freshly ground black
pepper, to taste

SAUCE

1 tablespoon unsalted butter

2 teaspoons all-purpose flour

1/2 cup Chicken Stock (see Index) or
canned broth

2 large egg yolks

1/3 cup heavy or whipping cream

Salt and freshly ground black
pepper, to taste

Pinch of freshly grated nutmeg

6 Pepperidge Farm puff pastry
shells, baked

3 tablespoons freshly grated Parme-
san cheese

Finely chopped fresh parsley for
garnish

1 Soak the sweetbreads in enough cold salted water to cover for 45 minutes. Rinse under cold running water and drain.

2 Soak the mushrooms in 1 cup lukewarm water for 2 hours. Drain, squeeze dry, chop fine, and set aside. Discard the soaking liquid or save for another use.

3 Bring 1 quart of water to a boil and add the lemon juice. Drop the sweetbreads into the water, cover, reduce heat, and simmer for 15 minutes. Remove from the water, drain, and cool until manageable.

4 Holding the sweetbreads under cold running water, remove all the membranes and tubules. Pat dry with paper towels. Cut the sweetbreads into ½-inch cubes.

5 Melt the butter in a medium-size skillet over medium heat. Add the mushrooms and onion and sauté for 10 minutes. Add the chicken and the sweetbreads and sauté, stirring, until heated through for another 2 to 3 minutes.

6 Add the stock, reduce the heat to low, cover, and simmer for another 5 minutes. Remove from the heat, season with salt and pepper, and set aside.

7 Preheat the oven to 350°F.

8 To make the sauce, melt the butter in a medium-size saucepan over medium-low heat. Sprinkle in the flour and cook, stirring, until the mixture foams, without letting it brown.

9 Remove from heat and beat in the stock, a little at a time, stirring until the mixture is smooth. Return to heat and simmer for 1 minute.

10 In a small bowl, beat the egg yolks with the cream. Whisk in some of the hot sauce. Stir this mixture into the remaining sauce. Stir over low heat for 3 to 4 minutes without allowing it to boil.

11 Stir the sweetbread mixture into the sauce. Season with salt and pepper and a pinch of nutmeg. Stir over low heat for 1 to 2 minutes.

12 Place the puff pastry shells on a buttered baking sheet. Fill with the sweetbread mixture. Sprinkle with Parmesan cheese and bake until the filling is lightly browned and bubbly, 10 minutes. Serve warm, sprinkled with parsley.

Serves 6

Soups

SUPI

Shchi is a meat soup, not the ordinary, unexcusably horrible meat soup, but a wondrous Russian meal made with various kinds of meat, egg, sour cream and herbs . . . It seems to me unthinkable to eat anything else after shchi.

— Knut Hamsun

In many ways, this was the most difficult chapter to write. Not because Soviet soups are inferior in quality to the other great soups of the world — in fact, it was just the opposite. We found it almost impossible to pick and choose among the hundreds of exotic and flavorful preparations from around the USSR. While we were confident that the most sophisticated lamb dishes were to be found in the Caucasus and Central Asia, the best pork dishes in the Ukraine and the Baltic states, and a thrilling variety of pilafs and rice dishes in Azerbaijan and Central Asia, it was extremely difficult to discriminate in this way between the great regional soups of the Soviet Union.

There are outstanding offerings from almost every corner of this vast nation — endless subtle variations of ruby-red borscht from the Ukraine; renowned Russian soups such as the wonderful clear fish soup, *ukha*, or the hearty cabbage soup, *shchi*; soups made with fragrant wild mushrooms from Byelorussia and Lithuania; and soups from Azerbaijan deliciously infused with saffron and other Middle Eastern spices. But, that's not all — Georgia and Armenia have a range of preparations that can top even these: Georgia is the home of *kharcho*, a soup of beef and rice, enlivened with a dozen local spices and made tart with tomatoes and sour plums; Armenia's flavorful lentil soups temptingly range from pungent and substantial to sweetish and delicate.

Enjoy the selection here; it reflects this nation's extraordinary diversity and richness to the full.

HOT SOUPS

Saffron Lamb Broth

Zaferanli Bulion

A rich lamb broth of intense color and flavor, enlivened by specks of saffron and sprinkled with fresh tarragon. Azerbaijanis sometimes add two or three chestnuts to each bowl. Rich, homemade chicken or beef stock can also be used for this recipe. Serve the broth in pretty ceramic cups.

6 cups homemade Lamb Stock (see Index)

1 large egg white

1 eggshell, crushed

1¼ teaspoons saffron threads, crushed in a mortar, plus about ¼ teaspoon whole saffron threads for garnish

Salt and freshly ground black pepper, to taste

Cooked chestnuts for garnish (optional)

Chopped fresh tarragon for garnish

1 Bring the stock to a simmer in a large soup pot over medium heat. Simmer for 3 minutes. Add the egg white and shell and raise the heat to medium-high. Bring to a boil, beating constantly with a wire whisk. When the stock boils, the egg white will start rising to the surface. At this point, turn off the heat and let stand for 5 minutes.

2 Line a colander with a double layer of dampened cheesecloth and strain the broth into a clean pot.

3 Stir the crushed saffron into 2 tablespoons stock in a small bowl and let stand for 5 minutes.

4 Season the stock with salt and pepper, stir in the diluted saffron, and simmer over low heat for 3 minutes.

5 Ladle the broth into cups and add a few chestnuts to each, if desired, plus a few saffron threads and fresh tarragon. Serve at once.

Serves 6 to 7

 ## Soup to Start

Old Russia—before Peter the Great—was a place of gargantuan feasts that boasted literally dozens of elaborately prepared dishes, stacked high on the endless banqueting tables of the courts. Among these no less than a third tended to be soups and broths accompanied by dozens of differently filled and whimsically shaped pies. Light, European-style first-course soups (consommés, clear soups, and soups puréed with cream) gained their first foothold in Russia through the courts of Catherine the Great, though their popularity peaked in the mid-nineteenth century. But while these pre-entrée soups became an important part of the aristocratic dinner ritual, they were never really incorporated into the culinary lifestyle of the urban middle classes or the Russian peasantry, both of whom preferred to stick to their Slavic traditions. Today first-course soups and consommés are enjoyed, especially chicken bouillon, a staple both at home and in restaurants, but they are invariably made more substantial by means of such accompaniments as quenelles, *pirozhki*, or larger pies such as *pirog* or *kulebiaka*.

Pomegranate Broth

Narli Bulion

Another broth from Azerbaijan, this one is refreshingly light yet tart, and studded with pomegranate seeds and fresh mint. With its subtle hint of the Middle East, it is an intriguing beginning to a meal.

5 cups Chicken Stock (see Index) or
canned broth
1⅓ cups fresh or bottled pomegranate juice

Salt and freshly ground black
pepper, to taste
½ cup pomegranate seeds for garnish
Chopped fresh mint for garnish

1 In a soup pot, bring the chicken stock to a simmer over medium heat.

2 Place the pomegranate juice in a small non-aluminum pan and reduce over high heat to ½ cup, 10 to 15 minutes. Stir the juice into the stock and season with salt and pepper.

3 Serve garnished with pomegranate seeds and mint.

Serves 6

Classic Russian Cabbage Soup

Shchi

In old Russia of the sixteenth and seventeenth centuries, there were endless varieties of *shchi* — *shchi* made with meat, with fish, kasha, barley, sorrel, and so on. Like borscht in the Ukraine, it was the main staple of a family's diet, rich and poor alike. Wealthier households would enjoy a rich stock made from meats or fish; poorer kitchens would prepare a *shchi* just from sauerkraut or cabbage.

My version is made with a combination of cabbage and sauerkraut, which are simmered in broth before they are added to the soup. Remember that *shchi*, like so many Slavic soups, tastes better on the following day — and even better on the day after that. So, make it in advance if you can, and don't bother with a main course. Although Russians eat their *shchi* with sour cream, it doesn't really need it, as it's already quite tart. Decide for yourself. Either a good German beer or a two to three year old Alsatian Riesling makes a perfect accompaniment and a slice of pumpernickel or rye bread is a must.

8 to 10 imported dried wild mushrooms (preferably porcini), well
rinsed

STOCK

3 pounds beef brisket
1½ to 2 pounds beef marrow bones
10 cups water
1 large onion
1 medium-size carrot, peeled
1 rib celery with leaves

1 parsnip, peeled
Bouquet garni (8 dill sprigs, 8
    parsley sprigs, 3 bay leaves,
    and 8 peppercorns tied in a
    cheesecloth bag)
Salt, to taste

SOUP

6 tablespoons (¾ stick) unsalted
    butter
4 cups shredded green cabbage
2½ cups packaged sauerkraut (not
    canned), rinsed under cold run-
    ning water and drained well
2 tablespoons tomato paste
1 medium-size carrot, peeled and cut
    into julienne
1½ cups chopped onions
1 rib celery, chopped

1 large purple turnip, peeled and
    diced
1 can (16 ounces) Italian plum
    tomatoes, drained, seeded, and
    coarsely chopped
Salt and freshly ground black
    pepper, to taste
1 large clove garlic, minced
Chopped fresh dill for
    garnish
Sour cream for garnish (optional)

1 Soak the dried mushrooms in 1 cup water for 2 hours. Drain the mushrooms, pat dry with paper towels, chop fine, and set aside. Discard the liquid or save for another use.

2 To make the stock, in a large soup pot, bring the meat, bones, and water to a boil over high heat, periodically skimming off the foam as it rises to the top. Add the remaining stock ingredients, and reduce the heat to low. Simmer, covered, until the meat is tender, about 2 hours.

3 Meanwhile, melt half the butter in a deep skillet over medium heat. Add the cabbage and sauerkraut and sauté for 10 minutes, tossing and stirring regularly. Add 1 cup hot stock (it doesn't have to be fully cooked) and the tomato paste. Cover and simmer over low heat for 35 to 40 minutes.

4 Melt the remaining butter in another large skillet and sauté the carrot, onions, celery, turnip, and mushrooms until soft and lightly browned, about 15 minutes.

5 When the stock is ready, strain it into a clean pot. Reserve the meat and discard the other solids.

6 Add the sauerkraut and cabbage, the vegetable mixture, and tomatoes to the stock. Season with salt and pepper, stir, and cook, covered, over medium-low heat for 20 minutes.

7 Cut the meat into bite-size pieces and add it to the soup, along with the minced garlic. Simmer for another 5 minutes.

8 Let stand for at least 15 minutes and preferably 24 hours before serving; refrigerate, covered, and reheat slowly if serving the next day. Serve garnished with dill and sour cream, if desired.

Serves 10

*S*hchi is the great soup of the Russian people; it is as rich and robust as the earth itself. But, there are few references to this dish in the literature of travel, so often written by Westerners in search of the exotic, the unusual, or the undiscovered. There is, however, one notable (and eccentric) exception to this, in Lewis Carroll's 1867 *Journal of a Tour in Russia.* Carroll offers an ironic, tongue-in-cheek narrative of his visit to Moscow and St. Petersburg, peppered with odd asides and much preoccupied with down-to-earth, everyday experiences.

The whole of the country from the Russian frontier to Petersburg was perfectly flat and uninteresting, except for the occasional apparition of a peasant in the normal fur cap, tunic and belt, and now and then a church with a circular dome and four little domes set round it, the tops painted green and the whole thing looking (as our friend said) very like a cruet-stand.

Carroll first tasted *shchi* (or *shtshee*, as he quaintly spelled it) at a station en route from Germany to St. Petersburg and found it "quite drinkable, though it contained some sour element, which perhaps is necessary for Russian palates." He noted that the "proper accompaniment" should be "a jug of sour cream to be stirred into it." Later, in Moscow, at the restaurant Moscow Traktir, he evidently becomes accustomed to the special taste of *shchi* and it features in his appreciative account of the "genuine Russian dinner" he enjoyed there.

"Borscht: The center of everything"
— Ukrainian Proverb

Although this crimson beet soup is eagerly adopted and sometimes even claimed as their own by the Russians, Poles, Lithuanians, and other nationalities (I even found a borscht recipe in a classic Italian cookbook), its strongest associations are with the Ukraine, where it's thought to have originated back in the fourteenth century. As you can imagine, the ingredients and methods of preparation vary greatly according to country, republic, city, and cook. However, the staple ingredient is always the luscious red beet that gives the dish its characteristic color and flavor, as well as its name borscht derives from the Old Slavonic (*brsh* — meaning, of course, "beet").

In a Ukrainian village home, borscht has always been more than just a soup; it usually constituted the mainstay of a family's whole diet. And justly so, for a proper borscht should include as many as twenty ingredients and ought to be thick enough for a spoon to stand up in it. Borscht was usually prepared in enormous quantities for the weeks ahead, and the capacious borscht pot sat right in the middle of the dining table, the great altar of domesticity. The whole family would assemble at meal times, each clutching his or her own wooden spoon with its distinctive marking. Meat from the borscht was the most desirable ingredient and in times of shortage was strictly distributed according to age and rank.

The women who prepared the soup had to be skillful cooks (in the Ukraine a woman's domestic qualities are judged by her borscht), and while we can buy borscht at the local supermarket, it's still worth the effort to prepare it in the best Ukrainian tradition.

Classic Ukrainian Borscht

Borshch

A proper Ukrainian borscht should include pork or ham and other meats — the more meat, the better — try making it with beef short ribs or pork ribs, adding some diced ham or smoked kielbasa at the end. Also important for a good borscht, is to prepare the stock and vegetables correctly, strictly observing the proper order in which the ingredients are added — there's nothing worse than soggy cabbage or undercooked potatoes. The amount of sugar included is a source of great dispute among borscht-lovers. Some like it sweet and mild, others, myself included, prefer it tart and zesty. Adjust the amount of sugar and lemon juice to suit your taste. You can't go wrong.

Like many Slavic soups, borscht should be served with sour cream, added separately but thoroughly mixed in by each diner. Borscht tastes better the next day, so make enough to enjoy the leftovers.

STOCK

1½ pounds beef chuck, shank, or flank

1 meaty ham bone (about 1 pound)

2 beef marrow bones (about 1 pound)

3 quarts water

1 onion

1 carrot, peeled

2 medium-size parsnips, peeled

1 rib celery with leaves

Bouquet garni (3 dill sprigs, 3 parsley sprigs, 4 bay leaves, and 10 black peppercorns tied in a cheesecloth bag)

Salt, to taste

SOUP

2 large beets (about 1¼ pounds)

4 medium-size boiling potatoes, peeled and cut into large pieces

1 pound fresh, ripe plum tomatoes, peeled and chopped, or 1 can (16 ounces) plum tomatoes, drained and chopped

Salt, to taste

¼ cup vegetable oil

1 large onion, chopped

1 large carrot, peeled and cut into julienne

1 large green bell pepper, cored, seeded, and diced

4 cups shredded green cabbage

¼ cup fresh lemon juice, or more to taste

3 tablespoons tomato paste

5 to 6 pitted dried prunes, chopped

1 teaspoon sugar, or to taste

Freshly ground black pepper, to taste

4 cloves garlic, minced

2 strips fried bacon, crumbled (optional)

3 tablespoons chopped fresh parsley, plus additional for garnish

3 tablespoons chopped fresh dill, plus additional for garnish

Sour cream

1 Preheat the oven to 375°F.

2 In a large soup pot, bring the meat, bones, and water to a boil over high heat, periodically skimming off the foam as it rises to the top.

3 Add the remaining stock ingredients and reduce the heat to low. Simmer, partially covered, until the meat is tender, at least 45 minutes.

4 Meanwhile, wash and dry the beets and wrap each one separately in aluminum foil. Bake the beets until tender, 1¼ hours.

5 Allow the beets to cool until manageable, then stem and peel them and cut into julienne or fine dice.

6 When the stock is ready, remove the beef, ham bone, and marrow bones, and set all but the marrow bones aside. Strain the stock through a fine sieve into a clean pot and discard all the solids.

7 Bring the stock to a boil, add the potatoes and tomatoes, and season with salt. Reduce the heat and simmer until the potatoes are almost tender, about 10 minutes.

8 While the vegetables are cooking, heat the oil in a large skillet over medium heat. Add the onion, carrot, and green pepper, and sauté over medium heat until the onion and green pepper are slightly softened, 5 minutes. Stir in the cabbage and continue to sauté the vegetables, stirring occasionally, until the cabbage is softened, 10 min-

utes more. Add the vegetables to the soup.

9 Sprinkle the beets with ¼ cup lemon juice and add them to the soup. Stir the soup and simmer, uncovered, for 5 to 7 minutes.

10 Add the tomatoes, tomato paste, and prunes. Season to taste with sugar, pepper, and additional lemon juice and salt, if desired. Simmer for another 7 minutes.

11 Cut the beef into bite-size pieces and scrape all the meat off the ham bone. Add both meats to the soup.

12 Remove the borscht from the heat and sprinkle with the minced garlic, bacon (if desired), and 3 tablespoons each parsley and dill. Let stand for at least 15 minutes before serving. Serve garnished with additional chopped fresh herbs and pass the sour cream.

Serves 12 to 14

Toil and Trouble

In the Ukraine, the women who prepared borscht, at one time, had to observe all the appropriate rituals and to watch out for omens. A coal dropped from the stove meant that a guest would arrive from far away; a borscht made on a Thursday signaled that the devil himself would come to bathe in it, a pot left forgetfully unturned during cooking betokened troubled times for the whole family.

Borscht with Apples and Beans

Chernihivskiy Borshch

Chernihov is a beautiful ancient Ukrainian city, home of a legendary folk warrior who was famous for his physical strength. So there must have been something special in the soup he ate!

This version, however, is somewhat lighter and healthier than the original strong-man food. The vegetables are not sautéed before being adding to the stock, and the beans, tart apples, and zucchini add an unexpected twist to a familiar — at least to us Russians — flavor. This borscht can also be vegetarian, in which case use 7 to 8 cups Vegetable Stock (see Index), and start with Step 2.

STOCK

*2 pounds beef chuck or shin, with
    the bone*

2 quarts water

1 small onion

1 carrot, peeled and quartered

1 leek (white part only), well rinsed

1 parsnip, peeled

1 rib celery with leaves

*Bouquet garni (6 parsley sprigs, 4 dill
    sprigs, 2 bay leaves, and 8 pepper-
    corns tied in a cheesecloth bag)*

Salt, to taste

SOUP

2 large beets (about 1¼ pounds)

*3 tablespoons white vinegar, or more
    to taste*

*2 large boiling potatoes, peeled and
    cut into wedges*

*2 cups coarsely grated green
    cabbage*

*1 pound fresh, ripe tomatoes,
    peeled, seeded, and coarsely
    chopped*

*2 medium-size tart apples (such as
    Granny Smith), cored, peeled,
    and cut into wedges*

2 small zucchini, cut into ½-inch dice

1½ cups cooked white beans

2 cloves garlic, minced

*Salt and freshly ground black
    pepper, to taste*

Sour cream

Chopped fresh dill for garnish

1 In a large soup pot, bring all the stock ingredients to a boil over high heat, periodically skimming off the foam as it rises to the top. Cover the pot, reduce the heat to low, and simmer until the beef is tender, 1½ hours.

2 Strain the stock through a fine sieve into a clean pot. Reserve the beef and discard the other solids.

3 Add the beets to the stock and cook over medium heat until tender, about 30 minutes. Remove the beets from the stock and cool until manageable. Peel the beets and cut into fine dice.

4 Return the beets to the pot along with 2 tablespoons vinegar, the potatoes, cabbage, and tomatoes. Simmer, partially covered, for 20 minutes.

5 Add the apples and zucchini, and continue simmering until the vegetables are tender, 15 minutes more.

6 Remove the meat from the bones and cut into bite-size pieces. Add it to the soup, along with the beans and garlic; season with salt and pepper and add more vinegar, if desired. Simmer for 5 minutes more.

7 Allow the borscht to stand at least 10 minutes before serving. Serve with sour cream sprinkled with dill.

Serves 8

Sour Cream

Most Slavic soups — such as borscht, *shchi*, *solianka*, and various mushroom soups — are traditionally served with sour cream (smetana). This not only slightly thickens the soup, but it provides just the right touch of tartness to enliven the root vegetables that provide the body of these soups. Many Slavs, myself included, will not eat a bowl of borscht without a good dollop of sour cream — indeed, we would rather make another trip to the store to replenish our sour cream stock than do without the smell, texture, and flavor of this chief-of-accompaniments. Remember that sour cream should always be added individually at the table, *never* premixed into the soup pot; otherwise it will curdle if the soup is reheated, and it will not produce the precise tart taste we crave. Sour cream also has to be well stirred into the soup — so don't let it sit on top of the bowl like a melting snowball. Pass the sour cream around in a pretty dish, sprinkled with chopped fresh dill and parsley.

My Mother's Super-Quick Vegetarian Borscht

Vegetariansky Borshch Moyei Mami

This is a frugal borscht my mother can whip up in just half an hour or so, and for my money it's as good as any thirty-ingredient borscht that takes half a day. It's more of a soup than classic Ukrainian borscht, which is a meal in itself. If you want to serve this borscht on the day it's made, allow at least 2 to 3 hours for the flavors to settle; or, easiest of all perhaps, make it the day before. If you are not a vegetarian, use chicken stock instead of vegetable. My mother adds the vegetables to the pot as she chops and grates them.

6 tablespoons (¾ stick) unsalted
    butter
1 large onion, finely chopped
1 large carrot, peeled and
    grated
1 large green bell pepper, cored,
    seeded, and cut into
    ¼-inch dice
3½ cups shredded green cabbage
1 medium-size beet, peeled and
    grated
1 small rib celery, cut into ¼-inch
    dice
½ tart apple, cored and cut into
    1-inch dice
2 medium-size boiling potatoes,
    peeled and cut into 1½-inch
    cubes

1 can (6 ounces) tomato paste
4 cloves garlic, minced
2 quarts Vegetable Stock, Chicken
    Stock (see Index for both),
    canned broth, or water
Bouquet garni (1 bay leaf and 8
    peppercorns tied in a cheesecloth
    bag)
1 teaspoon sweet Hungarian
    paprika
Salt and freshly ground black
    pepper, to taste
½ teaspoon sugar, or more to taste
1 tablespoon fresh lemon juice, or
    more to taste
Chopped fresh parsley for garnish
Chopped fresh dill for garnish
Sour cream

1 Melt the butter in a large soup pot over medium heat. Add the onion, carrot, and bell pepper and sauté until the onion and bell pepper are slightly softened, 5 minutes.

2 Stir in the cabbage, beet, and celery and continue to sauté, stirring and tossing occasionally, 10 to 15 minutes.

3 Stir in the apple, potatoes, tomato paste, and garlic, then add the stock and bouquet garni and bring to a boil. Reduce the heat and simmer, covered, for 20 minutes.

4 Add the paprika, salt and pepper, sugar, and lemon juice to taste. Let stand at least 2 to 3 hours, or overnight. Remove the bouquet garni before serving. Serve garnished with parsley and dill, and pass the sour cream.

Serves 8

Georgian Beef and Rice Soup

Kharcho

When I asked an old man, a celebrated cook in the Georgian community, for the recipe of his outstanding *kharcho*, I was gratified when he readily agreed to share it with me. "Take the meat," he said, "wash it, put it in a pot, and add everything else according to taste. . . ." The following is an reworked version of the old man's recipe!

The Georgians in Georgia use *tklapi*, a very tart dried sour plum roll to make the soup tart. Georgian emigrés substitute with tamarind concentrate (available at Indian groceries). If you can find neither, don't despair — use lemon juice instead. And note that the more herbs you put in, the better the soup gets.

1½ pounds boneless lean beef (flank
   or first-cut brisket)

7½ cups Beef Stock (see Index) or
   canned broth

3 tablespoons unsalted butter

2 medium-size onions, finely
   chopped

1 tablespoon all-purpose flour

2½ tablespoons tomato paste

6 large, fresh, ripe plum tomatoes,
   peeled, seeded, and finely
   chopped

¼ cup long-grain rice

¼ teaspoon dried tarragon

¼ teaspoon dried basil

¼ teaspoon dried mint

1½ teaspoons sweet Hungarian
   paprika

¼ to ½ teaspoon dried red pepper
   flakes

¾ teaspoon coriander seeds,
   crushed

¼ teaspoon ground fenugreek

2 teaspoons tamarind concentrate,
   diluted in ¼ cup hot stock, or 3
   tablespoons fresh lemon juice, or
   more to taste

3 large cloves garlic, crushed in a
   garlic press

¼ cup walnut pieces, ground in a
   food processor

Salt, to taste

1 cup mixed chopped fresh herbs
   (choose from tarragon, cilantro,
   parsley, basil, dill), or more to
   taste

About *Kharcho*

In the last twenty years or so, *kharcho* has become one of the most widely served soups in the whole USSR, rivaled only by Ukrainian borscht. You can find it everywhere, from the humble workers' cafeterias (*stolovaya*), which are as ubiquitous as hamburger joints in America, to the most exclusive Caucasian restaurants in Moscow and other major cities.

The recipe has undergone countless subtle and less subtle changes as it has winged its way around the Soviet Union. Most important is the tendency of the Russians to substitute lamb, which they envisage as more appropriate for a Caucasian dish, for the original beef. Personally, I prefer the lighter taste of the beef, but try it both ways and choose your favorite.

1 In a large soup pot, bring the meat and stock to a boil over high heat, periodically skimming off the foam as it rises to the top. Reduce the heat and simmer, partially covered, until the meat is very tender, about 1½ hours. Remove and reserve the meat.

2 Melt the butter in a medium-sized skillet over medium heat. Add the onions and sauté, stirring occasionally, until softened and colored, about 10 minutes.

3 Stir in the flour and cook, stirring, for 1 minute. Add about ½ cup of the stock and stir until smooth. Add the tomato paste and tomatoes. Whisk the contents of the skillet back into the pot. Add the rice and simmer, covered, for 10 minutes.

4 Add the remaining ingredients, except for the fresh herbs, and simmer until the rice is tender, another 10 to 15 minutes.

5 Remove the soup from the heat. Cut the meat into bite-size pieces. Add it to the soup along with ¼ cup of the fresh herbs, and let stand for 10 minutes. Right before serving, add the remaining fresh herbs.

Serves 8

Thick and Hearty Lamb Soup

Shurpa

This soup, loaded with chunks of lamb and autumnal vegetables, and generously spiced with cumin and chili pepper, is a trademark of Central Asian cuisine. It also works well with beef. Serve Steamed Cilantro Buns (see Index) alongside for a great cool weather lunch.

¼ *cup olive oil*

1½ *pounds stewing lamb, cut into 1½-inch chunks*

1 *cup chopped onions*

9 *cups Beef Stock (see Index), or canned broth*

1 *large purple turnip, peeled and cut into ½-inch dice*

1 *large zucchini, cut into ½-inch dice*

2 *carrots, peeled and cut into ½-inch dice*

2 *large green bell peppers, cored, seeded, and cut into strips*

1½ *pounds fresh, ripe plum tomatoes, peeled, seeded, and coarsely chopped*

1½ *teaspoons cumin seeds*

2 *small hot dried chili peppers*

1 *teaspoon coriander seeds, crushed*

1 *can (16 ounces) chick-peas, well drained*

Salt, to taste

2 *tablespoons white vinegar, or more to taste*

½ *cup chopped fresh cilantro for garnish*

1 Heat the oil in a heavy soup pot over high heat. Add the lamb and brown lightly, stirring occasionally, for 5 minutes. Add the onions and continue to cook until the lamb is thoroughly browned and the onions are softened and colored, about 7 minutes more.

2 Spoon off all the fat from the pot, then add the stock, and bring to a boil. Reduce the heat to low, cover, and simmer until the lamb is tender, about 1¼ hours.

3 Refrigerate the soup, uncovered, until the fat rises to the surface, about 40 minutes. Skim the fat away.

4 Bring the soup to a boil over medium heat and add the turnip, zucchini, carrots, peppers, tomatoes, cumin seeds, chilis, and coriander. Cook, covered, for 20 minutes. Add the chick-peas and cook for 10 minutes more.

5 Remove the chili peppers from the soup and add salt and 2 tablespoons vinegar. Taste and add more salt and vinegar, if desired. Let stand, covered, for 10 minutes.

6 Serve the soup garnished with plenty of cilantro.

Serves 6 to 8

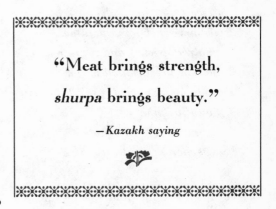

"Meat brings strength, *shurpa* brings beauty."

—Kazakh saying

Azerbaijani Meatball Soup

Kiufta Bozbash

In this Persian-influenced soup, the meatballs contain a wonderful surprise — they are stuffed with sour plums. If you have a source for dried sour cherries, you can also use them as a stuffing. The soup becomes a one-dish meal in Azerbaijan, when steamed Basmati rice is spooned into the bowl of soup.

MEATBALLS

6 ounces lean ground lamb

6 ounces lean ground beef

¼ cup long-grain rice

1 small onion, grated

1 large egg, lightly beaten

3 tablespoons chopped fresh parsley

¼ cup finely chopped fresh mint

Salt and plenty of freshly ground
   black pepper, to taste

12 pitted dried prunes, or 24 pitted
   dried cherries

SOUP

6 cups Lamb Stock or Beef Stock
   (see Index for both)

2 medium-size boiling potatoes,
   halved, peeled, and cut into wedges

2 tablespoons unsalted butter

1 medium-size carrot, peeled and cut
   into julienne

1 large onion, finely chopped

⅛ teaspoon ground turmeric

1 cup drained canned chick-peas

Salt and freshly ground black
   pepper, to taste

¼ teaspoon saffron threads, crushed
   in a mortar

2 tablespoons chopped fresh tarragon

2 tablespoons chopped fresh mint

Sumakh for garnish (optional)

Cooked Basmati rice (optional)

1 To make the meatballs, combine the lamb, beef, rice, onion, egg, parsley, mint, and salt and pepper in a large bowl. Mix thoroughly, cover, and refrigerate for 20 minutes.

2 Have a bowl of cold water ready. Divide the meat into 12 portions and form into balls. Dip your hands in the water to prevent the meat from sticking to your hands. Press a prune or 2 sour cherries into the middle of each ball and pinch the edges together. Roll the balls to make them smooth and slightly elongated.

3 To make the soup, bring the stock to a boil in a large soup pot. Add the potatoes and the meatballs, then reduce the heat to medium-low and cook, skimming, until

the potatoes are tender and the meatballs are cooked through, about 20 minutes.

4 Meanwhile, melt the butter in a small skillet over medium heat. Add the carrot and onion and sauté, stirring occasionally, until the onion is deep golden, about 15 minutes. Stir in the turmeric.

5 Carefully stir the contents of the skillet into the soup. Add the chick-peas and simmer for 5 minutes more. Add salt and plenty of pepper, if needed. Stir in the saffron, tarragon, and mint.

6 Serve at once, sprinkled with sumakh, if desired. Serve the rice on the side.

Serves 6

Winter Soups/Summer Soups

Most Soviet winter soups tend to be hearty, filling, and healthful. A properly thick homemade borscht, Georgian *kharcho* (with beans and rice), delicious Azerbaijani plum-stuffed meatball soup (*kiufta bozbash*), and the Russian spicy mixed meat soup *solianka*, all constitute a satisfying and unusual meal in themselves.

In the country and city alike, soup is never made for just one sitting, so the soup pot takes its place next to the samovar as one of the enduring symbols of hearth and home. As with any peasant cuisine, soup often is the main item of daily nourishment; often the meat from soups is fished out of the pot and served on fresh plates as a second course.

Summer soups, on the other hand, are light and refreshing. They make a perfect first course for an outdoor luncheon or, with a side salad, a simple but memorable luncheon with a friend. Tangy fruit soups from Lithuania, the just-right-on-a-hot-day yogurt soups of Central Asia, and Russian *okroshka* with raw mixed vegetables will surprise and delight your good-weather guests.

Lamb and Vegetable Soup with Homemade Noodles

Lagman

The Uzbek equivalent of borscht or *shchi*, *lagman* is a great favorite among Russians, who willingly endure long lines to get it at the popular Moscow restaurant, Uzbekistan. Here they sample *lagman* served in colorful Uzbek ceramic bowls, accompanied by freshly baked *non* (flat bread). *Lagman* is the name of the noodles added to the *vadzha* — the thick stew-like soup itself — which is made from lamb cooked with various vegetables and spices.

Of the many traditional methods of preparing the noodles, perhaps the most interesting is that of the Dungans, Chinese Muslims who settled in Uzbekistan. The Dungans add sesame oil to the noodle dough, then quickly stretch and fold the dough so that the finished *lagman* is one very long noodle, which is eaten with four chopsticks.

　　Lagman should be served in large bowls, accompanied by toasted pita, or better still, by *non* (see Index).

½ cup light olive oil

1 pound boneless lamb shoulder, cut into 1-inch cubes

2 medium-size onions, coarsely chopped

2 medium-size carrots, peeled and cut into thick strips or cubed

1 Asian eggplant, peeled and cut into small cubes

1 cup diced daikon (Asian radish), or black turnip

3 large tomatoes, peeled and coarsely chopped

2 medium-size Italian (pale green frying) peppers, cored and sliced

2 medium-size boiling potatoes, peeled and cubed

Salt and freshly ground black pepper, to taste

½ teaspoon coriander seeds, crushed

½ teaspoon black peppercorns

¾ teaspoon ground cumin

¾ teaspoon sweet Hungarian paprika

½ teaspoon hot Hungarian paprika

2 bay leaves

5 to 6 cups Lamb Stock, Beef Stock (see Index for both), or canned beef broth

2 cloves garlic, minced

1½ tablespoons red wine vinegar, or to taste

¼ cup finely chopped fresh cilantro, plus additional for garnish

3 tablespoons finely chopped fresh parsley, plus additional for garnish

Homemade Noodles (recipe follows)

1 In a large Dutch oven, heat the oil over medium heat until a light haze forms. Add the meat and brown it well on all sides, about 15 minutes. Remove with a slotted spoon and set aside.

2 Add the onions, carrots, and eggplant to the Dutch oven, and brown, stirring for 7 to 8 minutes.

3 Stir in the daikon, tomatoes, and peppers, and continue to cook over medium heat until the ingredients are well colored, 12 to 15 minutes.

4 Stir in the potatoes and cook to color slightly, 3 minutes. Spoon off all the excess oil and season the vegetables generously with salt and pepper. Add the coriander seeds, peppercorns, cumin, sweet and hot paprika, and bay leaves. Cook, stirring for 2 minutes.

5 Return the meat to the pot and stir to combine with the vegetables. Add 5 cups of the stock, bring to a boil, then reduce the heat to low and simmer, covered, until the meat is tender, about 45 minutes. Check the stock level after 30 minutes and if the soup is too thick add more. Remove the bay leaves and taste and correct the seasoning.

6 Add the garlic, vinegar, ¼ cup cilantro, and 3 tablespoons parsley. Remove from the heat and let stand for 10 minutes before serving.

7 Place some of the noodles into each serving bowl. Ladle in the soup and garnish with the remaining cilantro and parsley.

Serves 4 to 6

Homemade Noodles

Lagman

1¾ *cups all-purpose flour*
½ *teaspoon salt*
¼ *cup water*
1 *large egg, slightly beaten*
1 *tablespoon vegetable oil*

1 Sift the flour and salt together into a large bowl. Make a well in the center and pour the water, egg, and oil into it. Work the mixture with your hands, folding the flour over the egg and the water until they are completely incorporated.

2 Transfer the dough to a floured board. Using the heels of your hands, knead the dough until it is smooth and elastic, about 5 minutes.

3 Shape the dough into a ball and place it into a clean bowl. Cover with a damp kitchen towel and let stand at room temperature for 30 minutes.

4 On a large floured surface, use a floured rolling pin to roll out the dough into a rectangle slightly less than ⅛ inch thick. Trim the edges. Dust the dough lightly with flour and roll it up loosely, jelly-roll style. As you roll, make absolutely sure the dough isn't sticking to itself. With a sharp knife, cut the roll crosswise into thin strips. Spread out the noodles on a large plate or a clean cotton cloth and dust with flour.

5 Bring 2 quarts of salted water to a boil. Add the noodles and cook until tender, about 5 minutes.

Serves 6

Exotic Lamb, Chestnut, Quince, and Sour Plum Soup

Parcha Bozbash

I never cease to marvel at the ingenious combinations of flavors and the subtle aromatic seasoning of Azerbaijani cuisine. The particular flavor of this soup is imparted by quince and sour plums. Unfortunately, it's almost impossible to buy sour plums in the United States — though if you are near a Middle Eastern market, get a dried sour plum roll and and add a few pieces to the soup, instead of the prunes. Minced onion, sprinkled with the tart purple powder sumakh, is traditionally served in a separate bowl and added to the soup according to individual taste.

2 lamb shanks, about 1 pound each

7 cups Lamb Stock, Beef Stock (see Index for both), or canned broth

1 cup dried yellow split peas

1 pound fresh chestnuts

2 tablespoons unsalted butter

2 onions, quartered and sliced

½ teaspoon ground turmeric

Small pinch of ground cinnamon

1 small quince or apple peeled, cored, and cut into ¾ inch cubes

6 fresh prunes, as unripe as possible, cut into wedges

3 meaty fresh, ripe tomatoes, peeled, seeded, and chopped

½ teaspoon dried mint

½ teaspoon dried basil

1½ tablespoons fresh lemon juice

¼ teaspoon cayenne pepper

½ teaspoon saffron threads, crushed in a mortar

Salt and plenty of freshly ground black pepper

Chopped fresh mint for garnish

½ small red onion, minced and sprinkled with sumakh

1 In a large soup pot, bring the lamb and stock to a boil. Reduce the heat and simmer, covered, until the lamb shanks are tender, about 1½ hours. Remove the lamb shanks from the stock. Cool until manageable, then remove the meat from the bones, discarding the gristle and fat. Set the meat aside.

2 Refrigerate the stock, uncovered, until the fat rises to the surface, about 40 minutes. Skim the fat off.

3 Meanwhile, place the split peas and 3 cups water in a medium-size saucepan. Bring to a boil, then reduce the heat to low and simmer, covered, until the peas are tender but not mushy, about 40 minutes. Drain and set aside.

4 With a very sharp knife, make two crosswise incisions in the stem end of each chestnut. Cook the chestnuts in boiling water to cover for about 10 minutes.

5 Drain the chestnuts and cool until manageable. Remove their shells and skins, rinse, drain, and set aside.

6 In another large soup pot, melt the butter over medium heat. Add the sliced onions, turmeric, and cinnamon and sauté until the onion softens, about 10 minutes.

7 Add the defatted stock, the quince, prunes, and tomatoes. Simmer for 15 minutes.

8 Add the chestnuts, split peas, lamb, mint, basil, lemon juice, cayenne, and saffron and simmer for 10 minutes more. Adjust the seasoning, spicing the soup generously with salt and pepper.

9 Sprinkle with the chopped mint and serve with the minced red onion and sumakh on the side.

Serves 6 to 8

Spicy Mixed-Meat Soup

Solianka

I often serve *solianka* as a one-dish meal, in which case the amount of meats added can be increased. Remember, that wherever there are pickles, there must be vodka.

8 imported dried wild mushrooms,
    well rinsed
6 tablespoons (¾ stick) unsalted
    butter
3 large onions, coarsely chopped
1 cup diced cooked veal
1 cup diced cooked ham
1 cup diced Polish kielbasa or
    frankfurters
2 quarts Beef Stock (see Index) or
    canned broth
Bouquet garni (2 bay leaves and 8
    black peppercorns tied in a
    cheesecloth bag)
2 medium-size dill pickles, diced
2 tablespoons drained capers
10 to 12 small marinated mush-
    rooms, preferably My Mother's
    Marinated Mushrooms (see
    Index) but jarred is acceptable
1 can (16 ounces) Italian plum tom-
    atoes, drained, seeded, and
    chopped
2 tablespoons tomato paste
1 tablespoon all-purpose flour
12 Greek olives
¼ cup chopped fresh dill
¼ teaspoon dried marjoram
3 large cloves garlic, minced
¼ cup juice from dill pickle jar
Generous pinch of sweet Hungarian
    paprika
Salt and freshly ground black
    pepper, to taste
Lemon slices for garnish
Sour cream for garnish (optional)

About Solianka

There has been much debate among food historians about the origins of the name of this traditional Russian soup. Some say that it derives from the word *sol* (salt), because of the addition of salty pickles, olives, and capers. Others argue that the original name was *selianka*, which is related to the word *selo* (village), and thus points to the rural provenance of the dish. In addition, we now know that the version we have today using mixed meats and tomatoes came into being only in the nineteenth century. However, there's no debate at all about the soup's excellent taste!

1 Soak the mushrooms in ½ cup water for 2 hours. Drain the mushrooms and strain the liquid through a coffee filter. Set the mushrooms and soaking liquid aside.

2 Melt 4 tablespoons of the butter in a large soup pot over medium-low heat. Add the onions, veal, ham, kielbasa, and dried mushrooms and sauté over medium-low heat, stirring occasionally, 10 minutes.

3 Add the stock and soaking liquid and bring to a boil over high heat. Reduce the heat to low and add the bouquet garni, pickles, capers, and marinated mushrooms. Simmer, covered, about 10 minutes.

4 Meanwhile, melt the remaining 2 tablespoons of butter in a small skillet over low heat. Add the tomatoes and tomato paste and sauté, stirring, 5 to 7 minutes. Stir in the flour and continue to sauté for another minute.

5 Add a ladleful of the soup to the skillet, scrape the bottom with a wooden spoon, and whisk the mixture back into the soup.

Add the olives, dill, marjoram, garlic, pickle juice, and paprika. Stir the soup well, season with salt and pepper, and simmer, covered, over low heat for 10 minutes.

6 Remove the soup from the heat; remove the bouquet garni, taste, and correct the seasoning. Let stand for 10 minutes before serving.

7 Serve garnished with a slice of lemon on each serving and sour cream on the side, if desired.

Serves 6

My Mother's Chicken Soup with Dumplings

Kuriniy Bulyon s Kliotskami

Every mother has a recipe for a comforting soup intended to bring her child strength during the sundry ailments and afflictions of childhood; and every child out of childhood will swear by that remedial soup to the end of his or her days. This is my oath.

Although my mother is not the kind of cook who would knead her dough with time-consuming vigor and passion, nor does she clarify stocks and separate eggs, her recipes are always elegant, delicious, and, of course, super quick. In Moscow she was ceremoniously dubbed the "queen of soups." This "eat-it-it-will-make-you-better" soup is all of the above and much more.

DUMPLINGS
1 jumbo egg
3½ tablespoons all-purpose flour
Pinch of salt

SOUP
5 cups Chicken Stock (see Index), or
  canned broth
2 medium-size boiling potatoes,
  peeled and cut into ½-inch dice
8 baby carrots, peeled
1 large rib celery, sliced

Pinch of freshly ground black pepper
1 tablespoon finely chopped fresh
  dill (optional)

1 large fresh, ripe tomato, peeled,
  seeded, and coarsely chopped
Finely minced scallion (green onion)
  for garnish
Finely chopped fresh dill for
  garnish

1 To make the dumplings, break the egg into a small bowl, then add the flour, salt, pepper, and dill, if desired, and beat with a fork until smooth. Set the dumpling mixture aside.

2 In a soup pot, bring the chicken stock to a boil, then add the potatoes, carrots, and celery. Reduce the heat to low and simmer until the vegetables are tender, for 15 minutes.

3 Dip a teaspoon into cold water, scoop up about ½ teaspoon of the dumpling mixture and lower it carefully into the simmering soup. Repeat with the rest of the mixture, dipping your spoon into cold water before you make each dumpling. You should have about 8 to 10 dumplings.

4 Add the tomato, increase the heat to medium low, and cook until the dumplings rise to the surface, 5 to 7 minutes.

5 Season with salt and pepper, sprinkle with scallion and dill, and serve.

Serves 4 generously

Fish Soup à la Souvoroff

Ribniy Sup po Suvorovsky

This recipe comes from a legendary Moscow restaurant, Slavyansky Bazar, renowned in the nineteenth century for its authentic old Russian cuisine and its artistic clientele. Today the walls of the restaurant are embellished by portraits of the likes of Chekhov, Chaliapin, Tchaikovsky, and Stanislavsky — all faithful patrons. In fact, it was at this very restaurant, in 1898, that Stanislavsky had his famous twelve-hour conversation with Nemirovich-Danchenko, after which the Moscow Art Theater was born. Perhaps their soup, named for a legendary military hero, will inspire you to similar artistic visions.

3 tablespoons unsalted butter

1 large onion, coarsely chopped

1½ cups sliced fresh white mushrooms

1 carrot, peeled and cut in julienne

2 leeks (white part only), well rinsed and chopped

3 large, meaty fresh, ripe tomatoes, peeled and chopped, or canned tomatoes, drained and chopped

2 tablespoons tomato paste

1½ tablespoons all-purpose flour

6½ cups Fish Stock (see Index)

½ cup dry white wine

3 small boiling potatoes, peeled and cubed

Bouquet garni (2 bay leaves and 6 black peppercorns tied in a cheesecloth bag)

1 pound skinned whitefish fillets, cut into 1-inch pieces

3 small cloves garlic, crushed in a garlic press

3 tablespoons finely chopped fresh dill

3 tablespoons finely chopped fresh parsley

1 teaspoon sweet Hungarian paprika

Salt and plenty of freshly ground black pepper

Peeled lemon slices for garnish

1 Melt 2 tablespoons of the butter in a large, heavy soup pot, over medium heat. Add the onion and mushrooms and sauté stirring frequently until softened, about 10 minutes. If the mushrooms produce too much liquid, increase the heat to high and let it evaporate for 2 to 3 minutes.

2 Add the remaining tablespoon of butter, the carrot, and leeks and sauté, stirring until they soften, about 10 minutes more.

3 Stir in the tomatoes and tomato paste and cook, stirring frequently, for another 5 to 10 minutes. Sprinkle the flour on the vegetables and sauté, stirring, for 1 minute.

4 Gradually add the stock, stirring until well blended in.

5 Add the wine, potatoes, and bouquet garni. Bring to a gentle boil, then reduce the heat to low and simmer, covered, until the potatoes are almost tender, about 15 minutes.

6 Add the fish to the soup and poach it until just cooked through, about 5 minutes.

7 Stir in the garlic, dill, parsley, paprika, and salt and pepper. Remove the soup from the heat and let stand for a few minutes. Remove the bouquet garni before serving. Serve garnished with lemon slices.

Serves 6 to 7

 About *Ukha*

This fish soup, highly praised by Ivan the Terrible and by Antoine Carême (the great French chef) alike, is considered by authorities to be the oldest Russian soup.

Back in the twelfth century, though, *ukha* wasn't a clear fish soup—in fact it wasn't a fish soup at all, but could be prepared with anything from meat to cereals or mushrooms. At the lavish courts of the Czars and rich *boyars* (nobility) in the sixteenth and seventeenth centuries, as many as fifty different kinds of *ukha* would be served

between various pie dishes.

Later on, *ukha* became a sort of fisherman's broth made with three or more kinds of freshly caught fish, each of which made a distinct contribution to the soup's flavor. It was only in the nineteenth century, under the influence of French cuisine, that *ukha* became a clarified fish broth supporting tender morsels of poached fish.

Clear Salmon Soup

Ukha

A great favorite with my American friends because of its rich but light flavor, and its striking, almost minimal appearance, *ukha* makes a royal starter for French, American, and especially Japanese entrées. The version offered here is made with salmon, and in my opinion produces one of the most subtle and elegant of soups. To make properly strong soup — *navaristaya ukha* — you will have to make a stock from small freshwater fish (smelts are the best fish I can think of for this). The stock should be strained and further enhanced by salmon trimmings.

6 cups water
1½ pounds whole smelts, cleaned
    well
1 medium-size onion
1 large carrot, peeled and quartered
1 leek (white part only), well rinsed
1 small rib celery with leaves
1 parsnip, peeled
Bouquet garni, (4 parsley sprigs, 4
    dill sprigs, 2 bay leaves, and 4
    black peppercorns tied in a
    cheesecloth bag)
Salt and freshly ground white
    pepper, to taste

1 pound salmon trimmings, including
    heads, tails, and frames
¾ cup good dry white wine
3 small boiling potatoes
2 thin carrots, peeled
1 large egg white
1 eggshell, crushed
1 pound skinned salmon fillets, cut
    crosswise into 1½-inch pieces
5 tablespoons fresh finely chopped
    scallions (green onions), white
    bulb and 2 inches of green
Thin lemon slices for garnish

1 In a large soup pot, place the water, smelts, onion, quartered carrot, leek, celery, parsnip, bouquet garni, and salt and pepper, and bring to a boil over high heat, periodically skimming off the foam as it rises to the top. Cover the pot, reduce the heat, and simmer for 35 minutes.

2 Strain the stock through a fine sieve into a clean pot, pressing the solids with the back of a spoon to extract as much liquid as possible. Discard the solids.

3 Return the stock to the heat and add the salmon trimmings, wine, potatoes, and thin carrots. Bring to a boil, then reduce the heat to low and simmer, covered, until the vegetables are tender, about 25 minutes.

4 Strain the stock into a clean pot, discarding all the solids except for the potatoes and all the carrots. Rinse the potatoes and carrots being careful not to mash them, and set aside.

5 Return the stock to low heat and simmer for several minutes. Add the egg white and shell and increase the heat to medium-high. Bring to a boil, beating constantly with a wire whisk. When the stock boils, the egg white will start rising to the surface. At this point, turn off the heat and let stand for 5 minutes.

6 Line a colander with a double layer of dampened cheesecloth and strain the stock into a clean pot.

7 Add the fish fillets to the stock and poach over medium-low heat until cooked through, 5 minutes. Taste and adjust the seasonings.

8 Halve the reserved potatoes and cut into wedges. Cut the carrots into fine dice (if you have the patience, it's nice to cut the carrots into diamonds or stars).

9 Divide the fish fillets among 6 or 7 soup bowls. Add a few potato wedges and diced carrots to each bowl. Ladle the stock into the bowls, sprinkle with scallions, and garnish with lemon slices.

Serves 6 to 7

Byelorussian Wild Mushroom and Noodle Soup

Su Lapsha s Gribami

Make this soup a day in advance to allow the flavor of the mushrooms to come through. Add the noodles when you reheat the soup. For a special occasion, use Tiny Soup Dumplings Filled with Wild Mushrooms (see Index) instead of the noodles.

2 ounces imported dried mushrooms (such as Polish, porcini, or cèpes), well rinsed

2 quarts Chicken Stock (see Index), canned broth, or water

2 large boiling potatoes, peeled and cut into 1-inch cubes

Salt, to taste

3 tablespoons light vegetable oil

1 large carrot, peeled and cut into julienne

1⅓ cups finely chopped onions

1 leek (white part only), well rinsed and finely chopped.

1 tablespoon all-purpose flour

½ cup thin egg noodles

Freshly ground black pepper, to taste

Sour cream for garnish

3 tablespoons chopped fresh dill for garnish

1 In a large soup pot, bring the mushrooms and stock to a boil over high heat. Cover the pot, reduce the heat to low, and simmer until the mushrooms are tender, about 1 hour.

2 Remove the mushrooms with a slotted spoon, pat dry, chop fine, and set aside.

3 Bring the mushroom stock to a boil over high heat. Add the potatoes and salt, reduce the heat to low, and simmer, partially covered, until the potatoes are tender, about 15 minutes.

4 Meanwhile, heat the oil in a medium-size skillet, over medium heat. Add the carrot, onions, leek, and mushrooms. Sauté, stirring occasionally, until the

onion and leek are softened and dark gold, about 15 to 20 minutes.

5 Sprinkle the vegetables with flour, stir to blend, and sauté for 1 minute. Stir in a ladleful of hot stock and stir to blend.

6 Add the contents of the skillet to the soup along with the noodles, pepper, and more salt, if desired. Simmer until the noodles are tender, 5 to 7 minutes. Remove the soup from the heat and let stand for 10 minutes before serving.

7 Serve garnished with sour cream sprinkled with dill.

Serves 6

 # Three Wild Mushroom Soups

I think any Slav would agree that wild mushroom soup is one of the greatest pleasures of our cuisine — if I had my way I would include at least ten versions of the soup in this book! In the Soviet Union, mushroom-picking is still a popular national pastime, and there's nothing quite like an early morning search in the woods followed by the sound and the smell of a skillet of fresh sautéed chanterelles or porcini. Then there are the endless jars of pickled and marinated mushrooms and the strings of dried boletus that help keep body and soul together for the rest of the year.

On my recent visits back to the Soviet Union, loving relatives and friends loaded me up with garlands of dried mushrooms that I have had to negotiate past the quizzical glances of American customs officials. Fortunately for mushroom lovers here, imported Italian porcini and French cèpes (the same thing) are readily available. And Polish dried mushrooms can be found in Eastern European and Russian stores in most big cities.

Wild Mushroom Soup with Barley and Cheese

Gribnoy Sup s Perlovkoy i Sirom

I couldn't resist including this recipe, sent to me by a relative from Moscow, where it's made with local processed Gruyère cheese. Try it with Gruyère or white Cheddar for a sharper taste. If you are going to reheat it the following day, give it a good stir and warm it slowly over low heat. Although completely out of context, a couple of teaspoons of grated Parmesan added to each bowl before serving improves the flavor still further.

1 ounce imported dried mushrooms (such as Polish, porcini, or cèpes), well rinsed

7 cups water

3 tablespoons unsalted butter

2 cups sliced fresh white mushrooms

1 cup chopped onions

4 heaping tablespoons pearl barley

Salt and freshly ground black pepper, to taste

1 large carrot, peeled and cut into fine dice

1 large celery rib, cut into fine dice

1 large russet potato, peeled and cut into ½-inch dice

Bouquet garni (2 bay leaves and 4 black peppercorns tied in a cheesecloth bag)

¼ cup heavy or whipping cream

¾ cup grated Gruyère or white Cheddar cheese

Sour cream or freshly grated Parmesan cheese for garnish

Chopped fresh parsley or dill for garnish

1 Soak the dried mushrooms in 1 cup of the water for 2 hours. Drain the mushrooms, chop fine, and set aside. Strain the soaking liquid through a coffee filter and set aside.

2 Melt the butter in a large soup pot over medium heat. Add the white mushrooms and onion and sauté until the onion softens and the mushrooms give off their liquid, about 12 minutes.

3 Add the barley, dried mushrooms, the reserved soaking liquid, and the remaining

6 cups water to the soup pot and bring to a boil. Add salt and pepper, reduce the heat to low, cover, and simmer for 20 minutes.

4 Add the carrot, celery, potato, and bouquet garni and simmer until the barley is completely cooked and the vegetables are tender, 20 to 25 minutes. Remove the bouquet garni.

5 Add the cream and the Gruyère or Cheddar and simmer, stirring, until the cheese is melted, for about 5 minutes. Taste and adjust the seasoning.

6 Serve garnished with sour cream or Parmesan, sprinkled with fresh herbs.

Serves 6 to 8

Latvian Potato and Wild Mushroom Soup

Kartofelny Sup s Gribami

This is a potato soup to top all potato soups. Thick and creamy, it has the woodsy aroma of wild mushrooms that are enlivened by bacon cracklings and paprika. Serve it with Barley Skillet Bread (see Index).

1 ounce imported dried wild mushrooms (such as Polish, porcini, or cèpes), well rinsed
5½ cups water
Salt, to taste
6 medium-size russet potatoes, peeled and cubed

4 slices bacon, finely diced
1 small onion, finely chopped
⅔ cup heavy or whipping cream
Sweet Hungarian paprika, to taste
Freshly ground black pepper, to taste
Chopped fresh dill for garnish

1 Soak the mushrooms in 1 cup of the water for 2 hours. Drain the mushrooms and strain the liquid through a coffee filter.

2 In a large soup pot, bring the mushrooms, their soaking liquid, and the remaining water to a boil over high heat. Add salt, then reduce the heat to low and simmer, covered, for 30 minutes.

3 Add the potatoes, increase the heat to medium low, and cook until the potatoes are tender, about 15 to 20 minutes.

4 Remove from the heat. With a slotted spoon, remove the mushrooms. When they are cool enough to handle, chop them very fine.

5 Using the slotted spoon, transfer the potatoes to a food processor. Add 1 cup of the cooking liquid and process until puréed.

6 Whisk the potatoes back into the cooking liquid in the pot. You will have to stir them thoroughly with a fork or wire whisk until there are no lumps. Set aside.

7 In a small skillet, sauté the bacon until it renders its fat. Drain off all but 1 tablespoon of the fat, then add the onion and the mushrooms. Sauté, stirring occasionally, over medium-high heat until the mixture is well browned, about 15 minutes.

8 Return the soup to low heat. Add the cream and simmer gently for 2 minutes, until the soup is about to boil.

9 Stir in the sautéed onion, mushroom, and bacon mixture. Season with a few dashes of paprika and salt and pepper, then simmer for another 3 to 4 minutes.

10 Serve garnished with fresh dill.

Serves 6

Armenian Lentil and Apricot Soup

Vospapur

In this soup the dried apricots blend beautifully in color and taste with the red lentils (available in Middle Eastern shops and health food stores), which themselves become bright orange when cooked. This soup makes a great first course at a Thanksgiving meal.

3 tablespoons olive oil

1 large onion, finely chopped

2 large cloves garlic, finely chopped

⅓ cup dried apricots, chopped

1½ cups dried split red lentils,
   rinsed thoroughly

5 cups Chicken Stock (see Index) or
   canned broth

3 medium-size fresh, ripe plum
   tomatoes, peeled, seeded,
   and chopped

½ teaspoon ground cumin, or more
   to taste

½ teaspoon dried thyme

Salt and freshly ground black
   pepper, to taste

2 tablespoons fresh lemon juice, or
   more to taste

Chopped fresh parsley for
   garnish

1 In a large soup pot, heat the oil over medium heat. Add the onion, garlic, and dried apricots. Sauté, stirring occasionally, until the onion is soft, about 12 minutes.

2 Add the lentils and stock. Bring to a boil, then reduce the heat and simmer, covered, until the lentils are tender, about 30 minutes.

3 Stir in the tomatoes, cumin, thyme, and salt and pepper. Simmer, covered, for another 10 minutes.

4 Remove half the soup and purée it in a food processor. Return the purée to the pot. Stir a few times, then season the soup with the lemon juice and additional salt and pepper, if necessary. Simmer, stirring, for 2 to 3 minutes longer.

5 Serve sprinkled with parsley.

Serves 6

Lentil and Spinach Soup

Vospapur

It sometimes seems that there is a different lentil soup (*vospapur*) for every day of the week in Armenia. Accompany this spicy, aromatic variation with toasted pita bread triangles.

2 tablespoons vegetable oil

1 medium-size onion, finely chopped

3 garlic cloves, minced

¾ teaspoon ground cumin

½ teaspoon ground coriander

½ teaspoon hot Hungarian paprika

1⅓ cups brown lentils, rinsed
    thoroughly

1 package (10 ounces) chopped
    frozen spinach, thawed and
    squeezed dry

4½ cups Chicken Stock (see Index)
    or canned broth

1 can (16 ounces) Italian plum
    tomatoes, drained but juices
    reserved, chopped

Salt and freshly ground black
    pepper, to taste

1 tablespoon fresh lemon juice, or
    more to taste

1 Heat the oil in a soup pot over medium heat. Add the onion, garlic, cumin, coriander, and paprika and sauté, stirring, for 5 minutes.

2 Add the lentils and spinach and cook, stirring, for 2 minutes more.

3 Add the stock, tomatoes, and reserved tomato juices and bring to a boil. Reduce the heat to low, season with salt and pepper, and simmer, covered, until the lentils are tender, about 50 minutes.

4 Season with the lemon juice and additional salt and pepper, if needed. Let stand for 5 minutes before serving.

Serves 4

Moldavian White Bean Soup

Supa de Fasole

I like this soup thick and hearty, but you can vary the amount of water to achieve your desired consistency. As with so many hearty soups, nothing makes a better accompaniment than a loaf of sour dough rye bread.

1½ cups dried Great Northern
   beans, soaked overnight in water
   to cover and drained
7 cups water
1 meaty ham bone (about 1 pound)
1 rib celery with leaves
1 carrot, peeled
Bouquet garni (4 sprigs thyme, 4
   sprigs dill, 4 bay leaves, and 8
   black peppercorns tied in a
   cheesecloth bag)
2 medium-size boiling potatoes,
   peeled and cut into ¾-inch cubes

2 tablespoons unsalted butter
1 medium-size onion, finely
   chopped
2 cloves garlic, sliced
1 leek (white part only), well rinsed
   and chopped
Generous pinch of dried thyme
Salt and freshly ground black
   pepper, to taste
1 tablespoon red wine vinegar, or
   more to taste
Sweet Hungarian paprika

1 In a large soup pot, bring the beans, 5 cups of the water, the ham bone, celery, carrot, and bouquet garni to a boil over high heat, periodically skimming off the foam as it rises to the top. Cover the pot and reduce the heat to low. Simmer until the beans are tender, 1¼ hours or more, depending on the beans. Add more boiling water, a little at a time, if the beans absorb too much liquid before they are done.

2 Using a slotted spoon, remove and discard the ham bone, celery, carrot, and bouquet garni.

3 Remove about two-thirds of the beans and mash them thoroughly or purée them in a food mill with a medium disk. If you use a food processor, make sure you do not purée the beans too fine.

4 Return the beans to the pot and stir a few times. Bring to a boil over medium-high heat and add the potatoes. Reduce the heat to low and simmer until the potatoes are

almost tender, about 10 minutes.

5 Meanwhile, melt the butter in a small skillet over medium heat. Add the onion, garlic, and leek and sauté until the vegetables are just softened, about 8 minutes. Stir into the soup along with the thyme and salt and pepper. Stir well and simmer until the potatoes are tender, 5 to 10 minutes.

6 Add 1 tablespoon vinegar and let stand for 5 minutes. Taste again and adjust the vinegar, if necessary. Sprinkle each serving with a dash of paprika.

Serves 6

Red Bean Soup with Walnuts

Lobiani

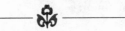

Red beans and walnuts are such an unmistakably Georgian combination that I think they should be put on the Georgian national flag — along with grapevines, of course. If you are going to reheat this delicious soup the next day, add a little more liquid, as it tends to thicken on standing.

1 pound dried red beans, soaked
    overnight in water to cover and
    drained
7 cups Chicken Stock (see Index) or
    canned broth
5 cups water
Salt, to taste
¼ cup olive oil
2 large onions, finely chopped
Freshly ground black pepper, to
    taste

½ cup walnut pieces, ground in a
    food processor
2 teaspoons coriander seeds, crushed
3 large cloves garlic, minced
¼ cup tarragon vinegar or more to
    taste
½ cup chopped fresh cilantro
¼ cup chopped fresh parsley

1 In a large soup pot, bring the beans, 5 cups of the stock, the water, and salt to a boil, periodically skimming off the foam as it rises to the top. Reduce the heat to medium, and cook the beans, uncovered, until tender, almost mushy, 1½ hours or more, depending on the beans. Add more boiling stock, a little at a time, if the beans absorb too much liquid before they're done.

2 Using a slotted spoon, remove the beans from the liquid and mash them thoroughly or purée in a food mill with a medium disk. If you use a food processor, make sure you do not purée the beans too finely.

3 Return the beans to the pot and stir a few times. Add a little stock if the soup seems too thick. Season with salt and pepper. Turn the heat to low and simmer while you prepare the next step.

4 Heat the oil in a medium-size skillet over medium heat. Add the onions and sauté, stirring occasionally, until golden, about 15 minutes.

5 Stir the onions and the oil in which it was sautéed into the soup. Simmer for another 5 minutes, then remove from the heat. Stir in the walnuts, coriander, garlic, and vinegar and let stand for 10 minutes before serving.

6 Serve sprinkled with plenty of fresh cilantro and parsley.

Serves 8 to 10

Moldavian Vegetable Soup

Supa de Zarzavaturi

This is a light yet satisfying vegetable soup made from those favorite Moldavian vegetables — peppers, tomatoes, and corn. Serve it with Moldavian Corn and Feta Cheese Bread (see Index).

5 tablespoons unsalted butter

1 cup chopped onions

5 cloves garlic, sliced

2 leeks (white part only), well rinsed and sliced

1 parsnip, peeled and cut into julienne

1 large rib celery, chopped

3 medium-size Italian (pale green frying) peppers, cored, seeded, and sliced

¼ teaspoon dried thyme

Generous pinch of dried marjoram

5 cups Vegetable Stock (see Index)

Bouquet garni (4 parsley sprigs, 4 thyme sprigs, 4 dill sprigs, 3 bay leaves, and 6 black peppercorns tied in a cheesecloth bag)

3 medium-size boiling potatoes, peeled and cut into large cubes

Salt and freshly ground black pepper, to taste

6 large fresh, ripe plum tomatoes, peeled and coarsely chopped

1 package (10 ounces) frozen corn kernels, rinsed in tepid water

2 tablespoons fresh lemon juice

3 tablespoons finely chopped fresh parsley, or more to taste

3 tablespoons finely chopped fresh dill, or more to taste

Sour cream

1 Melt the butter in a heavy soup pot over medium heat. Add the onions, garlic, leeks, parsnip, celery, and peppers. Sauté, stirring occasionally, until the vegetables are softened, about 20 minutes.

2 Stir in the thyme and marjoram. Add the stock and bouquet garni and bring to a boil. Let the liquid boil for a few minutes, then add the potatoes and salt and pepper. Reduce the heat to low and simmer, uncovered, for about 20 minutes.

3 Stir in the tomatoes and simmer until

the potatoes are tender, another 10 minutes. Add the corn and lemon juice and cook 3 to 4 minutes longer.

4 Remove the bouquet garni and taste and correct the seasoning, then let the soup stand for 15 to 20 minutes before serving.

5 Serve sprinkled with parsley and dill, pass the sour cream.

Serves 6

Tomato and Cilantro Soup

Chikhirtma iz Pomidorov

This version of *chikhirtma* is made with tomatoes and flavored with lots of cilantro. I promise it will be an enormous success — but don't let anyone tell you that it tastes Mexican. Make this soup when tomatoes are in season. It also tastes great chilled — though if you are going to serve it cold, omit the flour.

6 tablespoons (¾ stick) unsalted butter

3 medium-size onions, chopped

2 large cloves garlic, minced

10 medium-size fresh, ripe plum
    tomatoes, peeled and coarsely
    chopped

⅓ cup chopped fresh cilantro, plus
    additional for garnish

1 tablespoon all-purpose flour

4 cups boiling Chicken Stock (see
    Index), canned broth, or water

Salt, to taste

2 large egg yolks

¼ cup fresh lemon juice

Chopped fresh parsley for garnish

Freshly ground black pepper, to taste

1 Melt the butter in a soup pot over medium heat. Add the onions and garlic and sauté, stirring occasionally until well softened and lightly colored, about 10 minutes.

2 Stir in the tomatoes and cilantro and sauté, stirring frequently, for another 15 minutes. Sprinkle in the flour and cook for another minute, stirring.

3 Gradually stir in the hot stock and let it boil for about 1 minute. Reduce the heat to low, add salt, and simmer, uncovered, for 20 minutes, stirring once or twice.

4 Working in batches, purée the soup in a food processor until smooth. Return the soup to the pot and let it simmer, covered, for about 5 minutes. Remove from the heat.

5 In a bowl, whisk the egg yolks and lemon juice together until well blended. Gradually whisk in about 1 cup of soup until completely smooth.

6 Stir the egg yolk mixture back into the soup. Return the soup to the heat and simmer gently, uncovered, until the soup thickens, 3 minutes. Garnish with fresh parsley and cilantro and serve with plenty of freshly ground black pepper.

Serves 6

Yogurt, Spinach, and Sorrel Soup

Dovga

Delicious hot and cold yogurt soups are served all over the Caucasus and Central Asia. This version from Azerbaijan is one of the most interesting. Made with yogurt, rice, yellow peas, spinach, sorrel, and fresh herbs, it's tart and refreshing even in winter. If you omit the rice and peas, you can serve it cold, although, in this case, I don't think it works quite as well as the hot soup. Serve it to your most adventurous friends and let them guess what's in it. As *dovga* doesn't reheat well, make only as much as you are going to eat at one sitting.

4 cups Chicken Stock (see Index) or
    canned broth
3½ tablespoons long-grain rice
2 cups plain low-fat yogurt
1½ tablespoons all-purpose flour
Salt and freshly ground black pep-
    per, to taste
⅓ cup cooked yellow split peas
    (optional)
1 cup (loosely packed) finely chop-
    ped fresh spinach
2 cups finely chopped fresh sorrel
Pinch of sugar

3 tablespoons finely chopped scal-
    lions (green onions), white bulb
    and 2 inches of green
2 tablespoons finely chopped fresh
    dill
2 tablespoons finely chopped fresh
    cilantro
2 tablespoons unsalted butter
1½ teaspoons dried mint
⅛ teaspoon cayenne pepper, or more
    to taste
Sumakh for garnish (optional)

1 In a soup pot, bring the stock and the rice to a boil over high heat, then reduce the heat to low and simmer, partially covered, for 10 minutes.

2 In a large bowl, whisk the yogurt and flour until blended. Slowly whisk in about 1 cup of hot stock until completely smooth.

3 Whisk the yogurt mixture back into the pot. Add salt and pepper, then stir in the split peas, if using, the spinach, and sorrel. Simmer until the rice is tender, 8 minutes.

4 Add a small pinch of sugar to neutralize the acidity, then stir in the scallions and fresh herbs and simmer for 1 minute more. Remove from the heat.

5 Melt the butter in a small skillet over low heat. Stir in the mint and cayenne and remove from the heat.

6 Ladle the soup into serving bowls and swirl a little of the mint mixture into each

Think Soup

Many soups in this chapter are substantial enough to constitute an entire meal, especially when served with the right accompaniments. If you make the soup and the accompaniments the day before, then you can casually invite your friends to drop by for a late lunch after a visit to a museum or a walk in the park.

bowl. This will give the soup a mysterious Eastern aroma. Sprinkle with sumakh, if desired, and serve.

Serves 6

Georgian Egg and Lemon Soup

Chikhirtma

The second most prized Georgian soup after *kharcho*, *chikhirtma* is a lighter version of the egg and lemon soup so popular in Greece and the Middle East. This soup is loaded with spices and fresh herbs.

2 tablespoons unsalted butter

1 cup finely chopped onions

4 cloves garlic, sliced

1½ tablespoons all-purpose flour

6 cups boiling Chicken Stock (see Index) or canned broth

Salt and freshly ground black pepper, to taste

½ teaspoon coriander seeds, crushed

⅛ teaspoon ground fenugreek

⅛ to ¼ teaspoon dried red pepper flakes

3 large egg yolks

¼ cup fresh lemon juice

A few threads of saffron, crushed in a mortar and diluted in 1 tablespoon warm water

1⅓ cups shredded cooked chicken breast

2½ tablespoons finely chopped fresh cilantro for garnish

2½ tablespoons finely chopped fresh basil for garnish

2½ tablespoons finely chopped fresh mint for garnish

1 Melt the butter in a large soup pot over low heat. Add the onions and garlic and sauté, stirring occasionally, until softened but not colored, 5 minutes. Sprinkle in the flour and cook, stirring, for 1 minute.

2 Gradually stir in the hot stock. Increase the heat to medium and bring to a low boil, then reduce the heat to low and add the salt and pepper, coriander seeds, fenugreek, and pepper flakes to taste. Simmer, uncovered, for 5 minutes. Remove from the heat.

3 In a bowl, whisk the egg yolks and lemon juice together until well blended. Gradually whisk in about 1 cup of hot stock until completely smooth.

4 Stir the egg yolk mixture back into the soup. Return the soup to the heat and simmer gently, uncovered, without letting it boil, until the soup thickens, about 5 minutes. Stir in the saffron and chicken and serve garnished with the fresh herbs.

Serves 6

COLD SOUPS

Chilled *Kvass* Soup

Okroshka

I don't think there's anything more revitalizing on a hot summer's day than this ancient Russian soup made from *kvass*, our national drink. At first, I hesitated to offer this recipe thinking that no one would bother to find a source for *kvass* (see Notes on Ingredients). Now, with the growing interest in Russian food, I no longer think this the case. Although *kvass* is not easy to find, if you have a good source, this soup is well worth making.

4 hard-cooked egg yolks	*1 cup diced, cooked veal or ham*
1 teaspoon Dijon mustard	*1 cup diced, cooked frankfurters*
½ teaspoon sugar	*⅓ cup chopped scallions (green*
6 cups kvass	*onions)*
1 cup diced red radishes	*2 tablespoons chopped fresh dill*
1 large boiling potato, peeled,	*Salt and freshly ground black*
boiled, and diced	*pepper, to taste*
1½ cups diced, peeled cucumbers	*Sour cream for garnish (optional)*

1 In a soup tureen, mash the egg yolks with a fork. Stir in the mustard and the sugar and mix well. Gradually stir in the *kvass* to blend well. Refrigerate the soup for 1 hour.

2 In a large bowl, toss together the remaining ingredients, except the sour cream, to mix well.

3 Serve the *kvass* mixture from the tureen and pass the meat and vegetable mixture separately. The sour cream is a tasty optional accompaniment.

Serves 6

Estonian Chilled Cucumber Soup

Kholodniy Sup iz Ogurtsov

A refreshing cucumber soup of Karelian origin. Make sure it's thoroughly chilled before serving and follow it with the Estonian Cod Salad with Horseradish Sauce (see Index) for a hot weather luncheon.

2 tablespoons unsalted butter

1 small onion, finely chopped

7 medium-size firm Kirby cucumbers, peeled, seeded, and grated

1 cup chopped fresh dill, plus additional for garnish

3 cups Chicken Stock (see Index) or canned broth

Salt and freshly ground white pepper, to taste

1 cup sour cream

3 large egg yolks

¼ cup dry sherry

Grated zest of 1 lemon

1 Melt the butter in a soup pot over medium heat. Add the onion and sauté until softened but not colored, about 5 minutes.

2 Stir in the cucumbers and 1 cup dill, then cook, covered, until the cucumber has softened, 5 to 7 minutes.

3 Gradually stir in the stock. Bring to a boil, then reduce the heat to low. Add salt and pepper and simmer, covered, for 5 minutes.

4 Working in batches, purée the soup in a food processor until smooth. Return to the pot and simmer for 2 minutes, then remove from the heat.

5 In a bowl, whisk the sour cream with the egg yolks and sherry until blended. Stir in 1 cup of hot soup, then whisk the mixture back into the pot, stirring vigorously until smooth.

6 Stir in the lemon zest; then add more salt or freshly ground white pepper, if you wish. Cool, then refrigerate the soup for at least 4 hours.

7 Stir the soup before serving. Serve garnished with dill.

Serves 4 to 6

Cold Yogurt and Cucumber Soup

Katikli Shurpa

When traveling through Turkey recently in the sizzling August heat, I became convinced that yogurt-based drinks and foods are the best way to fight a summer thirst. The peoples of the Middle East, Central Asia, and the Caucasus, of course, have known this for generations — hence the incredible variety of summer yogurt soups in that part of the world.

4 cups plain low-fat yogurt
1⅓ cups ice water
Salt and freshly ground black
*   pepper, to taste*

3 medium-size firm cucumbers,
*   peeled, seeded, and finely diced*
2 small cloves garlic, minced.
12 fresh mint leaves, torn into pieces

1 In a large bowl, whisk the yogurt with the water until smooth. Season with salt and pepper.

2 Combine with the cucumbers and garlic and refrigerate for at least 45 minutes.

3 Stir in the mint and let stand for about 5 minutes before serving.

Serves 6

Sorrel and Spinach Soup

Zelyoniye Shchi

I always wanted to sample *potage Germini*, which sounded like something out of Balzac, suitable only for viscounts and fading beauties. Imagine my surprise, then, when I found out that it's nothing more than our sorrel *shchi*, eaten by villagers and children at their summer *dachas*. I think sorrel was the first herb I ever picked in the countryside; it was my grandmother who taught me to recognize its distinctive features and tart taste. All I did that week was pick sorrel and proudly offer it to *babushka* so she could make it into a wonderful, cool soup that we ate in the afternoon.

I'm offering here the traditional Russian version of the soup, with potatoes and hard-cooked eggs, garnished with sour cream. When sorrel is plentiful in the market, make it with 7 cups sorrel and no spinach.

2 tablespoons unsalted butter

1 small rib celery, chopped

1 medium-size onion, finely chopped

¼ cup chopped scallions (green onions)

3½ cups Chicken Stock (see Index) or canned broth

2 medium-size boiling potatoes, peeled and halved

4 cups (tightly packed) chopped sorrel

3 cups (tightly packed) chopped spinach

Salt and freshly ground black pepper, to taste

½ cup heavy or whipping cream

2 hard-cooked eggs, sliced, for garnish

2 small cucumbers, peeled and diced for garnish (optional)

Sour cream for garnish

1 Melt the butter in a large soup pot over medium heat. Add the celery and onion and sauté, stirring, until the onion is softened, about 7 minutes. Add the scallions and sauté for another 5 minutes.

2 Add the stock and bring to a boil. Add the potatoes, then reduce the heat to medium-low and simmer, partially covered, until the potatoes are tender, about 15 minutes. With a slotted spoon, remove the potatoes and set aside.

3 Bring the soup to a boil. Add the sorrel and spinach and cook until wilted, 3 minutes. Remove from the heat and add the salt and pepper.

4 Working in batches, process the soup in a food processor until the sorrel and spinach are finely minced. Transfer the soup to a tureen and stir in the cream. Cool, then refrigerate for 2 hours.

5 Dice the reserved potatoes and add them to the soup right before serving. Serve each soup portion garnished with 1 or 2 slices of egg, cucumbers, if you wish, and sour cream.

Serves 4

Cold Borscht

Kholodniy Borshch

This familiar classic is a must in my refrigerator in the dog days of summer. All you do is make plenty of liquid with beets and pass the rest of the ingredients in a bowl. Russian cold borscht is not nearly as sweet as the version served in this country — so adjust the amount of sugar to taste.

1½ pounds beets trimmed of all but
1 inch stems
9 cups water
¼ cup fresh lemon juice
2 tablespoons cider vinegar
1½ tablespoons sugar, or more to
taste
Salt and freshly ground black
pepper, to taste

3 large boiling potatoes, peeled,
boiled, and diced
4 medium-size Kirby cucumbers,
peeled, seeded, and diced
1 cup diced red radishes
3 hard-cooked eggs, chopped
1 cup chopped mixed scallions
(green onions), dill, and parsley
Sour cream for garnish

1 In a large pot, bring the beets and water to a boil, then reduce the heat to medium low and simmer, covered, until the beets are tender, 25 minutes or more, depending on their size.

2 Using a slotted spoon, remove the beets from the liquid and cool until manageable. Peel and grate the beets.

3 Stir the beets back into the liquid. Add the lemon juice, vinegar, sugar, and salt and pepper. Simmer for 15 minutes more. Adjust the amount of sugar to taste. Cool the soup, then refrigerate until ready to

serve, at least 2 hours.

4 In a large bowl, toss together the potatoes, cucumbers, radishes, eggs, and herbs to mix well.

5 Ladle the soup into bowls. Either spoon about 2 tablespoons of vegetable and egg mixture into each bowl or, as is the custom in Russia, serve it separately in a decorative serving dish. The sour cream should also be served on the side.

Serves 10

Estonian Bread Soup

Estonskiy Khlebniy Sup

When I asked Estonians about their national dishes, the first thing they mentioned was always their bread soup — of which, of course, there are dozens of varieties. This soup should ideally be made with sourdough black bread, but you can use a good pumpernickel. Serve it at the end, rather than the beginning of the meal, as it is really more of a dessert soup.

½ cup raisins

¼ cup plum brandy

5 cups water

½ cup sugar, or more to taste

6 slices black sourdough bread,
*   crusts removed, toasted*

2 small tart apples (such as Granny
*   Smith) peeled, halved, and sliced*

¾ cup pitted dried prunes

½ cup fresh cranberries

½ cup cranberry juice

1 piece (1 inch) cinnamon stick

Grated zest of 1 lemon

3 cloves

Whipped cream for garnish

1 Soak the raisins in the Calvados until plump, for 20 to 30 minutes.

2 In a soup pot, bring the water and ½ cup sugar to a boil over high heat. Add the bread, then reduce the heat to low and simmer until the bread just begins to dissolve.

3 Remove the bread with a slotted spoon and push it through a fine sieve. (You can also process it in a food processor, but for no more than two pulses. The bread should not be puréed.)

4 Stir the bread back into the pot. Add the raisins with their soaking liquid, apples, prunes, cranberries, cranberry juice, cinnamon stick, lemon zest, and cloves. Bring to a boil, then reduce the heat and simmer, covered, until the fruits are tender. Remove from the heat.

5 Taste the soup and add more sugar, if desired. Cool, then refrigerate for at least 1 hour.

6 Remove the cinnamon stick and cloves. Ladle the soup into serving bowls, and serve with whipped cream.

Serves 6

Apple Soup with Apple Dumplings

Yablochniy Sup s Klyotskami

Chilled fruit soups are very popular throughout Eastern Europe, where they are considered standard summer fare. This delicious Latvian soup with apple dumplings should be served at the end of a meal, topped with whipped cream or Crème Fraîche (see Index).

SOUP

5 large apples (such as Granny
    Smith), cored, peeled, and
    sliced
2½ cups water
2 cups Riesling wine
½ cup sugar
1 piece (2 inches) cinnamon stick

1 tablespoon grated lemon zest
1½ tablespoons raspberry jam
3 tablespoons unseasoned fine, dry
    bread crumbs
Juice of ½ lemon

DUMPLINGS

2 medium-size apples, peeled, cored,
    and grated
1¼ cups unseasoned fine, dry bread
    crumbs
2 tablespoons Calvados or apple
    brandy
2 tablespoons sugar

¼ teaspoon ground cinnamon
1 tablespoon grated lemon zest
1 large egg, lightly beaten
2 cups dry white wine
1 cup water
¼ cup sugar

1 Combine the sliced apples, water, Riesling, sugar, cinnamon stick, and lemon zest in a large soup pot. Bring to a boil over high heat, then reduce the heat to low and simmer, covered, until the apples are soft, about 15 minutes.

2 Stir in the raspberry jam, bread crumbs, and lemon juice, and simmer until the apples are almost mushy, 10 minutes. Remove the soup from the heat and cool slightly.

3 Place the soup in a food processor and pulse several times, but do not purée. Allow the soup to cool, then place in the refrigerator at least 2 hours.

4 To make the dumplings, combine the grated apples, bread crumbs, Calvados, sugar, cinnamon, lemon zest, and egg in a large bowl. Stir well to mix, then refrigerate the dumpling mixture for about 15 minutes.

5 In a large enameled saucepan, combine the wine, water, and sugar. Bring to a boil, stirring to dissolve the sugar. Reduce the heat to medium-low.

6 Using a melon baller, form the dumpling mixture into balls about 1 inch in diameter.

7 Drop the dumplings into the liquid and poach until they rise to the surface, about 3 minutes. Remove the dumplings with a slotted spoon, cool, and add to the soup. Return the soup to the refrigerator to finish chilling.

8 Serve 3 or 4 dumplings in each bowl of soup.

Serves 4 to 6

Sour Cherry Soup

Sup iz Vishni

A sumptuous dessert soup from nineteenth century Russia, that is delicious made with the summer's freshest sour cherries. You should not substitute canned cherries, though, as this alters the taste dramatically.

2 pounds fresh sour cherries

3 cloves

1 piece (1 inch) cinnamon stick

1⅓ cups water

2 cups sweet rosé wine

½ cup sugar, or more to taste

¼ cup fresh orange juice

1 tablespoon fresh lemon juice

Grated zest of 1 orange

Crème Fraîche for garnish (see Index)

1 Rinse and pit the cherries, reserving a handful of the pits. Set aside about 1 cup of the pitted cherries.

2 On a hard wooden surface, crush the reserved pits with a hammer or meat cleaver. Tie the crushed pits in a piece of cheesecloth along with the cloves and cinnamon stick.

3 In an enameled soup pot, combine the bag of crushed pits, the remaining cherries, the water, wine, and ½ cup sugar. Bring to a boil, stirring, then reduce the heat to low and simmer, covered, until the cherries are very soft, about 25 minutes.

4 Transfer the cherries and 1 cup of the liquid to a food processor. Purée until smooth.

5 Stir the puréed cherries back into the pot. Add the reserved cherries, the orange juice, lemon juice, and orange zest. Simmer over low heat until the cherries begin to soften and the mixture just begins to boil, 7 to 8 minutes.

6 Remove the soup from the heat and add more sugar, if you feel it's not sweet enough. Remove the bag of pits, cinnamon, and cloves. Cool, then refrigerate until ready to serve, at least 2 hours.

7 Serve garnished with crème fraîche.

Serves 6

Salads

---◆---

SALATI

Salads are recognized as an important part of the meal throughout the Soviet Union, yet their particular place in the meal remains uncertain. A salad is capable of making an appearance at almost any stage and sometimes, as in the United States, is a meal in itself.

In Russia, a fresh vegetable salad, dressed with sour cream, might be served as part of the *zakuska* spread, while a cooked vegetable or meat salad will accompany an entrée. In Central Asia, a whole array of tangy salads are served as mandatory accompaniments to a lamb pilaf. And in Moldavia, a salad of tomatoes, cucumbers, and peppers, sprinked with feta cheese is enjoyed throughout the entire meal.

The sophistication and finesse of western salad preparations have not yet penetrated the Soviet defense system, and the salads there remain simple and down to earth. Because of the enormous premium placed on fresh vegetables, many people prefer to eat them without any dressing at all, or just lightly sprinkled with oil and vinegar, or lemon juice.

In the more Europeanized parts of the USSR, the composed salad, made from combining cooked vegetables and dressing them with a creamy mayonnaise (which the Russians love almost as much as sour cream), reigns supreme. Salad Olivier (see the *zakuska* chapter for a delicious appetizer version), with chicken, potatoes, and a host of other ingredients, and *vinegret*, a ruby-colored salad of beets, potatoes, and pickles are the two mainstays in Russia. Frankly, a Russian would choose them above tomatoes, artichokes, leeks, and avocados.

To the south and east of the nation, where there are many more vegetables to choose from, the salads are a pleasure to look at and a wonderful reminder that the real success of a salad is a combination of luscious seasonal vegetables, a sprinkling of oil and vinegar and a good healthy appetite.

Shredded Chicken Salad with Cilantro

Salat iz Kuritsi s Kinzoy

L ots of deeply browned onions add a typically Russian flavoring, to this delightful chicken salad, while the fresh cilantro imparts a Caucasian touch. This recipe comes from Tamara Khanukashvili, a Georgian friend.

*3 pounds whole chicken breasts,
    well rinsed*
Salt
¼ cup light vegetable oil
2 cups chopped onions
*¾ cup walnuts, lightly
    toasted (see Note) and
    chopped*

*¼ cup finely chopped scallions
    (green onions)*
*¾ cup finely chopped fresh
    cilantro*
*1⅓ cups Homemade Mayonnaise
    (see Index)*
*Freshly ground black pepper,
    to taste*

1 Place the chicken breasts in a saucepan with enough water to cover. Bring to a boil, add ½ teaspoon salt, reduce the heat, and simmer until the chicken is cooked through, about 15 minutes. Drain the chicken and allow it to cool.

2 Remove and discard the skin. Remove the chicken from the bones and tear the meat into shreds. Place in a salad bowl and set aside.

3 Heat the oil in a medium-size skillet over medium-high heat. Sauté the onions, stirring, until deep golden, about 20 min-utes. Drain the onions and add them to the chicken. Cool to room temperature.

4 Add the walnuts, scallions, and cilantro to the chicken. Toss with the mayonnaise, and season with salt and pepper. Serve the salad at room temperature.

Serves 6

Note: To toast walnuts, preheat the oven to 350°F. Arrange the walnuts in one layer on a baking sheet. Toast, watching closely, until the nuts are fragrant and slightly more colored, about 5 minutes.

Estonian Cod Salad with Horseradish Sauce

Salat iz Treski s Khrenom

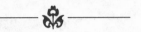

This zesty fish salad makes a lovely luncheon entreé. You can also try making it with haddock or halibut. Both the Slavs and the Balts have a weakness for poached fish dressed in a creamy horseradish sauce.

2 pounds cod fillets, cut into 2-inch
    pieces
Salt
2 tablespoons fresh lemon juice
¼ cup prepared horseradish,
    well drained
¾ cup sour cream
⅓ cup mayonnaise, preferably
    Hellmann's
Pinch of sugar

¼ cup very finely chopped onion
2 medium-size Kirby cucumbers,
    peeled and cut into small dice
3 tablespoons finely chopped
    fresh dill
Freshly ground black pepper,
    to taste
1 head Boston lettuce, leaves sepa-
    rated, rinsed, and patted dry
Cornichons for garnish

1 Place the cod fillets in a shallow enameled pan, add enough water to cover, and bring to a boil over high heat. Add ½ teaspoon salt, reduce the heat to low, and poach the fish until it just begins to flake, 3 to 4 minutes.

2 Drain the fish thoroughly and place it in a large bowl. Sprinkle with the lemon juice.

3 In a small bowl, combine the horseradish, sour cream, mayonnaise, sugar, onion, cucumbers, and dill. Mix thoroughly and season with salt and pepper. Toss the fish gently but thoroughly with this mixture, cover, and refrigerate for 45 minutes.

4 Arrange on a bed of lettuce and serve garnished with cornichons.

Serves 4 as a light first course

Crab and Rice Salad

Salat iz Risa i Krabov

Crab salad is a very prestigious dish in the Soviet Union. When making this simple but delicious dish, avoid the fake crabmeat that is now offered all over the country. It's far too sweet, and it ruins the whole point of a fine crab salad.

1 pound cooked lump crabmeat, picked over and coarsely shredded by hand
1 tablespoon fresh lemon juice
2 cups cooked long-grain rice (⅔ cup uncooked)

2 ribs celery, finely diced
2 medium-size Kirby cucumbers, finely diced
1 large dill pickle, finely diced
2 tablespoons chopped fresh dill
2 tablespoons snipped fresh chives

DRESSING AND GARNISHES

1 cup Homemade Mayonnaise (see Index)
2 tablespoons fresh lemon juice
2 teaspoons tomato paste
Salt and freshly ground black pepper, to taste

Boston lettuce leaves for garnish
2 cooked king crab legs, cut into 1 to 1½ inch pieces, for garnish
Parsley sprigs for garnish

1 In a large bowl, sprinkle the crabmeat with the lemon juice and let stand for 5 minutes.

2 Into the crabmeat stir the rice, celery, cucumbers, pickle, dill, and chives.

3 In a separate bowl, whisk together all the dressing ingredients.

4 Carefully toss the crab mixture with the dressing, keeping the ingredients intact. Season with salt and pepper. Cover and refrigerate for 1 hour.

5 On a decorative serving platter, arrange the salad on a bed of lettuce leaves. Garnish with crab legs and parsley sprigs.

Serves 6 to 8

Estonian Herring and Potato Salad

Rassolye

T his hearty salad contains the true flavors of the Baltic — salty fish, sour pickle, and tart, crispy apple. Serve on a cold evening with Homemade Riga Rye Bread and ice-cold vodka infused with caraway seeds (see the Index for the recipe page numbers).

1 salt (schmaltz) herring fillet
2 red-skinned potatoes, boiled and
    cut into ½-inch dice
3 canned beets, cut into ½-inch dice
⅓ cup minced onion
1 large tart apple, cored and cut
    into ½-inch dice
½ cup diced dill pickles
2 hard-cooked eggs, chopped
1 cup diced cooked ham or veal

DRESSING AND GARNISH
1 tablespoon whole-grain mustard
1 teaspoon dry mustard
1½ tablespoons cider vinegar
1⅓ cups sour cream
1 teaspoon prepared red horse-
    radish, drained
½ teaspoon sugar, or more to taste
Salt and freshly ground black
    pepper, to taste
1 hard-cooked egg, sliced, for garnish

A Cold Luncheon from the Baltic

Cold Veal Meat Loaf with Horseradish Sauce

Estonian Herring and Potato Salad

Cucumbers in Sour Cream

Riga Rye Bread

•

Aquavit

•

Alexandertort

• • •

◆◆

1 Soak the herring fillet in cold water to cover, covered, in the refrigerator for 6 to 8 hours or overnight.

2 Rinse the herring well, pat dry with paper towels, and cut into ½-inch cubes. Place in a large bowl and combine with the potatoes, beets, onion, apple, pickles, chopped eggs, and meats.

3 In a small bowl, whisk the mustards with the vinegar until smooth. Stir in the remaining dressing ingredients (through the salt and pepper) and blend well.

4 Add the dressing to the salad and toss until the ingredients are evenly coated.

5 Transfer to a serving bowl and serve garnished with sliced egg.

Serves 6

Moldavian Potato, Feta, and Scallion Salad

Salata de Cartofi cu Brinza

Just when you thought you'd run out of all the conceivable potato salad recipes, here is a treat from Moldavia for your next picnic. For additional color, you might enjoy adding roasted red pepper slivers.

6 medium-size red-skinned potatoes

⅓ cup olive oil

2 large cloves garlic, crushed in a garlic press

1 cup crumbled feta cheese, preferably Bulgarian

¼ cup finely chopped scallions (green onions)

3 tablespoons red wine vinegar, or more to taste

2 tablespons finely chopped fresh dill

Salt and freshly gound black pepper, to taste

8 imported black olives for garnish

1 Scrub the potatoes thoroughly under cold running water. Boil in lightly salted water until tender, 18 to 20 minutes. Cool until manageable and cut into ¾-inch dice.

2 In a large bowl, toss the potatoes with the olive oil and garlic and then cool to room temperature.

3 Add the feta and scallions to the pota-toes and drizzle with the vinegar. Add the dill and season to taste with salt and pepper. Toss all the ingredients together gently. Allow the salad to sit for 1 hour in order for the flavors to settle. Garnish with the olives and serve.

Serves 4

Russian Cooked Vegetable Salad

Vinegret

Synonymous with Russian, or rather, Soviet cuisine, *vinegret* imme-diately suggests herring, vodka, and black bread, a combination that inevitably puts any Russian in a party mood. Don't be put off by the canned peas called for in this recipe; they are a hot item in the USSR and cru-cial for many contemporary dishes.

1 large beet, with its skin, but
stemmed, washed, and dried, or
1 can (16 ounces) beets, drained
and cut into ½-inch dice
3 medium-size boiling potatoes, peeled
2 medium-size carrots, peeled
¾ cup chopped onion

3 medium-size dill pickles, cut into
½-inch dice
1 can (8½ ounces) peas, drained
¼ cup chopped scallions (green onions)
¼ cup finely chopped fresh dill
Salt and freshly ground black
pepper, to taste

DRESSING
1 teaspoon dry mustard
½ teaspoon sugar
3 tablespoons red wine vinegar

⅓ cup sunflower or corn oil
Salt and freshly ground black
pepper, to taste

1 If you are using a fresh beet, preheat the oven to 375°F.

2 Wrap the beet in aluminum foil and bake until tender, about 1¼ hours. When the beet is cool enough to handle, peel it, and cut it into ½-inch dice.

3 Meanwhile, cook the potatoes in lightly salted boiling water for 10 minutes. Add the carrots and cook until the vegetables are tender, but not mushy, about 10 minutes more. Let cool until manageable, then cut the vegetables into ½-inch dice.

4 In a large salad bowl, combine the potatoes, carrots, onion, pickles, peas, beet, scallions, and dill. Season with salt and pepper and toss gently, taking care not to crush the vegetables.

5 In a small bowl, whisk together the dry mustard, sugar, and vinegar. Whisk in the oil and season with salt and pepper.

6 Toss the salad with the dressing; taste and correct the seasoning. Cover and refrigerate for 30 minutes before serving.

Serves 4 to 6

Sauerkraut Salad "Provençal"

Kvashennaya Kapusta Provansal

This salad is called Provençal because of the olive oil, which used to be called "oil of Provence." There is hardly anything better for a winter buffet with cold cuts and, especially, ham.

2 packages (1 pound each) sauerkraut (do not use canned)

1 large sweet red apple, cored and
diced

½ cup seedless red grapes, each one
cut lengthwise in half

⅓ cup fresh cranberries

4 pickled or canned plums, drained
well, cut in half, and pitted

1 large carrot, peeled and
julienned

6 scallions (green onions), trimmed
and finely chopped

3 tablespoons chopped fresh dill

½ cup olive oil

½ teaspoon sugar, or more
to taste

1 Drain the sauerkraut thoroughly. Rinse under cold running water and squeeze the sauerkraut to remove any excess liquid.

2 In a large salad bowl, combine the sauerkraut with the apple, grapes, cranberries, plums, carrot, scallions, and dill

and toss well. Sprinkle with the sugar and toss with the oil. Taste and add more sugar, if desired. Cover and refrigerate overnight.

Serves 8

Tomato and Garlic Salad

Salat iz Pomidorov s Chesnokom

This is a great accompaniment to grilled meats, but do get the ripest and the meatiest tomatoes. In the Caucasus this salad is made with the local opal basil.

¼ cup best-quality red wine vinegar

2 large cloves garlic, crushed in a garlic press

5 medium-size fresh, ripe tomatoes, each cut into 8 wedges

⅓ cup finely chopped red onion

3 tablespoons extra-virgin olive oil

Salt and freshly ground black pepper, to taste

¼ cup slivered fresh basil, preferably opal

1 In a small bowl, combine the vinegar and the garlic and let stand for 30 minutes.

2 Place the tomatoes and onion in a salad bowl and sprinkle with the vinegar and garlic mixture. Toss with the olive oil and season with salt and pepper. Cover

and refrigerate for 30 minutes.

3 Sprinkle the salad with the basil and serve.

Serves 4 to 6

Cucumbers in Sour Cream

Salat iz Ogurtsov so Smetanoy

Serve this Slavic classic as a part of a Russian appetizer buffet. You can also try serving radishes in sour cream, in which case use 10 large red radishes and omit the capers.

> 5 large Kirby cucumbers, peeled and
>   sliced thinly
> 1 teaspoon salt
> ¾ cup sour cream
> 1 tablespoon white vinegar

> 2 tablespoons capers, drained
> 3 tablespoons finely chopped
>   fresh dill, plus additional dill
>   for garnish
> ¼ teaspoon sugar

1 In a medium-size bowl, toss the cucumbers with the salt and let stand for 1 hour. Drain thoroughly and pat dry with paper towels.

2 In a bowl, stir the sour cream with the vinegar, capers, dill, and sugar. Add the cucumbers and toss. Taste for seasoning and add salt, if desired. Cover and refrigerate for 1 hour.

3 Sprinkle with additional dill to serve.

Serves 6

My Mother's Salad Olivier

Salat Olivie po Retseptu Moyei Mami

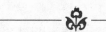

My mother's version of the Russian classic, which her American friends call "the best cole slaw they've ever eaten, makes a fine accompaniment to Russian Hamburgers."

2 cups shredded green cabbage

2 medium-size carrots, peeled and
    cut into julienne

1 large boiling potato, peeled,
    boiled, and cut into small dice

1 medium-size tart apple, peeled,
    cored, and diced

2 hard-cooked eggs, chopped

1 cup fresh or frozen green peas,
    cooked

Salt and freshly ground black
    pepper to taste

DRESSING

¾ cup Homemade Mayonnaise
    (see Index)

½ cup sour cream

1 tablespoon Dijon mustard

2 tablespoons fresh lemon juice

½ teaspoon sugar

Salt and freshly ground black
    pepper, to taste

1 Combine all the salad ingredients in a large bowl and toss well, being careful not to mash the ingredients. Season generously with salt and pepper.

2 In a bowl, thoroughly combine the dressing ingredients. Toss the salad with the dressing, cover, and refrigerate until ready to serve.

Serves 4 to 6

Green Bean
and Walnut Salad

Mtsvani Lobios Pkhali

This salad is a real winner among the seemingly endless repertoire of bean and walnut concoctions from Georgia. For a crunchier salad, serve it soon after adding the dressing; for a more piquant flavor, make it the day before, to allow the green beans to soak up the rich garlic, vinegar, and walnut flavors.

½ cup ground walnuts

2 medium-size cloves garlic, crushed
    in a garlic press

2 tablespoons red wine vinegar,
    or more to taste

1 tablespoon fresh lemon juice

1 tablespoon water

3 tablespoons olive oil

1 pound green beans, trimmed and
    cut crosswise in half

½ medium-size red onion, thinly sliced

¼ cup finely chopped fresh cilantro

Salt and freshly ground black
    pepper, to taste

1 In a small bowl, combine the walnuts, garlic, vinegar, lemon juice, water, and oil. Mix thoroughly. Let stand for 30 minutes.

2 Bring enough lightly salted water to a boil to cover the beans when added. Add the beans and boil until the beans are tender, about 7 minutes. Drain, refresh under cold running water, and drain again. Pat dry.

Bean Salads

Flavorful and nutritious bean salads hold a prominent place in the healthful cuisines of the Caucasus. Follow suit by combining white or red beans, chick-peas or lentils with chopped fresh plum tomatoes and red onions, a sprinkling of minced garlic and green chile pepper, and lots of fresh herbs. Toss with some lemon juice and good olive oil and delight in a healthy lunch.

3 In a salad bowl, combine the beans and the onion. Add the dressing, cilantro, and more vinegar, if desired. Season to taste with salt and pepper and toss well. Serve either chilled or at room temperature.

Serves 4

Pepper and Eggplant Salad

Salat iz Baklazhanov i Pertsov

Although not a part of the original recipe, roasting the peppers will make this Southern Russian eggplant salad truly special. The pickles provide a zesty accent, like capers do in Mediterranean recipes.

1 medium-size eggplant, about
    1¼ pounds, cut into
    ½-inch slices
Salt
5 tablespoons olive oil
1 small red onion, cut lengthwise in
    half, then thinly sliced
1 small green bell pepper, cored,
    seeded, and cut into strips
1 small red bell pepper, cored,
    seeded, and cut into strips

1 small yellow bell pepper, cored,
    seeded, and cut into strips
2 medium-size dill pickles, diced
2 cloves garlic, crushed in a garlic
    press
3 tablespoons fresh lemon juice
2 scallions (green onions), trimmed
    and finely chopped
⅓ cup finely chopped cilantro or
    parsley
Freshly ground black pepper, to taste

1 Place the eggplant slices in a colander and sprinkle generously with salt. Let stand for 30 minutes.

2 Preheat the oven to 425°F.

3 Rinse the eggplant slices well and pat dry with paper towels. Arrange the slices in one layer on a lightly oiled baking sheet. Brush the eggplant on both sides with 2 tablespoons of the oil and bake until golden brown, about 15 minutes on each side. Remove from the oven and let cool slightly.

4 In a salad bowl, combine the onion and bell peppers.

5 With a large knife, chop the eggplant slices fine. Add to the salad bowl along with the remaining 3 tablespoons oil, the pickles, garlic, lemon juice, scallions, and parsley. Mix thoroughly and season with salt and pepper. Cover and refrigerate for at least 1 hour.

Serves 6

Mushroom and Egg Salad

Salat iz Yaits i Gribov

Consider this lovely Russian salad next time you are looking for a new sandwich idea. It's great on a thick slice of sourdough rye accompanied by a crunchy deli pickle.

5 tablespoons vegetable oil

1 pound fresh white mushrooms,
  coarsely chopped

1 cup chopped onions

4 hard-cooked eggs, coarsely chopped

⅓ cup finely chopped fresh dill

¾ cup Homemade Mayonnaise
  (see Index)

2 tablespoons Dijon mustard

1 tablespoon fresh lemon juice

Salt and freshly ground black
  pepper, to taste

1 Heat 3 tablespoons of the oil in a medium-size skillet over medium heat. Raise the heat to high and sauté the mushrooms, stirring occasionally, until they throw off their liquid, reabsorb it, and are nicely browned, 15 minutes. Transfer the mushrooms to a salad bowl.

2 Heat the remaining 2 tablespoons oil in the skillet. Sauté the onions over medium heat, stirring occasionally, until deep golden, about 15 minutes. Transfer to the salad bowl along with the eggs and dill.

3 In a small bowl, whisk together the mayonnaise, mustard, and lemon juice. Toss the salad with this dressing and season with salt and pepper. Serve at room temperature.

Serves 6

Lima Bean
and
Spinach Salad

Salat iz Fasoli i Shpinata

This garlicky salad is a lucky hybrid of Armenian and Georgian salads discovered by successful Russian restaurateur, Grigori Furmanov, in New York, who has been even more successful ever since. Take it on your next picnic and discover why.

1 cup dried lima beans, soaked overnight in water to cover

⅓ cup extra-virgin olive oil

1 package (10 ounces) frozen
spinach

¾ cup walnut pieces

3 medium-size cloves garlic

3 tablespoons red wine vinegar

¼ cup finely chopped fresh parsley

¼ teaspoon ground coriander,
or more to taste

Small pinch of dried red pepper
flakes

Fresh lemon juice, to taste

Salt and freshly ground black
pepper, to taste

1 Drain the beans and place them in a saucepan, adding enough water to cover by at least 3 inches. Bring to a boil, reduce the heat to medium low, and cook until the beans are just tender, about 45 minutes. Make absolutely sure the beans are not overcooked.

2 Drain the beans thoroughly, place in a salad bowl, and toss with the olive oil. Set aside.

3 Cook the spinach in boiling, salted water until cooked through. Cool until manageable, then squeeze the spinach to remove any excess water.

4 Combine the spinach, walnuts, garlic, and vinegar in a food processor and process until smooth.

5 Gently stir the spinach mixture into the beans along with the parsley, coriander, and dried red pepper flakes. Season with lemon juice, salt, and pepper. Cover and refrigerate for 1 hour before serving.

Serves 4

Spinach and Yogurt Salad

Espinak Borani

A popular salad throughout the Caucasus and the Middle East, this can also serve as a dip with pita wedges. You can substitute mint or parsley for the cilantro.

2 bunches spinach, about 1½ pounds
in all, well rinsed and stemmed

⅓ cup finely chopped fresh cilantro

¾ cups plain low-fat yogurt

¼ cup fresh lemon juice

2 small cloves garlic, crushed in a
garlic press

¼ teaspoon sugar

Salt and freshly ground black
pepper, to taste

1 In a large saucepan, bring 3 cups of lightly salted water to a boil. Add the spinach and cook over medium-low heat until the spinach is tender, 2 to 3 minutes. Drain the spinach, cool until manageable, and squeeze the spinach to remove any excess water. Chop the spinach as fine as you can.

2 In a large bowl, combine the spinach with the cilantro, yogurt, lemon juice, garlic, and sugar. Mix thoroughly and season with salt and pepper. Cover and refrigerate for 1 hour before serving.

Serves 4

Yogurt and . . .

Vegetables dressed with yogurt make a refreshingly cool and tangy salad that goes perfectly with many summer entrées. Use it alone or for a richer flavor, mix the yogurt with a little heavy cream or sour cream. You can also add a couple of tablespoons of yogurt to your favorite vinaigrette. And don't forget to sprinkle on plenty of fresh herbs — mint, cilantro, and dill are appropriate choices.

Here are the vegetables that seem to have a natural affinity with yogurt:

Cucumbers • Red Radishes • Cooked Cauliflower • Cooked Green Beans • Cooked Spinach • Cooked Beets • Stir-fried Zucchini

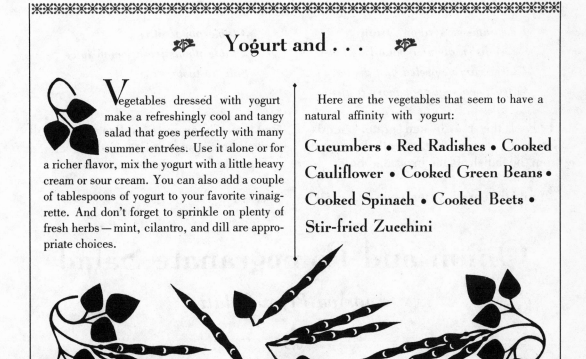

Asian Radish Salad

Turp Salati

This salad is from Central Asia, where it is made from the gorgeous, succulently sweet *margilan* radish, a rare treat, indeed. One closest in taste — although far inferior, alas — is the long white Asian (sometimes called Japanese or Chinese) radish daikon, available at Korean and other Asian-run vegetable markets. This salad is a traditional accompaniment to the Uzbek Lamb Pilaf (see Index).

1 medium-size daikon (Asian
    radish), about 1 pound
1 large carrot, peeled and grated
½ teaspoon sugar, or more to taste

3 tablespoons olive oil
2 tablespoons fresh lemon juice
Salt, to taste

1 Peel the radish and grate. Gently squeeze out some but not all the liquid from the radish. Place in a salad bowl.

2 Add the carrot, ½ teaspoon sugar, oil, and lemon juice and toss. Season with salt and add more sugar, if desired. Cover and refrigerate for at least 30 minutes.

Serves 4

Onion and Pomegranate Salad

Anor va Piyoz Salati

In Central Asia this salad of marinated red onions and pomegranate seeds is served as an accompaniment to savory pilafs and grilled meats. The sweet fruit complements the crisp onion perfectly.

2 large red onions, halved and sliced
Salt
¼ cup red wine vinegar
1 cup pomegranate seeds

¼ cup fresh or bottled pomegranate
    juice
⅓ cup chopped fresh Italian
    (flat-leaf) parsley

1 In a colander, toss the onion with 1 teaspoon salt. Allow to stand for 20 minutes. Drain thoroughly and pat dry with paper towels.

2 In a salad bowl, combine the onions with the vinegar, pomegranate seeds,

pomegranate juice, and salt, if needed. Cover and refrigerate for 2 to 4 hours. Add the parsley and toss right before serving.

Serves 6 as an accompaniment to pilafs or grills

Moldavian Tomato, Cucumber, and Pepper Salad

Salta de Patlagele, Castraveti si Ardei

T hroughout the Middle East and the Balkans, this basic salad of diced fresh vegetables accompanies every summer meal. It goes particularly well with grilled meats or fish.

4 medium-size firm ripe tomatoes,
    finely diced
5 small Kirby cucumbers, peeled and
    finely diced
2 Italian (pale green frying) peppers,
    cored, seeded, and finely diced
½ cup finely chopped red onion
¼ cup chopped fresh Italian (flat-
    leaf) parsley

¼ cup sunflower or olive oil
3 tablespoons red wine vinegar,
    or more to taste
Salt and freshly ground black
    pepper, to taste
4 ounces feta cheese, grated on the
    large disk of a grater

1 In a serving bowl, combine the tomatoes, cucumbers, peppers, onion, and parsley.

2 Whisk together the oil, 3 tablespoons vinegar, the salt, and pepper. Add the vinaigrette to the salad and toss to combine. Cover and refrigerate for 1 hour.

2 Taste the salad and correct the seasonings, if needed. Sprinkle with the feta (without tossing it into the salad). Serve at once.

Serves 4 to 6

Uzbek Tomato, Onion, and Pepper Salad

Achchik-Chuchuk

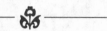

Serve this salad with a lamb pilaf or the Uzbek Lamb and Cumin Stew (see Index). The crunch of the peppers and onions and the sweetness of perfectly ripe tomatoes make it just the right accompaniment for either dish.

1 large onion, thinly sliced
Salt
2 large fresh, ripe tomatoes,
*   thinly sliced*
2 large green bell peppers,
*   thinly sliced*

Plenty of freshly ground black
*   pepper, to taste*
2 tablespoons red wine vinegar
3 tablespoons olive oil

1 Place the onion slices in a small bowl and toss with 1 teaspoon salt. Let stand for 25 minutes, then rinse under cold running water and pat thoroughly dry with paper towels.

2 Place the tomato, pepper, and onion slices in alternating layers in a shallow serving bowl, sprinkling each layer with salt and pepper. Sprinkle the vegetables with the vinegar and oil and toss gently. Cover and refrigerate for 1 hour before serving.

Serves 4

Russian Cuisine

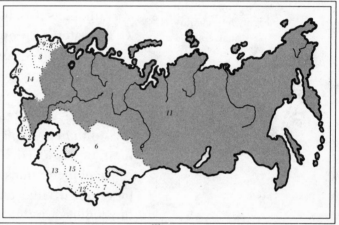

F rom Pskov in the west to the island of Sakhalin, a stone's throw from Hokkaido, Japan, the colossal Russian republic stretches some 16,000 miles (no less than a quarter of the way around the world), occupies three-quarters of the Soviet Union, and is home to about half of its people. Described in the atlas as the Russian Soviet Federated Socialist Republic, but affectionately known as "Mother Russia" to its Slavic children, the republic is a whole empire unto itself. It is sub-divided into sixteen autonomous republics, whose inhabitants range from blond Karelians (north of Leningrad), to the Eskimos of northeast Siberia, to Buddhist Buryats ranged along the Mongolian border.

The foods enjoyed by these peoples are as diverse and unusual as the landscapes they live in and the languages (some hundred of them) they speak. Depending on where you woke up on the Trans-Siberian Express, at mealtime you might find

1. ARMENIA
2. AZERBAIJAN
3. BYELORUSSIA
4. ESTONIA
5. GEORGIA
6. KAZAKHSTAN
7. KIRGHIZIA
8. LATVIA
9. LITHUANIA
10. MOLDAVIA
11. RUSSIA
12. TADZHIKISTAN
13. TURKMENIA
14. UKRAINE
15. UZBEKISTAN

your plate filled with dumplings (*pelmeni*), elegant Russian salmon in puff pastry, or even raw frozen reindeer. But the reindeer and Arctic fish are a little extreme and really not considered classic Russian cuisine.

The Feasts of Old Russia

Although Russia was culturally isolated from Western Europe until the time of Peter the Great (the late seventeenth century), there were, in fact, a good many foreign influences already at work in its cuisine. The Varangians, an ancient Scandinavian tribe that ruled over the region of Russia in the ninth century A.D., introduced the Russians to their much loved herring, and also to a cunning range of techniques (long known to the Vikings) for pickling, drying, and preserving foods throughout the endless winters. Then centuries of invasion and occupation by the Mongols, Tatars, and Ottoman Turks brought a whole shopping list of delicious foods that are now considered to be Slavic staples — noodles and dumplings (which the Turkic peoples had in their turn picked up from the Chinese), stuffed vegetables, tea (introduced as late as the seventeenth century) and that great symbol of Russian hearth and home, the samovar. Along with these came a veritable spice chest of seasonings, fermented milk drinks, olive oil, dried fruits, and lemons. We can paraphrase the well-known saying "Scratch a Russian and you'll find a Tatar" with "Bite into a Russian staple and you are sure to get a taste of the Orient."

The day-to-day fare of the Russian peasants

in those times, however, was sweet and sour and simple: The staples were grains of all sorts — rye, millet, wheat, and buckwheat, which were made into the sourdough breads and *kashas* (cereals) for which the region is famous — and the abundant resources of the woods, rivers, and lakes — mushrooms, berries, honey, and all kinds of fish.

By contrast, the exorbitant feasts of the Russian courts were the stuff of legend throughout Europe. Early accounts of Russia and the kingdom of "Muscovy," written by merchants and ambassadors from the West during the sixteenth and seventeenth centuries, offer a startling glimpse of the primitive, fledgling nation and its indulgent attitudes toward food and dining. In 1553 Richard Chanceler, on expedition from the king of England, described a royal feast given by the "barbarian" Muscovites and their king, "The Great Duke of Muscovy and Chief Emperor of Russia, John Basiliwich." The feast began with a ceremonial offering of bread and salt, which was supposed to keep order in the house. To this day *khleb i sol* (bread and salt) are considered the great tokens of Slavic hospitality — *khlebosolniy* (bread-and-salty) means a hospitable person in Russian. The affair proceeded with a staggering array of dishes (including a "young swan on a golden platter"), which were for the most part difficult for foreign travelers to identify.

Czars' feasts usually began with a roast, often a peacock complete with feathers and lavish decorations (the appetizer spread or *zakuska* table didn't

A welcoming Russian babushka proudly displays her window garden, which she planted in some of the local pottery.

Touching the rest of the dishes, because they were brought out in that order, our men can report no certainty; but this is true, that all the furniture and dishes and drinking vessels, which were then for the use of a hundred guests, were all of pure gold, and the tables so laden with vessels of gold, that there was no room for some to stand upon them.

— Richard Chanceler
Emissary to Muscovy
from King Edward
VI of England

really get going until the nineteenth century). They featured a great variety of hot and cold soup courses, accompanied by and interspersed with filled pies; half a dozen aspics (still very popular); huge, whole fish fancifully dressed up as dragons, which were sometimes so heavy that they had to be lifted by three burly servers; and platters of exotic birds. The variety of fowl, poultry, and game was particularly astonishing: grouse with pickled plums, larks with onions and saffron, partridges smothered in garlic sauce, hazel hens with ginger — the lists are endless. All the dishes were very well spiced with black pepper, saffron, cloves, ginger, garlic, cardamom, and other spices imported from the East that served the double function of preservatives and expensive status symbols. The portions uniformly enormous.

Though the variety and exoticism has been reduced today, with the Russians some things never change. Four hundred years later, and on another continent, the denizens of New York's Brighton Beach have built up a culinary Disney World, where table manners, quantity, and sheer indulgence seem modeled on the banqueting halls of old. When we go to a Brighton Beach restaurant with a large group of friends we usually order a table to be "spread." This means that when you arrive the table is loaded with two dozen cold appetizers, including the most sought-after Russian delicacies: caviars, an assortment of smoked fish, a platter of every imaginable cold cut, piquant minced vegetable caviars, eggplants in various disguises, huge bowls of pickles, and more. Just when you think you've eaten to the limit in come the hot appetizers: *pirozhki*, dumplings, stuffed cabbages, creamed mushrooms, and *blini*. Gorged and bemused, your eyes are scarcely able to follow the constant stream

of entrées that follow next. There's usually a sample of every main dish on the huge menu — kebabs, grilled sausages, chicken Kiev, and fried Cornish hens. Then fruit and ten kinds of pastry. And all this to the accompaniment of an electric organ incessantly thumping out rough-sounding arrangements of out-dated rock songs and a sprinkling of Jewish classics.

There's no doubt that what the Russians lacked in refinement and sophistication they have always made up for in sheer proportion. As one of Gogol's characters in *Dead Souls* said (making fun of French food), "If it's pork I want, I order a whole pig to be served at the table; if it's mutton, drag in the whole ram; if it's goose, then only a whole goose." As for table manners — I'm certain the Russians had almost no conception. In the days of Ivan the Terrible (the mid-sixteenth century), knives and forks were put out entirely for show, and the Czar and his rowdy *boyars* (noblemen) would attack the food with their bare hands and use their sleeves for napkins. Almost two hundred years later in the court of Peter the Great, things still had not changed very much. One of the best known books of the era was a manual of good manners for the young. Its recommendations and the literary style of their expression are simply hilarious. Young nobles were advised: "Cleanest not thy teeth with knives from the table, scratch not thy head during the repast, cutest not a loaf of bread by holding it against thy chest, and built thou not any fence of bones around thy plate."

But modernization and the wholesale adoption of European standards were just around the corner. Off came the long, flowing beards of the *boyars*. Off came their wives' Medieval braids and old Slavic headwear. Peter the Great instructed his court to attend "assemblies," or Russian-style "European Balls." And of course all this new premium placed on the values and customs of the West was reflected in the courtly kitchens. Peter's own tastes were actually rather simple, though he was reportedly willing to try almost anything once. The hearty foods of the German and Dutch burghers appealed to him most — smoked sausages and hams, schnitzels, *buterbrodi* (open-faced sand-wiches), and coffee all arrived in Russia at this time, and all came to stay. At one point, Peter became so fascinated by Dutch techniques of bread- and cheesemaking that he took lessons and learned how to do it himself.

The Baroque Age of Catherine the Great

The modernization and passion for the West that Peter the Great had set in motion was in full bloom in the splendid Baroque courts of the eighteenth century. Catherine the Great (the mid-eighteenth century), a Prussian princess who married and swiftly dispatched a Russian Czar, became the Queen of the Russian Enlightenment. Hers was an empire at the height of its strength, and her household was magnificent. This was also the moment of the first real Russian literature whose flowering paved the way for the genius of Pushkin. The great poet Gavrila Derzhavin, for example, was one of the first writers to celebrate the glories of everyday life in verse. And for him, everyday life seemed to revolved exclusively around the consumption of food. Even in his most straightlaced official odes to the Czarina, he managed to fit in robust and sensuous descriptions of food. And in poems such as "Invitation to Dinner" or "Various Wines," his culinary imagination ran riot as he basked in a paradise of "Rosy-cheeked pies, white cheese, red crawfish, amber caviar . . . glorious Westphalian hams, pilafs and pies, golden stertlets . . ."

Meals at the Imperial Palace were on an even grander scale. The dishes were endless: ten soups; various pâtés, terrines, and roulades; half a dozen or so poultry dishes; scrupulously prepared fish entrées — glazed salmon, perch with ham, crawfish soufflé; plate after plate of small fowl — partridges and truffles, pheasants with pistachios, woodcock salmi; roasts and salads; various smoked meats; savory tartlets and other dainties; and a cornucopia of sweets.

All these dishes were cooked by chefs brought in from France, Germany, and Holland, establishing a tradition of European culinary expertise that was crucial for Russian cuisine until the end of the nineteenth century. If a particular noble family couldn't afford such pricey human imports, they sent off their best young serf-chef to serve an apprenticeship with a Parisian master. Imperial dinners under Catherine were certainly grand, but the menus were also chaotic in the best Baroque tradition. In fact, the most sophisticated food of the era was cooked in the kitchens of the great noblemen. Best of all were dinners at Potemkin's, Catherine's chief minister and lover. He had ten chefs from many nations, and all his pots and pans were made of pure silver. One tureen was so massive that it could accommodate twenty buckets of water. Potemkin's chefs would use this enormous vessel to cook a fish soup with live stertlet that had been

Dinner with Potemkin

This is sample from the menu of one of Potemkin's epicurean feasts:

- Grouse Soup Infused with Chestnuts and Parmesan Cheese

- Grand Filet (of what meat exactly we are not informed) à la Sultan

- Cow's Eyes in Sauce (whimsically called "On Waking Up in the Morning")

- Upper Jaw of Calf (baked in ashes and garnished with truffles)

- Minced Calves' Ears

- Leg of Lamb

- Pigeons à la Stanislaus

- Goose (served "In Shoes" says the menu)

- Woodcock with Oysters

- Green Grape Gâteau

- Maiden's Cream

transported hundreds of miles in special tanks. No expense was spared. Gourmet geese were fattened to the brink of expiration to make *fois gras*; pigs ate the best walnuts and drank rich Hungarian wines; the hens were fed on truffle-filled porridge; and cinnamon bark blazed in the stove.

The Glories of the Nineteenth-Century Russian Table

B ut it was the nineteenth century that was the most glorious era of Russian culture and cuisine. As far as food is concerned, it was one long Belle Epoque. By the early 1800s, thanks in large part to Napoleon's military adventures, the nation had become completely infatuated with all things French. French was spoken in the aristocratic salons, every noble child worthy of the name had to have a French governess or tutor, and the wealthy would habitually dine on *consommé, poulardes, pâtés, vol-au-vents,* and *côtelettes de volailles*. The celebrated French chef, Marie-Antoine Carême, who created the famous Charlotte Russe (a dreamy dessert of ladyfingers, fruit purée, and cream), was the rage of St. Petersburg. Fortunes large and small were consumed to obtain good supplies of the best oysters, truffles, and pineapples.

Toward the middle of the century, however, there began in earnest a debate between the supporters of western influences and those who were calling for a return to the traditional Slavic culture that had had on enormous impact on the world of food — as well as on the literature, politics, and music of the day. In Tolstoy's *Anna Karenina*, the heroine's brother, Oblonsky, takes Levin (a character whose attitudes and appetite reflect Tolstoy's own) out to lunch. Oblonsky orders Flensburg oysters, soup Printanière, sauce Beaumarchais, and bottles of Chablis and Cachet Blanc to wash it all down. But Levin is unimpressed, claiming to prefer cabbage soup (*shchi*) and *kasha*, the very essence of Russian rural cuisine. A scornful waiter adds to the irony of the situation by inquiring whether Levin would like his *kasha* "à la Russe." When Oblonsky visits Levin on his estate a little while later, though, he is completely won over by the flavorful Slavic simplicity of the fare:

> *Although Stephan Arkadyevich [Oblonsky] was accustomed to very different dinners, he thought everything excellent: the herb brandy, and the bread, and the butter, and above all the salt goose and the mushrooms, and the nettle soup, and the chicken in white sauce, and the white Crimean wine — everything was delicious.*

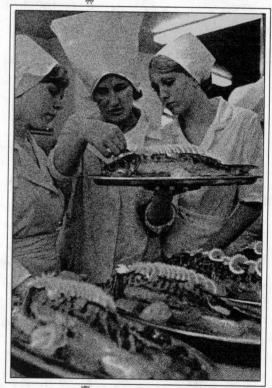

Exquisitely prepared fish is a tradition of classic Russian cuisine.

This was the kind of fare served at the tables of the country squires of Russia. While the peasants subsisted on *shchi* (to which a morsel of meat would be added only on major holidays), *kasha* (often eaten without the delicious butter), and the rye bread that was its perfect accompaniment, landowners — rich and modest alike — seemed to think of nothing but food.

In a land as vast as Russia, country estates could be many days distant from the nearest large city, so diversions were of great importance. Visit-

Their greatest concern lay in cooking dinner; even the aged aunt was invited to offer her advice. Everyone suggested his own favorite dish — soup with noodles or giblets, or tripe or brawn, red or/and white sauce . . . Concern for food was the primary and most important concern for the inhabitants of Oblomovka. What calves were fattened there every year for the festival days! What birds were reared there! What deep understanding, what hard work, what care was needed in looking after them. Turkeys and chickens for name-days and other solemn occasions were fattened on nuts. Geese were deprived of exercise and hung up motionless in a sack a few days before the festival so that they would get covered in fat. What stores of jams, pickles, biscuits. What meads, what kvasses were brewed at Oblomovka.

— Ivan Goncharov
Oblomov

ing one's neighbors and friends was the most important social ritual. And a visit would invariably include a meal. Page after page of nineteenth-century Russian literature is filled with leisurely, luminous descriptions of native Russian fare. The titans of Russian literature — Tolstoy, Dostoevsky, Gogol, and Chekhov — all lead tours round the sacred dining table without missing a dish.

Fish has always been the pride and joy of Russian cookery: the great Volga River, which arcs through the heartlands of Russia and tumbles into the Caspian Sea, has long been legendary for its sturgeons and stertlet. Yet even local rivers and provincial streams were teeming with fresh water fish: carps, perches, trout, pike, smelts, whitefish, bream, and dozens of others. These were pan-fried, steamed, braised with horseradish, baked with sour cream, or poached alive and served with a variety of flavorful sauces. Because meat and animal fats were forbidden on festival days (which number up to two hundred every year), Russian cuisine revolved around fish and mushrooms. On days that meat was allowed, in a typical middle-class household the fish was customarily followed by a roast — a good-size goose with cabbage and apples, a milk-fed suckling pig with horseradish, a saddle of mutton stuffed with kasha. These would be accompanied by pickled fruit, buckwheat kasha with wild mushrooms, and crunchy sauerkraut. And the habitual drinks were the centuries-old, lightly fermented *kvass*, vodka for men, and imported wines for special occasions. After dinner, glasses and decanters of all sizes and shapes would be fetched, and the company would round off their meal with homemade liqueurs and cordials, heady with the aroma of the berries and fruit from which they were made. Tea from the samovar would also be on hand along with a score of homemade preserves. The men would retire for a game of cards and sherry or Madeira, while the women continued to sip tea, chat, and play the piano.

Dining Out Nineteenth-Century Style

❧

While St. Petersburg was always more cosmopolitan and western, and filled with chic and elegant restaurants and cafés, Moscow took pride in its authentic *à la Russe* dining. Moscow, in fact, was by reputation a merchant city, supposedly uncorrupted by the false veneer of foreign manners. And in Moscow they really knew how to eat. One of the most popular establishments in the city at the end of the nineteenth century was the capacious Testov tavern, done up in the rustic style of a *traktir* — an old lower- and working-class eatery. The waiters, dressed in colorful folk costumes, rushed here and there bearing enormous portions of *blini* with smoked fish and caviar, oblong open pies with *visiga*, a dried sturgeon spine, fresh fish, eggs, and mushrooms, called *rasstegai*, which was Testov's trademark, or a spectacular twelve-tier *kulebiaka*, consisting of layers of sturgeon or salmon, rice, eggs, mushrooms, chicken, and game, with thin crêpes (*blinchiki*) between each layer to soak up the moisture and prevent the crust from getting soggy. The clientele was mixed, including nobility who knew how to eat well, millionaire merchants who knew how to spend their millions, and animated knots of artists, poets, and actors who knew little

A Foolish Frenchman

In his famous story *A Foolish Frenchman*, Anton Chekhov tells of a Frenchman who comes to Testov's. Seeing the monstrous, life-threatening portions of *blini* that a man next to him is about to devour, he thinks that the poor man is in the throes of some form of suicide or hideous self-mutilation. He is shocked at the sheer callousness of the waiters who are handing the poor man the weapons (the *blini*), without any sign of remorse, just to make a ruble. So in a fit of noble resolve, the Frenchman decides to save the man. He approaches the table but before he gets to finish his sentence, the happy customer tells the Frenchman that what he's ordered is, in fact, just a light breakfast — and complains about the small portions.

"Not only the climate, but even the stomachs here create miracles," gasps the Frenchman.

Eating Out

By and large Russians prefer to eat at home. When they do go out, it's usually to celebrate a special occasion. It's also common knowledge that if one really wants to eat well, one goes out for lunch, *na obed*, at which time the food will (with any luck) be freshly

Russians enjoy nothing more than their delicious bread, and they consume vast quantities of it. This young boy may very well devour this whole bublik himself!

of food and had little money anyway.

But eating on its own was seldom sufficient entertainment for a real Russian night out. Restaurant suppers would move on from Testov's to the infamous Gypsy club called Yar, where Pushkin had once been a regular. Here, the Gypsies would sing heart-rendering lyrics that made the Russians cry, or fiery ballads accompanied by dances that started out slowly and built to a wild crescendo. The Gypsies were passionate, lewd, and abandoned, providing just that thrill and danger (*ostriye oshusheniya*) without which a Russian party wouldn't be worthy of its name. When the guests could sing, dance, and drink no more, whoever was still standing would jump onto a sleigh with a Gypsy violinist and career around the frozen streets, making merry until they dropped. In the days following the Revolution, some of this uproarious nightlife could be enjoyed at the great Russian Gypsy restaurants of Paris. In Russia today the songs and laughter of the Gypsies are still immensely popular, and they have even been given their own theater, called *Romen*.

Eating Today

When it comes to eating and drinking in Russia, we must not forget the other side of the coin: the rather lean experience of most of the population, which does not, and has never, borne any resemblance to the excessive luxury and indulgence of the few in the Russia of the Czars. The contemporary supply problems of the Soviet economy have a long history. For centuries the Russian peasant, like his counterparts worldwide, often struggled to find enough basic nutrition to keep body and soul together. One account from the sixteenth century observes that in winter bread was sometimes made from dry stamped straw, that "in summer they make good shrift with grass, herbs, and roots," and that "barks of trees are good meat with them at all times." If the peasantry in the Soviet Union, especially in the colder, less productive north of Russia, often had a hard time of it with respect to food and resources, the revolutionary changes following 1917 offered them only mixed blessings.

The vast "collectivization" of farming pursued from the 1920s on has proved to be far less efficient than the authorities predicted at providing basic foodstuffs for the Soviet population at large. The sad legacy of this and other socialist policies has meant that the buying of food, especially in smaller cities, is a source of continual frustration and trauma. One must often stand on line for hours just to get a scrawny chicken or a fatty joint.

For the ordinary citizen, the ordeal of everyday provisioning is a narrative of Kafkaesque proportions. First of all, most of the shelves in most of the stores are empty for most of the time. Real (informed) buying thus commences when a delivery van is spotted some blocks from its predicted destination, and a line begins at a probable counter in a kind of panic of anticipation. In fact it really begins even before this, through the informal network of favors and old-boy networks known as *blat* (connections) — you find me a battery for my radio and I'll make sure you get some meat.

prepared. Evenings are reserved for entertainments or formal functions and the food is usually warmed-up lunch. The evening scene usually features a band or a show and the atmosphere can get quite seedy. Women rarely go out unaccompanied. In fact, when John and I took out my two pretty cousins last summer, it didn't take the men in our Central Asian cooperative restaurant long to realize that there were not enough "husbands" to go round (we had left their husbands in charge of the children at home), and I spent a good part of the proceedings fending off their spirited advances.

The main reason that restaurants are not as popular in Moscow as they are in New York is that they are so hard to get into. As with much else in the USSR, one needs to have some *blat* (connections). A pack of Camel or Marlboro cigarettes or a friend in the kitchen will mean good service and off-menu entrées. Failing this, the lines are enough to kill the most voracious appetite. Thankfully there are exceptions to all this in the new cooperative restaurants and in the special restaurants located in the artistic unions for writers, musicians, and actors.

The Hunt for Food in Moscow

When in Moscow you won't find a café or bistro on every block. But don't worry, you needn't starve. Here is our mini survival guide for the Western visitor.

- Go to the Central market, or to one of the smaller markets, and buy produce for sandwiches or nibbles. There will always be fresh tomatoes if you've got the rubles.

- Buy fresh bread as early as you can in the morning at your nearest bakery. Delicious Borodinsky sourdough black bread with coriander is one of the best things going in Moscow. And it's not too difficult to track down.

- If you're hungry in the middle of the day, go straight to the nearest international hotel. If you are not registered you will have to talk loudly in English and flaunt your raincoat, umbrella, Walkman, or some other western

In the workplace there is a rigidly hierarchic system of *zakaz*—take-home food packages. A humble *zakaz* might consist of a handful of cheap sausage slices and a couple of chunks of rock-hard candy; an average *zakaz* would feature better sausage and, say, some canned fish; and an upscale package might boast hot and cold smoked sturgeon, a jar of premium caviar, and a host of other delicacies.

At the zenith of this Soviet equivalent of insider trading, however, is the *zakritiy raspredelitel* (the "closed supply depot"). These are small, unmarked stores for Communist Party members (*apparatchiks*) and sundry hangers-on that redeem only special vouchers issued by various official organizations. Inside one of these places there are no commodities, no produce, no prices, and no labels—just a quiet flow of orders for the most lavish western and domestic products imaginable. Following the guarded proffering of a special coupon, the "After Eight Mints," the filet mignon, the smoked salmon, or whatever miraculously appears wrapped in newspaper or an anonymous-looking brown paper bag. Recipients tip their hats forward, pull up their lapels, put their heads down, and stride purposefully out of the "store." Fortunately in the nineties this party privilege is eroding quickly as a new free market system takes its place.

Everyday shopping, though, is still full of culinary paradoxes and eccentricities. Outside the system of official state shops and stalls, one could always visit the local private market—long the only real token of western-style enterprise in the USSR. Ambitious businessmen from the Caucasus and Central Asia travel thousands of miles to the urban markets of Russia, carrying with them nearly every vegetable under the sun—which they offer for sale at simply staggering prices. Recently a kilo (2.2 pounds) of strawberries was going for between a third and a quarter of the average monthly salary. I saw huge chunks of beef, free-range chickens and turkeys, three-day-old suckling pigs, homemade cheeses and other dairy produce, a myriad of pickles ranging from tiny chanterelles in a dill marinade to wild Caucasian onions, and all kinds of exotic spices—it's all there for people with enough rubles. But even if they haven't got much, people will buy a whole chicken for a dear visiting guest, oranges for an only child, and cottage cheese (believed to be good for the digestion) for the precious and much-respected *babushka* (grandmother).

No one goes shopping in the USSR without first sticking an *avoska* in their pocket. This is an expandable net bag, whose name derives from the Russian word *avos*, which means (approximately) "what if I'll be lucky." You can almost fit a camel into an *avoska*, which is just as well because shopping bags and shopping carts are not usually provided in the stores.

Hospitality

Hardships and bureaucratic complexities aside, the Russians are still obsessed with hospitality and no one is a guest without also sampling the day's cuisine. If anything, the culinary traumas of the Socialist century have brought about even more reverence for food and its rituals than was the case in the nineteenth century. It sometimes takes years for Soviet emigrés in the United States to understand

symbol (and if necessary a pack of Marlboros) as you pass the doorman, because he will be expecting an official guest pass. The Hotel Rossia, in Moscow, a stone's throw from Red Square, has a snack bar on every other floor where they serve tea, rolls, and light snacks that are quite edible. The Intourist Hotel on Gorky Street has several good eateries that technically serves guests only.

- Alternatively, always make sure that you tank up on enough victuals for half a day at every museum or gallery you visit. Almost all institutions of this type, from the gargantuan Hermitage Museum in Leningrad to the domestically scaled Photo-center on the inner ring road in Moscow, have a serviceable canteen or snackbar. Theaters and concert halls are also important oases in the culinary desert.

- Have your hotel front desk make reservations at one of the cooperative restaurants for dinner. This way you will probably be obliged to pay your bill in dollars, but it's worth the trouble and possible extra expense.

that a casual invitation to someone's home doesn't necessarily mean a full-scale meal. One young man, a recent arrival from Moscow, told me how he had been invited to a new friend's apartment, and to his horror had only been offered a bowl of Ben and Jerry's ice cream. "I wanted a plate of cutlets, and she offers me ice cream!" he moaned. Needless to say, that relationship didn't get very far. Anglo-Saxon hospitality seems quite arcane to the Russian mind. It will take a decade of culinary re-education for it finally to sink in that a dinner invitation for six means just that. No one in Russia would ever think twice about bringing along a few friends, or even someone with whom they just had an unfinished chat on the subway. And what's more, the kitchen would be ready for them and nobody would bat an eye. Even as I was testing recipes and proportions for this book, my mother would have been enormously upset if I didn't allow her to invite as many friends as suited her fancy to our innumerable dinner parties.

The hardships and inconveniences of daily life in Russia aside, an experience of genuine Slavic hospitality never fails to move and impress the western guest. Many Americans who have studied or worked in the USSR miss the warmth and camaraderie of the table more than anything else when they leave. No matter how cramped and confined the apartment (and they are almost *all* minuscule), there is always room for anyone who comes, and the table is always spread to overflowing with appetizers. Everyone raises their shot glasses (*ryumka*) filled with ice-cold vodka, and the meal begins

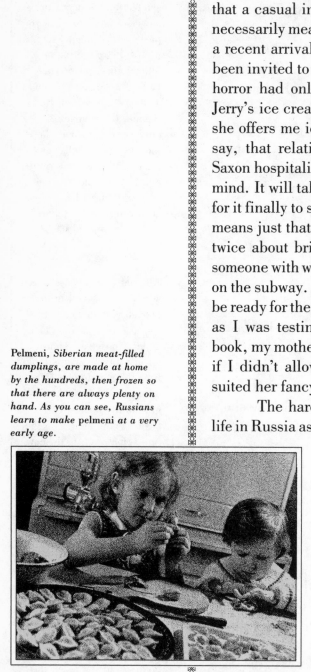

Pelmeni, *Siberian meat-filled dumplings, are made at home by the hundreds, then frozen so that there are always plenty on hand. As you can see, Russians learn to make* pelmeni *at a very early age.*

with a toast to "our meeting" (*so svidanyem*). As the conversation grows more animated, so the toasts arrive with accelerating speed — "for the lovely hostess," "For our most beloved guests," or for the outcome of this or that hotly debated political question.

The appetizers might be followed by a steaming bowl of chunky meat soup; the ancient fish soup (*ukha*); or in summer, by a crimson cold borscht or a tart sorrel *shchi*. Soups are accompanied by a large pie (*pirog*) filled with meat, cabbage, or wild mushrooms; or by diminutive, flaky *pirozhki* (savory filled pastries). The hostess knows full well that the main course (*vtoroye*) must be a real knockout because her guests will invariably have eaten so well before it arrives. It also requires the most ingenuity, since meat preparations are not, traditionally, a Russian forte. So our resourceful hostess will conjure up one or another of the favorite regional dishes — perhaps a spicy Georgian lamb stew, a chicken and fruit pilaf from Azerbaijan, or Jewish sweet and sour beef. Or she will stick to her Russian heritage by making chicken cutlets *Pozharsky*, moist and airy inside and crispy outside; or bake a juicy meat loaf filled with eggs and scallions; or she will wrap cabbage leaves around the best available ground meat and rice to make *golubtsi*, simmered in tomato sauce. A third option is to serve fish like they did so often in the good old days of the Czars: sturgeon in a robust sauce of tomatoes, mushrooms, olives, and pickles; a whole stuffed pike; gently poached whitefish in simple wine sauce; or cod baked under a piquant blanket of sharp cheese and mayonnaise.

After the main course, rustling up a dessert is a cinch. I have never met a Russian woman who couldn't bake like a dream. Perhaps an enticingly plump, sweet yeast dough *pirog* filled with fruit and sour cream; a Russian-style Napoleon with ten layers of pastry drenched in custard cream; or a refreshingly tart sour cream cake, *smetannik*, always a great hit. On the lighter side, maybe an apple Charlotte, or *kissel*, the ancient Russian gelatin-like dessert. Tea is invariably served with the sweets. A good strong dose arrives in a colorful ceramic pot, accompanied by a kettle of boiling water. Both liquids are poured into the cup, with the hostess taking care to inquire as to the strength desired. But as the Russians say, "Tea is not vodka — you can't drink too much of it." So out come the shot glasses again, and everyone lines up for the joke-telling marathons, poetry recitations, and political putdowns. At the first sign of a lull, the obligatory guitar is fetched and everyone breaks into song — a sentimental gypsy *romans*, a gay Russian folk song, or an impassioned social satire by the cult figure Visotsky. Everyone knows every song by heart. Everyone sings. Everyone has eaten and drunk sublimely. The sense of closeness and satisfaction around the table after one of these Russian meals is almost indescribable in English; we hope this book will reserve you a seat.

Lavish desserts are well loved in Russia, and a Russian woman who can't bake is practically unheard of.

Beef and Veal Dishes

GOVYADINA I
TELYATINA

Lost somehow between the penchant for pork in the west and the love of lamb in the east, the cow was never a central presence in any of the Soviet national cuisines. When ordering a beef or veal dish in a Soviet restaurant, you are likely to be confronted by a familiar vocabulary — that is, if you can construe the Cyrillic script or if you have your Berlitz primer handy: *bifshteks, antrekot, shnitsel, langet, eskalop, klops, gulash.* These names underline the fact that almost all the beef and veal preparations common in the USSR are imports from France, Germany, Austria, or Hungary. Even beef Stroganoff, Russia's main claim to fame among international beef dishes, is really another symptom of the national devotion to cubing their meat and disguising it under a sauce.

On a recent visit to my family in Moscow, I bought a spectacular fillet of beef from a private market (for a no less spectacular price) as a New Year's Eve treat. I left my purchase on the kitchen table for a few moments in order to make a telephone call, and when I came back my grandmother had chopped it up into small pieces and was half way through the preparation of a Jewish sweet and sour stew — a dish that works wonders with the kind of tough beef that needs to be braised forever, but that quite ruined my dream of seducing everyone with a gorgeously rare American roast. Apologizing for the impetuousness of our *babushka*, my mother reckoned that the closest most Russians have ever come to experiencing real rare roast beef was when they read Pushkin's *Eugene Onegin* — the lines in which he describes a meal eaten by a Europeanized dandy: rare roast beef, Limburger cheese, Strassburg pie, truffles, and pineapples.

Even though you are well advised to banish any lingering image of a succulent porterhouse steak or rare filet mignon while traveling in the Soviet Union, there's a good chance you won't even miss them if you have the opportunity to sample a beautifully marinated Georgian beef kebab (*basturma*), grilled to perfection on a charcoal fire, and basted with marinade to keep it moist and tender. Come to think of it, a richly satisfying plate of braised beef with horseradish, a top-of-the-line beef Stroganoff, or a fluffy stuffed meat loaf are nothing to frown at either.

As for veal, the Russians were never really partial to it, thinking it made neither ethical nor economic sense to kill young calves. But when veal finally arrived with so many other acquired tastes in the eighteenth and nineteenth centuries, some splendid recipes were devised, including ones offered in this chapter.

BEEF

Beef Stroganoff

Bef Stroganov

I think that at this point in history Americans probably are more familiar with good beef Stroganoff than the Russians because it's the quality of the beef that makes this dish excel. Although it seems like a culinary crime to cut up a filet mignon, the results are spectacular. You can also use filet mignon tips, which are cheaper and almost just as good — but nothing less. This recipe is what real beef Stroganoff should be — indulgent and restrained at once. Try using wild mushrooms, such as boletes or portabello, for an even nobler taste.

2 pounds filet mignon or filet mignon tips, cut into thin strips

3 tablespoons unsalted butter

¾ cup finely chopped onion

1 pound small fresh white mushrooms, caps only, wiped clean and halved

2¼ teaspoons all-purpose flour

⅓ cup Beef Stock (see Index) or canned broth

⅓ cup heavy or whipping cream

½ cup sour cream

2 teaspoons Dijon mustard

1½ tablespoons chopped fresh dill

1½ tablespoons chopped fresh parsley

Salt and freshly ground black pepper, to taste

1 Heat a large, heavy skillet, preferably cast iron, over high heat. Add the meat, a few pieces at a time, and quickly sear on all sides, stirring all the time with a wooden spoon, 3 to 4 minutes. If the meat throws off too much liquid, drain it off and set aside. Remove the meat from the skillet and set aside.

2 Melt the butter in a medium-size skillet over medium heat. Add the onion and sauté, stirring occasionally, until softened, about 5 minutes. Increase the heat to medium-high, then add the mushrooms and sauté, stirring frequently, until they are deeply colored, about 20 minutes. Turn the heat down to medium-low. Sprinkle in the flour and cook, stirring, for 1 minute.

3 Stir in the stock, heavy cream, sour cream, mustard, and the meat juices, if any. Simmer over low heat until the sauce thickens, about 5 minutes; do not allow to boil.

4 Return the meat to the skillet, stir to coat with the sauce, and heat for 1 minute. Stir in the dill, parsley, salt, and pepper, and serve at once.

Serves 4 to 6

Beef Stroganoff

It is not at all clear how this famous beef dish got the name Stroganoff, and if one of the members of the Stroganoff dynasty did give the dish his name, it isn't clear which one. The most outstanding gourmands in that family were Pavel Stroganoff, who lived in the late nineteenth century, and Alexander Stroganoff, who lived at the time of Catherine the Great.

Although the dish was most likely named after Pavel, it was Alexander who was notorious for his lavish feasts.

He fashioned his famous dinners after the Romans. The guests would recline comfortably at marble tables, wearing wreaths made of hothouse flowers, and be served by young boys in Roman tunics. Alexander's food was luxuriously restrained, an historical source informs us. The appetizer consisted just of caviar with a few rare vegetables and fruit, followed by a dish made of herring's cheeks (one plate required more than a thousand herrings). The lips of salmon, poached bear paws, and, perhaps, a roast wildcat followed. Then came cuckoo birds sautéed in butter and honey, halibut liver, and oysters, wild game, and "just a' few figs."

Besides the feasts, however, Alexander Stroganoff was a great patron of the arts without whose generosity Russia's passage into true enlightenment would have been difficult. He was an intimate friend with the greatest figures of the Russian eighteenth century, and not only financially endowed, but oversaw the construction of the monumental Kazan Cathedral, one of the best examples of St. Petersburg architecture.

Boiled Beef à la Russe

Varyonoye Miaso po-Russki

B oiled meats are just as popular in Russia today as they were a century ago when they were served at suppers accompanied by horseradish, mayonnaise, and mustards. As far as I'm concerned, nothing can be more simple and more satisfying than boiled beef, served hot or cold with a sweet and sour beet salad and lots of pickles. Serve this beef with horseradish and onion sauces and a plate of Crunchy Dill Pickles (see Index) or good deli pickles and boiled new potatoes.

1 pound beef marrow bones
2 quarts water
1 large onion, peeled and cubed
1 medium-size carrot, peeled and
    sliced
1 medium-size white turnip, peeled
    and cubed
2 ribs celery with leaves
2 cloves garlic, peeled
Bouquet garni (5 sprigs fresh
    parsley, 5 sprigs fresh dill, 8
    black peppercorns, and 2 bay
    leaves tied in a cheesecloth bag)

1 beef rump or bottom round
    roast, or piece of first-cut
    brisket (about 3 pounds)
Salt, to taste
Fresh dill sprigs for
    garnish
Onion and Honey Sauce (recipe
    follows)
Hot Horseradish sauce (recipe
    follows)

1 In a large pot combine the marrow bones, water, onion, carrot, turnip, celery, garlic, and bouquet garni. Bring to a boil over high heat, periodically skimming off the foam as it rises to the top.

2 Add the beef and salt, then return to a simmer. Reduce the heat to low and sim-

mer, covered, skimming as needed, until the beef is very tender, about 3½ hours.

3 If you are serving the beef cold, allow it to cool in the broth, then remove it from the broth and set aside while you prepare the sauces.

If you are serving the beef hot, remove

it from the broth immediately and allow it to cool slightly to ease the slicing.

4 Strain the stock and reserve for making the sauces.

5 To serve, cut the meat across the grain into ½-inch-thick slices. Arrange on a serving platter. If serving hot, spoon some stock on the meat. Garnish with dill sprigs and serve with the sauces on the side.

Serves 6

Onion and Honey Sauce
Lukoviy Vzvar

This is my rendition of a truly ancient traditional Russian sauce — or, rather, meat accompaniment — called *vzvar*, which is made from a vegetable or fruit such as onion, cabbage, or cranberry and made sweet and sour with vinegar and honey.

¼ cup vegetable oil

3 large Bermuda onions, quartered and thinly sliced

¾ cup broth from Boiled Beef à la Russe (see above), Beef Stock (see Index), or canned broth

1½ teaspoons Dijon mustard

1½ tablespoons honey

4 teaspoons cider vinegar

1 Heat the oil in a large nonstick skillet over medium heat. Add the onions and sauté, stirring occasionally, until colored and soft, about 20 minutes.

2 Add the broth, increase the heat to high, and cook until the liquid is reduced by half, about 7 minutes.

3 Stir in the mustard, honey, and vinegar, then reduce the heat to medium-low and simmer for another 10 minutes. Serve warm but not hot.

Makes about 2 cups

Hot Horseradish Sauce
Goryachiy Sous iz Khrena

Horseradish sauces, both hot and cold, are basic to Russian cuisine. They are used to dress boiled and braised meats and poached fish. I also like this sauce thickly spread on a smoky ham steak and baked in the oven for just a few minutes.

1½ tablespoons unsalted butter
1½ tablespoons all-purpose flour
1 cup broth from Boiled Beef à la Russe (see page 149), Beef Stock (see Index), or canned broth
¾ cup sour cream

½ cup prepared white horseradish, drained
Pinch of sugar, or more to taste
½ teaspoon white vinegar, or more to taste

1 Melt the butter in a small saucepan over medium-low heat.

2 Sprinkle in the flour and cook, stirring for 1 minute. Do not let the mixture brown.

3 Gradually add the broth, stirring constantly to avoid lumps. Add the sour cream, horseradish, sugar and vinegar. Taste and adjust the sugar, and vinegar, if desired. Stir and cook for a few minutes until heated through.

Makes about 2 cups

The time of Catherine the Great was the time of lavish feasts. The food at the palace was served on dishes of pure gold, decorated by the Empress's insignia made of large diamonds. Up to eighty dishes were served at court dinners. Her majesty, however, wasn't terribly fond of elaborate European dishes. One nineteenth-century historian notes, "She preferred boiled beef with pickled cucumbers and a sauce of smoked reindeer tongues."

Rustic Beef and Potato Stew

Podzharka

This richly brown and deeply flavored stew from my mother's repertoire will please even the most demanding of the recent "back to meat and potatoes" converts. Serve with crusty rye bread to soak up the gravy.

2½ pounds bone-in chuck steak

¼ cup vegetable oil

1 large onion, chopped

1 large carrot, peeled, cut lengthwise in half, then sliced crosswise into ¼-inch pieces

1 Italian (pale green frying) pepper, cored, seeded, and cut into strips

3 large cloves garlic, minced

Salt and freshly ground black pepper, to taste

1 teaspoon sweet Hungarian paprika

⅓ to ½ cup boiling Beef Stock (see Index) or canned broth

5 large boiling potatoes, peeled and quartered

2 tablespoons chopped fresh dill

2 tablespoons chopped fresh parsley

1 Trim the meat of most of the fat. Cut the meat into 1½-inch chunks, leaving some meat on the bones.

2 Heat the oil in a Dutch oven over medium heat. Add the onion and sauté until it begins to color, about 10 minutes.

3 Add the carrot and Italian pepper and continue to cook, stirring occasionally, until the vegetables are nicely browned,

about another 10 minutes.

4 Stir in the beef, garlic, salt and pepper, and ½ teaspoon of the paprika. Cook, stirring, over medium heat for 15 minutes. The meat and vegetables should be richly browned.

5 Reduce the heat to low and simmer, covered, stirring often, until the beef is tender, about 50 minutes. While the beef cooks, add stock, a few tablespoons at a time, only if the beef and vegetables stick to the bottom of the Dutch oven.

6 Add the potatoes, dill, parsley, more salt and pepper, and the remaining ½ teaspoon paprika. Cook, stirring, for 2 minutes.

7 Add just enough boiling stock to barely cover the potatoes. Let boil for a few min-utes, then cover, reduce the heat to medium-low, and cook until the potatoes are tender, about 20 minutes. Let the stew stand for 10 minutes before serving.

Serves 4

Note: To facilitate cutting the beef into small pieces, place it in the freezer for 20 minutes to firm up.

Piquant Georgian Beef Stew

Khalia

This simple, tart, and piquant beef dish, simmered with dried sour plums and traditional Georgian spices — coriander and fenugreek — is served in sizzling cast-iron skillets (*ketsi*) in Georgian restaurants.

3 tablespoons olive oil
1½ pounds stewing beef, cut into
    ½-inch cubes (see Note)
3 medium-size onions, finely chopped
¾ cup hot Beef Stock (see Index) or
    canned broth, or more as needed
2 teaspoons tamarind concentrate
    (see Note)
2½ tablespoons tomato paste
½ teaspoon hot Hungarian
    paprika
¾ teaspoon coriander seeds, crushed

¼ teaspoon ground fenugreek
1 teaspoon dried tarragon
Salt and freshly ground black
    pepper, to taste
3 large cloves garlic, crushed in a
    garlic press
¼ cup walnut pieces, finely chopped
    or coarsely ground
3 tablespoons chopped fresh cilantro
    leaves
Pinch of sugar, or more to taste

1 In large heavy skillet, preferably cast iron, heat the oil over medium-high heat. Add the beef and onions and cook, stirring, for 15 minutes. The meat will throw off quite a lot of liquid.

2 Combine ¾ cup hot stock with the tamarind concentrate and tomato paste in a bowl. Allow to stand until the concentrate dissolves, about 10 minutes, then stir well.

3 Add the mixture to the beef together with the paprika, coriander seeds, fenugreek, tarragon, and salt and pepper. Reduce the heat to low and simmer, covered, until the beef is very tender, about 1½ hours. Add more stock, a few tablespoons at a time, if the liquid in the skillet reduces too much. The liquid, however, should not be thin.

4 Stir in the garlic, walnuts, and cilantro and adjust the seasoning, adding sugar and more spices to taste, if desired. Simmer for 15 minutes more.

Serves 4

Note: To facilitate cutting the beef into small pieces, place it in the freezer for 20 minutes to firm up.

Tamarind concentrate is a tart paste, which Georgians in the United States substitute for dried sour plums. It can be purchased at Indian or Thai groceries or mail ordered (see Notes on Ingredients). If it isn't available, substitute 2½ tablespoons sugar-free plum butter, available at health food stores, mixed with 1 tablespoon lemon juice.

Braised Beef Stuffed with Horseradish

Trŏskinta Jautiena su Krienų Įdaru

This is one of the most delicious pot roasts I have ever tasted. The recipe is a variation on a popular nineteenth-century Lithuanian-Polish dish called "hussar's roast." The meat is stuffed with a horseradish mixture that beautifully enhances the rich flavors of the meat and sauce. If you wish, instead you can add the horseradish mixture to the pan juices 1 hour before the beef is ready. It makes a dish that is simpler, but just as good. The beef tastes even better the next day. Serve with Grated Potato Bake (see Index).

4 slices bacon, diced

2½ pounds beef bottom round or
　　chuck, in a thick piece

Salt and freshly ground black
　　pepper, to taste

2 medium-size onions, chopped
　　medium fine

1 large carrot, peeled and cut into
　　julienne

2 parsnips, peeled and cut into
　　julienne

1 rib celery, diced

2 tablespoons vodka

1 tablespoon white vinegar

¾ cup dry red wine

1 cup Beef Stock (see Index) or
　　canned broth

Bouquet garni (4 sprigs parsley, 4
　　sprigs dill, 1 bay leaf, 2 cloves,
　　and 8 to 10 black peppercorns
　　tied in a cheesecloth bag)

3 tablespoons unsalted butter

½ cup prepared white horseradish,
　　drained

2 tablespoons unflavored fine, dry
　　bread crumbs

1½ teaspoons sugar

1½ tablespoons all-purpose flour

1 Preheat the oven to 350°F.

2 In a large, heavy heatproof casserole or Dutch oven with a tight-fitting lid, sauté the bacon over medium heat until it renders its fat. Remove and discard the bacon.

3 Rub the beef with salt and pepper, then add it to the bacon fat and brown well on all sides over medium heat. Remove the meat to a plate. Add the vegetables to the casserole and sauté, stirring occasionally, until they begin to color, about 10 minutes. Return the beef to the casserole.

4 Combine the vodka and vinegar and pour over the meat. Add the wine, stock, and bouquet garni, and bring to a boil.

5 Place the casserole in the oven and bake, covered, for 1¾ hours, turning occasionally. When the meat feels almost tender when you test it with a skewer, remove the casserole from the oven, leaving

the oven on. Transfer the meat to a carving board.

6 Melt 1 tablespoon of the butter in a small saucepan, over low heat. Add all but 2 tablespoons of the horseradish to the saucepan and simmer, stirring, until hot. Stir in the bread crumbs and sugar and simmer for about 1 minute.

7 With a very sharp knife, make two lengthwise cuts through the meat as if you were cutting it into three equal layers, but cutting only five-sixths of the way through. Spread the horseradish mixture evenly between the cuts and tie the meat with kitchen string so it holds its shape.

8 Stir the remaining horseradish into the pan juices. Return the meat to the casserole and continue to bake, covered, for another 45 minutes. The meat is done when a knife inserted into its thickest part penetrates easily. Remove the meat to a cutting board, and cover with foil.

9 Strain the pan juices through a sieve into a small saucepan, pressing on the vegetables with the back of a spoon.

10 Melt the remaining 2 tablespoons butter in another small pan. Stir in the flour and cook for 1 minute. Add ½ cup of the pan juices and stir until blended. Whisk the mixture back into the remaining pan juices.

11 Cut the meat into slices across its length so each piece gets some of the horseradish mixture. Arrange the slices on a serving platter and spoon some of the sauce over. Pass the remaining sauce separately in a sauceboat.

Serves 6

Beef Shish Kebab

Basturma

Meat grilled on a skewer, called *basturma mtsvadi* in Georgian and *shashlik* in Russian (from *shashka*, meaning "sword") has truly become a symbol not only of Caucasian food, but of Soviet cuisine as a whole. It is a featured dish in the Russian restaurants of New York's Brighton Beach area, appropriately nicknamed "Little Odessa," and in the elegant Russian restaurants of Paris, as well as at a Georgian family picnic.

A friend once confessed to me that, in the course of his many misspent years, he had probably squandered the equivalent of an apartment and an automobile in rubles at one of the Moscow *shashlik* joints, *shashlichnaya* — whimsically called *Anti-Sovietskay* ("Anti-Soviet") by its intellectual habitués because it was right across the street from the Hotel Sovietskaya. I hoped he exaggerated, but the story points up the Muscovite passion for this juicy charcoaled meat and its tart *tkemali* (sour plum sauce) accompaniment.

My most vivid childhood recollection of *shashlik* is of an unbearably seductive odor wafting from the *shashlichnaya* at the Sokolniki amusement park. Unfortunately, the line used to outdistance the smell, so my desires for this delicious treat were usually unfulfilled.

Unlike Turks and Armenians, who favor lamb, Georgians prefer their *shashlik* to be made from a tender, marinated juicy sirloin of beef, grilled on long skewers over a charcoal fire, with a few vine leaves tossed in for extra flavor. Georgian chefs are especially proud when presenting the *basturma* on a platter colorfully decorated with vegetables and lemon wedges, with three skewers per plate arranged in a tripod. Serve it like the Georgians do, if you feel like making the evening especially memorable.

Eggplant kebabs and Sour Plum Sauce make a good accompaniment (see the Index for the recipe page numbers).

½ cup dry red wine, pomegranate juice, or sparkling water (see Note)

3 cloves garlic, crushed in a garlic press

1 small onion, grated

8 to 10 black peppercorns, crushed

Salt, to taste

2½ pounds boneless lean sirloin, cut into 1½-inch cubes

3 small onions, cut into wedges

3 green bell peppers, cored, seeded, and cut into wedges

¼ cup olive oil

GARNISHES

Radicchio or red kale leaves

2 tomatoes

2 lemons, cut into wedges

8 scallions (green onions), trimmed

1 long zucchini, cut into six 1-inch-thick slices

A Barbecue in the Mountains

• • •

Garlicky Farmer's Cheese Spread with Walnuts

Lavash or pita

•

Beef Shish Kebab

Sour Plum Sauce

Eggplant Kebabs

Green Bean and Walnut Salad

Tomato and Garlic Salad

Red wine from Tourraine

•

Rum Balls

1 In a large glass bowl, combine the wine, garlic, grated onion, peppercorns, and salt, then add the meat and toss to coat well. Refrigerate, covered, for 6 to 8 hours, turning the meat occasionally. Bring to room temperature before grilling.

2 Prepare hot coals for grilling until coated with white ash, or preheat the broiler.

3 Toss the onion and pepper wedges in a bowl with the oil.

4 Remove the meat from the marinade and string it on long metal skewers, alternating meat cubes with onion and pepper wedges and pushing everything closely together.

5 Grill or broil the skewers 4 inches away from the heat, turning frequently and sprinkling with the marinade every 3 minutes, 9 to 10 minutes for medium-rare, 12 to 13 minutes for medium.

6 To serve in a traditional way, line two serving platters with radicchio leaves or red kale. Cut into the tomatoes as though you are cutting them into quarters, but leave intact at the stem ends. Place one in the middle of each platter. Scatter lemon wedges and scallions on the platters. Stick the sharp end of each skewer into a zucchini slice. Place three skewers on each platter and bring the open ends together to form a tripod. Wrap the ends with a linen napkin to hold them together. Serve at once.

Serves 6

Note: Although it is traditional to marinate the beef in wine or vinegar, the truly experienced Georgian cooks suggest that they actually toughen, rather than tenderize, good beef. They recommend using sparkling water instead.

Pumpkin Moussaka

Titoumov Mussaka

For those familiar with Greek moussaka made from eggplant and topped with béchamel, this dish from Armenia, which is home to some of the best pumpkin dishes anywhere, will come as a wonderful new experience. Butternut squash can also be used instead of pumpkin.

3 pumpkins or butternut squash
  (2 pounds each)

3 tablespoons olive oil

1 medium-size onion, chopped

⅓ cup pine nuts (pignoli)

1½ pounds ground lean beef round

1½ tablespoons tomato paste

¼ cup canned beef broth or water

1 large fresh, ripe tomato, peeled
  and chopped

¼ cup chopped dried apricots

½ teaspoon ground cumin

¼ teaspoon ground allspice

⅛ teaspoon ground cinnamon

3 tablespoons finely chopped fresh
  parsley

Salt and freshly ground black
  pepper, to taste

5 tablespoons unsalted butter, cut
  into bits

1 cup milk

2 tablespoons all-purpose flour

Freshly ground white pepper, to
  taste

¼ cup unflavored dry bread crumbs,
  preferably coarse

¼ cup grated kefalotiri or Parmesan
  cheese (see Note)

1 Preheat the oven to 325°F. Butter two baking sheets.

2 Cut the pumpkins in half and scrape out the seeds. Place the pumpkins on the prepared baking sheets, cut side down, and bake until tender, about 1¼ hours. Leave the oven on.

An Armenian Supper

• • •

Pistachio nuts

Toasted pumpkin seeds

Mixed olives

Raki or Ouzo

•

Artichokes in Olive Oil

Pumpkin Moussaka

Okra and Tomatoes
in Olive Oil

Chilled young Tawny Port

•

Hazelnut Cake in Honey
Syrup

---

3 When the pumpkins are cool enough to handle, peel off the shells and cut the pulp into slices, ¼ inch thick. This can be done a day ahead.

4 Heat the oil in a large heavy skillet over medium heat. Add the onion and pine nuts and sauté, stirring, until the onion is soft but not browned and the pine nuts are lightly toasted, about 8 minutes.

5 Add the ground beef, turn the heat up to medium-high, and brown, breaking up the meat with a fork. Drain off all but 1 tablespoon of the fat.

6 Dilute the tomato paste in the broth and add to the skillet along with the tomato and apricots. Cook until the apricots have softened, 8 minutes. Remove from the heat, add the cumin, allspice, cinnamon, parsley, and salt and pepper.

7 Preheat the oven to 325°F. Butter a 14 × 9 × 2-inch baking dish.

8 Arrange half the pumpkin slices in an overlapping layer in the bottom of the prepared baking dish. Sprinkle with salt and 3 tablespoons butter. Spread the meat mixture evenly over the pumpkin with a rubber spatula. Arrange the rest of the pumpkin in a layer on top of the meat. Bake for 30 minutes.

9 While the moussaka is baking, prepare the sauce. Bring the milk just to a boil in a small saucepan over medium heat.

Remove immediately from the heat.

10 Melt the remaining 2 tablespoons butter over low heat in a medium-size saucepan. Add the flour and cook, stirring, for 2 minutes. Remove from the heat and add the milk, whisking vigorously until the mixture is smooth. Add salt and white pepper to taste and return to the heat. Simmer, stirring, for 10 minutes.

11 Remove the moussaka from the oven. Increase the oven temperature to 375°F.

12 Pour the sauce evenly over the moussaka and sprinkle with bread crumbs and cheese. Bake until the top is golden brown, about 15 minutes more. Remove from the oven and let stand for 5 minutes before serving. Cut into squares to serve.

Serves 6 to 8

Note: Kefalotiri is a tangy Greek grating cheese. It is available at Greek and some gourmet grocery stores.

Stuffed Meat Loaf

Farshirovanniy Rulet

This Russian meat loaf, stuffed with lots of scallions and chopped hard-cooked egg, is easy to prepare, pretty to look at, inexpensive, and, above all, extremely tasty.

3 tablespoons unsalted butter

1 large onion, finely chopped

3 slices white bread, crusts
    removed

⅓ cup milk

1¾ pounds ground lean
    beef round

2 large eggs, lightly beaten

¼ cup ice water

2 tablespoons sour cream

Salt and freshly ground black
    pepper, to taste

4 hard-cooked eggs, finely
    chopped

½ cup finely chopped scallions
    (green onions), greens only

4 tablespoons (½ stick) unsalted
    butter, melted

2 tablespoons mayonnaise,
    preferably Hellmann's

⅓ cup unflavored fine,
    dry bread crumbs, or more
    as needed

1 teaspoon sweet Hungarian
    paprika

½ teaspoon hot Hungarian
    paprika

1 Melt the butter in a small skillet over medium heat. Add the onion and sauté until lightly colored, about 12 minutes.

2 Meanwhile, soak the bread in the milk for 10 minutes. Squeeze the bread to remove any excess milk and crumble into a large bowl. Discard the milk.

3 Add the beef to the bread along with the onions and their cooking fat, eggs, ice water, sour cream, and salt and pepper. Knead until thoroughly blended. Set the meat loaf mixture aside.

4 In a second bowl, combine the hard-cooked eggs, scallions, and melted butter. Season lightly with salt and pepper and mix.

5 Preheat the oven to 375°F. Line a baking sheet with aluminum foil.

6 Spread the meat loaf mixture out on a large piece of waxed paper into a 12 × 10-inch rectangle. Spread the stuffing over the meat mixture, leaving a 1-inch border on all sides. Roll up like a jelly roll, starting on one long side. Peel back the waxed paper as you roll.

7 Place the roll, seam side down, on the prepared baking sheet. Spread with the mayonnaise, using a rubber spatula, and sprinkle generously with bread crumbs and with sweet and hot paprika.

8 Bake 1 hour. Cut into thick slices and serve at once.

Serves 6

Russian Hamburgers

Kotleti

I can say without fear of contradiction that this is what people in the Soviet Union today really eat. *Kotleti* has come to mean chopped-meat patties, but originally it meant cutlets. Humble *kotleti* are beautifully moist inside and crispy on the outside.

2 slices white bread, crusts removed

¼ cup milk

1½ pounds ground lean beef round

1 medium-size onion, grated

1 clove garlic, minced

¼ cup crushed or shaved ice or ⅓ cup ice water

1 large egg, separated

2 tablespoons chopped fresh parsley

2 tablespoons chopped fresh dill

Salt and freshly ground black pepper to taste

Unflavored fine, dry bread crumbs for rolling the kotleti

3 tablespoons vegetable oil, or more as needed

3 tablespoons unsalted butter, or more as needed

1 Soak the bread in the milk for 10 minutes. Squeeze the bread to remove any excess milk and crumble it into a large bowl. Discard the milk.

2 Add the beef to the bread along with the onion, garlic, ice, and the egg yolk. Stir to mix well.

3 Beat the egg white until frothy. Carefully add it to the meat mixture along with the fresh herbs and salt and pepper. Knead until thoroughly blended and fluffy.

4 Form the mixture into oval patties about 3 inches long. Place the bread crumbs on a plate. Roll the patties in the crumbs, flattening them lightly as you roll.

5 In a large, heavy skillet, preferably cast iron, heat 3 tablespoons each oil and butter over medium heat until the mixture foams. Add about four patties to the skillet and fry until richly browned on both sides. Reduce the heat to low, and cook, covered, for another 4 to 5 minutes. Prick a patty with the tip of a knife. If the juices still run red, cook a little more. Repeat the procedure with the rest of the patties, adding more oil and butter if necessary.

Serves 6

VEAL

Roast Veal
with Sour Cherries

Telyatina s Vishnyami

This and the recipe for Salmon Stuffed Veal with Caviar Sauce represent the best of nineteenth-century bourgeois Russian cooking. That is, they can be situated somewhere in between peasant dishes such as *shchi* and kasha and aristocratic, French-inspired haute cuisine.

Today, of course, either roast can be proudly presented at the most elaborate of formal dinners. This stunning preparation for veal with sour cherries shows the distinct influence of Austro-Hungarian cooking, somewhat less common in Russia than the French influence. If you can't find jarred sour cherries, substitute morello cherries. Bing cherries won't do for this dish.

*3½ to 4 pounds boneless veal loin,
    rolled and tied*
*2 cups jarred pitted sour cherries,
    drained but 1 cup syrup reserved
    (32-ounce jar sour cherries)*
½ lemon
*Salt and freshly ground black
    pepper, to taste*
*4 tablespoons (½ stick) unsalted
    butter, at room temperature*

*1½ cups Chicken Stock (see Index)
    or canned broth, or more, as
    needed*
Grated zest of 1 orange
⅓ cup Madeira
*⅛ teaspoon ground
    cinnamon*
Pinch of ground cloves
Pinch of ground cardamom

1 Preheat the oven to 400°F.

2 Make 12 to 14 slits, each ½ inch deep, in the veal with the tip of a knife and insert a cherry in each one. Set the remaining cherries aside.

3 Rub the veal with lemon and sprinkle with salt and pepper, then spread with the butter.

4 Place the veal in a roasting pan that is not too shallow and roast for 10 minutes. Reduce the oven temperature to 350°F.

5 Add the stock, remaining cherries, and reserved cherry syrup to the roasting pan. Cover the meat loosely with aluminum foil and roast, basting every 20 minutes, until the juices run clear when the meat is pierced with a skewer, about 1¾ hours.

6 Transfer the roast from the pan to a carving board. Cover with foil and let stand 10 minutes before carving.

7 Transfer the contents of the pan to a small saucepan and add enough stock to measure 2 cups. Add the orange zest, Madeira, cinnamon, cloves, cardamom, and salt and pepper. Bring to a boil over high heat and cook until reduced to approximately 1½ cups, about 5 minutes. Serve the veal sliced, accompanied by the sauce.

Serves 6 to 8

A Russian Dinner for a Special Occasion

Smoked salmon *buterbrodi*

Caviar Tartlets

Stolichnaya Cristal

•

Clear Salmon Soup

•

Roast Veal with Sour Cherries

Dilled new potatoes

Poached asparagus

Volnay

•

Charlotte Russe

• • •

Salmon Stuffed Veal with Caviar Sauce

Gastronomicheskaya Telyatina s Sousom iz Ikri

This recipe is adapted from a book by Elena Molokhovets, the queen of nineteenth-century Russian home cooking. Although the veal and salmon combination might sound unusual, the tiny pieces of salmon with which the veal is larded, and caviar added to the wine and cream sauce, provide a piquant accent to the delicate taste of the veal. Don't despair if you prefer not to add quality caviar to your sauce. It certainly adds a luxurious touch to the dish, but is not essential to it. You can either substitute lumpfish caviar or do without it altogether.

1 boneless veal shoulder roast (about 3 pounds), rolled and tied

4 ounces smoked salmon, cut into ½-inch dice

Salt and freshly ground black pepper, to taste

¾ teaspoon sweet Hungarian paprika

6 slices bacon

2 cups Chicken Stock (see Index) or canned chicken broth, or more as needed

⅔ cup good-quality dry white wine

⅓ cup heavy or whipping cream

4 tablespoons (½ stick) unsalted butter, at room temperature, cut into pieces

2 teaspoons grated lemon zest

2 tablespoons black caviar for garnish

Finely chopped fresh dill for garnish

1 Preheat the oven to 350°F.

2 Make about 20 deep slits all over the veal with the tip of a knife, and insert a salmon piece as deeply as you can into each one.

3 Place the veal in a roasting pan and rub with salt, pepper, and paprika. Wrap the bacon around the roast and pour 2 cups stock into the pan.

4 Roast the veal for 1¼ hours, then cover

loosely with aluminum foil and continue roasting until the juices run clear when the meat is pricked with a skewer, about 1 hour more. Remove the foil, then remove and discard the bacon. Place the veal on a carving board and re-cover with foil.

5 Pour the pan juices into a glass measuring cup and skim off the fat. If the liquid measures less than 1¼ cups, add stock. Place the juices in a saucepan along with the wine and cream. Bring to a boil over high heat and reduce to about 1 cup, about 5 minutes. Remove from the heat and beat in the butter a piece at a time. Add the lemon zest and stir until blended. Season with salt and pepper.

6 To serve, cut the veal into rather thin slices and divide among six plates. Spoon the sauce over the veal slices and dab each portion with about a teaspoonful of caviar. Sprinkle lightly with dill and serve at once.

Serves 6

Veal Cutlets with Chanterelles in Madeira Sauce

Telyatina s Lisichkami s Sousom iz Maderi

This recipe is my own creation, but is loosely based on two staple nineteenth-century Russian ingredients — wild mushrooms and Madeira. It's quick and easy to prepare, and unfailingly delicious. If you can't get hold of chanterelles, substitute boletes, morels, or portabello mushrooms. Don't use shiitake or oyster mushrooms, as they don't have a deep enough flavor.

Strange to say, by one of those twists of value that constantly occur between the culinary and the everyday worlds, cultivated mushrooms were actually more valued in old Russia than their wild relatives, which were picked and consumed by villagers and peasants. But don't be fooled!

This sauce will also work nicely with chicken fillets.

½ pound chanterelles, boletes, morels,
    or portabello mushrooms
5 tablespoons unsalted butter
4 boneless veal cutlets (about 5
    ounces each)
3 tablespoons all-purpose flour
¼ cup Madeira
⅓ cup Chicken Stock (see Index) or
    canned broth
¼ cup heavy or whipping cream

1½ tablespoons sour cream
½ teaspoon Dijon mustard
¼ teaspoon sweet Hungarian
    paprika
Salt and freshly ground black
    pepper, to taste
Generous pinch of freshly grated
    nutmeg
1 tablespoon finely chopped fresh
    parsley for garnish

1 Wipe the mushrooms with a damp paper towel. Cut the chanterelles or morels in half or, if using boletes or portabello, separate the stems from the caps and cut in thick slices.

2 Melt 2 tablespoons of the butter in a skillet over medium high heat. Add the mushrooms and sauté, stirring, until they throw off and reabsorb their moisture, about 12 minutes. Using a slotted spoon, transfer the mushrooms to a bowl and set aside.

3 Place the veal between two pieces of waxed paper and pound gently with the flat end of a meat pounder until thin. Dredge lightly in flour.

4 Melt the remaining 3 tablespoons butter in the skillet over medium heat. Add the veal and sauté for 2 minutes on each side. Remove to a plate.

5 Add the Madeira and stock to the skillet and bring to a boil over high heat. Reduce to about half, scraping the bottom of the skillet with a wooden spoon.

6 Add the cream and cook, stirring, for 3 minutes. Stir in the sour cream and mustard, turn the heat down to medium low, and cook, stirring, for 2 minutes more. Stir in the paprika.

7 Add the mushrooms to the sauce, stir, and season with salt, pepper, and nutmeg. Replace the veal in the skillet and turn several times to coat with the sauce. Heat for 1 minute. Serve at once, sprinkled with parsley.

Chanterelles, called *lisichki* (little foxes) in Russian, are my favorite mushrooms to pick. After a good late summer rain they appear in large orange-colored clusters, so all you have to do is kneel for a few minutes, then suppress your appetite until you bring them home and sauté them in butter.

Serves 4

Veal and Quince Stew

Tocana de Vitsel

A delicate aromatic veal stew from Moldavia that can be enjoyed on any occasion. Veal with quince is in my opinion one of those fortuitous culinary combinations that usually become clichés as soon as they are discovered. For some reason, though, this dish has not become widely known, at least not in the western hemisphere.

About Quinces

Quinces are one of the most fragrant fruits imaginable. They are available in the fall, and they store well in the refrigerator. As I am writing, the quinces in my refrigerator have been sitting there for over 2 months. Because quinces are always hard and because one doesn't usually eat them raw, it is sometimes difficult to tell when they are ripe. Ripeness does, however, make a difference when you cook with them, so when you buy them for immediate use, select quinces that are deep yellow and that give off the most intense aroma; smell is your best guide. When peeling and coring quinces use a very sharp knife, as the core tends to be very hard.

Add quince to meat or poultry stews or add to the pan juices when roasting pork or game. They will always add a special fragrant touch to your dishes.

8 tablespoons (1 stick) unsalted butter

2½ pounds boneless lean veal shoulder, cut into 1½-inch cubes

All-purpose flour for dusting the veal

2 medium-size onions, chopped

½ cup Beef Stock (see Index) or canned broth

½ cup fruity red wine

1 can (32 ounces) tomatoes, drained, seeded, and chopped

1 piece (1 inch) cinnamon stick

½ teaspoon sugar

Salt and freshly ground black pepper, to taste

2 quinces, cored, peeled, quartered, and sliced

2 tablespoons golden raisins

½ teaspoon sweet Hungarian paprika

1 tablespoon fresh lemon juice, or more to taste

Chopped fresh parsley for garnish

1 Melt 4 tablespoons of the butter in a large heavy casserole over medium heat. Dust the veal pieces with flour and brown a few at a time in the butter. With a slotted spoon, remove the veal to a plate.

2 Melt 2 more tablespoons of the butter in the casserole. Add the onions and sauté, stirring occasionally, until colored, about 12 minutes.

3 Stir in the stock and wine and bring to a boil, scraping the bottom of the casserole with a wooden spoon. Return the veal to the casserole along with the tomatoes, cinnamon stick, sugar, and salt and pepper. Reduce the heat to low and simmer, covered, until the veal is almost tender, about 1 hour.

4 Meanwhile, melt the remaining 2 tablespoons butter in a large skillet over medium heat. Add the quinces and raisins and sauté, stirring occasionally, until the quinces are soft and light golden in color, about 15 minutes.

5 Stir the quinces and raisins into the veal, adding paprika, lemon juice to taste, and more salt or pepper, if desired. Simmer for 45 minutes more.

6 Remove the cinnamon stick and serve, sprinkled with parsley.

Serves 6

Stuffed Breast of Veal

Horti Mise Ltsvats Brindzov

In this recipe from Armenia, the breast of veal is stuffed with aromatic rice pilaf and served with a sweet and tangy tomato and currant sauce. Ideally, you should use boned veal breast for this recipe, but if your butcher won't bone it for you, use a 7-pound breast of veal with bones. If some stuffing doesn't fit into the veal, bake it separately, covered, for about 40 minutes.

STUFFING

2 tablespoons olive oil

1½ cups long-grain rice

2¾ cups boiling Chicken Stock (see Index) or canned broth

Salt, to taste

3 tablespoons unsalted butter

1½ cups chopped onions

2 medium-size Italian (pale green frying) peppers, cored, seeded, and finely diced

½ cup tomato juice

¾ cup dried currants

⅓ cup finely chopped Italian (flat-leaf) parsley

½ teaspoon ground cinnamon, or slightly more to taste

½ teaspoon ground allspice

¼ teaspoon ground cloves

Freshly ground black pepper, to taste

4 pounds boneless breast of veal in one piece, trimmed of all fat, with a pocket cut for stuffing

Salt and freshly ground black pepper, to taste

¼ teaspoon ground cinnamon

1 tablespoon olive oil

¾ cup Chicken Stock (see Index) or canned broth

1 can (32 ounces) Italian plum tomatoes, drained and chopped

1 piece (2 inches) cinnamon stick

⅓ cup dried currants

2 teaspoons red wine vinegar, or to taste

1 To prepare the stuffing, heat the oil in a large heavy pot over medium heat. Add the rice and cook, stirring with a wooden spoon, about 5 minutes. Add the boiling stock and salt, then reduce the heat to low and simmer, covered, until all the liquid is absorbed, about 20 minutes. The rice should be very slightly hard to the bite.

2 Preheat the oven to 350°F.

3 Melt the butter in a medium-size skillet over medium heat. Add the onions and peppers and sauté, stirring occasionally, until they begin to soften and color very lightly, about 8 minutes.

4 In a large bowl, combine the rice, on-

ions and peppers, and remaining stuffing ingredients. Season to taste with salt.

5 Stuff the pocket in the veal breast somewhat loosely with the rice mixture. Sew up the pocket with a thick thread, or close with trussing skewers.

6 Rub the veal with salt, pepper, and about ¼ teaspoon cinnamon. Place in a roasting pan and brush with the oil. Roast for 2 hours, basting with the pan juices.

7 Add the stock, tomatoes, cinnamon stick, and currants to the roasting pan. Cover the veal loosely with foil and continue roasting for another hour. Remove the veal to a platter and let stand, covered with foil, for 20 minutes.

8 Remove the cinnamon stick from the sauce. Tip the roasting pan and skim the fat from the surface of the sauce, then add salt and pepper and vinegar to taste. (If the sauce seems thin, pour it into a small saucepan before seasoning and reduce over high heat to the desired thickness.)

9 To serve, either scoop the stuffing into a serving dish or cut the veal with stuffing intact, into serving pieces. Pass the sauce separately in a sauceboat.

Serves 6

Stuffed Veal Croquettes

Tabriz Kiufta

These delicious veal croquettes from Azerbaijan can also be made from ground lamb. The dish is also served in Iran, but there the croquettes are smaller and are simmered in tomato sauce.

STUFFING

4 tablespoons (½ stick) unsalted butter
1⅓ cups finely chopped onions
⅓ cup pine nuts (pignoli)
⅓ cup dried currants
¼ teaspoon ground cinnamon
¼ teaspoon ground cumin
⅛ teaspoon ground allspice
¼ cup finely chopped fresh parsley
Salt and freshly ground black pepper, to taste

CROQUETTES

2 slices white bread, crusts removed
⅓ cup milk
1 pound ground veal
2 large egg yolks
1 teaspoon sweet Hungarian paprika
3 tablespoons finely chopped fresh parsley (optional)
2 tablespoons ice water
Salt and freshly ground black pepper to taste
All-purpose flour for rolling the croquettes
2 large eggs, beaten
Unflavored fine, dry bread crumbs
3 tablespoons unsalted butter
3 tablespoons vegetable oil

1 To prepare the stuffing, melt the butter in a medium-size skillet over medium heat. Add the onions and sauté, stirring occasionally, until softened, about 8 minutes. Add the pine nuts and currants and continue to sauté, stirring until the currants are plump and swollen, about 7 minutes more. Off the heat, stir in the cinnamon, cumin, allspice, parsley, and salt and pepper. Set the stuffing aside.

2 To prepare the croquettes, soak the bread in the milk for 10 minutes. Squeeze the bread to remove any excess milk and crumble into a large ball. Discard the milk.

3 Add the veal to the bread along with the egg yolks, paprika, parsley, ice water, and salt and pepper. Knead thoroughly until smooth.

4 Have a bowl of ice water by you. Divide the veal mixture into 8 balls. Dipping your hands in the water, flatten each ball as much as you can. Place a heaping tablespoon of stuffing in the center of each circle, then bring the edges of the circle together over the filling and seal. Dip your hands in the water again and roll the patties between them to form oval croquettes.

5 Roll the croquettes lightly in flour, then dip into beaten egg and roll in bread crumbs.

6 Preheat the oven to 350°F.

7 Heat half each of the oil and butter in a heavy skillet over medium heat. Add half the croquettes and sauté until deep golden on all sides. Transfer to a baking sheet. Repeat with the remaining croquettes, using the remaining oil and butter.

8 Bake the croquettes until clear juice comes out when you prick one with a skewer, about 10 minutes.

Serves 4 to 6

Lamb Dishes

BARANINA

The Kirghiz poetry is filled with odes in the honor of sheep, the natives placing this animal on the highest pinnacle of their estimation — after their wives, and, indeed, sometimes before them. . . . As [their] ideas of poetry were . . . limited to songs about the beauty of a sheep and the delights of roast mutton, I fear that when he [Burnaby's guide] desired to tell her that she was the most beautiful of her sex, Nazar translated it as follows: He says "that thou art lovelier than a sheep with a fat tail"—this appendage being a great delicacy among the Tatars—"that thy face is the roundest in the flock, and that thy breath is sweeter to him than many pieces of mutton roasted over bright embers."

— Fred Burnaby
A Ride to Khiva

I'm not an expert in statistics, but I think it's safe to say that lamb is the meat most often consumed in the USSR. As you can tell from Fred Burnaby's amusing story, lamb is both the staple meat and a status symbol throughout the vast expanse of Soviet Central Asia. It's also the most popular meat in the Caucasus, and is widely enjoyed in Russia and the west of the USSR.

When a guest is invited to a party or a picnic in Central Asia or the Caucasus, the custom is to slaughter a lamb for the occasion. The chances are that it will be a spring lamb that has grazed on the most verdant mountain pastures and drunk nothing but spring water from mountain streams. Either the lamb is roasted whole on the spit, or the legs are cut up to make tender kebabs. The prime cuts of the lamb are seldom marinated, as their exquisite taste needs no encouragement.

Lamb is also enjoyed on less formal occasions, as the centerpiece of everyday meals. The shoulder and neck are used to make an endless variety of flavorful stews, the recipes for several of which I offer you here. The leg is roasted by Caucasians under a crust of herbs and spices; and grills might range from a humble but enticing dish of lamb kidneys or liver to the splendid Armenian rack of lamb, *karsky kebab*. Ground lamb is used to make various meatballs, patties (*keufteh*), and moussakas, or is used as a stuffing for vegetables. Hot and sweet peppers, cumin, coriander, cinnamon, and a dozen varieties of herbs in different combinations are teamed up with lamb in the Caucasus and Central Asia, making their lamb dishes some of the most exciting and tasty in the world.

Uzbek Lamb Kebabs

Sikh Kebab

In Uzbekistan, lamb kebabs are often marinated in a mixture of spices and vinegar, and during grilling, the lamb is sprinkled with salted water to assure juiciness. It is traditionally served with thinly sliced onions that are sprinkled with parsley. Grilled lamb kebabs are the number-one street food in Central Asia, filling the streets with an unbearably seductive aroma of grilled meat.

1 small onion, grated

1½ teaspoons cumin seeds

1 teaspoon coriander seeds, crushed

1 teaspoon fennel seeds

*1 teaspoon sweet Hungarian
    paprika*

½ teaspoon hot Hungarian paprika

3 tablespoons minced fresh cilantro

2 tablespoons minced garlic

3 tablespoons red wine vinegar

1 teaspoon salt

*2 pounds boneless lean lamb, cut
    into 1-inch cubes*

*Thinly sliced red onion, sprinkled
    with chopped fresh parsley*

1 In a glass or ceramic bowl, combine the grated onion, cumin, coriander, and fennel seeds, paprikas, cilantro, garlic, vinegar, and salt. Add the lamb and toss thoroughly to coat. Refrigerate, covered, for at least 12 hours and up to 24, tossing the lamb occasionally.

Marinades

Many Soviet chefs believe that acidic marinades add little or nothing to the taste of top-quality cuts of meat, such as legs of fresh lamb. They work wonders, though, when you want to tenderize a tougher cut of meat. In this case, the meat is left in the marinade for quite some time, and then grilled until well done. When prepared this way, you can actually taste the tanginess of the marinade. A cut such as lamb shoulder is perfect for this treatment, as well as easy on the pocketbook. Pomegranate juice, lemon juice, unripened grape juice, or vinegar are some of the favorite marinades in the USSR. Olive oil is not used as much as it is in the Middle East and the Mediterranean countries.

2 Prepare coals for grilling until coated with white ash, or preheat the broiler. Have a bowl of warm salted water ready for sprinkling the meat.

3 Remove the lamb pieces from the marinade and thread on long metal skewers, pressing them firmly together.

4 Grill or broil the lamb 4 inches away from the heat, turning and sprinkling with salted water every few minutes. Allow up to 10 to 12 minutes for pink lamb, and 15 minutes for well done. Serve immediately, accompanied by parsley-sprinkled sliced onions.

Serves 5 to 6

I n another version of Uzbek Lamb Kebabs, called *titrama*, the lamb is marinated in a pungent mixture of garlic, spices, and herbs. To make this marinade, process 1 onion, 12 cloves garlic, 1 large tomato, and a small bunch each of fresh parsley, cilantro, and basil in a food processor. Stir in ¼ cup olive oil and season with crushed coriander seeds, cumin seeds, hot and sweet Hungarian paprika, and salt. Marinate the meat in this mixture for just a few hours.

Pomegranate-Grilled Lamb Chops

Narli Kebab

T his is my adaptation of a sublime lamb preparation from Azerbaijan. The lamb is first tenderized in pomegranate juice, then the marinade is reduced to provide a healthful and tangy basting liquid.

1¾ cups fresh or bottled pome-
    granate juice
4 cloves garlic, crushed in a
    garlic press
6 black peppercorns, crushed
⅓ cup finely chopped fresh mint

Salt, to taste
8 rib lamb chops (each ¾ inch thick)
2 tablespoons olive oil
2 tablespoons pomegranate seeds for
    garnish (optional)
Mint leaves for garnish

1 Combine the pomegranate juice, garlic, peppercorns, chopped mint, and salt in a glass or ceramic bowl. Add the lamb chops and refrigerate for at least 4 hours and up to 12.

2 Prepare coals for grilling until coated with white ash, or preheat the broiler. Oil the grill or broiling rack.

3 Remove the chops from the marinade and set aside. Pour the marinade into a small saucepan and reduce over high heat to ⅓ cup, about 20 minutes.

4 Brush the chops with the marinade and the oil and grill or broil 3 inches from the heat, brushing twice with the remaining marinade. The Caucasians enjoy their meat well done, but you should grill it to a desired doneness — 5 minutes per side for medium-rare, 7 to 8 minutes of medium, and about 10 minutes for well done.

For a truly regal Azerbaijani mixed grill, serve Pomegranate-Grilled Lamb Chops, Ground Lamb on Skewers, and Chicken Kebabs. Grill several skewers of whole plum tomatoes and Italian peppers separately. The grill should be accompanied by red onions, thinly sliced and sprinkled with parsley; a small bowl of sumakh, and a plate of mixed fresh herbs. Mandatory is a plate of flatbread (*lavash*) or pita, which is wrapped around the meats, together with the onions and herbs.

5 Serve at once, garnished with pomegranate seeds, if desired, and mint leaves.

Serves 4

Roast Leg of Lamb with Vegetables

Skhvris Barkali Bostneulit

Although many seasoned chefs have turned against well-done lamb, that's the way they still do it in Georgia; and this is a place that produces some of the best roast lamb in the world. In this recipe, the leg of lamb is coated with the traditional spice mixture and roasted to perfection together with eggplants and tomatoes that have been tossed with olive oil, garlic, and cilantro. An accompaniment of Sour Plum Sauce is, in my opinion, a must.

A Georgian Dinner for American Friends

Cold Poached Vegetables with Walnut Sauce

•

Georgian Egg and Lemon Soup

•

Roast Leg of Lamb with Vegetables

Sour Plum Sauce

My Favorite Pilaf

Châteauneuf du-Pape

•

Strudel with Walnut Filling

Turkish Coffee

• • •

⅓ cup extra virgin olive oil, or more
    as needed
Georgian Spice Mixture (recipe
    follows)
1 leg of lamb (about 5½ to
    6 pounds)
3 large cloves garlic,
    slivered
Salt and freshly ground black
    pepper, to taste
2 large cloves garlic, minced
1 tablespoon finely chopped fresh
    cilantro
6 baby eggplants (about 3½
    inches long and 1 inch thick),
    stemmed and halved
    lengthwise
6 large fresh, ripe plum tomatoes,
    halved lengthwise
Sour Plum Sauce (see Index)

1 Add by the teaspoonful enough oil to the Georgian Spice Mixture to make a paste. Set aside.

2 Make slits all over the lamb with the tip of a knife and insert a garlic sliver in each. Rub the lamb with salt and pepper, then spread all over with the spice mixture. Refrigerate for 2 to 4 hours, bringing to room temperature before roasting.

3 Preheat the oven to 425°F.

4 Place the lamb, fat side up, in a shallow roasting pan and roast until the surface is brown and crusty, about 20 to 25 minutes.

5 While the lamb is roasting, combine the remaining olive oil, minced garlic, and cilantro in a large, shallow bowl. Add the eggplants and tomatoes and toss to coat with the oil. Set aside.

6 Reduce the oven temperature to 325°F. Continue roasting the lamb for 55 minutes for medium rare and 1½ hours for well done, which is preferred but not a must.

7 About 35 minutes before the roast is ready, add the vegetables to the roasting pan, scattering them, cut side up, around the lamb. Check in about 20 minutes and drizzle with additional olive oil if the vegetables look dry.

8 Remove the lamb from the oven, cover loosely with aluminum foil, and let rest for 20 minutes before carving. Serve surrounded by the roast vegetables. Pass the Sour Plum Sauce.

Serves 6

A variety of Georgian Dishes use *khmeli-suneli*, and each Georgian usually makes his or her own special blend. The constant spices are coriander and fenugreek, but the herbs may vary from dried parsley or dill to dried marigold petals, which give the mixture a yellowish hue. You may substitute the mixture for any Georgian recipe in this book that calls for coriander and fenugreek.

Georgian Spice Mixture
Khmeli-suneli

1 tablespoon coriander seeds
2 teaspoons dried parsley
1 teaspoon dried oregano
2 teaspoons dried tarragon
¼ teaspoon ground fenugreek

Grind the coriander seeds, parsley, oregano, and tarragon in a spice mill or coffee grinder until powdered. Transfer to a bowl and stir in the fenugreek. Store in an airtight container.

Makes about 2½ tablespoons

Lamb and Vegetables Baked in an Earthenware Casserole

Chanakhi

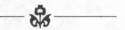

This is a mouthwatering and nutritious dish from Georgia, which is also extremely easy to make, providing you own a large unglazed earthenware casserole — a Römertopf clay pot is perfect. If you don't own one, I recommend that you make it item number one on your next birthday list. An old family friend swears that her whole life and diet has changed since I persuaded her to buy one; "Now," she says, "all I have to do is throw whatever ingredients I have into the Römertopf, put it in the oven, and forget about it — and it never fails to produce a dish that is flavorful perfection."

As this dish is actually a cross between a soup and a stew, serve it in large bowls or soup plates, with plenty of warm pita bread or *lavash* (see Index) to dip into the wonderful juices. I like to place the pot right on the table to tease the guests with the extraordinary aroma of lamb, vegetables, garlic, and fresh herbs — all blended and fragrant as only an earthenware-cooked dish can be.

3 pounds shoulder lamb chops

2 large cloves garlic, crushed in a garlic press

Salt, to taste

½ teaspoon hot Hungarian paprika

½ teaspoon sweet Hungarian paprika

5 large cloves garlic, finely minced

3 tablespoons finely chopped fresh cilantro, plus additional for garnish

6 baby eggplants (about 3½ inches long and 1 inch thick), stemmed

3 tablespoons finely chopped fresh parsley

3 large boiling potatoes, peeled and quartered

3 medium-size onions, sliced

Freshly ground black pepper, to taste

¾ cup tomato juice

½ teaspoon dried red pepper flakes

8 black peppercorns

2 tablespoons fresh lemon juice

6 fresh, ripe plum tomatoes, peeled and halved

Armenian Lamb and Vegetable Casserole

Kchuch

Named for a round earthenware pot, *kchuch*, is an Armenian cousin of *chanakhi*. Both are distantly related to Irish stew and more closely to the Turkish *güvetch*, a medley of vegetables and meats, slowly cooked until all the flavors are beautifully blended. The Armenian vegetables added to the lamb include tomatoes, Italian peppers, zucchini, onions, and string beans; a handful of dried apricots is also added to provide a typical faintly sweet Arme-

nian accent. The total proportion of vegetables should be equal to the amount of meat, for example 3 pounds vegetables for 3 pounds of lamb.

As one Armenian friend told me, to give an exact recipe for this simple dish would be to insult the intelligence of the cook. Just throw everything into the pot, spice with garlic, add plenty of herbs, some liquid, a bit of lemon juice, place it in the oven, and let the pot work its magic.

1 Trim off all the fat from the lamb and reserve.

2 Rub the chops with the crushed garlic, salt, and the hot and sweet paprika. Refrigerate for 1 hour, bringing to room temperature before cooking.

3 Have ready a large earthenware casserole with a tight-fitting lid. If unglazed, soak both casserole and lid in cold water

for 30 minutes (see Note).

4 Preheat the oven to 350°F.

5 Finely mince enough of the reserved lamb fat to make 1 tablespoon. Discard the rest. Mix with 2 pinches of salt, 1 teaspoon of the minced garlic, and 2 teaspoons of the chopped cilantro. Make several long, deep slits in each eggplant and stuff each one with a little of the fat mixture. This will make the eggplant moist and flavorful inside.

6 Arrange the lamb chops in the bottom of the casserole. Sprinkle with some of the parsley and some of the remaining cilantro and garlic. On top of the meat arrange a layer each of potatoes, eggplant, and onions, sprinkling each layer with garlic, fresh herbs, and salt and pepper.

7 Add the tomato juice, red pepper flakes, peppercorns, and lemon juice, then cover and cook in the oven for 50 minutes.

8 Add the tomatoes and cook, without stirring, for another 45 minutes.

9 Serve in large soup plates or bowls, sprinkled with fresh cilantro.

Note: When baking in a Romertöpf or other unglazed pottery, it is important to soak it in cold water for 30 minutes before each using so the clay absorbs the liquid. The ingredients will then be "steamed" for the first 15 or 20 minutes of cooking.

Serves 6

Lamb with White Beans and Tomatoes

Pastiner

ACaucasian Armenian dish, *pastiner* is made from cubed lamb, tomatoes, and one other vegetable, and finished in the oven. The recipe with white beans is an Armenian equivalent of chili — one of these dishes in which a little meat and some beans will stretch a long way to satisfy a hungry crowd, or feed a family for a few days. It produces a cassoulet-like dish with very little effort and a fraction of the expense. Its taste only improves with time, so you can refrigerate or freeze it. Serve with rice or bulgur and a salad.

2 cups dried white beans (white
    kidney, Great Northern, or baby
    limas), soaked overnight in
    water to cover and drained
Salt, to taste
3 tablespoons olive oil
2 pounds boneless lean lamb
    shoulder, cut into ½-inch dice
3 tablespoons unsalted butter
3 medium-size onions,
    chopped
½ to ¾ teaspoon hot Hungarian
    paprika
¾ cup Beef Stock (see Index) or
    canned broth
1½ tablespoons tomato paste
1 can (14½ ounces) Italian plum
    tomatoes, drained but juices
    reserved, chopped
1 green bell pepper, cored, seeded,
    and diced

1 small green chili pepper, cored,
    seeded, and diced (wear rubber
    gloves)
4 cloves garlic, peeled
1 teaspoon sweet Hungarian
    paprika, plus additional for
    garnish
1 tablespoon fresh lemon juice,
    or more to taste
Freshly ground black pepper,
    to taste
⅓ cup chopped fresh parsley, plus
    additional for garnish
Hot cooked rice or bulgur

1 In a large pot, bring the beans and 6 cups water to a boil over high heat, periodically skimming off the foam as it rises to the top. Add salt, reduce the heat to low, and cover the pot. Simmer until the beans are almost tender, about 40 minutes or more, depending on the beans.

2 Meanwhile, heat the oil in a large heatproof casserole over medium-high heat. Add the lamb and brown on all sides. Transfer the lamb to a plate and pour off the oil.

3 Add the butter to the casserole and melt over medium heat. Add the onions and sauté, stirring frequently, until softened and lightly colored, about 10 minutes. Return the lamb to the casserole and add salt, ½ teaspoon hot paprika, and the stock. Simmer the lamb, covered, over low heat until tender, about 1 hour.

4 Preheat the oven to 350°F.

5 Drain off the liquid from the lamb and degrease, if it seems fatty. Dilute the tomato paste in the liquid and return the mixture to the lamb.

6 Add the beans, tomatoes and their liquid, the green bell pepper, chili pepper, garlic, 1 teaspoon sweet paprika, remaining hot paprika to taste, 1 tablespoon lemon juice, pepper, and more salt if needed. Bring the mixture to a boil, then cover and place in the oven for 40 minutes.

7 Remove from the heat, add more lemon juice, if desired, and stir in the ⅓ cup parsley. Allow to cool for 10 to 15 minutes before serving.

8 Transfer the mixture to a serving dish and sprinkle with sweet paprika and additional parsley. Serve over rice or bulgur.

Serves 6 to 8 over rice

The Armenians are very casual about what they put in their lamb stews. In winter it might be dried beans, such as in this recipe; spring would bring tender spinach. In summer it might be a medley of tomatoes, eggplants, and green beans, while the fall is the season for pumpkin and squash: To the meat add 1 pound cubed pumpkin or butternut squash, lightly sautéed in butter, instead of the beans. Omit the peppers and use a dash of cinnamon and ground cumin for seasoning.)

Stir-Fried Lamb with String Beans and Tomato and Yogurt Sauce

Vochkhari Mise Tomatesov yev Madzounov

This superb preparation I once sampled in an Armenian home is actually a cross between two dishes, an Armenian string bean and lamb stew with yogurt sauce, and a Turkish dish called *iskander kebab,* in which grilled strips of lamb are served over hot pita bread and topped with tomato and yogurt sauces. In this recipe the lamb is quickly stir-fried and served on pita over a bed of string beans, and topped with the two sauces. You can play around with this recipe, using grilled lamb chops instead of the stir-fried leg of lamb or serving the beans on the side. The sauces, however, are essential to the dish.

GREEN BEANS

4 tablespoons (½ stick) unsalted
    butter
1 medium-size onion, quartered and
    sliced
1½ pounds green beans,
    trimmed and cut in half
    crosswise
1 clove garlic, minced

1 tablespoon fresh lemon juice
1 large fresh, ripe tomato, peeled,
    seeded, and chopped
¼ teaspoon hot Hungarian
    paprika
¼ teaspoon sweet Hungarian
    paprika
⅓ cup canned beef broth

TOMATO SAUCE AND LAMB

2 cups canned Italian plum
    tomatoes, drained but juices
    reserved
1½ tablespoons tomato paste
1 clove garlic, minced
¼ teaspoon dried red pepper flakes
2 tablespoons chopped fresh
    parsley
Salt and freshly ground black
    pepper, to taste

2 teaspooons red wine vinegar
¼ teaspoon sugar, or more
    to taste
1 teaspoon vegetable oil
1¾ pounds boneless lean leg of lamb,
    cut into strips (see Note)
1 cup plain low-fat yogurt
⅓ cup canned chicken broth

FOR SERVING

4 pita breads
2 tablespoons Clarified Butter
    (see Index)

¼ teaspoon hot Hungarian paprika
¼ teaspoon sweet Hungarian paprika
Chopped fresh parsley for garnish

1 Melt the butter in a large heavy skillet over medium heat. Add the onion and sauté until softened, 5 minutes. Add the beans and sauté, stirring, for 5 minutes. Stir in the garlic, lemon juice, tomato, hot paprika, sweet paprika, and the broth. Cover, reduce the heat to low, and simmer until the beans are very tender, about 30 minutes.

2 Meanwhile, prepare the tomato sauce:

Seed the canned tomatoes and mash well with a fork in a saucepan. Measure the reserved tomato liquid. If there is less than ¾ cup liquid, add water to measure that amount. Add the tomato liquid and tomato paste to the tomatoes, then stir in the garlic, red pepper flakes, and parsley. Simmer, uncovered, until the sauce thickens somewhat, about 15 minutes. Season with salt and pepper, vinegar, and sugar. Remove from the heat and keep warm.

3 Preheat the oven to 350°F.

4 Brush a heavy cast-iron skillet or wok with the oil, then heat over high heat until sizzling and stir-fry the lamb, a few pieces at a time, for about 5 to 6 minutes. Taste a strip of lamb and check for desired doneness. Season with salt and pepper, set aside, and keep warm.

5 Whisk the yogurt together with the chicken broth in a small saucepan. Heat over low heat, stirring, for 1 minute. Do not allow the yogurt to curdle. Set aside.

6 Arrange the pitas on a baking sheet, place in the oven, and bake until warm and slightly toasted, about 5 minutes.

7 Heat the clarified butter over low heat for 1 minute and stir in the hot and sweet paprika. Remove from the heat.

8 To serve, place a pita bread on a plate. Spoon some green beans on the pita and top with a serving of lamb. Sprinkle with parsley and pour about 2 tablespoons of tomato sauce over the lamb. Top with 2 tablespoons yogurt sauce and drizzle with some flavored butter. Serve at once.

Serves 4

Note: To facilitate cutting the lamb into strips, place it in the freezer for 20 minutes to firm up.

Stuffed Bulgur and Lamb Balls

Pohrov Keufteh

This is a typical Armenian dish, not found anywhere else in the Soviet Union. A combination of lamb and bulgur (called *keyma*) kneaded together and filled with spiced ground lamb is also popular in Lebanon and Syria, where it's known as *kibbe*. In those countries, however, the *kibbe* are usually fried, whereas Armenians often poach them in broth and serve them with yogurt and garlic sauce. Although *keufteh* are really delicious fried, poaching makes them much juicier. If serving the *keufteh* poached, accompany them with a bowl of stock to sprinkle on them, and the bowl of sauce. If serving them fried, just pass the sauce and serve with lemon wedges.

KEYMA

1 cup fine bulgur

½ cup boneless, very lean leg of
   lamb, ground three times

1 small onion, grated

Salt and freshly ground black
   pepper, to taste

Ice water

STUFFING

2 tablespoons unsalted butter

½ cup finely chopped onion

3 heaping tablespoons pine nuts
   (pignoli)

7 ounces ground lamb, not
   too lean

1 tablespoon tomato paste

¼ cup canned beef broth or water

⅛ teaspoon ground cinnamon

½ teaspoon sweet Hungarian
   paprika

¼ teaspoon ground cumin

⅛ teaspoon ground allspice

3 tablespoons finely chopped fresh
   parsley

2 tablespoons fresh lemon juice

Salt and freshly ground black
   pepper, to taste

FOR COOKING

½ cup Clarified Butter (see Index)
   for frying or 2 quarts Chicken
   Stock or Beef Stock (see Index
   for both) for poaching

Yogurt and Garlic Sauce (see Index)

1 In a fine sieve, rinse and drain the bulgur. Place in a bowl and add enough cold water to cover by 1 inch. Soak for 15 minutes. Drain, then wrap in a double layer of cheesecloth and press to squeeze out as much excess water as possible.

2 In a food processor, combine the bulgur, lamb, onion, and salt and pepper. Process, drizzling in 3 to 4 tablespoons ice water, until the mixture is smooth, about 30 seconds.

3 Transfer to a bowl and knead with your hands for another 4 to 5 minutes, sprink-

ling in a little ice water if the mixture begins to feel dry. You should have a very smooth paste. Sprinkle the *keyma* with another 1 tablespoon of ice water and refrigerate while making the stuffing.

4 To make the stuffing, melt the 2 tablespoons butter in a medium-size skillet over medium heat. Add the onion and pine nuts and sauté, stirring occasionally until the mixture is softened, about 8 minutes. Add the meat and cook until lightly browned, breaking it up with a wooden spoon. Stir in the tomato paste and ¼ cup stock and cook for 10 more minutes.

5 Turn off the heat and stir in the spices, parsley, lemon juice, and salt and pepper.

6 Have a bowl of ice water by you. Remove the *keyma* from the refrigerator and, dipping your hands in the water, shape into 16 balls. Take one ball and make a hollow in the middle. Holding your third finger in the middle, and your thumb on the outside, press the walls encircling the hollow until very thin. If the walls break, mend with your fingers, first dipping in water.

7 Place as much stuffing in the hollow as it will accommodate and press the opening together to close. Wet your hands with water and roll the ball between your palms into an egg shape.

8 Repeat with the rest of the *keyma* and stuffing, sprinkling the finished *keufteh* with ice water as you work to prevent the bulgur from drying out.

9 If frying the *keufteh*, heat the clarified butter in a large skillet over medium heat. Add the *keufteh* and fry until browned on all sides and heated through, 8 to 10 minutes. Or poach in a large pot of simmering stock for 10 minutes.

10 Serve with Yogurt and Garlic Sauce, accompanied by a bowl of stock to sprinkle over the *keufteh* if they were poached.

Serves 6

Uzbek Lamb Stew with Cumin Seeds, Coriander, and Bread

Zharkop

My grandmother, who lived in Uzbekistan for many years, had a wonderful repertoire of spicy Uzbek dishes, which she passed on to my mother, her daughter-in-law. As a child, I always felt that our household was special because we enjoyed these exotic preparations while next door and across the way other kids ate only *kotleti* (hamburgers) and potatoes.

In this stew, the lamb is simmered with well-browned carrots, onions, and green peppers, and is skillfully spiced with traditional Uzbek seasoning — cumin seeds (called *zira*), cayenne, and crushed coriander. Stale or toasted flat bread (*non*) is usually stirred into the stew in the last 2 to 3 minutes of cooking, but this is optional. Serve with Asian Radish Salad (see Index).

⅓ cup olive oil

1 pound lamb neck, trimmed of all fat and cut into serving pieces

1½ pounds boneless lean lamb shoulder, cut into 1-inch cubes

2 large onions, coarsely chopped

3 large carrots, peeled and julienned

2 large Italian (pale green frying) peppers, cored, seeded, and cut into strips

2 teaspoons tomato paste

4 to 6 black peppercorns

½ to ¾ teaspoon cumin seeds

1 teaspoon coriander seeds, crushed

½ teaspoon sweet Hungarian paprika

¼ teaspoon cayenne pepper, or more to taste

1 cup Lamb Stock, Beef Stock (see Index for both), or canned beef broth, or more as needed

4 large all-purpose potatoes, peeled and cut into 1½-inch cubes

4 cloves garlic, minced

Salt, to taste

¼ cup finely chopped fresh cilantro, plus additional for garnish

2 pita breads, toasted and quartered

1 In a large cast-iron pot or Dutch oven, heat the oil over medium-high heat until a light haze forms above it. Add the meat in batches and brown on all sides, stirring often. With a slotted spoon, remove the meat to a platter.

2 Add the onions, carrots, and peppers to the pot and sauté, stirring, until deeply colored, about 12 to 15 minutes. Drain off most of the fat.

3 Return the meat to the pot and stir in the tomato paste, peppercorns, cumin seeds, coriander seeds, paprika, cayenne, and ¾ cup stock. Reduce the heat to low, then cover and simmer until the lamb is tender, about 1 hour.

4 Stir in the potatoes and garlic. Add just enough stock to barely cover the potatoes. Add salt and simmer, covered, until the potatoes are tender, 20 to 25 minutes.

5 Stir ¼ cup cilantro and the bread into the stew and cook for 1 more minute.

6 Sprinkle with cilantro to serve.

Serves 4

Lamb and Vegetable Moussaka with a Topping of Feta

Musaca de Zarazavaturi cu Brinza

Abountiful moussaka from Moldavia made from tiny pieces of lamb, which are all but concealed in a cornucopia of vegetables and rounded off by a typically Moldavian feta cheese and sour cream topping. Traditionally, all the vegetables have to be sautéed separately, but it's less time consuming to bake them. The moussaka still takes a little time to prepare, but the vegetables and meat can be prepared a day in advance, so all you have to do is assemble and bake the moussaka on the day you serve it. Accompany the moussaka with a green salad, then sit back and watch it all disappear.

12 tablespoon olive oil

2½ pounds boneless lean lamb shoulder, cut into ½-inch cubes (see Note)

1½ cups chopped onions

1 cup undrained chopped canned Italian plum tomatoes

Salt and freshly ground black pepper, to taste

1½ teaspoons sweet Hungarian paprika

2 large eggplants (about ¾ pound each), stemmed and cut crosswise into ½-inch-thick slices

4 large fresh, ripe tomatoes, sliced not too thinly

3 large green bell peppers, cored, seeded, and sliced

3 large boiling potatoes, peeled and thinly sliced

3 tablespoons minced garlic

1 tablespoon dried thyme

⅓ cup chopped fresh parsley

1½ cups crumbled feta cheese, preferably Bulgarian

5 tablespoon unsalted butter, cut into small pieces

3 large eggs, beaten

1½ cups sour cream or plain yogurt

1 Heat 3 tablespoons of the oil in a deep skillet over medium heat. Add the lamb and onions and sauté, stirring occasionally, until the lamb is browned and the onions are richly colored, about 15 minutes. Add the canned tomatoes, salt and pepper, and ½ teaspoon paprika. Reduce the heat to low, then cover and simmer until the lamb is tender, about 1¼ hours.

2 Preheat the oven to 425°F.

3 Choose two baking sheets that can both accommodate the eggplants, fresh tomatoes, and green bell peppers and fit in the oven at the same time. Arrange the eggplants on one sheet and the fresh tomatoes and peppers on the other (it's okay if the vegetables overlap slightly). Sprinkle the vegetables with a total of 7 tablespoons olive oil. Bake until colored and soft, 10 to 12 minutes on each side. Remove from the oven and set aside. Reduce the oven temperature to 350°.

4 Heat the remaining 2 tablespoons oil in a large skillet over medium-high heat. Add the potato slices and sauté until light brown on both sides, about 15 minutes.

5 To assemble the moussaka, arrange all the potato slices on the bottom of a 14 × 10 × 2-inch baking dish (if you have one deeper than 2 inches, then use it). Sprinkle the potato layer with a little garlic, thyme, parsley, salt, and pepper. Scatter about 2 tablespoons of the feta over all.

6 Arrange half of the tomato, pepper, and eggplant slices in scant layers on the potatoes, sprinkling each layer with salt

In the Soviet Union, the most prized of all lambs is the fat-tailed sheep, creatures with enormous behinds that store the delicate, grainy fat used extensively for cooking in place of butter and oil. In parts of Central Asia a lamb dish that is too lean is considered an embarrassment, and will always be returned so that the cook can suffuse it with this delicious fat. When kebabs are made, squares of the fat are threaded on the skewer to keep the meat moist and juicy. It's also added to ground lamb dishes such as *lyulya kebabs* and lamb dumplings, and it's rendered to use as a base for frying.

and pepper, a scattering of garlic, thyme, parsley, and a little feta (reserve ½ cup for the topping). Top with all of the meat and onion mixture, spreading it evenly with a rubber spatula, and season particularly well. Repeat the tomato and pepper layers, continuing to season and add feta, and top with the remaining eggplant.

7 Dot the top with butter and bake for 50 minutes. Increase the temperature to 425°F.

8 In a bowl, whisk the eggs and sour cream until blended, then whisk in the remaining feta. Spread this mixture over the moussaka with a spatula and sprinkle all over with the remaining 1 teaspoon paprika. Bake for another 15 minutes until the top is brown and bubbly.

Note: To facilitate cutting the lamb into small pieces, place it in the freezer for 20 minutes to firm up.

Serves 8 to 10

Ground Lamb on Skewers

Lyulya kebab

A properly prepared *lyulya* calls for the choicest possible lamb delicately seasoned with spices and herbs, and most important of all — the whole secret of a good *lyulya* — vigorously kneaded into a very smooth, almost white, meat paste. *Lyulya kebab* are supposed to be grilled on special flat skewers that can support the ground meat; when grilling on regular skewers they sometimes fall off — so be careful! Serve wrapped in a pita with Sour Plum Sauce or Quick Tomato Sauce (see the Index for the recipe page numbers).

2 pounds boneless leg or shoulder of
    lamb with just a little fat, cut
    into 2 to 3 inch pieces
2 large onions
2 large cloves garlic, finely minced
½ teaspoon ground cumin
3 tablespoons finely chopped fresh
    mint
¼ cup finely chopped fresh parsley
¼ teaspoon cayenne pepper, or more
    to taste
Salt and freshly ground black
    pepper, to taste

4 to 5 tablespoons cold water
½ teaspoon sweet Hungarian
    paprika
Sumakh for garnish
Lavash or pita breads
Thin red onion rings
Fresh, ripe tomato quarters
Fresh herb sprigs (mint, cilantro,
    tarragon, and watercress)
1 bunch scallions (green onions),
    trimmed

1 If grinding the lamb yourself, quarter the onions, put the lamb, with the fat and onions, through a meat grinder twice. If the lamb was already ground by the butcher, grate the onion and add it to the meat.

2 Combine the ground lamb with the garlic, cumin, chopped herbs, cayenne, salt and pepper, and just enough water to give a firm consistency. Knead very thoroughly until smooth, then refrigerate for 30 minutes.

3 Have ready 6 long metal skewers, preferably flat. Wet your hands with cold water. Shape the lamb mixture into 3½-inch-long sausages around the skewers. The sausages should sit on the skewers tightly. Sprinkle with paprika and refrigerate for at least 20 minutes.

4 Prepare hot coals for grilling until coated with white ash, or preheat the broiler. Oil the grill or broiler rack well.

5 Grill or broil the kebabs 3 inches away from the heat, carefully turning to brown evenly on all sides, until well done, about 13 minutes.

6 Serve the kebabs on the skewers, sprinkled with sumakh and accompanied by *lavash* or pita breads, red onion rings, tomato quarters, fresh herbs, and scallions.

Serves 6

Lamb Shanks with Mashed Chick-Peas and Beans

Obgusht

This is a quintessential Persian-Azerbaijani home-style meal. *Obgusht* translates literally as "meat and water," and it consists of lamb shanks simmered in broth with chick-peas, potatoes, beans, and garlic. The broth is then poured off and served separately in bowls to which toasted *lavash* or pita is added. The meat and the beans are mashed together and spread on more bread. The dish is traditionally sprinkled with sumakh and accompanied by thinly sliced onion and mixed pickled vegetables (cauliflower, carrots, onions, etc.). It is not the prettiest of dishes, but it tastes great. Although, traditionally, all the ingredients have to be thoroughly mashed together, I am usually content to mash the chick-peas, beans, and potatoes, and to shred the lamb.

¾ cup chick-peas, soaked overnight in water to cover and drained

¾ cup Great Northern or baby lima beans, soaked overnight in water to cover and drained

Salt, to taste

2 lamb shanks (about 1 pound each)

1 large onion, quartered

½ teaspoon ground turmeric

5½ cups Lamb Stock, Beef Stock (see Index for both), or canned beef broth

4 cloves garlic, crushed in a garlic press

1½ tablespoons tomato paste

½ cup undrained chopped canned tomatoes

2 large boiling potatoes, peeled and cut into large cubes

Freshly ground black pepper, to taste

2 tablespoons finely chopped fresh cilantro

3 tablespoons finely chopped fresh parsley, plus additional for garnish

1 large pita bread, quartered and toasted

½ large Bermuda onion, halved, thinly sliced, and sprinkled with sumakh

Pita bread or lavash

8 sprigs fresh tarragon

8 sprigs fresh chives

8 sprigs fresh cilantro

1 In a large pot, bring the chick-peas, beans, and 2 quarts water to a boil over high heat, periodically skimming off the foam as it rises to the top. Reduce the heat to low, add salt, and cover the pot. Simmer until the chick-peas and beans are almost tender, about 1¼ hours, depending on the beans.

2 Meanwhile, trim and discard the excess fat from the lamb. Rinse the lamb and pat dry with paper towels.

3 Place the lamb and the onion in a soup pot, add the turmeric and stock, and bring to a boil over high heat. Reduce the heat to low and simmer, covered, skimming as needed, until the lamb shanks are tender, about 1¼ to 1½ hours.

4 Drain the chick-peas and beans. Add to the lamb shanks along with the garlic,

Caucasian Seasoning Map

 Although there are many similarities in the cuisines of the three Caucasian republics — Georgia, Armenia, and Azerbaijan — to me their flavors are quite distinct, largely because of the characteristic use of herbs and spices in each area. Where the Georgians would use coriander and fenugreek, the Armenians will add paprika, cinnamon, and allspice, while turmeric and saffron will go into almost every Azerbaijani dish. Here are the spices and herbs to have at hand, if you are seriously in-terested in preparing dishes from these regions.

Georgia: Ground fenugreek, coriander, hot and sweet paprika, chili peppers, garlic, cilantro, basil, parsley, and tarragon.

Armenia: Hot and sweet paprika, cinnamon, ground allspice, ground cumin, mild chilies, garlic, tarragon, basil, and parsley.

Azerbaijan: Saffron, turmeric, sumakh, ground cinnamon, ground allspice, dried fenugreek leaves, tarragon, basil, cilantro, chives, parsley, and mint.

---

tomato paste, tomatoes, and potatoes. Season with salt and pepper, cover, and simmer for 35 minutes, adding more liquid, if it seems to be reducing too much.

5 Remove from the heat and strain all the liquid into a clean pot. You should have about 4½ cups.

6 Remove the lamb from the bones and tear into fine shreds.

7 Mash the remaining solids with a potato ricer or masher, adding a few tablespoons of the liquid. It should be mashed, but not puréed. Stir in the 2 tablespoons cilantro and 3 tablespoons parsley.

8 Pour the liquid into soup bowls. Add 1 toasted pita quarter to each bowl and sprinkle with parsley.

9 Arrange the mashed mixture on a serving dish and top with shredded lamb. Serve sliced onions, pita, and fresh herb sprigs, separately. The mixture is eaten, wrapped in pita, together with a few sprigs of herbs and a little onion, accompanied by the soup.

Serves 4

Braised Lamb Shanks with Barley and Egg and Lemon Sauce

Vochkhari Mise Terbiyov

Although lamb shanks are usually braised in rich wine or tomato sauces, in this healthy Caucasian recipe they are cooked together with barley and served with an egg and lemon sauce spiked with saffron, coriander, and herbs. It really makes a superb one-dish meal, and Steps 1 through 7 can be prepared a day ahead.

4 lamb shanks (about ¾ pounds each)
Salt and freshly ground black pepper, to taste
2 to 3 tablespoons olive oil
1 medium-size onion, chopped
1 large rib celery, diced
1 tablespoon chopped celery leaves
2 large cloves garlic, minced
1 tablespoon grated lemon zest

Bouquet garni (6 sprigs parsley, 6 sprigs dill, 1 bay leaf, and 6 black peppercorns tied in a cheesecloth bag)
4 cups Lamb Stock, Beef Stock (see Index for both), or canned beef broth, or more as needed
1 cup pearl barley, rinsed and drained
Egg and Lemon Sauce (recipe follows)

1 Trim and discard all the fat from the lamb. Rinse and pat dry with paper towels, then rub all over with salt and pepper.

2 Heat 2 tablespoons of the oil in a Dutch oven over medium heat. Brown the lamb shanks well on all sides, about 12 to 14 minutes. Remove from the Dutch oven and set aside.

3 If necessary, add a little more oil to the Dutch oven. Add the onion and the celery, and sauté until soft and nicely colored, about 15 minutes.

4 Return the lamb shanks to the Dutch oven. Add the celery leaves, garlic, lemon zest, bouquet garni, and 4 cups stock. Season with salt and pepper, then bring to a boil. Reduce the heat to low and simmer, covered, for 1 hour.

5 Preheat the oven to 325°F.

6 Remove the Dutch oven from the heat and discard the bouquet garni. Tip the Dutch oven slightly and carefully skim off the fat. Drain the liquid from the pot and add enough stock to measure 3½ cups. Return the liquid to the Dutch oven.

7 Add the barley and bring to a boil, then cover and place the Dutch oven in the oven. Bake until the barley is completely cooked and the lamb shanks are tender, about 1¼ hours. (If you are making this dish in advance, strain out the cooking liquid. Return the lamb and barley to the Dutch oven and refrigerate, covered, overnight. Store the cooking liquid covered, in the refrigerator. To reheat, add ½ cup of the cooking liquid to the lamb and barley and place in a preheated 350°F oven for 20 minutes.)

8 With a slotted spoon, transfer the lamb and barley to a heated platter.

9 Strain and measure the liquid remaining. If you have more than ¾ cup, discard some liquid. If you have less, add some more stock.

10 Make the Egg and Lemon Sauce using the reserved cooking liquid.

11 Serve the lamb shanks over the barley, and either spoon the sauce over the lamb or pass it separately in a sauceboat.

Serves 4

Egg and Lemon Sauce
Terbiyeh

Popular in Armenia and throughout the Middle East, Egg and Lemon Sauce is tangy and smooth. You can also make it separately to serve with poached chicken or fish, or roast leg of lamb. If you do, substitute the lamb cooking liquid with the same amount of chicken broth (for chicken or fish) or beef broth (for lamb).

¾ cup lamb cooking liquid (see Step 9, above)

1 teaspoon cornstarch

1 tablespoon cold water

2 large egg yolks

3 tablespoons fresh lemon juice

Small pinch of sugar

¼ teaspoon saffron threads, crushed in a mortar and diluted in 1 tablespoon warm water

⅛ teaspoon ground coriander, or more to taste

Salt and freshly ground black pepper, to taste

1 tablespoon finely chopped fresh dill

1 tablespoon finely chopped fresh parsley

1 Bring the reserved lamb cooking liquid to a simmer in a small saucepan.

2 Meanwhile, whisk the cornstarch and water into a paste in a small bowl. Add the egg yolks and lemon juice and whisk until smooth. Whisk in about ¼ cup of the simmering liquid, then whisk the mixture back into the saucepan.

3 Add the sugar, diluted saffron, and the coriander to the sauce, then season with salt and pepper, if needed. Simmer, stirring, until the sauce thickens, about 5 minutes. Stir in the dill and parsley and serve immediately.

Makes about ¾ cup

Pork

Dishes

———— ❖ ————

SVININA

Pork was eaten by the Slavs long before beef became common or fashionable; and many a Russian will make no bones about his preference even today. Three hundred years or so ago, the *Domostroi*, the Russian bible of housekeeping, specified just how "the thrifty housewife" could stretch out her precious pig: The kidneys and feet should be properly stuffed; the liver should be chopped; the intestine stuffed with kasha; and the breast stewed. Not a morsel went to waste. Today the "humbler parts" are still used inventively. The feet and ears make *kholodets*, a delicious garlic-suffused jellied dish. The intestines are filled for sausages, and the fat is cured, often under a crust of black peppers. I must confess that when I'm offered a paper-thin, rosy slice of pork fat on a piece of black bread, its crust gently rubbed with garlic, I abandon all thoughts of cholesterol and happily eat it all up.

The ideal pig, however, the pig of a thousand culinary dreams, can be divided up according to the best recipes from around the republics. Garlicky pork sausage studded with pomegranate seeds from Georgia, satisfying pork and sauerkraut combinations from the Ukraine, pork chops braised with tart apples from the Baltic States, crispy roast suckling pig en-joyed throughout the USSR, and — the crown jewel of the Soviet pork repertoire — a succulent fresh roast ham suffused with garlic, which takes pride of place at the Easter table.

Although many Central Asians are secretly partial to a fine pork sausage, pork is officially forbidden by Islamic dietary laws. During the long years of invasion and occupation of the southern and western USSR by the Mongols and the Muslim Turks and Tatars, the consumption of pork in the Ukraine and Byelorussia, like the circulation of Cyrillic literature, became a symbol of resistance and an important focus in the preservation of national identity.

Pork is the real hero of the feast. Like a passionate youth it puts on different disguises on different occasions. But even clothed in the most elaborate attire its originality and genius is always revealed — whether we search it out under the drapes of a blood sausage, or in the sailor's jacket or liverwurst, under the rough mantle of country sausage, or in the mantilla of a frankfurter.

— Nikita Vsevoldovich Vselolzhsky,
Nineteenth-century St. Petersburg
gourmet and wit

Georgian Spicy Roast Picnic Shoulder with Pomegranate Sauce

Shemtsvari Ghoris Khortsi Brotseulis Satsebelit

This wonderfully spicy and garlicky roast pork is first marinated in *adzhika*, a traditional Georgian spice paste made of hot and sweet paprika, ground coriander, and fenugreek. The meat is then roasted until it almost falls off the bone. Traditionally, it is served with pomegranate sauce, although a sour plum sauce (*tkemali*) would also complement the roast well. Or, for a more fiery accompaniment, you can make an extra recipe for the spice paste.

This pork dish is usually served with red beans (*lobio*) in one form or another. I would suggest Red Beans with Walnut Sauce or Red Beans with Tamarind and Balsamic Vinegar. My Favorite Pilaf with Almonds, Raisins, and Orange Zest would complete the picture beautifully. (See the Index for the recipe page numbers.)

SPICE PASTE

3 tablespoons sweet Hungarian paprika
2 teaspoons hot Hungarian paprika
1 teaspoon ground coriander
½ teaspoon ground fenugreek
½ teaspoon ground cumin
½ teaspoon coarse (kosher) salt

1 picnic pork shoulder, 6 pounds
6 large cloves garlic, slivered
½ cup canned beef broth or water
Pomegranate Sauce (recipe follows)
Chopped fresh cilantro for garnish

A fiery red pepper paste, *adzhika*, is used extensively throughout Georgia. Add it sparingly to soups and stews, or spread it on lamb or beef before roasting to make a spicy crust. The recipe I give here is a simplified version made from powdered hot and sweet paprika and other spices. The original is made from fresh chili peppers and is hot enough to bring tears to your eyes from twenty feet.

1 In a small bowl, combine all the spices for the paste. By teaspoonfuls, add just enough cold water to get a medium-thick paste.

2 Remove the skin from the roast and trim off all but a thin layer of fat (this will keep the roast moist during cooking). Make deep slits all over the pork.

3 Add the garlic slivers to the spice mixture and stir to coat. Insert the coated garlic slivers, as deep as possible, into the slits in the roast. With a spatula, spread the remaining mixture all over the meat. Cover and refrigerate for at least 12 hours.

4 Preheat the oven to 400°F.

5 Place the roast on a rack in a roasting pan. Add the stock to the roasting pan and roast for 30 minutes. Reduce the oven temperature to 325°F and roast for another 3½ hours, basting with the pan drippings. Test the roast by pricking it with a skewer. When it is cooked, the skewer should slide in easily and the juices should run clear.

6 Remove the roast from the oven and let it stand for 15 minutes before carving. Carve the meat and arrange on a serving platter. Spoon the Pomegranate Sauce over the meat and sprinkle with cilantro.

Serves 6

Pomegranate Sauce

Narshrab

3½ *cups fresh or bottled pomegra-*
  nate juice
2 *cloves garlic, crushed in a garlic press*
⅛ *teaspoon dried red pepper flakes*
2 *tablespoons finely chopped fresh*
  cilantro
Salt, to taste
Pomegranate seeds

1 In an enameled saucepan, reduce the pomegranate juice over high heat to 1½ cups, about 20 minutes.

2 Stir in the garlic, pepper flakes, cilantro, and salt and allow to cool to warm or room temperature. Before serving the sauce, add a fistful of pomegranate seeds.

Makes about 1½ cups

Georgia and Armenia are two Christian nations in a Muslim area with a basically Middle Eastern style of cooking. But while pork is forbidden in the Middle East, Georgians and Armenians produce mouthwatering pork dishes flavored in a Middle Eastern idiom using hot and sweet paprika, cumin, coriander, pomegranate sauce, fenugreek, and fresh herbs.

Roast Pork Paprikash

Porc Prajita Cu Paprika

Moldavians have a special fondness for sauces and gravies, such as the one with this roast, generously spiced with garlic, herbs, and paprika. These sauces are really the essential part of the dish, especially when spooned over *mamaliga* — their beloved corn mush — which is a must with any Moldavian meal. Do try to make *mamaliga* at least once; but also remember that this delectable pork roast will taste almost as good with Garlicky Mashed Potatoes. (See the Index for the recipe page numbers.)

3 pounds boneless Boston butt, rolled
   and tied
4 cloves garlic, sliced
Salt and freshly ground black
   pepper, to taste
5 tablespoons unsalted butter
1 tablespoon Dijon mustard
3 small onions, coarsely chopped
1 Italian (pale green frying) pepper,
   cored, seeded, and quartered
4 fresh, ripe tomatoes, peeled and
   quartered

1 rib celery with leaves, cut into 4 pieces
1½ cups Beef Stock (see Index) or
   canned broth, or more as needed
2 teaspoons sweet Hungarian paprika
10 ounces fresh white mushrooms,
   wiped clean and sliced
1 scant tablespoon all-purpose flour
⅓ cup dry red wine
1 tablespoon fresh lemon juice
1 large clove garlic, minced
½ teaspoon dried thyme
2 tablespoons chopped fresh parsley

1 Preheat the oven to 350°F.

2 With a sharp knife, make deep slits all over the meat and insert the garlic slivers, as deep as possible, into the slits. Rub the meat with salt and pepper.

3 Melt 2 tablespoons of the butter in a large casserole over medium heat. Add the meat and brown it on all sides. Off the heat, spread the mustard over the meat with a spatula.

4 Add the onions, Italian pepper, tomatoes, celery, and stock to the casserole. Sprinkle the meat and vegetables with ½ teaspoon of the paprika and roast for 1¾ hours, turning the meat, and basting with the pan juices from time to time. Prick the meat with a skewer; if the juices run clear, the meat is done.

5 While the meat is roasting, melt 2 tablespoons butter in a small skillet over medium heat. Add the mushrooms and sauté, stirring occasionally, until the mushrooms throw off and reabsorb their liquid, about 12 minutes. Remove from the heat and reserve.

6 Remove the roast from the casserole, place on a cutting board, and cover with aluminum foil.

7 Strain the pan juices and skim off the fat. Return one-third of the roasted vegetables to the pan juices. Purée another one-third in a food mill or push through a fine sieve. Add the purée to the pan juices.

Discard the rest of the vegetables.

8 Melt the remaining 1 tablespoon butter in a small heavy saucepan over medium heat. Sprinkle in the flour and stir for 2 minutes. Whisk in the pan juices.

9 Add the wine, lemon juice, minced garlic, thyme, parsley and additional salt and pepper, if desired. Bring to a boil, then reduce the heat to low and simmer, covered, for another 10 minutes.

10 Stir in the mushrooms and the remaining paprika and simmer for 5 minutes more.

11 Carve the pork into thin slices and arrange on a serving platter. Pass the sauce separately in a sauceboat.

Serves 6 to 8

Roast Pork Loin with Caraway Seeds

Sviniacha Pechenia z Kminom

A simple and satisfying roast from the Ukraine, with just a hint of Eastern European flavoring in the caraway seeds. Serve with a good pilsner and Braised Sauerkraut with Wild Mushrooms and Bacon (see Index).

1 boneless pork loin (about 3
  pounds), tied
Salt and freshly ground black
  pepper, to taste
4 teaspoons caraway seeds
2 cups pearl onions

12 medium-size baking potatoes,
  peeled and quartered
⅓ cup Beef Stock (see Index) or
  canned broth
½ teaspoon sweet Hungarian
  paprika

1 Rub the pork loin with salt, pepper, and caraway seeds and let it stand for 30 minutes.

2 Meanwhile, preheat the oven to 400°F.

3 Drop the onions into boiling water for 1 minute. Rinse under cold running water and drain. Trim off the root ends, then cut an "X" in the root end and peel. Set aside.

4 Place the pork loin, fat side up, in a roasting pan and roast for 15 minutes. Reduce the oven temperature to 350°F.

5 Scatter the onions and potatoes around the pork and roast, basting with the stock.

After 1¼ hours, prick the roast with a skewer. If the juices run clear, the roast is done. If not, roast another 10 minutes and test again.

6 Fifteen minutes before the roast is ready, sprinkle the vegetables with paprika. When done, let the meat stand, covered with aluminum foil, for 15 minutes before carving.

7 Carve the meat and arrange on a serving platter, surrounded by the roasted vegetables.

Serves 6

Grilled Pork Chops with Garlic Sauce

Kostitsa de Porc La Gratar cu Muzhdei

An excellent Moldavian grill with the traditional garlic sauce, *muzhdei*. Moldavian Marinated Peppers and a simple vegetable salad are excellent accompaniments (see Index).

GARLIC SAUCE

8 cloves garlic, chopped

¼ teaspoon coarse (kosher) salt

¼ teaspoon hot Hungarian paprika

1 cup warm Beef Stock (see Index)
    or canned broth

2 tablespoons finely minced fresh
    parsley

1 tablespoon finely minced fresh dill

6 shoulder pork chops, ½ to ¾ inch
    thick, trimmed of most of the fat
    (about 3 pounds)

3 tablespoons olive oil

1 To prepare the sauce, in a mortar, pound the garlic, and salt and paprika into a smooth paste. If you don't have a mortar and pestle, purée in a food processor or mash in a bowl with the back of a large spoon.

2 Transfer to a small bowl and stir in the stock, parsley, and dill until well blended. Let the sauce stand at room temperature for at least 30 minutes.

3 Meanwhile, prepare hot coals for grilling.

4 When white ash appears on the surface of the coals, lightly pound the pork chops with the flat side of a meat cleaver. Brush the chops with the oil and grill, 3 inches from the heat, for 6 to 7 minutes on each side, sprinkling the meat with some of the sauce. When the meat is done, the juices should run clear when you prick a chop with a skewer.

Moldavian Summer Luncheon

Pickled Mixed Vegetable Caviar

Moldavian Marinated Peppers

Moldavian Corn and Feta Cheese Bread

•

Grilled Pork Chops with Garlic Sauce

Moldavian Potato, Feta, and Scallion Salad

Vermont apple wine

•

Strudel with Cheese Filling

• • •

5 Serve the chops with the remaining sauce on the side.

Serves 3 to 4

Pork Chops with Apples Braised in Beer

Svinina s Yablokami v Pive

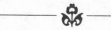

Baltic dishes are usually hearty yet possess a certain elegance. This one is adapted from a famous Latvian cookbook which endeavored to transform everyday fare into miniature feasts. Crispy Potato Bake or New Potatoes Braised in Sour Cream are perfect accompaniments (see the Index for the recipe page numbers).

4 center-cut loin pork chops, cut ¾
    inch thick (about 6 ounces each)
½ teaspoon ground ginger
Salt and freshly ground black
    pepper, to taste
3 tablespoons unsalted butter
1½ teaspoons all-purpose flour
¾ cup light beer
Pinch of granulated sugar

1 tablespoon grated lemon zest
2 cloves
1 medium-size onion, sliced and
    separated into rings
1 small tart apple (such as Granny
    Smith), peeled, cored, and cut
    into ⅛-inch-thick slices
1½ teaspoons (packed) dark brown
    sugar

1 Preheat the oven to 350°F.

2 Remove the excess fat from the pork chops and rub them generously with ground ginger, salt, and pepper.

3 In an ovenproof skillet just large enough to accommodate the pork chops in one layer, melt 2 tablespoons of the butter over medium heat. Dust the chops lightly with flour and brown in the butter for about 10 minutes, turning once after 5 minutes.

Remove the chops from the skillet and set aside.

4 Pour the beer into the skillet and bring to a boil. Stir in the granulated sugar, lemon zest, cloves, and additional salt and pepper. Return the pork chops to the skillet, cover, and bake for 20 minutes.

5 Meanwhile, melt the remaining 1 tablespoon butter in a small skillet over medium heat. Add the onion rings and sauté, stirring occasionally, until golden, about 15 minutes.

6 Remove the skillet from the oven and uncover. Arrange the sautéed onion over the chops and top with the apple slices. Spoon over some cooking liquid. Continue to bake, uncovered, until the apples are tender but not mushy, another 20 minutes, basting with the cooking liquid from time to time.

7 Preheat the broiler.

8 Sprinkle the brown sugar over the apples and place the skillet under the broiler for a few minutes, until you get a good glaze.

9 Place the pork chops, topped with the onions and apples, on individual plates and spoon some cooking liquid over them to serve.

Serves 4

Pork Chops Baked with Kasha and Wild Mushrooms

Svinina Zapechyonnaya s Kashei

An Old World treat from Byelorussia — juicy pork chops baked on a bed of kasha, flavored with wild mushrooms, onions, and bacon. It goes nicely with Sauerkraut Salad Provençal (see Index) and fresh pickles.

4 shoulder pork chops, cut ¾ inch
    thick (about 2 pounds)
½ teaspoon sweet Hungarian paprika
Salt, to taste
2 cups Beef Stock (see Index) or
    canned broth
1 ounce imported dried wild mush-
    rooms, preferably porcini, well
    rinsed

4 slices bacon, chopped
1 medium-size onion, chopped
1 cup whole kasha
    (buckwheat)
1 teaspoon caraway seeds
⅓ cup sour cream

1 Rub the pork chops with paprika and salt and set aside.

2 Bring 1 cup of the stock to a boil in a small saucepan over high heat. Remove from the heat, add the mushrooms, and soak for 1 hour. Remove the mushrooms from the soaking liquid, pat dry with paper towels, chop fine, and set aside. Strain the soaking liquid through a coffee filter and set aside.

3 In an heatproof casserole large enough to accommodate the pork chops in one layer, cook the bacon until it renders its fat. Using a slotted spoon, remove the bacon from the casserole and set aside.

4 Brown the pork chops well on both sides in the bacon drippings, about 15 minutes total. Drain on paper towels.

5 Pour off all but 2 tablespoons of the fat from the casserole. Sauté the onion in the remaining fat over medium heat until softened and colored, 8 minutes. Add the mushrooms, kasha, and caraway seeds and sauté, stirring, for 5 minutes more.

6 Preheat the oven to 325°F.

7 Combine the reserved mushroom soaking liquid with the remaining stock.

8 Season the kasha mixture with salt and stir in the reserved bacon pieces. Add the liquid and bring to a boil. Arrange the pork chops on top of the kasha and bake, uncovered, until the chops are tender and the kasha has absorbed all the liquid, about 25 minutes. Stir the sour cream into the kasha and serve immediately.

Serves 4

Hunter's Stew

Bigos

A Polish national treat, eagerly adopted by the Russians, Ukrainians, Lithuanians, and all other sauerkraut and sausage devotees. I think it puts the Alsatian choucroute to shame. Originally this dish was made from leftover game — hence the name "hunter's stew" — and is still supposed to be prepared from leftover meat. Of course, it's unlikely that anyone these days keeps this amount of cooked meats in their fridge, but if you do have any leftover meat, add it to the pot.

Bigos tastes much better when prepared ahead because it allows the flavors to settle properly. Steps 1 through 4 can actually be prepared even two days ahead. You should reheat the pork and ham mixture before adding it to the pot, however. Serve the *bigos* with peasant rye bread or good pumpernickel and a variety of mustards and horseradish. Vodka or good Czech or German beer seem to me the preferred libations. A hearty red wine or Alsatian Riesling, however, won't spoil the picture either.

This stew makes for a perfect meal after a long winter's walk, *après-ski*, or, of course, after hunting. It takes a little time to prepare, but it doesn't need anything else and will feed a crowd.

1 duck (4 pounds), rinsed inside and out and patted dry

7 tablespoons unsalted butter

1½ pounds boneless pork or veal, cut into 1½-inch cubes

1½ pounds thick ham steaks, cut into 1½-inch cubes

2 cups Chicken Stock (see Index), or canned broth

Salt and freshly ground black pepper, to taste

1½ cups coarsely chopped onions

2 cups shredded green cabbage

2 medium-size carrots, peeled and cut into julienne

4 pounds packaged (not canned) sauerkraut, rinsed and drained

1 large tart apple (such as Granny Smith), cored, peeled, and diced

1 ounce imported dried wild mushrooms (such as porcini), well rinsed

1 can (28 ounces) Italian plum tomatoes with their liquid, seeded and coarsely chopped

½ pound slab bacon, in 1 piece, rind removed

1½ pounds kielbasa, cut into 1-inch slices

⅓ cup Madeira

1½ teaspoons sugar, or more to taste

Bouquet garni (10 black peppercorns, 8 juniper berries, and 3 bay leaves tied in a cheesecloth bag)

1 Preheat the oven to 350°F.

2 Prick the duck all over with a fork, so the fat will run off during the cooking.

Place the duck in a roasting pan and roast until the juices run clear when you prick the thickest part of the thigh with a skewer, about 1 hour. Remove the duck from the oven, leaving the oven on. Set the duck aside.

3 Melt 3 tablespoons of the butter in a heatproof casserole over medium-high heat. Add the pork and brown very lightly on all sides. Add the ham, 1 cup of the stock, and salt and pepper. Cover and place the casserole in the oven for 1 hour (see Note). Remove from the oven and set aside. Reduce the oven temperature to 325°F.

4 Meanwhile, when cool enough to handle, remove the skin and bones from the duck. Cut the meat into 1-inch pieces.

5 In an ovenproof casserole large enough to accommodate all the ingredients, melt the remaining 4 tablespoons butter over medium heat. Add the onions and sauté, stirring occasionally, until softened, about 5 minutes. Add the cabbage and carrots and continue to cook, stirring, for 7 to 8 minutes.

6 Add the sauerkraut and cook, tossing and stirring, 10 minutes.

7 Stir the duck, the pork and ham and their cooking liquid, and the remaining stock into the casserole along with the rest of the ingredients and mix well. Season with salt and pepper and bring to a boil. Cover and bake in the oven until the meats are very tender, 1½ hours.

8 Remove the slab bacon and the bouquet garni to serve.

Serves 8 to 10

Note: If your oven is too small to accommodate the duck and pork and ham at the same time, cook the pork and ham on the top of the stove at a simmer, covered, for 1 hour.

Old World Fireside Supper

Calf's Liver Pâté on rye bread squares

Chopped herring on pumpernickel squares

Pepper Vodka

•

Hunter's Stew

Horseradish and an assortment of mustards

Alsatian Tokay Pinot Gris

•

Salad of mixed fresh greens

•

Cherry Sour Cream Cake

• • •

Pork and Prune Stew

Sviniacha Poliadvitsia z Slivkami

In the Ukraine, dried prunes have a wonderfully smoky flavor. The closest you can get to this flavor in the United States, I've found, is to soak the prunes in Chinese tea! Serve this stew with broiled new potatoes, sprinkled with melted butter, dill, and plenty of minced garlic.

½ cup very strong Lapsang
    Souchong tea
1⅓ cups pitted dried prunes, halved
3 tablespoons unsalted butter
3 tablespoons vegetable oil
2 large onions, coarsely chopped
2½ pounds boneless pork shoulder,
    cut into 1½-inch cubes
All-purpose flour for dusting the pork
¾ cup Beef Stock (see Index) or
    canned broth

½ cup dry red wine
Bouquet garni (2 bay leaves, 1-inch
    piece cinnamon stick, 6 black
    peppercorns, and 2 cloves tied in
    a cheesecloth bag)
Salt and freshly ground black
    pepper, to taste
4 cloves garlic, crushed in a garlic press
2 tablespoons red wine vinegar
Chopped fresh parsley for garnish

1 Bring the tea to a boil in a small saucepan over high heat. Pour over the prunes in a small bowl and let stand for 1 hour. Remove the prunes and set aside. Reserve half of the soaking liquid.

2 Heat half of the butter and half of the oil in a heavy heatproof casserole over medium heat. Add the onions, and sauté, stirring occasionally, until lightly colored, about 12 minutes. With a slotted spoon, remove the onions and set aside.

3 Meanwhile, preheat the oven to 350°F.

4 Heat the remaining butter and oil in the casserole over medium heat. Dust the pork cubes with flour and brown them, a few at a time, until deeply colored on all sides.

5 When all the pork is browned, return the onions to the casserole. Add the stock, red wine, bouquet garni, and salt and pepper. Bring to a boil, then cover and bake for 45 minutes.

6 Add the prunes, reserved soaking liquid, garlic, and vinegar to the casserole. Stir, then bake, covered, for 20 minutes.

Uncover and bake for 10 to 15 minutes longer until the cooking liquid thickens and reduces somewhat.

7 Remove the bouquet garni and adjust the seasoning. Sprinkle the stew with parsley, and serve immediately.

Serves 6

Georgian Pork Sausage

Kupati

I remember sitting in a restaurant in Batumi, a Georgian city by the Black Sea, and watching a man devour a huge plate of intriguing-looking sausages. Although I was always told never to talk to strange men in Georgia, my curiosity overcame my caution, and I timidly asked what he was eating.

He stared at me with open-eyed astonishment and said, "*Kupati*, of course."

"But what's that?" I retorted.

He looked at me helplessly, started to mumble a reply, and then suddenly snapped his fingers. Moments later a pile of *kupati* was in front of me, and I soon found myself digging in just like the stranger I had encountered. And all this to the cheers and encouragement of the other diners, whose fierce national pride was much moved by the spectacle of a young Russian's initiation into Georgia's noble cuisine. I can't describe what *kupati* are either — this is one of the foods you cannot explain. You must try for yourself.

Kupati should be stuffed into a sausage casing just like real sausages. So do try this, especially if sausage-making happens to be a favorite pastime. If not, the version given here, really a "quick *kupati*," is perfectly acceptable.

Kupati are equally good fried or grilled. I like them wrapped in thin bread, *lavash* or pita, accompanied by Pomegranate Sauce or Sour Plum Sauce (see the Index for the recipe page numbers).

8 ounces ground pork

6 ounces ground beef

6 ounces coarsely ground pork
    fatback

2 medium-size onions, finely chopped

3 large cloves garlic, finely minced

½ teaspoon ground coriander

¼ teaspoon ground allspice

¾ teaspoon hot Hungarian paprika

⅛ teaspoon ground cinnamon

3 tablespoons ice water

½ cup finely chopped fresh cilantro

Salt, to taste

½ cup pomegranate seeds, plus additional for garnish

2 tablespoons vegetable oil

2 tablespoons unsalted butter

1 small red onion, finely chopped for garnish

Chopped fresh parsley for garnish

1 In a large bowl, combine the meats, fatback, onions, garlic, spices, ice water, cilantro, and salt. Knead until the mixture is thoroughly blended. Gently stir in ⅓ cup pomegranate seeds taking care not to crush them. Refrigerate the mixture, covered, for at least 4 hours.

2 Form the meat mixture into sausages 3½ inches long, 1 inch thick.

3 Heat the oil and butter in a large skillet over medium heat. Add the sausages, a few at a time, and fry them until they are well browned on all sides and cooked

through, 10 to 12 minutes.

4 Combine the chopped red onion, additional pomegranate seeds, and chopped parsley. Serve the *kupati* garnished with this mixture.

Serves 6

Note: Kupati can also be cooked in a broiler or outdoors on a grill. Neither of these methods requires any cooking fats. Cooking time for broiled or grilled *kupati* is about 15 minutes.

Moldavian Meatballs

Perisoare a la Moldova

This meatball recipe from Moldavia is a real prize-winner among the endless variety of meatballs, from every corner of the Soviet Union, that I've been testing on family and friends for years. They're simmered in a garlicky sauce with red peppers, tomatoes, and other vegetables. Serve with *mamaliga* (Cornmeal Mush; see Index), polenta, rice, or noodles, and a salad. These meatballs taste better when prepared a day ahead.

MEATBALLS

1¼ pounds ground pork

8 ounces ground beef

1 medium-size onion, grated

2 cloves garlic, finely minced

¼ cup ice-cold milk

1 large egg, lightly beaten

3 tablespoons unflavored fine, dry bread crumbs

3 tablespoons finely chopped fresh parsley

SAUCE

4 cloves garlic, peeled

1 red bell pepper, cored, seeded, and cut into pieces

3 tablespoons vegetable oil

1 small onion, finely chopped

1 leek (white part plus 1 inch green), well rinsed, patted dry, and chopped

1 medium-size carrot, peeled and cut into julienne

1 small rib celery, finely chopped

1½ teaspoons all-purpose flour

1 cup Beef Stock (see Index) or canned broth

¼ cup dry red wine

1 cup canned Italian plum tomatoes, drained, seeded, and chopped

2 tablespoons tomato paste

¼ teaspoon sugar

1 teaspoon sweet Hungarian paprika

1 teaspoon hot Hungarian paprika

Salt and freshly ground black pepper, to taste

FOR FINISHING THE DISH

3 to 4 tablespoons unsalted butter

All-purpose flour for dusting the meatballs

1½ teaspoons sour cream

3 tablespoons chopped fresh parsley

2 tablespoons chopped fresh dill

1 In a large bowl, combine the ingredients for the meatballs. Knead until the mixture is thoroughly blended. Refrigerate, covered, while you make the sauce.

2 Mince the garlic and the red pepper in a food processor. Set aside.

3 Heat the oil in a Dutch oven over medium heat. Add the onion and sauté, stirring occasionally, until it begins to soften, about 5 minutes.

4 Add the leek, carrot, and celery and continue to sauté, stirring frequently, for

10 minutes. Stir in the minced peppers and garlic and sauté for 3 minutes more.

5 Sprinkle the flour over the vegetables. Add the stock, wine, tomatoes, tomato paste, sugar, sweet and hot paprika, and salt and pepper. Stir well, then cover and simmer for 15 minutes.

6 While the sauce is simmering, remove the meat mixture from the refrigerator. Have a bowl of cold water ready. Dipping your hands in the cold water to prevent the meat from sticking to your hands, make meatballs about 1½ inches in diameter.

7 Melt 3 tablespoons of the butter in

a large skillet over medium heat. Dust the meatballs with flour and brown them lightly on all sides in the butter.

8 Add the browned meatballs to the simmering sauce, stir gently, and continue to simmer, covered, for another 15 minutes.

9 Taste and correct the seasoning, then stir in the sour cream and fresh herbs. Remove from the heat and let stand for 5 minutes before serving.

Serves 6 to 8

Roast Stuffed Suckling Pig

Zharenniy Porosyonok

Suckling pig is one of the few Old World delicacies lavishly described by Gogol, Chekhov, and others in the nineteenth century, that is still being widely prepared in the Soviet Union today. Suckling pig is revered equally by the Russians, Ukrainians, Lithuanians, and especially by the Georgians, who often stuff it with their local cheese and roast it on a spit. For an authentically Georgian taste, rub the pig lightly with *adzhika*, a fiery hot pepper paste (see Index), and refrigerate for 24 hours before roasting. For a more traditional Russian flavor, stuff the pig with kasha stuffing and serve plenty of horseradish on the side. Not to be missed is the more substantial Lithuanian liver stuffing, and crunchy Homemade Pickles and marinated fruit—Marinated Pears in Honey (see the Index for the recipe page numbers) — are also welcome additions. Note that suckling pig usually has to be ordered from the butcher in advance, but it's definitely worth the planning and the wait.

1 suckling pig, 12 pounds, liver,
    heart, and lungs reserved if pre-
    paring the liver stuffing
2 teaspoons coarse (kosher) salt
2 teaspoons freshly ground black
    pepper
Russian Buckwheat Stuffing or
    Lithuanian Liver Stuffing
    (recipes follow)
¼ cup olive oil
1 small red apple
Fresh parsley or cilantro sprigs for
    garnish

1 Preheat the oven to 400°F.

2 Wash the pig thoroughly inside and out under cold running water. Pat dry with paper towels. Rub inside and out with coarse salt and pepper and let stand for 30 minutes.

3 Stuff the pig's cavity with the desired stuffing and sew up the opening.

4 Wrap pieces of aluminum foil around the pig's ears and tail so that they don't burn during the cooking. Brush the rest of the pig with oil and place it on a rack in a large roasting pan. Roast for 20 minutes, then reduce the oven temperature to 350°F and continue roasting for another 2½ hours, basting with the pan juices every 20 minutes.

5 Remove the foil from the ears and tail and continue to roast until the juices run clear when you prick the pig with a skewer, 20 to 30 minutes more.

6 Remove the stuffing to a serving platter, place a small apple into the pig's mouth, and serve, garnished with parsley or cilantro (if you are making it the Georgian way). Cut the pig lengthwise along the backbone. Cut each half crosswise between the ribs into 5 to 6 pieces.

Serves 6 to 8

Russian Buckwheat Stuffing
Nachinka iz Kashi

7 tablespoon unsalted butter
3 cups whole kasha (buckwheat)
6½ cups Beef Stock (see Index) or
    canned broth
Salt, to taste
2½ cups chopped onions
Freshly ground black pepper, to
    taste

1 Melt 3 tablespoons of the butter in a heavy pot over medium heat. Add the kasha and stir for 3 minutes. Add 6 cups of the stock and bring to a boil. Add salt, then reduce the heat to low, cover, and simmer until all the liquid is absorbed, about 20 minutes.

2 Meanwhile, melt the remaining 4 tablespoons butter in a large skillet over medium heat. Add the onions and sauté, stirring occasionally, until browned, about 20 minutes.

3 Add the onions to the kasha along with the remaining ½ cup stock and toss well. Season with freshly ground black pepper and additional salt.

Makes about 6½ cups stuffing

Lithuanian Liver Stuffing

Nachinka is Pechyonki po-Litovsky

Liver, heart, and lungs of the suckling pig, well rinsed and patted dried
½ pound calf's liver
1 pound ground veal
4 slices white bread, crusts removed
⅓ cup milk

½ cup bacon fat
2 medium-size onions, finely chopped
4 large eggs, separated
Pinch of freshly grated nutmeg
Salt and freshly ground black pepper, to taste

1 Bring 1 quart of water to a boil in a large saucepan over high heat. Add the pig's heart and lungs, then reduce the heat to low and simmer, uncovered, for 5 to 7 minutes. Add the pig's and calf's liver and simmer for another 10 minutes.

2 Drain the meats and grind in a meat grinder or a food processor. Combine with the ground veal in a large bowl. Set aside.

3 Meanwhile, soak the bread in the milk for 15 minutes.

4 While the bread is soaking, render the bacon fat in a medium-size skillet over medium heat. Add the onions and sauté, stirring occasionally, until they begin to color, about 10 minutes. Add the onions to the meats.

5 Remove the bread from the milk and, without squeezing, crumble it over the meat in the bowl. Mix in to the mixture along with the egg yolks, nutmeg, and salt and pepper.

6 Beat the egg whites with a wire whisk until they foam. Fold into the meat mixture.

Makes about 6 cups stuffing

Poultry and Game Dishes

PTITSA I DICH

Deliciously crispy chicken Kiev; gourmet chicken *tapaka* (tiny chickens pounded flat and fried to perfection); healthful chicken and vegetable stews from Armenia; classic Russian *pozharzky*, delicate croquettes made from ground chicken; juicy chicken kebabs from Azerbaijan; even a simple, finely poached free-range chicken on a country kitchen table — all these mouthwatering preparations bear witness to the cult status of chicken among the meats of the USSR. If the Soviets elected an animal leader (George Orwell notwithstanding) it would certainly be a noble farmyard chicken. No one — Balts, Uzbeks, Georgians, Russians — has a bad word to say against chicken, and many would be humbled before an especially fine bird as we in the West would laud a filet mignon.

If guests are expected, Russian mothers (or their special envoys) will plot for a week in order to track down the best poultry in town. They will loan their cars, they will trade precious concert tickets, they will go so far as to barter stockings or jeans from America. Anything so they can show off their skill with a lovingly prepared fresh chicken dish.

It's one of the great come-downs of emigration to find that chickens are two-a-penny in the United States, and that no one but the sick seems to think them prestigious. Soviet emigrés soon learn not to serve chicken at every dinner party, but it doesn't stop them from elaborating on their fabulous repertoire of chicken recipes for the family table. If you ask American Georgians or Armenians why chicken often enjoys such a mediocre reputation on this side of the Atlantic, they will invariably attribute it to factory-farming and the freezer. Every self-respecting Caucasian, they would say, not only buys directly from the farmer or the private market, but buys exclusively from a friend, or at the very least buys according to a strict ritual of family recommendations. As in other parts of the chicken-buying world, it is not considered unusual to make detailed enquiries about the diet and lifestyle of the prospective purchase, and if the answers are satisfactory and the price right, to take the live bird home under your arm. Only thus will you obtain lean, flavorful meat.

It's not surprising that Georgians, with their keen sense of good food, have a special flair for cooking chicken. They grill or roast them (accompanied by delicately spiced and well-textured walnut sauces — *satsivi* or *garo*); they fry them under a press (*tapaka*); and they stew them with a memorable sauce of herbs, tomatoes, and lemon juice (*chakhokbili*). All these preparations have become much sought-after favorites throughout the USSR.

Historic Presentations

In the western Soviet Union, roasted poultry has been appreciated for centuries. In the past, a simple household would have served a turkey, goose, or chicken, accompanied by fresh seasonal vegetables and they would have washed it down with jugs of beer or *kvass*. On the tables of the aristocracy, however, one could have sampled roast swan (a now forgotten Russian delicacy), larks, peacocks, even cuckoos.

Catherine the Great introduced more elaborate poultry and game dishes from Europe, including all kinds of terrines (a menu from one of her feasts mentions a mysterious "terrine with wings and green sauce"), roulades, and fancy sauces. Grigori Potemkin, Catherine's minister and lover, was known to have dissipated a small fortune to satisfy his craving for the best *foie gras*.

By the nineteenth century the high art of *côtelettes de volailles* — the preparation of dishes using choice breast meat — had arrived from France, and

Company's Coming

Here is a sample of poultry and game dishes served at a dinner given by Czar Alexei Mikhailovich (Peter the Great's father) in 1667:

Roast Woodcock Garnished with Plums

Roast Grouse on a Bed of Lemon

Roast Lemon Chicken (off the bone)

Chicken Pickled with Cucumbers

Turkey with Lavish Saffron Sauce

Roast Chicken (with and without onions)

Chicken in *ukha* (a traditional Russian soup)

Chicken with Kasha

Geese with Clove Sauce

Chicken Imbued with Lemon and Saffron

Kurnik (a flaky chicken pie)

Chicken *Piroghi*

soon became the rage of aristocratic cuisine. But Russian chefs, famous in this era for their inventive hybrids and elegant recombinations, interpreted *volailles* in their own distinctive way. *Voliay*, the Russian transcription, means "to roll"; so the technique of rolling chicken cutlets in bread crumbs was born, and this paved the way for such classics as Chicken Kiev and Chicken Croquettes Pozharsky. If the celebrity chefs of the great cities and courts were famously preoccupied in translating and adapting French cuisine, the tables of the vast provincial estates still boasted such Slavic favorites as plump roast goose with apples, duck stuffed with kasha, or turkey stuffed with a delectable bread mixture. Everywhere you looked in prerevolutionary Russia — in towns, cities, villages, and the remotest backwaters — chicken and poultry dishes reigned supreme.

Game

Moving beyond the farmyard, the western Soviets have also had a long passion for the hunt, an enthusiasm that is rendered unforgettably vivid in the great hunting scene of Tolstoy's *War and Peace*. The woods and forests of the Russian heartland once yielded an abundance of both big game — bear, moose, and wild boar — and small feathered game such as grouse, woodcock, and partridge. As in present-day northern Yugoslavia, we can expect a revival of traditional game preparations in a growing number of restaurants specializing in old Slavic fare. There are a few of these establishments in Moscow and environs, and others in the ancient Russian towns of Novgorod, Vladimir, and Suzdal. We look forward to this revival and offer you here your own private preview.

Chicken on Skewers

Juja kabab

Succulent pieces of grilled chicken, tenderized in a saffron and yogurt marinade. Grill a couple of skewers of cherry tomatoes separately. Serve this with Basic Steamed Saffron Rice with a Bread Crust (see Index).

1 chicken (4½ pound), boned (ask
   your butcher to do this for you),
   cut into 2-inch chunks
1½ cups plain low-fat yogurt
2 medium-size onions, finely chopped
4 cloves garlic, crushed in a
   garlic press
½ teaspoon hot Hungarian paprika

¾ teaspoon sweet Hungarian
   paprika
½ teaspoon crushed saffron threads,
   diluted in 1 tablespoon warm
   water
½ cup finely chopped fresh mint
   leaves
Salt, to taste

1 In a large glass or ceramic bowl, combine the chicken with the remaining ingredients and toss well. Cover and refrigerate for 12 hours, or overnight, turning a couple of times.

2 Prepare coals for grilling until coated with white ash, or preheat the broiler. Oil the grill or broiler rack.

3 Remove the chicken pieces from the marinade and shake off the excess. Thread the pieces onto long metal skewers. Since white meat will cook faster than dark meat, it is best to place each on separate skewers.

4 Grill or broil the chicken 3 inches from the heat, 10 minutes for white meat, 15 to 20 minutes for dark meat, turning the skewers several times. The juices should run clear when a piece of meat is pricked with a skewer.

Serves 3 to 4

The Azerbaijani Way

In Azerbaijan, where this recipe comes from, kebabs and many other meat and poultry dishes are traditionally accompanied by a plate of thinly sliced, sumakh-sprinkled sweet onions, a plate of fresh herbs, and flatbread (*lavash*). The kebabs are eaten wrapped in the *lavash* together with some onion and a few herb sprigs.

Grilled Chicken with Garlic and Walnut Sauce

Kotmis Garo

This dish always reminds me of Georgian gardens surrounded by lush vines — a vat of young homemade wine buried in the ground waiting to be drunk, a table loaded with cold appetizers, and men with startling mustaches patiently grilling the chickens (which they were probably given by a next-door neighbor in exchange for a round of homemade cheese).

As with so many of the best Georgian dishes, the sauce accompanying the chicken is prepared with walnuts and is superb. For a better-tasting chicken, throw a vine leaf or two into your coals. Serve accompanied by sprigs of fresh tarragon, mint, and cilantro, and with a simple vegetable salad, such as Tomato and Garlic Salad (see Index). Using a free-range chicken, which is what is done in Georgia, will make this dish truly special.

*2 chickens (2½ pounds each),
    quartered, well rinsed, and
    patted dry*
*Salt and freshly ground black
    pepper, to taste*
½ cup olive oil
¾ cup fresh lemon juice
3 cloves garlic, minced
*8 sprigs fresh tarragon,
    stems crushed with the back
    of a knife*
*Garlic and Walnut Sauce
    (recipe follows)*

1 Rub the chicken pieces thoroughly with salt and pepper.

2 Combine the olive oil, lemon juice, garlic, tarragon, and additional salt and pepper in a shallow dish. Add the chicken and turn to coat with the marinade. Cover and refrigerate for at least 6 hours, turning occasionally.

3 Prepare the coals for grilling until coated with white ash, or preheat the broiler. Oil the grill or broiler rack.

4 Remove the chicken from the marinade and, without drying, grill or broil it 3 to 4 inches from the heat, turning a few times and basting with the marinade. The chicken is ready when the juices run clear when the thickest part of the thigh is pricked with a skewer, after about 30 minutes.

5 Serve the chicken with th sauceboat.

Serves 6 to 8

Garlic and Walnut Sauce

Garo

1½ cups walnut pieces
5 cloves garlic, peeled
½ cup chopped fresh cilantro
1 cup Chicken Stock (see Index) or
*   canned broth, warm (not hot)*
3 to 4 tablespoons fresh lemon juice

Salt, to taste
¼ teaspoon ground coriander
¼ teaspoon ground
*   fenugreek*
¼ teaspoon cayenne pepper
½ teaspoon ground turmeric

1 In a food processor, combine the walnuts, garlic, and ¼ cup of the cilantro. Process until the walnuts are finely ground.

2 Transfer to a bowl and stir in the stock, lemon juice to taste, salt, coriander,

fenugreek, cayenne, turmeric, and the remaining cilantro. Let the sauce stand at room temperature, covered, for at least 2 hours before serving.

Makes about 2 cups

Chicken Kiev

Koteleti po Kievski

Although chicken Kiev is one of the best-known Russian (or Ukrainian) classics, its history and origins are almost completely obscure. The dish probably started life as a version of the French *côtelettes de volailles*

(stuffed chicken cutlets), but how the noble city of Kiev came to lend its name to the dish is not clear, especially as chicken Kiev does not really blend in with the much heartier dishes typical of Ukrainian cuisine.

In a properly prepared chicken Kiev, the breast is boned and stuffed with butter in such a way that the wing bone remains attached. I give an easier version made from boneless chicken breast halves stuffed with herb-flavored butter. Chicken Kiev should be served immediately from the frying pan so a delicious hot spring of butter will spurt out as the meat is cut.

12 tablespoons (1½ sticks) unsalted
  butter, at room temperature
2 tablespoons finely chopped
  fresh dill
1½ tablespoons fresh lemon juice
Freshly ground white pepper,
  to taste
6 whole skinless, boneless chicken
  breasts (about 8 ounces each),
  halved

Salt, to taste
All-purpose flour for rolling
  the chicken
2 large eggs, beaten, for dipping
  the chicken
Homemade fine, dry bread crumbs
  for breading the chicken (about
  2 cups; see box)
Vegetable oil for deep frying

1 Blend the butter with the dill, lemon juice, and a healthy amount of white pepper.

2 On a plate, shape the butter into twelve 1-inch-long "fingers." Cover the plate with plastic wrap and refrigerate until completely firm, at least 2 hours.

3 Place each chicken breast half between two sheets of waxed paper and pound with the flat side of a meat pounder until very thin, taking great care not to rip the meat. If the meat should tear, just press it together until it sticks.

4 Sprinkle the flattened breasts with salt and place a butter "finger" lengthwise on each. Tuck in the ends, and roll the breast

Making Bread Crumbs

To prepare bread crumbs, remove the crusts from a day-old loaf of Italian or French bread. Cut into thin slices and dry in a 325°F oven until completely dried, 10 to 15 minutes. Process in the food processor. For chicken Kiev, Russians prefer coarse-textured bread crumbs.

up. Secure with a toothpick and make sure there are no visible openings or tears in the meat, so the butter has no way of leaking out during cooking.

5 Dip the rolls in flour, then into the beaten egg, then roll in bread crumbs, making sure they are thoroughly coated.

6 Place the breaded rolls on a platter, cover with plastic wrap, and refrigerate for at least 4 hours.

7 When ready to cook, preheat the oil in a deep-fryer to 350°F.

8 Drop four of the chicken rolls into the hot oil. Fry until deep golden, about 8 minutes. Transfer to paper towels to drain, and keep warm in a low oven, or on a heated platter. Repeat the procedure with the rest of the chicken. Serve immediately.

Serves 6 to 8

Chicken Croquettes Pozharsky

Pozharskiye Kotleti

These fluffy, delicate ground chicken and veal croquettes are traditionally accompanied by smothered mushrooms. I often serve Mushrooms Sautéed with Madeira (see Index) alongside.

3 slices whole-wheat bread, crusts removed
⅓ cup heavy or whipping cream
1 pound ground chicken breast meat
¾ pound ground veal
1 small onion, minced
9 tablespoons unsalted butter, at room temperature
2 large egg yolks
2 tablespoons Madeira

2 tablespoons chopped fresh dill (optional)
Salt and freshly ground black pepper, to taste
1 large egg white
About 1⅓ cups unflavored fine, dry bread crumbs
2 eggs, beaten, for dipping the chicken
4 tablespoons light vegetable oil

1 Soak the bread slices in the cream for 10 minutes. Squeeze the bread to remove any excess cream. Then discard all but 3 tablespoons of the cream.

2 In a food processor, combine the bread, cream, chicken, veal, onion, 3 tablespoons butter, the egg yolks, Madeira, dill (if using), and salt and pepper. Process for 3 to 4 pulses until well blended but not puréed. Transfer to a large bowl.

3 Beat the egg white until it holds stiff peaks. Gently fold it into the meat mixture. If the mixture seems too loose to form into croquettes, cover, and refrigerate to firm up, 1 hour.

4 Have a bowl of cold water ready. Dip your hands in the cold water to prevent the meat from sticking to your hands. Shape the meat mixture into 12 oval croquettes.

5 Sprinkle the bread crumbs on a cutting board or other flat surface. Dip the croquettes into the beaten egg, then roll them in the crumbs to coat well.

6 Heat 2 tablespoons of the remaining butter and 2 tablespoons of the oil in a large skillet. Fry six of the croquettes over medium heat until crispy and brown, 12 to 15 minutes. The juices should run clear when a croquette is pierced with a fork. Repeat with the rest of the croquettes, adding more butter and oil as needed. Serve immediately.

Serves 6

A Literary Dish

One of the unfailing duties of every Russian food historian is to contribute a piece of research to the great legend of chicken Pozharsky. The reason for this is that this dish was originally immortalized in a versified letter, dispatched by Alexander Pushkin in the early nineteenth century, in which the author advises a friend to sample the cutlets at Pozharsky's (tavern) in the city of Torzhok.

You should be aware that Pushkin's status in the Soviet Union tops even the veneration reserved for Shakespeare or the Beatles in Britain. Almost every fact of his life is committed to memory by Russian school children and the tavern in Torzhok is flooded by droves of Pushkin devotees.

In view of all this, I felt obliged to provide at least one of the many authentic versions of the Pozharsky legend. It's my favorite: Alexander I made a stopover at Pozharsky's and sat down to lunch. He ordered veal cutlets. To Pozharsky's horror, he was out of veal. His wife suggested that he trick the Czar by serving his chicken croquettes rolled in bread crumbs. The Czar was delighted with his meal. Emboldened, the Pozharskys acknowledged their fraud, but the Czar gave them a medal instead of a reprimand, and put "Pozharsky" chicken straight on the royal menu.

Stuffed Chicken Breast with Morels

Kurinoye File so Smorchkami

This recipe is adapted from a Russian cookbook written in the 1840s. According to the cookbook dried morels were so common in the kitchen that they were tossed into the pan by the fistful to add body and flavor. Don't we wish this were the case in the nineties!

2 cups Chicken Stock (see Index) or
    canned broth
1 ounce dried morels, well rinsed
1 whole skinless, boneless chicken
    breast (about 1¼ pounds), halved
7 ounces ground chicken meat
1 large egg, slightly beaten
2 tablespoons finely chopped fresh
    parsley

1 tablespoon finely chopped fresh
    dill
Salt and freshly ground black
    pepper, to taste
⅓ cup dry white wine
½ cup heavy or whipping cream
2 tablespoons unsalted butter,
    chilled, cut in pieces
2 teaspoons dry vermouth

1 Bring ½ cup of the chicken stock to a boil and pour over the morels in a heatproof bowl. Soak for 1 hour. Drain, then chop fine. Strain the soaking liquid through a coffee filter and set aside.

2 Place each chicken breast half between two sheets of waxed paper and pound with the flat side of a meat pounder until thin.

3 In a small bowl, combine the ground chicken, egg, 1 tablespoon of the parsley, the dill, and 2 tablespoons of the chopped

morels. Season with salt and pepper and mix well.

4 Place half the filling along the long side of each breast half, tuck in the ends, and roll up. Secure with a toothpick.

5 Place the chicken rolls in a medium-size saucepan and add the morel soaking liquid, the remaining broth, the wine, and the remaining morels. Bring the liquid to a boil, then reduce heat to low, partially cover, and poach the chicken until cooked through, 20 minutes. With a slotted spoon, remove the chicken to a heated platter.

6 Over medium-high heat, reduce the poaching liquid to ⅓ cup, 15 minutes. Add the cream and cook for 7 minutes more.

7 Off the heat, whisk in the butter and

vermouth until well blended. Stir in the remaining parsley and season with salt and pepper.

8 To serve, cut the rolls into ½-inch slices and spoon the sauce over them.

Serves 2

Chicken Paprika

Kuritsa s Paprikoy

Some Hungarian staples, such as this rich chicken stew with bell peppers and paprika, migrated into western Russia across the Carpathian mountains, bringing with them a satisfying piquancy and bite. This tastes even better the next day, so I always prepare Steps 1 to 4 the day before. Serve with buttered egg noodles, rice, or *mamaliga*, Moldavian Cornmeal Mush (see Index).

2 tablespoons unsalted butter

1 large onion, chopped

3 tablespoons sweet Hungarian paprika, plus additional for garnish

3 tablespoons vegetable oil

1 chicken (3¼ pounds), cut into serving-size pieces, well rinsed, and patted dry

1 large green bell pepper, cored, seeded, and cut into strips

1 large red bell pepper, cored, seeded, and cut into strips

4 large fresh, ripe tomatoes, peeled, seeded, and coarsely chopped

Salt and freshly ground black pepper, to taste

¼ teaspoon dried marjoram

1 cup Chicken Stock (see Index) or canned broth

2 tablespoons sour cream

3 tablespoons heavy or whipping cream

1 tablespoon chopped fresh parsley for garnish

1 Melt the butter in a large Dutch oven over medium-low heat. Add the onion and sauté, stirring occasionally, until softened, about 5 minutes.

2 Add the 3 tablespoons paprika and stir until the onions turn reddish brown.

3 In a large skillet, heat the oil over medium heat until it sizzles. Brown the chicken on all sides. You will probably have to do this in batches to get the pieces nicely browned. Drain on a paper towel.

4 Transfer the chicken to the Dutch oven with the onions. Add the peppers and cook over medium heat, stirring, for 5 minutes. Stir in the tomatoes, salt and pepper, marjoram, and the stock, then reduce the heat to low, cover the pot tightly, and simmer until the chicken is very tender, about 40 minutes.

5 Meanwhile, in a small bowl, whisk together the sour cream and heavy cream.

6 With a slotted spoon, transfer the chicken to a heated platter.

7 Whisk a little of the hot sauce into the sour cream mixture, then add the mixture to sauce in the Dutch oven. Reduce over high heat until slightly thickened.

8 Serve the chicken with the sauce spooned over it, sprinkled with a little paprika and parsley.

Serves 4 to 6

Chicken with Herbs and Tomatoes

Chakhokbili

The name of this Georgian dish, *chakhokbili*, derives from the word *khokhobi*, which means "pheasant" in Georgian. But although this dish was evidently made with pheasant at one time, today either chicken or lamb is used. *Chakhokbili* is a refreshing, slightly tangy fricassee, with tomatoes, garlic, lemon juice, and lots of fresh herbs. Double the recipe and serve at a large dinner party — it's healthy, simple, and inexpensive. Serve with a steamed rice pilaf or bulgur pilaf.

4 tablespoons (½ stick) unsalted butter

1 chicken (4½ pounds), cut into
    12 to 16 pieces, well rinsed and
    patted dry

6 cloves garlic, crushed in a garlic
    press

3 large onions, coarsely chopped

10 fresh, ripe plum tomatoes, peeled
    and quartered

⅓ cup dry white wine

¼ cup fresh lemon juice

6 tablespoons chopped fresh basil,
    plus additional for garnish

5 tablespoons chopped fresh
    cilantro

5 tablespoons chopped fresh
    parsley

2 tablespoons chopped fresh tarragon

8 black peppercorns

1 bay leaf

Salt and freshly ground black
    pepper, to taste

1 Melt the butter in a large Dutch oven. Add the chicken pieces, a few at a time, and brown on all sides over medium heat. Replace all the chicken in the Dutch oven.

2 Stir the garlic and onions into the chicken. Reduce the heat to medium-low, cover tightly, and cook without stirring for 15 minutes. The chicken will release quite a lot of juice.

3 Add the tomatoes, wine, ¼ cup lemon juice, half the herbs, all the peppercorns, the bay leaf, and salt and pepper. Simmer, covered, until the chicken is tender, about 35 minutes.

4 Stir in the rest of the herbs and simmer for 10 minutes more.

5 Taste and correct the seasoning. Remove the bay leaf. Sprinkle with fresh basil, and serve at once.

Serves 6

Chicken with Okra

Bamiyov Hav

I must confess that I didn't taste okra until quite recently. For some reason, I would only cast suspicious glances at it in Indian and Middle Eastern markets, and could never bring myself to give it a try. But when I finally did, I was extremely surprised to recall that I had actually tasted it dozens of times as a child—but always in a vegetable stew, where its looks were disguised. This stew comes from Armenia and will please both the eye and the palate. Serve it with steamed or boiled rice or with a bulgur pilaf (see Index).

10 ounces fresh okra
¼ cup white wine vinegar
¼ cup olive oil
1 chicken (3½ pounds), cut into 8 pieces, well rinsed, and patted dry
2 small onions, quartered and thinly sliced
3 cloves garlic, sliced
1⅓ cups Chicken Stock (see Index) or canned broth

1 can (16 ounces) Italian plum tomatoes, chopped, juice reserved
2 tablespoons fresh lemon juice
¼ cup dry white wine
Salt and freshly ground black pepper, to taste
¼ cup chopped fresh parsley

1 Stem the okra pods and rinse in a colander under cold running water. Drain well. In a bowl, combine the okra with the vinegar and let stand while preparing the chicken.

2 Heat the oil in a large ovenproof casserole over medium heat until it sizzles. Add the chicken and lightly brown, turning it to brown evenly. With a slotted spoon, transfer the chicken to a platter.

3 Preheat the oven to 350°F.

4 Drain off all but 1 tablespoon of the oil from the casserole and sauté the onions and garlic over medium-low heat until softened but not browned, about 8 minutes.

5 Stir in the chicken stock, tomatoes and juice, lemon juice, and wine. Bring to a boil, then reduce the heat and let simmer for several minutes.

6 Return the chicken to the casserole, season generously with salt and pepper, cover, and place in the oven until the chicken is tender, about 30 minutes.

7 Drain the okra and stir it into the casserole. Add more seasoning if necessary and continue to bake, covered, until the okra is tender but not overcooked, another 10 minutes.

8 Remove the casserole from the oven, transfer the chicken pieces to a heated platter and cover with aluminum foil.

9 Place the casserole over high heat and reduce the sauce until it thickens, about 5 to 7 minutes. Stir in the parsley and spoon the sauce over the chicken.

Serves 4

Crispy Fried Cornish Hen

Tapaka

W hen I was growing up, this crispy chicken dish was my very favorite. Moscow always suffered (and still suffers) from a shortage of poultry. As a very special treat, my grandmother would stand on line for many hours if she heard news on the grapevine of "chicken in town." She would arrive home triumphantly brandishing a bird, which she cooked especially for me.

The name *tapaka* derives from the heavy iron skillet (*tapa*) with its weighted lid, under which the marinated chicken is flattened and then fried. This achieves a firm, golden crust. *Tapaka* chicken is traditionally accompanied by Spinach in Yogurt Sauce (see Index). You should serve as many hens as you have guests.

CORNISH HEN

1 Cornish game hen (about ¾ pound), well rinsed and patted dry

1 large clove garlic, crushed in a garlic press

2 teaspoons fresh lemon juice

Pinch of sweet Hungarian paprika

Salt

3 tablespoons Clarified Butter (see box, facing page)

Freshly ground black pepper, to taste

GARNISHES AND ACCOMPANIMENT

Romaine or Boston lettuce leaves

Scallions

Red onion rings

Red radishes

Cherry tomatoes

Sour Plum Sauce (see Index)

1 With a meat cleaver, poultry shears, or a very sharp knife, split open the breast of the Cornish hen. Carefully remove the breastbone. Cover the hen with waxed paper and pound with the flat side of the cleaver or a meat pounder to flatten.

2 Combine the garlic, lemon juice, paprika, and about ¼ teaspoon salt. Rub over the hen and refrigerate it, covered for at least 2 hours or as long as overnight.

3 Heat the clarified butter in a heavy cast-iron skillet over medium heat.

4 Brush the garlic off the hen, then place the hen in the skillet, skin side down. Cover the bird directly with something flat (such as an ovenproof plate) and place a heavy object (such as a brick, a workout weight, or a smaller iron skillet) on top so the hen is firmly pressed down.

5 Cook until the skin is deep golden and crispy, about 20 minutes. Turn the bird, re-weight, and cook on the other side for about 15 minutes. Pierce a thigh with a skewer. The hen is ready when the juices run clear.

6 Serve on a bed of lettuce, garnished with the fresh vegetables, and accompanied by Sour Plum Sauce on the side.

Makes 1 serving

Clarified Butter

Melt 8 tablespoons (1 stick) unsalted butter (or more if needed) in a small saucepan over low heat. When the butter forms a white foam on the surface, remove the pan from the heat and let stand until the milk solids settle on the bottom, 3 to 5 minutes. Carefully pour off the clear butter, leaving the solids in the saucepan. Strain the solids through several layers of cheesecloth to remove as much of the clarified butter as possible. Eight tablespoons of butter yields about 6 tablespoons when clarified. Clarified butter will keep in the refrigerator for up to three weeks.

Turkey Stuffed with Fruit and Almond Pilaf

Amich

This Armenian dish is always a hit at my all-American Thanksgiving dinner. I must admit that my pumpkin dishes are Armenian as well! You can also try this wonderful rice stuffing of dried fruit and almonds with chicken, in which case use about one-third of the stuffing recipe to stuff a 3½- to 4-pound chicken. Gravy is not an Armenian or Russian phenomenon, but do follow the old American impulses and whip up a light gravy that would complement the fruity stuffing.

STUFFING

Salt, to taste

2½ cups uncooked long-grain rice

8 tablespoons (1 stick) unsalted
   butter

2 cups chopped onions

2 cups chopped dried apricots,
   preferably Californian

1½ cups golden raisins

1 cup dried currants

1½ cups whole blanched almonds

Grated zest of 3 oranges (reserve
   the oranges)

Freshly ground black pepper,
   to taste

TURKEY

1 turkey (12 to 14 pounds), rinsed well

3 oranges, reserved from preparing
   the stuffing

Salt and freshly ground black
   pepper, to taste

¼ cup olive oil

4 tablespoons (½ stick) unsalted
   butter

3 tablespoons unsalted butter, melted

¼ cup canned chicken broth

1 Bring 4 quarts water to a boil in a large pot and let boil for about 2 minutes. Add salt. Pour in the rice in a thin, steady stream. Let boil, stirring once or twice, for 7 or 8 minutes. The rice should still be slightly hard to the bite. Drain the rice in a colander and rinse with cold water.

2 Set the colander containing the rice over a pot of fresh boiling water. Wrap a linen or cotton (not terry cloth) kitchen towel around the lid of the pot and cover the pot tightly. Steam the rice until almost tender, but still slightly firm, 25 minutes. Transfer to a bowl.

3 While the rice is steaming, melt the 8 tablespoons butter in a large skillet over medium-low heat. Add the onions and sauté, stirring occasionally, until they wilt, about 5 minutes. Stir in the dried fruits and almonds and cook gently until the fruits are soft and plump, about 15 minutes.

4 Stir the sautéed mixture and the butter in which they cooked into the rice. Season with salt to taste and add the orange zest. Stir well. Refrigerate until ready to use, if making the stuffing a day ahead.

5 Remove the giblets and neck from the bird's cavity and save for another use. Rinse the insides of the turkey and pat dry. Halve the reserved oranges and rub the cavity with the halves. Season the turkey inside and out with salt and pepper and squeeze some orange juice on the outside.

6 Stuff the neck area loosely with some of the stuffing and fold the neck skin under the body. Pack the body cavity loosely with some of the remaining stuffing. Sew or skewer the opening closed. Transfer the remaining stuffing to a buttered ovenproof casserole and set aside.

7 Preheat the oven to 425°F.

8 Heat the oil and the 4 tablespoons butter in a small saucepan over low heat until the butter melts.

9 Brush the turkey all over with the butter and oil. Arrange the turkey on a rack of a roasting pan and roast, uncovered, for 30 minutes.

10 Reduce the oven temperature to 325°F. Cover the turkey loosely with aluminum foil and roast, basting every 20 minutes, until the juices run clear when the fleshy part of the thigh is pricked with a skewer, about 3 hours. If the turkey is not browning enough, 30 minutes before the roast should be done, raise the oven temperature to 450°F, and roast, uncovered, for the remainder of the cooking time.

11 Half an hour before the turkey is ready, drizzle the remaining stuffing with the melted butter and broth and bake, covered until the turkey is ready. Transfer the turkey to a carving board, cover with aluminum foil, and let stand for 15 minutes.

12 Remove the string or skewer from the cavity opening and spoon the stuffing onto a serving platter. Carve and serve the turkey with stuffing and gravy, if desired.

Serves 8 to 10

Turkey Breast with Apple and Tomato Purée

Indeika s Tomatno-Yablochnim Pyure

I found the original version of this *nouvelle cuisine*–sounding recipe in an 1855 so-called *Gastronomic Almanach* put together by a Russian chef, Alexander Radetsky, who was once the maitre-d' to Prussian Prince Maximilian of Leuchtenberg, the husband of Czar Nicholas's daughter. Radetsky was much criticized by Slavophiles in his time for advocating an ostentatiously French cuisine. But French or not, this recipe was too good to pass up, so *voilà*, a (delicious) serving of culinary controversy for your next dinner party.

4 tablespoons (½ stick) unsalted butter

3½ pounds boneless turkey breast, rolled and tied

1 large tart apple (such as Granny Smith), peeled, cored, and thickly sliced

2 large meaty, fresh, ripe tomatoes, peeled, seeded, and quartered

1½ cups Chicken Stock (see Index) or canned broth, or more as needed

Bouquet garni (4 sprigs parsley, 4 sprigs dill, 2 bay leaves, 3 cloves, and a ½-inch piece cinnamon stick tied in a cheesecloth bag)

Salt and freshly ground black pepper, to taste

¼ cup dry sherry

¼ teaspoon ground cardamom

Pinch of freshly grated nutmeg

1 Preheat the oven to 350°F.

2 Melt the butter in a large skillet over medium heat. Add the turkey breast and brown on all sides for about 10 minutes. Transfer to a roasting pan.

3 Add the apple, tomatoes, chicken stock, and bouquet garni to the roasting pan. Sprinkle the turkey with salt and pepper and roast for 10 minutes.

4 Reduce the oven temperature to 325°F. Cover the turkey loosely with aluminum foil and cook for 50 minutes, opening the foil and basting the turkey breast with pan juices every 15 minutes or so.

5 Add the sherry to the pan and cook until the juices run clear when you prick the meat

with a skewer, about another 30 minutes. Remove the turkey breast from the pan and set aside, covered with foil.

6 Remove the bouquet garni from the pan. Transfer the pan juices to a food processor and add the cardamom and nutmeg. Process for 2 to 3 pulses, until smooth but not overpuréed.

7 Transfer the sauce to a saucepan and bring to a boil over high heat. Cook until slightly reduced, about 2 minutes.

8 Slice the turkey and serve either with the sauce spooned over or served separately in a sauceboat.

Serves 6

Roast Goose Stuffed with Cabbage

Kepta Zasis su Kopustais

Roast goose with apples, potatoes, or cabbage (or all of the above, as in this recipe) often crowned the nineteenth-century holiday table in Russia, the Ukraine, or Lithuania. Today geese are still widely available in the USSR, imported from Hungary, and continue to be a holiday favorite. This Old World holiday recipe comes from Lithuania.

1 goose (8 to 10 pounds)

2 cups chopped onions

6 cups coarsely shredded green cabbage

3 cups packaged (not canned) sauerkraut, drained, rinsed, and squeezed dry

1 large, tart apple (such as Granny Smith), cored and chopped

1 cup chopped pitted prunes

½ teaspoon sugar, or more to taste

¾ cup Chicken Stock (see Index) or canned broth

Salt and freshly ground black pepper, to taste

2½ teaspoons sweet Hungarian paprika

2 teaspoons caraway seeds

6 large boiling potatoes, peeled and quartered

5 medium-size tart apples (such as Granny Smith), cored and quartered

1 Remove the giblets and the neck from the bird's cavity and save for another use. Remove all the fat from the cavity and set aside. Rinse the goose under cold running water and pat dry.

2 Chop the reserved fat and place in a large, heavy skillet. Cook the fat over low heat until it is completely rendered, 10 to 15 minutes. Remove the cracklings and all but 4 tablespoons of the fat and save for another use.

3 Add the onions and cabbage to the fat in the skillet and sauté, tossing and stirring, over medium heat until they begin to color and reduce in size, about 15 minutes.

4 Stir in the sauerkraut, chopped apples, prunes, sugar, and ½ cup of the stock.

A Country Estate Dinner

Herring in Mustard Sauce

Vodka

•

Byelorussian Wild Mushroom and Noodle Soup

•

Roast Goose Stuffed with Cabbage

Honey Marinated Pears

Chilean Cabernet Sauvignon

•

Russian Tea

Twig Cookies

• • •

Reduce the heat to low and cook, covered, stirring occasionally, about 20 minutes. Remove from the heat and set aside. You should have about 7 cups of stuffing.

5 Preheat the oven to 425°F.

6 Rub the goose inside and out with salt, pepper, 1 teaspoon of the paprika, and the caraway seeds. Stuff the goose with as much stuffing as will comfortably fit without packing. Sew or skewer the opening closed. Place the remaining stuffing in an ovenproof casserole and set aside.

7 Place the goose, breast side up, in an oval roasting pan large enough to accommodate the potatoes and apples later. Roast for 20 minutes.

8 Prick the skin of the goose all over with a fork to release the fat during cooking and roast for another 15 minutes.

9 Reduce the oven temperature to 325°F and prick the goose again. Roast, basting twice, for another 30 minutes.

10 Remove and discard all but 3 tablespoons of the accumulated fat. Place the potatoes and quartered apples around the goose and drizzle with the fat. Continue roasting, basting the goose, potatoes, and apples once or twice, for another 45 minutes to 1 hour. The goose is ready when the juices run clear when the fleshiest part of the thigh is pricked with a skewer.

11 Forty-five minutes before the goose is ready, add the remaining ¼ cup stock to the reserved stuffing and bake, covered, together with the goose.

12 Transfer the goose to a carving board. Remove the string or skewer from the cavity opening. Cover the bird with aluminum foil and let stand for 15 minutes.

13 To serve, arrange the apples and potatoes on a separate platter and sprinkle with the remaining paprika.

Serves 6

Braised Quail with Walnut and Pomegranate Sauce

Fesindjan

A subtle and exotic Persian-influenced dish that crowns the formidable repertoire of fine stews served over rice pilafs in the republic of Azerbaijan. In Azerbaijan, this stew is made with a wild game bird, called *kashkaldak* (a kind of wild duck), for which quail makes a good substitute. Although the traditional Persian way is to cook this dish with duck, I would certainly recommend quail, if available. Note that quail will cook much faster than duck, and you will end up with more sauce. Serve with Basic Steamed Saffron Rice with a Bread or Potato Crust (see Index).

8 quail (¾ pound each) or 2 duck-
    lings (4 pounds each)
¼ cup vegetable oil
3 medium-size onions, coarsely chopped
¾ teaspoon ground turmeric
1 cup Chicken Stock (see Index) or
    canned broth
2¾ cups ground walnuts
3 cups fresh or bottled pomegranate
    juice

2 tablespoons fresh lemon juice
1½ teaspoons sugar
1 piece (1 inch) cinnamon stick
¼ teaspoon ground cardamom
Salt and freshly ground black
    pepper, to taste
¾ cup pomegranate seeds for
    garnish
Fresh mint leaves for garnish

1 With a meat cleaver, poultry shears, or very sharp knife, halve each quail, removing the backbone, or quarter each duckling, if using. Rinse well and pat dry with paper towels.

2 Heat the oil in a Dutch oven over medium heat and brown the birds well on all sides, in batches, if necessary. Set aside. If you are cooking duck, pour off all but 2 tablespoons of fat (quail are leaner and will not release additional fat).

3 Add the onions to the drippings in the Dutch oven and sauté, stirring occasionally, over medium heat for 5 minutes. Stir in the turmeric and continue to cook until the onions turn golden, about 12 minutes.

4 Add the chicken stock and cook, scraping the bottom of the Dutch oven with a wooden spoon, for 3 minutes. Stir in the walnuts and pomegranate juice and heat until the sauce is barely boiling. Reduce the heat to low and simmer the sauce, uncovered, for 20 minutes.

5 Stir in the lemon juice, sugar, cinnamon, cardamom, salt, and pepper. Return the birds to the casserole and mix well to coat with the sauce. Simmer, covered, until the birds are tender, about 30 minutes for quail, 1½ hours for duck.

6 Meanwhile, preheat the oven to 350°F.

7 Uncover the casserole and place in the oven for 15 minutes. Remove and if serving duck, skim off the fat.

8 Serve sprinkled with pomegranate seeds

Exotic Azerbaijani Feast

Herbed Feta

Fresh herb sprigs

Lavash **or pita bread**

•

Yogurt, Spinach, and Sorrel Soup

•

Basic Steamed Saffron Rice with Potato Crust

Braised Quail in Walnut and Pomegranate Sauce

Rose Sherbet

•

Amarone from Veneto

Saffron Pudding

Turkish Coffee

• • •

and garnished with mint leaves.

Serves 4

Pheasant Georgian Style

Fazan po-Gruzinski

This recipe for pheasant braised with fruit, walnuts, and wine was very popular in nineteenth-century France, where it was called *faison à la georgienne*. My version, however, is adapted from a nineteenth-century Russian cookbook. Serve with Basic Steamed Saffron Rice with a Potato or Bread Crust (see Index).

1½ cups seedless red grapes,
    or as needed
2 pheasants (about 3 pounds each),
    ready to cook
5 tablespoons unsalted butter
1½ cups walnut halves, toasted (see
    Index)
1 cup Chicken Stock (see Index) or
    canned broth
¾ cups fresh tangerine juice
1 cup Beaujolais Nouveau (which is
    a substitute for young Georgian
    wine)

½ cup strong green tea
⅓ cup port
1 bay leaf
6 sprigs fresh thyme, tied together,
    or ½ teaspoon dried thyme
    (use as a last resort)
Salt and freshly ground black
    pepper, to taste
1½ cups peeled tangerine
    wedges

1 In a food processor, purée the grapes. Press through a fine-mesh sieve and measure ¾ cup of the grapes. Set aside.

2 Rinse the pheasants under cold running water and pat thoroughly dry.

3 Preheat the oven to 350°F.

4 In a Dutch oven large enough to accommodate both pheasants and all the liquids and other ingredients, melt the butter over medium heat. Brown the pheasants, one at a time, well on all sides.

5 Return the first pheasant to the pot. Add the walnuts, chicken stock, tangerine juice, wine, green tea, port, and puréed grapes, and bring to a boil. Add the bay leaf, thyme, salt, and pepper; cover and place in the oven. Cook for 25 minutes.

6 Add the tangerine wedges and continue cooking until the pheasants are tender, about 15 to 20 minutes.

7 Remove the pheasants from the Dutch oven and transfer to a rimmed baking sheet. Turn the oven temperature up to 375°F and roast the pheasants until the skin is just slightly crisp, 7 to 10 minutes.

8 While the pheasants are in the oven, remove the bay leaf and thyme sprigs from the sauce. Place the sauce over high heat and reduce it by half, about 10 minutes.

9 Serve the pheasants, passing the sauce separately in a sauceboat.

Serves 6

Once Upon a Time

An old Georgian legend tells of a young prince who went hunting for pheasant in an unknown land. He killed a bird, but as he recovered it, he saw that the bird had already been cooked in the hot spring into which it had fallen. On this spot the prince founded the city of Tbilisi (which means "hot waters"), the present-day capital of Georgia. It's not surprising, then, that the Georgians always prepare pheasant with a special reverence and flair.

Rabbit Baked in Clay with Wild Mushrooms and Sour Cream

Pechenya Zayach'i

It seems to me that where the French use shallots and wine the Slavs use mushrooms and sour cream; so that the sour cream sauce of rustic Slavic dishes is almost an equivalent of the *bourguignonne* of the French. Anyway, this is a delicious, yet simple recipe from Byelorussia, which can also be made with chicken or goose. It is, however, essential that you bake it in clay, as this preserves the flavor better than anything else. The Byelorussians serve this dish with *deruni*, their excellent Potato Pancakes (see Index).

6 imported dried wild mushrooms
    well rinsed
4 slices bacon, diced
2 rabbits (3 to 3½ pound each),
    each cut into 6 serving pieces
6 tablespoons (¾ stick) unsalted
    butter
2 medium-size onions, coarsely
    chopped
1 parsnip, peeled and cut into
    julienne
2 cups Chicken Stock (see Index) or
    canned broth

Bouquet garni (8 sprigs parsley, 2
    bay leaves, and 6 black pepper-
    corns tied in a cheesecloth bag)
Salt and freshly ground black
    pepper, to taste
1 pound fresh wild mushrooms
    (boletes, chanterelles, morels,
    or portabello)
¼ cup heavy or whipping cream
3 tablespoons sour cream
¼ cup dry vermouth
Chopped fresh parsley for garnish
    (optional)

1 Soak the dried mushrooms in ½ cup water for 1 hour. Drain, pat dry with paper towels, chop fine, and set aside. Reserve the soaking liquid for another use.

2 In a large skillet, fry the bacon over medium heat for about 5 minutes. When it has rendered its fat, remove the bacon with a slotted spoon and set aside to drain on paper towels.

3 Add the rabbit, a few pieces at a time, to the bacon drippings and brown on all sides over medium heat. Transfer the browned pieces as they are done to a large unglazed earthenware casserole with a lid (a Romer-töpf is perfect).

4 Wipe out the skillet and melt 4 tablespoons of the butter in it over medium heat.

Add the onions, parsnip, and dried mushrooms, and sauté, stirring occasionally, until the vegetables are softened and lightly colored, about 10 minutes.

5 Meanwhile, preheat the oven to 350°F.

6 Add the stock and bouquet garni to the skillet. Bring to a boil, and boil for 1 to 2 minutes.

7 Add the sautéed vegetables and stock, the reserved bacon, and salt and pepper to the casserole with the rabbit. Bake, uncovered, for 45 minutes.

8 Wipe the fresh mushrooms clean with a damp paper towel. Separate the stems from the caps, if the mushrooms are large, and slice both not too thin.

9 Wipe out the skillet again and melt the remaining 2 tablespoons butter in it over medium heat. Add the mushrooms and sauté until they throw off and reabsorb their liquid, about 12 minutes.

10 Check the rabbit and, if it's tender, remove the pieces to a heated platter with a slotted spoon. Do not turn off the oven.

11 Remove the bouquet garni from the sauce and discard. Press the sauce through a sieve or pass through a food mill. Transfer to a saucepan and heat over medium-low heat for 2 minutes. Combine the heavy cream and the sour cream in a small bowl.

Whisk a little of the sauce into the cream mixture, then whisk the cream mixture into the sauce in the pan. Whisk in the vermouth and cook for 5 minutes more, without allowing it to boil.

12 Return the rabbit to the casserole and stir in the sautéed mushrooms and the sauce. Bake, uncovered, for 7 minutes more.

13 Serve the rabbit directly from the casserole, sprinkled with a little parsley, if desired.

Serves 6

Fish Dishes

RIBA

I'm sure every seafood aficionado would agree that the secret of a great fish dish does not lie in a complex sauce or an elaborate preparation. They are only supporting players, while the star of the show is certainly the fish itself, straight from the water and possessing its own fresh flavor and texture. For any cook dedicated to recreating ethnic recipes outside the country of origin, the fish course is always the most difficult. No food is more specific to an area than seafood. So, when it comes to capturing all the true tastes of seafood from the Soviet Union, it is almost impossible.

The Russian rivers and lakes teem with dozens of varieties of freshwater fish: pike, perch, eel, carp, tench, bream, tiny smelts, and many others for which there are no English equivalent. From Lake Sevan in Armenia comes a delicate pink salmon trout, which the Armenians call *ishkhan*, meaning "prince." From the Baltic Sea come plump herring, that are lightly cured in salt and eaten with a dollop of sour cream. The Black Sea is home to some of the tastiest fish in the world. My favorite is the grey mullet (*kefal*), with its firm, white flesh panfried to perfection.

If Lake Sevan counts princes among its offspring, the Caspian Sea is mother to kings and queens. Its spectacular sturgeon and whitefish varieties are some of the most sought after fish in the world, prized as much for their caviar as for their lush, meaty flesh.

Travelers to the countries of the Soviet Union have made special mention of their fisheries since ancient times. Herodotus noted the abundance of sturgeon in the Dnieper River (in present day Ukraine), the merchants of Ancient Greece founded colonies on the shores of the Black Sea, which they dubbed the "hospitable sea" because of its abundance of fish. Over the centuries foreign visitors to Russia reported amazing tales of feasts with dozens of fish courses and featuring fish so huge that three men couldn't lift them and so fancifully decorated that they looked more like dragons and birds. Others were impressed by the staggering variety of fish at the Russian markets, writing of "lamprey marinated with pepper and bay leaves, mounds of perch reaching up to the roof, frozen fish lined up in the snow, silvery salmon with bright red slashes across them." These superb natural resources, together with nearly six months worth of Lenten days combined to make Russian fish cuisine one of the best in the world.

By the nineteenth century, the Lenten menu had become extra-ordinarily rich and varied. To begin a dinner, there might be a cold sturgeon with creamed horseradish, herring in every guise, or a whole fish in a piquant aspic. Then, perhaps, a clear fish soup accompanied by *kulebiaka*, (a layered fish pie) or a hearty *solianka* (chowder), laden with pickles, capers, and olives. Main course choices included sterlet (a small variety of sturgeon), poached in Champagne; or, for a more rustic dish, a bream stuffed with kasha. For the connoisseur there were turbot livers, herring cheeks, crawfish soufflés, while those with simpler tastes and thinner wallets enjoyed fish teamed with such favorite Russian ingredients as wild mushrooms, sour cream, pickles, and robust tomato sauces.

Sadly many of the stars in this fish heaven have fallen since the Revolution, as food standards and distribution declined. But a tradition of great fish cookery remains. New recipes have been developed and old ones adapted to suit the prevailing supply. People now get out their fishing rods and simply indulge in one of Russia's favorite and most rewarding pastimes.

The recipes in this chapter will give you an authentic taste of classic Russian fish preparations and a tempting glimpse of ethnic recipes as well.

Estonian Fried Smelts

Kalavorm

Served as a snack with beer, these very tasty, crisp, tiny fish are the Estonian equivalent of popcorn. They are sprinkled with vinegar and consumed with great gusto. I don't advise using frozen smelts for this dish.

¾ cup rye flour

⅓ cup all-purpose flour

1 teaspoon salt, or more to taste

2 teaspoons caraway seeds
   (optional)

1 cup vegetable oil for frying

2 pounds fresh smelts, heads
   and tails left on, cleaned, rinsed,
   and patted dry

Apple cider vinegar or lemon juice

1 On a large plate, combine the rye and white flours, salt, and caraway seeds and mix well.

2 Heat the oil in a large heavy skillet over medium-high heat until very hot but not smoking.

3 Roll the smelts in the flour mixture, and fry, a few at a time, until crisp and golden, about 1 minute on each side. Drain on paper towels.

4 Serve with vinegar.

Serves 4 to 6 as a snack

Fish with Mushrooms and Crabmeat in Ramekins

Riba s Krabami i Gribami v Gorshochke

In this Russo-French recipe, sautéed fish, crabmeat, and mushrooms are baked in a delicate cream and Cognac sauce. It makes a substantial hot appetizer or luncheon dish. If you don't have individual 1-cup ramekins, you can bake this dish in a medium-size ceramic or earthenware casserole.

*5 tablespoons unsalted butter, or
    more if needed*
*16 large fresh, white mushroom
    caps, wiped clean and sliced*
*1 pound delicate white-fleshed fish
    fillets (such as flounder or sole),
    cut into 1-inch pieces*
*1½ cups lump crabmeat, picked over
    and flaked*
¼ cup Cognac
3 tablespoons dry sherry

1½ cups heavy or whipping cream
*Salt and freshly ground black
    pepper, to taste*
Pinch of freshly grated nutmeg
*1½ teaspoons fresh lemon juice, or
    to taste*
*½ cup Béchamel Sauce
    (see Index)*
*2 tablespoons freshly grated
    Parmesan cheese*

1 Melt 2 tablespoons of the butter in a large skillet over medium heat. Add the mushrooms and sauté until they throw off and reabsorb their liquid, 12 to 15 minutes. Remove the mushrooms from the skillet and set aside.

2 Preheat the oven to 400°F.

3 Melt the remaining 3 tablespoons butter in the same skillet and sauté the fish fillets until opaque on both sides, 6 to 7 minutes. Remove the fish from the skillet and set aside.

4 Melt another tablespoon of butter if needed, then add the crabmeat to the skillet and sauté, stirring, until heated through, about 3 minutes. Remove from the skillet.

5 Add the Cognac and the sherry to the skillet and reduce by half over high heat. Add the cream and reduce by half.

6 Return the fish, mushrooms, and crabmeat to the skillet. Season to taste with salt, pepper, nutmeg, and lemon juice, and stir gently.

7 Divide the mixture between four 1-cup ramekins. Spoon 2 tablespoons béchamel over the top of each and sprinkle with Parmesan. Bake until golden and bubbly, about 7 minutes.

8 Serve in the ramekins.

Serves 4

Sturgeon Kebabs

Shashlik iz Osetrini

———— ❧ ————

With its firm, thick, meatlike flesh, sturgeon lends itself perfectly to grilling. Sturgeon kebabs are a specialty in many Russian restaurants in both the United States and the USSR. If you can't get sturgeon, substitute swordfish, which is not as delicate in flavor but is similar in texture. For a more refined dish, make salmon kebabs, using salmon steaks rather than fillets. The Russians brush the fish with sour cream before grilling, but olive oil can be substituted.

2 pounds sturgeon steaks,
    at least 1 inch thick,
    cut into 1½-inch
    cubes

Salt and freshly ground black
    pepper, to taste
¼ cup fresh lemon juice
¾ cup sour cream or ½ cup olive oil

GARNISHES
Whole scallions, trimmed
Fresh cilantro or parsley sprigs

Tomato quarters
Lemon wedges

1 Rub the fish cubes all over with salt and pepper. Place them in a large glass baking dish, sprinkle with lemon juice, and let stand for 30 minutes.

2 Prepare coals for grilling until covered with white ash, or preheat the broiler. Oil the grill or broiler rack.

3 Thread the fish on large skewers.

Brush with sour cream or olive oil and grill or broil 3 inches away from the heat, turning from time to time. The fish should be ready in about 10 minutes.

4 Serve garnished with scallions, cilantro sprigs, tomato quarters, and lemon wedges.

Serves 4

Baked Sturgeon with Russian Sauce

Zapechonnaya Osetrina pod Russkim Sousom

There isn't one definitive recipe for "Russian sauce" for fish, but it is usually a tomato-based sauce with mushrooms and piquant additions such as olives, pickles, capers, and sometimes marinated mushrooms. Sturgeon or swordfish are about the only fish that can stand up to such a gutsy sauce.

3 tablespoons light vegetable oil

½ pound fresh, white mushrooms, wiped clean and sliced

4 tablespoons (½ stick) unsalted butter

1 medium-size onion, finely chopped

1 small parsnip, peeled and finely chopped

1 small carrot, peeled and grated

1 tablespoon tomato paste

1½ tablespoons all-purpose flour

1⅓ cups Fish Stock (see Index)

½ cup dry white wine

2 large, meaty, fresh, ripe tomatoes, peeled, seeded, and chopped

1 bay leaf

6 black peppercorns

½ cup chopped dill pickles

12 pitted Greek olives

1½ tablespoons capers, drained

2 tablespoons fresh lemon juice, or to taste

Pinch of sugar, or to taste

Salt and freshly ground black pepper, to taste

4 sturgeon or swordfish steaks (7 to 8 ounces each)

1 tablespoon olive oil

Chopped fresh parsley for garnish

1 Heat the oil in a medium-size skillet over medium-high heat. Add the mushrooms and sauté, stirring frequently, until they throw off and reabsorb their liquid, 12 to 15 minutes. Set aside.

2 Melt the butter in a large, heavy saucepan over medium heat. Add the onion, parsnip, and carrot and sauté, stirring frequently, until limp, about 10 minutes.

3 Add the tomato paste and cook, stirring, until bubbly, about 3 minutes.

4 Stir in the flour and cook for 1 minute. Add the fish stock and wine and stir until smooth. Add the tomatoes, bay leaf, and peppercorns, cover, and simmer the sauce until the flavors are blended, about 15 minutes.

5 Add the pickles, olives, capers, sautéed mushrooms, lemon juice, sugar,

The flesh of the caviar (that is to say, of the caviar-producing) sturgeon has a delicate flavor, such as one rarely finds in a cartilaginous fish. It can easily be passed off as veal. We must, however, admit that the nations of today do not show the same enthusiasm for this flesh as did the peoples of classical times. The latter used to garland with flowers not only the sturgeon but also those who served it and those who brought it to the table to the sound of flutes. In Greece, according to Athenaeus, the sturgeon was regarded as the best fish for a banquet.

— Alexander Dumas
Dictionary of Cuisine

and salt and pepper to the sauce. Simmer for 3 to 4 minutes more.

6 Preheat the oven to 375°F.

7 Place the fish steaks in a glass or enameled baking dish. Rub with salt and pepper and brush with the olive oil. Bake until the fish is just opaque, about 8 minutes, turning once.

8 Remove the bay leaf. Pour the sauce over the fish and bake until the sauce is bubbly, 5 to 7 minutes longer. Serve at once, garnished with parsley.

Serves 4

Baked Fish with Eggplant and Pomegranate Sauce

Tevzi Badrijanit Brotseulis Tsvenshi

Serve this great Georgian recipe in spring or summer. The traditional pomegranate sauce complements both the fish and the eggplant beautifully. Accompany it with a rice pilaf and Spinach in Yogurt Sauce (see the Index for the recipe page numbers).

1 red snapper or striped bass (about 4 to 6 pounds), head and tail left on, cleaned, rinsed, and patted dry

Salt and freshly ground black pepper, to taste

2 cloves garlic, crushed in a garlic press

1 cup olive oil, or more as needed

2 medium-size eggplant (about ½ pound each), sliced ½ inch thick

3 cups fresh or bottled pomegranate juice

¼ cup finely chopped red onion

2 cloves garlic, minced

¼ teaspoon dried red pepper flakes

¼ cup chopped fresh basil

¼ cup chopped fresh cilantro

1 Preheat the oven to 375°F.

2 Rub the fish with salt, pepper, the crushed garlic, and 3 tablespoons of the olive oil and place in a baking dish. Let stand for 15 minutes.

3 Bake the fish until opaque throughout, 10 minutes for every inch of the thickness of fish, measured at the thickest part, 40 minutes to 1 hour, depending on the size of the fish. The fish should be browned and crispy on top.

4 Meanwhile, place the eggplant slices in a colander and sprinkle them with 2 teaspoons salt. Let stand for 30 minutes. Rinse the eggplant thoroughly and pat dry with paper towels.

5 Pour the remaining oil into a heavy skillet. If the oil is less than 1 inch deep, add more oil. Heat the oil over medium-high heat. Fry the eggplant slices, a few at a time, until deep golden on both sides, about 15 minutes. Drain on paper towels.

6 Reduce the pomegranate juice over high heat to about 1⅓ cups, 10 to 15 minutes. Stir in the onion, minced garlic, red pepper flakes, basil, and cilantro and season with salt. Allow the sauce to cool to warm temperature.

7 Serve the fish surrounded by eggplant slices and pass the pomegranate sauce in a sauceboat.

Serves 4 to 6

Whole Salmon in Aspic

Zalivnaya Lososina

Fish in aspic is truly a quintessential Russian dish, a mandatory part of the appetizer or supper buffet. In this recipe, a whole salmon is served in a light white wine aspic, beautifully garnished with vegetables and caviar-filled zucchini cups. To make the dish, you need a large fish poacher and an oval serving dish for the fish.

Serve with Horseradish Mayonnaise or Dill Mayonnaise (see the Index for the recipe page numbers).

COURT BOUILLON

4 cups Fish Stock
  (see Index)
2 cups dry white wine
2 leeks (white part only),
  well rinsed and chopped
1 medium-size onion,
  chopped

1 large carrot, peeled and chopped
1 rib celery, chopped
10 sprigs fresh dill
10 sprigs fresh parsley
1 bay leaf
Salt, to taste

SALMON AND ASPIC

1 whole salmon
  (4 to 5 pounds),
  head and tail left on,
  cleaned and rinsed

2 large egg whites, beaten
2 eggshells, crushed
2 envelopes unflavored gelatin
¼ cup fresh lemon juice

GARNISH

1 small lemon, thinly sliced
1 cucumber, thinly sliced
2 large zucchinis, about 7 inches
  long and 1½ to 2 inches thick

Carrot slices
Fresh parsley sprigs
2 to 3 ounces salmon caviar

1 Combine all the court bouillon ingredients in a fish poacher large enough to hold the salmon. Bring to a boil, then reduce the heat to low, and simmer, covered, for 25 minutes.

2 Tie the salmon to the poaching rack and gently lower it into the simmering liquid. Add enough water just to cover the fish. Bring to a simmer and poach 10 minutes for every inch of the thickness of the fish, measured at the thickest part, 20 to 30 minutes.

3 Carefully remove the fish from the poaching liquid, cool, and refrigerate while preparing the aspic.

4 Strain the poaching liquid and reduce over high heat to about 5 cups. Add the egg whites and shells to the liquid and bring to a boil over high heat, beating constantly with a wire whisk. When the egg whites rise to the surface, turn off the heat and let stand for 5 minutes. Line a colander with a dampened double layer of cheesecloth and strain the liquid into a clean pot.

5 Sprinkle the gelatin over the lemon juice and let stand to soften for 5 minutes.

6 Stir the gelatin mixture into the clarified poaching liquid and cook over medium heat, stirring, until the gelatin is dissolved. Cool and refrigerate until the aspic mixture is syrupy, 30 minutes.

7 Remove the fish from the refrigerator, untie it from the rack, and carefully remove the skin from the body. Transfer the fish to a deep oval serving dish.

8 Pour about 1 cup of the aspic into the serving dish. Using a tablespoon, coat the fish with some of the remaining aspic. Refrigerate the fish until the aspic is set, 45 minutes to 1 hour. Do not refrigerate the remaining aspic (see Note).

9 Meanwhile, prepare the garnish. Cut the lemon and cucumber slices in half. Partially peel the zucchinis, leaving stripes of green at ½-inch intervals. Cut each zucchini crosswise into four pieces. Scoop out three-quarters of the pulp from each piece with a small spoon. Be sure to leave a bottom on each cup.

10 When the aspic on the fish is set, dip the lemon and cucumber slices in the remaining (unrefrigerated) aspic and place them on the salmon in alternating rows to resemble fish scales.

11 To decorate the serving dish, dip the carrots and parsley sprigs in aspic and place them attractively around the fish. Spoon a thin layer of aspic into the serving dish and on the fish. Place the zucchini cups around the fish. Refrigerate until the aspic is set, 1 to 1½ hours.

12 Apply one more coating of aspic to the fish and chill. Before serving, spoon the caviar into the zucchini cups.

After-Theater Buffet

Salad Olivier in Tartlets

Pirozhki with a Meat Filling

Eggs Stuffed with Mushrooms

Lemon Vodka

•

Whole Salmon in Aspic

Horseradish or Dill Mayonnaise

Cucumbers in Sour Cream

Australian Chardonnay

•

Lavish Chocolate Meringue Cake

• • •

Serves 8 as part of a buffet

Note: If the aspic begins to set too much, reheat it over low heat, then refrigerate until just syrupy.

Steamed Salmon with Sorrel and Spinach Sauce

Lososina s Sousom iz Shchavelya i Shpinata

Spring Dinner à la Russe

• • •

Wild Mushroom Caviar on toast points

•

Cold Borscht

•

Steamed Salmon with Sorrel and Spinach Sauce

Poached baby vegetables

White Burgundy

•

Strudel with a Rhubarb Filling

Sorrel, which grows in great abundance in the Russian countryside, has always been a staple ingredient in the peasant kitchens, but somehow never made it into the Russian haute cuisine, perhaps because it was considered too common. I am thrilled that sorrel made such a successful appearance in the post-nouvelle culinary scene, even though I miss paying just a few kopeks for a huge bunch to the *babushkas* who sell it all over Moscow. This recipe, which delights both the eye and the palate, will please food trendies and nostalgic Russians alike.

*4 salmon steaks (about 6 ounces
   each), skinned and boned
Salt and freshly ground black
   pepper, to taste
¼ cup light olive oil
3 tablespoons fresh lemon juice
2 teaspoons capers, drained
Sorrel and Spinach Sauce
   (recipe follows)*

1 Rub the salmon steaks with salt and pepper. Combine the oil, lemon juice, and capers in a shallow bowl. Add the salmon and turn to coat with the marinade. Refrigerate for 1 hour.

2 Remove the salmon steaks from the marinade and arrange them in a steamer set over simmering water. Cover and steam until opaque throughout, 6 to 7 minutes.

3 To serve, divide the sauce among four plates and place the salmon on top.

Serves 4

Sorrel and Spinach Sauce

Sous iz Shchavelia i Shpinata

2 cups (tightly packed) rinsed, drained, and chopped sorrel
1 cup (tightly packed) rinsed, drained, and chopped spinach
Salt
2 cups heavy or whipping cream

½ cup dry white wine
2 tablespoons unsalted butter, cold, cut into small pieces
Freshly ground black pepper, to taste
Fresh lemon juice, to taste (optional)

1 Scald the sorrel and spinach in boiling salted water for 2 minutes. Rinse under cold water, drain, and squeeze thoroughly dry.

2 Mince the sorrel and spinach in a food processor, together with ⅓ cup of the cream.

3 Combine the remaining 1⅔ cups cream and wine in a medium-size saucepan. Boil over high heat until reduced by half, about 7 minutes. Add the sorrel and spinach and cook for 2 minutes more, stirring.

4 Off the heat, stir in the butter, a piece at a time, whisking after each addition until thoroughly incorporated. Season the sauce with salt and pepper to taste. Add some lemon juice, a ½ teaspoon at a time, if a tarter flavor is desired.

Makes about 1½ cups

Cold Tuna in Walnut Sauce

Tevzi Satsivi

The Georgians prepare this dish with cold poached sturgeon or lake trout. After a few experiments, I discovered that grilled tuna and *satsivi* sauce is a match made in heaven. Serve it as a summer entrée or appetizer.

1½ pounds fresh tuna steaks, cut
    into 1½-inch cubes
¼ cup olive oil

SAUCE AND GARNISH
1⅓ cups walnut pieces
3 large cloves garlic
¼ teaspoon coarse (kosher) salt
2 tablespoons unsalted butter
1 medium-size onion, finely chopped
2¼ teaspoons all-purpose flour
1¼ cups Chicken Stock (see Index)
    or canned broth
1½ tablespoons tarragon vinegar
¼ teaspoon hot Hungarian paprika
½ teaspoon ground coriander

Salt and freshly ground black
    pepper, to taste

Small pinch of ground
    cinnamon
1 teaspoon dried tarragon
¼ teaspoon saffron threads, crushed
    in a mortar and diluted in 1
    tablespoon warm water
3 tablespoons finely chopped fresh
    cilantro
Walnut pieces for garnish
Fresh cilantro sprigs for garnish

1 Preheat the broiler.

2 In a bowl, toss the tuna with the olive oil. Arrange the fish cubes on a rack in a broiler pan and broil, 4 inches from the heat for 4 minutes. Turn and broil for 3 to 4 minutes more. Season with salt and pepper and let cool to room temperature.

3 To prepare the sauce, grind the 1⅓ cups walnuts, garlic, and salt in a food processor. Set aside.

4 Melt the butter in a medium-size saucepan over medium-low heat. Add the onion and sauté until it just begins to soften, about 5 minutes.

5 Sprinkle in the flour and stir to blend for 1 minute. Gradually add the stock, stirring constantly. Return the heat to low and stir until the mixture thickens slightly, 1 to 2 minutes.

6 Stir in the ground walnut mixture and the remaining ingredients through the chopped cilantro. Simmer the sauce over low heat, stirring frequently, for about 10 minutes. Remove from the heat and cool to room temperature.

7 Pour the cooled sauce over the fish, cover, and refrigerate for several hours or overnight. Serve garnished with walnut pieces and cilantro sprigs.

Serves 6 as a light entrée or 8 as an appetizer

Backyard Luncheon from the Caucasus

• • •

Cold Cucumber and Yogurt Soup

•

Cold Tuna in Walnut Sauce

Cold Bulgur and Vegetable Pilaf

Pepper and Eggplant Salad

Vouvray Demi Sec

•

Apricot Mousse

• • •

Grilled Trout with Tarragon

Forel s Estragonom

The sweetest and most delicate-tasting trout are abundant in the Armenian lakes and Georgian mountain brooks of the Caucasus. This fish tastes best grilled outdoors. Serve on a bed of tarragon sprigs garnished with pomegranate seeds, if available.

2 cloves garlic, minced

¼ teaspoon coarse (kosher) salt

½ cup extra virgin olive oil

¼ cup fresh lemon juice

*6 to 8 sprigs fresh tarragon, leaves
chopped, stems crushed with the
back of a knife*

*Freshly ground black pepper,
to taste*

*4 brook trout (about ¾ pound
each), heads and tails left on,
cleaned, rinsed, and patted dry*

*Pomegranate seeds for garnish
(optional)*

*Fresh tarragon sprigs for
garnish*

1 Using the back of a spoon, mash the garlic and salt to a paste in a shallow glass or ceramic dish. Whisk in the oil, lemon juice, chopped tarragon sprigs, and pepper.

2 Add the fish to the marinade and turn to coat completely. Cover and refrigerate for 30 minutes.

3 Prepare coals for grilling until covered with white ash, or preheat the broiler. Oil the grill or broiler rack.

4 Remove the fish from the marinade, reserving the marinade, and make a few crosswise incisions in the skin to prevent it from breaking during grilling.

5 Grill or broil the fish 2 to 3 inches away from the heat, basting lightly, with the reserved marinade. After 5 minutes, turn the fish and grill until opaque throughout, 5 to 6 minutes more.

6 Serve garnished with pomegranate seeds and tarragon sprigs.

Serves 4

Lunch by the Lake

Rice Stuffed Grape Leaves

•

Grilled Trout with Tarragon

**Braised Leeks with Egg and
Lemon Sauce**

Long Island Fumé Blanc

•

Watermelon

• • •

Mushroom-Stuffed Fillets of Flounder

Rizhskoye Telnoye

This is an updated Latvian version of an old Russian dish in which mushroom-stuffed flounder fillets are served in a delicate, velvety wine and cream sauce. Serve it with Two-Colored Cauliflower and Beet Purée Bake (see Index).

4 thin flounder fillets (about 5 ounces each)

Salt and freshly ground black pepper, to taste

3 tablespoons unsalted butter

10 ounces fresh, white mushrooms, wiped cleaned and chopped

2 tablespoons finely chopped fresh parsley

3 tablespoons heavy or whipping cream

¾ cup Fish Stock (see Index), or as needed

¾ cup dry white wine, or as needed

SAUCE

1 tablespoon unsalted butter

2¼ teaspoons all-purpose flour

1 cup fish poaching liquid

2 tablespoons dry white wine

1 large egg yolk

3 tablespoons heavy or whipping cream

1½ teaspoons fresh lemon juice, or more to taste

Salt and freshly ground black pepper, to taste

1 tablespoon chopped fresh parsley

1 Place the fish fillets between two sheets of waxed paper and flatten with the flat side of a knife or a mallet, taking care not to tear the flesh. Rub the fillets with salt and pepper and set aside.

2 Melt the butter in a medium-size skil-let over medium heat. Add the mushrooms and sauté, stirring, until softened and lightly colored, 10 minutes.

3 Stir in the parsley and cream and cook for 3 to 4 minutes more. Season with salt and pepper.

4 Reserve 2 tablespoons of the mushroom mixture. Divide the remaining mixture among the fish fillets, spreading it evenly over each. Roll up the fillets carefully, securing each with a toothpick.

5 Place the fish rolls in a medium-size nonreactive skillet that holds them comfortably. Add the reserved mushrooms. Pour in the fish stock and the wine so the liquid barely covers the fish. It might be more or less than the specified amount, depending on the size of your skillet. Bring the liquid to a boil, then reduce the heat to low and simmer, covered, until the fish flakes when gently tested with a fork, about 7 minutes.

6 Carefully transfer the fish to a heated platter and keep warm.

7 Reduce the poaching liquid over high heat to 1 cup, 5 to 7 minutes.

8 To prepare the sauce, melt the butter in a small saucepan over low heat. Add the flour and stir to blend for 1 minute.

9 Gradually add the poaching liquid, then the wine, stirring with a wooden spoon until the sauce has thickened.

10 In a small bowl, whisk together the egg yolk and cream until well blended.

11 Add a little of the hot sauce to the egg yolk mixture, stir to blend, then whisk the mixture back into the sauce. Add the lemon juice and salt and pepper. Continue cooking the sauce over low heat until it thickens, 10 minutes. Stir in the parsley.

12 Spoon the sauce over the fish and serve immediately.

Serves 4

Carp with Vegetables and Mushrooms

Karpis su Daržovėmis ir Grybais

This is an extremely tasty carp dish from Lithuania that just smacks of *Mittel Europa*. The carp is poached in a special court bouillon and dressed with a vegetable, mushroom, and cream sauce. In addition to being delicious, this is one of the most inexpensive fish dishes you can make.

1 carp (about 4 pounds), filleted
  but trimmings reserved
3½ cups water
1 onion, quartered
1 parsnip, peeled
2 small carrots, peeled
2 ribs celery with leaves
1 bay leaf
4 black peppercorns
4 teaspoons white vinegar
1 leek (white part only), well
  rinsed and chopped
⅓ cup chopped onion
½ cup fresh, white mushrooms,
  the smallest you can find,
  wiped clean and halved
½ cup heavy or whipping
  cream
⅓ cup sour cream
Salt and freshly ground black
  pepper, to taste
Pinch of sugar, or to taste
1 tablespoon chopped fresh dill

1 In a large, heavy soup pot, combine the carp trimmings, water, quartered onion, parsnip, 1 carrot, 1 celery rib, the bay leaf, peppercorns, and vinegar. Bring to a boil over high heat, skimming off the foam as it rises to the top. Reduce the heat to low and simmer for 35 minutes.

2 Strain the stock through a double thickness of dampened cheesecloth, discarding the solids. Pour the stock into a clean pot. Reduce over high heat to 2 cups, if necessary.

Friday Night Supper

My Mother's Chicken Soup
with Dumplings

•

Carp with Vegetables and
Mushrooms

Potato Pancakes

Sweet and Sour Beet Salad

New Zealand Sauvignon Blanc

•

Cranberry Apple Pie

• • •

3 Cut the carp fillets crosswise into 2- to 3-inch serving size pieces. Cut the remaining celery and carrot into neat ½-inch dice.

4 Add the fish, diced celery and carrot, leek, the chopped onion, and mushrooms to the stock. Bring to a low boil over medium heat, then reduce the heat to low and simmer, uncovered, until the carp is opaque throughout and flakes easily with a fork, about 5 minutes. Remove the fish with a slotted spoon and keep warm.

5 Reduce the poaching liquid to 1 cup over high heat. Reduce the heat to low. Add the cream and the sour cream and season with salt and pepper and a little sugar. Bring to a simmer over low heat. Simmer,

without boiling, for 15 minutes. Stir in the dill and spoon the sauce over the fish.

Serves 4

Cod Moscow Style

Treska po Moskovski

This cod dish is something that the people of Moscow prepare on an everyday basis, making do with what little they have in the way of ingredients — a frozen cod fillet, a couple of onions, some mayonnaise, and a packet of processed cheese. Mundane as it sounds, I personally couldn't eat enough of it. In fact, following my return from a recent visit to Moscow, it was one of the first dishes I made, curious to discover if it would hold its charm. And it did!

For a more "authentic" taste, try the processed Gruyère called Valio, which is imported from Scandinavia.

2 pounds cod fillets, cut into 8 pieces
Salt and freshly ground black
    pepper, to taste
3 tablespoons fresh lemon juice
5 tablespoons unsalted butter
All-purpose flour for rolling the
    fish

2 large onions, cut into rings
½ cup mayonnaise, preferably
    Hellmann's
¾ cup grated Gruyère or white
    Cheddar cheese
Chopped fresh parsley and dill for
    garnish

1 Preheat the oven to 375°F.

2 Rub the fish fillets with salt and pepper and place in a shallow dish. Sprinkle with lemon juice and let stand for 15 minutes.

3 Melt 3 tablespoons of the butter in a large skillet over medium heat. Roll each fish fillet lightly in the flour and fry until just opaque, 3 to 4 minutes on each side. Transfer the fish to an ovenproof casserole.

4 Wipe out the skillet and melt the remaining 2 tablespoons butter over medium heat. Add the onion rings and sauté, stirring occasionally, until golden, about 20 minutes.

5 Spread the mayonnaise on the fish with a rubber spatula. Place the onions on top and sprinkle with the cheese.

6 Bake until the surface is well browned and bubbly, 10 to 15 minutes. Serve hot or cold, sprinkled with fresh herbs.

Serves 4 to 6

Moldavian Fish, Tomato, and Red Pepper Casserole

Peste cu Ardei si Paradais

In Moldavia, this robust fish casserole is prepared from carp and other freshwater fish, but it also works well with cod, halibut, or red snapper. Although feta is not part of the original recipe, I like to sprinkle the top with it, because it complements the tomato and red pepper flavor beautifully.

Serve this casserole with *mamaliga* (Moldavian Cornmeal Mush), polenta, or rice and a Moldavian Tomato, Cucumber, and Pepper Salad (see the Index for recipe page numbers). Unfortunately, the excellent Moldavian wine is almost impossible to buy in the United States, so try a substantial white of your choice.

A Seventeenth Century Nobleman's Fast-Day Fare

This is a partial list of the dishes served at a nobleman's (*Boyarin*) house on a fast day in 1656. No mean fast, if you ask me!

Cabbage with sturgeon

Caviar with onions

Caviar, salted and pressed

Fried spine of sturgeon

Steamed herring

Smoked salmon with lemon

Steamed pike sterlet

Steamed bream

Boiled backs of whitefish

Fried carp

Ukha of pike

Pirog with fish and sauerkraut

Kulebiaka with beans

(and many more!)

2½ pounds firm, white-fleshed fish fillets (such as carp, pike, cod, perch, halibut, or red snapper)

Salt and freshly ground black pepper, to taste

6 tablespoons olive oil

⅓ cup fresh lemon juice

2 teaspoons finely chopped fresh chives

1 small red bell pepper, cored, seeded, and cut up

3 cloves garlic

2 leeks (white part only), well rinsed and sliced

7 to 8 large, fresh, white mushrooms, wiped clean and sliced

5 medium-size fresh, ripe plum tomatoes, peeled, seeded, and chopped

1 cup dry white wine

¼ cup chopped fresh Italian (flat-leaf) parsley

2 tablespoons chopped fresh dill

¼ teaspoon dried red pepper flakes

¾ cup crumbled feta cheese, preferably Bulgarian

1 Rub the fish fillets with salt and pepper and place in a large glass or enameled baking dish. Combine 3 tablespoons of the olive oil, the lemon juice, and chives and pour the mixture over the fish. Let marinate for 30 minutes.

2 Meanwhile, mince the bell pepper with 1 clove of the garlic in a food processor. Set aside.

3 Heat the remaining 3 tablespoons oil in a medium-size skillet over medium heat. Add the leeks and mushrooms and sauté, stirring occasionally, until softened and colored, about 15 minutes.

4 Stir in the tomatoes, wine, and bell pepper mixture and continue to sauté until slightly reduced, about 15 minutes.

5 Meanwhile, preheat the oven to 375°F.

6 Finely mince the remaining garlic. Top

the fish in the baking dish with the sautéed vegetables and sprinkle with the minced garlic and herbs. Season with the red pepper flakes and salt and pepper and bake, uncovered, until the fish is opaque throughout, about 15 minutes.

7 Sprinkle the casserole with feta and bake until the cheese is bubbly and lightly browned, another 10 minutes or so.

Serves 6 to 8

Haddock and Scalloped Potatoes

Zapekanka iz Ribi i Kartofelya

Fish and potatoes in one form or another is the staple diet throughout the Baltic area. This is a satisfying one-dish meal from Latvia, which can also be made from cod or hake. Serve with a green salad and crusty fresh rye bread.

4 large baking potatoes in their skins, well scrubbed

7½ tablespoons unsalted butter

1 pound haddock or cod fillets, cut into 1-inch pieces

All-purpose flour for rolling the fish

2 large onions, sliced

½ pound fresh, white mushrooms, wiped clean and sliced

Salt and freshly ground pepper, to taste

¾ teaspoon sweet Hungarian paprika

3 tablespoons chopped fresh dill

2 large eggs, lightly beaten

1⅓ cups half-and-half

1½ tablespoons unflavored, fine, dry bread crumbs

1 Boil the potatoes in their skins in salted water until tender, but not over-cooked, 20 to 25 minutes. Drain and cool until manageable.

2 Peel the potatoes and slice ¼ inch thick.

3 Melt 3 tablespoons of the butter in a large heavy skillet over medium heat. Roll the fish pieces lightly in flour and fry until golden and opaque throughout.

4 In another skillet, melt 3 tablespoons of the butter over medium heat. Add the onions and mushrooms and sauté, stirring occasionally, until the onions are colored and the mushrooms have thrown off and reabsorbed their liquid, 15 minutes.

5 Preheat the oven to 350°F.

6 Line an attractive 9-inch-round oven-proof casserole with three-quarters of the potato slices. Sprinkle the potato layer with salt, pepper, ¼ teaspoon paprika, and half the dill. Spread a layer of mushrooms and onions over the potatoes and season again with salt, pepper, ¼ teaspoon paprika, and the remaining dill.

7 Place all the fish in a layer in the casserole. Season with salt and pepper. Arrange the remaining potatoes in a circle along the edges of the casserole.

8 Whisk together the eggs and half-and-half and pour over the casserole. Sprinkle the fish with bread crumbs and the remaining ¼ teaspoon paprika, and dot with the remaining 1½ tablespoons butter. Bake until the top is lightly browned, about 20 minutes. Serve directly from the casserole.

Serves 4

Zesty Fish Casserole

Ribnaya Solianka

This dish is really a soup, and it is the fish version of the Spicy Mixed Meat Soup. Although it uses such Mediterranean ingredients as tomatoes, capers, olives, and garlic, it nevertheless has an emphatically Russian flavor, achieved by the addition of dried mushrooms and pickles. As with bouillabaisse or a hearty chowder, a second course is totally unnecessary. Serve it with *pirozhki* (see Index) or a good black bread.

½ ounce imported dried wild mushrooms (such as Polish, porcini,
   or cèpes), well rinsed
6 tablespoons (¾ stick) unsalted
   butter
1 parsnip, peeled and diced
1 medium-size carrot, peeled and
   diced
1 large onion, coarsely chopped
1 tablespoon tomato paste
Pinch of sugar
2½ cups Fish Stock (see Index)
1 cup drained, chopped canned
   tomatoes
2 cloves garlic, minced
4 black peppercorns
2 bay leaves

¼ cup dill pickle brine
1½ pounds mixed firm, white-fleshed
   fish fillets (such as sturgeon,
   halibut, swordfish, or haddock),
   cut into ½-inch pieces
⅓ cup diced dill pickles
Salt and freshly ground black
   pepper, to taste
1½ tablespoon small capers, drained
8 pitted Greek olives
Generous pinch of sweet Hungarian
   paprika
1 tablespoon fresh lemon juice, or
   to taste
Lemon slices for garnish
Chopped fresh parsley for garnish
Chopped fresh dill for garnish

1 Soak the mushrooms in 1 cup water for 1½ hours. Drain the mushrooms, pat dry, and coarsely chop. Strain the liquid through a coffee filter, reserving ½ cup.

2 Melt the butter in a medium-size soup pot over medium heat. Add the mushrooms, parsnip, carrot, and onion, and sauté, stirring occasionally, until the onion is softened and colored, about 15 minutes.

3 Stir in the tomato paste, sprinkle in the sugar, and sauté, stirring, 2 to 3 minutes.

4 Add the fish stock, reserved mushroom soaking liquid, tomatoes, garlic, peppercorns, bay leaves, and pickle brine. Bring to a boil, then reduce the heat to low and simmer, covered, for 20 minutes.

And there's nothing in the world, brothers, that I'd rather do than fish. Don't give me bread, just let me sit with a hook and line, by God! . . . There's no greater pleasure than to fish for chub where the current is strong. You cast a seventy-foot line without a sinker, using a butterfly or a beetle, so that the bait floats on the surface; you stand in the water with your pants off and let it go with the current and smack! the chub jerks it! Only you've got to be on the lookout that it doesn't snatch your bait away, the damned creature. As soon as it tugs at your line, you must give it a pull; don't wait. What a lot of fish I've caught in my time!

— Anton Chekhov
Daydreams

5 Add the fish, pickles, and salt and pepper to taste. Simmer, covered, until the fish is almost tender, 5 minutes.

6 Add the capers, olives, paprika, and lemon juice to taste and simmer, covered, for about 10 minutes more. Allow to stand for 15 minutes before serving.

7 Serve garnished with the lemon slices and a sprinkling of parsley and dill.

Serves 4 to 5

Russian Fish Cakes

Ribniye Kotleti

When I was growing up in Moscow, we practically lived on cod, which was then cheaper and more readily available than meat. These cod cakes, flavored with lots of sautéed onions, still remain a great favorite of mine. Serve them hot, with Hot Horseradish Sauce, or cold, with Dill Mayonnaise (see the Index for recipe page numbers).

6 tablespoons vegetable oil
1 cup finely chopped onions
½ cup milk
3 slices white bread, crusts removed
1½ pounds cod fillets, cut into 2-inch pieces
1 small onion, quartered
1 large egg, lightly beaten

2 tablespoons chopped fresh dill
2 tablespoons fresh lemon juice
Salt and plenty of freshly ground black pepper, to taste
1 tablespoon unsalted butter
Unflavored fine, dry bread crumbs for rolling the fish cakes

1 Heat 3 tablespoons of the oil in a medium-size skillet over medium heat. Add the chopped onions and sauté, stirring occasionally, until deep golden, about 15 minutes. Transfer to a large bowl and set aside.

2 In a small bowl, pour the milk over the bread and let soak for 5 minutes.

3 Meanwhile, process the fish together with the quartered onion in a food processor until ground, but not puréed. Transfer to the bowl with the sautéed onions.

4 Squeeze the bread to remove any excess milk. Crumble the bread and add it to the large bowl along with the egg, dill, and lemon juice. Season with salt and pepper and knead well to blend. Cover and refrigerate to firm up, about 1 hour.

5 Form the fish mixture into 3-inch oval patties.

6 Heat the remaining 3 tablespoons oil and the butter in a large, heavy skillet. Roll the patties in bread crumbs to cover completely. Fry over medium heat until golden, about 4 minutes on each side. Drain on paper towels. Serve hot, warm, or cold.

Serves 6

Crawfish Boiled in Beer

Raki v Pive

Those who think crawfish, or crayfish, is an exclusively Cajun treat will be surprised to find out that they are the most popular crustaceans in Russia, where lobsters and shrimp have not been spotted since the Revolution. In the nineteenth century, crawfish were prepared in a great variety of ways, but today they are mostly enjoyed boiled, by every summer vacationer who likes fishing. Eating crawfish is one of those rare occasions when a Russian will give up vodka for beer (eating *vobla*, a salty dried fish, is another such occasion). In this recipe, the crawfish-beer bond is intensified. Any Russian would agree that a Czech pilsner is the ideal beer, with (or without) the crawfish. But save it for drinking and use the cheapest available beer for cooking the crawfish. You'll need slightly more than a six-pack.

3 quarts beer

2 onions, quartered

2 tablespoons coarse (kosher) salt

4 bay leaves

20 black peppercorns

1 bunch fresh dill

6 cloves

2 tablespoons dill seed

1 piece (1 inch) fresh ginger

2 pounds live crawfish

1 In a large pot, bring the beer to a boil over medium-high heat. Add the onions, salt, bay leaves, peppercorns, dill, cloves, dill seed, and ginger and cook for 15 minutes.

2 Rinse the crawfish in cold water and add half of them to the boiling liquid. Cook until the crawfish are red, about 5 to 6 minutes.

3 Remove the cooked crawfish to a platter with a slotted spoon; cover loosely with aluminum foil. Cook the remaining crawfish. Serve at once.

Serves 3 to 4

Baltic Cuisine

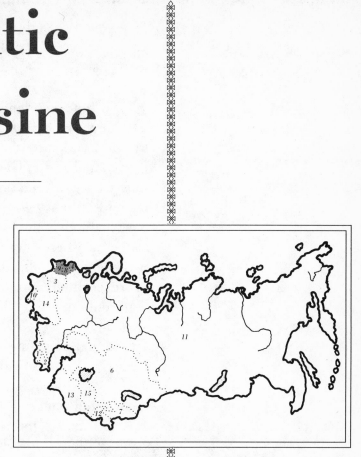

The three Baltic republics, Estonia, Latvia, and Lithuania, form a vivid green fertile crescent hugging the eastern extremity of the Baltic Sea. The people of the Baltic Republics are maritime and agricultural folk, who enjoy the highest standard of living in the USSR. Virtually untouched by the Mongol and Tatar invasions, the present-day territory of the Baltic states has been fought over by Scandinavians, Germans, Poles, and then by the Russians who finally took over in 1940. Yet through all the vicissitudes of their complicated past, the Baltic peoples have maintained an unyielding sense of independence, and have enjoyed a strong cultural affinity with northern Europe—which can be felt in their cuisine. It's certainly true that when you visit Vilnius, Riga, or Tallinn (the capitals of Lithuania, Latvia, and Estonia, respectively), or one of the nearby fortified medieval towns, you can easily think yourself on the Baltic coast of Sweden, Denmark, or Germany.

1. ARMENIA
2. AZERBAIJAN
3. BYELORUSSIA
4. ESTONIA
5. GEORGIA
6. KAZAKHSTAN
7. KIRGHIZIA
8. LATVIA
9. LITHUANIA
10. MOLDAVIA
11. RUSSIA
12. TADZHIKISTAN
13. TURKMENIA
14. UKRAINE
15. UZBEKISTAN

A Trip to Lithuania

My first experience of the Baltic was a wonderful summer-long sojourn in Vilnius where I was on location for the shoot of a children's film in which I had a part. The work was hard and the hours were long, but even this couldn't dampen my fascination for the river of twisting cobbled streets that flowed through the Old Town, the ornate Gothic Cathedral where I heard my first Catholic mass, and perhaps above all, the cozy, comforting atmosphere, so different from the pulsating urban rhythms that would drum me through the day in the heart of Moscow.

In the evening we would do the rounds of the attractive, domestically scaled local cafés and eateries that seemed to us the height of European chic and elegance. I can still remember the polite and efficient professionalism of the waiters. For a troup of luxury-starved Muscovite youngsters it was like the sweetest dream come true to be confronted with an almost unbelievable array of tempting dishes, and to be able to *choose* between them. There were huge trays of carefully decorated open-faced sandwiches; steaming soups served from rustic ceramic pots; a dozen kinds of entrées, each attractively garnished with color-coordinated vegetables. Then, best of all, there were the unending varieties of pastries: miniature tartlets filled with jellied fruits, decadent cream puffs, tiny eclairs, chewy almond cookies, pastry

A group of performers dressed in ancient costumes keep Lithuanian customs alive at the Open-Air Museum outside of Vilnius.

horns brimming with buttercream — all served with generous helpings of sumptuous whipped cream, the likes of which, I was certain, had never even been rumored about back in Moscow.

As I was only nine years old at the time, my favorite hang-out was a children's café called the *Little Gnome*. It was filled with all sorts of beautiful, hand-crafted toys, and eating there was like a day trip to paradise. Main courses were artfully designed in the shape of buildings, animals, and flowers; the cakes were decorated with fairy-tale characters; and drinking one of the enormous selection of milkshakes made from the rich local ice cream (wild strawberry was my favorite) was heaven itself. My grandmother used to joke that I grew a whole inch that summer — "somewhat in the stomach, but mostly in the eyes!"

On weekends we made excursions to the many historic towns in the vicinity, wandered in mossy pine and oak forests and picnicked on one or another of the startlingly green meadows that dot the Lithuanian countryside. We would take our baskets and jars and indulge in the pre-eminent Russian sport of mushroom and berry picking. Our two quarries, though, are much-loved staples in the Baltic just as they are throughout the Slavic world. In the early summer we found tiny delicious wild strawberries — the prince of berries in fragrance and taste — and later came ripe raspberries, huge blueberries (the Baltic "national" berry) and half a dozen other varieties the English names of which I still haven't discovered. Not surprisingly, the Balts make wonderful berry and fruit tarts, fine berry soups, and as in other Slavic nations, a delicious traditional custard-like berry dessert, thickened with potato starch, called *kissel*.

Tallinn of Old

Tallinn's picturesque Lower Town is strewn with charming old buildings, the most venerable of which date back to the thirteenth century (when the Danes were in charge) and the fourteenth century when the Teutonic knights bought into the area and filled it with castles and forts. There are noble burghers' mansions, craftsman's guilds, a Romanesque convent, and some fabulous examples of northern gothic architecture of which the Great Guild is outstanding. Not far from the center, completing the gallery of styles, is the Baroque Kadriorg Palace (1718–24) with its park and elegant Swan Lake. But Tallinn does not have a monopoly on Estonian culture and history. Just over a hundred miles southeast of the capital is the sadly ravaged city of Tartu (there was a terrible fire in 1775, and much destruction by the occupying Germans in World War II), whose university has for more than half a millennium been one of the great centers of learning in Northern Europe.

Because Baltic summers are cool and rainy the mushroom season starts in mid-July, a month earlier than in Russia. Lithuanian mushrooms were so abundant that we picked nothing but the youngest and firmest boletes, disdainfully ignoring the less sought-after species. On one trip I can distinctly recall a gaggle of kindergarten children, no more than four years old, strewn across a field, proudly calling out the names of the mushrooms they had found. A Slavic child learns the names of mushrooms very early. Often unable to consume the bountiful gifts of the Lithuanian woods, we transformed our hotel room into a cottage preservation industry, turning our trophies into pickles, jams, marmalades, syrups, and compotes. Throughout the next winter my entire family enjoyed the fruits (or berries, rather) of my hard summer work.

Visiting Estonia

Although the Baltic republics, like the Scandinavian nations, share many geographical, historical, and cultural similarities, each has its own distinct traditions, and cuisine that are zealously preserved by the local inhabitants. Estonia to the north is perhaps the most Scandinavian in feeling. It is also the smallest of the Soviet republics in population. The capital, Tallinn (which means "Danish city"), is a vibrant old walled Hanseatic trading town some seventy or so kilometers from the Finnish capital of Helsinki across the Bay of Finland. Its walls are punctuated by a string of towers and bastions, of which one of the most formidable is the fifteenth century "Kiek-in-de-Kök" (Peak-into-the-

Kitchen) that offers teetering views over the ancient rooftops and into the neighborhood kitchens — where the authorities not unreasonably presumed they would be able to monitor most of the important goings-on in the city.

The Estonians are by nature honest, direct, and somewhat stern, and their climate is rather unforgiving, with a long dark winter and a short summer that is often cold and rainy. Although they care enormously about their land, by and large the agricultural conditions are not favorable. In consequence the most important natural assets in the republic are the fisheries — both in the Baltic Sea and in the abundant freshwater lakes. Not surprisingly the cuisine reflects the qualities of both land and people. The Estonian diet is frugal and simple, consisting mostly of fish, dairy products, and grains. City cuisine is more sophisticated, the bountiful Finnish coffee table and the Swedish smörgasbord having made their way into Estonian *haute cuisine* during the nineteenth century. These additions, among others, attest to the strong influence of the German and Scandinavian kitchens.

To an unaccustomed palate, Estonian cooking might well seem a bit bland. Spices are almost never used and country cooks rarely even include onions. But when you get used to the farm-fresh mildness of the cuisine you soon begin to appreciate the real meaning of basic food. This is truer than ever when measured against other regions of the Soviet Union today, where the quality of the food supply has taken a nose dive in response to adverse economic conditions. Despite shouldering their own burden of difficult change, the Estonians maintain the highest standards of freshness and quality in the country. Whether it's perfect boiled new potatoes,

a simple cod fillet poached in milk, a bowl of juicy blueberries mounded with cream, or a delicious Estonian boiled dinner (*tukhlinnott*), the taste of home-cooked dishes is as vivid and natural as the Estonian forests, waters, and meadows themselves.

Yet the apparent blandness of Estonian cuisine is deceptive for another reason: their skill in using salt. Salt, of course, has traditionally kept the whole Baltic region going through the long, hard winters. For generations the staple Baltic and North Atlantic fishes — herring, smelts, sardines, anchovies, and cod — were preserved in salt by pickling or drying (in the case of cod). Yet the Estonians have a special flair for incorporating their salty fish into mouthwatering dishes, whether as a simple accompaniment to boiled potatoes or as a base for other, more daring, combinations. Combining fish and meat, for example, is an Estonian specialty. Their famous salad called *rassolye* is similar to the Scandinavian *sillsalad*, but the Estonian version also includes cooked meats whose flavors deliciously offset the taste of the fish and mingle with a refreshing combination of potatoes, beets, pickles, and apples. Order a simple pork patty at a local restaurant and there might be another surprise: a filling of mashed anchovies. And a popular national dish, *kalapirukat*, is a closed pie made of rye flour, containing bacon fat, pork, and pickled smelts. Watch out for the motto of Estonian cuisine: eat, drink, and be surprised!

A view of Tallinn, the old walled capital of Estonia.

Latvian and Lithuanian Cuisine

The cuisines of Latvia and Lithuania have much in common with Estonian cooking. They make extensive use of Baltic, North Sea, and freshwater fish. They feature hearty porridges and gruels made from rugged crops that can withstand the fierce Baltic winters — earthy cracked rye, nutty-flavored barley, oats, millet, and bran (wheat and buckwheat grow in all three states, but they do much better in the more temperate climates of Byelorussia and the Ukraine). Sturdy vegetables that can be stored for a long time — cabbage, rutabagas, turnips, kohlrabi, beets, potatoes (which arrived in the Baltic region one hundred years before they reached Russia); dried legumes such as peas and lentils; and a great variety of dairy dishes are other shared staples. The three small Baltic republics, in fact, produce some twenty percent of the total Soviet dairy supply.

Despite their ties with the Scandinavian nations, the Latvians and Lithuanians are essentially Slavic peoples whose real culinary heritage is shared with other Slavic groups — Russians, Ukrainians, Byelorussians, and Poles. Foodwise this means a preponderance of borscht, dumplings, sour cream, *kissel*, pancakes, and filled pies.

Lithuanian food has long been held in great esteem by the Russians. As far back as the fourteenth and fifteenth centuries the Lithuanian state was a powerful player in the European arena. Its courts and castles had a reputation for luxury and good living and its trade routes stretched all the way to the Near East. These mercantile links encouraged the development of new culinary ideas, and the Lithuanians have borrowed much from eastern

Land of Amber

Lithuania is, by far, the largest repository of amber in the world — nearly ninety percent of the total supply. Amber pendants and jewelry have been found dating back to before the second millennium B.C. At times throughout history, European and Middle Eastern cultures felt amber was so precious that they sent merchants and traders thousands of miles to seek it out. Assyrians, Phoenicians, and Greeks all craved amber in ancient times. The Greeks called it "elektron" — meaning "the substance of the sun" — from which we also derive our word "electricity." What we now know to be a magnificent time-sculpted fossilized tree resin, was thought in those days to be everything from condensed sea foam to the tears of a weeping god.

cuisines — a great range of spices, sweet and sour flavors, noodles, and dumplings. There is almost as great a range of stuffed dishes in Lithuania as there is in Armenia — *zepelinai* (potato dumplings stuffed with meat or liver); *koldunai* (which are similar to Ukrainian *vareniki*); *veretinai* (potato-filled dumplings). Then there is that great Central European staple, stuffed cabbage, plus pot roast stuffed with horseradish, whole fish stuffed with sauerkraut, and *ristinai* (stuffed beef or pork rolls).

If the Estonians and Latvians look mostly to the "gifts of the sea" — as they call seafood in Russia — the Lithuanians, famous for their hunting since the Middle Ages, exploit to the full the rich resources of their forests and woods. Smoked wild boar from the region was a money spinner back in the fifteenth century, when it was a luxury export to Germany and other western European countries. Specially prepared wild game is more difficult to find these days, though it is already beginning to make a welcome comeback as the Baltic economies begin to look to the West. At country restaurants you can find tender, rosy, smoked hams (*skilandis*) and smoked goose, the favorite domestic bird. *Bigos*, a magnificent hunter's stew of sauerkraut and half a dozen varieties of meat that should properly include boar, venison, wild duck, and various smoked sausages, is a real throwback to the culinary splendors of the Lithuanian courts. But *bigos* tastes pretty regal even when made from more modest domestic meats.

Bigos, tall, elegant yeast cakes called *babas*, and more than a dozen other dishes reflect the culinary heritage that Lithuania shares with its neighbor, and sometime mortal enemy, Poland. Perhaps their major common bond is the Catholic church.

Lithuania is also famous for its bees. If ancient historical documents are to be believed, alcoholic meads fermented from golden Lithuanian honey were once exported to far-off Britain. In towns and villages throughout the republic one can still sample a slightly fermented, nonalcoholic honey drink called *krupnikas*. The drink is fragrant with ginger, cinnamon, and cloves, and the Lithuanians sometimes spike it with a good dose of brandy to remind themselves of old times. (Lithuanians now export a honey-infused vodka bearing the same name.)

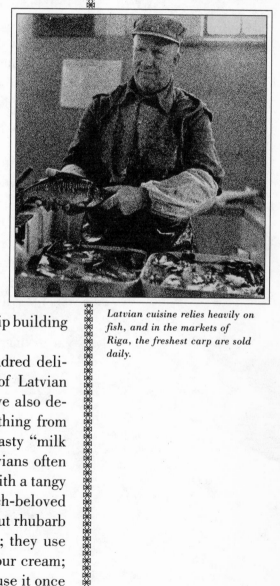

Latvian cuisine relies heavily on fish, and in the markets of Riga, the freshest carp are sold daily.

The Latvian state is tucked in between Estonia to the north and Lithuania to the south, and its culture is the most mixed in the region. It has a large Russian population, and sizable minorities of Byelorussians, Poles, and Germans. In the later nineteenth century almost half the population of Riga, the capital, was German. Latvia has a large light industrial sector, a vigorous ship building industry, and is famous for its fisheries.

Fish and potatoes each in a hundred delicious disguises lie at the very heart of Latvian cuisine. But from the Germans they have also developed a passion for sausages — everything from dark blood sausages and liverwurst to tasty "milk frankfurters." Like most Slavs, the Latvians often have a craving for that little something with a tangy flavor. And time and again it's the much-beloved rhubarb that comes to the rescue. They put rhubarb in their refreshing compotes and *kissels*; they use it for pies which are then topped with sour cream; they add it to buttermilk soup; and they use it once

more for crispy salads with tart apples and more sour cream.

If my favorite dairy product in Estonia is a jug of fresh cream, in Latvia the superb sour milk dishes are irresistible, and the native resourcefulness and invention with them is almost endless. Cottage cheese, sour cream, buttermilk, and a type of mild yogurt called *skabs piens* find their way into almost every meal. Sometimes a casserole that already contains a good dose of sour cream or cottage cheese is served with additional buttermilk on the side. No Latvian family lunch or dinner would be complete without a traditional dish of smothered yellow peas and bacon, served with a rustic ceramic jug of buttermilk. More time-honored still is a peasant dish with truly ancient origins called *putra*. This translates roughly as cereal — but it's much more than that, consisting of a grain product (usually barley) magically combined with a goodly helping of cottage cheese and sour milk. The dish is then left to ferment (or "ripen" as the Latvians put it) for about a day. This basic version is called *skaba putra*, but there are hosts of others including *vets putra* that includes potatoes and salt pork. For the Latvians dairy foods are a high art.

Although the Baltic states offer us a cuisine that seems to ring of its Eastern and Western neighbors, almost every dish has a flavor nuance that is purely the region's own. The vivid freshness of the coastal sea air and the gentle, lush pastures and lakes of the interior produce ingredients that are honest and straightforward in taste. Baltic cuisine has clearly won me over.

Vegetable Dishes

OVOSHCHI

In the western and northern regions of the Soviet Union (the Baltic states, European Russia, the Ukraine), vegetable preparations have always been very simple and unpretentious, as befits the predominantly rural ways of the vast Russian countryside. But the overwhelming fact of life facing the vegetable lover today in the northern republics of the USSR is the sheer difficulty of obtaining fresh produce, a difficulty that by Western standards would amount to a major supply crisis, especially of quality vegetables in the major urban centers. In fact, it's almost impossible to find fresh food for all but a few months in the summer. With the recent liberalization of private markets in Moscow and elsewhere, a bizarre economic situation has taken hold in which a few people are able to make a vast profit while the majority of consumers are left shell-shocked by astronomical "free-market" prices.

This "deluxe" private market economy has a tendency to reinforce the attitude of simple reverence bestowed on a handsome, unblemished potato or a splendid, juicy carrot. Someone who has just paid as much as a day's salary for a pound of new potatoes will probably want the family to savor them perfectly boiled and served up simply with a pat of butter. City dwellers in particular crave the unadorned natural flavor of their hard-won vegetables, and shy away from dressing them up in unaccustomed finery with sauces and sundry accompaniments. Perhaps this is the only real advantage of the new market system in the USSR — when one can find and afford fresh vegetables at the market, they are at least guaranteed to have come straight from the soil, and they will almost certainly have no added chemicals or preservatives.

The same story of scarcity and

Dill Millionaires

Anyone working in the private food sector in Russia enjoys a tremendously privileged life-style. I have relatives in Moscow who have achieved an exceptionally high standard of living through the private sale of bunches of dill at a small Moscow market. They run three cars in a city in which even a rusty old Lada is looked on with the admiration we would accord a Ferrari. Indeed, their small patch of herb-growing land on the outskirts of town probably has as much relative worth as an equivalent acre in the middle of downtown Tokyo. And this is just a livelihood built on dill; for choice vegetable produce, the stakes are higher still.

over-valuation accounts for the enormous popularity and sheer snob value of a simple commercial can of green peas. Canned produce will often be proudly featured on restaurant menus and even displayed stacked like artwork in the home.

Around the Soviet Union

The situation is entirely the reverse in the Caucasus, the Crimea, and Central Asia, where there is, in fact, a whole shadow economy developed around the export of food and vegetables to Moscow, Leningrad, and other less fortunate northern cities. The cuisines of Georgia and Armenia feature a luscious palate of vegetables similar in range to the most fertile parts of the Mediterranean — eggplants, dozens of kinds of legumes prepared in an almost endless variety of ways, sun-blessed tomatoes of incredible sweetness that can easily make a satisfying meal in themselves, fuzzy okra, summer squashes (best just fried in butter), slender, flavorful leeks, and more. There are many overlaps in the preparation of their vegetables among the Georgians, Armenians, and Azerbaijanis, and these methods, in turn, have much in common with Middle Eastern techniques. In Armenia vegetables are simmered in olive oil and a tomato-based sauce, and then eaten hot or cold. The Georgians like to dress their vegetables with walnuts. And all three of the Caucasian republics feature delicious dishes called *borani* (vegetables with yogurt sauce) and *chikhirtma* (vegetables with egg sauce).

Sometimes vegetables will be simmered together in a tempting mélange that is usually made in quantities sufficiently huge to supply the whole family for a week or more. The Caucasus region also produces a wide variety of excellent peppers (ranging from sweet to devilishly hot) that are stuffed or roasted. Chili peppers are strung and dried on the rafters for winter consumption much as they are in the American Southwest.

Perhaps the most exciting of these combinations is found in the festive *Echmiadzin dolma* — a fabulous array of Armenian stuffed mixed vegetables, named for the religious center of the nation. It's not surprising, then, that most of the dishes in this chapter come from the Caucasus area.

In the Slavic heartland of Western USSR (the Ukraine and Byelorussia) and in the Baltic, where the climate is far more restrictive, there is a marked preference for rugged root vegetables that can sustain the cold of the winter. Turnips, potatoes, carrots, rutabagas, and beets are prepared in many imaginative ways, often teamed up with such Slavic staples as sour cream, bacon, or sautéed onions. These dishes are certainly at their best next to a warming winter roast.

Although plump luscious fruits hold first place in Central Asia, the region is also famed for its superb vegetables, which are equally infused with a unique dulcet flavor — delicious sweet jade radishes, exotic yellow carrots from Uzbekistan, dozens of exquisite varieties of onions from Tadzikstan, finely textured pumpkins used in pilaf and as stuffing for dumplings and pastries,

and an abundance of unusual legumes — tiny peas (*noot*), mung beans (*mash*), chick-peas (*nookhat*). In Central Asia, however, vegetables also play second fiddle to the meat — especially to lamb, with which they are often combined in spicy soups or stews, and to the ever-popular and versatile rice, which reigns supreme in all five of the Central Asian republics.

Taken together, these exciting, healthful recipes from the republics offer a host of suggestions for vegetable accompaniments, luncheon and dinner dishes, and party platters.

Asparagus with Egg, Garlic, and Lemon Sauce

Dznepeg Havkitov, Skhtorov, yev Limonov

Although there are plenty of Russians today who have never seen fresh asparagus, before it was "introduced" into Russia from Germany in the eighteenth century, asparagus grew wild all over the country and was avidly consumed by roaming boars, as one historical source informs us. It is even more ironic that, despite its almost complete absence in city stores, asparagus still maintains a highly visible presence in recent Soviet cookbooks. This excellent, gutsy preparation comes from Armenia.

5 tablespoons unsalted butter

2 large cloves garlic, crushed in a
    garlic press

2 pounds fresh asparagus

3 tablespoons fresh lemon juice

1 hard-cooked egg, finely chopped

Salt and freshly ground black
    pepper, to taste

2 teaspoons finely chopped fresh
    tarragon

1 Melt the butter in a small skillet over low heat. Off the heat, stir in the garlic; keep warm while you cook the asparagus.

2 Cut off the tough lower stems of the asparagus and discard. Place the asparagus in a shallow pan and add just enough water to cover. Bring to a boil over medium-high heat and cook, uncovered, until the asparagus is tender, 3 to 5 minutes, depending on the thickness. Drain and pat dry with paper towels.

3 Stir the lemon juice and egg into the

garlic butter. Place the asparagus in a serving dish and toss with the sauce. Season to taste with salt and pepper, sprinkle with tarragon, and serve.

Serves 4 to 6

Make a Wish

In Russia, the appearance of the first vegetable or fruit of the season is always a major event, and known to the whole town in a matter of minutes. After a long winter of cabbage and potatoes, what can be sweeter than the crunch of a spring cucumber or a tender green lettuce leaf! When eating the first fruit or vegetable of the season, or tasting one for the first time, it is customary in Russia to make a wish. It makes this joyous moment even more significant.

Artichokes in Olive Oil

Tzitayoughov Gangar

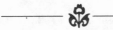

The Armenians who remained on the Turkish side of the USSR border prepare artichokes with great gusto. This is a cold dish that fits perfectly with grilled fish or goes solo as a filling appetizer.

6 tablespoons fresh lemon juice,
*   or more to taste*
6 large artichokes
⅓ cup olive oil
Salt, to taste
12 pearl onions, peeled
2 medium-size boiling potatoes,
*   peeled and cut into ½-inch dice*
1 large carrot, peeled and diced

2 cloves garlic, finely minced
¼ to ½ teaspoon sugar, or more
*   to taste*
1 cup fresh or frozen green peas
Freshly ground black pepper,
*   to taste*
2 tablespoons chopped fresh dill
Lemon wedges for garnish

1 Partially fill a medium-size bowl with cold water and add 3 tablespoons of the lemon juice.

2 Cut off all but about ¼ inch of the stem from the artichokes. Snip off the hard outer leaves and pull off the remaining leaves to within ⅜ inch of the hearts. Trim off about ½ to 1 inch (depending on size) from the top. With a spoon, scoop out the chokes. As you are preparing the artichokes, drop the trimmed ones into lemon-water to prevent them from discoloring.

3 Place the artichokes in an enameled pot and add enough water to cover them by 1½ inches. Add the remaining 3 tablespoons lemon juice, the olive oil, and salt and bring to a boil.

4 Add the onions, potatoes, carrot, and garlic and simmer, uncovered, until the vegetables are tender, about 20 minutes.

5 Stir in ¼ teaspoon sugar and the peas and cook for another 5 minutes. Remove from the heat and taste and correct the seasoning, adding the pepper and more lemon juice, salt, or sugar if desired. Allow to cool to room temperature in the liquid.

Today artichokes have become the stuff of dreams and legends in the Soviet Union, mostly known through descriptions as an exotic representation of the West. They were introduced into St. Petersburg from Holland in the early eighteenth century, but after the Revolution they completely disappeared from the stores.

6 Transfer the vegetables and about half of the liquid to a serving bowl, sprinkle with dill, and serve with lemon wedges on the side.

Serves 3 to 6

Chick-Peas and Swiss Chard

Nivig

Swiss chard is called "horse's sorrel" in Russian. Since I had never come across chard in Moscow, I had great difficulty in interpreting this recipe when it was enthusiastically offered to me by an old Armenian woman in the Yerevan market. Chard was out of season when we met, so she couldn't point it out to me. I completely forgot about the recipe, until, some months later, someone used horse's sorrel as a substitution for grape leaves in the preparation of *dolma*. I realized that it was Swiss chard, tried the woman's recipe myself at home, and was delighted with its delicacy and flavor. This dish is usually served cold or at room temperature.

1 pound Swiss chard, rinsed and drained

3 tablespoons light olive oil

1 small onion, cut in half, then sliced

1 clove garlic, sliced

1 cup canned or cooked chick-peas, drained

1 large, meaty, fresh, ripe tomato, peeled, seeded, and chopped

2 tablespoons water

2 tablespoons fresh lemon juice

Salt and freshly ground black pepper, to taste

1 Remove and discard the white stems from the Swiss chard and chop the leaves coarsely.

2 Heat the olive oil in a large nonstick skillet over low heat. Add the onion and garlic and sauté gently until the onion is softened but not colored, about 5 minutes.

3 Add the chick-peas and tomatoes and cook, stirring, for 5 minutes. Add the Swiss chard and water, cover, and simmer until the chard is wilted, 3 minutes.

4 Remove the skillet from the heat. Stir in the lemon juice and salt and pepper. Allow to cool to room temperature before serving.

Serves 4

Chick-Pea and Onion Stew

Piezly Nukhat

This is a tasty poor man's dinner from Tadzhikistan, served over a bowl of steamed rice. Tadzhik onions are perhaps the largest and the sweetest in the USSR. Steps 1 and 2 can be prepared a day ahead.

1 cup dried chick-peas, soaked overnight in water to cover and drained

3 cups Vegetable Stock (see Index) or water

⅓ cup vegetable oil

4 large Bermuda onions, about 2½ pounds in all, peeled and cut into wedges

2 large fresh, ripe tomatoes, peeled, seeded, and cut into chunks

¼ teaspoon dried red pepper flakes

½ teaspoon coriander seeds, crushed

½ teaspoon saffron threads, crushed in a mortar and diluted in 1 tablespoon warm water

½ teaspoon ground cumin

½ teaspoon sweet Hungarian paprika

⅛ teaspoon ground cinnamon

Salt, to taste

1 Cover the chick-peas with water and bring to a boil. Allow to boil for 3 minutes, and then drain. When cool enough to handle, rub the chick-peas between your fingers to remove the skins. Place the chick-peas in a colander and rinse under cold running water.

2 In a large pot, combine the chick-peas and the stock. Bring to a slow boil, cover, and cook over low heat until almost soft, 1¼ hours. Drain off all but ⅔ cup cooking liquid.

3 Heat the oil in a Dutch oven over medium heat until sizzling. Add the onions in batches and cook, stirring occasionally, until lightly colored, about 12 minutes. Add them to the chick-peas as they brown.

4 Add the tomatoes, red pepper flakes, coriander seeds, saffron, cumin, paprika, cinnamon, and salt and simmer, covered, until the chick-peas are completely tender, about 35 minutes. Taste and correct the seasoning and serve.

Serves 6

Mash Mush

Mashkitchiri

I n Uzbek, *mash* means mung beans. Familiar to health food enthusiasts and well known to connoisseurs of Indian cuisine as the principle constituent of *dahl*, mung beans are a staple legume throughout Central Asia. *Mashkitchiri* is a wonderfully satisfying vegetarian meal of vegetables, mung beans, and rice, jazzed up with hot paprika and cumin seeds. Mung beans are readily available at health food stores.

¼ cup vegetable oil

1¾ cups chopped onions

2 small carrots, peeled and diced

1 boiling potato, peeled and cubed

3 fresh, ripe tomatoes, peeled and
　　coarsely chopped

¾ teaspoon cumin seeds

¼ to ½ teaspoon hot Hungarian
　　paprika

Salt and freshly ground black
　　pepper, to taste

4½ cups boiling Chicken Stock
　　(see Index) or water

¾ cup mung beans, soaked over-
　　night in salted water to cover
　　and drained

1 cup long-grain rice

Chopped fresh cilantro for garnish

1 Heat the oil in a large pot over medium-high heat, until a light haze forms above it. Sauté the onions until they begin to color, 5 to 7 minutes.

2 Add the carrots and potato and sauté until they just begin to brown, about 10 minutes. Stir in the tomatoes, cumin seeds, paprika, and salt and pepper.

3 Add 1½ cups of the boiling stock and let boil for 3 to 5 minutes. Stir in the mung beans, reduce the heat to low, cover, and cook the

mung beans until tender, 40 minutes.

4 Meanwhile, in a medium-size saucepan, combine the rice with the remaining 3 cups boiling stock. Let boil for 2 minutes. Reduce the heat to low and cook, covered, until all the liquid is absorbed and the rice is tender, about 20 minutes.

5 Stir the rice into the mung bean mixture. Serve sprinkled with cilantro.

Serves 4 to 6

Red Beans with Tamarind and Balsamic Vinegar

Lobio Tkemali

Tamarind concentrate from India, Chinese chili paste, and Italian vinegar combine forces in this close approximation of a splendid Georgian cold bean dish, usually made with local tart plum paste (*tkemali*). The New York Georgian community has ingeniously found the perfect substitute in tamarind paste for these hard-to-find Caucasian sour plums. If you can't find tamarind paste (available in Indian or Middle Eastern stores), use 2 tablespoons unsweetened plum butter (available in health food stores), plus 2 tablespoons fresh lemon juice.

1⅓ cups small red beans, soaked overnight in water to cover and drained

1 onion, peeled

1 medium-size carrot, peeled

About 3 inches celery rib

Salt, to taste

5 pitted dried prunes

¼ cup balsamic vinegar

2 teaspoons tamarind concentrate or 2 tablespoons unsweetened plum butter

1 teaspoon Chinese chili and garlic paste

⅓ cup best-quality olive oil

¾ teaspoon coriander seeds, crushed

¼ teaspoon ground fenugreek

¼ cup finely chopped fresh cilantro leaves, plus additional for garnish

Red onion rings for garnish

1 Combine the beans with the onion, carrot, and celery in a soup pot. Add enough water to cover the beans by 3 inches and bring to a boil. Add salt, then reduce the heat to low, cover, and cook the beans until tender but not mushy, about 55 minutes or more, depending on the beans.

2 Meanwhile, combine the prunes and balsamic vinegar in a nonreactive small saucepan and simmer for about 15 minutes. Remove the prunes with a slotted spoon, reserving the vinegar. Finely chop the prunes. Add the tamarind concentrate to the vinegar and let stand until dissolved, about 10 minutes. Stir well and set aside.

3 Drain the beans and discard the onion, carrot, and celery. Place the beans in a serving dish and allow them to cool.

4 In a small bowl, whisk together the diluted tamarind mixture, the chili paste, and the olive oil. Add the chopped prunes, coriander seeds, and fenugreek.

5 Toss the beans with the tamarind mixture. Taste and correct the seasoning and stir in the ¼ cup cilantro. Refrigerate, covered, for at least 2 hours before serving. Serve garnished with the additional cilantro and the onion rings.

Serves 4 to 6

White Bean Plaki

Lupia Plaki

In Armenia and the Middle East, *Plaki* is the name for one of the essential preparations for vegetables or fish. *Plaki* usually denotes a vegetable or fish stew prepared with olive oil, tomatoes, onions, and spices. When warm, *plaki* can be served as a side dish or a vegetarian entrée over bulgur or rice. Served cold, it takes its place in the Armenian *meza* spread.

1½ cups dried baby lima beans or
    Great Northern beans, soaked
    overnight in water to cover and
    drained
Salt, to taste
2 medium-size carrots, peeled
    and cut into fine dice
1 large rib celery, cut into fine dice
½ cup finely chopped onion
½ cup canned Italian plum tomatoes,
    drained and chopped

2 tablespoons tomato paste
⅓ cup olive oil
6 cloves garlic, halved, plus
    2 cloves minced
Juice of 1 lemon, or more to taste
1 teaspoon sweet Hungarian paprika
¼ teaspoon hot Hungarian paprika
2 tablespoons chopped celery
    leaves
⅓ cup finely chopped fresh parsley,
    plus additional for garnish

1 Place the beans in a large pot and add enough water to cover the beans by 1 inch. Bring to a boil, add the salt, then reduce the heat to medium-low, cover, and cook the beans until they are almost done, but still slightly hard to the bite. It should take anywhere from 35 to 50 minutes or more, depending on the beans.

2 Add the carrots, celery, onion, tomatoes, tomato paste, olive oil, and garlic halves and cook, uncovered, until the beans and vegetables are tender, another 25 to 35 minutes. Be sure, though, not to overcook the beans.

3 Add the lemon juice, sweet and hot paprika, celery leaves, ⅓ cup parsley, and the minced garlic, and simmer for 10 minutes more. Taste and correct the lemon juice and seasoning. Serve either warm or cold, garnished with additional parsley.

Serves 4 to 6

Cabbage Baked with Feta

Verza cu Brinza

A lively and unusual way to dress up cabbage. Make sure you fry the cabbage well, as this really brings out its best qualities. I found the original recipe for this dish in a Moldavian cookbook, and it has been a favorite ever since.

1 firm head green cabbage (about 2½ pounds), cored and finely slivered

3 tablespoons unsalted butter

2 tablespoons vegetable oil

¼ cup sour cream

2 large eggs

¼ cup finely chopped fresh dill (optional)

Salt and freshly ground black pepper, to taste

1⅓ cups finely crumbled or grated feta cheese, preferably Bulgarian

½ cup unflavored, coarse, dry bread crumbs

1 to 2 teaspoons sweet Hungarian paprika

5 tablespoons unsalted butter, melted

1 Blanch the cabbage in boiling water for 2 minutes. Drain and pat dry with a linen or cotton (not terry cloth) kitchen towel.

2 Heat the 3 tablespoons butter and the oil in a large skillet over medium heat. Add the cabbage and sauté, stirring and tossing frequently, until the cabbage is nicely browned, 15 to 20 minutes. Cool the cabbage until it is easy to handle.

3 Preheat the oven to 375°F.

4 In a small bowl, whisk together the sour cream and eggs. Mix thoroughly with the cabbage. Add dill, if desired, and season to taste with salt and pepper. Transfer the mixture to an earthenware casserole dish.

5 Combine the feta with the bread crumbs. Sprinkle the mixture over the cabbage. Sprinkle with paprika and melted butter and bake until bubbly and the top is browned, about 15 minutes.

Serves 6

Sweet and Sour Red Cabbage

Kislosladkaya Krasnaya Kapusta

This recipe comes from my friend Garry Muller, an American chef who has a better understanding of Russian food than most Russians. The red cabbage, braised with apples, dried currants, apple cider, and fruity vinegar, makes a perfect accompaniment to roast duck, goose, or pork.

5 tablespoons unsalted butter
1¼ cups chopped onions
1 large, firm head red cabbage
    (about 3 pounds), shredded
7 tablespoons fruit vinegar
    (such as raspberry, cherry, or
    apple cider)
¾ cup Chicken Stock (see Index) or
    canned broth

1 large tart apple (such as
    Granny Smith), peeled,
    cored, and thinly sliced
½ cup dried currants
⅓ cup apple cider
5 cloves
Generous pinch of freshly grated nutmeg
Salt and freshly ground black
    pepper, to taste

1 Melt the butter in a large Dutch oven over medium heat. Add the onions and sauté, stirring occasionally, until softened, 5 to 7 minutes.

2 Add the cabbage and cook, stirring and tossing, for about 10 minutes. Add the vinegar and stock, then reduce the heat to low and cook, covered, for 20 minutes.

3 Add the remaining ingredients, cover, and simmer for about 1¼ hours. Adjust the seasoning, adding more salt or vinegar if desired, and serve.

Serves 6

Spicy Carrots with Cumin Seeds

Sabzi Piez

Braised carrots, onions, sweet and hot paprika, and lots of cumin seeds is one of the most emphatically Uzbek combinations. It's used as a base for beef and lamb stews, and is added to the *zirvak*, the meat component of *palov*, the famous Central Asian rice pilaf. The carrots and onions are well browned in very hot oil (in Uzbekistan they use a cottonseed oil or special sesame oil, but it's hard to find an equivalent here) and a little water is added. The dish is then slowly braised, exuding in the process the unbearably tempting odor of cumin.

I find that as a side dish, *sabzi piez* fits well with a robust chicken or meat dish, so long as it doesn't have a spice flavor that would clash with the cumin.

¼ *cup olive oil*

2 *medium-size onions, coarsely*
    chopped

1½ *pounds carrots, peeled and cut*
    into 1½ × ¼-inch sticks

1 *teaspoon cumin seeds*

½ *teaspoon sweet Hungarian paprika*

¼ *teaspoon hot Hungarian paprika*

2 *teaspoons tomato paste*

3 *cloves garlic, unpeeled*

Salt, to taste

¼ *cup canned beef broth or water,*
    or as needed

1 Heat the oil in a large skillet over medium-high heat until a light haze forms above it. Add the onions and sauté, stirring, until they begin to color, about 5 minutes. Add the carrots and continue to sauté, stirring until the onions and carrots are well colored, 12 minutes.

2 Reduce the heat to low. Stir in the cumin seeds, sweet and hot paprika, tomato paste, garlic, and salt. Add enough broth to barely cover the vegetables. Simmer, covered, stirring occasionally, until the carrots are tender and the liquid has reduced, about 30 minutes. Remove and discard the garlic and serve the dish at once.

Serves 4 to 6

Carrot Baba

Morku Apkepas

This Lithuanian vegetable baba is almost as sweet and delicate as the real thing (a yeast baba or babka, that is). Serve it with a basic roast chicken or even to accompany the Thanksgiving turkey.

6 tablespoons (¾ stick) unsalted
  butter
½ cup finely chopped onion
2 pounds carrots, peeled and grated
1 large tart apple (such as Granny
  Smith), peeled and cut
  into chunks
½ cup sour cream
6 tablespoons (¾ stick) unsalted
  butter, melted
2 large egg yolks, beaten

2 slices white bread, crusts
  removed
⅓ cup heavy or whipping
  cream
¾ teaspoon ground ginger
½ teaspoon ground cardamom
1 teaspoon sugar
Salt and freshly ground black
  pepper, to taste
½ cup unflavored, fine, dry
  bread crumbs

1 Melt 4 tablespoons of the butter in a large skillet over medium heat. Add the onion and sauté until soft, about 7 minutes. Add the carrots, and cook, stirring, until softened, about 10 minutes.

2 Place the carrots and onion in a food processor. Add the apple and process until finely minced but not puréed. Transfer to a large bowl and set aside.

3 Preheat the oven to 350°F. Butter a 9-inch-round baking pan.

4 In a bowl, whisk the sour cream, melted butter, and egg yolks, together.

5 Soak the bread in the cream for 5 min-

utes. Mash into the sour cream mixture. Add the ginger, cardamom, sugar, and salt and pepper. Add this mixture to the carrot mixture and mix well.

6 Melt the remaining 2 tablespoons butter in a small saucepan. Add the bread crumbs and sauté until golden, about 2 minutes.

7 Pour the carrot mixture into the prepared pan. Top with the bread crumbs and bake until lightly golden, 30 minutes.

Serves 6

Two-Colored Cauliflower and Beet Purée Bake

Zapenka iz Tsvetnoy Kapusti i Svyokli

I found this dish in an obscure Soviet cookbook, where it stood out among scores of almost identical recipes. When trying it out, I resorted to a little "measure of the eye," and after a few attempts, it finally came out perfectly.

2 large beets
2 small heads cauliflower (about 1
    pound each)
Salt, to taste
2 large egg yolks
3 tablespoons sour cream
1 tablespoon heavy or whipping
    cream

Freshly ground black
    pepper, to taste
1 clove garlic, minced
2 teaspoons cider vinegar
1 tablespoon sweet vermouth
3 tablespoons unsalted butter

1 Preheat the oven to 375°F.

2 Remove the stems from the beets. Wash and dry them and wrap each one in aluminum foil. Bake the beets until tender, about 1¼ hours.

3 While the beets are baking, break the cauliflowers into florets. Boil in plenty of salted water until tender, about 10 minutes. Drain.

4 In a food processor, process the cauliflower at low speed until finely minced but not puréed. Add the egg yolks, sour cream, and cream and process until completely incorporated. Season with salt and pepper.

5 Remove the beets from the oven. Re-duce the oven temperature to 325°F. Allow the beets to cool until manageable, then peel and cut into chunks. Clean the processor, and process the beets at low speed. Transfer to a bowl and add the garlic, vinegar, and vermouth. Season with salt and pepper and mix well.

6 Arrange half the cauliflower in a layer in a greased rectangular baking dish that is at least 2 inches deep. Use a rubber spatula to spread a layer of the beets on top. Top with a layer of cauliflower and smooth with the spatula. Dot with the butter and bake until bubbly, 30 minutes.

7 Serve at once, taking care not to mash the purées together.

Serves 6 to 8

Fried Eggplant Slices

Tapkvats Simpoug

This is a simple Caucasian staple that I am more than willing to have three times a day. Although the eggplant slices are delicious on their own, the dish can be even further enhanced by one of the following sauces: Walnut Sauce (from the Cold Steamed Vegetables recipe), Yogurt and Garlic Sauce, Quick Tomato Sauce, or Pomegranate Syrup (see the Index for recipe page numbers). If you wish, the eggplant slices can also be brushed with oil and baked at 425°F for about 20 minutes, instead of fried. Serve warm or at room temperature.

3 medium-size eggplants (about ¾ pound each), not more than 3 inches thick

Coarse (kosher) salt

Olive oil

Chopped fresh basil or cilantro for garnish

1 Wash and stem the eggplants. Cut into ½-inch slices. Place in a colander and toss with a generous amount of coarse salt. Let stand for 30 minutes.

2 Rinse the eggplant slices and pat thoroughly dry with paper towels.

3 Heat about ½ inch of oil in a large skillet over medium heat for about 2 minutes. Add as many eggplant slices as will comfortably fit in the skillet in one layer. Sauté until golden brown, 5 to 7 minutes, then turn the eggplant and brown on the other side. Remove the slices with a slotted spoon and drain on paper towels. Repeat the process until all the eggplant is cooked, adding more oil as needed.

4 Sprinkle the eggplant with chopped basil or cilantro and serve with one or more sauces of choice.

Serves 6 to 8 as an appetizer or side dish

Eggplant Kebabs

Badrijan Kebab

These skewers of delicious eggplant stuffed with a mixture of lamb fat or salt pork, garlic, and cilantro (making them temptingly flavorful and moist inside) are a mandatory affair at Caucasian barbecues.

3 ounces salt pork
2 large cloves garlic
1 level teaspoon coarse (kosher) salt
6 to 8 sprigs fresh cilantro, stemmed
¼ to ½ teaspoon cayenne pepper

8 baby eggplants, about 4 inches long and no more than 2 inches thick
Olive oil for brushing the eggplants

1 Prepare coals for grilling until covered with white ash, or preheat the broiler. Oil the grill or broiler rack.

2 With a sharp knife, finely mince the salt pork together with the garlic, salt, cilantro, and cayenne to taste until the ingredients are blended.

3 Wash and stem the eggplants. Pat thoroughly dry. With a sharp knife, make a lengthwise slit in the eggplant, cutting approximately one-third of the way into the eggplant, and leaving about ½ inch uncut on each end. Insert a little of the salt pork mixture into each slit.

4 Thread the eggplants lengthwise on long metal skewers, two on each skewer. Brush with olive oil. Grill or broil the eggplants, turning from side to side (not slit side down) until soft, 25 to 30 minutes.

Serves 4

Eggplants Astrakhan Style

Baklazhani po-Astrakhanski

This is an old family recipe that the family "archivist," Aunt Nadia, entrusted to me some years ago, along with old family pictures, the family coat-of-arms, and nineteenth-century postcards of my paternal grandmother's villa in Astrakhan on the banks of the great Volga river. The addition of apple and pickles gives this dish a delicious sweet-tart flavor.

2 medium-size eggplants (about 2 pounds in all)
Coarse (kosher) salt
6 tablespoons vegetable oil, or more as needed
3 large onions, coarsely chopped
2 pounds meaty, fresh, ripe tomatoes, peeled, and finely chopped

1 large tart apple (such as Granny Smith), peeled, cored, and chopped
2 large dill pickles, diced
Salt and freshly ground black pepper, to taste
1½ tablespoons red wine vinegar

1 Wash and stem the eggplants. Pat thoroughly dry. Cut the eggplants into medium-size cubes. Place the cubes in a colander and toss with a generous amount of coarse salt. Let stand for 30 minutes.

2 Rinse the eggplants under cold running water and pat thoroughly dry on paper towels.

3 Heat 3 tablespoons of the oil in a large skillet over medium heat. Add the onions and sauté, stirring occasionally, until they begin to turn golden, 12 minutes. With a slotted spoon, transfer the onions to a Dutch oven with a tight-fitting lid.

4 Add the remaining 3 tablespoons oil to the same skillet and brown the eggplant cubes, a few at a time, transferring the browned ones to the Dutch oven.

5 Add the tomatoes, apple, and pickles (and more oil if needed) to the eggplants and the onions. Stir the vegetables over medium-high heat for about 10 minutes. Reduce the heat to very low and season with salt and pepper; cover and simmer for 2½ hours, stirring from time to time.

6 Add the vinegar and additional salt and pepper, if needed. Serve either at room temperature or cold.

Serves 8

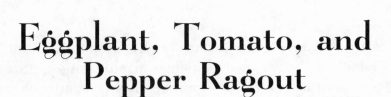

Eggplant, Tomato, and Pepper Ragout

Adzhapsandali

There are two versions of this dish. One, called *adzhapsanda*, comes from Central Asia and is made by steaming layers of lamb, eggplant, onions, peppers, and tomatoes for a long time in a pot, which is placed in a larger pot of water. This version, however, is called *adzhapsandali* and comes from Georgia. The same vegetables (minus the lamb) are placed in layers in a pot and simmered for a long time to produce an absolutely mouth-watering result.

1 large eggplant, about 1¾ pounds

Coarse (kosher) salt

⅓ cup light olive oil, or as
needed

2 large onions, sliced into rings

4 large Italian (pale green frying)
peppers, cored, seeded, and cut
into rings

½ cup canned Italian plum tomatoes, drained

Sugar (optional)

8 medium-size meaty, fresh plum
tomatoes, peeled and sliced

¾ cup finely chopped mixed fresh
herbs (such as Italian or flat-
leaf parsley, cilantro, and basil)

6 cloves garlic, minced

Salt and freshly ground black
pepper to taste

1 Wash and stem the eggplant. Cut into ⅜-inch slices. Place in a colander and toss with the salt. Let stand for 30 minutes.

2 Rinse the eggplant and pat thoroughly dry with paper towels.

3 Heat ¼ cup of the oil in a large skillet over medium-high heat until it sizzles. Add the eggplant slices and sauté until they are golden brown on both sides, 10 minutes. Remove from the skillet to paper towels to drain.

4 Add the remaining oil to the skillet and sauté the onions and peppers, tossing and stirring over high heat until they are nicely browned, about 15 minutes. Set aside.

Perfect Ending

To me one of the simplest and most delightful conclusions to a meal with a Mediterranean accent, is a plate of lus-ciously ripe persimmons, peeled, sliced and garnished with mint sprigs.

5 Pass the canned tomatoes through a sieve, and taste. If they are acidic, sprinkle them very lightly with sugar as you add them to the casserole (about 1 medium pinch sugar for each tomato layer, see Step 6).

6 In a large heavy casserole with a flat bottom, arrange the eggplants, fresh to-matoes, and onions and peppers in layers, sprinkling each layer with herbs, garlic, salt and pepper, and the puréed tomatoes. Cook, covered, over a low heat, without stirring, for 1½ hours. Serve slightly warm, or cold.

Serves 6

Eggplant
Stuffed with Walnuts

Badrijani Nigvzis Satenit

This is a truly knockout eggplant dish from Georgia given to me by a superb Georgian emigré cook called Venera (which translates as "Venus"). Make sure you find the tenderest and firmest eggplants.

8 small eggplants, no more than 4
    inches long and 2 inches wide
1 teaspoon coarse (kosher) salt
½ cup walnut pieces
2 large cloves garlic
4 sprigs fresh cilantro
3 tablespoons finely chopped
    onion
1 small rib celery, finely chopped

½ teaspoon hot Hungarian paprika
5 tablespoons tarragon vinegar
3 tablespoons finely chopped fresh
    parsley
3 tablespoons water
Salt and freshly ground black
    pepper, to taste
⅓ cup olive oil, plus additional for
    the eggplants

GARNISHES
Cilantro sprigs
Red onion rings

Pomegranate seeds

1 Stem the eggplants and cut them lengthwise in half. Place them in a colander, sprinkle with coarse salt, and let stand for 30 minutes.

2 Rinse the eggplants thoroughly and pat dry with paper towels.

3 In a food processor, grind the walnuts together with the garlic and cilantro.

Transfer the mixture to a bowl.

4 Add the onion, celery, paprika, vinegar, parsley, water, and salt and pepper. Stir well.

5 Select a skillet large enough to accommodate all of the eggplants, or use two skillets (in which case increase the amount of oil). Heat the oil over medium heat. Add

◆◆◆

the eggplants and sauté on both sides until they feel soft when pricked with a fork, about 15 minutes. Cool the eggplants until manageable. Scrape off about 1 tablespoon of the pulp from each half. Reserve for another use.

6 Spread the eggplant halves generously with the walnut mixture. Place on a serving platter, cover, and refrigerate for at least 2 hours or overnight.

7 Serve garnished with cilantro sprigs, red onion rings, and pomegranate seeds.

Serves 4 to 8

Georgian Green Beans

Lobio Kverstkhit

The Georgians are blessed with a superb overabundance of delicious bean recipes. In this dish, the beans are infused with garlic and vinegar, to which a beaten egg is added. This type of preparation, featuring beans, eggplant, or spinach, is common throughout the Caucasus. Don't be fooled into thinking that the recipe will produce something like scrambled eggs — the eggs just bind the beans together in a wonderful, delicate sauce.

2 pounds green beans, trimmed

Salt, to taste

3 tablespoons unsalted butter

1 large onion, cut in quarters, then thinly sliced

1½ teaspoons red wine vinegar

3 tablespoons canned chicken broth or water

2 cloves garlic, minced

3 tablespoons finely chopped fresh cilantro

3 large eggs, beaten

Fresh ground black pepper, to taste

1 tablespoon chopped fresh parsley leaves (for garnish)

1 Drop the beans into a large pot of salted boiling water and blanch them for 3 minutes. Drain the beans and refresh under cold running water. Drain again thoroughly and pat dry with paper towels.

2 Melt the butter in a 9-inch skillet over medium heat. Add the onion and sauté, stirring occasionally, until transparent, 5 to 7 minutes.

3 Stir in the beans and sauté, stirring, for 5 minutes more. Stir in the vinegar, broth, garlic, and salt and pepper, and cook for another 10 minutes. Add the cilantro.

4 Add half the eggs and stir quickly with a wooden spoon until they begin to set, about 2 minutes. Pour in the rest of the eggs, then reduce the heat to low, cover, and simmer for 5 minutes without disturbing until the eggs are set.

5 Sprinkle with parsley and serve at once.

Serves 6 to 8

The green beans common in the Soviet Union are slightly different from the common ones available in the United States. They are flat, broad, and fleshy, with young beans inside. This variety, sold frozen as broad beans, is sometimes available fresh at farmer's and ethnic (Italian and Greek) markets.

Green Beans with Ground Lamb

Lobio Khortsit

A Caucasian equivalent of spaghetti and meatballs, this is a hearty dish that can easily double as an entrée or as a side dish to roast chicken or pork. In both cases it is usually served over steamed rice or bulgur pilaf. Although the recipe I give calls for cooking the *lobio* on top of the stove, for a more rustic flavor and feel you can combine the beans and lamb in an earthenware casserole and prepare Step 4 in a 375°F oven, baking the beans until they are tender. Note that throughout the Caucasus and the Middle East it is customary for the beans to be cooked "well done."

2 pounds green beans, trimmed
3 tablespoons olive oil
1 medium-size onion, finely
    chopped
10 ounces ground lamb
3 tablespoons unsalted butter
1 can (16 ounces) Italian plum to-
    matoes, drained but liquid re-
    served, seeded, and chopped

3 cloves garlic, crushed in a garlic
    press
½ teaspoon hot Hungarian
    paprika
⅛ teaspoon ground cinnamon
⅛ teaspoon ground cumin
Salt, to taste
¼ cup finely chopped fresh Italian
    (flat-leaf) parsley or cilantro

1 Wash the beans and cut crosswise in half. Pat dry and set aside.

2 Heat the olive oil in a large heavy skillet over medium heat. Add the onion and sauté until it begins to color, 7 minutes. Add the lamb and brown, breaking it up with a fork, 10 minutes more.

3 Melt the butter in another large skillet, over medium heat. Add the beans and sauté, stirring, for 10 minutes.

4 Stir in the meat and onion, the tomatoes and their liquid, the garlic, paprika, cinnamon, and cumin. Season with salt. Cook, covered, until the beans are very tender, about 20 minutes. Uncover and cook for 15 more minutes.

5 Sprinkle with parsley and serve.

Serves 8 over rice or bulgur

Ground meat and vegetable dishes simmered in tomato sauce and jazzed up with local spices, are some of the most popular home-style fare in the Caucasus, just like chili is in the American Southwest. These dishes are filling, inexpensive, and easy to prepare. Okra, zucchini, fried eggplant slices, fried potato slices, or spinach can be substituted for the green beans in this recipe if you wish. Serve over rice or a bulgur pilaf for a satisfying lunch.

Braised Leeks with Egg and Lemon Sauce

Terbiyov Bras

I first tasted this tangy, refreshing leek preparation in Armenia as an accompaniment to poached trout. The egg and lemon sauce will also work nicely with poached tender carrots or braised celery root.

12 fresh slender leeks (about 2¼
    pounds), trimmed of all but 1
    inch of green tops
7 tablespoons olive oil
1½ cups Chicken Stock (see Index),
    canned broth, or water

¼ teaspoon sugar
Salt, to taste
1 teaspoon all-purpose flour
¼ cup fresh lemon juice
1 large egg
1 tablespoon finely chopped fresh dill

1 To remove any sand, soak the leeks in cold water to cover for 15 minutes. Rinse thoroughly and pat dry with paper towels.

2 Heat the oil in a large saucepan over medium heat. Add the leeks and sauté, tossing frequently, until they just begin to soften. Add the stock, sugar, and salt and bring to a gentle boil. Reduce the heat to low, and simmer, covered, until the leeks are tender, about 20 minutes. With a slotted spoon, transfer the leeks to a bowl.

3 Reduce the cooking liquid over high heat to ¾ cup, 7 minutes.

4 In a small bowl, beat the flour together with 1 tablespoon of cold water until

thoroughly blended. Whisk in some hot cooking liquid, then whisk the flour mixture into the remaining hot liquid.

5 In another bowl, beat the egg with the lemon juice. Whisk in about a ladleful of the hot cooking liquid and whisk back into the saucepan. Cook over low heat, stirring, until the mixture thickens, 3 minutes.

6 Off the heat, return the leeks to the saucepan and turn to coat them with the sauce. Allow the dish to cool to room temperature.

7 Stir in the dill before serving.

Serves 4 to 6

Mushroom Tokana

Tocana de Ciuperci

Tokana is a Moldavian stew suffused with garlic, fresh tomatoes, and sweet paprika. It is traditionally eaten with *mamaliga*, a delicious local cornmeal mush. This recipe offers a vegetarian *tokana* featuring mushrooms. For an authentic taste, try to use wild mushrooms, or at least a combination of wild and cultivated, as commercially produced mushrooms are almost unavailable in the USSR (though paradoxically considered a delicacy just for this reason). Serve over Moldavian Cornmeal Mush (see Index).

1½ pounds fresh mushrooms (such
    as boletes, portobello, cremini,
    white, or a combination)
5 tablespoons sunflower oil
1½ tablespoons fresh lemon juice
1 large onion, coarsely chopped
1 medium-size red bell pepper,
    cored, seeded, and diced
3 large fresh, ripe tomatoes, peeled,
    seeded, and coarsely chopped

2 large cloves garlic, sliced
1 teaspoon sweet Hungarian paprika
¼ teaspoon dried thyme
½ teaspooon fennel seeds
2 teaspoons all-purpose flour
¾ cup dry white wine
Salt and freshly ground black
    pepper, to taste
3 tablespoons finely chopped fresh
    parsley

1 Trim the mushrooms, separating the stems from the caps, and wipe thoroughly with a damp paper towel to remove any traces of dirt. Cut the mushrooms into ½-inch pieces. (If the mushrooms are young and firm, you can use the stems, too.)

2 Heat 4 tablespoons of the oil in a large skillet over high heat. Add the mushrooms and sauté, stirring constantly, until the

mushrooms are browned, about 7 minutes. Sprinkle with the lemon juice and set aside.

3 Heat the remaining oil in a Dutch oven over medium-high heat. Add the onion and bell pepper and cook, stirring, until the onions are lightly colored, 7 to 8 minutes. Stir in the tomatoes, garlic, paprika, thyme, and fennel seeds and cook, stirring continually, for 3 to 4 minutes.

4 Turn the heat down to medium and sprinkle in the flour. Add the wine and stir to blend. Season to taste with salt and pepper, then reduce the heat to low and simmer, covered, for 12 to 15 minutes.

5 Add the mushrooms, stir, and simmer for about 10 minutes longer.

6 Correct the seasoning, sprinkle with parsley, and serve.

Serves 6

Sautéed Mushrooms with Madeira

Gribi s Maderoy

Madeira has been a prized ingredient in Russian *haute cuisine* since the middle of the nineteenth century, though its popularity in noble and merchant households as a drink dates back to Peter the Great. Traditionally, Madeira has been combined with mushrooms and sour cream to produce a quintessentially Russian sauce that still delights the Russian palate, especially in combination with Pozharsky croquettes, *kotleti* (Russian hamburgers), or other ground meat dishes (see the Index for recipe page numbers).

3 tablespoons unsalted butter
¼ cup chopped shallots
1½ pounds fresh, white mushrooms, wiped cleaned and sliced
⅓ cup Madeira
¼ cup heavy or whipping cream

2 tablespoons sour cream
Salt and plenty of freshly ground black pepper, to taste
Generous pinch of freshly grated nutmeg
3 tablespoons finely chopped fresh parsley (optional)

1 Melt the butter in a large skillet over medium heat. Add the shallots and sauté, stirring occasionally, until they begin to brown, about 10 minutes.

2 Add the mushrooms and sauté, stirring, until they begin to throw off their liquid. Turn the heat up to high and cook, tossing and stirring, until the liquid is reabsorbed, about 12 minutes. Continue to sauté over high heat, stirring, until the mushrooms are nicely browned, about 3 minutes more.

3 Stir in the Madeira and cream and quickly stir until they are somewhat re-duced. Turn the heat down to low, stir in the sour cream, and simmer for another 3 minutes. Season with salt, pepper, and nutmeg. Serve garnished with parsley, if desired.

Serves 4

Mushroom Julienne

Gribnoy Zhulien

Although in French *julienne* refers to a particular process of cutting, in Russia today it signals a specific dish — poultry, ham, or mushrooms in white sauce baked in individual ramekins or cocotte pans — similar to the French *au gratin*. The ingredients, however, are chopped in a way that can vaguely resemble julienne, but not always. *Zhulien* was traditionally a late supper dish, and still in Moscow today you can find it at many restaurants and on the intermission menus of theaters and concert halls. It is also served as an appetizer, but I find the dish quite sufficient for supper or lunch, accompanied by a salad and a glass of wine.

4 tablespoons (½ stick) unsalted
   butter
2 small onions, finely
   chopped
2 pounds fresh, white mushrooms,
   wiped clean and coarsely
   chopped
1½ tablespoons dry vermouth
⅔ cup sour cream

¾ cup Béchamel Sauce (see Index)
⅓ cup finely snipped fresh chives
Generous pinch of freshly grated
   nutmeg
½ teaspoon dried fennel seeds
Salt and freshly ground white
   pepper, to taste
¾ cup grated Gruyère cheese

ge heavy skillet, melt the butter
m heat. Sauté the onions, stirring occasionally, until they begin to
color, about 8 minutes.

2 Add the mushrooms and sauté, stirring, until they begin to throw off their
liquid. Turn the heat up to high and cook,
stirring frequently, until the liquid is reabsorbed, about 15 minutes. Continue to
cook the mushrooms over high heat until
nicely browned, about 3 minutes.

3 Stir in the vermouth and cook for 3
minutes.

4 Preheat the oven to 425°F.

5 Turn the heat down to low and stir in
the sour cream, ½ cup of the béchamel,
the chives, nutmeg, fennel seeds, and salt

and pepper. Mix well. Allow the mixture to
heat for 3 minutes.

6 Divide the mushrooms among four
ovenproof ramekins. Spread about a tablespoon of the remaining béchamel on top of
each portion and sprinkle liberally with
Gruyère.

7 Bake for 15 minutes, until bubbly and
the tops are well browned.

Serves 4

Okra and Tomatoes in Olive Oil

Loligov Bamia

I n combination with steamed rice or bulgur pilaf, this lovely okra dish from
the Caucasus is best next to a succulent roast lamb. If you like your okra
slightly *al dente,* simmer the tomatoes first and add the okra in the last 7
minutes of cooking.

1½ pounds fresh okra

5 tablespoons fresh lemon juice, or
more to taste

⅓ cup best-quality olive oil

1 medium-size onion, quartered and
sliced

3 large, meaty, fresh, ripe tomatoes,
peeled, seeded, and coarsely
chopped

½ cup canned chicken broth or
water

¼ to ½ teaspoon sugar

Salt and freshly ground black
pepper, to taste

⅓ cup chopped fresh parsley

1 Rinse and drain the okra and trim off the stems. Sprinkle with 2 tablespoons of the lemon juice and set aside.

2 Heat the olive oil in a deep skillet or a Dutch oven over medium heat. Add the onion and sauté, stirring occasionally, until translucent, about 5 minutes.

3 Add the okra and tomatoes and cook, stirring, for about 5 minutes. Add the broth and the remaining 3 tablespoons lemon juice, ¼ teaspoon sugar, and salt and pepper. Reduce the heat to low, and cook, covered, until the okra is tender but not overcooked, 15 to 20 minutes.

4 Off the heat, stir in the parsley. Taste for seasoning, adding more lemon juice or sugar if desired and serve at once.

Serves 6

Smothered Red Peppers Paprikash

Lecho

This is a Hungarian dish that is sold in cans throughout the Soviet Union, and that the Russians dearly love as their own — unlike many other Eastern European conserves that are still consumed, but without special passion. I devised this recipe for those occasions when a Russian or Polish store is not within easy reach. It took me a few attempts to realize that these peppers could actually be eaten in a civilized fashion (as a relish or side dish for grilled meats) rather than plucked straight from the skillet.

3 tablespoons vegetable oil

2 medium-size onions, cut in half
   and thinly sliced

1 scant teaspoon sweet Hungarian
   paprika

6 large red peppers, cored, seeded,
   and cut into medium-thick strips

3 canned Italian plum tomatoes,
   drained and finely chopped

2 teaspoons tomato paste

⅓ cup chicken broth, or more if
   needed

Salt and freshly ground black
   pepper, to taste

1½ tablespoons red wine
   vinegar

⅛ teaspoon sugar, or more
   to taste

1 Heat the oil in a large skillet over medium heat. Add the onions and sauté until softened but not colored, 5 to 7 minutes. Stir in the paprika and toss with the onions until they are deeply colored.

2 Add the peppers and continue to sauté, stirring occasionally, for another 10 minutes. Do not allow the vegetables to brown.

3 Stir in the tomatoes, tomato paste, broth, and salt and pepper. Allow the mixture to boil, reduce the heat, cover, and simmer the peppers until very tender, about 30 to 35 minutes, adding more liquid, a little at a time, if it evaporates.

4 Off the heat, stir in the vinegar and sugar and allow the mixture to cool.

5 This can be served warm, at room temperature, or cold.

Serves 4

Garlic Mashed Potatoes

Kartofelnoye Pyure s Chesnokom

When I was researching this book in Moscow during the last few years, this recipe must have been offered to me by as many as a dozen different people, each one claiming it as their own special preparation for mashed potatoes. I wish I had the time to thank them all separately for their collective culinary knowledge, because this dish really is one of the best ways I know to cook potatoes.

> 2 pounds Idaho potatoes, peeled and
>   quartered
> Salt, to taste
> 7 tablespoons unsalted butter, cut
>   into pieces, at room temperature

> ½ cup sour cream
> 3 large cloves garlic, finely
>   minced

1 Cook the potatoes in plenty of salted boiling water until tender, about 25 minutes. Drain thoroughly.

2 Mash the potatoes, using a potato ricer or a vegetable mill.

3 Stir in 5 tablespoons of the butter, the sour cream, and garlic. Season to taste with salt and beat the potatoes until fluffy. Let stand for 1 hour.

4 Preheat the oven to 350°F.

5 Transfer the mashed potatoes to a buttered round ovenproof casserole, dot with the remaining 2 tablespoons butter, and bake until heated through and the top is golden, about 15 minutes.

Serves 6

Potato Pancakes

Deruni

Known as *deruni* or *dranniki* (both words derive from the verb "to tear into shreds"), potato pancakes are a national obsession in Byelorussia and the neighboring Ukraine. The women in these parts seem to make them day and night (not the greatest task in my view, especially if there's no food processor around), just to observe the time-honored custom that no meal is complete without a pile of hot fresh potato pancakes. Serve with sour cream, bacon cracklings, or sautéed onions.

2 pounds new potatoes, peeled

1 medium-size onion, grated

1 small carrot, peeled and grated

⅓ cup all-purpose flour

¼ cup milk

1 large egg, lightly beaten

¼ teaspoon baking powder

Salt and freshly ground black
pepper, to taste

Light vegetable oil for frying

1 Grate the potatoes coarsely by hand or in a food processor using a coarse grating blade. Squeeze the mixture in a clean linen or cotton (not terry cloth) kitchen towel to remove any excess moisture. Let the mixture stand for 5 minutes and squeeze again. Rinse the potatoes in several changes of cold water. Drain and squeeze again to remove as much moisture as possible.

2 In a bowl, combine the potatoes with the onion and carrot and stir well with a fork. Sprinkle on the flour and mix in. Add the milk, egg, baking powder, and salt and pepper, and mix thoroughly.

3 Heat about ½ inch of oil in a large heavy skillet over medium-high heat. Drop the potato mixture by tablespoonfuls into the oil and press gently with a spatula to flatten. Fry until golden brown on both sides. Transfer to drain on paper towels (if necessary, keep the fried *deruni* warm in a 200°F oven). Repeat the process with the remaining potato mixture. Serve at once.

Serves 4 to 6

New Potatoes Braised in Sour Cream

Molodaya Kartoshka Tushonaya v Smetane

To this basic Salvic recipe, you can add sautéed onions and bacon; ½ ounce reconstituted dried wild mushrooms, sautéed in butter; ½ cup crumbled feta cheese; or 1 small tart apple, peeled and diced. These ingredients should be added with the sour cream in Step 2.

2 pounds new potatoes, the smallest
 available
½ cup chicken broth or water
1 cup sour cream

Salt, to taste
3 cloves garlic, minced
½ cup chopped fresh dill

1 Parboil the potatoes in salted boiling water for 8 minutes. Drain thoroughly.

2 Transfer the potatoes to a heavy heat-proof casserole. Add the broth, sour cream, and salt and bring to a gentle boil. Reduce the heat to low, cover, and simmer, uncovering to stir occasionally, until the potatoes are very tender. Five minutes before the potatoes are finished cooking, stir in the garlic.

3 Toss with the dill and serve.

Serves 4

Grated Potato Bake

Kugelis

A potato pudding from Lithuania, tender and airy inside and crispy on the outside. As you can tell from the name, there are definite affinities with the Jewish kugel, which is, of course, made without the bacon. Serve with sour cream, sautéed onions, or lingonberry preserves.

¼ pound sliced bacon,
 diced
2 large onions, finely chopped
3 pounds new potatoes,
 peeled
1 cup light cream or half-and-
 half

3 large egg yolks, slightly
 beaten
Salt and freshly ground black
 pepper, to taste
2 large egg whites
4 tablespoons (½ stick) unsalted
 butter

1 Sauté the bacon in a medium-size skillet over medium heat until it renders its fat. Remove from the skillet and drain on paper towels.

2 Pour off all but 2 tablespoons of the fat from the skillet. Add the onions and sauté, stirring occasionally, over medium heat until deeply colored, about 15 minutes. Remove from the heat and set aside.

3 Grate the potatoes coarsely by hand or in a food processor using a coarse grating blade. Wash in several changes of water. Squeeze the potatoes well in a clean linen or cotton (not terry cloth) kitchen towel to remove as much liquid as possible. Rinse and squeeze again.

4 In a large bowl, thoroughly combine the potatoes, sautéed onions, bacon, cream, and egg yolks. Season generously with salt and freshly ground black pepper.

5 Preheat the oven to 375°F.

6 Beat the egg whites until stiff. Gently fold into the potato mixture, using a rubber spatula. Carefully transfer the mixture to a well-buttered round 10-inch baking dish or heavy ovenproof skillet. Dot the top with butter.

7 Bake until the top is browned and crispy and the potatoes are tender, 45 minutes to 1 hour.

Serves 6 to 8

Paprika Fries

Zharennaya Kartoshka s Paprikoy

D espite the fact that the Russians eat potatoes far more frequently than those fortunate enough to have a more varied food supply, no one ever seems to tire of fried potatoes. This recipe comes from my mother, who claims she could eat fried potatoes three times a day.

6 medium-size baking potatoes, scrubbed and patted dry
¼ cup light vegetable oil

1½ teaspoons sweet Hungarian paprika, plus additional for garnish
Salt, to taste

1 Cut the potatoes in half lenthwise and cut each half into 4 wedges.

2 In a large, heavy skillet, heat the oil over medium heat. Add the potatoes and cook, stirring frequently until the potatoes are well-colored and soft, about 25 minutes.

3 Sprinkle on the paprika and salt and cook, stirring, for 5 minutes more. Serve at once, sprinkled with additional paprika.

Serves 4

Fried Potatoes with Wild Mushrooms

Zharennaya Kartoshka s Gribami

This is the quintessential Russian *dacha* dish, and many a Russian would kill for it when away from home. Nowhere are the passions of the Russian soul more generously exposed — love for the countryside associated with mushroom picking, a feeling of coziness and comraderie, all the good sentiments of a cherished land. For me the dish never fails to evoke the happiest memories of childhood — of my last summer days at the *dacha*, the height of the mushroom season, a lingering sadness at twilight on Sunday evening with the prospect of returning to Moscow drawing near.

Fortunately, I usually now spend my summers in Vermont with Russian friends, and we can hunt mushrooms as often as we like. We fondly gather up our findings, take them home, and fry them with lots of onions, potatoes, and a touch of sour cream. I must confess that we often eat straight from the skillet, drink vodka from the bottle, and get progressively nostalgic for home by the mouthful. You will understand that cultivated mushrooms just won't do here!

Introducing the Potato

There are several legends concerning the potato's migration to Russia. Some say that like so many comestibles and commodities, it was brought in by Peter the Great in the seventeenth century; others say it was there already, having somehow arrived from North America by an undefined route. Then there are those who maintain that there were no potatoes to speak of until the time of Catherine the Great in the eighteenth century. Contrary to what one might think,

though, the potato was not an instant success, many peasants preferring to stick to the more familiar turnips and rutabagas. But by the nineteenth century it had become a ubiquitously popular staple, particularly in Byelorussia, where a family is often quite content to eat potatoes in different disguises for breakfast, lunch, and dinner.

¾ pound fresh wild mushrooms (such as chanterelles or small boletes)

2 tablespoons unsalted butter

4½ tablespoons vegetable oil

4 medium-size boiling potatoes, peeled and cut into 1½ × ¼-inch sticks

Salt and freshly ground black pepper, to taste

1 cup finely chopped onions

3 tablespoons sour cream

1 Wipe the mushrooms with a damp cloth. Separate the stems from the caps. (The small chanterelles can be left whole.) Cut the stems in half crosswise. Cut the smaller caps in half and the larger ones in quarters.

2 Melt the butter in a medium-size skillet over medium heat. Add the mushrooms and cook, tossing and stirring, until they throw off and reabsorb their liquid, about 12 minutes. Set aside. Wipe out the skillet.

3 Heat 3 tablespoons of the oil in a large skillet over medium heat. Add the potatoes and cook over medium heat for about 5 minutes. Scrape under the bottom layer with a wooden spoon and stir so that the cooked potatoes are on top. Cook the potatoes in this fashion until they are cooked through and deep golden, about 20 minutes. They might stick to the bottom of the skillet a little, so keep scraping them off. Season with salt and pepper.

4 While the potatoes are cooking, heat the remaining oil in another skillet. Add the onions and sauté over medium heat until deeply colored, about 15 minutes.

5 Stir the mushrooms, onions, and sour cream into the potatoes, and toss everything together well. Cook over low heat until the sour cream is heated through, 2 minutes. Serve at once.

Serves 3 to 4

Pumpkin Fritters

Oladyi s Tikvoy

Serve these as a breakfast dish with sour cream, honey, or jam, or as a side dish with a delicate stew, in which case reduce the amount of sugar to ¾ teaspoon.

1½ cups canned solid-pack pumpkin
2 large eggs
¾ cup buttermilk
2 tablespoons unsalted butter, melted
¼ teaspoon salt

1 tablespoon sugar
½ teaspoon baking soda
¾ cup all-purpose flour
Vegetable oil for frying the
*   fritters*

1 Combine the pumpkin, eggs, buttermilk, and melted butter in a large bowl and beat well with a fork.

2 Sift together the dry ingredients and gradually add them to the bowl, beating well until blended. You can also use a food processor to mix the batter.

3 Heat about 2½ teaspoons oil in a large skillet over medium heat, making sure it's evenly distributed over the skillet. Drop the batter by heaping tablespoonfuls into the skillet, adding as many as will fit comfortably. Fry on both sides until golden, 3 to 4 minutes.

4 Repeat the procedure until all the batter is used up, adding more oil as needed.

Makes about 18 fritters to serve 4

Spinach in Yogurt Sauce

Borani

I n the West, spinach is frequently teamed with cream, but in the Caucasus and the Middle East yogurt is considered its natural partner. And in my opinion, it's a better choice, as the tartness of the yogurt provides just the right accent to the bland spinach leaf. Simple and basic, this is one of my favorites. Make sure to take great care when adding the yogurt or it will curdle before you know it.

Borani

O ne of the most common vegetable preparations in the Caucasus and throughout the whole Middle East is *borani*. It can be prepared with almost any vegetable and can be served either hot or cold. My favorite vegetables for making *borani* are spinach, green beans, and okra, although fried eggplant slices, poached cauliflower, or beet greens also work nicely. Cook the vegetables in butter with some onion, garlic, and a dash of hot and sweet paprika. The yogurt should be added at the very end and heated very carefully, if you are serving the *borani* hot.

5 tablespoons unsalted butter

1 medium-size onion, quartered, then thinly sliced

2 large cloves garlic, sliced

2 bunches spinach (about 2 pounds), rinsed thoroughly, patted dry, stemmed, leaves coarsely chopped

½ cup plain low-fat yogurt, or more, to taste

Salt and freshly ground black pepper, to taste

1 Melt the butter in a large, heavy skillet over medium heat. Add the onion and garlic and sauté until softened and transparent, about 7 minutes.

2 Add the spinach and cook, stirring and tossing until the spinach is wilted, about 5 minutes.

3 Remove from the heat and stir in the yogurt and salt and pepper. Return to very low heat and cook stirring, until the yogurt is heated through, 1 minute. Serve at once.

Serves 4

Braised Sauerkraut with Bacon and Wild Mushrooms

Solianka s Gribami

The Slavic way with sauerkraut, in my opinion, far surpasses even the best German and Alsatian preparations in which the cabbage, though often lavishly adorned with all kinds of wurst and sundries, is still usually left to cook on its own. In this recipe the cabbage is skillfully combined with smoky bacon, wild mushrooms, Madeira, and tomato paste; it will make one of the best accompaniments to a pork dish that you have ever tasted.

1 ounce dried wild mushrooms (such as Polish, porcini, or cèpes), well rinsed

6 ounces smoky bacon, diced

¾ cup chopped onion

2 cups shredded green cabbage

2 pounds packaged (not canned) sauerkraut, thoroughly rinsed and drained

½ cup chicken or beef broth

2 tablespoons Madeira

2 teaspoons caraway seeds (optional)

2 tablespoons tomato paste

½ teaspoon sugar, or more to taste

Freshly ground black pepper, to taste

1 Soak the mushrooms in 1 cup water for 1 hour. Drain the mushrooms and pat them dry with paper towels. Chop the mushrooms medium fine. Strain the soaking liquid through a coffee filter and set aside.

2 In a large Dutch oven, sauté the bacon over medium heat for 10 minutes.

3 Drain off all but 3 tablespoons of the bacon fat. Add the onion and mushrooms to the pot and sauté, stirring frequently, over medium heat until the onion begins to turn golden, about 10 minutes.

4 Add the cabbage, toss well, and continue to sauté until the cabbage wilts and begins to color, 10 minutes.

5 Add the sauerkraut and sauté, stirring,

for 5 minutes. Add the reserved soaking liquid, the broth, Madeira, caraway seeds (if desired), and tomato paste. Stir and bring to a low boil, then reduce the heat to low. Add the sugar and pepper, stir well, and simmer, covered, for 45 to 50 minutes. Serve hot.

Serves 4 to 6

Cold Steamed Vegetables with Walnut Sauce

Postneuli Nigvzis Sotsibelit

This version of a Georgian recipe (remember that the Georgians are prepared to dress almost anything in a walnut sauce) makes a great buffet dish and is a real treat for those who love crispy baby vegetables. The sauce also works well as a dip with raw vegetables.

WALNUT SAUCE

¾ cup walnut pieces

2 large cloves garlic

½ small dried chili pepper, seeded

6 small sprigs cilantro

⅛ teaspoon coarse (kosher) salt

1¼ cups Chicken Stock (see Index) or canned broth

½ teaspoon saffron threads, crushed in a mortar and diluted in 1 tablespoon warm water

¼ teaspoon sweet Hungarian paprika

¼ teaspoon ground coriander

¼ teaspoon ground fenugreek

1 tablespoon red wine vinegar

VEGETABLES

1½ pounds mixed vegetables (such as small new potatoes, baby carrots, asparagus, green beans, cauliflower florets, wax beans)

Salt and freshly ground black pepper, to taste

1 To make the sauce, process the walnuts, garlic, chili pepper, cilantro, and coarse salt in a food processor until pulverized.

2 Transfer to a medium-size saucepan, add the chicken broth and slowly bring to a simmer, stirring. Add the saffron, paprika, coriander, fenugreek, and more salt if needed and stir without allowing the mixture to boil, for 3 to 4 minutes. Remove from the heat and stir in the vinegar. Cool and refrigerate, covered, until ready to use.

3 Fill a large pot with 2 inches of salted water and fit with a steamer basket. Bring the water to a boil and steam each vege-

table separately to desired doneness. Refresh under cold running water. Drain well. Pat dry with paper towels and refrigerate, covered, until ready to use, but no more than 1 day.

4 To serve, place a bowl with the walnut sauce in the center of a serving platter. Arrange the vegetables attractively around the bowl.

Serves 8

Vegetarian Medley

Güvetch

The recipe below is for a "complete" *güvetch*, which is to say that it includes all of the prescribed vegetables. You can certainly omit or substitute a few, but you should definitely keep the eggplants, tomatoes, potatoes, okra, and green beans. As with so many dishes in this book, *güvetch* improves in taste and texture if it's made a day in advance. To risk a departure from my culinary region, I must admit that *güvetch* is outstanding over steamed couscous. But it's also excellent with rice or bulgur pilaf. Serve warm or cold, but not hot.

2 small eggplants (about ¾ pound
    total)
Coarse (kosher) salt
About ¾ cup olive oil, or as needed
2 medium-size Bermuda onions, cut
    into quarters, then sliced
2 medium-size carrots, peeled,
    quartered lengthwise, and cut
    into 1½-inch strips
2 ribs celery, chopped
8 medium-size fresh, ripe plum
    tomatoes, peeled, seeded, and
    halved
Bouquet garni (6 sprigs fresh thyme,
    6 sprigs fresh parsley, 6 sprigs
    fresh dill, and 1 bay leaf tied in
    a cheesecloth bag)

2 large baking potatoes, peeled and
    cut into large cubes
Vegetable Stock (see Index)
    or water
6 ounces fresh okra, stemmed
½ pound fresh green beans,
    trimmed
1 large zucchini, cut into large
    dice
4 cloves garlic, sliced
Salt and freshly ground black
    pepper, to taste
1½ cups drained canned or cooked
    chick-peas or white beans
2 teaspoons red wine vinegar
1 teaspoon sugar, or more
    to taste

1 Wash and stem the eggplants. Cut into 1-inch cubes. Place in a colander and toss with coarse salt. Let stand for 30 minutes.

2 Meanwhile, heat about 2 tablespoons of the oil in a large skillet over medium heat. Add the onions and sauté, stirring occasionally, until softened, about 7 minutes. If you are going to cook the *güvetch* in the oven, transfer the onions to a large earthenware casserole with a lid that can accommodate all the vegetables. If you are cooking it on top of the stove, transfer them to a large pot.

3 Add the carrots and the celery to the skillet, toss to coat with oil, and cook, covered, until the carrots begin to soften, about 10 minutes. Add them to the onions.

4 Add oil to the skillet to a depth of ½ inch. Rinse the eggplant and pat thoroughly dry with paper towels. Add to the oil and cook, stirring occasionally, until deep golden on all sides and softened, 15 minutes. Transfer them to the casserole.

5 If cooking the *güvetch* in the oven, preheat the oven to 375°F.

6 Add the tomatoes, bouquet garni, potatoes, and enough stock to barely cover the vegetables. Place the *güvetch* in the oven or cook on top of the stove over medium heat for 10 minutes. Reduce the oven temperature to 325°F or reduce the burner heat to low. Simmer, covered, for 40 minutes.

7 Add the okra, green beans, zucchini, 3 of the garlic cloves, and salt and pepper. Cover and simmer for another 35 minutes.

8 Off the heat, stir in the chick-peas, vinegar, sugar, and remaining garlic and simmer for 5 minutes more. Taste and correct the seasoning and remove the bouquet garni. Cool, cover, and refrigerate.

9 Bring to room temperature or rewarm before serving. Serve either warm or at room temperature.

Serves 8 to 10 people as a side dish

Güvetch

Throughout the entire Balkan region, from southern Romania to western Turkey, where the dish's name originates, *güvetch* designates an artfully complex mélange of root and green vegetables slowly simmered together to produce one of those dishes that are referred to as "basic" — in the very best sense of the word. Before I tasted my first real *güvetch* in Odessa on the Black Sea, I thought that the term actually referred to a similarly named packet of frozen vegetables (tomatoes, green beans, and okra) imported into Russia from Bulgaria. And, despite a few protests to the contrary, I later discovered that a rather random combination of vegetables quickly thrown together at the last minute is far from constituting an authentic *güvetch*. The real thing requires a few tricks and a little time, but the end result is well worth the effort, especially as *güvetch* is usually made in large quantities to last for several days. It also tastes much, much better when cooked in an earthenware casserole; but if you don't have one large enough, you can easily cook it on top of the stove.

Zucchini-Cheese Patties

Kabak Mucver

The Turkish name for this dish, which I first tasted in western Anatolia, is *kabak mucver*. But it is even better in Armenia where it is made with aged and salty local sheep's cheese, *chanakh*, for which the Greek kasseri makes a good substitute. The patties should be eaten slightly warm, accompanied by Yogurt and Garlic Sauce.

3 zucchini (about 8 ounces each),
    peeled and grated
Salt
1½ tablespoons unsalted
    butter
¾ cup finely chopped onion
6 ounces kasseri cheese,
    grated

½ cup all-purpose flour
2 large eggs, beaten
Freshly ground black pepper,
    to taste
Light vegetable oil for frying
Yogurt and Garlic Sauce (see
    Index)

1 In a colander, toss the zucchini with 1 teaspoon salt. Let stand for 30 minutes. Rinse thoroughly under cold running water. Drain and squeeze the zucchini to remove the excess water and pat dry on paper towels. Place the zucchini in a bowl.

2 Melt the butter in a large skillet over medium heat. Add the onion and sauté, stirring, until softened, about 7 minutes. Cool slightly, then add the onion, cheese, and dill to the zucchini in the bowl. Stir well to combine.

3 Beat the flour together with the eggs

and add to the zucchini mixture. Mix well and season with salt and pepper.

4 Measure enough oil into a large skillet to come up about ½ inch. Heat the oil until very hot. Drop about 1½ tablespoons of the batter into the skillet for each patty, spacing them about 1 inch apart. Pat the patties lightly with a spatula to flatten. Fry until golden on both sides.

5 Cool and serve with the Yogurt and Garlic Sauce.

Serves 6

STUFFED VEGETABLES

Eggplant Stuffed with Meat

Missov Simpoghi Dolma

Plump eggplants take well to stuffing and lamb is a traditional stuffing ingredient. I offer two different versions here. The first, *keyma*, is a traditional variation. The second, *tas kebab*, comes from the Ararat Dardanelles, a superior Armenian restaurant in Manhattan. Both are delicious.

3 tablespoons olive oil

2 eggplants (about 1 pound each),
    stemmed and halved lengthwise

Salt and freshly ground black
    pepper, to taste

Keyma *or* tas kebab *for stuffing the
    eggplants (recipes follow)*

1½ cups tomato juice

½ teaspoon sweet Hungarian
    paprika

2 tablespoons lemon juice

2 large fresh, ripe tomatoes, peeled
    and sliced

Parsley sprigs for garnish

1 Heat the olive oil over medium heat in an ovenproof casserole large enough to accommodate all the eggplant in one layer. Add the eggplants, cut side up, and sauté until the shells are softened, about 10 minutes. Remove the eggplant and pour off half the remaining oil from the casserole. Allow the eggplants to cool until manageable.

2 Preheat the oven to 350°F.

3 Hollow out each eggplant half, leaving a ¼-inch-thick shell all around. Sprinkle the shells generously with salt and pepper. Reserve the eggplant pulp for another use.

4 Stuff the eggplants with either the *tas kebab* or *keyma* stuffing. Place the stuffed eggplant halves in the casserole.

5 In a small bowl, mix together the tomato juice, paprika, lemon juice, and a sprinkling of salt and pepper. Pour the mixture over the eggplants. Top each half with some of the tomato slices and bake, basting occasionally with the cooking liquid, until the eggplants are tender and the stuffing is cooked through, about 45 minutes.

6 Arrange the eggplant on a serving platter and garnish with the parsley.

Serves 4

Ground Lamb Stuffing

Keyma

3 tablespoons olive oil
12 ounces ground lamb
¼ cup pine nuts (pignoli)
4 canned Italian plum tomatoes, drained, seeded, and finely chopped
¼ to ½ teaspoon sweet Hungarian paprika
¼ teaspoon hot Hungarian paprika

1 tablespoon tomato paste
⅛ teaspoon ground allspice
Small pinch of cinnamon
⅓ cup beef broth or water
Salt and freshly ground black pepper, to taste
¼ cup finely chopped fresh parsley

1 Heat the oil in a large heavy skillet over medium heat. Add the lamb and sauté, breaking up the pieces with the back of a spoon, until it is no longer pink, about 10 minutes.

2 Add all the remaining ingredients except the parsley, cover, and simmer until cooked through, 20 minutes. Stir in the parsley before stuffing the vegetables.

Makes enough to stuff 2 large eggplants

Lamb Stewed in Tomato Sauce

Tas Kebab

1 pound boneless lean leg of lamb,
    cut into ¾-inch cubes
Salt and freshly ground black
    pepper, to taste
1½ tablespoons all-purpose flour
1 tablespoon unsalted butter
2 tablespoons olive oil
1 cup chopped onions
2 cloves garlic, minced
2 medium-size fresh, ripe tomatoes,
    peeled and finely chopped
1 tablespoon tomato paste
½ cup Lamb Stock (see Index) or
    canned beef broth
1 bay leaf
¼ teaspoon dried thyme
½ teaspoon sweet Hungarian
    paprika
½ teaspoon hot Hungarian
    paprika
¼ cup finely chopped fresh parsley

1 Sprinkle the lamb pieces with salt and pepper and dust with the flour. Set aside.

2 Heat the butter and olive oil over medium-high heat in a large heavy skillet. Add the lamb and sauté, stirring, until brown on all sides, about 10 minutes. Add the onions and continue to cook, stirring,

Vegetables to Stuff

In the Soviet Union, the following vegetables are favorites for stuffing. Once you choose a vegetable, select a complementary stuffing—ground meat; flavored rice or bulgur; barley or buckwheat with wild mushrooms; finely chopped vegetables simmered in tomato sauce; millet and bacon cracklings; and cheese are just some of the possibilities. Stuff the vegetables and bake them in the oven, drizzled with olive oil, or simmer them on top of the stove in a flavorful sauce. Let your imagination be your guide.

Artichokes

Cabbage leaves

Eggplants

Green and red bell peppers

Mushroom caps

Onions

Potatoes

Swiss chard

Tomatoes

Yellow squash

Zucchini

until the onions are colored, about 10 minutes more.

3 Stir in the garlic, tomatoes, and tomato paste and cook, stirring, for about 5 minutes. Add the stock, bay leaf, thyme, sweet and hot paprika, chopped parsley, and additional salt and pepper, if desired. Reduce the heat to low and simmer, covered, until the meat is tender, about 1 hour. Remove the bay leaf.

Makes enough to stuff 2 large eggplants

Stuffed Vegetables
Dolma

Stuffed vegetables are commonly served throughout the USSR in one or another of their tempting varieties. These *dolma* (stuffed dishes) were first introduced into Russia by the Turks. While the Slavs were busy fending off Ottoman military incursions, they seemed happy to absorb the culinary influences of their invader. Ukrainian stuffed cabbage, *holubtsi* (which means "little doves") clearly shows how a Middle Eastern dish is cunningly adapted to Slavic tastes by using local ingredients: cabbage leaves, pork for stuffing, and sour cream for flavoring.

The very best Soviet stuffed dishes, however, are still found in the Caucasus. The Armenian art of vegetable stuffing is as refined as any in the world. Any vegetable or fruit that can be hollowed out or wrapped around a filling can be used for *dolma*. There are appetizer *dolmas* of peppers and grape leaves stuffed with an aromatic mixture of rice, pine nuts, dried fruit, currants, and spices; the spectacular *Echmiadzin dolma* — a colorful bounty of seasonal vegetables stuffed with meat and rice and simmered in a tart sauce; or an exotic dish of stuffed apples and quinces, called *Ashtarak dolma*.

For those unfamiliar with these delights, they will come as a true surprise and a wonderful discovery — their healthy, colorful, and tasty combination of flavors fits into almost any menu, and seduces the most discerning guests equally as it pleases at the family table.

Vegetable-Stuffed Zucchini with Feta Cheese Sauce

Dovlecei Umplut cu Zarzavaturi

This typical Moldavian dish of zucchini stuffed with various vegetables under a piquant feta cheese sauce makes a delightful vegetarian entrée. The stuffing and sauce also work well with green bell peppers or yellow squash. This dish can also be served cold.

6 large zucchini

6 tablespoons olive oil

3 medium-size carrots, peeled and
  cut into ¼-inch dice

2 cups chopped onions

2 ribs celery, cut into ¼-inch dice

2 tablespoons tomato paste

3 tablespoons chopped fresh parsley,
  plus additional for garnish

2 tablespoons chopped fresh dill

Salt and freshly ground black
  pepper, to taste

1¾ cups tomato juice

¾ teaspoon sugar, or more to taste

1½ tablespoons cider vinegar

1 cup crumbled feta cheese, prefer-
  ably Bulgarian

1 Rinse the zucchini and pat dry with paper towels. Cut the zucchini lengthwise in half. Using a melon baller scoop out the pulp, leaving a ¼-inch shell. Chop the pulp and set both pulp and shells aside.

2 Heat 4 tablespoons of the oil in a large skillet over medium heat. Add the carrots and sauté, stirring occasionally, about 5 minutes. Add the onions, celery, and zucchini pulp and sauté, stirring, until all the vegetables are soft and colored, about 20 minutes. Stir in the tomato paste and sauté for 3 to 4 minutes more.

3 Off the heat, stir in 3 tablespoons parsley and the dill and season with salt and pepper.

4 In a flat-bottomed heatproof casserole that will accommodate all the zucchini in one layer, heat the remaining 2 tablespoons oil over medium-high heat. Add the zucchini shells and sauté until the shells are browned, 8 to 10 minutes.

5 Sprinkle the insides of the zucchini shells with salt, and stuff loosely with the vegetable mixture. (Add any leftover stuffing to the cooking sauce, see Step 7.)

6 Meanwhile, preheat the oven to 375°F.

7 Mix the tomato juice with the sugar, vinegar, and salt and pepper. Pour over the zucchini and bring to a boil over medium-high heat. Place in the oven and bake, basting occasionally with the cook-

ing liquid, until the liquid reduces and the zucchini are tender, about 45 minutes. Sprinkle with the feta cheese and bake until the top is browned, 10 minutes longer.

8 Sprinkle with parsley before serving.

Serves 6

Stuffed Cabbage

Golubtsi

This version of the familiar Eastern European classic comes from an American gourmet of Russian stock, so it goes by its Russian name instead of the Ukrainian *holubtsi*. The cabbage rolls are topped with béchamel sauce and Parmesan cheese, and finished in the oven. You can, however, omit the béchamel and Parmesan and serve the *golubtsi* with sour cream on the side — this is how it's usually done in Russia.

STUFFING

1 tablespoon unsalted butter

1 large onion, chopped

6 ounces ground beef

6 ounces ground pork

½ cup long-grain rice

2 tablespoons ketchup

⅓ cup canned beef broth or water

2 tablespoons chopped fresh dill

2 tablespoons chopped fresh parsley

Salt and freshly ground black pepper, to taste

CABBAGE AND SAUCE

12 to 14 large green cabbage
*   leaves*

Salt, to taste

¼ cup vegetable oil

¼ cup all-purpose flour

2 cups Beef Stock (see Index)
*   or canned broth, or more*
*   if needed*

3 tablespoons tomato paste

2 tablespoons ketchup

1½ teaspoons (firmly packed) brown
*   sugar, or more to taste*

Freshly ground black pepper, to
*   taste*

¾ cup thin Béchamel Sauce (see
*   Index)*

¼ cup freshly grated Parmesan
*   cheese*

1 Melt the butter in a small skillet over medium heat. Add the onion and sauté, stirring occasionally, until lightly colored, about 10 minutes.

2 In a large bowl, combine the meats, onion, and remaining stuffing ingredients. Knead until the mixture is thoroughly blended. Set aside.

3 Scald the cabbage leaves in a pot of salted boiling water for about 5 minutes. Drain thoroughly and pat dry with paper towels.

4 With a sharp knife, cut out the tough center vein from each cabbage leaf. Divide the stuffing into equal portions. Place a

Moldavian Stuffed Cabbage

Stuffed cabbage is a favorite throughout the Soviet Union and it is prepared in a great variety of ways. One of my favorite preparations comes from Moldavia, where it is made with pickled cabbage leaves, producing a wonderful tart yet sweet dish, perfect for a winter evening. Lacking a whole pickled cabbage, I stuff the meat into fresh cabbage leaves and add sauerkraut to the cooking liquid.

Prepare the stuffed cabbage as directed in the *golubtsi* recipe. Sauté the rolls in oil and add 1½ cups drained fresh (in bags, not canned) sauerkraut and a 16-ounce can of chopped plum tomatoes to the cooking liquid. Simmer for 1½ hours, then adjust the amount of sugar to taste. Serve sour cream on the side and accompany the dish with a good Alsatian Riesling.

portion on the base of each leaf, tuck in the sides, and roll the leaves up, tucking in the sides firmly as you roll.

5 In a large heatproof casserole or Dutch oven that will accommodate all the rolls, heat the oil over medium heat for 1 minute. Spread the flour on a plate and roll the cabbage rolls in it, then place them in the casserole, seam side down. Brown the rolls on all sides until deeply colored, about 15 minutes.

6 Heat the stock in a small saucepan over medium heat. Stir in the tomato paste, ketchup, and sugar, then season with salt and pepper. Add the mixture to the casserole. The liquid should cover the rolls completely (if it doesn't just add more stock). Bring to a boil over high heat, then reduce the heat to low, cover, and simmer for 25 minutes.

7 Meanwhile, preheat the oven to 375°F.

8 Increase the heat under the casserole to high, uncover, and let the liquid boil until it is somewhat reduced, about 5 minutes. Place the casserole in the oven and bake, uncovered, until the liquid reduces even further, about 15 minutes.

9 Spread the béchamel evenly over the rolls, sprinkle with the grated Parmesan, and bake, uncovered, until the top is nicely browned, 10 minutes longer. Serve the cabbage rolls at once.

Serves 4 to 6

Mixed Stuffed Vegetables

Echmiadzin Dolma

The town of Echmiadzin, with its ancient cathedral, is the seat of the Catholicos, the head of the Armenian Orthodox church, and is the religious capital of Armenia. I often serve this namesake dish during the summer — the combination of zucchini, peppers, and eggplants looks extremely festive on the platter, and the stuffing, which I make from mixed pork and beef with rice and heaps of fresh herbs, is wonderfully flavorful. A fresh garden salad complements the dish perfectly. And it is usually served with a yogurt sauce.

STUFFING

½ pound ground pork

¾ pound ground beef

½ cup long-grain rice

4 canned Italian plum tomatoes,
  drained and finely chopped

1 cup finely chopped onions

⅓ cup ice water

1 teaspoon sweet Hungarian paprika

1 cup mixed finely chopped fresh
  herbs (such as mint, basil,
  cilantro, parsley, or dill)

Salt and freshly ground black
  pepper, to taste

VEGETABLES AND SAUCE

8 medium-size fresh, ripe tomatoes

4 baby eggplants

4 small zucchini

4 large Italian (pale green frying)
  peppers

Salt, to taste

2 beef marrow bones, about 1 pound

½ cup Italian plum tomatoes,
  drained and finely chopped

1 small quince, diced (optional)

1 small tart apple (such as Granny
  Smith), diced

Juice of ½ lemon

Chopped fresh parsley (for garnish)

Chopped fresh mint (for garnish)

Yogurt and Garlic Sauce (see Index)

1 In a large bowl, combine all the stuffing ingredients. Knead until the mixture is thoroughly blended.

Autumn Harvest Luncheon

Lentil and Spinach Soup

•

Mixed Stuffed Vegetables

Yogurt and Garlic Sauce

Herbed Basmati Rice Pilaf

Retsina

•

Sour Cherry Meringue Pie

• • •

2 Cut the stem ends off the fresh tomatoes and scoop out the pulp with a melon baller, leaving a ¼-inch shell. Similarly, cut the stem ends off the eggplants and zucchini and scoop out the pulp using an apple corer. Core, seed, and derib the

Italian peppers. Sprinkle the insides of the tomatoes and zucchini with salt. Reserve the various pulps for another use.

3 Stuff the vegetables compactly with the stuffing, up to about ¼ inch from the tops, as the stuffing will expand during the cooking.

4 Arrange the eggplants, zucchini, and marrow bones (which will make the broth flavorful) in the bottom of a 4-quart stock pot. Place the peppers and tomatoes on top. Add the chopped tomatoes, quince, if using, the apple, lemon juice, and salt. Place a plate over the vegetables, and weight it down with a small heavy bowl. Add enough water to cover and bring to a quick boil. Reduce the heat to low, cover, and simmer until the vegetables and fruit are cooked through, about 45 minutes to 1 hour.

5 Allow the vegetables to cool just slightly in the broth, then remove carefully with a slotted spoon and arrange on a serving platter. Spoon the chopped apple and quince over the vegetables, and sprinkle with 5 to 6 tablespoons of the broth and with fresh herbs.

6 Serve with the Yogurt and Garlic Sauce on the side.

Serves 6 to 8

Roasted Red Peppers Stuffed with Feta

Ardei Rosii Umplut cu Brinza

———— ❧ ————

The combination of red peppers with a zesty feta, butter, and garlic mixture is unmistakably Moldavian and unfailingly delicious. These peppers should be served cold as an appetizer, or luncheon or supper dish. You can also fill hollowed out cherry tomatoes with the stuffing for a delectable summer hors d'oeuvre.

6 large red bell peppers, cored,
    seeded, and deribbed
½ pound feta cheese, preferably
    Bulgarian, crumbled into pieces
6 tablespoons (¾ stick) unsalted
    butter, at room temperature
4 ounces cream cheese, at room
    temperature
3 cloves garlic, chopped
2 tablespoons chopped fresh chives
2 tablespoons chopped fresh
    parsley
¼ cup finely chopped walnuts
½ teaspoon sweet Hungarian
    paprika
1 tablespoon extra virgin olive oil

1 Preheat the broiler.

2 Broil the peppers on a baking sheet, 2 inches from the heat, turning several times, until the peppers are softened and the skins are blistered and charred, about 20 minutes. Wrap the peppers in a clean linen towel and let steam for 15 minutes. Keeping the peppers whole, peel of the skins.

3 Combine the remaining ingredients except the oil in a food processor and process until smooth.

4 Stuff the peppers with the feta mixture as compactly as you can. Arrange on a serving platter, drizzle with the olive oil and refrigerate for at least 1 hour before serving.

Serves 6

Late Summer Vegetarian Buffet

Eggplants Stuffed with Walnuts

Roasted Red Peppers Stuffed with Feta

White Beans *Plaki*

Cold Bulgur and Vegetable Pilaf

Phyllo Turnovers with Spinach and Tahini Filling

White Zinfandel

•

Fruit and Berry Compote

Butter Cookies

• • •

Stuffed Apples and Quinces

Ashtarak Dolma

Yet another delectable stuffed dish from the Caucasus. Make this in the fall when ripe, sweet-smelling quinces are available. Quince pulp is tough, so it should be removed, carefully, with a sharp knife.

Salt, to taste

¼ cup long-grain rice

4 small tart apples (such as Granny Smith)

4 small quinces

4 tablespoons fresh lemon juice

6 ounces lean ground lamb shoulder

6 ounces lean ground beef

1 medium-size onion, finely chopped

½ cup canned Italian plum tomatoes, well drained and chopped

1 large egg, slightly beaten

¼ cup finely chopped fresh mint, plus additional for garnish

3 tablespoons finely chopped fresh basil, plus additional for garnish

Freshly ground black pepper, to taste

½ cup dried apricots, preferably California

8 pitted dried prunes

¼ teaspoon ground cinnamon

2 cups Beef Stock (see Index) or canned broth, or more if needed

Yogurt and Garlic Sauce (see Index)

1 In a saucepan, bring 2 cups of salted water to a boil. Add the rice and cook, covered, over high heat until almost cooked but still hard to the bite, 15 minutes. Drain well.

2 Cut the stem ends off the apples and quinces, and reserve. With a sharp knife, scoop out the pulp, leaving a ½-inch shell in each fruit. Sprinkle the insides with 1 tablespoon of the lemon juice and salt and set aside.

3 In a large bowl, combine the meats, onion, tomatoes, egg, ¼ cup mint, 3 tablespoons basil, and the rice. Season with salt and pepper, then knead, until the mixture is thoroughly blended.

4 Preheat the oven to 350°F.

5 Spoon the stuffing into the fruits and cover with the reserved stem ends. Arrange them in a flat-bottomed, ovenproof casserole large enough to accommodate the fruits in one layer. Scatter the dried fruits and the apple and quince pulp around the stuffed fruits. Combine the remaining 3 tablespoons lemon juice and the cinnamon with 2 cups stock. Pour around the stuffed fruits, adding more stock as needed to almost cover. Cover the casserole and bake until the fruits are tender, about 1 hour.

6 Carefully lift the fruits from the liquid with a slotted spoon and arrange them on a serving platter. Spoon the cooking liquid and dried fruit over them and sprinkle with additional chopped herbs. Pass the Yogurt and Garlic Sauce.

Serves 4

Stuffed Pumpkin

Titoumi Dolma

This spectacular Armenian pumpkin recipe can be the centerpiece of any Thanksgiving table. The pumpkin is stuffed with rice, apples, raisins, and sour cherries, then baked. To serve, cut into wedges and serve with the stuffing.

1 pumpkin (about 4 pounds)

1½ cups long-grain rice

2 large tart apples (such as Granny Smith), peeled, cored, and diced

½ cup golden raisins

½ cup dried sour cherries (available at specialty food stores)

8 tablespoons (1 stick) unsalted butter, melted

1 tablespoon sugar, or more to taste

¾ teaspoon ground cinnamon, or more to taste

Salt, to taste

¼ cup hot water

1 Cut out the stem end of the pumpkin in a circle about 4 inches in diameter. Reserve. Scoop out the seeds with a large spoon and rinse the inside of the pumpkin carefully. Pat dry. With a grapefruit spoon or other small spoon, or with a melon baller, scoop out as much flesh as possible around the pumpkin, being careful not to penetrate the skin. Chop the flesh and set aside.

2 In a large saucepan, bring 3 quarts of salted water to a boil. Add the rice and cook, covered, over high heat until almost cooked but still slightly hard to the bite, 15 minutes. Drain well.

3 Meanwhile, preheat the oven to 325°F.

4 In a large bowl, combine the rice with the chopped pumpkin, apples, raisins, dried cherries, and the melted butter. Season with sugar, cinnamon, and salt, and mix thoroughly.

5 Spoon the stuffing loosely into the

Stuffed Squash

You can also make this delicious and original dish in individual portions, using acorn squash halves. Just hollow them out, chop the squash, combine it with the rice stuffing, and refill the shells. Cover with aluminum foil and bake until tender, about 1 hour.

pumpkin, sprinkle with the hot water, and close tightly with the reserved "lid." Place the pumpkin on a baking sheet and bake until the pumpkin is tender when you prick it with the point of a knife, about 2 hours. Cut into wedges and serve.

Serves 8

Rice-Stuffed Grape Leaves

Yalanchi Sarma

If you are tired of the often soggy, uninspiring stuffed vine leaves sold at delis or produced from the can, then try this Armenian version with pine nuts, dried currants, and delicate seasoning. The Armenian cooks I know prefer the *Orlando* or *Yergat* brands of vine leaf.

1 jar (16 ounces) vine leaves (grape
    leaves), preserved in brine
6 tablespoons olive oil
1 cup finely chopped onions
½ cup long-grain rice
2 tablespoons tomato paste
3 tablespoons dried currants
Juice of ½ lemon
¾ cup water
Salt, to taste
¼ cup toasted pine nuts (pignoli; see
    box, next page)
½ teaspoon sugar
½ teaspoon ground allspice
¼ teaspoon ground cinnamon
5 tablespoons finely chopped fresh
    parsley
1½ cups Yogurt and Garlic Sauce
    (see Index)

Meat-Stuffed Grape Leaves

Grape leaves stuffed with meat is a very
popular dish in the Soviet Union,
where it is prepared often in the Caucasus
and Central Asia. To prepare it, follow the
instructions for Rice-Stuffed Grape Leaves,
but use the stuffing from Mixed Stuffed Vegetables, using either a combination of beef
and pork, or beef and lamb. Meat stuffed
grape leaves should be cooked in chicken or
beef stock for 35 to 40 minutes. Serve the
dish with Yogurt and Garlic Sauce.

1 Trim the stems from the leaves. Scald
the leaves in boiling water for 1 minute.
Rinse under cold running water, then drain
thoroughly. Set aside until ready to use.

2 Heat the oil in a medium-size saucepan over medium heat for 1 minute. Add
the onions and sauté, stirring occasionally, until they just begin to color, about 5
minutes. Add the rice, tomato paste, currants, and lemon juice and stir for 1 to 2
minutes. Add the water and salt and bring
to a boil. Reduce the heat to low and simmer, covered, just until the rice has absorbed all the liquid, about 15 minutes.
The rice should be slightly hard to the bite.

3 Off the heat, stir in the pine nuts,

sugar, allspice, cinnamon, and parsley,
until thoroughly mixed.

4 To stuff, place a leaf, dull side up, on
a flat surface. Place about a teaspoon of the
stuffing near the stem end. Turn the sides
in and roll up into a neat "package." Press
the end of the leaf into the roll; it should
adhere easily. Repeat with the remaining
leaves and stuffing.

5 Line the bottom of a casserole with a
few leaves so the stuffed leaves won't stick
to the bottom during cooking. Arrange the
stuffed leaves side by side in two or three
layers. Cover with a plate, and, holding
the plate tightly in place, add enough
salted water to cover.

6 Bring quickly to a boil over high heat. Reduce the heat, cover, and simmer for 25 to 30 minutes.

7 Remove the stuffed leaves carefully from the liquid with a slotted spoon. Cool to room temperature.

8 Arrange the stuffed leaves on a serving platter and serve with the Yogurt and Garlic Sauce.

Makes about 35 stuffed leaves, to serve 8 to 10 as an appetizer

Toasting Pine Nuts

To toast pine nuts, preheat the oven to 350°F. Spread the pine nuts in one layer on a baking sheet and toast, stirring once or twice, until the pine nuts are golden, about 5 minutes. Watch the nuts closely during the toasting to prevent them from burning.

Baltic Stuffed Potatoes

Farshirovanniy Kartofel po-Pribaltiyski

These potatoes, stuffed with wild mushrooms and sprats, are substantial enough to constitute a luncheon entrée. Sprats are available at many supermarkets, but you can use good-quality sardines instead.

6 imported dried wild mushrooms (such as porcini), well rinsed
4 large baking potatoes
Salt and freshly ground black pepper, to taste
6 tablespoons (¾ stick) unsalted butter
½ cup chopped onion

8 large canned sprats, or 4 large sardines, packed in oil
¼ cup sour cream
2 tablespoons fresh lemon juice
3 tablespoons finely chopped fresh dill
1¼ cup freshly grated Parmesan cheese

1 Soak the dried mushrooms in 1 cup water for 2 hours. Remove the mushrooms from the soaking liquid, pat dry with paper towels, chop fine, and set aside. Discard the liquid or save for another use.

2 Preheat the oven to 400°F.

3 Scrub, rinse, and dry the potatoes. Bake until tender when you pierce them with a knife, about 1¼ hours. Lower the oven temperature to 375°F.

4 When the potatoes are cool enough to handle, cut a slice off the top of each and scoop the pulp into a bowl, leaving a ¼-inch shell. Sprinkle the potato shells with salt and pepper and set aside. Mash the potato pulp and reserve.

5 Melt 2 tablespoons of the butter in a small skillet over medium heat. Add the onion and mushrooms and sauté, stirring occasionally, until lightly colored, about 10 minutes.

6 Mash the sprats with the back of a fork in a large bowl. Add the potato pulp, sauteéd onion and mushrooms, sour cream, lemon juice, dill, and salt and pepper, and mix thoroughly.

7 Stuff the sprat mixture into the reserved potato shells. Top each with a tablespoon of the remaining butter and sprinkle with Parmesan. Bake until the potatoes are hot and the tops are lightly browned, 15 minutes. Serve immediately.

Serves 4

Georgian Cuisine

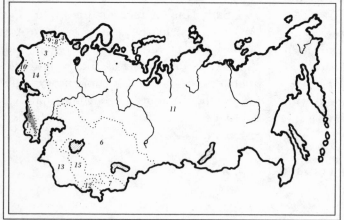

1. ARMENIA
2. AZERBAIJAN
3. BYELORUSSIA
4. ESTONIA
5. GEORGIA
6. KAZAKHSTAN
7. KIRGHIZIA
8. LATVIA
9. LITHUANIA
10. MOLDAVIA
11. RUSSIA
12. TADZHIKISTAN
13. TURKMENIA
14. UKRAINE
15. UZBEKISTAN

There's really no doubt that of all the republics, Georgia is the most popular among Soviet people. Many factors contribute to their fascination with this exotic and foreign yet inviting land. Its exhilarating scenery pits the dramatic Caucasus mountains against long, luxurious plains and great, turbulent rivers. And, the celebrated Black Sea coast attracts thousands of vacationers and dignitaries, many of whom, including Khruschev and Stalin (Georgia's most infamous son), had dachas in the breathtaking seaside town of Pitsunda.

Georgian lifestyle is the envy and marvel of many Soviets. Always the most independent of the republics, it's rumored to have produced an unlikely number of underground millionaires. A particularly extravagant Georgian woman once told me how she used to fly all the way from Tbilisi, the Georgian capital, to Moscow (over a thousand miles) just to satisfy her craving for certain deluxe chocolates available only in the official stores.

Most of the time, though, it's the Russians who travel to Georgia to experience its unique atmosphere, and just as important, to sample its outstanding cuisine. The excellence of any cuisine depends in great part on the quality of a region's fresh products. The abundance of culinary ingredients in subtropical Georgia is unparalleled in the USSR and matched in Europe only by the most fecund regions of the Mediterranean. The fertile soil produces acres of luscious citrus fruits, pomegranates, walnuts, figs, corn, beans, and herbs; and the region's ancient ways of cattle breeding and cheese making provide superb meat and dairy products.

These mouth-watering natural riches, along with unique and time-honored culinary methods, make Georgian cuisine the most sought after in the entire Soviet nation. Sophisticated Muscovites and initiated visitors alike prize Moscow's numerous Georgian restaurants above all others. But the best place to experience the full flavor and the distinctive setting of a Georgian meal is undoubtedly in the republic itself, and particularly in Tbilisi, justly considered the culinary capital of the USSR. Nowhere else in the world can you taste such piquant aromatic sauces; have your meats marinated and grilled to such perfection; or enjoy such a variety of local cheeses and breads, sometimes combined in the famous cheese pie called *khachapuri.* To top it all, Georgian dishes offer great nutritional value. Simply grilled meats, sauces made exclusively from vegetables, fruits, and nuts, and the renowned Georgian yogurt—*matsoni*—exist in a healthy alliance with the sprightly mountain air.

A Proud Culture

A visit to Georgia, however, is much more than a pure indulgence of the senses. Georgia has one of the most ancient cultures in Europe and the Near East, dating back to Jason's legendary quest for the Golden Fleece, which ended up in Colchis, to the east of the Black Sea. Georgia also has a fascinating written language, which has been traced back to the fifth century (some four hundred years before the development of the Cyrillic script) and which is apparently based on Aramaic, the language of Christ. As a child, I was often intrigued by the sinuous script of Georgian bottle labels, as dense and enticing as the filigrees of vines and branches in the background. The high point of Georgian literary culture came in the eleventh and twelfth centuries when Shota Rustăveli, whose humanistic ideals preempted some of the concerns of the Western European Renaissance, wrote *The Knight in a Tiger's Skin.* Most impressive of all, perhaps, are the sumptuous examples of Byzantine architecture, painting, and metalwork that still survive in most parts of the republic — compelling testimonies of a powerful indigenous culture much given to religious ritual and ceremony as well as secular celebrations.

The term "Georgian" is actually rather confusing, because more than fifteen Caucasian nations inhabit the full extent of Georgian territory. The landscape alternates between mountains and lowlands and historically there was little communication among regions, so many languages and traditions have remained unchanged — in some cases for thousands of years. This accounts both for the regional differences in Georgian cuisine and for the longevity of their culinary traditions. The Khartleli people who live in and around Tbilisi consider themselves the purest Georgians. They tend to disparage the other nationalities, vaunting their own blood, culture, and cuisine above all the rest.

Unparalleled Hospitality

The essential trait that unites all of these peoples is their almost obsessive dedication to hospitality, now legendary throughout the USSR. My father, who could sometimes be misanthropic in his attitude toward guests and society in our small Moscow apartment, would return from one of his seemingly compulsive trips to the Georgian Highlands loaded down with foodstuffs given to him by the families he had stayed with. I still remember eagerly unpacking rows of fragrant tangerines; round after round of stringy *suluguni* cheese; packets of *khmeli-suneli* (an exotic blend of dried spices and herbs required for many of the best Georgian dishes); *basturma* (a smoked spicy beef); and tall green bottles of homemade Isabella wine, made from young Concord-type grapes.

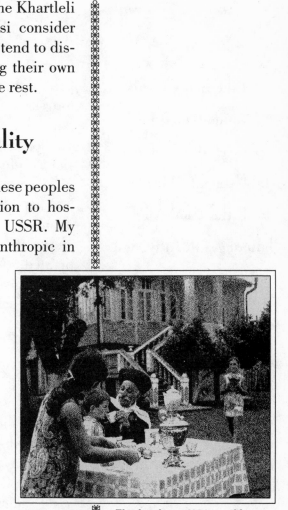

This handsome 107-year-old Georgian serves tea from a samovar to his young guests.

But my father brought back more than these tantalizing foods. Georgian hospitality used to take hold of him, and for weeks after his return we would find him practically dragging people in off the streets for food, conversation, and drinks. I often remember being kept awake for half the night by the conviviality in the next room. Pushkin aptly noted that in Georgia, a guest becomes a "holy person."

"Like many of his
compatriots, he
possessed an inborn
'table-talent.' He spoke
all the Caucasian
languages fluently, and
the toasts he made
never needed a
translation."

—Fazil Iskander
The Goatibex Constellation

Once you're actually in the republic, the rituals and expectations of hospitality are endless. Once, one of my friends was traveling through a Georgian village with some of his colleagues. They paused for a few moments to photograph a medieval fortress, when a mini-bus pulled up beside them. Several people leaped out and cordialities and introductions were exchanged—followed by an explosion of pleasure from the Georgians. They were a film crew from Tbilisi, on location for a shoot, and had actually been searching for just this group of strangers in order to share their lunch. "Without guests the whole meal loses its point," they explained. "Now we can make toasts and talk loudly about ourselves and listen to your stories. We've known each other so long, we've nothing new to say." A table, chairs, crates of wine, and what was more of a feast than a luncheon were miraculously fetched from the mini-bus. There were skewers of marinated beef aching for the grill, crispy fried chickens (*tapaka*), heaps of salads dressed with vinegar and ground walnuts, and vast bunches of fresh herbs. Needless to say, no one got up for a good many hours.

A Georgian festive meal is more like a full-scale social event than simply an occasion for eating. Georgians are always coming up with excuses for getting together—whether it's for the birth of a first-born son, perhaps, or for the opening of the season's first vat of homemade wine.

A Toast for Everything

The reputation of the Georgians for chatter, wit, and repartee has both a historical precedent in their splendid tradition of rhetoric, which dates back to the fourth century, and a less formal outlet, with its own long history, in the numerous and exuberant toasts proposed at a Georgian table. A person's popularity in the community will often depend on his (it's only the men who make toasts) ability to speak in this situation. And, it's this type of person who is usually chosen as *tamada*, chief toast-maker or master of ceremonies. He is either the oldest or most famous of the company, or the man best known for fine toasts and grand delivery. When the *tamada* speaks, no one is allowed to eat, and he also dictates how much the guests should drink. Of course, one of the most important qualities of a good *tamada* is an ability to hold liquor well and to remain (relatively) sober throughout the whole meal.

There are many traditional toasts and a fairly well-established order of proposal. A customary opening toast is "For our victory," a throw-back to Georgia's warrior epoch. Then whole families are enumerated with special reverence reserved for the toast "To the dead." When salutations are made to a guest, he is passed a horn — *kanzi* — containing about one and a half liters of wine, which he is expected to down without faltering and then to replace upended on the table before proposing a response. Women usually keep to a separate end of the table and spend more time running back and forth to the kitchen than keeping pace with the consumption of the men.

Nothing contributes more to the festival spirit of a Georgian meal than the quality of the regional wines — the smooth Kinzmarauli, the full-bodied Kakhetinian, or the semi-dry fragrant Akhasheni — which are Georgia's most sought-after exports.

Georgians drink like only Georgians can. They are so tough! Their wines don't travel very well — but on the spot they're exquisite. A good Kakhetinian is equal to any Burgundy. Wine is stored in *marans* — massive vats dug into the ground, which are opened with great ceremony. Recently a Russian dragoon toppled in, and was sadly drowned in Kakhetinian.

— Alexander Pushkin
Voyage to Arzrum

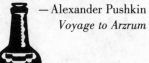

Abkhasia: Land of the Long-Lived

Abkhasia is a golden triangle of rugged land at the eastern edge of the Black Sea and to the west of Georgia. Legend has it that the Abkhasians were entertaining guests and so arrived late when God was distributing land. Feeling sorry for the tall, noble people, God raked together a few rock-strewn scraps of land and created for them an arduous, makeshift country.

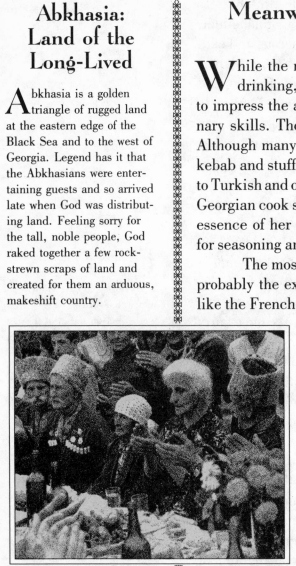

In Georgia, this dinner was held to celebrate the 140th birthday of Khfar Lasuria (center). Her 100-year-old son, Tarkuk (on her right), helped plan the festivities. Perhaps if you pay proper attention to the Georgian recipes in this book, you too may celebrate birthdays way into your second century.

Meanwhile, in the Kitchen

While the men spend many hours talking and drinking, the women are hard at work trying to impress the assembled company with their culinary skills. Their range of choices is vast indeed. Although many staple dishes, such as pilaf, shish kebab and stuffed vegetables (*dolma*) can be traced to Turkish and other Middles Eastern origins, a good Georgian cook seems effortlessly able to capture the essence of her homeland with an unfailing finesse for seasoning and subtle flavors.

The most significant feature of the cuisine is probably the extensive use of piquant sauces. Unlike the French tradition of stock- and cream-based sauces, the Georgians make theirs almost exclusively from fruits, vegetables, and nuts. The most common is a delicious aromatic sauce with many variations made from ground walnuts, garlic, and herbs that is diluted with vinegar, stock, or pomegranate juice. Another uses slightly tart fruit or vegetables such as wild plums or tomatoes, which are cooked slowly until condensed and then spiced with garlic, pepper, and herbs. The same sauce can be served with a variety of meats, but the dish is always named for the sauce used, such as *satsivi*, a walnut sauce, or *chakhokbili*, a tomato sauce.

If meat is not combined with a sauce, it's either marinated and grilled on skewers outside (the Georgians love family picnics), as in the famous *shashliks*, or stewed with fruits or vegetables. Fish is not as common as meat, but the most appreciated is undoubtedly the sweet-tasting trout abundant in the swift mountain streams of the Georgian Highlands.

It's impossible to imagine a Georgian kitchen without huge bunches of aromatic herbs. These are invariably used in cooking or for garnishing and decoration, but they are also often eaten just as is. Herbs grow in great variety and abundance in Georgia. Fortunately, many are available in Chinese, Korean, and Italian groceries in the United States. But others are what the Georgian emigré community sadly refer to as "lost tastes." Herbs commonly used in Georgian cooking that are readily available here are cilantro (fresh coriander), mint, chives, scallions, parsley, basil (preferably opal), tarragon, and chives. When preparing a Georgian recipe, be generous with herbs, especially cilantro.

Spices are less prominent than herbs. In general, the flavor of Georgian dishes is subtle and only mildly pungent, rather than hot and spicy. Favorite spices are crushed coriander seeds, mild paprika, fenugreek, and turmeric. In eastern Georgia red peppers are more valued than they are in the west, and in Abkhasia they enjoy a spicy sauce called *adzhika*, made from red chili peppers, salt, and herbs. But always remember that if you're generous with the herbs, be careful with the spices; they should enhance but never overpower a dish's flavor.

Georgians often eat their sauces with bread alone — a tribute as much to their baking as to their sauce making. Nowhere is the regional distinction in the republic more evident than in its breads. In the east they produce a fine, crusty bread made from yeast dough and baked on the sides of a large pitcher similar to the Indian tandoor oven. In the west the

The Abkhasians, though, have taken an ample revenge on nature. Here amid chestnut and boxwood slopes and between groves of wild persimmon, pomegranate, and walnut trees, you might come across a sprightly old woman of 120, or a dozen male dancers, singers, and musicians, all over 90. The miraculous longevity of the Abkhasians is the result of a whole recipe of factors: the climate; daily exercise; regular, moderate consumption of food and drink; and the outstanding dietary value of the local produce and local preparations. Nuts (a mash of chestnuts, almonds, pecans, and hazelnuts, and beechnuts is a favorite dish), berries, garlic, raw and lightly cooked vegetables, small amounts of unfatty meat, seasonal fruits, a low-alcohol wine, *abista* (a cornmeal mush), and the life-giving fermented milk drink, *matzoni*, are the principal constituents of the Abkhasian diet. We should all take note. You will find that much of the healthfulness and vitality of this astonishing land comes through in the recipes we offer from Georgia, Armenia, and Azerbaijan. Eat well and live long!

most notable bread, called *mchadi*, is made from corn flour and fried in flat clay pans (*ketsi*). Throughout the Republic, *ghome*, a kind of polenta made from white corn flour, is often substituted for bread. The Georgians love to tuck a piece of cheese into it and let it melt from the heat of the *ghome*.

Cheeses are ubiquitous and substantial enough to constitute a whole meal on occasion. There are two basic types, neither readily available in the United States: a delicious salty, stringy cheese, *suluguni*, with a texture similar to mozzarella; and a variety of goat cheeses, related to feta but generally a little less salty. Cheeses are frequently eaten hot, either boiled in milk with herbs, roasted, or fried. My own favorite is a plateful of golden *suluguni* wheels, gently fried in butter, accompanied by a ripe tomato salad and washed down with a good dose of fruity Isabella wine.

There are few striking Georgian desserts, in part because of the variety of beautifully presented fresh fruits that always adorn the table after a meal. Some sweets are concocted from nuts and honey, but there is nothing like the fascination with desserts common in Armenia or the Middle East, with their exquisite phyllo pastries and gorgeous halvah.

The real conclusion to a Georgian meal, however, is not edible. I'm referring to the extraordinary singing, which even to me, a trained musician, is almost a miracle. In most European countries the folk songs are usually monophonic or have a simple counterpoint. But these mountain people produce after-dinner songs for as many as eight voices. Well-fed if not gorged, after perhaps four hours at table, your consciousness is thankfully raised by the songs, and the final impression of the feast is of a high-spirited camaraderie better than any *digestif*.

Rice and Grains

RIS I KRUPI

Flavorful grains may have only recently dazzled American palates, but they have, from time immemorial, sat at the heart of Soviet eating. What's more, I think it's fair to say that they've often been prepared in more fascinating ways than those dreamed up by even the most imaginative post-nouvelle chefs.

Buckwheat cooked with richly browned onions and wild mushrooms; nutty bulgur studded with a cornucopia of vegetables and herbs; Moldavian cornmeal mush enlivened with tangy feta and moistened with melted butter; hearty barley and bacon casserole from the Baltic; Ukrainian millet and pumpkin baked with honey — these are just a few of the tasty and surprising grain preparations from around the republics.

As in the Far East, rice, too, is central to a whole way of life in parts of the USSR — it's use provides an endless source of folklore and wisdom, and its methods of preparation are an important form of national self expression. To me, the great rival traditions of pilaf wizardy in Central Asia and in Azerbaijan are two of the highest forms of culinary art. A Central Asian pilaf is a rich combination of deeply browned lamb, carrots, onions, rice, and pungent spices, all simmered together in a special pot, while the Azerbaijanis make their pilaf in the old Persian manner — the aromatic basmati rice is steamed with a crunchy crust and accompanied by a variety of stews, which include such exotic ingredients as pomegranate juice and chestnuts, and which are subtly perfumed with a bouquet of spices.

While the people of the exotic East feast on pilafs, *kasha* has been the enduring staple of Slavic life. The word *kasha*, however, does not always designate buckwheat as it does in the United States. This Slavic name was brought to America by Jewish emigrés at the beginning of the twentieth century. *Kasha* in Russian refers to most kinds of grains, usually when they are cooked to the consistency of a porridge. Thus, you can have oatmeal *kasha* in the morning, buckwheat *kasha* with your dinner, or a millet *kasha* as a late night supper.

One Russian saying, though, really says it all: "*shchi da kasha, pishcha nasha*" — "*shchi* and *kasha*, that's our real food."

Rice and Lamb Pilaf

Kovurma Palov

elow is the basic preparation for lamb pilaf as made in Tashkent, capital of Uzbekistan, and taught to me by my many Uzbek friends. To the simple *zirvak* of lamb, carrots, and onions, you can add either one of a combination of the following: 1 large quince, cored, peeled, and diced; 1½ cups partially cooked or canned chick-peas; 1 cup raisins; about 15 to 20 cloves garlic; 1½ cups diced fresh pumpkin.

Serve with Uzbek Tomato, Onion, and Pepper Salad; Asian Radish Salad; or Marinated Onion and Pomegranate Salad (see the Index for recipe page numbers).

¼ cup light olive oil

¼ cup light vegetable oil

2 pounds lamb shoulder with some fat and just a few bones, cut into 1½-inch chunks

1 pound carrots, peeled and cut into thick strips

3 large onions, cut into ¼- to ½-inch dice

½ teaspoon hot Hungarian paprika

½ teaspoon sweet Hungarian paprika

¼ teaspoon ground turmeric

2 teaspoons cumin seeds

Salt, to taste

½ cup water

2 cups medium-grain rice, rinsed and drained

1 whole medium-size head garlic, outer layer of skin and stem removed

2¾ cups boiling water

1 Heat the oils in a large, heavy, preferably oval-bottomed casserole, over medium heat for about 7 minutes, until a light haze forms above it. Carefully add a lamb bone to the oil, let it brown on all sides, and remove.

2 Turn the heat up to high, add the lamb, and remaining bones and brown, stirring frequently for about 10 minutes. Add the carrots and onions, stir well, and cook over high heat, stirring, until the onions are slightly colored, about 10 minutes more. Stir in the hot and sweet paprika, turmeric, cumin seeds, and salt. Then add the ½ cup water. Bring to a boil, then reduce the heat to medium low, cover, and simmer until the meat is tender, about 25 minutes.

3 Flatten the surface of the meat mixture with a large slotted spoon. Pour the rice evenly over the meat, and bury the garlic head in it. Flatten the surface of the rice.

4 Place a heavy plate over the rice and pour in the boiling water in a steady stream. (Placing a plate over the rice will ensure that the rice and meat will not mix while you pour in the water). Remove the plate carefully, turn the heat up to high, and let the water boil vigorously until it all boils off, about 15 to 20 minutes.

5 Gather the rice into a mound and make 6 or 7 holes in it with the back of a wooden spoon. Reduce the heat to very low, cover the pot tightly and let the pilaf steam until the rice is tender, about 20 to 30 minutes. Remove from heat and let stand for about 10 minutes.

6 To serve, spread the rice on a large serving platter and arrange the meat, vegetables, and garlic in a mound over it. Serve with any of the suggested salads.

Serves 6

An Uzbek Pilaf Dinner

Assorted Nuts

•

Rice and Lamb Pilaf

Uzbek Tomato, Onion, and Pepper Salad

Onion and Pomegranate Salad

Chinese Radish Salad

Central Asian Flatbreads

Portuguese Garrafeira

•

Poached Quince with Whipped Cream

Green Tea

• • •

Uzbek Pilaf

Palov

It is said that, while swooping through Central Asia, Alexander the Great summoned a local soldier and bid him prepare a dish that would be proper nurture to a fighting man, an inspiration in taste, easily transportable, and made from fresh local ingredients. The soldier brought back his best pilaf.

Long described in the region as the "food that feeds many,"pilaf (*palov* in Uzbekistan) is probably the richest and most distinctive of all the foods of Central Asia. Specially prepared with lamb or other meats, which are combined with rice and aromatic spices and then steamed, a great pilaf is a truly memorable culinary experience.

Like so many of the sumptuous foods of Central Asia, pilaf is not just a dish but a way of life. This is especially true in Uzbekistan, the real spiritual homeland of *palov*. Here it is both a powerful symbol and an essential element of *dastarkhan* — the exotic and generous Central Asian hospitality ritual that has entertained guests in this vast region for millenia. Pilaf is always present on the most important family and religious occasions — weddings, the birth of a child, the long-awaited visit of a valued guest, or, more modestly, on the occasion of a simple weekend gathering of good friends.

Although every Uzbek woman knows how to prepare pilaf, and is some-times allowed to make it on weekdays, the preparation of a "serious" lamb pilaf is reserved for the men. In fact, according to ancient tradition, a young boy must learn all the subtleties of pilaf-making before he comes of age — that is, before he turns sixteen. On the occasion of more important, weekend meals the men will often gather separately to "perfume" the pilaf with pungent spices and local extras, while the women sip tea together and enjoy various confections, which are considered "feminine" foods.

The Pilaf Ritual

The actual business of preparation is, as you can already imagine, treated almost with the sanctity of a religious ceremony, and the cook (*oshpaz* in Uzbek) is regarded more as a magician than menial. The best pilaf makers are famous throughout the republic, and their skills are carefully passed from generation to generation, ensuring venerable dynasties of pilaf wizards. There are even annual pilaf-making contests in Uzbekistan, where young talents are discovered and old masters have the chance to prove their skills.

When the men set out to make a pilaf, first, at the crack of dawn, they go off to market, where they search out the best and freshest ingredients. Their primary concern, of course, is the lamb itself. In Central Asia, pilaf is always made with the meat and fat from a recently slaughtered fat-tailed sheep, using a piece that includes some bone and some of the prized fat. (Alas, I usually have to forgo the fat when I make the dish in the United States.) Together with the meat, two other key ingredients, carrots and onions, constitute the heart of a pilaf, which is called *zirvak*, and to which the rice is added later.

The rice itself is no less important than the *zirvak*. Of the many kinds of rice (mostly short and medium grain) available in Central Asia, the best loved (and the most costly) is called *dezira*. It's slightly pink in color, and has just the right starch content for a perfect result. Then, of course, there are the spices. Uzbek markets are filled with row upon row of neatly portioned aromatic spices, whose thousand colors match the gorgeous polychrome of the national costumes and which send up a heady scent that could seduce the gods. For pilaf, however, only a few choice spices are needed: cumin seeds (*zira*), which give it a highly distinct flavor, unlike any other Middle Eastern rice dish; two doses of ground red peppers, mild and hot; and *barbaris* (barberries) — tiny, dark purple dried berries that have a sharp, sour taste. Ground barberries produce a rich, reddish powder called *sumakh*, which is used extensively in the cuisine of the Middle East. I have rarely seen whole barberries for sale outside of the Soviet Union, so you have to leave them out when cooking at home — unless you are able to stock up during visits to the USSR, which is what I try to do. However, you can make an

When in Uzbekistan

In Uzbekistan the stranger had better be aware of the high premium placed on a specially prepared pilaf. My grandmother, a Russian architect and designer, often used to tell the story of a business trip she made to Tashkent (the capital of Uzbekistan), which included a meeting with some top local officials. When she arrived for the appointment, she found that the conference room was set up for a pilaf banquet. At the timid suggestion that she wasn't particularly hungry, and thought it best to get down to work, the minister of transport went bright red in the face and growled to his subordinates that the pilaf should be "thrown into the ditch at once." Needless to say, my grandmother soon realized that refusing a pilaf was no way to do business in Centra Asia.

authetic *pilaf* even without barberries.

Traditionally, pilaf is made in a huge, oval cast-iron pot, hung over a charcoal fire set in a clay fireplace. Nowadays, however, even when a pilaf is made indoors on the stove, the pot (*kazan*) is still extremely important. It must be heavy enough so it can sustain high heat without burning the meat, and it must have an oval bottom so the meat and rice can be correctly distributed.

(I've experimented with regular pots, and the results, believe me, are not exactly the same — the pot is definitely part of the magic.) A proper *kazan* also has to be well greased by constant use — it should never be washed with water, or, God forbid, actually scrubbed and scoured. The Uzbeks just wipe it carefully with an oiled cloth; and they will insist and I will second this — that the older the *kazan*, the better the pilaf.

When the pilaf is finished, the rice is carefully scooped out and heaped onto traditional blue and white ceramic platters, and the *zirvak* is mounded on top of the rice. The pilaf is accompanied by cupfuls of hot green tea served in special cup-bowls (*piala*) and eaten with various salads and pickles — pickled garlic and onion, tomato and peppers, radish salad, and others. Even in today's Uzbekistan the pilaf is eaten with the fingers and not cut-lery. And just in case you think such traditions have died in the emigré communities around the world, I was half shocked and half amused recently when, on meeting an Uzbek family at home in New York, the husband ate the pilaf he had made with his fingers, and then cupped his hand, filled it with more pilaf, and offered it to his wife!

Of course, infinite varieties of pilaf are prepared throughout Central Asia, and each region will argue wildly that it is the best. Profound differences in taste are achieved by a fiercely or less fiercely browned *zirvak*; by altering the proportion of meat, carrots, and rice; and by particular additions to the *zirvak*. Remember, also, that while my description is as faithful as possible to the best ingredients and preparations found in Uzbekistan, a very good pilaf can still be made in the States — especially as your pot gets old and you learn the magic of pilaf!

Chicken Pilaf with Nuts and Candied Orange Peel

Bairam Polo

This is a spectacular pilaf from the Central Asian republic of Tadzhikistan, where the language, culture, and cuisine are Persian, rather than Turkic. This pilaf, which is supposed to be very sweet, is often served at weddings and holidays to assure a sweet life for the years to come. I reduced the amount of sugar in this recipe to make it suitable for more casual occasions.

Zest of 3 large oranges, cut into
    ¼-inch-wide strips
¼ cup olive oil
1 chicken (3½ pounds), well rinsed,
    patted dry, and cut into serving-
    size pieces
3 large onions, sliced into
    rings
½ teaspoon ground turmeric
Small pinch of cinnamon

Salt and freshly ground black
    pepper, to taste
4¾ cups water
6 tablespoons (¾ stick) unsalted
    butter, cut into pieces
2 cups long-grain rice
¾ cup sugar
⅔ cup slivered almonds
⅔ cup shelled pistachio nuts

1 Blanch the orange zest in boiling water for 1 minute. Rinse under cold running water and blanch once more for 1 minute. Place in a colander to drain and set aside.

2 Heat the oil over medium-high heat in a large, heavy casserole. Add the chicken pieces, a few at a time, turning them to brown evenly on all sides. Remove the chicken pieces to a heated platter and drain off all but 2 tablespoons of oil. Add the onions to the casserole and sauté until light golden, about 10 minutes. Stir in the turmeric, cinnamon, and salt and pepper, then return the chicken to the casserole. Add 4 cups of the water and bring to a boil. Reduce the heat to low, cover, and simmer until the chicken is almost tender, about 30 minutes.

3 Turn the heat up to high and let the liquid boil, uncovered, for 1 minute. Stir in 4 tablespoons of the butter and the rice, reduce the heat to low, and simmer, covered, until the rice is tender and all the liquid is absorbed, about 20 minutes.

4 Meanwhile, make the syrup. Combine the sugar and the remaining ¾ cup water in a small saucepan. Bring to a boil, stirring, then reduce the heat to low and cook until the sugar is completely dissolved, about 5 minutes.

5 Melt the remaining 2 tablespoons of butter in a medium-size skillet over medium-low heat. Add the nuts and the orange zest and stir for 4 to 5 minutes. Add the syrup and cook until the syrup is somewhat reduced, about 10 minutes.

6 To serve, spoon the rice and the chicken onto a decorative serving platter and mix with two-thirds of the nut mixture. Scatter the rest of the mixture over the pilaf.

Serves 6

My Favorite Pilaf

(with Almonds, Raisins, and Orange Zest)

Plov s Mindalyom, Izyumom i Apelsinovoy Tsedroy

I am not sure whether this recipe comes from Armenia or Azerbaijan, and I don't remember who gave it to me, but I know I can fall back on it at any time, and I always keep the ingredients at hand. Its subtle combination of flavors never fails to impress! As a side dish, it can be served with almost any entrée, although it seems to overshadow them all.

4 tablespoons (½ stick) unsalted
    butter
1 cup grated carrots
⅓ cup slivered almonds
Grated zest of 2 oranges
⅓ cup golden raisins
¼ teaspoon ground
    turmeric

1½ cups long-grain rice
3 cups boiling Chicken Stock
    (see Index), canned broth,
    or water
Salt, to taste

1 Melt the butter in a heavy 2-quart saucepan over medium-low heat. Add the carrots and stir over medium heat for about 5 minutes. Stir in the almonds, orange zest, raisins, and turmeric, and continue to stir for another 3 to 4 minutes. Add the rice and keep on stirring until the rice is well coated with the butter and takes on some color, 2 minutes.

2 Pour in the boiling stock in a steady stream and let boil for about 2 minutes.

Add salt, reduce the heat to very low, cover tightly, and simmer until all the liquid is absorbed, 15 to 20 minutes. Let stand, covered, for 10 minutes.

3 Fluff the rice with a fork, transfer to a serving platter, and stir gently before serving.

Serves 4 to 6

Rice and Mushroom Pilaf

Plov s Gribami

Whenever this pilaf appears at Russian dinner parties, the hostess always claims she invented it herself. Perhaps I will be the one to get the credit for posterity, since I might be the first one to record it on paper. It also works very well if you use barley instead of the rice.

*1 ounce dried wild mushrooms,
  preferably porcini, well rinsed*

9 tablespoons unsalted butter

2½ cups chopped onions

*1 pound fresh white mushrooms,
  wiped clean and sliced*

*2 medium-size cloves garlic,
  minced*

¼ cup sour cream

1 cup long-grain rice

1½ cups water

*Salt and freshly ground black
  pepper, to taste*

*3 tablespoons chopped fresh
  dill*

1 Soak the dried mushrooms in ⅔ cup water for 2 hours. Remove the mushrooms from the soaking liquid, pat dry with a paper towel, chop fine, and set aside. Strain the soaking liquid through a coffee filter and set aside.

2 Melt 4 tablespoons of the butter in a large skillet. Sauté the onions over medium heat, stirring occasionally, until nicely browned, about 25 minutes.

3 Meanwhile, in another skillet, melt 4 more tablespoons of the butter and sauté the dried and fresh mushrooms until golden also about 25 minutes. Toward the end add the garlic and sour cream, stir, and cook for 3 to 4 minutes longer.

4 While the onions and mushrooms are cooking, combine the rice, water, mushroom soaking liquid, and the remaining 1 tablespoon butter in a large saucepan and bring to a boil over high heat. Add salt, then reduce the heat, cover, and simmer until the rice has absorbed all the liquid, about 20 minutes.

5 Stir the mushrooms and the onions thoroughly into the rice, add salt and pepper, and heat for about 5 minutes. Transfer to a serving bowl and sprinkle on the dill.

Serves 4 to 6

Azerbaijani Pilafs

Azerbaijani cuisine is, perhaps, the most distinctive and yet least known of all three Caucasian republics. Having been a part of Persia (Iran) for over two centuries, to a great extent Azerbaijan shares the splendid ancient tradition of Persian cooking. Even a humble meal is a feast for the eyes and the palate, always possessing a subtle balance of flavors and a touch of the exotic.

But the most tempting dishes of all are the sumptuous pilafs in which the ingredients are not simmered together as in Central Asia, but are prepared separately and mixed either at the table or during the last stages of cooking. The contents of one of these extravaganzas will always include steamed basmati rice, brightened with saffron, and side dishes of chicken, meat, or wild game. Although the range of flavors in a pilaf is wide, the trademarks of Azerbaijani cuisine are the faintly sweet and delicately tart flavorings. To achieve this the Azerbaijanis often use pomegranate juice — a kitchen stable in that part of the world — dried lemons, sour plums, and the juice of unripe grapes, called *abgora*. The sweet element comes from fresh and dried fruit, such as apricots, quince, raisins, sour cherries, and persimmons. A heartier, home-style pilaf will often include legumes, chestnuts, pumpkin, or squash.

But certainly, rice is the most important element of a pilaf and much attention is paid to its preparation. The only rice used for pilaf is the aromatic basmati and the Azerbaijanis spare no time and trouble to bring out the full glory of its taste.

First, the rice is carefully picked over, soaked in salted water, and rinsed. Soaking and rinsing help wash out the extra starch that makes the rice sticky when cooked. The Azerbaijanis claim that it also washes away the extra calories, which is why, they explain, they can consume such gigantic portions of rice and never experience a sense of overeating. The prepared rice is then boiled until almost tender and carefully rinsed once more. Then the actual steaming begins. The bottom of a large copper pot is lined with a layer of flat bread, potatoes, or some of the rice that has been bound with eggs. This is the *kazmag*, a deliciously crunchy crust that prevents the basmati rice from burning and constitutes the most sought-after element of the pilaf. A little water is added, the prepared basmati rice is gathered in a mound on top of the *kazmag*, and then it is slowly steamed until the grains are tender but perfectly intact. One potential drawback of steaming basmati rice in this fashion is that it tends to get rather dry. To remedy this, the rice is mixed with lots of butter, which, no doubt restores the lost calories, but makes the rice deliciously moist.

Serving the pilaf is also a serious affair. Part of the rice is spooned onto a decorative platter, the rest is colored with saffron and placed on top of the white rice, with the broken pieces of *kazmag* scattered on top. So the pilaf proudly presides at the center of the table surrounded by the seductive smells of dishes of stew, platters of fresh herbs, a bowl of yogurt to spoon on the savory stews, and the bright purple sumakh powder to add just an extra tart touch.

The taste of properly prepared basmati rice is truly unique and unforgettable and the Azerbaijani way of serving it is festive and inviting. *Khoshgäldiz* — welcome!

Basic Steamed Saffron Rice with a Crust

(Pilaf with *Kazmag*)

Azerbaijan Plovi

This is the basic preparation of an Azerbaijani basmati rice pilaf. For the *kazmag*, the delicious crust on the bottom of the pot, you can choose bread, potatoes (my favorite), or rice bound with eggs. Serve this pilaf as a side dish with your favorite entrée, or in a traditional Azerbaijani way with one or more of the toppings that follow.

2 cups basmati rice (see Note)
Salt
Bread Crust, Egg Crust, or Potato
    Crust (recipes follow)
1 cup (2 sticks) unsalted butter, or
    more as needed, melted

¼ cup water
½ teaspoon saffron threads, crushed
    in a mortar
Pomegranate seeds, candied fruit, or
    fresh mint leaves for garnish

1 Place the rice in a fine sieve and rinse thoroughly under cold running water to remove as much starch as possible. Place the rice in a large bowl and add enough lukewarm water to cover it by about 1 inch. Add about 1 teaspoon salt and let the rice soak for 1 hour. Drain the rice and rinse well under cold running water.

2 Bring 3 quarts water to a boil in a large pot and let boil for about 2 minutes. Add salt. Pour in the rice in a thin, steady stream. Let boil, uncovered, stirring once or twice, 7 to 8 minutes. The rice should be almost cooked but still slightly hard to the bite.

Drain the rice thoroughly and rinse under cold running water. Drain again.

3 Mix 4 tablespoons of the butter and the ¼ cup water and pour it into a large, flat-bottomed, heatproof casserole with a tight-fitting lid. Spread the butter mixture evenly on the bottom of the casserole. Place the desired crust in the casserole, making sure it covers the bottom completely. Heat the casserole over medium heat for 5 minutes. Place half the rice in the casserole, sprinkle with another 4 tablespoons of the butter, top with the remaining rice, and sprinkle with another

A Perfect Pilaf

Making a perfect steamed basmati rice pilaf takes a little practice. Here are a few useful tips.

• Choose a very large pot with a heavy bottom for steaming the pilaf. If the rice is too crowded in a pot, it will not steam through properly.

• When boiling the pilaf in water, make sure you don't overcook or undercook it. The grains should be almost tender but still just slightly al dente — 7 to 8 minutes should do it.

• Don't leave the pilaf unattended; keep tasting the grains.

• Midway through the steaming, check the amount of steam, and add a few tablespoons of water, if it seems insufficient. Also, taste some rice from the top. If it doesn't seem to be cooking properly, carefully stir the rice with a spatula, so that the rice that was on the top of the pot is placed on the bottom.

---

4 tablespoons of the butter. Gather the rice into a mound and make 6 to 7 holes with the handle of a wooden spoon. Wrap the casserole lid in a linen or cotton (not terry cloth) kitchen towel to absorb the steam during cooking. Tie the ends together over the top. Cover the casserole tightly, making sure that no steam can escape during cooking. Reduce the heat to very low and steam the rice, stirring once or twice, until tender, 40 minutes.

4 In a small bowl, stir the saffron into the remaining 4 tablespoons of the butter and let stand for 5 minutes.

5 Remove the rice from the heat and let stand, covered, for 5 minutes. Place 1 cup of the rice in the bowl with the saffron butter and toss until bright yellow.

6 Arrange the rest of the rice on a decorative serving platter. Remove the crust with a metal spatula. Break it into pieces and scatter them, along with the saffron rice, over the white rice. Decorate, if desired, with pomegranate seeds, candied fruit, or mint leaves. Served with the desired topping.

Serves 6

Note: If you are making the Egg Crust, increase the amount of rice to 2½ cups. The amount of water remains the same.

Bread Crust
Lavashli Kazmag

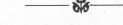

Enough lavash, *pita bread, or flour tortillas to cover the bottom of a large casserole*

If you are using pita, split each bread into two rounds. After spreading the melted butter evenly over the bottom of the casserole (Step 3 above), line with the bread. Proceed with the remainder of the basic steamed rice recipe.

Makes enough for 1 pilaf crust

Toppings for Basic Steamed Saffron Rice with a Crust

The five topping recipes included here are just a few of the traditional toppings for basic steamed rice pilaf. Pilafs with toppings make particularly splendid company or party dishes. They are not difficult to prepare and if you make the topping, or toppings, a day ahead, the flavors will have a chance to mellow. All that you'll have to do on the day you are serving is to make the rice. Then sit back and enjoy.

The topping recipes that follow are:

Lamb Stew with Chestnuts and Pomegranates

•

Meatballs in Pomegranate Sauce

•

Lamb, Herb, and Black-Eyed Pea Stew

•

Beef and Eggplant Stew

•

Cornish Game Hen with Dried Fruit

• • •

Egg Crust
Jumurtali Kazmag

This classic Persian crust is actually made with rice, which is mixed with beaten eggs.

4 large eggs
1 cup precooked Basic Steamed Saffron Rice with a Crust (see page 368, through Step 2)

Beat the eggs in a large bowl and mix with the rice. Spread the mixture evenly over the butter on the bottom of the casserole (Step 3, page 368). Proceed with the remainder of the basic steamed rice recipe.

Makes enough for 1 pilaf crust

Potato Crust
Kartofli Kazmag

These crispy, browned potato slices, scattered on the saffron pilaf, disappear before anything else, always leaving me to regret that the bottom of my casserole is not large enough to accommodate more.

2 to 3 boiling potatoes, peeled and
thinly sliced

Salt, to taste

Place the potato slices as close together as possible over the melted butter on the bottom of the casserole (Step 3, page 368). Do not overlap. Sprinkle the potatoes with salt. Proceed with the remainder of the basic steamed rice recipe.

Makes enough for 1 pilaf crust

Lamb Stew with Chestnuts and Pomegranates

Nar Kaurma

Exotic to a western palate, *nar kaurma* is really the Azerbaijani equivalent of a simple meat-and-potato affair. In fact, traditional Azerbaijani cookbooks often suggest that potatoes can be substituted for chestnuts, and lemon juice for pomegranate juice. But in this case don't be tempted, even if chestnuts and pomegranates don't grow in your garden.

1 pound large fresh chestnuts

¼ cup light vegetable oil

2 onions, chopped

1½ pounds boneless leg or shoulder
of lamb, cut into 1½-inch chunks

¼ teaspoon ground turmeric

¼ teaspoon saffron threads, crushed
in a mortar

½ teaspoon ground cinnamon

½ teaspoon dried mint

1½ cups ground walnuts

1 cup fresh or bottled pomegranate juice

2 tablespoons tomato paste

1½ cups Chicken Stock (see Index)
or canned broth

3 tablespoons fresh lemon juice

½ teaspoon sugar, or more to taste

Salt and freshly ground black
pepper, to taste

Basic Steamed Saffron Rice with a
Crust (see page 368)

¼ cup chopped fresh mint for garnish

1 Preheat the oven to 425°F.

2 Cut an X on the flat side of the chestnuts with a sharp, small knife. Spread the chestnuts in an even layer on a baking sheet and roast until tender, about 20 minutes. Cool until manageable and peel off the shell and the inner skin. Set aside.

3 Heat the oil in a heavy casserole over medium heat and sauté the onions until golden, about 15 minutes. Raise the heat to high, add the meat and the turmeric, and brown the meat well on all sides, stirring, about 10 minutes.

4 Stir in the saffron, cinnamon, mint, walnuts, pomegranate juice, tomato paste, and the stock. Bring to a boil, reduce the heat to low, cover, and simmer until the lamb is completely tender, 1½ hours.

5 Add the lemon juice, sugar, salt and pepper, and the reserved chestnuts. Simmer for 10 minutes more. Serve over Basic Steamed Saffron Rice with a Crust, garnished with the fresh mint.

Serves 6

Meatballs in Pomegranate Sauce

Fesinjan Kyufta

T his sauce gives an ordinary meatball an intriguing allure right out of the Arabian Nights. The meatballs are quite spicy, so I don't add spices to the sauce.

MEATBALLS

¾ pound lean ground sirloin

½ pound lean ground shoulder or leg of lamb

1 medium-size onion, grated

1 large egg, lightly beaten

2 to 3 tablespoons ice water

¼ cup unflavored fine, dry bread crumbs

¼ teaspoon ground allspice

¼ teaspoon hot Hungarian paprika

1 teaspoon dried mint

Salt and freshly ground black pepper, to taste

¼ cup all-purpose flour

5 tablespoons unsalted butter

SAUCE

1/3 cup Lamb Stock or Beef Stock
   (see Index for both), or canned
   beef broth
1 1/2 cups fresh or bottled
   pomegranate juice
Salt and freshly ground black
   pepper, to taste
1/4 cup pomegranate seeds

Basic Steamed Saffron Rice with a
   Crust (see page 368)
1/4 cup finely chopped fresh mint
   leaves for garnish
Pomegranate seeds for
   garnish

1 Combine the ground meats, onion, egg, ice water, bread crumbs, spices, mint, and salt and pepper in a large bowl. Mix thoroughly, cover, and refrigerate for 20 minutes.

2 Shape the chilled meat mixture into meatballs the size of an apricot. Spread the flour on a plate and roll the meatballs lightly in it.

3 Melt the butter in a large, heavy skillet over medium heat. Add the meatballs and cook until browned on all sides, about 15 minutes. Remove to a plate and set aside.

4 Pour the stock and the pomegranate juice into the skillet and turn the heat up to high. Scrape the bottom of the pan with a wooden spoon and let the liquid boil for about 5 minutes. Season to taste with salt and pepper, then add the browned meat-

Pilaf Banquet

Tahini and Hazelnut Dip

Crudites

Assorted olives

Lavash or pita bread

•

Basic Steamed Saffron Rice
with a Crust

Lamb, Herb, and Black-eyed
Pea Stew

Cornish Hen with Dried Fruit

Meatballs in Pomegranate
Sauce

Yogurt and Garlic Sauce

Sliced onions, sprinkled with
sumakh

Lemon Sherbet

Cru Beaujolais

•

Almond and Pistachio Paklava

"Mulberry" Cookies

balls and the pomegranate seeds. Reduce the heat to low, cover, and let simmer for 15 minutes.

5 Place the Basic Steamed Saffron Rice on a platter and arrange the meatballs around the sides or heaped on top of the rice; or serve them in a separate dish. Garnish with pomegranate seeds and chopped mint.

Serves 4 to 6

Beef and Eggplant Stew

Badrijan Kourma

This hearty stew of beef, eggplants, carrots, and chick-peas is served over pilaf in the Central Asian republic of Tadzhikistan, whose cuisine is another influenced by Persian cooking. This stew is more robust, however, than the Azerbaijani ones. Although I serve it with the Basic Steamed Saffron Rice with a Crust, it will also stand up to a side dish of potatoes.

1 large eggplant, about 1½ pounds
⅓ cup vegetable oil
2 cups coarsely chopped onions
3 medium-size carrots, peeled and
    sliced diagonally, ¼-inch thick
1 pound boneless beef chuck, cut
    into 1-inch cubes
½ teaspoon ground turmeric
½ teaspoon sweet Hungarian
    paprika
1 teaspoon cumin seeds, or more
    to taste
¼ teaspoon cayenne pepper, or more
    to taste
2 cups Beef Stock (see Index) or
    canned broth
3 large tomatoes, peeled, seeded,
    and coarsely chopped
Pinch of sugar
Salt, to taste
1 can (16 ounce) chick-peas, drained
3 tablespoons chopped fresh parsley
Basic Steamed Saffron Rice with a
    Crust (see page 368)

1 Preheat the oven to 375°F.

2 Pierce the eggplant all over with a small knife and bake on a baking sheet until soft, about 45 minutes. Cool until manageable, cut in half, scoop out the pulp, and set aside.

3 Heat half the oil in a large heavy skillet over medium heat. Add the onions and carrots and sauté until colored and softened, about 15 minutes.

4 In a heavy casserole, heat the rest of the oil over medium-high heat, and brown the meat on all sides, stirring occasionally, about 10 minutes.

5 Add the sautéed vegetables, turmeric, paprika, cumin seeds, cayenne, and the eggplant pulp to the casserole. Cook, stirring, for 2 minutes.

6 Add the stock, tomatoes, sugar, and salt, and bring to a boil. Reduce the heat to low, cover, and simmer until the meat is tender, about 1¼ hours.

7 Add the chick-peas, taste and correct the seasoning, if necessary, and cook for 10 more minutes. Serve sprinkled with parsley to accompany the Basic Steamed Saffron Rice.

Serves 6 over rice

Lamb, Herb, and Black-Eyed Pea Stew

Sabzi Kaurma

Mahnaz Salmassi, who gave me this recipe, says this dish is the way to a man's heart. "If an Azerbaijani girl does not know how to prepare it, she better just marry an American." But even for those not involved in matrimonial schemes, this tangy, aromatic stew is a real treat. The selection and amount of herbs can be varied according to taste, but I suggest you try the original version first. Beef can be used instead of lamb with equal success.

¾ cup black-eyed peas, soaked overnight in water to cover
6 tablespoons vegetable oil
1 medium-size onion, chopped
1¼ pounds stewing lamb or beef, cut
   into 1-inch cubes
¼ teaspoon ground turmeric
3 cups Beef Stock (see Index),
   or canned broth
¼ teaspoon saffron threads,
   crushed in a mortar and diluted
   in 2 tablespoons of the Beef Stock
Salt and freshly ground black
   pepper, to taste
3 cups tightly packed chopped
   spinach

3½ cups tightly packed chopped
   Italian (flat-leaf) parsley
5 bunches of scallions (green onions),
   green part only, finely chopped
⅓ cup fresh lemon juice, or more
   to taste
Generous pinch of sugar
¼ cup finely chopped fresh
   cilantro
2 tablespoons dried fenugreek leaves
   (available at Middle Eastern and
   Indian groceries; optional)
Basic Steamed Saffron Rice with a
   Crust (see page 368)
Yogurt and Garlic Sauce
   (see Index)

1 Drain the black-eyed peas. Place in a pot with 4 cups water and bring to a boil. Reduce the heat to low, cover, and simmer until almost tender, 45 to 50 minutes. Drain and set aside.

2 Heat 3 tablespoons of the oil in a heavy casserole. Add the onion and sauté over medium heat until golden, about 15 minutes.

3 Raise the heat to high and add the meat and turmeric and brown on all sides, stirring.

4 Add the stock and saffron; season with the salt and pepper. Lower the heat and simmer, covered, until the meat is tender, about 1½ hours.

5 While the meat is simmering, heat the remaining 3 tablespoons of oil in a large skillet. Add the spinach, parsley, and scallions and sauté, stirring, over medium heat until softened, about 10 minutes. Reduce the heat to low, cover, and cook, stirring occasionally, for 15 minutes more.

6 Add the spinach mixture, the black-eyed peas, lemon juice, sugar, cilantro, and fenugreek to the meat. Taste and adjust the seasoning. Simmer for another 20 minutes to blend the flavors. Serve over Basic Steamed Saffron Rice with a Crust, accompanied by Yogurt and Garlic Sauce.

Serves 8

Cornish Game Hen with Dried Fruit

Shirin Juja

The name of this dish literally means "sweet chicken" in Azerbaijani, and enticing combinations of meat, sweet and sour dried fruit, and exotic spices are hallmarks of the region. Just double the recipe for a large buffet.

4 Cornish game hens (about 1 pound each), halved, well rinsed, and patted dry
Salt and freshly ground black pepper, to taste
1 teaspoon sweet Hungarian paprika
6 tablespoons (¾ stick) unsalted butter
½ cup slivered almonds
¾ cup coarsely chopped dried apricots, preferably Californian
½ cup dried currants
½ cup golden raisins

¼ teaspoon ground turmeric
¼ teaspoon ground cinnamon
½ teaspoon ground ginger
1 tablespoon grated orange zest
1⅓ cups Chicken Stock (see Index) or canned broth
1 teaspoon honey
1 tablespoon fresh lemon juice, or more to taste
⅛ teaspoon saffron threads, crushed in a mortar
Basic Steamed Saffron Rice with a Crust (see page 368)

1 Preheat the oven to 350°F.

2 Place the Cornish hens between two pieces of waxed paper and gently pound with the flat side of a meat cleaver or a meat pounder to flatten. Rub with salt, pepper, and paprika.

3 Melt 4 tablespoons of the butter in a large nonstick skillet over medium heat.

Add as many Cornish hen halves as will easily fit and brown well on both sides until deep golden and crisp. Repeat with the rest of the hens.

4 Transfer the hens to a rimmed baking sheet, sprinkle with the butter in which they were browned, and place them in the oven until the juices run clear when the meat is pricked with a skewer, about 20 minutes.

Transfer to a heated platter and keep warm.

5 Meanwhile, melt the remaining 2 tablespoons butter in a small skillet over medium heat. Add the almonds and toast, stirring, for 2 minutes. Add the dried fruit, spices, and orange zest and reduce the heat to low. Sauté, stirring occasionally, for 5 minutes.

6 Stir in the stock and honey and cook, uncovered, until the liquid reduces somewhat and the fruit is plump, about 15 minutes. Add the lemon juice and saffron. Remove from the heat and let stand for 3 minutes. Stir.

7 Arrange the Cornish hens over a mound of the Basic Steamed Saffron Rice and spoon the dried fruit sauce over them, or serve it separately.

Serves 6 to 8

Lamb, Raisin, and Bean Pilaf

Lobia-Chilov Plov

I n this recipe and the one for Festive Basmati Pilaf with a Pumpkin Crust, the rice and topping are mixed together during the final cooking stages, producing enticing one-dish meals.

1 cup dried white (navy, pea, or
  Great Northern) beans, soaked
  overnight in water to cover
2 cups basmati rice
Salt
¼ cup olive oil, or more if needed
1½ pounds boneless leg or shoulder
  of lamb, cubed
¾ cup chopped onion
½ teaspoon saffron threads, crushed
  in a mortar
2 tablespoons warm water
Freshly ground black pepper, to taste

1 cup Lamb Stock, Beef Stock (see
  Index for both), or canned beef
  broth
¼ teaspoon ground cinnamon
¼ teaspoon ground turmeric
¼ teaspoon freshly grated nutmeg
15 tablespoons unsalted butter, melted
½ cup raisins
10 pitted dates
¼ cup water
Bread Crust (see page 369), Potato
  Crust, or Egg Crust (both page
  370)

Pilafs

R ice, claimed Brillat-Savarin, "softens the fiber and diminishes the courage. We may refer to the Hindu, who live almost exclusively on rice, and who have been subjugated by anyone who chose to conquer them." We should refer Brillat-Savarin in turn to the tribesmen of Central Asia, who have for centuries eaten rice-based dishes as their most important staple. And we can say, at least, that rice prepared as a pilaf seems to have had just the opposite effect with the sturdy, tenacious peoples of Central Asia.

According to one account both the word *pilaf* (Persian *pilau*, Uzbeki *palov*) and the dish pilaf have migrated mightily in the course of the centuries, turning up as far from their probable point of origin in Central Asia, as the African *pellao*, and the Carolinian purloo. This is a remarkable testimony to the importance and endurance of this rice-based food as a key staple throughout the rice-growing world.

1 Drain and rinse the beans well. Drain again, and place in a large saucepan. Add 3 cups water to the beans and bring to a boil. Reduce the heat to low and simmer, covered, until tender but not mushy, about 1 hour. Skim often.

2 Meanwhile, place the rice in a fine sieve and rinse thoroughly under cold running water to remove as much starch as possible. Place the rice in a large bowl and add enough lukewarm water to cover it by about 1 inch. Add 1 teaspoon salt and let the rice soak for 1 hour. Drain the rice and rinse well under cold running water. Drain again.

3 Drain the beans and set aside.

4 Heat the oil in a large, heavy skillet over medium-high heat. Brown the lamb well, a few pieces at a time, on all sides. Remove the lamb to a heated platter.

5 If necessary, add more oil to the skillet. Add the onion and sauté over medium heat until light golden, 10 minutes.

6 Dilute ¼ teaspoon of the saffron in the 2 tablespoons warm water. Return the lamb to the skillet, season with salt and pepper, and add ¾ cup of the stock, the diluted saffron, cinnamon, turmeric, and nutmeg. Bring the liquid in the skillet to a boil, then reduce the heat to low, cover, and simmer until the meat is tender and the liquid has evaporated, about 1½ hours.

7 Meanwhile, heat 3 tablespoons of the melted butter in a small skillet over medium-low heat. Add the raisins and dates and stir until the fruit is softened, about 10 minutes. Remove from the heat and set aside.

8 Bring 3 quarts water to a boil in a large pot and let boil for about 2 minutes. Add salt. Pour in the rice in a thin, steady stream. Let boil, stirring once or twice, for 7 to 8 minutes. The rice should be almost cooked but still slightly hard to the bite. Drain the rice thoroughly and rinse under cold running water.

9 Mix 4 tablespoons of the melted butter and the ¼ cup water and pour into a large, heatproof, flat-bottomed casserole with a tight-fitting lid. Place the desired crust in the casserole, making sure it covers the bottom completely. Spread 1 cup of the rice evenly over the crust, then add a few pieces of meat, a cupful of beans, and some raisins and dates. Repeat with some more of the rice, and the rest of the meat, beans, raisins, and dates. Top with the remaining rice. Drizzle another 4 tablespoons melted butter and the remaining ¼ cup stock on top, and gather the layers (except for the crust) into a mound. Make 6 to 7 holes in it with the handle of a wooden spoon. Wrap the casserole lid in a linen or cotton (not terry cloth) kitchen towel to absorb the steam during cooking. Tie the ends together over

the top. Cover the casserole tightly, making sure that no steam can escape during cooking. Cook over medium-high heat for 5 minutes, then reduce the heat to very low and steam the pilaf without disturbing it for 40 minutes.

10 In a small bowl, stir the remaining ¼ teaspoon saffron into the remaining 4 tablespoons melted butter and let stand for 5 minutes.

11 Remove the pilaf from the heat and let stand, covered, for 5 minutes. Remove 1 cup of the rice from the pilaf, add it to the saffron butter, and toss until bright yellow.

12 Spoon the pilaf onto a decorative platter and spoon the saffron rice on top. Break the crust into pieces and scatter on top of the pilaf. Serve at once.

Serves 4 to 6

Festive Basmati Pilaf with a Pumpkin Crust

Kham Doshma Pilaf

As *kham doshma pilaf* uses such fine autumnal ingredients as pumpkin and chestnuts, it makes a wonderful alternative for Thanksgiving weekend — you can save the leftover turkey for another occasion. Although not a hundred percent authentic, veal or beef fits just as well in this delicate concoction.

12 to 14 large fresh chestnuts

2 cups basmati rice

Salt

3 tablespoons olive oil

1⅜ cups (2¾ sticks) unsalted butter,
    melted

1½ pounds boneless lamb, veal, or
    beef (use only the best cuts), cut
    into 1½-inch cubes

¾ cup Beef Stock (see Index), or
    canned broth

Freshly ground black pepper, to taste

⅓ cup golden raisins

12 dried apricots, preferably
    California

12 pitted dried prunes

¼ cup water

About 6 medium-thick slices fresh
    pumpkin, or enough to cover the
    bottom of a large, flat-bottomed
    casserole, peeled

½ teaspoon saffron threads, crushed
    in a mortar

1 Preheat the oven 425°F.

2 Cut an X on the flat side of the chestnuts with a sharp, small knife. Spread the chestnuts out in an even layer on a baking sheet and roast until tender, about 20 minutes. Cool until manageable and peel off the shell and inner skin. Set aside.

3 Place the rice in a fine sieve and rinse thoroughly under cold running water to remove as much starch as possible. Place the rice in a large bowl and add enough lukewarm water to cover it by about 1 inch. Add 1 teaspoon salt, stir, and let the rice soak for 1 hour. Drain the rice and rinse well under cold running water. Drain again.

4 Heat the oil and 2 tablespoons of the melted butter in a large heavy skillet over medium heat. Brown the pieces of meat gently, a few at a time, on all sides. Return all the meat to the skillet and add the stock. Reduce the heat to low, cover, and let simmer until the meat is almost tender,

about 1½ hours. Remove from the heat and season to taste with salt and pepper.

5 In another skillet, heat 4 tablespoons of the melted butter over medium-low heat. Add the raisins, apricots, prunes, and chestnuts and stir until the fruit is softened, about 10 minutes. Remove from the heat and set aside.

6 Bring 3 quarts water to a boil in a large pot and let boil for about 2 minutes. Add salt, then pour in the rice in a thin, steady stream. Let boil, uncovered, stirring once or twice, 7 to 8 minutes. The rice should be almost cooked but still slightly hard to the bite. Drain the rice thoroughly and rinse under cold running water.

7 Mix 4 tablespoons of the melted butter and ¼ cup water and pour into a large flat-bottomed casserole with a tight-fitting lid. Arrange the pumpkin slices snugly on the bottom of the casserole, then add half of the rice. Drizzle 4 tablespoons butter over the rice. Add the meat and a few tablespoons of the cooking liquid. Arrange the dried fruit and chestnuts on the meat. Spoon the remaining rice on top and drizzle with 4 tablespoons of the butter and a few more tablespoons of the cooking liquid. Gather the layers (not the pumpkin) into a mound and make 6 to 7 holes in it with the handle of a wooden spoon. Wrap a linen or cotton (not terry cloth) kitchen towel around the casserole lid to absorb the steam during cooking. Tie the ends together over the top. Cover the casserole tightly, making sure that no steam can escape during cooking. Cook over medium-high heat for 5 minutes, then reduce the heat to very low and steam the rice, without disturbing, for 40 minutes.

8 Stir the saffron in the remaining 4 table-spoons melted butter in a small bowl and let stand for 5 minutes.

9 Remove the pilaf from the heat and let stand, covered, for 5 minutes. Remove a ladleful of the rice to the bowl with the saffron butter and toss until bright yellow.

10 Arrange the pilaf on a decorative serving platter and spoon the saffron rice on top. Scatter the pumpkin slices on top of the pilaf. Serve at once.

Serves 4 to 6

Herbed Basmati Rice Pilaf

Sabzi Plov

Azerbaijanis are reputed to grow the best herbs in the Soviet Union and they use them generously in their cooking. This aromatic green pilaf is traditionally served with fish in Azerbaijan and makes one of the most delectable side dishes I know.

2 cups basmati rice
Salt
1 cup finely chopped scallions (green onions), green part only
1½ cups chopped fresh parsley

¾ cup chopped fresh dill
3 tablespoons chopped fresh cilantro
¼ cup vegetable oil
6 tablespoons (¾ stick) unsalted butter, melted

1 Place the rice in a fine sieve and rinse thoroughly under cold running water to remove as much starch as possible. Place the rice in a large bowl and add enough lukewarm water to cover it by about 1 inch. Add 1 teaspoon salt, stir, and let the rice soak for 1 hour. Drain the rice and rinse well under cold running water. Drain again.

2 Bring 3 quarts of water to a boil in a large pot and let boil for about 2 minutes. Add salt, then pour the rice in a thin, steady stream. Let boil, uncovered, stirring once or twice, 7 to 8 minutes. The rice should be almost cooked but still slightly hard to the bite. Drain the rice thoroughly and rinse under cold running water.

3 In a large bowl, mix the rice with the scallions and herbs.

4 Heat the oil in a large heatproof flat-bottomed casserole with a tight-fitting lid.

Spread a layer of the herbed rice evenly on the bottom of the casserole. Add the remaining rice in a mound on the bottom layer and make 6 to 7 holes in the rice with the handle of a wooden spoon. Pour the butter over the rice. Cook over medium heat for about 5 minutes. Wrap the casserole lid in a linen or cotton (not terry cloth) kitchen towel to absorb the steam during cooking. Tie the ends together over the top. Cover the casserole tightly, making sure that no steam can escape during cooking. Reduce the heat to very low and steam the rice without disturbing it, for 40 minutes.

5 To serve, spoon the rice into a decorative serving platter. Remove the crust that formed in the bottom of the casserole with a metal spatula, break into pieces and scatter on the rice.

Serves 6

Cold Bulgur and Vegetable Pilaf

Itch

Although the Armenians insist on calling this tabbouleh-like dish a pilaf, it can pass as salad. Either way, it should end up served next to grilled fish or meat.

1 can (32 ounces) Italian plum
    tomatoes
½ cup olive oil
2 cups chopped onions
2 cups fine bulgur
¼ cup fresh lemon juice, or more
    to taste
Salt and freshly ground black
    pepper, to taste

1 small hot red pepper, cored,
    seeded, and finely diced
1 large red bell pepper, cored
    seeded, and cut into ½-inch dice
1 large red onion, chopped
8 scallions (green onions) trimmed
    and finely chopped
½ cup finely chopped fresh
    parsley

1 Drain the tomatoes, reserving the liquid, and chop fine or process for one or two pulses in a food processor. Combine with the reserved liquid and set aside.

2 Heat the oil in a deep skillet or 3-quart saucepan over medium heat. Add the onions and sauté until they just begin to soften, about 5 minutes. Stir in the tomatoes and the liquid and bring to a boil.

3 Place the bulgur in a large bowl and pour in the onion and tomato mixture. It should cover the bulgur by about ½ inch.

Add some boiling water if it doesn't. Add the lemon juice and salt and pepper, then cover tightly and let stand for 40 to 45 minutes, until the liquid is completely absorbed.

4 Add the remaining ingredients and toss well. Correct the seasoning, and add more lemon juice, if desired. Let stand for 10 to 15 minutes before serving. Serve either cold or at room temperature.

Serves 8

Bulgur Pilaf with Tahini Sauce

Tahiniyov Pilav

This recipe was adapted from a wonderful Armenian vegetarian cookbook, *Classic Armenian Recipes: Cooking without Meat,* by Alice Antressian and Mariam Jebejian. The nutty flavor of the bulgur is further enhanced by an even more nutty tahini sauce.

3 tablespoons olive oil
½ cup chopped onion
2 carrots, peeled, and cut into
    fine dice
1 medium-size green bell pepper,
    cored, seeded, and finely
    diced

SAUCE
2 cloves garlic, crushed in a garlic
    press
⅛ teaspoon salt
2 teaspoons fresh lemon juice
½ cup tahini

1 medium-size red pepper, cored,
    seeded and finely diced
1 cup medium or coarse bulgur
2¼ cups Chicken Stock (see Index)
    or canned broth
Salt, to taste
1 cup well-drained canned chick-peas

¾ cup Chicken Stock (see Index) or
    canned broth
Chopped Italian (flat-leaf) parsley
    for garnish

1 Heat the oil over medium heat in a heavy saucepan. Add the onion, carrots, and bell peppers, and sauté, stirring, about 7 minutes.

2 Add the bulgur and stir for 2 minutes. Add the stock and salt and bring it to a boil. Then, reduce the heat to low, cover the pan, and simmer for 10 minutes.

3 Stir in the chick-peas and simmer, covered, until the bulgur is tender, 10 to 15 minutes more. Remove from heat and let stand, covered, for 10 minutes.

4 To make the sauce, combine the garlic, salt, lemon juice, and tahini in a medium-size bowl. Gradually whisk in the stock. The mixture should be slightly thicker than heavy cream.

5 Stir the pilaf gently but thoroughly. Arrange it on a serving platter and sprinkle

Bulgur

A bulgur pilaf is a versatile and flavorful grain side dish. To prepare a bulgur pilaf for four people, simply sauté the flavoring ingredients in a little butter or oil, stir in 1 cup coarse or medium ground bulgur, and add about 2¼ cups of boiling stock or water. Simmer for 15 minutes and serve.

Armenians like to add the following flavorings to a bulgur pilaf: pine nuts and dried currants; onions and tomatoes; diced zucchini and red bell peppers; scallions; fresh basil; and toasted sesame seeds.

with parsley. Spoon the sauce over the pilaf or pass separately.

Serves 4 to 5

Moldavian Cornmeal Mush

Mamaliga

Made from stone-ground, bright orange, local cornmeal, *mamaliga* is as essential to Moldavian and Romanian cuisine, as rice is to the Chinese. For breakfast, it is eaten fried with a slice of bacon; at lunch, it is sprinkled with feta cheese and baked; at dinner, it is served as a base for a hearty stew; and for dessert, slices of *mamaliga* are topped with confectioners' sugar or jam.

Mamaliga tastes very much like the newly popular Italian polenta, although the Moldavians insist that it is far superior, especially when made with their own cornmeal. Vigorous stirring is the key to a good, smooth *mamaliga*, and every Moldavian housewife has a long wooden spoon for this purpose. Traditionally, it has to be made in a heavy u-shaped pot but I find that molding it in an oval bowl is much easier.

3½ cups water

Salt, to taste

1 cup stone-ground yellow cornmeal

5 tablespoons unsalted butter, cut into bits

8 tablespoons (1 stick) unsalted butter, melted, for serving

1 Combine the water and salt in a heavy saucepan and bring to a boil. Add 2 tablespoons of the cornmeal in a steady stream and whisk until the water returns to boiling. Gradually add the rest of the cornmeal, stirring constantly. Reduce the heat to low and cook the mixture, covered, until thickened and cooked through, 10 minutes.

2 Add in the butter, a piece at a time, stirring constantly. Continue stirring until the mixture leaves the sides of the pan, about 5 minutes more.

3 Transfer the *mamaliga* to a medium-size oval bowl and flatten the surface with a wet spoon. Let stand for 5 minutes.

4 Invert the *mamaliga* onto a plate and sprinkle with the melted butter.

Serves 6 to 8

Some Favorite Traditional Ways to Serve Mamaliga

- Sprinkle the *mamaliga* with 1 cup crumbled feta cheese and bake in a 400°F oven until the feta is golden and bubbly, 10 minutes. Serve with melted butter.

- Cut the *mamaliga* into ¼-inch-thick slices, dredge in cornmeal, and fry in butter. Serve for breakfast with fried bacon.

- Mix hot *mamaliga* with 1½ cups kasseri cheese, transfer to a rectangular casserole, drizzle with 4 tablespoons melted butter that has been mixed with 3 to 4 cloves of crushed garlic, and bake in a 375° F oven until the top is browned, 12 minutes.

- Place a thin slice of German ham and a thin slice of sharp cheese between two slices of *mamaliga*, dip in beaten egg, and fry in butter until golden.

Kasha and Wild Mushroom Casserole

Zapekanka iz Grechnevoy Kashi s Gribami

A delectable rustic Slavic winter dish, this casserole is perfect as a side dish for stews or as a vegetarian entrée. Any form of pickle is a welcome addition.

1 ounce imported dried wild mushrooms, preferably porcini, well rinsed

8 tablespoons (1 stick) unsalted butter

1 cup whole kasha (buckwheat)

Salt, to taste

2 large onions, chopped

10 ounces fresh white mushrooms, wiped clean and sliced

1 cup sour cream

½ cup chicken broth

The Meaning of Kasha

So central is *kasha* to the Slavic peoples that the Russian language abounds with metaphorical expressions based on this resonant word. Six hundred years or so ago, the word *kasha* meant "feast," and the ancient chronicles tell many tales of wondrous *kasha* given by various rulers. *Kashas* were also important ritual foods at weddings, christenings, and funerals. They were eaten at peace treaty signings, giving rise to the expression which is still current: *S nim kashi ne svarish* — You can't make kasha with him (you won't get anywhere with this fellow). Other

kasha sayings include: *U nego v golove kasha* — He's got kasha in his head (he's all mixed up). *Zavarilas' kasha:* A kasha got cooked up (some confusion began). *Raskhlyobivat' kashu:* To spoon out the kasha (to straighten out the confusion). *Kashi maslom ne isportish:* You can't spoil kasha with butter (you can't have too much of a good thing).

1 Soak the dried mushrooms in 2 cups tepid water for 2 hours. Remove the mushrooms from the soaking liquid, pat dry with a paper towel, chop, and set aside. Strain the liquid through a coffee filter, transfer to a saucepan, and bring to a boil. Reduce the heat and keep at a bare simmer while preparing the next step.

2 Melt 2 tablespoons of the butter in an ovenproof medium-size casserole over medium heat. Add the kasha and stir for 3 to 4 minutes. Add the simmering liquid and salt, then reduce the heat, cover, and simmer until the liquid is absorbed, 15 to 20 minutes.

3 Meanwhile, melt another 4 tablespoons butter in a large skillet. Add the onions and sauté over medium heat for 5 minutes. Add the fresh and the wild mushrooms and sauté, stirring, until nicely colored, 15 to 20 minutes.

4 Preheat the oven to 375°F.

5 Stir the mushroom and onion mixture into the kasha. Blend together the sour cream and stock and add to the kasha. Stir well, then dot the top of the casserole with the remaining 2 tablespoons butter and bake until the top is lightly browned, 15 to 20 minutes. Serve at once.

Serves 4 to 6

Millet with Pumpkin

Pshonnaya Kasha s Tikvoy

When I was a child we were served this *kasha* for our kindergarten breakfasts. Like most Russian children, I hated breakfast-type *kasha* with a passion. For my mother, on the other hand, this was the food of the Gods and the kind-hearted nannies gave her my portion when she came to pick me up. Today, while I have no fond memories of that kindergarten, I try to have this *kasha* for breakfast as often as I can.

6 tablespoons (¾ stick) unsalted
    butter, or more if desired
1½ cups diced, peeled, fresh
    pumpkin

2¾ cups milk
1 cup hulled millet seeds
Small pinch of salt
1 tablespoon honey, or more to taste

1 Preheat the oven to 325°F.

2 Melt the butter in an ovenproof casserole, over medium-low heat. Add the pumpkin and sauté, stirring, until the pumpkin just begins to soften, about 5 to 6 minutes. Add the milk and bring to a gentle boil.

3 Place the millet in a large, heavy skillet and stir over medium-high heat until the seeds turn golden, about 5 minutes. Combine with the pumpkin, then add the salt and the honey and stir until it is dissolved. Reduce the heat to low, cover, and cook until the liquid is almost absorbed but the millet is still moist, about 15 minutes.

4 Place the covered casserole in the oven and bake until the millet is dry, 25 to 30 minutes. Add more butter, if desired, fluff the millet with a fork, and serve.

Serves 6

Central Asian Cuisine

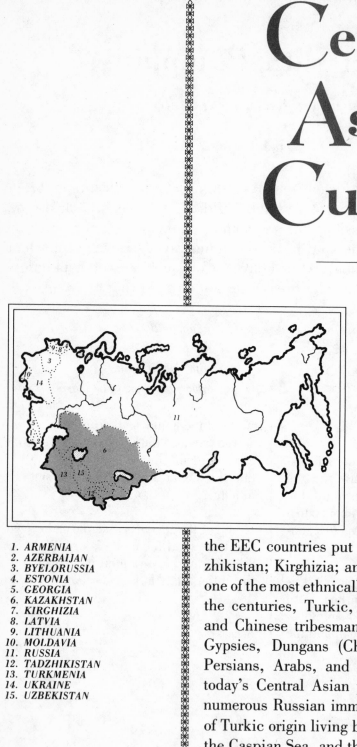

O nce known as the fabled Tatary, the vast semi-arid expanse of Soviet Central Asia is today unevenly divided among five republics: Kazakhstan, to the north, which is larger than the other four combined (and larger than all the EEC countries put together); Turkmenia; Tadzhikistan; Kirghizia; and Uzbekistan. This area is one of the most ethnically diverse in the world. Over the centuries, Turkic, Mongolian, Hun, Iranian, and Chinese tribesman have been augmented by Gypsies, Dungans (Chinese Muslims), Indians, Persians, Arabs, and Jews. But the majority of today's Central Asian population, apart from the numerous Russian immigrants, are Altaic peoples of Turkic origin living between the southern Urals, the Caspian Sea, and the spectacular Pamir mountains where the Soviet Union meets Afganistan and China.

Soviet Central Asia was the cradle of some of the earliest civilizations in the present day territory of the USSR. Astonishing irrigation systems were already watering the arid deserts of Uzbekistan and Turkmenia, south of the Aral Sea in the kingdom of Khorezm, as early as the seventh century B.C. The famous Silk Route stretched all the way from China to the eastern Mediterranean. Its fabulous processions of caravans carried fabrics and exotic spices from east to west and spawned rich trading towns, such as Samarkand and Bukhara, along the way. Following the conquests of Alexander the Great in the fourth century B.C., many fine Greek cities flourished in the region. These were mostly plundered and abandoned during the next millenium; but Samarkand became a magnificent city once more as the capital of the great empire forged by the Mongol warrior Tamerlane. Today it is still the proud site of gorgeous blue-tiled ancient mosques and other Islamic monuments, as well as Tamerlane's splendid mausoleum.

Though now almost entirely sedentary, the population of Soviet Central Asia, until recent times, used to be made up of a mixture of nomadic and semi-nomadic groups, mixed with city-dwelling Sarts and a few Russian colonists. The steppe and the desert, little water, and intermittently productive soil are the overriding physical determinants of everyday life in the region. But the land supports silver poplars, willows, plane trees, desert saksaul, and walnut and mulberry trees. There is also a profusion of vines, producing, according to one account of Turkmenia, grapes "of many kinds, white, green, and purple in color [that] vary considerably in

shape. Some are almost as large as plums, while the grape that is cultivated most is green and bottle-shaped, longer than any I have seen elsewhere; cut in half, it would make two grapes of ordinary size." Apricots, almonds, pistachios, giant pumpkins, "yellow and blue-black figs," sour pomegranates, pears, and the famous apples of Kazakhstan — all are picked and carefully stored in lofts and jars, and sometimes in the cool ground. All make their way into pilafs or desserts, where their outstanding quality and flavor render the foods of Central Asia not so much dishes to be consumed as delicacies to be savored.

One of the most notable features of Central Asia is its vast flocks of sheep, which turn the semi-desert landscape white as they are herded by tough highland shepherds from their summertime mountain pastures to the valleys and lowlands for the winter. These Karakul and Astarkhan sheep, with their handsome, curly fleeces, are pretty much a life-support system in themselves for the Central Asian peoples, providing milk and cheese, meat, and warm woolen clothing.

In the Bazaars

The Central Asian bazaars are justly as famous as those of Istanbul and Cairo. Here you can find a cornucopia of exotic fruits and spices, meat sold conveniently by the piece, fine sweetmeats and freshly blanched almonds, vendors selling herb fritters and a dozen other compelling fast foods. Old accounts of the bazaars tell of "Afghan Gypsies," "velvet-capped Tatars," "Hindu money changers,"

and purple-haired Bukharan silk dyers; and of a tempting profusion of syrups, ices, teas, and milk-based refreshments. And amid all this teeming energy you could hear gentle lute music and gaze at gorgeously costumed puppet shows. Some of this vibrant spectacle and tradition can still be glimpsed in the bazaars and local markets. The Turkmen hill folk still don their vast, shaggy fur hats and elaborate costumes; and fragments of the great Islamic culture that once flourished in the region are visible at every turn.

Uzbek and Tadzhik women still wear tunics and dresses made according to traditional designs, a fantasy of bright, colored stripes. And they still wear their hair in a multitude of long, intricate braids, which further enhances the finery of their costumes. The men, by contrast, wear quilted robes that supposedly keep them cool in the over-100-degree heat. Everyone wears a *tyubeteika*, a little head cap, usually in black with a white design. The *tyubeteika* is something of a status symbol; and although you might not be able to tell them apart at first glance, their cost can vary from one to a hundred or more rubles — the more expensive kinds having a pure silk lining and delicate, hand-picked motifs.

The fare of the markets is as legendary as the people themselves. You can find just about every kind of dried and fresh fruit imaginable. There are melons, grapes, figs, and over a dozen varieties of raisins alone. There are row upon row of unusual spices and dried herb mixtures, and wonderful

These two Tadzhik women are dressed in traditional fashion, complete with tunics, tyubeteikas, *and beautiful, long braids.*

radishes, light jade in color and sweet as honey. In Kazakhstan, you can find luscious apples the size of soccer balls.

Shopping in the market is a serious affair and is, in fact, often performed in a slow and rather dignified fashion. The local buyer will invariably handle and closely examine every item on the list. Serious faces will be made, the eyes rolled back and forth in elaborate expressions of fine judgment and connoisseurship. Most serious of all is the art of purchasing meat, which, like the preparation of a *plov* (pilaf), is reserved for the men.

Culinary Specialties

While there are many similarities among the various markets of Central Asia, the five Soviet republics all have notable specialties and culinary emphases. The nomadic, desert peoples of Turkmenia, for example, enjoy a diet made up almost exclusively of meat and milk products. They prepare meat dishes from camels, horses, lamb, and *dzeiran*, a mountain goat that makes an outstanding kebab. Meats are usually simply boiled or grilled and served without accompaniment. Perhaps the favorite dish of the Turkmenians is *kavardak* — lamb cut into large chunks and simmered in huge clay pots over coals made from the *saksaul* plant, a fern renowned for its aromatic properties, from the Karakum Desert. Meats are often dried in the desert sun so that they will endure for as long as the shepherd's great wanderings. Turkmenians drink *chal*, the fermented milk of camels and sheep. Fish dishes are rare in the region except among those who live along the Caspian Sea. Here sturgeon, whitefish, and snapper are popular ingredients for flavorful soups, pilafs, and kebabs. These people also make an outstanding fish dumpling, called *balik borek*.

The inhabitants of Kazakhstan and Kirghizia have also been traditionally nomadic. Most of the dishes of the area are very simple and rarely call for the kind of sophisticated kitchen utensils employed by a more sedentary population. As in Turkmenia the staples are simple, boiled meats, especially lamb and horse meat. The highly spiced horse meat sausage, *kazi*, is delicious; and the national dish, *besh barmak* (meaning "five fingers," as it is eaten with your hands), which combines homemade noodles, boiled lamb, and a lamb broth served separately, is a regional obsession. The eating of meat in Kazakhstan and Kirghizia constitutes a ritual in itself. Portions are scrupulously assigned according to familial hierarchy. A guest will always get the head of the animal, and particular cuts go to designated family members. The cuisine of these regions also bears fascinating traces of Chinese culinary traditions, which were imported by the Dungans and Uighurs. And the many Koreans who inhabit Kazakhstan have also contributed generously to the cuisine of their adopted home.

The most refined of the cuisines of Central Asia are undoubtedly those of Tadzhikistan and Uzbekistan. They are the product of many profound influences, including Persian (especially in Tadzhikistan), Chinese (steamed dumplings, steamed buns, fried noodles), Afghani, and even Indian. Extensive use is made of vegetables and fruits, including pumpkin, squash, turnips, radishes, eggplants, and tomatoes. Legumes such as kidney beans,

The best way to cut a melon is to cut off a piece from the top (this used to be done with special swords by the men of Central Asia), and then, holding the top piece in place so that the melon remains intact, to cut the remaining melon vertically into slices. When you remove the top that holds the pieces together, the melon should fall apart into beautiful, even slices.

The melons of Uzbekistan are renowned throughout the Soviet Union.

chick-peas, and lentils also figure in many dishes. Mung beans, called *mash* in Uzbekistan, are a great favorite. As in parts of China, steaming is perhaps the preferred way of preparing vegetables and dough products. And as in India, clay ovens (*tandir*) are used for baking the region's excellent breads. Many kinds of popular kebabs are made on special iron grills, called *mangal*. Finally and magnificently, reigning supreme over all other dishes in the region, is the delectable rice pilaf, unquestionably one of the most creative methods of preparing rice anywhere.

Virtually all known fruits and spices can be found in Uzbekistan — including no less than a thousand varieties of melon alone. Each variety often bears a name clearly indicating its special quality. These include *obi navvat* (which means "sweeter than sugar") and *non-gusht* ("bread and meat"). And their diversity of shapes, colors, and textures seem to outdo even these exotic names. In parts of Central Asia the Muslims believe the melon to be a holy fruit — and the design on its skin to be the writing of Allah.

It's little wonder, then, that rich folklore and elaborate rituals center on the melon. In Central Asia it is said that "earth is the melon's mother, the sun its father, and water its guardian." The poets of the East used to write beautiful odes to the fruit, dubbing it the "wonder of the East." In the autumn there is a colorful melon-tasting feast, the *kavum sayli*, which fills the air with the intoxicating fragrance of these magnificent fruits. Locals will buy up small mountains of melons when they are at their best to make enough compotes, jams, jellies, and syrups to last throughout the year. And in winter, such is the rarity of the melon in the more northerly parts of the Soviet Union, that they are sold in Moscow and Leningrad by migrant Uzbeks for up to a quarter of the average monthly salary. A melon is certainly the best "souvenir" that you can bring back from Central Asia at Christmastime.

Besides produce, flat breads (*non*), spicy *manti* (Uzbek lamb dumplings), walnut-filled pastries (*samsa*), and a delicious variety of milk drinks, many of them clabbered like the famous "cooler" *ayran*, are just some of the many other temptations of the region.

Beyond the Bazaars

As if they had anticipated the impossible temptation of so many mouthwatering foods and spices, street vendors hawk their wares at almost every corner. You can sample delicious *samsa* — filled, round pies that come with scallions or other herbs (in which case they are called *kuk samsa*), or with lamb, pumpkin, or mashed chick-peas. Or you can try the splendid large-size dumplings, *manti*, or their spicy, smaller relatives, *chuchvara*. At some point you'll surely sample a refreshing *ayran*, the time-honored way to quench a hot-weather thirst. *Ayran*, a yogurt-based drink, used to be served from containers made from sheep's stomachs (*torsuk*), which kept it at the right temperature as efficiently as any modern thermos. Then, as now, the taste of the cold, almost imperceptibly sour and slightly vis-

Tajiks

The Tajiks say that they are the oldest people in the land. They plant wheat, flax, and melons. They have long, resigned faces, and exhaust themselves in tending irrigation ditches. They keep fighting partridges and do not know how to look after horses.

In the valley above the Tajik village, we come to a camp. . . . Their yurts had domed white roofs, and the sides were painted with lozenges, scrolls, and chequers in every conceivable color, like a field of chivalry. Horses were grazing in a meadow of cornflowers, and there were white-leavened willows along the stream. We saw a fat-tailed sheep with a tail so big it had to be strapped to a cart. Outside the yurts, some women in purple were carding wool.

This is the time of year when the farmers and nomads, after a season of acrimony, are suddenly the best of friends. The harvest is in. The nomads buy grain for the winter. The villagers buy cheese and hides and meat. They welcome the sheep onto their fields: to break up the stubble and manure it for autumn planting.

— Bruce Chatwin,
The Songlines

Be attentive and receptive to guests. A true man expresses his dignity not only in combat, but in how he treats his fellow humans. You can be dying from fatigue, but never let it show to a guest. Always be modest about yourself and curious about the guest.

— Old Kazakh saying

cous liquid is enough to cool the most volcanic and market-vexed brow. And if you need to sit awhile to let the sights and tastes settle, you can always find a *chaikhana* (teahouse), with its abundance of characterful old men languidly sipping their green tea and gossiping about the day's business and the prospects for tomorrow.

More than anything else it is *dastarkhan* — the ancient Muslim hospitality ritual — that unites the immense land area of Soviet Central Asia and its kaleidoscope of traditions and produce. Whenever guests arrive, even if they are complete and utter strangers, they will always be offered a *piala* (cup-bowl) of piping hot green tea; a loud, dignified *torge shiginiz* ("welcome," in the Kazakh language); and a special hospitality tray divided into sections and loaded with delicacies such as *kishmish* (raisins), *uryuk* (dried apricots), dried chick-peas, pistachios, almonds, *navat* (sugar crystals), and *khalva* (halvah). In the older villages people still sit on low benches pulled up to an equally low, round table. And one can imagine them sitting there, patiently yet with visible anticipation, for only after a guest has finished his tea is it permissible to ask where he comes from, who he is, and what his business is: "Take my bread and salt and tell me the whole truth," as the old Kazakh saying puts it.

Dumplings and Noodles

IZDELIYA IZ TESTA

I am a true dumpling devotee — I adore them, whether they are Japanese *gyoza*, Korean *mandu*, Turkish *manti*, Siberian *pelmeni*, or Native American cornmeal dumplings. I could easily live a long happy life just on *dim sum*. And, if Marco Polo had done nothing else besides introducing Europeans to the Chinese way of noodle and dumpling making, as far as I'm concerned, it would have been more than enough to secure his immortality.

In every part of the Soviet Union, the native cooks excel in their own special preparations — pilafs in Central Asia, borscht in the Ukraine, grills in Azerbaijan. But stuffed dumplings — thin noodle dough wrapped around a choice morsel of food — are equally at home in every corner of this enormous culinary map. The noodle dough is pretty much the same throughout the Soviet Union, since what's needed are the most basic of ingredients: flour, water, and sometimes an egg or two. But after the dough is kneaded well, allowed to rest, and thinly rolled out, the national character of the dumpling comes to the fore in the manner of filling and the method of cooking.

The Central Asians, who are geographically close to China, steam their dumplings like the Chinese, but fill them with lamb according to the Turkic tradition. The Armenians also fill their dumplings with lamb and call them by the same name that they do in Central Asia (*manti*), but they then bake them in a tomato-flavored broth. The Siberians fill their *pelmeni*, a combination of pork, beef, and (sometimes) lamb. They make them by the hundreds, storing them in a cellar or outside in the freezing ground. But if there was a dumpling contest in the USSR, then the grand prize would have to be awarded to the Ukrainians, for whom plump dumplings called *vareniki* are truly a national obsession. Dozens of fillings and toppings and many hours of hard work go into the preparation of their native treat.

But the story does not end with filled dumplings — there are also "drop" dumplings, made from either grains or potatoes, eggs, and other flavorings, cooked in boiling water. These are easier to prepare and usually make wonderful accompaniments to stews, soaking up a rich home-style gravy. And then, of course, there are the plain homemade noodles, no mean treat in themselves.

Unfortunately there aren't too many shortcuts to making filled dumplings; the dough can be mixed in a food processor and rolled out in a pasta machine, of course, but time-saving tips pretty much end there. Once you

get the hang of it, though, filling dumplings is quite fun. Either invite a few
friends over for a nice gossip session,
turn on your favorite TV show, or play
a good Verdi opera. Dumplings, as the

Siberians realized centuries ago, are
a food made for the freezer, and in my
opinion, no freezer should be without
a good stock of them.

Ukrainian Filled Dumplings

Vareniki

Vareniki are made with simple noodle dough and can be filled with
almost anything, from sauerkraut to sour cherries. But it's nice to serve
them with two or more toppings for variety. These might include sour
cream, deeply browned onions, bacon cracklings, or, if the filling is sweet,
confectioners' sugar or Crème Fraîche (see Index). While boiling is a traditional way of cooking *vareniki*, they can also be fried in vegetable oil.

NOODLE DOUGH

2 cups unbleached all-purpose
    flour
Salt

2 large egg yolks
1 tablespoon vegetable oil
7 to 8 tablespoons water

1 large egg white, lightly beaten
1 recipe Potato, Cheese, Sauer-
    kraut, or Cherry Filling
    (recipes follow)

4 tablespoons (½ stick) unsalted
    butter

1 In a food processor, blend the flour and
½ teaspoon salt. With the motor running,
add the egg yolks and the oil through the

feed tube, then pour in the water, in a
slow, steady stream, until the dough forms
a ball around the blade. Transfer the

dough to a floured surface and knead until smooth, about 2 minutes. Cover with a linen or cotton (not terry cloth) kitchen towel and let stand for 30 minutes.

2 Divide the dough in half and shape into two balls. Keep one ball covered with the towel. On a floured surface with a floured rolling pin, roll out the dough to a very thin sheet, about 1/16 inch thick (if making the Cherry Filling, roll out slightly thicker to prevent tearing during cooking), making sure it doesn't tear. With a round cookie cutter, cut out circles about 3 inches in diameter. Gather the scraps together into a ball and set aside, covered.

3 Have a bowl with the egg white by you. Place a heaping teaspoon of the desired filling in the middle of each circle. Fold the dough over the filling to form a semi-circle. Brush the edges with the egg white and press the edges firmly together with the tines of a fork to seal. Place the *vareniki* as they are made on a lightly floured large baking sheet about 1 inch apart and keep covered with a damp cloth.

When you have finished making this batch of *vareniki*, roll out the second ball of dough and make a second batch. Add the leftover scraps of dough to the scraps left from the first batch, knead into a ball, and roll out for a final batch of *vareniki*.

4 Meanwhile, in a large pot, bring 6 quarts of salted water to a boil (or divide the water between two pots).

5 Reduce the heat to medium so the water simmers and carefully lower half the *vareniki* into the water. Boil, stirring occasionally with a wooden spoon to prevent sticking, until they rise to the surface, and are cooked through, 6 to 7 minutes. With a slotted spoon, carefully remove the *vareniki* to a colander and drain thoroughly. Transfer to a deep serving bowl and toss with half the butter.

6 Cook the rest of the *vareniki* in the same way.

Makes 50 to 55 vareniki (serves 4 people as an entrée)

Potato Filling
Nachinka z Kartopli

Richly browned onions or bacon cracklings or sour cream make a good accompaniment for *vareniki* with this filling.

> 6 tablespoons (¾ stick) unsalted
>   butter
> 1 medium-size onion, finely
>   chopped
> 3 large boiling potatoes, peeled,
>   boiled, and mashed
> ¼ pound farmer's cheese
> 2 ounces Colby or other mild
>   Cheddar cheese, grated
> Salt and freshly ground black
>   pepper, to taste

Happiness Is Plenty of Vareniki

Patsuk opened his mouth, stared at the vareniki, *and opened his mouth wider still. At that moment, a verenik jumped out of the bowl, splashed into the cream, flipped over and leapt straight up into his mouth. Patsuk ate it, opened his mouth again, and another verenik went through the same performance. The only trouble he took was to munch it up and to swallow it.*
—Nikolai Gogol
Christmas Eve

This is how one of Gogol's characters, a sorcerer, put his precious magic gift to use. I often wish dumpling magic would come true for me. But, alas, I not only have to use a fork like everyone else, but I also have to go through the pains of preparation. The only alternative is buying frozen *vareniki*, known in this country by their Polish name, *pierogi*, or to pop into one of New York's Ukrainian or Polish diners — but the result in either case, though often tasty and well made, is not as good as the real thing.

Vareniki can be easily frozen, so if you happen to be in the mood, you should always make more than you can possibly eat at a single sitting. But remember, *vareniki* are one of the most beguiling "just one more" foods, and any estimate you might make of the total number required to satisfy your company should be doubled at least, if you don't want to disappoint.

Sometimes, when there's an old Hollywood classic on TV, I resolve not to be idle while I watch it and set out on a dumpling marathon. I recall that it wasn't much different back in the USSR. Once I spent a month with relations in Odessa during the premiere of a thirteen-part spy thriller (well, okay, the sides were changed around a little). We were all eating the *vareniki*, which had been mass produced by the hundreds, and I still had a doggy-bag full to take on the train back to Moscow.

1 Melt the butter in a small skillet over medium heat. Add the onion and sauté, stirring occasionally, until nicely browned, about 15 minutes. Remove from the heat and let cool slightly.

2 In a large bowl, combine the potatoes and cheese. Add the sautéed onion along with the cooking fat and mix well. Season with salt and pepper, then use to fill the *vareniki*.

Makes enough to fill 50 to 55 vareniki

Cheese Filling

Sirna Nachinka

This filling can be either sweet or savory, so add salt or sugar accordingly. Serve with sour cream and confectioners' sugar, if sweet.

> 2 cups farmer's cheese
>
> 1 large egg yolk
>
> 3 tablespoons sugar for sweet
>   vareniki *or* salt, to taste, for savory
>
> ½ teaspoon vanilla sugar for sweet
>   vareniki *(optional; see page 473)*

In a large bowl, combine all the filling ingredients and mix thoroughly. Use as a filling for *vareniki*.

Makes enough to fill 50 to 55 vareniki

If you are lucky enough to own a pasta machine, you can certainly use it to roll out dumpling dough. It won't necessarily save time, but it will give you a perfectly smooth, thin dough. Working in small batches, roll out the dough as you would for ravioli or tortellini, using the smooth rollers of the machine.

Sauerkraut Filling

Nachinka z Kvashenoyi Kapusti

In any recipe calling for sauerkraut, be sure to buy the freshest available — straight from the barrel or the kind sold in plastic bags works best. Serve sautéed onions as an accompaniment, along with the bacon from the recipe.

3 slices bacon, diced

1 large onion, chopped

3½ cups packaged (not canned)
sauerkraut, rinsed and squeezed
thoroughly dry

1½ tablespoons tomato
paste

2 teaspoons sugar

⅓ cup chicken or beef
broth

1 Sauté the bacon in a large skillet over medium heat until it renders its fat. Remove the bacon and reserve. Drain off all but 2 tablespoons fat.

2 Add the onion to the skillet and sauté, stirring frequently over medium heat until nicely browned, almost 15 minutes. Turn the heat up to medium-high, add the sauerkraut, and sauté, stirring, until sof-tened and cooked throughout, 10 to 15 minutes. Stir in the tomato paste, sugar, and broth. Reduce the heat to low, then cover and simmer for 20 minutes. Remove from the heat and cool to room temperature before using to fill *vareniki*. Use the reserved bacon as a topping.

Makes enough to fill 50 to 55 vareniki

Cherry Filling
Nachinka z Vishni

This filling is simply glorious. The Ukrainians use sour cherries from their gardens, without even bothering to remove the pits. But if you can't find fresh sour cherries, use jarred imported cherries, available at some supermarkets and specialty food stores.

Place the cherry-filled *vareniki* in a serving bowl, top with a dollop of sour cream, or Crème Fraîche (see Index), pour some juice over them, and top with a few cherries. They shouldn't be served very hot.

4 cups pitted fresh or jarred sour
cherries

½ cup sugar for fresh cherries,
¼ cup for jarred

Cherry juice, if necessary

¼ cup cherry liqueur

1 tablespoon cornstarch

1 If you are using fresh cherries, mix them with the ½ cup sugar and leave in a warm place for several hours until they begin to give off their juice. Strain the juice. You should have about 2 cups. If less, add canned or bottled cherry juice.

If you are using canned cherries, drain them thoroughly and reserve 2 cups of the syrup. Mix the canned cherries with the ¼ cup sugar. Reserve several cherries for garnish.

2 In a small saucepan, bring the reserved juice or syrup to a boil over medium-high heat. Let boil until reduced to about 1 cup. Remove from the heat, stir in the liqueur, and let cool to room temperature. Reserve to pour over the filled and cooled *vareniki*.

3 Toss the cherries with the cornstarch. Fill each *varenik* with 2 fresh or 4 canned cherries, sealing especially tightly.

Makes enough to fill 50 to 55 vareniki (serves 6 for brunch, 8 for dessert)

Cheese Dumplings

Sirni Halushki

This is a wonderful dish full of childhood memories. I often serve *halushki* as a pasta course, just as I would Italian gnocchi. In this case, they can be sprinkled with Parmesan cheese instead of the traditional sour cream. *Halushki* can also be served as dessert dumplings. Just increase the amount of sugar to ⅓ cup and serve with fresh berries and Crème Fraîche (see Index).

3 large eggs

1 pound farmer's cheese

⅓ cup farina (cream of wheat; not instant)

¼ cup all-purpose flour

1 teaspoon sugar

Salt, to taste

3 tablespoons instant flour (such as Wondra) for rolling out the dough

4 tablespoons (½ stick) unsalted butter, cut into pieces

Sour cream or freshly grated Parmesan cheese

1 In a large bowl, lightly beat the eggs. Thoroughly mix in the farmer's cheese, farina, all-purpose flour, sugar, and salt. Refrigerate, covered, for 30 minutes.

2 In a large pot, bring 2 quarts of water to a boil over medium-high heat.

3 Sprinkle your work surface with the instant flour. Roll one-third of the farmer's cheese mixture into a long roll about 1 inch thick. With a sharp knife, cut the roll diagonally into 1½-inch pieces. Repeat with the rest of the mixture. Drop the dum-plings into the boiling water and cook until they rise to the surface and are cooked through, 3 to 4 minutes. You will probably have to do this in batches.

4 With a slotted spoon, remove the dumplings to a colander and drain well.

5 Transfer the dumplings to a serving bowl, toss with the butter and serve with the sour cream or Parmesan cheese on the side.

Makes 30 to 35 halushki

Siberian Meat-Filled Dumplings

Pelmeni

Delicious Siberian meat-filled dumplings, *pelmeni*, are really what frozen food is all about. Made by the hundreds, at one time they were stored outside in huge bags throughout the seemingly endless Siberian winters. In Russia today, *pelmeni* are served in special *pelmeni* parlors called *pelmennaya*, and are a very popular fast food. Street *pelmeni* are, however, much inferior to the homemade variety, which should contain two kinds of meat and be lovingly shaped by hand (although you can find commercial "*pelmeni* makers" in the USSR). Eating *pelmeni* also takes a special skill, and I've often heard tough Russians brag about how many *pelmeni* they were able to consume at a sitting — it can get up to a hundred.

Pelmeni can be served in beef or chicken broth as a first course, or they can be fried in butter, which is less authentic but truly delicious. Traditional accompaniments for *pelmeni* are sour cream, perhaps sprinkled with dill or white vinegar. I actually like mixing the two.

DOUGH

3 cups sifted unbleached all-purpose
  flour
1 scant teaspoon salt

1 large egg
1 cup cold water

FILLING

¾ pound ground beef
½ pound ground pork
2 medium-size onions, finely chopped

¼ cup crushed ice
Salt and freshly ground black
  pepper, to taste

Salt, to taste, for cooking the
  pelmeni
1 large egg white, lightly beaten

4 tablespoons (½ stick) unsalted
  butter, cut into pieces

1 In a food processor, blend the flour and salt. With the motor running, add the egg, through the feed tube, then pour in the water, in a slow, steady stream, until the dough forms a ball around the blade. Transfer the dough to a floured surface and knead until smooth, about 2 minutes. Cover with a linen or cotton (not terry cloth) kitchen towel and let stand for 30 minutes.

2 In a large bowl, combine all the filling ingredients, stirring until they are thoroughly mixed.

3 Divide the dough in half and shape into two balls. Keep one ball covered with the towel. On a floured surface, with a floured rolling pin, roll out the dough to a very thin sheet, about 1/16 inch thick, making sure it doesn't tear. With a round cookie cutter, cut out 2-inch circles.

4 In a small saucepan, bring 2 cups of salted water to a boil over high heat.

5 Have a bowl with the egg white near you. Place a scant teaspoon of filling toward the bottom of one circle. Fold the empty half of the dough over the filling to form a semi-circle. Brush the edges with the egg white and press the edges firmly together with the tines of a fork to seal. Fold the ends of the semi-circle firmly together over the filled portion and press them against the dumpling. Boil the one dumpling for 10 minutes to taste the filling for seasoning; *pelmeni* should be well seasoned.

6 Fill and shape the remaining rounds, arranging dumplings as they are made on a lightly floured baking sheet, about 1 inch apart. At this point, *pelmeni* are usually frozen. Cover the baking sheet with aluminum foil or plastic wrap and place in the freezer until they are completely frozen. When frozen, transfer the *pelmeni* to a plastic bag.

7 To cook the *pelmeni*, bring 6 quarts of salted water to a boil in a large pot (or divide the water between two pots). Drop in half the *pelmeni* and cook, stirring occasionally with a wooden spoon to prevent sticking, until they rise to the surface and are thoroughly cooked through, about 8 minutes. With a slotted spoon, carefully remove the *pelmeni* to a colander and drain well. Transfer to a deep serving bowl and toss with some of the butter.

8 Cook the remaining *pelmeni* the same way.

Makes 100 pelmeni *(serves 6 to 8)*

Uzbek Steamed Lamb Dumplings

Manti

These juicy lamb dumplings are my personal favorite. Serve them as a main course, topped with Yogurt and Garlic Sauce and plenty of black pepper. In Uzbekistan, these *manti*, consumed prodigiously, are cooked in special, deep, multileveled steamers (which every Uzbek housewife brings to the States when she emigrates). Chinese bamboo steamers make an excellent substitute. The proper texture for the meat is very important. The Uzbeks actually chop it fine by hand. It can be coarsely ground instead, but make sure you don't grind it too fine or else the meat will clump together.

1 recipe dough for Vareniki *(see page 401)*

FILLING

1½ pounds boneless shoulder or leg of lamb, coarsely ground
2 medium-size onions, finely chopped
⅓ cup Lamb Stock (see Index) or canned beef broth
½ cup chopped fresh cilantro

1 to 2 teaspoons freshly ground black pepper
Salt, to taste
8 tablespoons (1 stick) unsalted butter, cut into 24 pieces
Yogurt and Garlic Sauce (see Index)

1 On a floured surface with a floured rolling pin, roll out one ball of dough to a very thin sheet about ⅟₁₆ inch thick. With a round cookie cutter cut out 4-inch circles from the dough. Roll out the second ball of dough and continue cutting out circles until you have 24.

2 In a large bowl, thoroughly combine the lamb, onions, stock, cilantro, pepper, and salt.

3 Have a bowl of cold water near you. Mound 2 tablespoons of the filling in the center of each circle. Top each with a piece of butter. Fold the sides up and around the filling. Wet your fingers in cold water and pinch the edges together on top.

4 Bring water to a depth of 2 inches to a boil in the bottom of a regular steamer, or in the bottom of a large wok or other pot, if you are using a Chinese multilevel bamboo steamer. Grease the metal steamer top well. Add as many *manti* as will fit comfortably, without touching, to the steamer top (or tops). Steam, tightly covered, about 20 minutes, reversing the position of the multilevel tops halfway through the steam time. Remove the *manti* to a plate and keep warm, covered. Steam any remaining *manti* the same way.

5 Serve the *manti* with the Yogurt and Garlic Sauce spooned over the top.

Makes 24 manti (serves 6)

Tiny Soup Dumplings filled with Wild Mushrooms

Ushki

These delightful little dumplings, whose Russian name means "little tears," are served in the traditional Ukrainian borscht made for Christmas Eve, or in wild mushroom soup or a simple broth or consommé. If you like them as much as I do, make them slightly larger than directed and serve them with a simple cream sauce, as you would tortellini. If you serve this *ushki* in Wild Mushroom Soup (see Index), just omit the noodles.

2 ounces imported dried wild
    mushrooms, preferable porcini,
    well rinsed
¼ cup vegetable oil
1 cup finely chopped onions
Salt and freshly ground black
    pepper, to taste

¼ cup unflavored fine, dry bread
    crumbs
2 large egg whites, lightly
    beaten
½ recipe dough for Vareniki (see
    page 401)

1 Soak the mushrooms in 2 cups water for 2 hours. Remove the mushrooms from the soaking liquid, pat dry with paper towels, chop very fine or mince in a food processor, and set aside. Strain the soaking liquid through a coffee filter, setting aside 3 tablespoons and reserving the rest for another use.

2 Heat the oil in a small skillet over medium heat. Add the onions and sauté, stirring occasionally, until light golden, about 10 minutes. Add the mushrooms and sauté, stirring, for 5 minutes. Add 2 tablespoons of the mushroom soaking liquid and cook for 10 minutes longer. Remove from the heat and let cool about 10 minutes.

3 Season the mushroom mixture with salt and pepper, add the bread crumbs and 1 of the egg whites, and mix well.

4 On a floured surface with a floured rolling pin, roll out the dough to a very thin sheet about ¹⁄₁₆ inch thick. With a pizza cutter or a large, sharp knife, cut the dough into 1-inch squares.

5 Have a bowl with the remaining egg white near you. Place a heaping ¼ teaspoon of filling near one corner of each square. Moisten the edges of the square with egg white. Fold the dough in half to form a triangle and firmly press the edges together with the tines of a fork to seal. Bring the opposite corners of the triangle together and pinch to seal. Place the *ushki* as they are made on a lightly floured large baking sheet and cover with a linen or cotton (no terry cloth) kitchen towel.

6 In a large pot, bring 4 quarts salted water to a boil over high heat. Or bring a pot of soup to boil.

7 Drop the *ushki* into the boiling water or soup and boil until tender, 4 to 5 minutes. Boil only as many as you need at a time and freeze the rest (see page 408, Step 6).

Makes 45 to 50 ushki

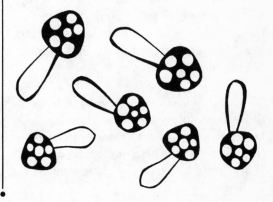

Armenian Dumplings Baked in Broth

Monti

Another excellent recipe for lamb-filled dumplings, this one from Armenia. These are baked and then moistened at the end with tomato-flavored broth. Serve with Yogurt and Garlic Sauce.

3 tablespoons olive oil
¾ pound ground lean lamb
½ cup finely chopped onion
2 cloves garlic, minced
¼ cup finely chopped fresh parsley,
*   plus additional for garnish*
Salt and freshly ground black
*   pepper, to taste*
1 recipe dough for Vareniki *(see*
*   page 401)*

3 tablespoons tomato paste
4 cups Beef Stock or Chicken Stock
*   (see Index for both), or canned*
*   broth*
6 tablespoons (¾ stick) unsalted
*   butter, melted*
½ teaspoon hot Hungarian
*   paprika*
Yogurt and Garlic Sauce (see Index)

1 Heat the oil in a medium-size skillet over medium-high heat. Add the lamb, onion, and garlic and sauté, chopping up the meat with a fork, until the lamb is cooked through, about 10 minutes. Off the heat, add the parsley and salt and pepper. Set the filling aside.

2 On a floured surface with a floured rolling pin, roll out one ball of dough, to a very thin sheet, about ¹⁄₁₆ inch thick. Trim the edges with a pizza cutter or a large, sharp knife and cut the dough into 1½ inch squares.

3 Preheat the oven to 350°F. Lightly butter 1 or 2 large, shallow roasting pans.

4 Have a bowl of cold water near you. Put about ¾ teaspoon of filling on each dough square. Moisten two opposing points of each square with water and pinch them together over the filling. Leave the ends of the *monti* open. As each *monti* is made, place it in the prepared roasting pan and cover with a slightly damp linen or cotton (not terry cloth) kitchen towel to keep them from drying out. You should have about 50 *monti*.

5 Bake the *monti* until light brown, about 15 minutes.

6 Meanwhile, in a large saucepan dilute the tomato paste in the broth. Season with salt and pepper and bring to a boil over medium heat. Pour half the broth over the *monti* and bake for another 10 minutes. Pour in the remaining broth and bake until the *monti* have absorbed some of the liquid, about 15 to 20 minutes more.

7 Melt the butter in a small saucepan over low heat. Off the heat, stir in the hot paprika.

8 Place the *monti* and some liquid in individual serving bowls. Drizzle with some of the butter and sprinkle with parsley. Serve the Yogurt and Garlic Sauce on the side.

Makes about 50 monti *(serves 4)*

Barley-Shaped Pasta, Russian Style

Barli Pasta s Gribami

As you can probably tell from the title of this dish, this is a Russianized recipe, using an American product, Goodman's Toasted Barley Shape. I tasted it in several emigré homes in New York and found it very Russian and very delectable. It makes a great accompaniment to hearty winter stews or roasts.

5 tablespoons vegetable oil
1½ cups finely chopped
onions
10 ounces mushrooms, cleaned
and chopped
8 ounces Goodman's Toasted Barley
Shape

½ cup canned chicken broth
¼ cup heavy or whipping cream
Salt and freshly ground black
pepper, to taste

1 Heat 2 tablespoons of the oil in a medium-size skillet over medium heat. Add the onions and sauté until well browned, about 15 minutes. Remove from the skillet and set aside.

2 In the same skillet, heat the remaining 3 tablespoons of oil over medium-high heat. Add the mushrooms and sauté until they are golden, about 15 minutes.

3 In a large pot, bring 2 quarts of salted water to a boil. Add the toasted barley shape and cook until just tender, about 8 minutes. Drain well in a colander.

4 Add the chicken broth and cream to the pot and bring to a boil. Add the cooked toasted barley shape, mushrooms, onions, and salt and pepper and mix well. Cover and simmer over low heat until the liquid is absorbed and the flavors are blended, about 7 minutes.

Serves 4

Pasta Russa

One of my favorite pasta sauces is the one I have created based on a combination of favorite Russian flavors — wild mushrooms, lots of deeply browned onions, cream, and Madeira. To make it, brown the onions in oil and remove them from the skillet. Cook your favorite wild mushrooms in the same skillet, then remove them. Add some Madeira and cream to the skillet and reduce to half. Return the mushrooms and onions to the skillet, add salt and pepper, a dash of sweet paprika, and some chopped parsley. Serve over fresh fettuccine or angel hair pasta. Divine!

Pasta, Lamb, and Feta Cheese Casserole

Ghiymya Hinkal

A totally new twist for pasta lovers — homemade pasta diamonds, topped with subtly seasoned ground lamb, then sprinkled with feta, finished in the oven, and served with a Yogurt and Garlic Sauce with Cinnamon.

2 tablespoons olive oil

1 cup chopped onions

¾ pound boneless lean lamb
  shoulder, ground

1 medium-size fresh ripe tomato,
  peeled and finely chopped

1 clove garlic, crushed in
  a garlic press

3 tablespoons pine nuts (pignoli),
  toasted (see Index)

1½ teaspoon sweet Hungarian
  paprika

⅛ teaspoon ground allspice

¼ teaspoon ground cinnamon

¼ teaspoon cayenne pepper

Salt, to taste

5 tablespoons finely chopped fresh
  parsley

½ recipe dough for Vareniki (see
  page 401)

¾ cup crumbled feta cheese,
  preferably Bulgarian

1 cup plain low-fat yogurt

2 cloves garlic, minced

½ teaspoon ground cinnamon

1 Heat the oil in a large heavy skillet over medium heat. Add the onions and sauté, stirring occasionally until golden, about 10 minutes.

2 Increase the heat to medium-high and add the ground lamb. Sauté, breaking up the meat with a fork until the meat is cooked through, 10 minutes. Stir in the tomato, garlic, and pine nuts, then turn the heat down to medium-low and sauté, stirring, for 7 to 8 minutes. Add the spices, including the salt, and sauté for 5 minutes more. Off the heat, stir in 3 tablespoons of the parsley and set aside.

3 On a floured surface with a floured rolling pin, roll out the dough into a very thin square about ¹⁄₁₆ inch thick. With a pizza cutter or a large, sharp knife, cut the dough into 1-inch diamonds. Gather the scraps into a ball, reroll, and cut out more pasta.

4 In a large pot, bring 4 quarts salted water to a boil over high heat.

5 Preheat the oven to 375°F. Lightly butter a medium-size ovenproof casserole.

6 Add the pasta to the boiling water, stirring with a wooden spoon to prevent sticking, and cook until the pasta rises to the surface, about 3 minutes. Drain thoroughly in a colander and place in the prepared casserole.

7 Top the pasta with the meat, sprinkle with the feta cheese, and bake until heated through and the top is bubbly, about 10 minutes.

8 In a small bowl, combine the yogurt and garlic. Stir well to mix, and let stand about 15 minutes. Just before serving, swirl in the cinnamon.

9 Sprinkle the casserole with the remaining 2 tablespoons parsley and serve the yogurt sauce on the side.

Serves 4

Apple and Noodle Kugel

Kugel iz Lapshi s Yablokami

This is a wonderfully comforting Jewish dish from Lithuania that is ideal for brunch, but goes down just as well for dessert. I make it with a greater percentage of apples than noodles, but you adjust the amounts, if you wish.

4 cups cooked wide egg
    noodles
3 large eggs, lightly beaten
4 tablespoons (packed) light brown
    sugar
6 medium-size tart apples (such as
    Granny Smith), peeled and
    cored
2 tablespoons fresh lemon juice

½ cup raisins
¼ cup slivered almonds
1 tablespoon ground
    cinnamon
2 tablespoons unflavored fine, dry
    bread crumbs
4 tablespoons (½ stick) butter,
    melted

1 Preheat the oven to 375°F.

2 In a large bowl, mix the noodles with the beaten eggs and 2 tablespoons of the sugar. Set aside.

3 Grate the apples into another bowl and sprinkle with the lemon juice. Add the remaining sugar, raisins, almonds, and cinnamon and mix well. Let stand for 10 minutes.

4 Butter a round baking dish and sprinkle with some of the bread crumbs. Arrange one third of the noodle mixture on the bottom and top with half the apple mixture. Repeat the layers, finishing with the remaining noodles. Sprinkle the top with the remaining crumbs and drizzle with the melted butter. Bake until the top is golden brown, about 50 minutes.

5 Cool slightly and serve.

Serves 4

Breads and Savory Pies

KHLEBA I PIROGHI

All over the world, people derive a special pleasure from the taste of a good loaf of bread; but none perhaps treat bread with such reverence as the Slavs. Together with salt, bread is the ancient symbol of Slavic hospitality, an integral part of a hundred rituals and ceremonies. As far back as the time of Peter the Great, special laws were passed to regulate the quality of bread. Breadmakers who sold loaves smaller than those stipulated under the law, or whose bread wasn't properly baked through, were rounded up and summarily beaten.

In the 1940s, the Russians doubled the already profound value placed upon bread due to their terrible experiences during World War II. For long months it was the only food available, and even then it was strictly rationed. My relatives still have vivid recollections of youngsters in the 1950s being yelled at by war veterans or grouchy *babushkas* for casually tossing a fragment of a sticky bun into the trash can. A living testimony to the honor of bread can be found in the Moscow Museum of Bread, with its old manuscripts, ancient breadmaking tools, reproductions of various breads, and an especially poignant room devoted to World War II. I once saw a whole book detailing a hundred imaginative uses for leftover bread.

A Good Russian Loaf

As you can see, a Russian house without bread is as unthinkable as a house without walls. In normal times, bread is consumed in incredible amounts by the Russians. When I have Russian guests, I buy enough bread for all and then three times more. Often my visitors will devour a whole loaf each at a single sitting, spreading it thickly with butter, complaining that the quality of bread is so bad outside Russia, and apologizing between mouthfuls that they haven't eaten more. I must admit that I often now pine for the flavor of Russian bread—those rich, dark, nutty, slightly sour, nicely moist rectangular loaves. I wouldn't trade them for the most perfect French baguettes. Unfortunately, these are nearly impossible to reproduce at home as the grind and quality of the flour and the ovens are very different in Russia.

When John and I arrived in Moscow at the beginning of our last visit, my father drove us straight to the bakery (*bulochnaya*) to buy some bread for breakfast. These are usually self-service affairs, the breads temptingly exposed on wooden shelves so they can be poked and prodded for freshness with a large fork provided for the purpose. The Russians have had to endure sad declines in the quality of much produce during the last century, but one thing that has never surrendered to lower standards is their beloved bread. In addition, the State has long subsidized the price, so a loaf costs just a few cents—though this will no doubt change as the country moves toward a market economy.

In a bakery, one can buy several varieties of dark (*chorniy*) bread, though most people's favorite is *borodinsky*, a dark-brown, slightly sweet-tasting loaf that is studded with coriander seeds. Almost all of the dark bread is sourdough; indeed, the first Slavic breads were prepared from a base called *zakvaska*, which was allowed to "sour," or ferment, for several days before being added, little by little, to other batches of dough to produce the loaves. Bakeries also sell fine oblong white loaves, delicious savory crescents (*rogaliki*), huge bagels sprinkled with poppy seeds (*bubliki*), and a host of plump buns (*bulochki*), which are either plain or filled with jam or poppy seeds.

And Throughout the USSR

Slavs are not alone among Soviets in their passion for bread. In the Caucasus and Central Asia, bread-making is carried on in an outside clay oven, similar to the Indian *tandoori*, and appropriately called *tandir* in Central Asia, *tonir* in Armenia, and *tone* by the Georgians. Unlike Slavic breads, which are baked in a slow-baking stove to yield large, dense loaves, the tandoori-type oven is hot enough to make a wonderfully chewy flatbread, with a distinct smoky aroma in less than ten minutes.

In Armenia and Azerbaijan, the most common bread is the almost paper-thin *lavash*, which comes in large sheets and is used tortilla-like for wrapping around food. Another favorite is *pide*, one of the many variations on pita. A particularly delicious bread in Georgia is called *deda puri* ("mother's bread"). This one is not flat, but long and slightly crooked, somewhat resembling a saber. In Tbilisi, the capital, you see proud, mustached men carrying big bags of the bread—presumably to their mothers'.

The staple bread in Central Asia comes in a large, plump circle and is called *non*. It has an indentation in the middle that usually features an attractive design poked out with a special forklike instrument, the *chikech*. *Non* can be flavored with scallions, onions, sesame seeds, or with the great local favorite, lamb fat cracklings. Working people in the region will sit down to a basic meal of fresh *non* and half a luscious melon. They will tell you that nothing could taste better.

But breads are not the only masterpieces that come out of the Russian and ethnic ovens. Nearly each region of the Soviet Union has an impressive repertoire of savory filled pies and pastries. Small and large, baked or fried, with dozens of inventive fillings, these wonderful creations are the true treasures of the Soviet home.

Caucasian Thin Bread

Lavash

Like tortillas in Mexico, *lavash* is an indispensable component of any Caucasian meal. It is so thin that it is mainly used for wrapping around pieces of local cheese, grilled meats, or simply sprigs of fresh mint, tarragon, cilantro, or local opal basil.

I have noticed that *lavash* is catching on in this country. It is "imported" from California, where it is mass produced by Armenian bakeries, and is often available in quality food stores in large cities.

This bread keeps extremely well in an airtight container. If you freeze it, wrap it first in aluminum foil. Just heat it in the oven before serving.

2 teaspoons active dry yeast
½ teaspoon sugar
1 cup lukewarm water (105°
  to 115 °F)
½ teaspoon salt

3¼ to 3½ cups unbleached all-
  purpose flour
2 tablespoons unsalted butter,
  melted

1 In a large bowl, combine the yeast, sugar, and water, and let stand until foamy, about 5 minutes. Stir in the salt.

2 Add 3¼ cups of the flour, 1 cup at a time, mixing well after each addition with a wooden spoon.

3 Transfer the dough to a floured surface and knead until smooth and elastic, about 10 minutes, adding enough of the remaining flour to prevent sticking. Shape the dough into a ball and place in a large bowl. Drizzle with the melted butter and turn to coat with the butter. Cover with a linen or cotton (not terry cloth) kitchen towel and let rise in a warm, draft-free spot until doubled in bulk, about 2 hours.

4 Punch the dough down and divide into six pieces. Shape each into a ball and flatten into 1-inch-thick rounds. Cover with a towel and let stand at room temperature for 30 minutes.

5 Preheat the oven to 450°F. Place a large, heavy-duty baking sheet in the oven to heat for 5 to 10 minutes.

6 On a floured surface with a floured rolling pin, roll out one of the pieces of dough into a 12 × 10-inch rectangle. Carefully remove the baking sheet from the oven. Drape the rolled-out dough over the rolling pin and unroll it onto the baking sheet. Bake in the lower third of the oven until the bread is slightly bubbly and browned, 5 to 6 minutes. Remove from the baking sheet to the work surface, sprinkle with cold water, and cover with a towel. Repeat with the rest of the dough. When all the breads are baked, wrap in aluminum foil and let stand for 30 minutes.

Makes 6 breads

Note: if you like the breads crispy, don't sprinkle them with water or wrap in foil. Just let the breads cool on a rack.

Central Asian Flatbreads

Non

B aking has been a major preoccupation in Central Asia since ancient times, and the way with bread has changed very little through the centuries. Everyone lucky enough to own a private house equips it with a *tandir*, a cylindrical clay oven used mainly for baking *non*, which is baked by sprinkling rounds of dough with water and slapping them onto the walls of the *tandir.* In this country, many emigrés from that part of the world, acquire baking tiles or stones, which helps to reproduce the taste of their cherished bread. Lacking these, however, you can still make great flatbread. Simply preheat your oven well, and use a well-heated, heavy-duty baking sheet or the back of a cast-iron skillet or earthenware casserole. Enjoy the *non* while it's still hot.

2½ cups lukewarm water (105° to 115°F)

1 package active dry yeast

1½ teaspoons sugar

1 tablespoon vegetable oil

¾ teaspoon salt

4 to 4½ cups unbleached all-purpose flour

2 cups whole-wheat flour

½ cup minced onion

1 teaspoon minced garlic

1 In a large bowl, combine ¼ cup of the water, the yeast, and sugar and let stand until foamy, about 5 minutes.

2 Add the rest of the water, the oil, and the salt, then gradually add 4 cups of the all-purpose flour and all the whole-wheat flour, 1 cup at a time, mixing well after each addition with a wooden spoon.

3 Transfer the dough to a floured surface and knead until smooth and elastic, about 10 minutes, adding enough of the remaining all-purpose flour to prevent sticking.

4 Shape the dough into a ball, place in a buttered bowl and turn to coat. Cover with a linen or cotton (not terry cloth) kitchen towel and let rise in a warm, draft-free place until doubled in bulk, about 1½ hours.

5 Divide the dough into eight pieces and shape each piece into a ball. On a floured surface with a floured rolling pin, roll out each ball into a round about 7 inches in diameter. With a pastry brush, brush each round with cold water. Cover with a towel and let stand for 30 minutes.

6 Meanwhile, preheat the oven to 500°F. Place a heavy-duty baking sheet in the oven to heat for 15 minutes.

7 Wet your hands in cold water and make an indentation in the center of each dough round about 2 inches in diameter. With a fork, prick all over the indentation in a circular fashion. Sprinkle with the onion and garlic.

8 Carefully remove the baking sheet from the oven. Sprinkle the rounds lightly with cold water and place on the baking sheet. Bake in the lowest part of the oven until the breads are light golden and baked through, 12 to 15 minutes. Remove from the oven, wrap in a clean, damp kitchen towel, and let rest for 10 minutes.

Makes 8 loaves

The Riga Rye Bread

Rizhsky Khleb

This Latvian bread is praised by some Russians even more than their wonderful native Russian bread. It can be eaten straight from the oven, but I like it better the next day.

2 packages active dry yeast

1 teaspoon sugar

1¼ cups lukewarm water (105° to 115°F)

¼ cup barley malt or dark honey

3 tablespoons unsalted butter, melted

2 teaspoons salt

1 tablespoon caraway seeds

3 cups unbleached all-purpose flour

1½ cups rye flour

1 In a large bowl, combine the yeast, sugar, and ¼ cup of the water. Let stand until foamy, about 5 minutes.

2 Add the remaining water, the barley malt, 1 tablespoon of the melted butter, salt, and caraway seeds to the yeast mixture. Add the all-purpose flour and all but ¼ cup of the rye flour, 1 cup at a time, stirring well after each addition with a wooden spoon. Cover the bowl with a linen or cotton (not terry cloth) kitchen towel and let the dough stand for about 5 minutes.

3 Transfer the dough to a floured surface and knead until smooth and elastic, about 10 minutes, adding enough of the remaining rye flour to prevent sticking.

4 Shape the dough into a ball and place

in a large bowl. Drizzle with the remaining 2 tablespoons melted butter and turn to coat. Cover with a kitchen towel and let rise in a warm, draft-free spot until doubled in bulk, about 1½ hour.

5 Punch the dough down, divide it in half, and knead each half briefly. Shape each half into an oval loaf, place on a buttered baking sheet, cover, and let rise for about 30 minutes.

6 Meanwhile, preheat the oven to 375°F.

7 Bake the bread for about 45 minutes, until the crust is dark brown and the loaves sound hollow when tapped with a knuckle. Cool on a rack.

Makes 2 small loaves

Tahini Rolls

Tahiniov Gata

These delicious Armenian rolls make wonderfully unusual breakfast or coffee rolls. The recipe makes eight very large rolls, but you can easily make them smaller if you wish.

1 package active dry yeast
2½ tablespoons sugar
¼ cup lukewarm water (105° to 115°F)
½ cup milk, at room temperature
½ cup water, at room temperature
1 large egg, beaten
10 tablespoons (1¼ sticks) unsalted
    butter, melted

¼ teaspoon salt
3¼ cups unbleached all-purpose
    flour, or more as needed
1 cup tahini
¾ cup (packed) light brown sugar
1 large egg yolk, beaten with 1 tea-
    spoon milk

1 In a small bowl, combine the yeast, ½ tablespoon of the sugar, and the lukewarm water. Let stand until foamy, about 5 minutes.

2 In a large bowl, combine the milk, water, egg, 8 tablespoons of the melted butter, the salt, and the remaining sugar. Add the yeast mixture and mix well. Add 3¼ cups of the flour, 1 cup at a time, stirring well after each addition with a wooden spoon.

3 Transfer the dough onto a floured surface and knead until smooth and elastic, about 10 minutes, adding more flour as necessary to prevent sticking. Place the dough in a large bowl. Drizzle with the

remaining 2 tablespoons melted butter and turn to coat. Cover with a linen or cotton (not terry cloth) kitchen towel and let rise in a warm, draft-free spot until doubled in bulk, 1 to 2 hours.

4 Punch the dough down and divide into eight balls. Let rest, covered, about 10 minutes.

5 On a floured surface with a floured rolling pin, roll each ball into a round about 8 inches in diameter. Brush each round with 2 tablespoons tahini and sprinkle with about 1½ tablespoons brown sugar. Roll the rounds up, jelly-roll style. Pull and twist each roll to form a twisted rope. Roll each rope into a pinwheel, tucking the outer end underneath. Place the rolls on a buttered baking sheet, cover, and let rise for about 30 minutes.

6 Meanwhile, preheat the oven to 375°F.

7 Brush the rolls with the egg wash and bake until golden brown, about 35 minutes. Serve warm.

Makes 8 large rolls

Steamed Cilantro Buns

Yutangza

If this recipe sounds Chinese, it's because it comes from the Uighurs, Chinese Muslims, many of whom settled across the border in Uzbekistan. I sampled these tasty and unusual buns at Yakimanka, a privately owned Uzbek restaurant in Moscow. Located in a classicist eighteenth-century building on the bank of the Moscow River, Yakimanka serves extremely delicious home-style Central Asian food, prepared by the Uighur chef, Mohamed Khodzha (*khodzha*, meaning "noble"), and his beautiful young wife, Anna Akhmedovna. Mohamed, the son of a well-known Chinese revolutionary and a father of ten, doesn't speak any Russian, and prays daily, before making his meals. He was a well-known chef in Uzbekistan's capital, Tashkent, when he was invited to take up the job in Moscow, which, in the private food industry, is equivalent in pay and prestige to that of a high-ranking politician.

Mohamed prepares these traditional Uighur buns especially for the Oriental tourists who frequent the restaurant.

1 package active dry yeast

2 teaspoons sugar

½ cup lukewarm water (105° to 115°F)

½ cup milk, at room temperature

½ teaspoon salt

8 tablespoons (1 stick) unsalted butter, melted

3 to 3½ cups unbleached all-purpose flour

1 cup finely chopped fresh cilantro

1 In a large bowl, combine the yeast, sugar, and water and let stand until foamy, about 5 minutes.

2 Stir in the milk, salt, and 2 tablespoons of the butter and mix well with a wooden spoon. Stir in 3 cups of the flour, 1 cup at a time, stirring well after each addition.

3 Transfer the dough to a floured surface and knead until smooth and elastic, about 8 minutes, adding enough of the remaining flour to prevent sticking.

4 Shape the dough into a ball. Place in a buttered bowl and turn to coat. Cover with a linen or cotton (not terry cloth) kitchen towel and let rise in a warm, draft-free spot until doubled in bulk, about 1½ hours.

5 Punch the dough down and knead briefly. Divide into sixteen parts and shape each into a ball.

6 On a floured surface with a floured rolling pin, roll out one ball to a round about 1/16 inch thick. Brush generously with melted butter and sprinkle all over with cilantro. Fold in the edges of the round so they meet in the center and roll into a smooth bun between the palms of your hands. Repeat with the remaining balls of dough.

7 Place the buns on a buttered baking sheet, brush lightly with melted butter, and let them rise, covered, for about 20 minutes.

8 In a bamboo or metal steamer set over simmering water, steam as many buns as will fit without touching, partially covered, until cooked through, about 20 minutes. Steam the rest of the buns.

9 Serve slightly warm.

Makes 16 buns

Farmer's Cheese Loaf

Tvorozhnaya Bulka

A lovely, sweetish bread from the Baltic, excellent with butter and jam. For a fluffy, delicate texture, the dough has to rise twice, once as a sponge and then again after it is kneaded.

2 packages active dry yeast

½ cup plus 1 teaspoon sugar

1 cup milk, scalded and cooled to
   lukewarm (110° to 115°F)

3¼ to 4 cups unbleached all-purpose
   flour

6 tablespoons (¾ stick) unsalted
   butter, at room temperature

2 large eggs

½ pound farmer's cheese

2 tablespoons rum

Grated zest of 1 lemon

½ teaspoon salt

2 tablespoons unsalted butter,
   melted

1 large egg yolk, beaten with 1
   teaspoon milk

Confectioners' sugar

1 In a large bowl, combine the yeast, 1 teaspoon sugar, and milk. Let stand until foamy, about 5 minutes. Stir in about 2 cups of the flour and beat with a wire whisk until smooth. Cover with a linen or cotton (not terry cloth) kitchen towel and put in a warm place. Let stand until doubled in bulk, 1 hour.

2 In a medium-size bowl with an electric mixer, beat the 6 tablespoons butter and ½ cup sugar until light and fluffy. Beat in the eggs, then the farmer's cheese. Beat in the rum, lemon zest, and salt.

3 Stir the butter mixture into the risen batter. Gradually stir in another 1¼ cups of the flour, stirring continually, until you have a rather soft dough. Transfer the dough to a floured surface and knead until smooth and elastic, 5 to 10 minutes, adding enough of the remaining dough to prevent sticking.

4 Shape the dough into a ball and place in a large bowl. Drizzle with the melted butter and turn to coat. Cover, and let rise in a warm, draft-free spot, until doubled in bulk, 1½ hours.

5 Punch the dough down and shape it into one oval loaf. Place the loaf on a buttered baking sheet, cover, and let rise for 30 minutes.

6 Meanwhile, preheat the oven to 350°F.

7 Brush the loaf with the egg wash and bake until nicely browned, about 50 minutes.

8 Cool on a rack. Dust the loaf with confectioners' sugar.

Makes 1 large loaf

Moldavian Corn and Feta Cheese Bread

Kukuruzniy Khleb s Brinzoy

This bread is excellent with stews and soups, or simply with a slice of feta cheese or smoked ham, which is the way it is often enjoyed in Moldavia. It is a very savory corn bread, indeed.

2 cups crumbled feta cheese
½ cup sour cream
2 large eggs, lightly beaten
2 cups milk
6 tablespoons (¾ stick) unsalted
    butter, melted

2 cups yellow cornmeal, preferably
    stone ground
¾ cup unbleached all-purpose flour
½ teaspoon sugar
2 teaspoons baking powder
½ teaspoon baking soda

1 In a large bowl, stir together the feta cheese, sour cream, eggs, milk, and melted butter.

2 Sift the dry ingredients together and stir into the feta mixture. Blend thoroughly. Cover and let stand for 15 minutes.

3 Meanwhile, preheat the oven to 375°F. Butter a 13 × 9-inch rectangular baking pan.

4 Transfer the batter to the prepared pan and bake in the middle rack of the oven until light golden brown and firm to the touch, 35 to 40 minutes. Serve warm.

Serves 6 to 8

Moldavian Corn and Cheese Bread

Cut this savory bread into slices, top with crumbled Bulgarian feta, and bake in a 375°F oven until the feta is bubbly. Top with a roasted red pepper and pass around as an appetizer.

Barley Skillet Bread

Yachmennaya Lepyoshka

Breads made from slightly sweet, aromatic barley flour are favored by Afghans and Indians, Celts and Scandinavians alike. This flatbread, although it could almost come from Central Asia, is a traditional Estonian staple. Normally it is eaten straight from the oven, slathered with butter, honey, or — more traditionally — lingonberry preserves. I, however, find that it tastes even better the next day.

4 tablespoons (½ stick) unsalted
    butter, melted
1½ cups barley flour
½ cup unbleached all-purpose
    flour
⅓ cup whole-wheat flour
2 tablespoons (packed) brown
    sugar

½ teaspoon salt
½ teaspoon baking powder
1 teaspoon caraway seeds (optional)
1 large egg, beaten
1 cup buttermilk
2 tablespoons vegetable oil

1 Preheat the oven to 375°F. Brush an 8 or 9-inch cast-iron skillet with 2 tablespoons of the butter.

2 Sift the dry ingredients and caraway seeds (if using) together in a large bowl.

3 Whisk together the egg, buttermilk, and vegetable oil. Add the dry ingredients and mix until blended. Do not overmix. You will have something between batter and dough.

4 Spoon the mixture into the skillet and smooth the top with a rubber spatula. Drizzle the remaining butter over the top.

5 Bake until golden brown and a cake tester comes out clean, 50 minutes. Serve slightly warm.

Serves 6

Russian Pie with Fish, Mushrooms, and Rice

Kulebiaka

One of the most sumptuously elaborate creations of Russian cuisine is the *kulebiaka*, an oblong pie filled with layers of choice fish, dilled rice, wild mushrooms, thin crêpes, and *vesiga* (the dried spine marrow of sturgeon). Unfortunately a true multilayered *kulebiaka*, as it was prepared in the nineteenth century on country estates and in the famed Moscow taverns (*traktirs*), is but a memory that still lives on in the pages of Russian literature.

In Russia today, *kulebiaka* is a generic name for an oblong-shaped pie, filled with meat or cabbage. In the West, it's best known through the French variation *coulibiac* — salmon in puff pastry. The version I am offering here will provide a happy compromise. I forgo the time-consuming crêpes and the unavailable *vesiga*, and the fish I recommend is turbot, one of my favorites.

1 cup Fish Stock (see Index)

1 cup dry white wine

2 pounds turbot fillets, cut into 1½-inch cubes

3 tablespoons light vegetable oil

1 cup finely chopped onions

10 ounces fresh wild mushrooms (such as portobello, cremini, or shiitake), or fresh white mushrooms, cleaned and thinly sliced

1½ cups cooked long-grain rice

½ cup chopped fresh dill

Salt and freshly ground black pepper, to taste

1 recipe Yeast Dough, Sour Cream Pastry (see Index for both), or 2 sheets commercial puff pastry

3 tablespoons unflavored fine, dry bread crumbs

4 hard-cooked eggs, chopped

6 tablespoons (¾ stick) unsalted butter, melted

⅓ cup fresh lemon juice

1 large egg white, lightly beaten

1 large egg yolk, beaten with 1 teaspoon milk

1 Combine the fish stock and wine in a deep skillet and bring to a gentle boil over medium heat. Add the fish and poach until opaque, 5 to 7 minutes. With a slotted spoon, remove the fish to a bowl and allow to cool. Reserve the poaching liquid for another use.

2 In the skillet, heat the oil over high heat. Add the onions and sauté, stirring, until they soften slightly and just begin to color, 5 minutes. Add the mushrooms and stir the mixture quickly until the mushrooms give off and reabsorb their liquid, about 10 minutes. Set aside to cool.

3 In a bowl, combine the rice with the dill and season lightly with salt and pepper.

4 Preheat the oven to 375°F. Lightly butter a large baking sheet.

5 Divide the dough or pastry into two pieces. On a floured surface, with a floured rolling pin, roll out one piece to a 14 × 9-inch rectangle. (If you are using puff or sour cream pastry, refrigerate the piece you are not working with.) With a sharp knife, trim away the edges to form an oval shape. Drape the dough over the rolling pin and transfer it carefully to the prepared baking sheet. Reserve the trimmings.

6 Sprinkle the bread crumbs evenly over the dough. Arrange half the dilled rice evenly over the crumbs, leaving a 1½-inch border all around. Spread half the mushroom mixture over the rice and season with salt and pepper. Then sprinkle half the

Russian Fish Supper Traktir Style

Assorted smoked fish

•

Lemon Vodka

•

Fish Soup à la Souvoroff

•

Kulebiaka

•

Pouilly Fumé

•

Russian Berry Custard

• • •

chopped eggs over the rice. Arrange the fish on top of the eggs, season, then top with layers of the remaining mushrooms, eggs, and rice. Season each layer with salt and pepper. Pat the filling into a more compact shape.

7 Whisk together the melted butter and

lemon juice and pour it slowly and evenly over the filling.

8 Roll out the remaining piece of dough to slightly larger than the first piece. Place the top crust over the layered bottom crust and trim it to the shape of the bottom crust. Fold up the edge of the bottom crust to seal the *kulebiaka* and crimp decoratively.

9 Gather together the leftover scraps of dough and roll out thin. Cut out decorative shapes. Prick the *kulebiaka* with the tip of a sharp knife in six evenly spaced places. Brush the decorations with the egg white and arrange the top crust. Press gently to adhere. Brush with the egg yolk wash. If you are making the *kulebiaka* with yeast dough, allow it to rest for 20 minutes before baking.

10 Bake in the middle of the oven for 15 minutes. Reduce the oven temperature to 350°F and bake until deep golden, 25

to 30 minutes more. Allow to cool slightly. Cut the *kulebiaka* in thick slices and serve.

Serves 6 to 8

The kulebiaka must make your mouth water, it must lie there before you, naked, shameless, a temptation! You wink at it, you cut off a sizable slice, and you let your fingers just play over it, this way, out of excess of feeling. You eat, the butter drips from it like tears, and the filling is fat, juicy, rich, with eggs, giblets, onions . . .

— Anton Chekhov
The Siren

Tatar Wedding Pie

Gubadia

Tatar cuisine is especially well known in Russia for its baked goods, which is the pride of any Tatar.

On a recent visit to Moscow I discovered a wonderful cooperative (privately owned) Tatar café with a vast repertoire of delectable savory and sweet pies. I made it a habit to go there for lunch and befriended the director, who introduced me to the staff, who were brought especially from Kazan, the capital of the Tatar autonomous republic. The baking chef happily shared her recipes with me.

Here is a favorite Tatar pie — with layers of meat, rice, chopped eggs, and raisins (the Tatars also add *kort*, sweet, dry cottage cheese). It is traditionally served for weddings and big banquets. The recipe below will serve four as an appetizer or a light first course. (Double the recipe and make two pies for a buffet, or four small 4-inch individual pies for a lunch or supper main course.)

4 tablespoons vegetable oil
½ pound ground beef
Salt and freshly ground black
*   pepper, to taste*
1 large onion, chopped
3 hard-cooked eggs, finely chopped
½ recipe Yeast Dough (see Index)

8 tablespoons (1 stick) unsalted
*   butter, melted*
½ cup cooked long-grain rice
⅓ cup raisins
1 large egg yolk, beaten with 1
*   teaspoon milk*

1 Heat 2 tablespoons of the oil in a medium-size skillet over medium-high heat. Add the ground beef and sauté, breaking up the beef with a fork, until it is cooked through, about 12 minutes. Season with salt and pepper and transfer to a plate. Wipe out the skillet.

2 Heat another 2 tablespoons of the oil in the skillet over medium heat. Add the onion and sauté, stirring occasionally, until well browned, about 15 minutes. Remove from the heat and combine with the chopped egg.

3 Preheat the oven to 350°F. Lightly butter a 9-inch round baking pan.

4 On a floured surface with a floured rolling pin, roll out half the dough into a 10-inch circle. Line the prepared baking pan with the dough so it covers the rims of the baking dish and hangs over slightly.

5 Layer the filling in the crust in the following order, sprinkling each layer with some of the melted butter: Meat, rice, and egg and onion. Top with the raisins.

6 Roll out the other half of the dough into a 9-inch circle. Place it on top of the filling, fold the top and bottom edges together, and crimp decoratively. Let the pie stand, covered with a linen or cotton (not terry cloth) kitchen towel, for 15 minutes before baking.

7 Brush the top of the pie with the egg

wash, pierce in several places with a sharp knife, and bake until the pie is golden brown and a cake tester comes out clean, about 40 to 45 minutes. Serve warm.

Serves 4

Savory Strudels

Vertuta

Savory strudels are a Balkan and Moldavian specialty. They make great appetizers, snacks, or buffet dishes. For those willing to adventure beyond packaged phyllo dough, I've included a homemade strudel dough recipe in the dessert chapter of this book.

8 sheets phyllo dough, thawed and handled according to the instructions on the package or ½ recipe homemade strudel dough (see Sweet Strudels in Index)

8 tablespoons (1 stick) unsalted butter, melted

⅓ cup unflavored, fine, dry bread crumbs

1 recipe Feta Cheese and Potato or Wild Mushroom Filling (recipes follow)

1 Preheat the oven to 375°F. Butter a baking sheet well.

2 Stack the phyllo sheets on top of one another on the prepared baking sheet, brushing each sheet first with about 2 teaspoons of the melted butter, then sprinkling it with bread crumbs (or follow Steps 1 through 6 in the Sweet Strudels recipe, then sprinkle the dough with bread crumbs). Place the filling in a compact row lengthwise down the phyllo, 2 inches from the edge. Roll up like a jelly roll and tuck in the ends. Turn the strudel seam side down and brush with the remaining butter.

3 Bake until golden brown, about 35 minutes. Let cool about 20 minutes, then slice.

Serves 6 to 8

Feta Cheese and Potato Filling

Nachinka iz Brinzi i Kartofelya

3 medium-size boiling potatoes,
  boiled, peeled, and mashed
1½ cups grated feta cheese
4 tablespoons (½ stick) unsalted
  butter, melted

2 tablespoons sour cream
2 large egg yolks, beaten
¼ cup finely chopped fresh parsley

In a bowl, combine the mashed potatoes, feta cheese, melted butter, sour cream, egg yolks, and parsley and mix well.

Makes enough to fill 1 strudel

Wild Mushroom Filling

Nachinka iz Gribov

1 ounce imported dried wild mushrooms, well rinsed
6 tablespoons (¾ stick) unsalted
  butter
2 pounds fresh white mushrooms,
  wiped clean and sliced
1 pound fresh wild mushrooms (such
  as shiitake, portobello, chanterelles), wiped clean and sliced

⅓ cup dry vermouth
½ cup sour cream
⅓ cup unflavored, fine, dry bread
  crumbs
¼ cup snipped fresh chives
¼ teaspoon freshly grated nutmeg
Salt and freshly ground black
  pepper, to taste

1 Soak the dried mushrooms in 1 cup water for 2 hours. Drain the mushrooms, pat dry, and chop fine. Reserve the soaking liquid for another use.

2 Melt the butter in a large skillet over medium heat. Add the fresh and dried mushrooms, and sauté, stirring until they begin to throw off liquid, 5 to 7 minutes. Turn the heat up high and continue to sauté, stirring occasionally, until all the liquid evaporates. Turn the heat down to medium and sauté for another 5 minutes.

3 Stir in the vermouth, turn the heat up to high, and let boil for 5 minutes. Remove from the heat and stir in the sour cream, bread crumbs, chives, nutmeg, and salt and pepper. Allow the filling to cool before filling the strudel.

Makes enough to fill 1 strudel

Crimean Lamb Pie

Chebureki

I was a *chebureki* junkie as a child in Moscow. So was my schoolfriend Sheida, who was a Turkish girl living at the nearby embassy. Every day after school we ran across the street to the *cheburechnaya* (*chebureki* joint), frequented exclusively by taxi and truck drivers, where for sixteen kopeks (about twenty-five cents) you could buy two beautifully golden, large, deep-fried pies, which exuded an impossibly seductive smell. Together among the throng of taxi drivers, we learned all the necessary skills to consume them like experts. Cutting them with a knife was forbidden. You had to break them in half carefully, without losing a drop of the hot broth inside, and then eat each half separately, holding it with both hands. Our ritual would end with a trip to the fruit store for a glass of tomato juice or, if we felt rich, grape juice, which the saleswoman generously (and illegally) diluted with water so she could make more money off it. Upon my return to Moscow after a long absence, I was horrified to find out that our *cheburechnaya* had been closed down and was due to be replaced by a cooperative (privately owned) café. The only *chebureki* available now are also cooperative, at fifty kopeks apiece. No thanks! Although the homemade *chebureki* are far superior to the ones I remember, I still miss them terribly.

1 recipe noodle dough for Vareniki
(see Index)
½ pound ground lamb
¼ pound ground sirloin
2 cloves garlic, minced
2 medium-size onions, finely
chopped
¼ cup chopped fresh cilantro

Salt and freshly ground black
pepper, to taste
3 tablespoons unsalted butter,
melted
⅓ cup ice water
Vegetable oil for deep frying

1 Divide the dough into twelve equal pieces and shape them into balls. Let stand, covered with a linen or cotton (not terry cloth) kitchen towel for 15 to 20 minutes.

2 Meanwhile, make the filling. Combine the lamb, sirloin, garlic, onions, and cilantro in a bowl. Season with salt, and very generously, with ground black pepper.

3 On a floured surface with a floured rolling pin, roll out the dough into rounds, about 3 inches in diameter. Brush each one with melted butter, stack them on top of each other and let stand, covered with a towel, for about 15 to 20 minutes more. Roll out each round some more and then pull the sides of each until they are about 6 inches in diameter, taking care not to tear the dough.

4 Mix the ice water into the filling and divide the filling into twelve equal portions.

Place a filling portion on one side of each round of dough. Fold the other half over the filling and press the edges together. Trim the edges even with a sharp knife and seal with the tines of a fork.

5 Heat the oil in deep fryer to 375°F.

6 Fry the *chebureki* until deep golden, 3 to 4 minutes on each side. Drain on paper towels. Serve at once.

Makes 12 chebureki *(serves 6)*

Armenian Pizza

Lachmanjun

This dish, prepared by Armenians who settled in Turkey, became our favorite snack on our many visits to Turkey. The recipe comes from Vartouhi Papazian, an Armenian from Greece.

CRUST

1 package active dry yeast

¼ teaspoon sugar

1¼ cups water

¼ cup vegetable oil

½ teaspoon salt

3¼ to 3½ cups unbleached all-purpose flour

TOPPING

10 ounces lean lamb, finely ground

2 medium-size onions, finely chopped

1 green bell pepper, cored, seeded, and finely chopped

2 tablespoons tomato paste

½ cup canned Italian plum tomatoes, drained and chopped

1 teaspoon minced garlic

¼ cup finely chopped fresh parsley

1 teaspoon sweet Hungarian paprika

¼ teaspoon hot Hungarian paprika

Salt and freshly ground black pepper, to taste

1 In a large bowl, combine the yeast, sugar, and water and let stand until foamy, about 5 minutes. Stir in 2 tablespoons of the oil and the salt.

2 Add 3¼ cups of flour, 1 cup at a time, mixing well after each addition with a wooden spoon. Transfer the dough to a work surface. Coat your hands with some of the remaining oil and knead the dough until it is completely smooth and elastic,

adding just enough of the remaining flour to prevent sticking.

3 Shape the dough into a ball and place it in a large bowl. Drizzle with the rest of the oil and turn to coat. Coat with a linen or cotton (not terry cloth) kitchen towel and let rise in a warm, draft-free place until doubled in bulk, about 1 to 1½ hours.

4 Meanwhile, make the topping. In

another large bowl, combine all the topping ingredients and mix well.

5 After the dough has risen, divide the dough into eight equal pieces and shape each one into a ball. Place the balls on a floured surface and let rest, covered with a towel, for about 10 minutes.

6 Preheat the oven to 450°F. Lightly oil two large baking sheets.

7 On a floured surface with a floured roll-ing pin, roll out each piece of dough into a round about 4 inches in diameter. Divide the topping into eight parts and spread over the entire surface of each circle.

8 Arrange the *lachmanjuns* on the prepared baking sheets and bake in the lower third of the oven until the topping and the dough are nicely browned, about 15 minutes.

Makes eight 4-inch pies

Phyllo Turnovers

Bourek

Buttery phyllo triangles have become extremely popular cocktail fare in this country. They come in all kinds of guises in Turkey and Armenia, where they are an absolute must at any sit-down or buffet event.

1 package (1 pound) phyllo dough, about 24 sheets, thawed and handled according to the instructions on the package

1 cup (2 sticks) unsalted butter, melted (or more as needed)
1 recipe Cheese or Spinach and Tahini filling (recipes follow)

1 Preheat the oven to 350°F. Butter two large baking sheets.

2 Place one sheet of dough on a clean surface and brush with melted butter. (The other sheets should be covered with a damp cloth to prevent them from drying.) Fold the sheet lengthwise into thirds.

Brush again with butter. With one short end facing you, place a heaping tablespoon of the filling in the center of the strip, about 1½ inches from the bottom. Fold the lower corner across the filling into a triangle. Continue folding until the strip is used up.

3 Repeat with the rest of the phyllo and filling, placing the finished triangles on the prepared baking sheet, seam side down. Refrigerate any that don't fit on the baking sheet until you are ready to bake them.

4 Brush the triangles with the remaining butter and bake in the middle of the oven until puffy and golden brown, about 30 minutes. Serve hot.

Makes 24 turnovers.

Cheese Filling

Bourek Banirov

½ *pound kasseri or kefalotyri cheese, grated*
½ *pound mozzarella, grated*
6 *ounces cottage cheese*
3 *tablespoons unsalted butter, softened*
2 *large egg yolks, lightly beaten*
⅓ *cup finely chopped fresh parsley*
Salt and freshly ground black pepper, to taste

Combine all the ingredients in a bowl and mix well. Taste and adjust the seasoning.

Makes enough to fill 24 turnovers

Spinach and Tahini Filling

Bourek Spanakhov yev Tahiniov

3 *packages (10 ounces each) chopped frozen spinach, thawed*
6 *tablespoons (¾ stick) unsalted butter*
3 *tablespoons olive oil*
1 *cup chopped onions*
6 *tablespoons tahini*
⅓ *cup unflavored fine, dry bread crumbs*
⅓ *cup finely chopped fresh parsley*
Salt and freshly ground black pepper, to taste

1 Drain the thawed spinach in a colander and squeeze out as much liquid as possible.

2 Heat the butter and oil in a large skillet over medium heat. Add the onions and sauté, stirring occasionally, until very lightly colored, about 10 minutes. Add the spinach and cook, stirring, for about 15 minutes, until the mixture is dry and the spinach has cooked through. Transfer into a bowl and let cool to room temperature.

3 Add the rest of the ingredients and mix well. Taste and correct the seasoning.

Makes enough to fill 24 turnovers

Estonian Ham and Cheese Rolls

Rogaliki s Vetchinoy i Sirom

These rolls are great cocktail fare that come from the most Westernized republic. Buy good-quality imported ham for them and have it sliced thick rather than thin.

½ recipe Yeast Dough (see Index)
24 slices ham, each 3 inches square
¼ cup freshly grated Parmesan
  cheese

4 tablespoons (½ stick) unsalted
  butter, melted
2 large egg yolks mixed with 1
  teaspoon milk

1 Preheat the oven to 350°F. Butter two large baking sheets.

2 On a floured surface with a floured rolling pin, roll out the dough to an 18 × 12-inch rectangle. With a sharp knife, cut out twenty-four 3-inch squares.

3 Place one ham slice on each square of dough. Place about ½ teaspoon of the Parmesan in the middle of each ham

square and drizzle with about ½ teaspoon melted butter. Starting at one corner, roll each square into a neat roll.

4 Arrange the rolls, seam side down, on the prepared baking sheets, spacing well apart, and brush with the egg wash. Bake until the rolls are golden brown, about 40 minutes.

Makes 24 rolls (serves 8 to 12)

Tatar Meat Pies

Beliashi

Although these succulent open meat pies should be made from proper yeast dough, my mother has been successfully making them for years from Pillsbury buttermilk biscuits. She keeps a few packs of those in her refrigerator, and "in the event of the slightest guest," as my grandmother used to put it, she is in top hospitality form in only fifteen minutes. She also always brings *beliashi* to parties, which makes her not only a popular hostess, but a popular guest.

2 containers (10 biscuits each)
Pillsbury buttermilk
biscuits
1 pound ground sirloin
1 large onion, grated
¼ cup finely chopped fresh parsley
or dill
⅓ cup ice water
Salt and plenty of freshly ground
black pepper, to taste
Vegetable oil for deep frying

1 Open the containers of biscuits, separate the biscuits, and let stand for 15 minutes.

2 In a large bowl, combine the meat, onion, parsley, and water. Knead well with your hands to mix and season with salt and pepper.

3 Heat the oil in a deep fryer to 375°F.

4 Pat the biscuits between your fingers, flattening them as much as possible. Place a scant 1 tablespoon of the filling in the middle of each and moisten the edges with cold water. Fold the edges toward the middle, leaving about a ¾-inch hole in the middle. Press the edges to make sure they stick so the pies won't open during cooking.

5 Fry the *beliashi*, three or four at a time, open side down first, until golden brown, about 4 to 5 minutes on each side. Transfer to paper towels to drain and keep warm while the remaining *beliashi* are cooking.

Makes 20 beliashi

Georgian Cheese Pie

Khachapuri

In the restaurants and *khachapuri* parlors of Georgia, the pie is made from a dough that combines local yogurt, eggs, and flour, or from yeast dough. The shape and the fillings vary from region to region.

Here, I am giving the standard homemade version, made from a dough that is similar to strudel dough and two authentic and delicious fillings. One is a combination of cheeses, which most resemble the local string cheese *suluguni*; the other is made from red beans. For the dough, you can also use frozen Pepperidge Farm puff pastry sheets, in which case roll it out to a thickness of ⅛ inch and cut out squares of the dimensions indicated in the recipe. This recipe was given to me by Venera Batashvili, whose wonderful *khachapuri* is sold in Russian shops in New York.

*2½ cups unbleached all-purpose
    flour*
¾ teaspoon salt
1 large egg
3 tablespoons vegetable oil
*½ cup club soda, or more as needed,
    at room temperature*

*12 tablespoons (1½ sticks) unsalted
    butter, melted*
*1 recipe Cheese or Red Bean Filling
    (recipes follow)*

1 Sift the flour and salt into a large bowl, and make a well in the middle. Pour in the egg, oil, and club soda and stir into the flour, adding more club soda, if necessary, to make a rather soft dough. Transfer the dough to a floured board and knead until smooth and elastic, about 10 minutes. Shape the dough into a ball, cover with a linen or cotton (not terry cloth) kitchen towel, and let stand for 1 hour.

2 Divide the dough into four parts and shape each one into a ball. Let stand, covered for 15 minutes.

3 Preheat the oven to 350°F. Butter two large baking sheets.

4 On a floured surface, roll out one of the balls to an ⅛-inch-thick square. Brush the dough with some of the melted butter. Dip your fingers in melted butter and pull the edges of the dough in different directions, stretching it evenly until it is almost transparently thin. Don't worry if the dough tears, as you will be folding it up. With a sharp knife, trim the edges of the dough to form an even square. Fold the square in half, brush the surface generously with melted butter, and fold in half again crosswise, to form a smaller square. It should be approximately 6 to 7 inches. If it isn't, pull it out slightly to fit the dimensions.

5 Brush the square with butter. Shape one-fourth of the filling into a ball and place in the center of the square. Fold in the corners of the square like an envelope. With your palm, flatten the pie so it is about 1 inch thick. Brush the top with melted butter, and carefully transfer to a prepared baking sheet.

6 Repeat the procedure with the rest of the dough and filling.

7 Bake the pies in the middle of the oven until golden brown; about 35 minutes. Serve warm.

Makes 4 pies, to serve 8

Georgian Pizza

I think of *khachapuri* as the Georgian equivalent of pizza. I first tasted it in Sukhumi, the capital of the Abkhasian region on the Black Sea, whose two most famous attractions were a zoo with exotic monkeys and a well-known *khachapuri* parlor called Nartia. My mother and I had just disembarked from a cruise ship, having already eaten a filling dinner on board. We decided, nevertheless, to adventure in this unknown new town — not usually advisable for unaccompanied women — to try to locate some of the famous cheese pies and to enjoy a nightcap.

Winding through the narrow cobbled streets, we finally found our grail. The Nartia was crammed with local men shouting their incessant orders for vast piles of the pies, smoking, laughing, and gesticulating. We waited at the counter in the hope of attracting some attention, but in vain. Finally, my mother had an inspiration: She started addressing me in English, and while I was wondering if she'd gone crazy, we heard a rally of whispers — "See to the foreigners at once!"

A table was cleared within seconds, and we were swiftly served a hearty selection of the enormous boat-shaped pies, open in the middle, with *suluguni* cheese sizzling provocatively inside. We were entertained all evening with wine and conversation and returned, proud of our success, to the ship.

Imagine our embarrassment when we strolled about the deck next morning, discussing our ruse in perfect Russian, and ran straight into two men who had been particularly attentive to us the previous night. Still, I would never have sacrificed the delicious new taste of *khachapuri* for a few awkward stares.

Cheese Filling

Nachinka iz Sira

10 ounces mozzarella cheese, grated

8 ounces feta cheese, preferably
    Bulgarian, crumbled

6 ounces cottage cheese

8 tablespoons (1 stick) unsalted
    butter, at room temperature, cut
    into small pieces

1 large egg

Salt, to taste (optional)

In a large bowl, combine all the ingredients except the salt and mix well. Taste and season with salt, if necessary.

Makes enough to fill 4 pies

Red Bean Filling

Nachinka iz Fasoli

1 cup dried red beans, soaked over-
    night in water to cover

Salt and plenty of freshly ground
    black pepper, to taste

¼ cup olive oil

1¼ cups finely chopped onions

½ cup finely chopped fresh cilantro

1 Drain the beans and place them in a saucepan along with enough fresh water to cover by at least 2 inches. Bring to a boil, add salt, and reduce the heat to medium low. Cook the beans, partially covered, until almost mushy, about 1½ hours.

2 While the beans are cooking, heat the oil in a medium-size skillet over medium heat. Add the onions and sauté, stirring occasionally, until dark brown, about 15 to 20 minutes.

3 When the beans are done, drain them well and mash. Add the sautéed onions and their cooking fat and the cilantro. Season generously with black pepper and salt. Cool to room temperature.

Makes enough to fill 4 pies

Open-Faced Cheese Pies, Adzharian Style

Adzharuli Khachapuri

This mouth-watering *khachapuri*, which resembles an open calzone, is the version that's often served in *khachapuri* parlors throughout Georgia. It's a boat-shaped open pie, usually filled with a pungent goat's cheese. A mixture of chèvre and farmer's cheese gives a good approximation. In Georgia a fresh egg is often baked on top of the *khachapuri*.

DOUGH

1 package active dry
    yeast
¼ teaspoon sugar
¾ cup lukewarm water (105° to
    115°F)
2 tablespoons vegetable oil

2¼ to 2½ cups unbleached all-
    purpose flour
½ teaspoon salt
Cornmeal for dusting the baking
    sheet

FILLING

1⅔ cups chèvre, crumbled
1⅔ cups farmer's cheese
6 tablespoons (¾ stick) butter, at
    room temperature, cut into
    pieces

Salt, to taste
1 teaspoon chopped fresh cilantro
    (optional)

1 In a large bowl, combine the yeast, sugar, and ¼ cup water. Let stand until foamy, about 5 minutes.

2 Add the remaining water, the oil, 2¼ cups flour, and salt and mix well with a wooden spoon.

3 Transfer the dough to a floured surface and knead until smooth and elastic, 5 to 10 minutes, adding enough of the remaining flour to prevent sticking. Shape the dough into a ball and place it in a buttered bowl, turning to coat. Cover the dough with a linen or cotton (not terry cloth) kitchen

Pies

With both *pirog* and *pirozhki*, there is no real rule of thumb for how to choose which crust to use. It depends on the filling, the shape of the pie, and the context in which it is served. But here are my suggestions (see the Index for the recipe page numbers).

• The plain Yeast Dough, somewhat similar to brioche, is the most traditional crust to use for *piroghi* and *kulebiaka*. It's on the substantial side and pies made with it are good to serve as entrées. Accompanied by a bowl of soup, they provide a hearty meal. I would reserve Yeast Dough for the cool months of the year when it is time for serious baking.

• Quick Yeast Dough is a great favorite with Russian women, myself included. It's flakier and lighter than Yeast Dough, but makes a crust substantial enough to hold a filling without getting soggy. Its great advantage is that it can be prepared at absolutely the last moment.

• Sour Cream Pastry is very savory, buttery, and delicate, making for lighter pies, which are great to serve as an appetizer, or a party or light supper dish.

• I love pies made with puff pastry, but it's a bit too delicate to hold a large amount of moist filling. It is great for *pirozhki*, but just about works for *kulebiaka*.

---

towel and let rise in a warm, draft-free place until doubled in bulk, about 1½ hours.

4 Thirty minutes before you bake the *khachapuri*, preheat the oven to 500°F. Lightly oil a heavy-duty baking sheet and sprinkle it with cornmeal.

5 Punch the dough down and divide it into four pieces. Shape each into an oval and let stand, covered, for 10 minutes.

6 Meanwhile, mix all the filling ingredients together with a fork.

7 Roll out one oval to a boat shape and trim to 8 inches long and about 5½ inches wide in the middle. Spread one-fourth of the filling over the dough, leaving a 1-inch border all around. Bring the edges of the boat in to create a standing border. Pinch the two long ends and cut off the excess. Gently transfer the *khachapuri* to the baking sheet.

8 Repeat the procedure with the remaining dough and filling.

9 Bake the *khachapuri* in the lower third of the oven until the crust is golden brown and the filling is bubbling and lightly colored about 12 minutes.

Makes 4 khachpuri *(serves 4)*

Savory Filled Pastries

Pirozhki

One of the traditional Russian favorites, *pirozhki* are ideal finger foods or accompaniments for soups. When making *pirozhki*, try using at least two different fillings. It's a good idea to place the meat and cabbage fillings in the freezer for about 25 minutes to make them more compact. Baked *pirozhki* freeze well. Reheat in a 325°F oven for 20 to 25 minutes.

1 recipe Quick Yeast Dough, Sour Cream Pastry (see Index for both), or 2 sheets commercial puff pastry

1 recipe Potato filling (recipe follows), Meat Filling (see page 453), Cabbage Filling (see page 454), or ½ recipe of each of two fillings

1 large egg yolk, beaten with 1 teaspoon milk

1 Preheat the oven to 350°F. Lightly butter two large baking sheets.

2 Divide the dough or pastry into three pieces. Refrigerate the pieces you're not working with. On a floured surface with a floured rolling pin, roll out one piece of dough to a thickness of slightly more than ⅛ inch. With a 3-inch cookie cutter or top of a drinking glass, cut out rounds from the dough. Flatten each round slightly between your fingers and place a heaping

Other Fillings for Pirozhki

- Chopped scallions and hard-cooked eggs, seasoned with salt and pepper, and moistened with melted butter
- Ground cooked veal and finely chopped sautéed mushrooms, mixed with a little white sauce or sour cream
- Cooked dilled rice and chopped hard-cooked eggs
- Cooked dilled rice, flaked sautéed fish, and hard-cooked eggs
- Ground cooked calf's liver and lots of deeply browned onions

teaspoon of the filling in the middle. Fold the edges up so they meet in the center and press together firmly to seal. Press the sealed edges lightly against the *pirozhok* and pat into an oval shape. Place on the baking sheet, seam side down.

3 Repeat with the remaining dough and filling, gathering the leftover scraps of dough into a ball, reroll, and cut out as many more rounds as possible. Space the *pirozhki* 1 inch apart on the baking sheet. (If all the *pirozhki* don't fit on two baking sheets, bake them in batches, keeping the unbaked ones refrigerated.) Brush with the egg wash and bake in the middle of the oven until golden brown, 25 to 30 minutes. Serve warm.

Makes about 45 to 50 pirozhki

Potato Filling
Kartofelnaya Nachinka

3 tablespoons vegetable oil

2 large onions, finely chopped

4 large boiling potatoes, boiled and
    mashed

½ cup farmer's cheese

4 tablespoons (½ stick) unsalted
    butter, melted

Salt and freshly ground black
    pepper, to taste

Pie Puzzled?

As you can probably see, the names of the pies are defined by their shape and size, whereas the fillings and types of pastry or dough can be used interchangeably. The recipes are set up to offer a range of possibilities for pastries and fillings. They are all thoroughly delectable, try them all and pick your own favorites. I've added stress marks to help you with the pronunciations.

Pirozhók is singular for a small filled oval pastry.

Pirozhkí is the plural.

Piróg is singular for a large rectangular, square, or round pie that can be sweet or savory, depending on the filling.

Piroghí is the plural.

Pierógi is the Polish word for dumplings. Don't confuse it with *piroghi*.

Kulebiáka, known in the States by its French title *coulibiac*, is an oblong pie, traditionally filled with fish.

---

1 Heat the oil in a small skillet over medium-high heat. Add the onions and sauté, stirring occasionally, until well browned, about 15 minutes.

2 Combine the onions with the rest of the ingredients in a bowl and mix well.

Makes enough to fill 45 to 50 pirozhki

Large Savory Filled Pie

Pirog

The word *pirog* derives from the Russian word *pir*, meaning "feast." Not surprisingly, the dish is the Russian party food par excellence. This recipe makes a large pie. Halve the recipe for a smaller number of people, or make two pies with different fillings. Serve as part of a buffet, an accompaniment to soups, or a lunch or supper entrée.

1 recipe Yeast Dough, Quick Yeast Dough, or Sour Cream Pastry (see Index for all recipes)

¼ cup unflavored fine, dry bread crumbs

1 recipe Rice and Fish filling (recipe follows), Meat Filling (see page 453), or Cabbage Filling (see page 454)

1 large egg yolk, beaten with 1 teaspoon milk

1 Preheat the oven to 375°F. Lightly butter an 18 × 12 × 1-inch baking sheet.

2 Divide the dough into two slightly uneven pieces. On a floured surface with a floured rolling pin, roll out the larger piece of dough to a 14 × 10-inch rectangle. Drape it over the rolling pin and transfer it to the baking sheet. (There should not be an overhang.)

3 Sprinkle the surface of the dough with the bread crumbs and spread the filling evenly over the crumbs, leaving a 1½-inch border all around.

4 Roll out the second piece of dough to a 12½ × 8½- rectangle. Place over the fill-

ing, fold up the edges of the bottom crust, and press to seal. Crimp decoratively with the tines of a fork. Brush the top with the egg wash. If you are making the *pirog* with yeast dough, allow it to rest for 20 minutes before baking.

5 Bake the *pirog* in the middle of the oven until the crust is golden and baked through (cover loosely with aluminum foil if the crust is browning too quickly), 40 to 45 minutes.

6 Serve warm or at room temperature, cutting the pie into 3-inch squares before serving.

Makes 1 large pirog *(serves 10)*

Savory Pies

An old Russian saying goes like this (allowing for a little poetic license to find the rhyme):

People's houses would seem like sties

Were it not for their tasty pies.

You should believe every word of it. Crusty filled pies, both sweet and savory, are one of the glories of Slavic cuisine with the *pirog*, a large pie filled with all kinds of meats, fish, mushrooms, or cabbage as the star of many a homemade Russian meal.

All the great Russian writers are keenly observant when it comes to the health of the *pirog*. In fact, in *Dead Souls* by Nikolai Gogol, one infatuated character dished out precise instructions for making his beloved pie:

"In one corner put the cheeks and dried spine of a sturgeon, in another put some buckwheat, and some mushrooms and onions, and some soft roe . . . yes . . . and some brains, and something else as well . . . Yes, and see to it that the crust is well browned on one side and a trifle less on the other. As for the underneath . . .

see that it's baked so that it's quite . . . well not to the point of crumbling but so that it will melt in the mouth like snow and not make any crunching sound." Petukh smacked his lips as he spoke.

Delicious pies, of course, can be made from puff or short pastry, but the Russian genius for baking comes into its own with yeast dough. I can usually tell just from looking at a woman whether or not she makes good dough. It's a talent you're born with, there's no doubt about that. With all my kitchen gadgets and fresh ingredients, surrounded by a whole library of baking books and tart-making tips, and after seeing *babushkas* at work a hundred times, I still can't do it like the best of them, especially when they're inspired by some special occasion. My envy for their plump, fragrant dough, as light as a goose-feather pillow, the crust a golden brown perfection, simply knows no bounds.

But the *pirog* is not the only triumph of the Russian oven. Try some of the diminutive, flaky pies called *pirozhki*, which seem to disappear in the Russian home just as the

best homemade chocolate-chip cookies vanish in seconds from American kitchens. Larger, deep-fried *pirozhki* are still the favorite street food in the USSR. Then there are *vatrushki*, cheese-filled open tartlets that come sweet or savory; *kulebiaka*, an oblong pie with fish, rice, mushrooms, and other fillings; and the old Moscow treat, *rasstegai*, an open pie with a fish filling that is invariably served with the traditional clear fish soup, *ukha*.

As the Russian empire expanded in the nineteenth century, so the filled-pie repertoire was augmented by butter-rich savory phyllo triangles from Armenia; the Tatar *cheburek* — a deep fried lamb-filled pie; Georgian cheese-bread (*khachapuri*); and Moldavian strudels filled with feta.

All the pies in this chapter can be served as accompaniments to soup, as fun party dishes, or just as snacks. The more substantial ones make excellent lunch or dinner entrées.

A Rustic Russian Luncheon for Eight

Herring in Sour Cream Sauce

•

My Mother's Marinated Mushrooms

•

Beet Caviar with Walnuts and Prunes

•

Pumpernickel bread

•

Vodka

•

Shchi

•

Meat-Filled *Pirog*

•

Russian Cranberry Mousse

• • •

Rice and Fish Filling for Pirog

Nachinka iz Risa i Ribi dlya Piroga

With a green salad and a glass of white wine, a fish *pirog* is a great light dinner. Serve sour cream or a cream sauce of your choice on the side.

7 tablespoons unsalted butter
1½ pounds white-fleshed fish fillets (such as halibut, haddock, bass, snapper, or turbot), cut into 1-inch cubes
1½ cups chopped onions
10 ounces fresh white mushrooms, wiped clean and chopped
1 cup cooked long-grain rice
3 hard-cooked eggs, chopped
¼ cup chopped fresh dill
3 tablespoons unsalted butter, melted
3 tablespoons chicken broth
3 tablespoons sour cream
1 tablespoon fresh lemon juice
Salt and freshly ground white pepper, to taste

1 Melt 4 tablespoons of the butter in a

large skillet over medium heat. Add the fish and sauté on all sides until opaque throughout, 5 to 7 minutes. Transfer to a large bowl with a slotted spoon.

2 In the skillet, melt another 3 tablespoons of the butter over medium heat. Add the onions and sauté, stirring occasionally, until softened, about 5 minutes. Add the mushrooms and sauté, stirring, until the mushrooms have thrown off and reabsorbed their liquid and are lightly colored, about 15 minutes.

3 Add the mushrooms to the fish along with the rice, eggs, and dill. Toss gently.

4 In a small bowl, whisk the melted butter, broth, sour cream, and lemon juice to blend well. Toss the fish mixture gently with this sauce, and season with salt and pepper.

Makes enough to fill 1 pirog

Two Popular Pie Fillings

Dve Nachinki dlya Pirogov i Porozhkov

The two savory fillings that follow can be used with great success in *pirozhki*, a *pirog*, or *kulebiaka*. For convenience sake, make an extra batch of filling and freeze it until ready to use.

Meat Filling

Myasnaya Nachinka

A very savory filling made particularly tasty by lots of deeply browned onions. Pies with this filling make a good entrée. You can also use leftover chicken or turkey instead of the beef.

3 tablespoons vegetable oil
3 large onions, finely chopped
2 pounds boiled beef chuck, ground
4 hard-cooked eggs, chopped
⅓ cup beef broth
3 heaping tablespoons sour cream
1½ tablespoons all-purpose flour
*2 tablespoons chopped fresh dill
   (optional)*
2 tablespoons chopped fresh parsley
*Salt and freshly ground black
   pepper, to taste*

1 Heat the oil in a medium-size skillet over medium-high heat. Add the onions and sauté, stirring frequently, until well browned, about 15 minutes.

2 In a large bowl, combine the onions,

beef, and remaining ingredients. Stir until well blended.

Makes enough to fill 45 to 50 pirozhki, 1 pirog, or 1 kulebiaka

Cabbage Filling

Kapustnaya Nachinka

I simply don't understand people who don't like cabbage, but even they will change their mind once they taste a traditional Russian cabbage pie. Some Russian cooks use a combination of cabbage and sauerkraut for this filling.

*1 head (about 3 pounds) green
   cabbage, finely chopped
3 tablespoons unsalted butter
3 tablespoons vegetable oil
4 hard-cooked eggs, finely chopped*

*Salt and freshly ground black
   pepper, to taste
2 tablespoons chopped fresh dill
   (optional)*

1 Blanch the cabbage in boiling salted water for 3 minutes. Drain well and squeeze the cabbage to remove any excess liquid.

2 Heat the butter and oil in a large skillet over medium heat. Add the cabbage and cook, stirring, until soft and colored, 15 to 20 minutes.

3 Remove from the heat and stir in the remaining ingredients. Cool to room temperature.

Makes enough to fill 45 to 50 pirozhki, 1 pirog, or 1 kulebiaka

Ukrainian Cuisine

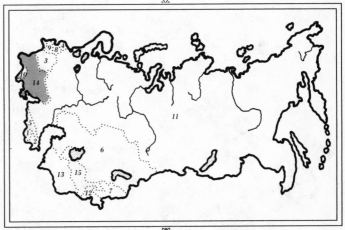

I 'll never forget how I got my first taste for Ukrainian food. A skinny, pale, city-bound child, growing up in a cluttered apartment in the heart of old Moscow, my initiation into the earthen, homey cuisine of this hulking western re-public was actually through literature. One frozen night my parents went out with some friends, leaving me in the care of neither a babysitter (unheard of in Moscow) nor, on this occasion, my *babushka* (grandma). Instead, they dropped a tattered volume of Nikolai Gogol's short stories, *Evenings on a Farm Near Dikanka* on the kitchen table and made a beeline for the front door. A perfect strategy! I found the book, took it to my room, and bundled up under a thick blanket, I devoured the whole collection, quiet as a lamb and good as gold.

There were spooky tales of fang-toothed *kolduni* (sorcerers); funny stories about seductive mermaids and beefy cossacks; endless descriptions of the local markets, bulging with colorful produce,

1. ARMENIA
2. AZERBAIJAN
3. BYELORUSSIA
4. ESTONIA
5. GEORGIA
6. KAZAKHSTAN
7. KIRGHIZIA
8. LATVIA
9. LITHUANIA
10. MOLDAVIA
11. RUSSIA
12. TADZHIKISTAN
13. TURKMENIA
14. UKRAINE
15. UZBEKISTAN

"His cheeks blushed
like a poppy-flower.
He's now a beet,
not an onion."

— Nikolai Gogol
Evenings on a Farm Near Dikanka

and countless feasts and celebrations; and above all, long, luxurious paragraphs detailing the robust peasant foods of Gogol's native Ukraine. They certainly wanted me to amuse myself, but my parents actually got more than they bargained for. Such was the power of Gogol's intense folkloric imagination that for months I refused to sleep with the light off, terrified that some spirit might emerge from behind my piano to torment me. And in the daytime, I would pester my mother to prepare roast suckling pig, or plump goose with steaming cabbage, or, at the very least, some of those sweet dumplings (*vareniki*) provocatively stuffed with fresh sour cherries whose hot juice left the mouth tingling with pleasure.

My poor mother, all she could come up with in the meatless and fruitless Russian winter was a vegetarian borscht. And while this was a magnificent effort of Muscovite improvisation, it revealed the tendency of the Russians to appropriate Ukrainian cuisine (and other Soviet cuisines) for their own — in the process lending it a kind of awkward sophistication.

In fact, a dish such as chicken Kiev, which is so strongly associated with the Ukraine, is not typically Ukrainian at all. It's actually an early twentieth-century invention designed to upgrade a "provincial" food to Russo-Gallic gourmet standards. Likewise, the immensely popular Ukrainian borscht became a Soviet "national" dish, constantly undergoing cunning revisions and local adaptions as the recipe traveled, and losing in the process many of its essential characteristics such as fat and garlic. Both dishes nowadays supposedly represent Ukrainian fare in every city-center restaurant in the USSR (as well as in every "Russian" restaurant in the West); but they actually offer a faint, even misleading, impression of their real roots in the Ukraine.

Perhaps this is one of the reasons why my childhood cravings were strangely disappointed when I had the opportunity to visit some Ukrainian cities a few years later. Although I did manage to taste the more popular dishes, I was soon forced to the same conclusion: that the essence of this cuisine is often lost in busy urban centers. It was only at the end of my trip, when I was hiking with a group of geologists and stayed over for several nights in village homes, that I realized just how Ukrainian food is wedded heart and soul to the land, to the homestead, and to the small hamlet and its ancient traditions.

Food Fit for a Cossack

The word *Ukraine* actually means "border" or "frontier," and the country shares four international boundaries—with Romania, Czechoslovakia, Hungary, and Poland. The Ukraine has been plundered, settled, and fought over by all these nations and others besides. Although the capital, Kiev, was the birthplace of Orthodoxy in 988 (when the old pagan idols were cast into the Dnieper River by Prince Vladimir), the religious faith of the Ukrainians was also contested by Muslims, Tatars, and Turks from the south, and by Catholic Poles and Lithuanians from the north and the west.

And the story is the same for food. Although the Ukrainians fended off their enemies with some success, they absorbed a large number of alien cooking habits and ingredients while violently rejecting others, yet always endeavoring to maintain their own social and religious customs. The faintly exotic and enormously versatile eggplant, for exam-

When you arrive we'll give you melons such as you've never tasted in your life, I think; and you'll find no better honey in any village in the world—I'll take my oath on that—it's as clear as a tear or a costly crystal. . . . And what pies my old woman will feed you on! What pies, if only you knew—simply sugar, perfect sugar—the butter fairly melts on your lips when you begin to eat them. Really, when you come to think of it, there's nothing these women can't do! Have you, friends, ever tasted pear kvass flavored with sloes, or raisin and plum vodka? Or rice soup with milk? Good heavens, what dainties there are in the world . . . they're too good for words. Only last year . . . but how I'm rambling on! Just come, make haste and come and we will give you such good things that you'll talk about them to everyone you meet.

—Nikolai Gogol,
*Evenings on a Farm
Near Dikanka*

ple, was rejected wholesale in all but the southern extremities of the Ukraine until the twentieth century because of its association with the Ottoman domination. On the other hand, both *vareniki* and stuffed cabbage (*holubtsi*), which were originally imported from Turkey, have been considered essential elements of Ukrainian cuisine for generations.

Among meat dishes, the vigorous consumption of pork or oven-roasted boar — the only food, proverbially, that could satisfy the mighty appetite of a cossack — actually became a symbol of resistance to the Muslims, to whom pork was of course forbidden.

Bigos (savory stewed sauerkraut with sausage or pork) is actually Lithuanian or Polish in origin, while the western Ukrainian penchant for sticky-sweet strudels, breaded meats, and the whole range of tarts and cheesecakes is a carryover from the Austro-Hungarian glory days. But whenever Ukrainians borrowed and adapted a recipe, they always made it uniquely their own.

Ukrainian food is one of the great rustic cuisines of the world — honest, spontaneous, often solid and heavy, and yet always possessing a natural subtlety and a taste as rich and hearty as the soil itself. This food is somehow unsuited to the restaurant, for it is "home-style cooking" in the original and the best sense of the phrase — meant for families, for homecomings, and for holy days.

Even more than in most of the regions of Europe, Ukrainian cuisine is intimately linked to the land. Culinary artifice and invention have not intervened as dramatically as in, say, Burgundy or Emilia-Romagna, where the palate is constantly seduced by richness and refinement, though Ukrainian soil is no less fertile and productive than that of these more famous farming areas. In the end, there's probably more kinship between Ukrainian fare and the hearty foods of the Germanic and North Slavic peoples.

Appropriately, the most potent symbol of the republic is its almost bright, black soil (*chernozem*), which stretches away in the seemingly infinite steppe lands between the Carpathian and the Ural mountains. The bulk of the Ukraine, which is the second largest "country" in Europe after Russia, is taken up by grasslands and humus-rich arable fields; and in the past, when a Ukrainian left his native country, he always carried off a handful of soil as both trophy and memorial, for it was mixed with his adopted soil on his grave.

A Land of Many Grains

As its reputation as "the breadbasket of Europe" suggests, the predominant crops of Ukraine are various grains: rye, wheat, millet, oats, and the staple buckwheat, which produces a dark, pungent flour. The characteristic foods are therefore *kasha* (hot cereal), breads, dumplings, and cakes — all of which are prepared in such a variety of ways as to rival the prodigal inventiveness of Italians with pasta and the Chinese with rice. Breadmaking in particular has been raised to an art in the Ukraine, revealing a startling range of shapes, tastes, and textures for every conceivable occasion: Weddings, funerals, christenings, name days, and religious festivals all require their own special breads. Most impressive is the *korovai*, a gigantic head-high wedding bread so fantastically decorated with flowers, sheaves, animals, and other even more elaborate

Food inhabits Ukrainian national consciousness more fully than in almost any other part of the USSR. This is partly because the country is so overwhelmingly agricultural, but there's more to it than that. Every aspect of its rich folklore is suffused with references to food. In bygone days, for example, if you wanted to catch a witch, you were advised to wrap a tasty slab of cheese in some cloth and somehow tie it onto your shirt where it should dangle throughout Lent. On the Saturday before Easter, all the witches of the neighborhood would supposedly appear and beg for the cheese.

motifs, that you can often see these baked sculptures on view in the museums of folk art along with colorful embroidered towels and delicately ornate Easter eggs.

Bread is treated by the Slavs with such enormous respect that *khlib* (bread) and *sil* (salt), the most enduring ancient tokens of hospitality, should always be presented to guests upon their arrival. And in the old days, a guest who actually brought bread into a house could never properly be refused entertainment — which was often a real nuisance as each and every village had its own skilled "gate-crasher."

When dough isn't baked, it's usually either boiled or fried in the familiar forms of dumplings or fritters. I'm absolutely convinced that there must be as many different kinds of these delicious morsels as there are days of the year — though I must admit I've never counted. Skimming through Ukrainian cookbooks makes me smile at their extraordinary inventiveness in the naming of their dough products: *pampushki, halushki, shuliki, bootziki* — affectionate nonsense diminutives, which are untranslatable even into Russian.

The methods of preparation are as varied as the names. These "little doughy delights" can be made from different kinds of flour, with or without fillings, and flavored with anything from diced pork fat to honey and poppyseeds — a favorite Ukrainian combination. Although all of the varieties are delicious, the only recipe that has successfully traveled outside its

Delicious homemade dumplings are offered for sale Ukrainian-style, from a festively decorated, handcrafted bowl.

native republic is that for *vareniki*, the ceaselessly versatile, semicircular dumplings made from thinly rolled noodle dough and filled with those most dear and familiar tempters of the Slavic palate: cottage cheese, sauerkraut, chopped liver, sautéed mushrooms, potatoes, or fresh fruit (no seafood, please).

Besides its formidable grains, central Ukraine is alive with a whole spectrum of sumptuous fruits and vegetables. Outstanding are the deep-red, honey-sweet beets and the plump white cabbages. Both are ~~lovingly~~ prepared for star roles in soups and salads during the summer months and brined for the winter — the cabbage to make savory sauerkraut and the beets to produce a beet *kvass*, the ruby-colored fermented liquid that is used in turn to make the famed Ukrainian borscht throughout the cold season.

Like other Slavs, Ukrainians are not known for simply prepared red meats, such as lamb or beef.

Vegetables for sale are lavishly displayed at a Ukrainian market.

Instead they adore their sausages, gorgeous plump poultry, abundant freshwater fish, and pork, which is considered the national meat as much for its fat as its flesh. Indeed, pork fat is put to work somewhat obsessively in the cuisine, mostly for frying, but it's also eaten smoked or salted, and it's even added to some of the rural desserts. Now much more figure and health conscious, I remember with a mixture of horror and nostalgia how as a child I used to down large chunks of snowy-white salted lard smeared onto thick slices of sourdough bread and accompanied by hot boiled potatoes with sour cream, garlic, and dill.

The fringes of the republic are very different

from the grain-rich core. To the north are marsh-lands and forests; the ~~romantic~~ Carpathian high-lands and foothills rise dramatically to the west, yielding strong-flavored mushrooms and succulent berries; while along the Black Sea coast and the Sea of Azov, a buoyant climate and the ripe produce are reminiscent of the Mediterranean. In particular, Odessa and the Crimean seaports enjoy a much more cosmopolitan, seaside cuisine.

But wherever you travel in the Ukraine, from the rich uplands of Volhynia in the west to the old Cossack lands along the mighty Dnieper River, from Kiev in the north to the Crimea in the south, you will find the miracles of this republic's cuisine. Whole-some wheat, beautiful barleys, unbelievable beets, and lush vegetables are harvested, prepared, and variously combined as only real people of the land know how. With a colorful cultural revival in the air in the early 1990s, we are destined to hear much more about this fascinating nation that links Russia to the center of Europe. Enjoy your first taste!

Brunch and Tea Dishes

ZAVTRAKI I CHAI

Leisurely breakfasts and brunches and late afternoon teas are the most pleasant meals to be enjoyed in the Soviet Union today, since they require few hard-to-come-by ingredients and relatively little preparation time. Instead, they rely on the time-honored traditions of hospitality and culinary ingenuity — both of which, thank goodness, are still in abundant supply.

As in other parts of the world (John's London mornings, kicked off with brimming platefuls of eggs and bacon, come most readily to mind), breakfast is often considered the most important meal of the day. One Russian culinary maxim offers the rationale for this, warning as it does against the perils of late eating: Eat your breakfast yourself, share lunch with a friend, and give your supper to an enemy. Russian breakfasts, then, are usually substantial, even on busy weekday mornings. They might include *tvorog*, Russian cottage cheese topped with jam; eggs; buttermilk; cold cuts; black and white breads; hot cereal (*kasha*); and tea — which is more common than coffee. It is also not unusual to find breakfasters in the USSR skillfully modifying and warming up leftovers from the night before. One American friend simply could not believe that he had been served herring and potatoes at nine o'clock in the morning.

Best of all, though, is the long, lazy weekend brunch, a well-respected family tradition that draws everyone together in most Soviet households. These occasions will include a variety of little pancakes or fritters (*oladyi*); *syrniki* — sweet cheese patties; *blinchiki* — mouthwatering filled crêpes; and freshly baked rolls and buns eaten with fruity homemade preserves. When reinvented in the American kitchen, this brunch fare can really sparkle. So be sure to use some of these suggestions if you're looking for novel ideas for the weekend table.

Teatime

The tea ceremony is, of course, a highly important and long-standing tradition in both the western (European) and southern (Muslim) parts of the USSR. The samovar itself (*samovar* literally means "self-boiler") has for generations been a symbol of Russian hospitality in the West. Although there are few places where authentic samovars are still used today, they have become much-prized collector's items; and beautiful examples of nineteenth-century metalwork can be found both in local museums and in private homes all over the Soviet Union. Almost every

Moscow apartment is adorned with a modern electric samovar, however — eagerly wheeled out for foreign guests — which keeps the tea warm while both brewing and between cups. (Often it is given as a gift to parting guests together with a special red-cheeked doll wearing a quilted skirt — *baba na chainik*, the "teapot woman.") Yet as quintessentially Russian as they may seem, both the samovar and the tea it so deliciously serves in fact traveled beyond the Urals from the east — the samovar from Persia in the eighteenth century, and tea via Mongolia a century before.

Although not nearly as formal as in the days of the Czars, an invitation to afternoon tea (*k chayu*) in Russia is still quite a serious affair, like as not to be overly supplied with tempting sweet and savory tidbits. With the food supply situation so difficult these days, tea invites are rapidly replacing sit-down dinners. Frankly, I don't consider this such a great loss, as I would much rather sample the fruits of the Russian genius for baking than tug on a piece of tough beef for which my hosts had probably stood in line for half a day. Tragically, even the institution of tea is under threat by virtue of the sheer scarcity of quality teas in Soviet stores. Anyone traveling to Russia today soon discovers that a tin of Earl Grey is one of the most pleasing presents to give.

And in Central Asia

Much more exotic, if at the same time rather less filling than a Russian tea ceremony, is the tea ritual of Central Asia, which begins rather than ends a meal. Although black tea is sometimes served at a guest's special request, green tea (sworn by in the region as the most effective summer cooler) is the traditional beverage. Tea is brewed in splendid orange and white ceramic pots, and served in *piala*s, bowl-shaped ceramic cups. The first cup is customarily poured back into the pot to assure the desired strength. Curiously enough, the more a guest is respected and honored, the smaller the amount of tea he receives. This way it doesn't get cold so quickly, and the host's hospitality can be measured out by his attentiveness to the refills. If you don't feel like sipping your tea in batches, however, you can always ask for tea "without respect," in which case you will get a full cup and simultaneously acquire a reputation for being a rude guest.

When you arrive for a meal in Central Asia you will invariably find a table spread with the customary accompaniments for tea — bowls of freshly picked fruit, halvah and other exotic sweets, and *kiyem*, beautiful, translucent fruits in syrup. Sugar is rarely served in this part of the USSR. In the Caucasus, where Turkish-style coffee is favored over tea, one can savor a startling variety of delicate small cookies, as well as pastries in syrup, nut and honey confections, and various kinds of homemade halvah.

Walnut-Stuffed Prunes

Chernosliv s Orekhami

In Russia these wonderful prunes always seem to turn up as an appetizer (without the whipped cream, of course). But a friendly weekend brunch is really the occasion to show them off at their most seductive and winning. The play of color between the black of the prunes and the white of the whipped cream offers exciting possibilities for serving and presenting.

½ cup full-bodied red wine

1 cup water

3 tablespoons sugar

20 large pitted prunes

2 cloves

20 large walnut pieces

½ cup heavy or whipping
  cream

1 tablespoon raspberry or cherry
  liqueur

1 In a small saucepan, combine the wine, water, and sugar. Cook, stirring, over medium heat until the sugar dissolves, 1 to 2 minutes. Add the prunes and cloves and cook over medium-low heat until the prunes swell, 25 minutes.

2 Drain the prunes, reserving about ¼ cup of the liquid. Cool the prunes, then stuff each with a walnut piece and arrange on a serving platter. Spoon the reserved liquid over the prunes.

3 Whip the cream with the liqueur until stiff. From a pastry bag fitted with a decorative tip, pipe the cream over the prunes.

Serves 4

Central Asian Tea Party

For a highly original and exotic tea party that is also healthful and simple to prepare, try the following menu of nuts, dried and fresh fruit, exotic sweets, and green tea. In Central Asia this kind of tea gathering would be a ladies-only event. The women would politely consume their sweet dainties, accompanied by a good dose of chatter and gossip, while the men devoured an elaborate lamb pilaf, washing it down, in turn, with giant shots of vodka and their own raucous banter.

Green tea

Bowl of fresh fruit (persimmons, pomegranates, peaches or apricots, and two varieties of grapes and two of melons)

Unsalted almonds

Unsalted pistachios

Dried apricots

Golden raisins

Dates

Sugar crystals

Halvah

Hazelnut Crescents

Almond and Pistachio Baklava

Quince or Fig Preserves

Peasant Breakfast

Krestianskiy Zavtrak

A hearty breakfast hash from the Ukraine, *krestianskiy zavtrak* features an eye-opening combination of pumpernickel, smoked bacon and sausage, and fried eggs. Serve this hash with Paprika Fries (see Index) for a winter brunch.

5 tablespoons unsalted butter

2 cups ½-inch dice of day-old
    pumpernickel bread, preferably
    German

4 ounces smoky bacon, chopped

¾ cup finely chopped onion

3 cups ½-inch dice of smoked
    kielbasa or bratwurst

Salt and freshly ground black
    pepper, to taste

8 large eggs

Finely chopped fresh dill for garnish

1 Melt 4 tablespoons of the butter in a large skillet over medium heat. Sauté the bread cubes in batches until golden brown and crispy. Transfer to a bowl and set aside. Wipe out the skillet.

2 Fry the bacon in the skillet over medium heat until it renders its fat. Add the onion and sauté until it begins to color, about 8 minutes. Add the kielbasa and cook, stirring, until the onion and kielbasa are nicely browned.

3 Melt the remaining 1 tablespoon butter in a medium-size nonstick skillet over medium heat. Add one-fourth of the kielbasa mixture and one-fourth of the bread to the skillet and distribute evenly with a wooden spoon. Cook for 1 minute.

4 Break 2 eggs into the skillet. Cook for 2 minutes, stirring the whites gently with a thin spatula. When the whites are almost set and the yolks are still runny, reduce the heat to low, cover the skillet, and cook for 1 minute, or to desired doneness. Slide the hash and the eggs onto a plate.

5 Repeat with the remaining ingredients to make three more portions.

6 Serve immediately, sprinkled with dill.

Serves 4

Omelet with Feta and Scallions

Omlete cu Brinza si Ciapa Verde

A particularly delicious omelet from Moldavia. Throughout the Soviet Union omelets are not usually folded, but you can do it the Western way too. Serve with hot pita and a good dollop of yogurt or sour cream.

6 ounces feta, preferably
   Bulgarian
⅓ cup finely chopped scallions
   (green onions)
1½ teaspoons sweet Hungarian
   paprika, plus additional paprika
   for garnish

6 large eggs
⅓ cup milk
Salt and freshly ground black
   pepper, to taste
2 tablespoons unsalted butter
2 tablespoons chopped fresh dill for
   garnish

1 If the feta is too salty, soak in cold water for 30 minutes. Drain well and crumble into fine pieces. Combine in a bowl with the scallions and paprika and set aside.

2 In a large bowl, whisk the eggs with the milk, salt, and pepper until frothy.

3 Melt the butter in a 10-inch omelet pan over medium heat. When the butter bubbles rapidly, add half of the egg mixture and stir until it just begins to set. Continue cooking until the eggs are almost completely cooked, running a thin spatula around the edges to prevent sticking, about 1½ minutes.

4 Sprinkle half of the feta mixture on the omelet, then reduce the heat to very low, cover, and cook for 1 minute more. Slide the omelet onto a plate, folding over, if desired.

5 Repeat with the remaining ingredients to make one more omelet.

6 Serve at once, lightly sprinkled with paprika and dill.

Serves 2

Herb Omelet

Sabzi Kyukyu

The Persian-Azerbaijani dish *kyukyu* is something of a cross between an omelet and a pancake. This is the most popular *kyukyu*, made with lots of fresh herbs and served as an appetizer or side dish. I find it an ideal buffet brunch dish, especially as it can be made the night before. It can be served either warm or at room temperature and is traditionally accompanied by Yogurt and Garlic Sauce (see Index).

If making *kyukyu* for a large number of people, you can bake it in a well-buttered rectangular baking dish in a 350°F oven. It should take about 30 minutes.

Breakfast in the Meadow

Herb Omelet

Georgian Cheese Bread

Kasseri and feta cheeses

Mixed olives

Fresh tomatoes and cucumbers

Pita bread

Chilled Yogurt Drink

Tahini Buns

Coffee and strong tea

• • •

6 large eggs, well beaten

*2 cups finely chopped
   spinach*

*1 cup finely chopped scallions
   (green onions)*

*1 cup finely chopped
   fresh parsley*

*½ cup finely chopped
   fresh dill*

*3 tablespoons finely chopped
   fresh cilantro*

*¼ cup finely chopped
   walnuts*

¼ teaspoon ground turmeric

*Salt and freshly ground black
   pepper, to taste*

3 tablespoons vegetable oil

1 In a large bowl, combine the eggs, spinach, scallions, herbs, walnuts, turmeric, and salt and pepper. Mix well.

2 Heat the oil over medium heat in a 10-inch skillet. Add the egg mixture and cook until it just begins to set, about 5 minutes. Reduce the heat to low, cover, and cook until the *kyukyu* is completely set, about 15 minutes more.

3 Without removing the skillet from the heat, cut the *kyukyu* into eight wedges with a metal spatula or a dull knife. Carefully turn each wedge and cook, covered, until the second side is lightly colored, about 5 minutes more.

4 Transfer to a serving platter and cool to warm or room temperature.

Serves 4 to 6

Smoked Whitefish Omelet

Kutum Kyukyu

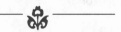

This omelet is considered very prestigious in Azerbaijan, where it is made with local smoked whitefish (*kutum*) and lots of fresh herbs. The Azerbaijanis use cilantro, but this can overpower the delicate taste of the whitefish, so I prefer to use a combination of dill and chives. It can be served either warm or at room temperature and is traditionally accompanied by melted saffron butter. You can serve it either as a brunch entrée or as an appetizer.

1 tablespoon all-purpose flour
½ teaspoon baking powder
5 large eggs
Salt and freshly ground black
*   pepper, to taste*
2 tablespoons unflavored fine, dry
*   bread crumbs*
⅓ cup finely chopped fresh dill
¼ cup finely snipped fresh
*   chives*

1 tablespoon fresh lemon juice
3 tablespoons unsalted butter
¾ cup finely chopped onion
8 ounces hot-smoked whitefish,
*   flaked, about 2 cups*
¼ teaspoon saffron threads, crushed
*   in a mortar*
8 tablespoons (1 stick) unsalted
*   butter, melted*
Lemon slices for garnish

1 Sift together the flour and baking powder into a large bowl. Add one of the eggs and whisk until blended. Add the remaining eggs and salt and pepper and whisk until frothy. Fold in the bread crumbs, dill, chives, and lemon juice. Set aside.

2 Melt the 3 tablespoons butter in a 10-inch heavy skillet over medium heat. Add the onion and sauté until softened, about 7 minutes. Stir in the fish and sauté, stirring, for 2 minutes more.

3 Preheat the broiler.

4 Pour the egg mixture over the fish, separating the fish with a spatula so the eggs cover the bottom of the skillet. Reduce the heat to low and cook until the bottom and sides of the eggs are cooked but the center is still loose, about 7 to 8 minutes, shaking the skillet occasionally to prevent sticking.

5 Place the skillet under the broiler, about 6 inches from the heat, and cook until the omelet is set on top and light golden, about 2 minutes. Do not overcook.

Allow the omelet to cool slightly.

6 To make saffron butter, infuse the melted butter with the saffron and let stand for 10 minutes. Stir.

7 To serve, run a knife around the edge of the skillet to loosen the omelet. Invert the omelet onto a platter. Cut into wedges or diamond shapes and serve with lemon slices and saffron butter on the side.

Serves 4

Farmer's Cheese Patties

Sirniki

This traditional Russian breakfast dish has been tremendously popular with Western tourists in the USSR. In fact many visitors have reported that the best meal to be had in Moscow is the breakfast buffet (the "Swedish Table" — *Shvedskiy Stol* — as the Russians call it) at the Intourist Hotel, which features these patties. *Sirniki* is also the only Russian dish that

I've seen requested in the "You Asked For It" section of *Gourmet* magazine.

These "little fried cheesecakes," as a friend once described them, are perfect for a family breakfast or a formal brunch. Steps 1 and 2 can be prepared the evening before, so all you have to do is fry them up and serve with lashings of sour cream and preserves (lingonberry, black currant, and raspberry are the Russian choices).

¼ cup brandy

⅓ cup raisins

1 pound farmer's cheese (do not substitute cottage cheese)

2 large egg yolks, beaten

1½ tablespoons sour cream

⅓ cup all-purpose flour, plus 1 tablespoon for dusting the patties

2 tablespoons uncooked cream of wheat (not instant)

3 tablespoons sugar, or more to taste

1 tablespoon vanilla sugar (see box)

¼ teaspoon salt

4 tablespoons (½ stick) unsalted butter

1 In a small saucepan, bring the brandy to a boil. Off the heat, add the raisins and soak for 30 minutes. Drain and dry with paper towels. Set aside.

2 Press the farmer's cheese through a fine sieve. Combine it in a large bowl with the raisins, egg yolks, sour cream, ⅓ cup flour, cream of wheat, sugar, and vanilla sugar. Mix thoroughly and add salt. Cover and refrigerate overnight.

3 Form the cheese mixture into twelve round flat patties about 3½ inches in diameter. Dust the patties on both sides with the 1 tablespoon flour.

4 Melt the butter in a large nonstick skillet over medium heat. Add as many patties as will comfortably fit and fry until deep golden on both sides.

Vanilla Sugar

I always keep a canister of vanilla-scented sugar to add to cakes, compotes, and other desserts. Just bury a large vanilla bean in a 2 to 3 pound container of sugar and store for at least 1 week before using.

5 Repeat with the remaining patties. Serve at once.

Serves 4 to 6

Apple Pancakes

Oladyi s Yablokami

In my experience, Russian pancakes, even the unraised ones, are usually much more delicate in taste and texture than their American counterparts. This recipe for small, ethereal pancakes comes from Latvia, where pancakes resemble the Swedish *plätter*. Try them if you are in the mood for adventuring beyond an instant-cooking cereal or some pancakes-from-the-box affair. Since melted butter is already added to the batter, you shouldn't need any more for frying. If the pancakes stick, however, add about ½ teaspoon of melted butter to the pan before frying. Serve with sour cream, honey, or jam.

2 large tart green apples (such as
   Granny Smith), cored and
   peeled
1½ tablespoons vanilla sugar (see
   box, preceding page)
1 tablespoon fresh lemon juice
3 large eggs, separated
½ cup milk
1 cup half-and-half or light
   cream

3 tablespoons unsalted butter,
   melted, plus additional melted
   butter for frying the pancakes
   if needed
1 cup plus 3 tablespoons unbleached
   all-purpose flour
½ teaspoon salt
½ teaspoon baking soda
¼ teaspoon white vinegar
Confectioners' sugar

1 Quarter the apples and slice thinly crosswise. Toss in a bowl with the vanilla sugar and lemon juice and let stand while preparing the batter.

2 In a large bowl, beat together the egg yolks, milk, half-and-half, and butter. Sift together the flour and salt, then whisk into the egg yolk mixture until smooth. In a tablespoon, combine the baking soda and the vinegar and stir into the batter. Let stand at room temperature for 30 minutes.

3 Fold the apples into the batter, making sure they are evenly distributed.

4 Beat the egg whites until stiff and fold them into the batter.

5 Heat a heavy, preferably cast-iron, 5-inch skillet over medium heat. Pour about 3 tablespoons of the batter into the skillet and cook until golden brown on both sides, about 3 to 4 minutes in all.

6 Repeat with the remaining batter, keeping the cooked pancakes warm in a 225°F oven.

Makes about 14 pancakes (serves 4)

Buttermilk Fritters

Oladushki

This favorite breakfast treat is as popular with Russians as vodka. And the splendid domestic aroma from the frying pan is as familiar to any Russian child as is the smell of popcorn at a movie house to his or her American counterpart. Serve with jam, honey, or sour cream.

2 eggs, separated
1½ cups buttermilk
1 tablespoon vegetable oil, plus
    additional oil for frying

1 cup unbleached all-purpose flour
1½ tablespoons sugar
¼ teaspoon salt
½ teaspoon baking soda

1 In a large bowl, combine the egg yolks, buttermilk, and the 1 tablespoon vegetable oil. Mix well.

2 Sift the dry ingredients together and gradually add them to the buttermilk mixture, beating until well blended. Let the batter stand for 1 hour.

3 Just before frying the fritters, beat the egg whites until they hold stiff peaks and carefully fold them into the batter.

4 Heat a scant tablespoon of oil in a large nonstick skillet over medium heat. For each fritter, drop about 1½ tablespoons of the batter into the skillet. You should be able to fit in 4 or 5 at a time. Fry on both sides until golden, 3 minutes each side.

5 Repeat with the remaining batter, keeping the cooked fritters warm in a 225°F oven.

Makes about 20 fritters (serves 4)

Filled Crêpes

Blinchiki

In the Jewish community in the U.S., *blinchiki* are known as blintzes. In Poland and the Ukraine, they are called *naliesniki*. *Blinchiki* are the unraised, filled cousins of the Russian *blini*. Whatever you know them as, they are usually filled with meat, cheese, or fruit and served accompanied by sour cream.

2 large eggs, lightly beaten
1 large egg yolk, lightly beaten
1 cup milk, at room temperature
1 tablespoon sugar for a sweet filling,
    ½ teaspoon for a savory filling
Large pinch of salt
1⅓ cups unbleached all-purpose
    flour

½ cup club soda
4 tablespoons clarified butter (see
    Index)
1 recipe Meat, Sweet Farmer's Cheese,
    or Apple Filling (recipes follow)
About 1½ tablespoons vegetable oil
Confectioners' sugar, if using a
    sweet filling

1 In a large bowl, whisk together the eggs, egg yolk, milk, sugar, and salt. Gradually add the flour, continuing to whisk until the batter is smooth. (This can be done in a food processor.) Let stand at room temperature for 30 minutes, then stir the club soda into the batter.

2 Heat a crêpe pan or a 7-inch nonstick skillet over medium heat. When it's very hot, brush the skillet with about ½ teaspoon of the clarified butter.

3 Remove the pan from heat. Measure out about 2½ tablespoons of the batter and quickly pour it into the pan. Quickly rotate and tilt the pan until the batter covers the bottom completely. Fry on one side until golden, about 1 minute. Turn, and fry on the other side for 10 seconds more. It should be paler than the first side. Remove and set aside. Repeat with the rest of the batter.

4 Place a *blinchik* on a cutting board, well-browned side up, and place 2 heaping tablespoons of the filling in a row slightly below center. Fold the closest end up over the filling, then fold both sides in toward the center and roll up as you would an egg roll. Repeat with the remaining *blinchiki*.

5 Heat the oil in a larger skillet over medium heat. Add as many *blinchiki* as fit comfortably and fry on both sides until golden, about 5 minutes.

6 Repeat with the rest of the *blinchiki*, keeping the cooked ones warm in the oven. Sprinkle *blinchiki* with a sweet filling with confectioners' sugar before serving.

Makes about 18 blinchiki (serves 6)

Meat Filling

Myasnaya Nachinka

This filling can be made from either beef, chicken, or turkey. *Blinchiki* with meat is a great Russian favorite for lunch or a light supper. They are served hot, accompanied by sour cream.

> 2 tablespoons vegetable oil
> 1 cup chopped onions
> 1½ pounds cooked beef or chicken, ground
> 2 tablespoons canned chicken broth
> 2 tablespoons sour cream
> Salt and freshly ground black pepper, to taste

1 Heat the oil in a small skillet over medium heat. Add the onions and cook,

stirring occasionally, until deeply browned, about 15 minutes.

2 In a large bowl, mix the onion thoroughly with the remaining ingredients.

Makes enough to fill 18 blinchiki

Sweet Farmer's Cheese Filling

Tvorozhnaya Nachinka

If you prefer, add 1 cup of well-drained canned sour cherries to this classic filling instead of raisins. Serve *blinchiki*, sprinkled with confectioners' sugar and with sour cream on the side.

> 1½ pounds farmer's cheese
> ¼ cup sugar, or more to taste
> 3 heaping tablespoons sour cream
> ½ cup raisins (optional)

1 Process the farmer's cheese, sugar, and sour cream in a food processor, until smooth.

2 Transfer to a bowl, add the raisins, if desired, and mix well.

Makes enough to fill 18 blinchiki

Apple Filling

Yablochnaya Nachinka

Serve *blinchiki* with this Lithuanian filling slightly warm for brunch or dessert. Pass a bowl of crème fraîche to dollop on. Don't feel confined to using only apples. Substitute apricots, peaches, or a favorite berry.

5 tablespoons unsalted butter
9 tart apples (such as Granny
    Smith), cored, peeled,
    and sliced

⅓ cup (packed) light brown sugar
¼ cup brandy
½ teaspoon ground cinnamon
    (optional)

1 Melt 2 tablespoons of the butter in a large skillet over medium heat. Add as many apples as fit comfortably, and sauté, stirring occasionally, until soft, about 15 minutes. Repeat with the rest of the apples, adding more butter as needed.

2 Return the apples to the skillet, stir in the brown sugar and brandy and cook, stir-

ring, over high heat, until the brandy reduces by half, about 5 minutes.

3 Transfer the apples to a bowl and add cinnamon, if desired. Let the filling cool to lukewarm before filling the *blinchiki*.

Makes enough to fill 18 blinchiki

Mushroom Crêpe Torte

Blinchatiy Pirog s Gribami

In Russia *blinchatiy pirog* is usually eaten in February, that is around the time of the Butter Festival, *Maslenitsa*, which is when *blini* and *blinchiki* are traditionally made. The leftover *blini* are often stacked together with a filling between the layers, and then baked. This makes a really splendid brunch dish — especially as the crêpes and the filling can be made the previous day so that all you have to do is bake the *pirog* just before the guests arrive. Either *blinchiki* or *blini* (see Index) can be used for this dish. When making *blinchiki* for this dish, use ½ teaspoon sugar and cook them in an 8-inch skillet. Serve with sour cream or crème fraîche.

1 ounce imported dried mushrooms,
    preferably porcini, well rinsed
1 cup water
2 pounds fresh white mushrooms
7 tablespoons unsalted butter
1¼ cups finely chopped onions
3 tablespoons dry vermouth
Salt and freshly ground black
    pepper, to taste
½ cup heavy or whipping
    cream

2 tablespoons sour cream
1¼ cups grated Gruyère cheese
3 tablespoons chopped fresh dill
14 blinchiki (see page 476), fried on
    both sides
2 tablespoons unsalted butter
½ cup Béchamel Sauce (see Index)
3 tablespoons unflavored fine, dry
    bread crumbs

1 Soak the dried mushrooms in the water for 2 hours. Drain the mushrooms, pat dry, chop fine, and set aside. Reserve the soaking liquid for another use.

2 Wipe the fresh mushrooms clean with a damp paper towel. Slice thinly.

3 Melt 5 tablespoons of the butter in a large skillet over medium-high heat. Add the onions and chopped dried mushrooms and sauté, stirring, for about 7 minutes. Add the fresh mushrooms and toss until they begin to give off their juices. Raise the heat to high and continue to sauté, stirring until the juices are reabsorbed, 15 minutes. Reduce the heat to medium and sauté the mushrooms for another 5 minutes.

4 Add the vermouth, turn the heat up to high, and cook for 2 to 3 minutes. Season the mushrooms with salt and pepper and stir in the cream, sour cream, and ¾ cup of the Gruyère, mixing it in well with a wooden spoon. Reduce the heat to low and cook until the cream thickens, another 5 minutes. Taste and correct the seasoning. Remove from the heat and set aside.

5 Preheat the oven to 400°F.

6 Grease an 8-inch round cake pan with 1 tablespoon of the butter. Place 1 crêpe in the pan and spread it with about 1 tablespoon of the filling. Continue doing this with the rest of the crêpes and the filling until they are used up, topping the last crêpe.

7 Mix the béchamel sauce with the remaining ½ cup Gruyère and spread over the torte. Sprinkle with the bread crumbs and dot with the remaining 1 tablespoon butter. Bake until the top is browned and bubbly, about 15 minutes. Serve at once.

Serves 4 to 6

Poppy Seed Roll

Makivnek

A great favorite in all of the western USSR, this roll is splendid for coffee or tea parties. One word of warning: It will disappear so quickly that you better make two or three at once, especially if you are expecting friends to visit.

2 cups poppy seeds

Milk

½ cup sugar

3 tablespoons honey

½ cup golden raisins

5 tablespoons chopped
    almonds

Grated zest of ½ lemon

2 tablespoons butter, melted

2 large egg whites

½ recipe Sweet Yeast Dough (see
    Index)

1 large egg yolk, beaten with
    1 teaspoon milk

1 In a medium-size saucepan over medium heat, scald the poppy seeds in enough milk to barely cover for 2 to 3 minutes. Drain off all but a few tablespoons of the milk.

2 In a food processor, grind the poppy seeds with the remaining milk. Combine in a bowl with the sugar, honey, raisins, almonds, lemon zest, melted butter, and egg whites and mix well.

3 On a sheet of floured waxed paper with a floured rolling pin, roll out the dough to a 12-inch square about ¼ inch thick. Spread the filling on the dough, leaving a ½-inch border all around, and use the waxed paper to help roll up the cake as you would a jelly roll. Let stand, covered with a linen or cotton (not terry cloth) kitchen towel for 25 to 30 minutes.

4 Meanwhile, preheat the oven to 350°F.

Lightly butter a jelly-roll pan.

5 Place the roll on the prepared pan and brush with the egg wash. Bake until nicely

browned, about 45 minutes. Cool before serving.

Serves 8

Saffron Bun

Krendel s Shafranom

Baltic version of the traditional pretzel-shaped bun or *krendel*, this dish is perfect for breakfast or afternoon tea. I like it toasted with the freshest butter and homemade preserves.

1 package active dry yeast

½ cup plus 1 teaspoon granulated sugar

1½ cups half-and-half or light cream, scalded and cooled to warm

5½ cups unbleached all-purpose flour, plus additional flour as needed

1 large egg, beaten

2 large egg yolks, beaten

4 tablespoons (½ stick) unsalted butter, melted and cooled slightly

¾ teaspoon saffron threads, crushed in a mortar and diluted in 2 tablespoons warm milk

1 teaspoon vanilla extract

1 teaspoon rum extract

¾ cup raisins

½ cup candied fruit

TOPPINGS

1 large egg yolk beaten with 1 teaspoon milk

½ cup sliced almonds

Confectioners' sugar

1 In a large bowl, combine the yeast, the 1 teaspoon granulated sugar, and the half-

and-half. Let stand until foamy, about 5 minutes.

2 Gradually add half the flour to the yeast mixture, beating until smooth. Place the sponge in a warm draft-free place and let stand until bubbly and doubled in bulk, 1 hour.

3 In a second large bowl, beat the egg

Russian Brunch Buffet

Meat-Filled Crêpes

My Mother's Salad Olivier

Saffron Bun

Walnut-Stuffed Prunes

Cranberry Drink

•

Farmer's Cheese Patties

•

Coffee and Tea

• • •

---

and egg yolks, ½ cup granulated sugar, butter, saffron mixture, and the extracts with an electric beater until smooth.

4 Stir the raisins and candied fruit into the sponge and then add the egg mixture. Add the remaining flour, ½ cup at a time, mixing well after each addition, until you have a sticky dough.

5 Transfer the dough to a floured surface, sprinkle it with additional flour, and knead until you have a smooth, elastic dough, 5 to 8 minutes, adding more flour if necessary.

6 Place the dough in a large buttered bowl, turning it to coat with the butter. Cover and set in a warm, draft-free place until doubled in bulk, about 1½ hours.

7 On a large floured surface, roll the dough into a long sausage about 3 inches thick and 36 inches long. Place on a large buttered baking sheet and turn the ends in toward the center to form a large "pretzel." Cover and let stand for 40 minutes.

8 Preheat the oven to 350°F.

9 Brush the *krendel* with the egg wash and sprinkle with the almonds, pressing them in slightly so they adhere. Bake in the middle of the oven until golden brown, 45 minutes.

10 Remove from the oven and cool on a rack. Allow to stand for 4 to 6 hours. Serve sprinkled with confectioners' sugar.

Serves 12

Open Cheese Tartlets

Vatrushki

The Russian equivalent of cheese Danish pastries are called *vatrushki*. They are ubiquitously available at Russian coffee shops, where they vary in quality from virtually inedible to absolutely sublime. If you are offered them at a private home, then the scale begins with sublime and extends well beyond any culinary adjective. Along with *sirniki*, *vatrushki* are highly popular with visiting tourists, who seem genuinely to admire the Russian way with cheese. The filling can be either sweet or savory; if the latter, then you might serve the *vatrushki* as an accompaniment to borscht. To make a savory filling, omit the sugar, vanilla extract, and raisins, and add salt to taste.

1 pound farmer's cheese, pressed
   through a sieve
3 tablespoons sugar
2 large egg yolks, lightly
   beaten
2 tablespoons sour cream

1 tablespoon all-purpose
   flour
2 teaspoons vanilla extract
½ cup raisins
½ recipe Yeast Dough
   (see Index)

EGG WASH
1 egg yolk, beaten with 1 teaspoon
   milk

1 In a large bowl, combine the farmer's cheese, sugar, egg yolks, sour cream, flour, vanilla, and raisins. Mix thoroughly.

2 On a lightly floured surface with a floured rolling pin, roll out the dough to ½-inch thickness (you can divide it into two parts, if preferred).

3 With a cookie cutter, cut out rounds 4 inches in diameter. Gather up the scraps, reroll, and cut out as many more rounds as possible. Pressing firmly with your thumbs, make an indentation in the middle of each round, leaving about a ¾-inch border. Spread 2 tablespoons of the filling in the indentation.

4 Place the *vatrushki* on a greased baking sheet, giving them enough room to expand. Cover with a cloth and let stand in a warm, draft-free place for 20 minutes.

5 Preheat the oven to 350°F.

6 Pinch the edges of the rounds upward

to make sure the filling doesn't spread too much during baking. Brush the *vatrushki* with the egg wash and bake until lightly browned, about 25 to 30 minutes. Cool to warm on a rack.

Makes about 15 vatrushki

Hazelnut Crescents

Fundukli Sheker Churek

A refined and delicate cookie from the Caucasus, just right with a demitasse of strong Turkish coffee on a lazy afternoon. There are two ways of shaping this cookie. If you have a crescent-shaped cookie cutter, just roll out the cookie dough and cut out the cookies. If not, you will have to shape each one by hand.

1 cup (2 sticks) unsalted butter
⅔ cup confectioners' sugar, plus
  additional for sprinkling
1 teaspoon grated lemon zest
1 teaspoon vanilla extract

1 large egg yolk
1½ cup toasted blanched hazelnuts,
  ground
2 cups sifted unbleached all-purpose
  flour

1 In a large bowl, beat the butter and sugar with an electric mixer until light and fluffy.

2 Add the lemon zest, vanilla extract, and egg yolk, and stir well. Slowly add the hazelnuts and flour, mixing as you add.

Gather the dough into two balls, wrap in plastic wrap, and refrigerate for 1 hour.

3 Preheat the oven to 350°F.

4 With a lightly floured rolling pin, roll out each ball of dough to ¼ inch thick on a lightly floured surface. Cut out the cookies with a crescent-shaped cookie cutter. Or break small pieces of dough and form them into crescents, ¼ inch thick and about 2 inches long.

5 Place the shaped cookies on two bak-

ing sheets, about 1 inch apart. Bake until pale golden, about 20 minutes. Allow the cookies to cool on the baking sheet, then sprinkle generously with confectioners' sugar.

Makes about 3 dozen

Butter Cookies

Koorabie

These butter cookies, popular throughout the Turkish Middle East, are so rich they literally melt in your mouth. When I was a child they used to be my very favorite snack — especially those that I bought from a delicatessen next door to the famous Prague Restaurant in the center of Moscow, a store that now remains just about the only place where you can find a halfway decent version of takeout food.

10 tablespoons clarified butter (see Index), melted and chilled until slightly hardened
4 tablespoons solid vegetable shortening, melted and cooled
¾ cup confectioners' sugar, plus additional for sprinkling

1 teaspoon vanilla extract
¾ teaspoon almond extract
1¾ cups unbleached all-purpose flour, sifted
¾ teaspoon baking powder

1 Preheat the oven to 325°F.

2 Divide the butter and the shortening between two bowls. Add an equal amount of sugar to each bowl and beat with an electric mixer. Add the vanilla extract to one

bowl and the almond extract to the other.

3 Sift the flour and the baking powder together thoroughly. Add half the flour, about ¼ cup at a time, to one bowl, beating well after each addition. In the same fashion, add the rest of the flour to the other bowl.

4 Divide the dough in one bowl into twelve to fourteen round balls. Flatten each one into a ½-inch-thick patty. Place on an ungreased baking sheet about 2 inches apart.

5 Divide the other dough half into four pieces and roll each out about ½ inch thick. Divide each roll into three parts and

shape each part into an S shape. Place on the baking sheet.

6 Bake the cookies until light golden, about 20 minutes. Cool the cookies on a rack.

7 Just before serving, sprinkle the cookies with the confectioners' sugar.

Makes about 2 dozen cookies

Estonian Rye Cookies

Ruiskatut

These popular Estonian (actually Karelian) cookies are often served with cocktails or used as a base for canapés. I like them spread with cream cheese and a little lingonberry preserves.

8 tablespoons (1 stick) unsalted
    butter, at room temperature
⅓ cup (packed) light brown sugar
1 cup rye flour

3 tablespoons milk
¾ cup unbleached all-purpose flour
1 teaspoon baking powder
½ teaspoon salt

1 In a large bowl, beat the butter and sugar with an electric mixer until light and fluffy.

2 Sift the dry ingredients together and gradually add to the butter mixture. Beat in the milk and mix well. Wrap the dough

in plastic wrap and refrigerate for 1 hour.

3 Preheat the oven to 375°F and butter two baking sheets.

4 Roll the dough out ¼ inch thick. Using a cookie cutter, cut out 1½-inch rounds.

Place on the baking sheet about 2 inches apart. Gather up the scraps, reroll, and cut out as many more rounds as possible. Prick the cookies all over with a fork.

5 Bake until light brown, 8 to 10 min-utes. Cool on racks and store in an airtight container.

Makes about 3 dozen cookies

Ukrainian Doughnuts

Pampushki

Popular as *ponchiki* in Russian or *pampushki* in Ukrainian, these doughnuts give off a marvelous aroma from the kiosks where they're sold throughout the USSR. The taste is closer to the Italian *zeppole* than to American doughnuts, only these are filled with jam. My Ukrainian friends insist on homemade rose jam or tart red currant jam.

1 package active dry yeast
3 tablespoons plus 1 teaspoon granulated sugar
1 cup warm milk
1 large egg
2 large egg yolks
1 tablespoon rum
6 tablespoons (¾ stick) unsalted butter, melted

Grated zest of ½ lemon
Pinch of salt
3¼ to 3½ cups unbleached all-purpose flour
1 cup rose petal, red currant, or apricot jam
Vegetable oil for deep frying
½ cup confectioners' sugar

1 In a small bowl, combine the yeast, the 1 teaspoon of sugar, and ¼ cup of the milk. Let stand until foamy, about 5 minutes.

2 In a large bowl, beat the egg, egg yolks, 3 tablespoons of sugar, rum, 4 tablespoons melted butter, and the salt with an electric mixer for 1 minute. Add the remaining ¾ cup milk, the yeast mixture, and lemon zest. Turn off the mixer and add 3¼ cups of the flour, 1 cup at a time. Transfer the dough to a floured surface and knead until it is smooth, but not too thick, about 10 minutes. Add just enough of the remaining flour to prevent sticking.

Tea from the Samovar

Cabbage-Filled *Pirozhki*

Assorted *Buterbrodi*

Ukrainian Doughnuts

Poppy Seed Roll

Chocolate Covered Cheese Confections

•

Russian Tea

• • •

3 Transfer the dough to a large bowl. Drizzle with the remaining 2 tablespoons melted butter and turn to coat. Cover with a linen or cotton (not terry cloth) kitchen towel and let rise in a warm, draft-free place until doubled in bulk, 1½ hours.

4 When the dough has risen, punch it down with your fist and divide into two equal balls. Keep one covered while you roll out the first. On a floured surface, roll out one ball to a thickness of ¼ inch. With a 3-inch cookie cutter, cut out rounds, transferring them to buttered baking sheets as you make them. Repeat with the remaining ball of dough. Gather up the scraps, roll them out, and cut out as many more rounds as possible. Let rise, covered, for about 40 minutes.

5 Place 1 teaspoon jam in the center of each round. Fold the dough over the filling and pinch the edge together securely. Roll the *pampushki* gently between the palms of your hands to give them a round shape.

6 In a deep fryer or deep, heavy skillet, pour in oil to the depth of 2 inches. Heat to 350° to 370°F.

7 Carefully drop a few *pampushki* into the hot oil and fry until nicely golden, about 4 minutes or less on each side. Remove to drain on paper towels.

8 When all the *pampushki* are made and dried, sprinkle them generously with sifted confectioners' sugar. Serve warm or at room temperature.

Makes about 25 pampushki

From the Pantry

---◆---

DOMASHNIYE ZAGOTOVKI

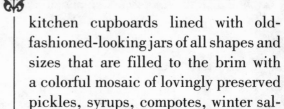

When I travel to the Soviet Union during the winter, friends shake their heads and wonder how on earth I am going to survive without fresh fruit and vegetables. But in many ways, winter is my favorite time to go to Moscow. The December sun's reflection is gorgeous on the crisp snow-blanketed city. The neo-classical buildings of my native Arbat look more romantic than ever, immaculately dressed in white; and Red square, floodlit by night, with a scatter of flakes fluttering down, is one of the most splendid visions on earth.

As far as food is concerned, I always look forward to the sight of kitchen cupboards lined with old-fashioned-looking jars of all shapes and sizes that are filled to the brim with a colorful mosaic of lovingly preserved pickles, syrups, compotes, winter salads in vinegar, jams, and relishes.

My anticipation begins even on the way to the airport. I imagine the authentic peasant fare of Russia — a platter of steaming *kasha* accompanied by crunchy sauerkraut with apples and lingonberries; piquant marinated chanterelles, suffused with garlic and dill; soused apples whose magnificent flavor can only be attained with the tart *antonovka* apple (the very thought of which brings tears to the every emigré's eye);

Jam and Jealousy

. . . jam was being made on the terrace by a method new to Agafya Mikhailovna, without the addition of water. Kitty had introduced this new method, which had been in use in her home. Agafya Mikhailovna to whom the task of jam-making had always been entrusted . . . had nevertheless put water with the [berries], maintaining that the jam could not be made without it. She had been caught in the act, and now was making jam before everyone, and it was to be proved to her conclusively that jam could be well made without water.

Agafya Mikhailovna, her face flushed and angry, her hair untidy and her thin arms bare to the elbows, was moving the preserving pan over the brazier with a circular motion, looking darkly at the raspberries and devoutly hoping they would stick and not cook properly. The princess, conscious that Agafya Mikhailovna's anger must be chiefly directed at her, as the one responsible for the raspberry jam-making, tried to appear to be absorbed in other things and not interested in the jam, and so talked of other matters, but cast stealthy glances in the direction of the stove.

Leo Tolstoy
— *Anna Karenina*

and cucumbers pickled and marinated in more ways that can be recalled.

Once there, I sometimes find myself hoping to catch a cold just so that I can drink tea loaded with the thick raspberry preserves my father makes, and that he reserves strictly for the ill. "Put a few teaspoons in your tea, and you'll sweat out your cold by the next morning," he says. The healthy must make do with gooseberry, sour cherry, black currant, peach, or apricot preserves.

Of course, all this bounty is the result of warm weather work. If one visits the Soviet Union toward the end of the summer, there is scarcely a family from Tallinn to Tbilisi that is not engaged in the most beloved national domestic chore. The ripest and the most unblemished fruits and vegetables are picked fresh from the tree, or bought at the local market, and every apartment, terrace, and backyard is transformed into a makeshift preserving factory. The Russians have a special way with cucumber pickles. First they set them in jars lined with fragrant oak leaves, black currant leaves, horseradish root, and dill weed. The pickles are then either submerged in a salt brine, or if a more sweet-and-sour flavor is desired, drowned in a vinegar marinade. In the Crimea, huge wooden tubs are prepared for pickled watermelons, a national treat, while in Georgia, life is unthinkable without the tart plum sauce *tkemali*, generously spiked with garlic and half a dozen fiery spices. In Central Asia, luscious, sun-kissed figs, aromatic quinces, and the miraculous local melons are all preserved for winter, set like precious jewels in a translucent syrup. Grapes and apricots are dried in the sun to be offered to a dear guest as part of the *dastarkhan*, a time-honored hospitality offering.

Preserving, however, is really not just another diversion, and its delicious fruits are not just another way to tickle the taste buds. Only in America, and perhaps a small handful of other countries, can one readily obtain quality fresh fruits and vegetables throughout the whole year. In most other places, eating is organized around the notion of seasonal produce. That means when fruit and vegetables come in, they are tantalizingly tasty, abundant, and cheap, but they have to be kept somehow for the winter. In many colder countries, preserving these precious seasonal treasures, was often the only way to keep alive in the hungry winter months. So, salt, sugar, and vinegar, with the aid of natural chemical processes, were vital for the lifegiving supply of energy and vitamins. For Russians, the pantry is at the very heart of the kitchen.

Russian Sauerkraut

Kislaya Kapusta

The crunchy delight stored on every balcony of every Russian apartment house every winter has little to do with the soggy horror story that passes as sauerkraut in this country. To make the taste and the look even livelier, the Russians add lingonberries (for which I have substituted cranberries here), apples, and carrots. I remember many occasions when, after having bought some at a market, I came home with an empty plastic bag, such was my craving to eat it all right there on the spot. If you are not as impulsive, try serving it as you would a winter salad, with cold cuts, ham, or other pork dishes.

The All-Time Favorite

Sauerkraut is the number-one staple throughout Russia, the Ukraine and Lithuania. As it is made in huge quantities for the winter, a sauerkraut is used generously in these regional cuisines, the more so as fresh cabbage is not always available. In the United States, however, I have always considered properly pickled crunchy sauerkraut to be such a treat that I don't often cook with it.

5 pounds green cabbage, shredded
   (should be about 16 cups),
   1 large whole cabbage leaf
   reserved
4 large carrots, peeled and grated
1 cup fresh lingonberries or cranberries, picked over and rinsed
2 medium-size tart apples (such as
   Granny Smith), cored and cut
   into ½-inch dice
3½ tablespoons coarse (kosher) salt
1 teaspoon sugar

1 Combine the shredded cabbage with the carrots, lingonberries or cranberries, and apples in a very large bowl or bucket. Use your fingers to toss thoroughly with the salt and sugar, making sure it is evenly distributed. Let stand for 1 hour.

2 Transfer the vegetables and the accumulated liquid into a 2-gallon jar with a wide mouth or a small nonreactive bucket. Cover with the reserved cabbage leaf. Place a saucer on the cabbage leaf and weight with a large can filled with water or a small workout weight. The cabbage should be completely submerged in liquid. Place a double layer of clean wet cheesecloth over the mouth of the jar and tie securely with kitchen string. Place in a well-ventilated place, at about 65° to 70°F.

3 Every day for the next four days, remove and rinse out the cheesecloth. Before replacing it, remove any scum that might appear on the cabbage leaf and top of the shredded cabbage. Then pierce the shredded cabbage to the bottom of the jar in several places to release the gases. Also, make sure the cabbage is totally submerged in brine. If it isn't, add enough water to cover. Taste the cabbage, and if it seems well on its way to fermentation, transfer it to a cooler spot (a garage or dry basement might be ideal). The sauerkraut will take a total of 10 to 12 days until it is fully fermented. Be sure to check and taste it daily.

4 After that time, transfer the sauerkraut to individual sterilized jars, add the brining liquid, and seal. It will keep for up to 3 months in the refrigerator.

Makes about two 1-quart jars

Sweet and Sour Beet Salad

Salat iz Marinovannoy Svyokli

Pickled beets are very popular in the European part of the Soviet Union and make a colorful and piquant accompaniment to a winter roast. You can also use baby beets, whole or halved, for this recipe.

2 pounds medium-size beets
¾ cup white vinegar
½ cup water
⅓ cup sugar

Salt and freshly ground black pepper, to taste
Dill sprigs for garnish

1 Preheat the oven to 375°F.

2 Wrap the beets individually in aluminum foil and bake until tender, 1 hour or more, depending on size.

3 While the beets are baking, prepare the marinade. Combine the vinegar, water, and sugar in a small nonreactive saucepan and bring to a boil. Remove from the heat.

4 Cool the cooked beets until manageable, peel, and cut into thick strips. Arrange in a large glass bowl, pour the marinade over them, and season with salt and pepper. Cover and refrigerate for at least 12 hours.

5 Serve garnished with dill sprigs.

Serves 8

My Mother's Marinated Mushrooms

Marinovanniye Gribi Moyei Mami

Although these savory mushrooms can keep in the refrigerator for up to one month, they usually disappear as soon as we make them. For a real treat, try this recipe with your favorite wild mushrooms, which is how it is done in Russia. Serve them in a rustic crock, accompanied by squares of black bread and, even more to the point, with a shot of vodka.

1½ pounds small fresh, white
    mushrooms
2 tablespoons fresh lemon juice
¾ cup water, or more as needed
Coarse (kosher) salt, to taste
¾ cup tarragon vinegar
8 black peppercorns

3 bay leaves
½ teaspoon sugar
4 cloves garlic, sliced
12 sprigs fresh dill with stems,
    coarsely chopped
1 tablespoon olive oil

1 Wipe the mushrooms thoroughly with a damp paper towel and trim the stem ends.

If some mushrooms are large, cut them in half lengthwise. Sprinkle with lemon juice

Dried Mushrooms

Sushoniye Gribi

The August mushroom picking season around all of the western USSR is something everyone looks forward to, because it promises strings of pungent dried mushrooms, an essential Slavic ingredient, for the winter to come. If you are a mushroom picker, it is absolutely ludicrous to pay the steep prices for the imported porcini or cèpes, when you can just as easily do it yourself (but remember, never prepare mushrooms unless they have been clearly identified as safe for eating, either by a mushroom expert or with the aid of a reliable guidebook). The best mushrooms to dry for our purposes (which is to say for Slavic and Baltic cuisines) are most kinds of boletus, those with the brownish caps and spongelike texture under the caps. Some people insist on drying only the caps. I, however, use at least a part of the stem.

To dry the mushrooms: Wipe thoroughly with a damp paper towel. Separate the caps from the stems, trim about ½ to ¾ inch off the stems, and cut the caps in half, if they are large. Using a large-holed needle, thread the mushrooms onto heavy-duty kitchen string, leaving a 1-inch space between the mushrooms. Spread the string flat, either on a covered radiator or in a barely warm oven, with just the pilot light on. Keep them there until they have dried, making sure they don't touch each other, about 12 to 24 hours. Then, hang the thread in a dry well-ventilated place for several days. Transfer the mushrooms to an airtight plastic container. They will keep for the whole winter.

and let stand for 10 minutes.

2 Place the mushrooms in a medium-size nonreactive saucepan and add the water; if it doesn't cover the mushrooms, add more. Bring to a boil, then add salt, reduce the heat, and simmer, uncovered, for 10 minutes. With a slotted spoon, remove the mushrooms from the liquid. Rinse under cold running water and set aside. Strain the cooking liquid through a coffee filter and measure out ¾ cup.

3 Return the ¾ cup mushroom liquid to the saucepan along with the vinegar, peppercorns, bay leaves, and sugar. Bring to a boil, then reduce the heat to medium low and cook, covered, for about 5 minutes. Cool to room temperature.

4 Place the reserved mushrooms in a 1-quart jar, scattering the garlic slices and dill sprigs between layers. Add the cooled marinade and top with the oil. Cover and refrigerate. The mushrooms will be ready to eat in 4 to 6 hours, but will get better and better if left for up to a week. They will keep for up to 1 month.

Makes 1 quart

Armenian Mixed Pickles

Turshi

Serve these in a pretty ceramic bowl as part of a Middle Eastern buffet instead of the usual olives. I like these pickles very crunchy, but you can blanch the cauliflower and carrots before pickling.

3 cups cauliflower florets

3 tablespoons plus 1 teaspoon salt

3 large carrots, peeled and cut diagonally into ¼-inch-thick slices

3½ cups water

1½ cups white vinegar

1 tablespoon sugar

10 black peppercorns

3 ribs celery, cut into 2-inch pieces

6 Italian (pale green frying) peppers, as small as possible, cored, seeded, and cut in half lengthwise

1 small hot chili pepper, seeded and sliced thinly

8 large cloves garlic, sliced

6 sprigs fresh dill

1 In a small bowl, toss the cauliflower with ½ teaspoon salt. In another small bowl, toss the carrots with ½ teaspoon salt. Let stand for 1 hour.

2 Meanwhile, in a medium-size non-reactive saucepan, combine the water, 3 tablespoons salt, the vinegar, sugar, and peppercorns and bring to a boil. Remove from the heat and let cool slightly.

3 Drain the cauliflower and carrots, pressing down lightly to squeeze any excess liquid from them. Combine with the celery and Italian peppers. Place half of the chili pepper slices, garlic, and dill sprigs on the bottom of each of two sterilized 1-quart jars. Arrange half the vegetables in each jar and pour the marinade over. Seal the jars and keep in a cool, dry place, or on a bottom shelf of the refrigerator. The pickles should be ready in about a week. These will keep for several months in the refrigerator.

Makes 2 quarts

Cranberry-Horseradish Relish

Klyukva s Khrenom

In Russia this relish is made from lingonberries, which are slowly becoming a culinary favorite in this country. However, it is also excellent with cranberries, so do consider it for your next Thanksgiving.

3½ cups fresh cranberries, picked over and rinsed
¾ cup sugar

2 tablespoons red wine vinegar
3 heaping tablespoons prepared white horseradish

1 In a food processor, chop the cranberries coarsely.

2 Transfer to a bowl, add the rest of the ingredients, and toss well. Transfer to jars and store on the lowest shelf of the refrigerator. The relish will keep for up to 1 month.

Makes about 1 quart

Moldavian Red Pepper Relish

Salat iz Marinovannikh Pertsev

Peppers in one guise or another accompany almost every meal in Moldavia. These are especially good with grilled fish. You can use a combination of red, orange, and yellow peppers for an even prettier relish.

◆◆

6 medium-size red bell
　　peppers, cored and
　　seeded
¾ cup water
½ cup white vinegar
2 bay leaves
2 teaspoons sugar

8 black peppercorns
Coarse (kosher) salt
5 small onions, thinly
　　sliced
6 sprigs fresh dill
3 cloves garlic, sliced
3 tablespoons olive oil

1 Blanch the peppers in a pot of boiling water for about 5 minutes. Drain and rinse under cold running water. Slice the peppers rather thin.

2 In a medium-size nonreactive saucepan, combine the water, vinegar, bay leaves, sugar, peppercorns, and salt and bring to a boil over medium heat. Boil, uncovered, for 3 minutes.

3 Place the peppers, onions, dill, and garlic in a 12-ounce jar. Add the marinade and cool to room temperature.

4 Stir in the olive oil, cover, and refrigerate for at least 12 hours. The relish will keep for up to 1 month.

Makes one 12-ounce jar

Pickled Mixed Vegetable Salad

Salat iz Marinovannikh Ovoshchey

In Russia this colorful Balkan-influenced salad is consumed vigorously throughout the winter when fresh vegetables are scarce. Here, however, it is unusual and different enough to accompany cold meats for those impromptu lunches or suppers.

1 medium-size green cabbage

2 tablespoons coarse (kosher) salt

½ cup water

½ cup white vinegar

12 black peppercorns

1 tablespoon sugar

1 large carrot, peeled and cut into
    julienne

3 medium-size red bell peppers,
    cored, seeded, and cut into
    julienne

2 onions, thinly sliced

2 green tomatoes, seeded and diced

2 small dried hot red chili peppers

3 whole cloves garlic, sliced

2 tablespoons vegetable oil

1 In a bowl, toss the cabbage with the salt and let stand for 1 hour.

2 Meanwhile, in a nonreactive saucepan, combine the water, vinegar, peppercorns, and sugar and bring to a boil. Remove from the heat and let cool.

3 Drain the cabbage and squeeze to get rid of any excess liquid. In a large bowl, toss thoroughly with the carrot, red peppers, onions, and green tomatoes. Add the chilies and garlic and toss well.

4 Add the oil to the marinade and toss well with the vegetables. Let stand for 1 hour, then place the salad in a sterilized 2-quart jar. Seal the jars and refrigerate. It is ready to eat now, but will taste better the next day.

Makes 2 quarts

Sterilizing Jars

If you are planning to store pickles or preserves for more than a month, you will have to keep them in sterilized glass containers to prevent them from spoiling.

To sterilize the containers, wash them thoroughly in very hot water. Bring a large kettle of water to a boil. Place the jars upright in a large pot and add in the lids and rings. Pour the boiling water into the pot over and into the jars. Cover and let stand for 10 minutes. Using tongs, carefully remove the jars, pouring out the water. Invert and dry briefly on a clean kitchen towel. Remove the lids and rings and dry briefly on the towel. Fill and seal the jars while they are still hot, handling them as little as possible.

Sour Power

The Russian peasant lives on sours . . . To satisfy this taste for sours, the quantity of cucumbers raised here is quite surprising: every market-place in the kingdom displays heaps of them from side to side . . . the poor seldom use them until prepared in something of the following fashion:

A cask . . . is strewed with a layer of fresh oak-leaves in the bottom. Over this, a layer of cucumbers is placed; after which, more leaves — then cucumbers again — and so on till the vessel is full. A pickle of salt and water is now poured in, till the whole be well saturated; and so strong is the compound, that, when stored in a cold place, the cucumbers will keep a whole year in their briny element. Eaten in moderation, the cucumber thus prepared will be found a very tolerable relish, even by the stranger.

— Robert Brenner
Excursions into the
Interior of Russia

Crunchy Dill Pickles

Solyoniye Ogurtsi

In the late summer, *babushkas* all over Moscow sell the traditional Russian cucumber-pickling ingredients — oak and black currant leaves, horse-radish roots and leaves, and dill stalks. In the Ukraine, this pickling bouquet also includes caraway seeds. Add any or all of these, if they are available, for an aroma of the Russian countryside.

25 Kirby (pickling) cucumbers (each about 4 inches long)

12 dill plants, with the seed heads (if unavailable, substitute large dill stalks)

2 pieces (each ½ inch) horseradish root

8 cloves garlic, cut in half

12 black peppercorns

5 tablespoons coarse (kosher) salt

1 thick slice rye bread, preferably sourdough

1 Trim both ends of the cucumbers and wash well to remove any traces of soil. Drain and dry with paper towels.

2 Arrange the cucumbers upright in a 1 gallon jar with a wide mouth, interspersing them with the dill, horseradish, garlic, and peppercorns.

3 In a nonreactive saucepan, combine the salt with 2 quarts water. Bring to a boil, stirring until the salt is completely dissolved. Pour the mixture over the cucumbers; it should cover them completely. Let cool for 10 minutes.

4 Put the bread over the cucumbers and place a saucer inside the jar. Place a weight such as a small workout weight or a can on the saucer. Cover the mouth of the jar with a dampened cheesecloth and tie with a kitchen string. Let the cucumbers stand in a dry but warm spot for 2 days,

rinsing the cheesecloth every day. Remove the bread, cover again with cheesecloth, and let stand for another 3 days.

5 Transfer the cucumbers and the brine to a clean jar and refrigerate. The pickles will keep for up to a month.

Makes 25 pickles

Note: To make quick pickled cucumbers, which are even crunchier, reduce the amount of salt to 4 tablespoons and omit the rye bread. These will be ready to eat after 24 hours, although they will be at their best after 2 days. These won't keep for more than a week.

Pomegranate Syrup

Narshrab

An absolutely indispensable ingredient in Caucasian and Middle Eastern cuisine, this can be served on its own with grilled fish or meats, or used to flavor meat or chicken stews, compotes, or sauces.

4 cups fresh or bottled pomegranate juice

3 tablespoons sugar

1 In a small saucepan, combine the pomegranate juice and sugar and bring to a boil over medium heat, stirring until the sugar dissolves completely, 2 to 3 minutes. Boil until the juice reduces to 1½ cups, 15 to 20 minutes.

2 Cool, then transfer the syrup to a clean bottle or jar. Refrigerated, the sauce will keep indefinitely.

Makes about 1½ cups

Georgian Sour Plum Sauce

Tkemali

This tart sauce, made from a special dark red tart *tkemali* plum, is a true gem of the Georgian kitchen. The best way to reproduce the flavor is to use slightly unripe fresh prunes and add lemon juice.

1½ pounds unripe fresh prunes
¾ cup finely chopped fresh cilantro
5 large cloves garlic, crushed in a
 garlic press
1½ teaspoons crushed coriander
 seeds

¼ teaspoon ground fenugreek
¼ to ½ teaspoon dried red pepper
 flakes
¼ cup fresh lemon juice, or to taste
Salt, to taste
1 tablespoon olive oil

1 In a large nonreactive saucepan, combine the prunes and enough cold water to barely cover. Bring to a boil, then reduce the heat to low and simmer, covered, until the prunes are soft, 10 to 15 minutes.

2 Drain the prunes, then pit and put them through a food mill. Return the prunes to the saucepan. Add the cilantro, garlic, coriander seeds, fenugreek, red pepper flakes to taste, ¼ cup lemon juice, and salt. Bring to a boil and heat for 2 to 3 minutes, then remove from the heat. Taste and add more lemon juice, if desired.

3 Cool the sauce to room temperature and transfer to a sterilized 1-quart jar. Top with the oil, seal, and refrigerate. The sauce should stand for at least 4 to 6 hours before serving. *Tkemali* will keep for up to 2 months in the refrigerator.

Makes about 3 cups

Honey-Marinated Pears

Marinovanniye Grushi s Myodom

There is hardly anything better to accompany roast poultry or game, or even lamb or pork. You can also try this marinade with other fruit, such as cherries, grapes, and plums.

6 medium-size firm Barlett
*   pears, peeled, cored, and*
*   quartered*
Juice from ½ lemon
1 cup honey

2¼ cups water
¾ cup cider vinegar
1 piece (1 inch) cinnamon stick
3 cloves

1 Place the pears in a large bowl, sprinkle them with the lemon juice, and let stand for 5 minutes.

2 In a large nonreactive saucepan, combine the honey and water and bring to a boil over medium heat, stirring until the honey is completely dissolved, 5 minutes.

3 Add the pear quarters to the pan in one layer and cook at a medium boil until the pears are just tender, about 5 minutes. With a slotted spoon, transfer the pears to a bowl and reserve.

4 Add the vinegar and spices to the syrup and bring to a boil, stirring. Reduce the heat to low and simmer for about 5 minutes. Remove from the heat and allow the marinade to cool to room temperature, then strain it.

5 Pour the pears into a sterilized 1-quart jar and pour half of the marinade into the jar. Seal the jar and refrigerate for 3 to 4 days, by which time the pears should be ready to eat. The pears will keep for up to 3 weeks in the refrigerator.

Makes 1 quart

Fig Preserves

Vareniye iz Inzhira

Although fresh figs are scarce and expensive in this country, it is truly worthwhile to take advantage of the brief period when they are available to preserve them in syrup. Offer fig preserves to your guests on a winter afternoon with a cup of unsweetened green tea.

3 pounds fresh green or purple figs
5 cups sugar
4 cups water
½ cup chopped walnuts
¼ cup fresh lemon juice

1 Wash the figs and carefully peel off the skins. (You can also leave the skins on, but the texture of the preserve will be less delicate.)

2 In a large nonreactive saucepan, combine the sugar and the water. Bring to a boil, stirring until the sugar is dissolved. Add the figs, stirring to coat them with the syrup. Reduce the heat and simmer for 10 minutes. Remove from the heat and let stand for 10 to 12 hours or overnight.

3 Return the saucepan to medium-low heat and simmer the figs, stirring carefully, until the mixture thickens, 20 to 25 minutes. Stir in the walnuts and the lemon juice and simmer for another 5 minutes.

4 Divide the preserves between two

Russian preserves are much thinner than the American or French varieties, with chunks of fruit or whole berries floating in a fragrant thick syrup. These are habitually offered as surprise presents: "These are from our *dacha*, what a crop our cherry tree gave this year." Then a whole diary's worth of fond summer memories will come flooding from the happy present-giver. If you are the fortunate receiver, remember that what you have to give back is a good dose of patience and attention, such is the Russians' love of their countryside.

sterilized 1-quart jars. Seal the jars and let cool completely. Store in a cool dark place or on the lowest shelf of the refrigerator. The preserves will keep several months in the refrigerator.

Makes 1½ quarts

Preserving Childhood

When I was a child, my cousins and I went on wild strawberry picking marathons. Returning from the woods, our mouths and hands would be smudged red and purple. Hardly able to stand from so much kneeling, we would beg *babushka* to make our favorite preserves from all our hard-won little trophies. With the seriousness of an alchemist she measured equal amounts of berries and sugar into a huge copper basin, and as the intoxicatingly sweet smelling mixture was brought to a boil, we eagerly awaited our share of the tasty foam (*penki*) that we were allowed to skim off the preserve. After that point, we lost all interest in the activity and made our way toward the prickly gooseberry bush, only to emerge an hour later all scratched and torn, but satisfied, as only eight year olds can be, with the results of our next harvest.

Quince Preserves

Vareniye iz Aivi

Unfortunately, quinces are too rare in this country to use for making huge quantities of preserves. However, we are not spoiled by a great abundance of good-quality commercial quince preserves (the ones imported from Greece and Turkey are, for some reason, quite awful), so being the quince enthusiast that I am, I still make my own.

4 cups sugar
3½ cups water
2 pounds quinces, cored, peeled and
  cut into thin slices

1 piece (3 inches) cinnamon stick
2 cloves
2 tablespoons fresh lemon juice

1 In a large nonreactive saucepan, combine the sugar and the water. Bring to a boil over high heat, stirring constantly until the sugar is completely dissolved.

Add the quinces and spices and reduce the heat to low. Simmer, stirring occasionally, until the fruit is tender and the liquid has thickened, about 1 hour. Remove from the heat and let stand 10 to 12 hours or overnight.

2 Remove the spices, then bring the preserves to a simmer over low heat and simmer until the mixture has thickened even further, about 15 minutes. Stir in the lemon juice and simmer for 2 to 3 minutes longer.

3 Pour into five sterilized 8-ounce jars. Seal the jars and store on the lowest shelf of the refrigerator. The preserves will keep for several months.

Makes five 8-ounce jars

Homemade Cottage Cheese

Tvorog

The salty cottage cheese with large curds sold in this country has very little resemblance to the smooth, creamy, slightly sour-tasting Russian *tvorog*. Here is the easiest and the most successful method for making it at home. This recipe can be used any time farmer's cheese is called for in this book. First, though, allow it to drain for 24 hours.

½ gallon whole milk

3 tablespoons sour cream

1 Place the milk and sour cream in a large container. Let stand, uncovered, in a warm place (the oven with a lit pilot light is fine) until the milk curdles, 48 hours.

2 Line a fine sieve with several layers of cheesecloth. Carefully separate the curds from the whey as much as you can and place the curds in the sieve. Allow to drain over a large bowl for 2 hours.

3 Place a large plate over the curds, and arrange a weight, such as a water-filled jar, on the plate. Place in the refrigerator and let drip until the curds are dry, 8 hours or overnight. Allow less time for a creamier *tvorog* or more for farmer's cheese.

Makes about 1 pound

Feasts and Holidays

PRAZDNIKI

The Soviet Union is such a gargantuan country, comprising such a great variety of people, each with their own distinctive religions and customs, that it is rich with traditional holidays and ritual celebrations. You could spend just one week in the USSR and enjoy a whole calendar year of feasts and festivities — public and private; religious and secular — from the plain and popular to the strange and esoteric.

Even after the Revolution, when religion had been disdained (following Marx) as the "opium of the people" and the government tried to bring order and homogeneity to the entire nation, many local ethnic traditions somehow survived. There are the unique Bear Dances with their shamanistic rites performed on hunting holiday among the indigenous people of western Siberia; the old dating-dance rituals of mountainous Daghestan in the northern Caucasus (such events are almost the only way of getting young people together so deep are the valleys and so tall are the hills in this remote region). In far-flung Slavic villages there are still many traces of Russia's pagan past, including riotous dances and bonfires, wreathmaking, and skinny-dipping to celebrate Ivan's Eve at the end of June.

Remarkable, too, are the mosque services and lavish feasts that mark the end of the six-week fast of Ramadan, the great Islamic holiday that is celebrated throughout Central Asia. And the Jewish people of the USSR, scattered here and there across the entire nation, have shown great endurance and fortitude in an often hostile climate by honoring the whole range of traditional Jewish holidays. Today traditional holidays are beginning to flourish with more vigor as the Soviet people seek to rediscover their ethnic identities and their religious pasts.

Reasons to Celebrate

Of course, since no nation willingly passes up an opportunity for making merry, during the leaner times in this century the official Soviet state holidays became excuses for partying and abandon. The anniversary of the October Revolution and May Day (the day of honor for the workers and the peasants) are marked with astonishing civic pomp and urban fancy dress. Whole cities are cloaked with red banners and flags, illuminated at night by spotlights and fireworks, and trampled on all day by parade after parade — the military, the unions, the Young Pioneers. The fountains seem to flow with vodka. May 9th commemorates the victory over the Germans and the streets are filled with bemedaled old war cronies swapping anecdotes about the Second World War. Most women eagerly await International Women's Day on March 8th. On this day and this day only, virtually the entire Soviet Union momentarily abandons its hardened patriarchal ways. You can see men lining up in the shopping queues, cooking, cleaning house, and running to and fro with bunches of mimosas, the emblem of the holiday, for their mothers, wives, and

As in most other countries, the official New Year in the Soviet Union is the first of January. But in some Islamic regions people also celebrate *Nouruz*, the Persian New Year, which falls on the first day of spring. *Nouruz* is a joyous celebration of the renewal of life. Green is the favorite color of the *Nouruz* festivities and young green sprouts of wheat, which everyone grows in flower pots for the occasion, are the symbol of the holiday.

co-workers.

State holidays in the USSR — Yuri Gagarin's (the first man in space) Birthday, Teacher's Day, Aviation Worker's Day, Railwayman's Day, etc. — are all celebrated with speeches, fireworks, and propaganda, having replaced the saints' days celebrated in pre-Revolutionary Russia.

And the domestic celebrations? Well, these are similar to social get-togethers the world over — presents and a cake with candles for a birthday, a huge banquet for the defense of a university thesis, graduation balls. Brides are customarily dressed in a white dress and veil, but although some couples still go in for a church service, it is more common to find the wedding group laying flowers at the Tomb of the Unknown Soldier (every big city has one).

Happy New Year

By far the most important nationwide celebration is that reserved for the New Year. Because religious ceremonies have been officially discouraged, New Year festivities took on many of the rituals of Christmas: Grandfather Frost (*ded moroz*) brings a huge Christmas tree (*yolka*) home for the family, and with his granddaughter, the Snow Maiden (*snegurochka*) makes a guest appearance at the customary children's feast on New Year's Day. While the kids are reluctantly packed off to bed on New Year's Eve, impatient to gather their presents from under the tree in the morning, the adults get together to drink champagne and enjoy the delicacies specially made for the occasion. Since it is virtually impossible to do any shopping on New Year's Eve itself, preparations begin early. Anything that can be stored or preserved is saved for the party. Caviar is a must, and will be accompanied by smoked sturgeon and salmon, a special roast (usually a goose or a turkey), beautiful fruit from far-off regions, and an elegant selection of pastries and cakes. When the clock on the Kremlin tower strikes twelve, the New Year begins, and everyone drinks and dances until dawn. The festive spirit usually comes to an end on January 13, the old calendar New Year, a day that is also celebrated by Russians. The tree is taken outside, always with sadness and regret, and the working year begins in earnest.

Food Fests

Food, of course, is central to all festivities, and sometimes there are special celebrations for particular dishes or harvests. The first batch of new, unaged feta cheese features in a late spring festival in Moldavia. The hills of Georgia resound with feasts and merrymaking for the first October wines. In the Ukraine, Christmas is celebrated with an elaborate twelve-dish meal; the Russian Butter Festival brings delicious buttery *blini*; Armenians will congregate around a spring lamb to celebrate any important occasion, in Azerbaijan the focal point is always a ritual pilaf, and for Passover there is the traditional gefilte fish.

The recipes and feast day ideas I offer here are really just a drop in the festival ocean. Do try them out on the appropriate day; but I'm sure you'll find that these special dishes are so delicious and tempting that you will want to enjoy them more than once a year.

BUTTER FESTIVAL
Maslenitsa

Maslenitsa, the equivalent of Mardi Gras, comes the last week before the great Lent that precedes Easter. Depending on the date of Easter, it takes place sometime in late February. Although it coincides with the beginning of Lent, it was never really a church festival, relating instead to the pagan celebration of the dawn of spring and the burial of winter. Accordingly, in the past, *Maslenitsa* was one of the merriest and wildest celebrations of the whole calendar year. With Lent approaching (the leanest and most austere time in the Orthodox year), this was literally the last opportunity to have fun and make merry; and the Russians traditionally indulged in it with the same zealousness and excess that they would then give to their religious exercises during Lent. It was also the last occasion when rich foods could be prepared and enjoyed, since the Lenten laws forbade all meat and dairy products.

The name *Maslenitsa* derives from *maslo*, meaning "butter," and the foods eaten during this week were as fatty and buttery as can be. *Maslenitsa* was also the name of the pagan deity who ruled over the winter season. Elaborate, homemade figures of the *Maslenitsa* were taken to all the festivities and paraded around. And on the last day of the week they were ceremoniously burned on top of huge bonfires — the fires being a form of tribute to the sun, which would warm the world in the months to come. The celebrations and diversions were wild and fantastic. Great cities and tiny hamlets alike were transformed into amusement parks. There were mime shows, clowns, troops of traveling artists. People would slide down specially constructed slopes of ice. For the gentry there would be masked balls and afternoon parties. For everyone else it was a time of family visits, wrestling matches, and circuses.

Nothing, though, was more characteristic of the festival than its foods — and the most important food was the rich, spongy *blini*, drowned in melted butter and topped with a whole kaleidoscope of traditional Russian delicacies: caviar, smoked salmon and sturgeon, tiny pickled smelts, piquant sardines, herring in a dozen sauces, and heaps of sour cream to top it all. For tea and desserts, the *blini* would be loaded with homemade jams and preserves. Leftover *blini* were stacked with fillings in between and baked to make tall *blini* pies. On every street corner fresh *blini* were hawked by raucous vendors; and they would grace every fireside dinner and restaurant table, rich and poor alike. The sheer quantity of *blini* consumed during the Butter Festival is almost unimaginable — it was as if people were eating for the whole year and not just the Lenten weeks ahead. Fifteen to twenty was standard; but a healthy appetite could get through as many as three dozen. In rural areas there were even *blini*-eating contests, in which as many *blini* as possible were consumed without pausing or drinking. The loser would have to pay for everyone else's *blini*.

The Butter Festival itself is still properly honored only in the more remote Russian villages, but making and eating plenty of *blini* during that week has remained a strong tradition, even in the cities, to this day.

Russian Pancakes

Blini

Plump, delicate *blini* are one of the best things Russian cuisine has to offer, especially when enhanced by caviar, smoked fish, and other delicacies. Preparing good *blini* is more than just whisking all the ingredients together. In this recipe, which comes from a friend of my mother's, the batter is made in three steps. First, there is the sponge of milk, flour, and yeast; then more flour is added, along with butter, oil, and seasonings; then hot milk is added, which gives the *blini* an especially delicate texture. The batter has to rise a total of three times, and needless to say, the results are spectacular. Frying the *blini* takes a bit of practice as well: Traditionally, the skillet is oiled with a potato dipped in oil, which prevents there being too much oil in the skillet. Then just the right amount of batter must be poured into the skillet, which you immediately tilt to spread the batter evenly. "The first *blin* is always lumpy," the Russians say. After three or four you'll feel like a pro.

4¼ cups milk

5 teaspoons sugar

2 packages active dry yeast

3 cups unbleached all-purpose flour

1 teaspoon salt

2 tablespoons light vegetable oil, plus additional for frying

3 tablespoons unsalted butter, melted

4 large eggs, separated

1 small potato, halved

1 In a small saucepan, scald 3 cups of the milk over low heat. Transfer to a large bowl and cool to lukewarm (105° to 115°F).

2 Add 1 teaspoon of the sugar and the yeast to the milk, stir, and let stand until foamy, about 5 minutes.

3 Whisk in half the flour until smooth. Place the sponge, covered, in a warm place until doubled in bulk, about 1 hour.

4 Beat in the remaining flour, the salt, 2 tablespoons oil, the butter, and the remaining sugar. Set aside to rise, covered, until doubled in bulk, about 45 minutes.

5 In a saucepan, bring the remaining 1¼ cups milk just to a boil, remove from the heat, and beat into the batter.

6 Beat the egg yolks well and stir into the batter.

7 In a separate bowl, beat the egg whites until they form soft peaks and fold into the batter.

8 Let rise once more in a warm place, covered, for about 45 minutes.

9 Dip a potato half into oil and rub over the bottom of a 5- or 7-inch crêpe pan or nonstick skillet. Heat the pan over medium heat for 1 minute. Pour about ¼ cup of batter into the pan and very quickly tilt and rotate the pan so the batter covers the entire surface in a very thin layer. Cook until the underside is golden, about 1 minute. Turn and cook for 30 seconds more (see Note).

10 Repeat with the rest of the batter, greasing the pan with the oiled potato before making each *blin* and sliding each as it is made into a heatproof deep serving dish. Keep the cooked *blini* covered with aluminum foil, in a 275°F oven.

Makes about 30 blini *(serves 8 to 10 as an appetizer, 4 to 6 as an entrée)*

Note: Be sure to taste the first *blin* since this is a good time to make adjustments. Add more milk if the batter seems thick, or more flour if it's too thin. You can also add more sugar or salt.

Butter Festival Blini Feast

Blini with . . .

Black and salmon caviars

Herring in Mustard Sauce

Herring in Sour Cream Sauce

Assortment of smoked fish

Wild Mushroom Caviar

Mixed Vegetable Caviar

Melted butter

Sour cream

Chopped scallions

Chopped hard-cooked eggs

Flavored Vodkas

•

Jam

•

Russian Tea

Buckwheat *Blini*

Grechneviye Blini

This version is considered the classic Russian *blini* in the United States, although in the Soviet Union it's not prepared nearly as often as are the regular *blini*. I find that buckwheat *blini* have a somewhat more frugal taste and a drier texture than regular *blini*, and that they are nicely complemented by sour cream and caviar.

Blini

As well as being perhaps the most popular of Russian dishes, both in the USSR, and far afield, *blini* are one of the most ancient Slavic foods, dating back to the pre-Christian era. Some say that *blini* were part of a solar cult, deriving their golden disk-like shapes from the sun itself. Because of their association with early spring festivities, including the ritual burial of winter and the remembrance of dead ancestors, *blini* are, in Russia (though not in the other Slavic countries), traditionally eaten during the spring Butter Festival and at funerals.

1¾ cups milk

2 teaspoons sugar

1 package active dry yeast

¾ cups buckwheat flour

¾ cups unbleached all-purpose flour

½ teaspoon salt

3 tablespoons unsalted butter, melted

2 tablespoons vegetable oil, plus additional for frying

3 large egg yolks

2 large egg whites

1 small potato, halved

1 In a small saucepan, scald the milk over low heat. Transfer to a large bowl and cool to lukewarm (105° to 115°F).

2 Add 1 teaspoon of the sugar and the yeast to the milk, stir, and let stand until foamy, about 5 minutes.

3 Whisk in the buckwheat and all-purpose flours, salt, sugar, butter, the 2 tablespoons oil, and the egg yolks until smooth.

On Human Frailty: An Object Lesson for the Butter Festival by Anton Chekov

Counselor Semyon Petrovich Podtikin sat himself down at the table, covered his chest with a napkin, and wriggling with impatience, waited for the *blini* to arrive . . . Neatly ranked in the middle of the table were lines of tall, slender bottles — three kinds of vodka, a Kiev cordial, Rhine wine, and even a pot-bellied bottle filled with the concoction of the Benedictine Brotherhood. Arranged around the drinks in artistic disorder were heaps of herring in mustard sauce, pickled smelts, sour cream, black caviar (3 rubles and 40 kopeks per pound), smoked salmon, etc. Podtikin salivated at these images of plenty . . . His eyes became buttery, and his face was convulsed with desire . . .

"How can you take so long?," he frowned, turning to his wife, Katya. "Hurry!"

Finally the kitchen maid appeared with the *blini* . . . Risking a severe burn, Semyon Petrovich grabbed at the two topmost (and hottest) *blini*, and deposited them, plop, on his plate. The *blini* were deep golden, airy, and plump — just like the shoulder of a merchant's daughter . . . Podtikin glowed with delight and hiccuped with joy as he poured hot butter all over them. Then, as if to further inflame his appetite with pleasurable anticipation, he slowly, painstakingly, spread them with caviar. To the few patches not covered with caviar, he applied a dollop of sour cream . . . All that was left to eat, don't you think? But no! Podtikin gazed down at his own creation and was still not satisfied. He reflected a moment and then piled onto the *blini* the fattest piece of salmon, a smelt, and a sardine, and only then, panting and delirious, he rolled up the *blini*, downed a shot of vodka, and opened his mouth. . . .

But at this very moment he was struck by an apoplectic fit.

Let rise in a warm place, covered, until doubled in bulk, about 1 hour.

4 In a separate bowl, beat the egg whites until they form stiff peaks and fold into the batter.

5 Dip a potato half into oil and rub over the bottom of a large nonstick skillet. Heat the pan over medium heat for 1 minute. Drop the batter by tablespoonsful into the skillet, spacing 1 inch apart. Cook until the undersides are golden, about 1 minute. Turn and cook for 30 seconds more. Transfer to a heatproof plate.

6 Repeat with the remaining batter, greasing the skillet with the oiled potato before each batch. Keep the cooked *blini*, covered with aluminum foil, in a 275°F oven.

Makes about 4 dozen small blini *(serves 10 as an appetizer)*

EASTER

Paskha

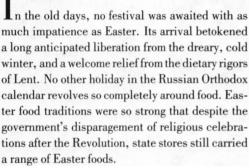

In the old days, no festival was awaited with as much impatience as Easter. Its arrival betokened a long anticipated liberation from the dreary, cold winter, and a welcome relief from the dietary rigors of Lent. No other holiday in the Russian Orthodox calendar revolves so completely around food. Easter food traditions were so strong that despite the government's disparagement of religious celebrations after the Revolution, state stores still carried a range of Easter foods.

These dishes are some of the richest imaginable, as if all the cooks in the land were trying their hardest to make up for all the butter, cream, and eggs they had abandoned during Lent. Eggs, of course, are the most important symbol of Easter (standing for the renewal of life itself) and the first food to break the fast. There is an Easter ritual, still performed in villages and country towns, of rolling eggs on the ground, a kind of Russian Easter golf. But this is not just a game — an egg that touches the earth is supposed to impregnate it and give it new fertility. Egg-painting is another notable Slavic ritual. In the Ukraine beautifully painted eggs, called *pysanki*, have made a significant contribution to the national folk art heritage.

In Russia, the nobility would have their eggs specially gilded, vying with each other both in cost and visual extravagance. The country folk, on the other hand, used natural vegetable dyes — beets for red, onion skins for a deep golden-brown. I must say, I find these simply decorated eggs more moving than the most gorgeous examples.

At our house during Easter, my Russian friends mingle with John's art world friends, and everyone brings an imaginatively colored and designed egg. We wouldn't trade our collection for the Czar's Fabergés (especially since painted eggs are traditionally believed to have impressive magical powers — they can recover lost objects, quench a fire, or find prosperity). Eggs, then, are still today the first concern of the Easter preparations. They are prepared for the Thursday before Good Friday so that they can be taken to church for a blessing.

The second Easter priority, and the most anxiety-ridden of all, is the *kulich*, the tall, spectacular Easter coffee cake. A proper *kulich* should be sinfully rich and feather light at the same time. To achieve this difficult combination, the Easter cook might use up to thirty eggs, a pound of butter, and as many as three risings for the flavorful yeast dough. Once the *kulich* is tucked away in the oven, all door-slamming, sneezing, and loud chatter in the vicinity is strictly forbidden for fear of a collapsed cake and a ruined Easter. All you're allowed to do while the *kulich* is baking is sit quietly, take in the aroma, and count the hours before Easter Sunday.

The third ritual food is *paskha* (which is also the Russian word for Easter), a luscious cheese mold which is spread on the *kulich* on Sunday. *Paskha* is made from pot cheese, butter, and egg yolks, and flavored with lots of vanilla, lemon zest, and perhaps almonds and raisins. All the ingredients are blended together, and the mixture is pressed into a special pyramid-shaped mold that has a hole in the bottom, like a flower pot. The *paskha* is weighted down and left in the refrigerator to compress. After it is unmolded, it is fancifully decorated with nuts and candied fruits, and the traditional letters XB (which stand, in Cyrillic script, for "Christ has risen") made from nuts or candied fruit are pressed into the sides. Both the *kulich* and the *paskha* are taken to church for a blessing on the Thursday or Friday before Easter.

When the ritual foods have been prepared, the savory items of the Easter meal are made ready. Here the cook has a freer hand. Easter breakfast, served after church, is set in advance and usually features cold dishes — sausages of all kinds, ham, cold game, and smoked fish are popular choices. The hot lunch on Easter Sunday will certainly include a pork dish, perhaps a roast ham or a suckling pig, and a roast turkey. Sometimes there's a roast leg of lamb as well. A man named Repnin, who was the Russian ambassador to Poland during the reign of Catherine the Great, was renowned for his opulent feasts and once produced an Easter celebration with a whole spring lamb (to signify the *agnus dei*), four wild boars (for the seasons), and twelve deer with gilded horns for the twelve months). He also served 365 *kulichs* and *babas*, and 52 barrels of wine!

Late on Saturday evening, the congregation heads off for the local church service. Although no one in my family practiced the Russian Orthodox faith, Easter was the one service we always attended. This was true throughout Moscow and elsewhere, for the Easter service is a movingly unique combination of passion and austerity. It lasts many hours and culminates in a winding procession, the *kresniy khod*. Home at last, the table is beautifully set and decorated with flowers and garlands. The painted eggs add bright splashes of color. Proudly presiding over everything are the tall *kulich*, topped with a red rose, with the *paskha* next to it. The eggs are broken and kisses exchanged. *"Khristos voskres"* (Christ has risen). *"Voistinu voskres!"* (Indeed he has!) is the reply.

Baked Fresh Ham

Buzhenina

Fresh ham is, for my money, the most delicious cut of pork available. Serve it for a festive occasion, with Kasha and Mushroom Casserole, Sauerkraut Salad Provençal, and Honey-Marinated Pears (see the Index for the recipe page numbers). If you wish to make a gravy (which the Russians don't usually do), degrease the pan juices, thicken with about 1½ tablespoons of flour, and add a bit of stock.

1 fresh ham (about 8 to 10 pounds)
⅓ cup Dijon mustard
⅓ cup (packed) dark brown sugar
Salt, to taste

1 cup light beer
1 cup apple cider
3 cloves
2 bay leaves
Freshly ground black pepper, to taste

1 Preheat the oven to 325°F.

2 With a sharp knife, score the skin of the ham in a diamond pattern.

3 Mix together the mustard, brown sugar, and salt and spread all over the ham.

4 Place the ham on a rack in a roasting pan, add the remaining ingredients, and roast, basting with the juices, until a meat thermometer registers 170°F or the juices run clear when you insert a skewer into the thickest part of the roast, about 3 hours.

5 Let the roast stand, covered with foil, for 15 minutes.

6 Carve into thin slices and serve with gravy, if desired.

Serves 10

Easter Coffee Cake

Kulich

This spectacular recipe for *kulich* comes from Tatiana Ziritskaya, who emigrated to this country many years ago via China. *Kulich* will keep on the lowest shelf of the refrigerator for up to a week.

½ cup milk

1½ tablespoons honey

2 tablespoons vegetable oil

4½ cups unbleached all-purpose flour, sifted twice

1 package active dry yeast

⅓ cup lukewarm water (105° to 115°F)

9 large egg yolks

1 cup sugar

½ teaspoon freshly grated nutmeg

¼ teaspoon ground cardamom

1 teaspoon vanilla extract

2 tablespoons Cointreau

2 tablespoons brandy

Grated zest and juice of 1 orange

1½ large vanilla beans, split lengthwise

12 tablespoons (1½ sticks) unsalted butter, melted and cooled to lukewarm

½ cup golden raisins

½ cup finely chopped almonds

½ teaspoon almond extract

1 large egg white

1 In a medium-size saucepan, bring the milk to a boil over medium heat. Remove from the heat and add the honey and oil, stirring until the honey is dissolved.

2 Gradually add ½ cup of the flour, beating until the mixture is completely smooth. Cool to lukewarm.

3 In a large bowl, add the yeast to the water, stir, and let stand until foamy, about 5 minutes.

4 Add the milk and flour mixture to the yeast and stir until smooth. Cover with a linen or cotton (not terry cloth) kitchen towel and let rise in a warm place until the sponge doubles in bulk, about 1 hour.

5 In a second large bowl, beat the egg yolks and the sugar until thick and pale yellow. Add the nutmeg, cardamom, vanilla extract, Cointreau, brandy, orange zest, and orange juice and beat for few more seconds.

6 Scrape out the seeds from the vanilla beans and add them to the yolk mixture. Add the butter, raisins, almonds, and almond extract.

7 With a clean dry beater, beat the egg white until it forms soft peaks and fold it into the egg yolk mixture.

8 Combine the yolk mixture with the risen sponge and mix gently but thoroughly. Using an electric mixer, gradually beat in the remaining 4 cups flour until you have a very smooth, loose dough. Transfer the dough to a clean, well-greased bowl, cover with plastic wrap, and let rise in a warm place until doubled in bulk, 1½ hours.

9 Cut two 1½-inch strips of parchment paper, each long enough to be molded down one side, then across the bottom and up the opposite side of a clean 2-pound coffee tin. The ends should extend above the top of the tin. Butter the tin and the strips, then set them into the tin crisscross to each other. Fold the ends over the outside of the tin.

10 Punch the dough down and place it in the tin. Let rise again, covered, until doubled in bulk, about 45 minutes.

11 While the dough is rising, preheat the oven to 325°F.

12 Bake the *kulich* until it is golden brown and a cake tester comes out clean, about 1 hour to 1 hour 10 minutes. Cool slightly, then carefully lift the *kulich* from the tin by pulling up on the ends of the parchment strips. Remove the parchment and let the *kulich* cool on a rack.

Makes 1 cake (serves 8)

Easter Cheese Mold

Paskha

When made from homemade cottage cheese, *paskha* is at its best. The homemade cheese is smooth, creamy, and has just the right, slightly sour taste. If using farmer's cheese, try to use Friendship brand, available at most supermarkets. Serve *paskha* with slices of Easter Coffee Cake (see the preceding page).

2 pounds Homemade Cottage Cheese
   (see page Index) or farmer's
   cheese
1½ cups sugar
8 ounces cream cheese, at room temperature, cut into pieces
6 large hard-cooked egg yolks,
   crumbled
1½ cups heavy or whipping cream
¾ cup ground almonds
Grated zest of ½ lemon
1 teaspoon lemon extract
½ teaspoon vanilla extract
1 large vanilla bean, split lengthwise
½ cup golden raisins
Chopped candied fruit for
   decoration

1 In a large bowl, combine the cottage cheese or farmer's cheese, sugar, cream cheese, and egg yolks, stirring to mix.

2 In batches, process the mixture in a food processor, adding an equal amount of cream to each batch, until completely smooth. Transfer back to the bowl.

3 Stir in the ground almonds, lemon zest, lemon extract, and vanilla extract. Scrape the seeds from the vanilla bean and add them to the cheese mixture along with the raisins. Mix thoroughly.

4 Line a clean, unused 8-cup flower pot with a double layer of rinsed and squeezed-dry cheesecloth. Spoon the cheese mixture into the lined pot, then fold the ends of the cheesecloth neatly over the

Russian Easter Luncheon

Easter eggs

Assorted cold meats and
sausages

Assortments of mustards

Flavored Vodkas

•

Baked Fresh Ham

Hot Horseradish Sauce

Kasha and Mushroom Casserole

Sauerkraut Salad Provençal

Honey-Marinated Pears

Alcoholic Sparkling Cider
from Normandy

•

Easter Coffee Cake

Easter Cheese Mold

Meringue Cookies

• • •

top. Place a saucer on the cheesecloth, then a 2-pound weight, such as a can, on the saucer. Put the flower pot in a bowl large enough for the liquid to drain into. Refrigerate for at least 12 hours.

5 Empty the bowl. Unmold the *paskha* onto a serving plate and carefully remove the cheesecloth. Decorate with candied fruit, pressing some of the fruit into the *paskha* to form the letters XB, which stands for *Khristos voskres* ("Christ has risen").

Serves 8

Meringue Cookies

Merengi

These delicious cookies are a great way to utilize the egg whites that are left over from preparing *kulich*. Double or triple the recipe and give them to friends as an Easter treat.

1 cup slivered almonds
4 large egg whites, at room
    temperature

1 cup confectioners' sugar
½ cup ground almonds
½ cup chopped dates

1 Preheat the oven to 350°F.

2 Spread the slivered almonds on a baking sheet and toast until lightly colored, 3 to 5 minutes.

3 Reduce the oven temperature to 300°F.

4 Beat the egg whites with an electric mixer in a large bowl until foamy. Gradually add the sugar, continuing to beat until the whites are stiff and shiny, about 10 minutes.

5 Gently but thoroughly, fold in the toasted and the ground almonds and the dates.

6 Drop the meringues by tablespoonful on an ungreased large baking sheet, spacing 1 inch apart. Bake until the cookies are golden and dry, about 25 to 30 minutes.

Makes about 3 dozen

PASSOVER

Pesach

For the many Jewish people all over the Soviet Union, celebrating religious holidays are not just a matter of honoring a tradition or an excuse to have a good time. It is, rather, a matter of preserving their identity and bringing up their children as Jews in a foreign and often hostile environment. Keeping kosher and conducting religious services was, and still is, difficult, sometimes impossible, because many cities don't have an active synagogue. But services are conducted in private homes, children attend clandestine Hebrew classes, and dietary laws are honored to the best of people's abilities, even when buying basic foodstuffs requires a miracle in itself.

Of all the Jewish holidays, Passover, which commemorates the deliverance of the Jews from the Egyptians and their exodus from Egypt, has a special educational significance. Although most Jewish holidays are spent in the synagogue, Passover is really a home holiday, designed to bring families, and especially those with young children, together. The Passover ceremony is called *seder*, which means "order" (of rituals) in Hebrew. It is usually conducted by the head of the family with all the other family members reading from the *Haggadah*, the Passover book, and the youngest member reading a series of questions that pertain to the meaning of the holiday.

The centerpiece of the Passover table and the seder ceremony is the seder plate, a divided dish that accommodates all the symbolic foods: *matzo* (for the cakes the Israelites hastily baked during their flight from Egypt; *maror* (a bitter herb, usually horseradish, for the bitterness of slavery);

haroset (a mixture of fruits and nuts, symbolizing the mortar from which the Israelite slaves made bricks in Egypt); *z'roa* (a shank bone recalling the Paschal lamb); and a fresh green herb which is dipped in salt water (the herb standing for spring and the salt water for tears).

In the Jewish communities of the USSR, the preparations for Passover and the special meal begin early. My friend Raisa Arievna Amiranova, who grew up in a Turkmenian city called Mara, where her father was the architect of the local synagogue, recalls how Passover preparations were made there. As early as the preceding fall (Passover is in spring), kosher Passover wine was made from the best grapes of the season. Several weeks before the holiday, special Passover flour would be ground for the *matzos* ("We would never touch store-bought *matzos*," said Raisa). When it came time to make the *matzos*, men kneaded the dough on huge outdoor tables, working up to a hundred pounds of flour a day. The women, meanwhile, would be preparing rice for the Passover pilaf, removing every trace of foreign grains (*khomez*). Just before the holiday itself, the house would be scrubbed and cleaned to rid it of all the remnants of leavened products — unleavened *matzo* is the only bread that can be eaten at Passover. Only then did the preparation of the Passover meal proceed. This would include *gefilte* fish and the Passover chicken pilaf with apples and quince.

As the seder meal ends, the Soviet Jews raise their glasses and say what all the Jews say around the world, "Next year in Jerusalem."

Haroset

My favorite part of the Passover meal is the matzo, spread with *haroset* and horseradish. This recipe for *haroset* comes from my friend Tamara, who possesses a wealth of Georgian Jewish recipes.

1 sweet red apple, cored, peeled,
*　and cut into pieces*
1 pear, cored, peeled, and cut into
*　pieces*
½ cup walnut pieces
½ cup blanched almonds
½ cup hazelnuts, toasted and skinned
*　(see page 5, Steps 1 and 2)*

½ cup raisins
½ cup pitted dates
⅓ cup sweet kosher wine
1½ tablespoons honey

Working in batches, if necessary, mince all the ingredients in a food processor. Transfer to a bowl.

Makes about 3½ cups

Gefilte Fish

Farshirovannaya Riba

This is a fabulous recipe for gefilte fish, in which a whole fish skin is stuffed with ground fish, matzo, and lots of sautéed onions, and baked on a bed of vegetables with a sweet and sour tomato sauce. It is also traditional Friday night fare in Soviet Jewish households. Serve with horseradish.

1 whole whitefish (about 5 pounds),
    scaled, fins and gills removed,
    and gutted

1 sheet matzo

3 tablespoons light vegetable oil

2 large onions, finely chopped

1 small onion, grated

1 large egg

1 large egg yolk

1¾ teaspoons sugar

Salt and freshly ground black
    pepper, to taste

1 medium-size carrot, peeled and
    sliced

1 small parsnip, peeled and cut into
    small dice

½ rib celery, cut into small dice

6 sprigs fresh dill

6 sprigs fresh parsley

1¾ cups tomato juice

4 teaspoons red wine vinegar

2 bay leaves

10 black peppercorns

3 allspice berries

Watercress, for garnish

1 Roll the fish against a cutting board to loosen the skin. Crack through the backbone just below the head and just above the tail. With a dull knife, loosen the skin on the fish, and gently begin pulling it off in one piece, toward the tail, loosening it as you go. You should have the whole fish skin with head and tail attached. Rinse the skin thoroughly and set aside.

2 Remove the fish flesh from the bones.

Every woman experienced in preparing gefilte fish will advise you to taste a tiny bit of the ground fish mixture to determine the correct amount of seasoning. And for many it has indeed become a mechanical gesture when making the fish. This is, however, not recommended under any circumstance due to the hazard of food poisoning, which can result from tasting uncooked fish. Instead, poach a meatball-size piece and taste for seasoning.

Cut into pieces and grind it, in batches, in a food processor, just until finely chopped, taking care not to purée it.

3 Break the matzo into pieces and soak in water to cover for 10 minutes. Squeeze the matzo to remove any excess moisture.

4 Heat 2½ tablespoons of the oil in a medium-size skillet over medium heat. Add the chopped onions and sauté, stirring occasionally, until golden, about 15 minutes.

5 Preheat the oven to 350°F.

6 In a large bowl, combine the ground fish, matzo, sautéed onion, grated onion, egg, and egg yolk, half the sugar, and salt and pepper. Mix until thoroughly blended.

7 Stuff the fish mixture into the fish skin. It should resemble a whole fish when stuffed. There is no need to sew or skewer the fish closed.

8 Scatter the carrot, parsnip, celery, dill, and parsley in an ovenproof casserole that can accommodate the fish. Place the stuffed fish, seam side down, on the vegetables and brush with the remaining ½ tablespoon oil. Bake, covered, until the fish is lightly browned, about 10 minutes.

9 Add the tomato juice, vinegar, bay

leaves, peppercorns, allspice, the remaining sugar, and salt. Continue baking the fish, covered, basting with the sauce for another 50 minutes. Allow to cool in the sauce and refrigerate for at least 2 hours before serving.

10 To serve, remove the fish from the sauce, arrange on a bed of watercress, and decorate with the cooked carrot slices.

Serves 6

Chicken Soup with Walnut Balls

Tsvniani Khenaghi

As a special Passover treat the Jews of Georgia prepare these delicious soup dumplings from walnuts, eggs, and matzo meal. Serve a few in the soup and save some for later. They are delicious cold, accompanied by a piquant sauce. The oregano in this recipe should really be fresh.

WALNUT BALLS
1½ cups finely ground walnuts
¼ cup minced onions
3 large eggs, beaten
⅓ cup matzo meal
1½ tablespoons chopped fresh
    oregano

Salt and freshly ground pepper,
    to taste
1 large egg white, whisked until
    frothy

7 cups Chicken Stock
    (see Index)

½ cup chopped mixed dill, cilantro,
    and parsley

1 In a large bowl, combine all the walnut ball ingredients.

2 Bring 2 quarts of salted water to a boil. Have a bowl of cold water by you. Dipping your hands in the water, shape the walnut mixture into 2-inch balls. Drop them into the boiling water, and cook until cooked through, 10 minutes. Remove the balls with a slotted spoon and keep warm.

3 Heat the chicken stock. Ladle into soup bowls, add three walnut balls to each bowl and add garnish with fresh herbs.

Serves 6

Bukharian Chicken Pilaf with Apples, Raisins, and Quince

Tovuk Palov

This recipe was given to me by a member of a large community of Bukharian Jews in New York City. Their forefathers originally settled in the ancient city of Bukhara in present-day Uzbekistan, after a century-long sojourn in Persia, and their cooking is a wonderful blend of Sephardic, Persian, and Central Asian cuisines.

¼ cup vegetable oil, or more if needed

2 chickens (about 2 pounds each), each cut into 6 pieces, well rinsed and patted dry

2 cups chopped onions

3 large carrots, peeled and cut into fine dice

1 large tart apple (such as Granny Smith), peeled, cored, and cut into large dice

1 large quince, peeled, cored, and cut into large dice

1¼ cup raisins

1 teaspoon cumin seeds

¼ teaspoon ground cinnamon

4 cups Chicken Stock (see Index) or canned broth

Salt and freshly ground black pepper, to taste

2 cups long-grain rice

1 Heat half of the oil over medium heat in a large, heavy skillet. Add as many chicken pieces as will fit and brown on all sides. Set aside while you brown the remaining chicken, adding more oil, if needed.

2 Heat the remaining oil over medium heat (about 2 tablespoons) in a large, heavy casserole. Add the onions and carrots and sauté until the onions are lightly colored, about 10 minutes. Add the apple and quince and sauté, stirring occasionally, for 10 minutes more.

3 Add the chicken, raisins, cumin seeds, cinnamon, ½ cup of the stock, and the salt and pepper to the casserole. Cover and simmer for 20 minutes.

4 Add the rice and the remaining stock and let boil over high heat until most of the liquid is absorbed, about 10 minutes. Gather the chicken and rice into a mound and poke in it several large holes with the handle of a wooden spoon. Cover tightly, reduce the heat to low, and place an asbestos pad under the casserole. Steam the rice until it is completely tender, about 30 minutes.

5 Allow the pilaf to stand for 10 minutes before serving. Spoon the rice onto a serving platter and arrange the chicken on top.

Serves 6

Passover Meal from Around the Soviet Union

The Passover meal I serve at my house reflects the incredible diversity of cooking styles among the Soviet Jews. Wherever they settled, Lithuania, Moldavia, Georgia, or Central Asia, they adopted the cooking styles of the region while giving the recipes a completely new context. Thus, my Gefilte Fish from Moldavia has a sweet and tangy tomato sauce, typical of the area; the chicken soup from Georgia has their characteristic walnut theme; and the main course from Central Asia is, of course, a splendid pilaf.

Gefilte Fish

•

Chicken Soup with Walnut Balls

•

Bukharian Chicken Pilaf with Apples, Raisins, and Quince

Kosher Pouilly Fumé

•

Almond Raspberry Torte

• • •

Almond-Raspberry Torte

Mindalniy Tort s Malinoy

Vegetable oil for greasing the
*   parchment*
Matzo meal for sprinkling the
*   parchment*
6 large egg yolks
1 cup plus 2½ tablespoons sugar
4 large egg whites

1½ cups ground blanched almonds
⅓ cup potato starch
1 teaspoon grated lemon zest
1½ cups raspberries, plus additional
*   for decoration*
1 tablespoon Cognac
⅓ cup raspberry jam

1 Preheat the oven to 350°F. Line the bottom of a 9-inch springform pan with baking parchment. Oil lightly and sprinkle with matzo meal.

2 In a large bowl, beat the egg yolks with 1 cup of sugar until the mixture is pale yellow and forms a ribbon when the beaters are lifted.

3 With a clean, dry beater, beat the egg whites until they hold stiff peaks in another large bowl.

4 Gently fold one-third of the egg whites into the yolk mixture, then fold in the rest, alternating with the almonds, potato starch, and lemon zest.

5 Pour the batter into the prepared pan and bake for 20 minutes. Reduce the temperature to 325°F and bake until a cake tester comes out clean, 20 to 25 minutes more.

6 Remove the cake from the oven and let cool for 15 minutes. Remove the sides of the pan, carefully invert the cake, and peel off the parchment. Let cool completely. Cut the cake horizontally, into two layers.

7 Purée the raspberries in a food processor. Strain through a sieve to remove the seeds. Add 2 tablespoons of the sugar and the Cognac. Place one cake layer on a platter, cut side up, and spread with the raspberry filling. Top with the other layer, cut side down.

8 In a small saucepan, combine the jam with the remaining ½ tablespoon of sugar. Heat, stirring, for 5 minutes. Press through a sieve to remove as many seeds as possible. Brush the jam glaze over the top and sides of the cake. Decorate with the reserved raspberries and refrigerate until the glaze is set, at least 1 hour.

Serves 8

UKRAINIAN CHRISTMAS
Rizdvo

If I could attend the best seasonal festivities in the whole of the Soviet Union, I would certainly choose Russia for Easter and the Ukraine for its splendid Christmas celebration, which is full of symbolic meaning and deeply rooted in ancient traditions. The Ukrainians celebrate Christmas on January 7, the Orthodox calendar Christmas Day, but the most important moment of the whole celebration is certainly the *Svyata Vechera* (the Holy Supper), a spectacular feast that takes place on Christmas Eve and that, like so many other Orthodox festival meals, is preceded by a day of fasting. The meal itself, although far from frugal, is a Lenten one, not permitting any meat or dairy products.

In the Ukraine, the festivities begin with the appearance of the first star in the eastern sky on Christmas Eve. In the old days crowds of boys and girls, carrying a wooden Star of Bethlehem with a lighted candle in the middle and enormous sacks, would run outside into the crisp night air. They'd sing the traditional Christmas carols, *koliadki*, near their neighbors' windows and be rewarded with various edible treats especially prepared for

the occasion. As this carol — collected by Nikolai Gogol, a great connoisseur of his native Ukrainian folklore demonstrates — the words were often most explicit:

> "Kind one, good one
> Give us a dumpling,
> A heap of kasha
> And a ring of sausage."

By midnight everyone would be assembled in one of the striking onion-domed churches, sporting their best embroidered shirts, for the moving Christmas service. By about 2 A.M. families drifted back to their homes, which had been white-washed and scrubbed clean for the occasion. There they would eat, relax, and enjoy the decorations, which did not include our customary Christmas tree, but rather sheaves of wheat or rye placed under the icon of the Virgin and Child. This Ukrainian Christmas symbol, called *didukh* (grandfather), is a carry-over from the Ukraine's pre-Christian past and another reminder of this country's deep reverence for grains.

Although many of the rituals are no longer practiced today, the festive, traditional meal is still very much a part of a Ukrainian Christmas. The holiday table is covered with a crisp white tablecloth, under which is hidden a handful of hay, preferably the first hay from the summer harvest (symbolizing the manger in which Christ was born) and some garlic cloves (expected to bring good health to the family throughout the coming year). Candles are lit, one on the *kolach* (three braided loaves, graduated in size and stacked like a wedding cake one on top of the other) and one on the window to invite a passing stranger to share the holiday meal. Once a prayer is said, and the greeting "*Khristos rodivsya*" (Christ was born) is exchanged, the family is ready to begin the most meaningful meal of the year. This meal consists of twelve dishes (each standing for one of the twelve apostles) of which everyone must have at least a little taste.

In some families, the first dish to break the fast is *kutia*, a ritual dish of wheat berries, poppy seeds, nuts, dried fruits, and honey; in others it closes the meal. Next comes another ritual offering, a piece of *kolach* with honey, a tribute to good harvests and the richness of the native soil. This is followed by several fish courses, perhaps carp or pike in aspic with a pungent horseradish sauce, or herring, and also by a bowl of light vegetarian borscht with diminutive mushroom-filled dumplings. Then come the traditional favorites of stuffed cabbage with a grain and mushroom stuffing and *vareniki* filled with potatoes or sauerkraut. These are followed by a half dozen delectable sweet courses, including a splendid multi-layered Christmas cake with poppy seeds, dates, and nuts; Poppy Seed Roll and Honey Cake, both traditional tea time treats; *uzvar*, a ritual dried-fruit compote spiced with cinnamon and cloves; and delicate twig cookies, an Eastern European specialty. The sweets are made far in advance and in huge quantities so that there is enough for the coming week, which is a happy time of family reunions, parties, and visits from friends. But the *Svyata Vechera* is strictly a family celebration, and not only the people but also the domestic animals get to participate. They are offered a little of each dish, for they, too, participated in the miracle of the birth of Jesus.

With the exception of *kutia*, perhaps, all the Christmas dishes are enjoyed in the Ukraine all year round, for in Ukraine, the rhythms of domestic life, so closely linked with the native soil, are inseparable from the cycles of the Orthodox Church. And on Christmas Eve, the story of the birth of Christ is movingly evoked through the symbols of the Ukraine's own agrarian past.

Ritual Wheat Berry Cereal

Kutia

The most sacred of all Slavic ritual dishes, *kutia*, is a cereal of wheat berries, poppy seeds, honey, and dried fruit, that is served only at religious festivals of great importance. I actually tasted my first *kutia* at a Ukrainian home in the United States. Because this is a Lenten dish, milk should not be used in preparing it. But, if you are not an observant Eastern Orthodox, you can substitute milk as it makes a more flavorful dish. It can be served chilled, as a dessert, or hot, as a breakfast cereal.

1½ cups wheat berries (available at health food stores), soaked in lukewarm water to cover for at least 24 hours and drained
4½ cups water or milk, or more as needed
¾ cup poppy seeds
⅔ cup slivered almonds

½ cup honey
⅔ cup chopped dry apricots
½ cup raisins
Small pinch of salt
Cinnamon for garnish

1 Combine the wheat berries and water or milk in a medium-size heavy pot and bring to a boil over high heat. Reduce the heat to low, cover, and simmer until the wheat berries are very tender, 3 hours or more, depending on the quality of the wheat. Add more liquid, as needed, to keep the wheat berries covered by 1 inch.

2 Meanwhile, in another pot, scald the poppy seeds in boiling water to cover for 1 minute. Drain well, then add lukewarm water to cover and soak for 30 minutes. Drain the poppy seeds again.

3 Grind the poppy seeds in a food processor and set aside.

4 Preheat the oven to 350°F.

5 Spread the almonds on a baking sheet and toast until very light golden, 3 to 5 minutes. Set aside. Reduce the oven temperature to 325°F.

6 Drain off the cooking liquid from the wheat berries into a glass measuring cup. Discard all but ½ cup. Add the honey to the liquid and mix well.

7 In an ovenproof casserole, mix the wheat berries, honey, poppy seeds, almonds, apricots, raisins, and salt. Bake the *kutia*, uncovered, for 20 minutes.

8 Remove the casserole from the oven,

cover, and let stand for 15 minutes. Either serve warm as hot cereal, or chill and serve in dessert glasses. Sprinkle with cinnamon.

Serves 8

Stuffed Cabbage with Rice and Mushroom Filling

Holubtsi z Rizhom i Hribami

You can substitute barley or buckwheat for the rice in this vegetarian version of the Slavic classic. Serve the *holubtsi* with sour cream if you're not an observant Eastern Orthodox.

STUFFING AND CABBAGE

1 ounce imported dried mushrooms, well rinsed

1½ cups long-grain rice

2 cups water

Salt, to taste

8 tablespoons vegetable oil

1½ cups chopped onions

10 ounces fresh white mushrooms, wiped clean and chopped

2 tablespoons chopped fresh dill

Freshly ground black pepper, to taste

12 to 14 medium-size cabbage leaves

¼ cup all-purpose flour

1 cup Vegetable Stock (see Index)

1 can (28 ounces) crushed Italian plum tomatoes, with their liquid

2 tablespoons apple cider vinegar

1 teaspoon sugar

Bouquet garni (4 sprigs each dill and parsley, 1 bay leaf, and 8 black peppercorns tied in a cheesecloth bag)

1 Soak the mushrooms in 1 cup water for 1 hour. Drain the mushrooms, dry, chop finely, and set aside. Strain the soaking liquid through a coffee filter.

2 Combine the rice, 2 cups water, and the soaking liquid in a large pot and bring to a boil. Add the salt, reduce the heat to low, cover, and simmer until the rice is almost tender and the liquid is absorbed, about 15 minutes. Remove from heat.

3 Heat 3 tablespoons of the oil in a large heavy skillet over medium heat. Add the onions and the dried mushrooms and sauté, stirring, until the onions are deeply browned, about 15 minutes. Add to the rice and wipe out the skillet.

4 Heat 2 tablespoons of the oil in the same skillet over medium-high heat. Add the fresh mushrooms and sauté until they are golden brown, about 15 minutes. Add the mushrooms and dill to the rice. Season with salt and pepper and mix well.

5 Preheat the oven to 350°F.

6 Scald the cabbage leaves in salted boiling water for about 5 minutes. Drain thoroughly and pat dry with paper towels.

7 With a sharp knife, cut out the tough center vein from each leaf. Divide the stuffing evenly among the leaves, placing it toward the base of each leaf. Tuck in the sides, and roll the leaves up, pressing in the ends firmly as you roll.

8 In a large ovenproof casserole or Dutch oven that can accommodate all the rolls, heat the remaining 3 tablespoons oil over medium heat. Roll the stuffed rolls in flour and brown over medium heat on all sides, about 15 minutes. Add the stock and tomatoes and bring to a boil.

9 Stir in the remaining ingredients. Bake, uncovered, until the cabbage is tender, about 40 minutes. Remove the bouquet garni before serving.

Serves 4 to 6

Ukrainian Christmas Cake

Perekladenets

This is the traditional Ukrainian Christmas dessert. Rich and satisfying, it consists of four thin layers of yeast dough, each slathered with a typically Ukrainian filling — poppy seed, date, and walnut.

1 recipe Sweet Yeast Dough (see
  Index)
1 recipe Poppy Seed Filling (recipe
  follows)
1 recipe Date Filling (recipe follows)
1 recipe Walnut Filling (recipe
  follows)
1 egg yolk, beaten with 1 teaspoon
  milk

1 Divide the dough into four equal pieces. On a floured surface with a floured rolling pin, roll out one piece of dough into a 13 × 9-inch rectangle. It will be rather thin. Drape the rolled-out dough around a rolling pin and transfer to a large baking sheet. Keep the remaining dough covered.

2 Spread the poppy seed filling on the dough, leaving a ½-inch border on all sides.

3 Roll out a second piece of dough in the same fashion and place on top of the poppy seed filling. Spread with the date filling.

4 Roll out a third piece of dough and place on the date filling. Spread with the walnut filling.

5 Roll out the remaining dough to a rectangle 1 inch larger on all sides than the others. Place over the walnut filling and, bending the edges down, press them securely together with the edges of the bottom layer.

6 Cover with a paper towel and let stand in a warm, draft-free place until it has risen somewhat, about 30 minutes.

7 Meanwhile, preheat the oven to 350°F.

8 Prick the cake with a fork in several places. Brush with the egg wash and bake until cooked through, 50 minutes to 1 hour. Cool completely on a rack. This cake is better if allowed to rest for a day before serving. Wrap it in aluminum foil and place on the lowest shelf of the refrigerator.

Serves 10

Poppy Seed Filling
Nachinka z Maku

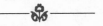

This is an easy-to-make poppy seed filling that uses commercially available Solo poppy seed filling, available in many supermarkets (look in the international section on the shelf with kosher products) and popular in many Ukrainian, Jewish, and Eastern European households. The filling for this cake requires only one egg white; but if you are using it to make a strudel, you should use two.

1 large egg white
2 cans (12½ ounces each) Solo
  brand poppy seed filling

In a large bowl, whisk the egg white until frothy. Stir in the poppy seed filling and mix well.

Makes enough to fill 1 Christmas Cake layer

Date Filling
Nachinka z Daktiliv

2 packages (8 ounces each) pitted
    dates, chopped
1½ cups good-quality apricot
    preserves

In a medium-size bowl, stir the dates and preserves well to mix.

Makes enough to fill 1 Christmas Cake layer

Walnut Filling
Nachinka z Voloskikh Horikhiv

3 large egg whites
¾ cup sugar
1 teaspoon vanilla extract
½ pound walnut pieces, ground

1   In a large bowl, beat the egg whites with an electric mixer until soft peaks just begin to form. Add the sugar and vanilla extract and beat until incorporated.

2   Stir in the walnuts and mix thoroughly.

Makes enough to fill 1 Christmas Cake layer

Honey Cake
Medivnik

T his fragrant, rich, and flavorful honey cake is truly one of the symbols of the Ukrainian homestead. Allow plenty of time for the simple goodness of this cake to come out; like so many dishes from this part of the world, it gets progressively more flavorful during the first three or four days of its life. But don't wait for Christmas to enjoy it.

Ukrainian Twelve-Dish Christmas Eve Supper

Ritual Wheat Berry Cereal

•

Christmas bread with honey

•

Herring in Mustard Sauce

•

Whole Salmon in Aspic

•

My Mother's Super-Quick Vegetarian Borscht with Tiny Soup Dumplings Filled with Wild Mushrooms

•

Ukrainian Filled Dumplings with Sauerkraut and Potato

Stuffed Cabbage with Rice and Mushroom Filling

•

Ukrainian Christmas Cake

•

Honey Cake

•

Poppy Seed Roll

•

Dried Fruit Compote

•

Twig Cookies

4 large eggs, separated

1 cup sugar

1 cup vegetable oil

1 cup honey (see Note)

3 tablespoons instant coffee powder, diluted in ¼ cup hot water and cooled

4 cups unbleached all-purpose flour

2½ teaspoons baking powder

1 teaspoon baking soda

1 teaspoon ground cinnamon

½ teaspoon ground cardamom

¼ teaspoon ground cloves

Pinch of salt

Grated zest of ½ orange

½ cup dark raisins

½ cup chopped dried apricots

½ cup chopped walnuts

1 Preheat the oven to 350°F.

2 In a large bowl, beat the egg yolks and the sugar with an electric mixer until the mixture is pale yellow and forms a ribbon when the beaters are lifted. Continuing to beat, slowly pour in the oil, honey, and coffee.

3 Sift the flour, baking powder, baking soda, cinnamon, cardamom, cloves, and salt into a large bowl. Beat slowly into the egg mixture, just until smooth.

4 With clean, dry beaters, beat the egg whites until soft peaks form. Fold one-third of the whites into the batter, then fold in the rest.

5 Gently but thoroughly fold in the orange zest, raisins, apricots, and walnuts.

6 Pour the mixture into two buttered 9 × 5 × 3-inch loaf pans. Bake until a skewer inserted in the center comes out clean, about 1¼ hours.

7 Let the cakes cool for about 10 minutes, and then remove from the pans and cool on a rack. Wrap in a plastic wrap and keep on the lowest shelf of the refrigerator for at least 24 hours for the flavors to settle.

Makes 2 loaves

Note: If your honey is too thick, heat it slowly over low heat and allow to cool to room temperature.

Dried Fruit Compote

Uzvar

Along with being a Slavic ritual dish, Dried Fruit Compote is also one of the favorite wintertime desserts in the USSR. Spike it with a good dose of brandy, if you wish, and serve with whipped cream, crème fraîche, or vanilla ice cream.

1½ pounds mixed dried fruit (such
    as apples, pears, figs, pitted
    prunes, and apricots)
5 cups water
2 tablespoons honey
3 tablespoons sugar, or more to taste

1 piece (2 inches) cinnamon stick
3 cloves
1 small vanilla bean, halved
    lengthwise
2 tablespoons fresh lemon juice, or
    more to taste

1 In a nonreactive saucepan, combine the dried fruit and water and bring to a boil over medium heat.

2 Add the honey, sugar to taste, cinnamon stick, and cloves and stir until the sugar and honey are dissolved, 2 to 3 minutes.

3 Scrape the seeds from the vanilla bean into the compote and then add the bean. Reduce the heat to low and simmer, covered, for 1½ hours.

4 Add the lemon juice to taste. Cool and refrigerate until cold before serving.

Serves 6

Twig Cookies

Khrustiki

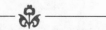

These delicious deep-fried cookies are a favorite Eastern European treat. Although many purists would insist on a traditional bow tie shape, you can make an easier shape of your own choice.

2 large eggs
1 large egg yolk
1 tablespoon heavy or whipping
    cream or water
3 tablespoons sugar
1 teaspoon brandy
1 teaspoon dark rum

1¾ to 2 cups unbleached all-purpose
    flour
½ teaspoon baking soda
⅛ teaspoon salt
Vegetable oil for deep frying
Confectioners' sugar for sprinkling

1 In a large bowl, beat together the eggs, egg yolk, cream, sugar, brandy, and rum.

2 Sift the dry ingredients together and stir gradually into the egg mixture. Knead briefly into a smooth dough. Divide in half.

3 On a floured surface with a floured rolling pin, roll out each dough half to a thickness of ⅛ inch. Cut into 6 × ¾-inch strips.

4 In a deep fryer, heat the oil to 375°F.

5 Make a 1-inch slit 2 inches from one end of each strip. Push the opposite end of the strip into the slit, pulling it out slightly on the other side. Repeat with the remaining dough.

6 Deep-fry the *khrustiki*, a few at a time, turning once, until golden, about 3 minutes. Drain on paper towels and cool completely.

7 Sprinkle generously with confectioners' sugar before serving.

Makes about 2½ dozen **khrustiki**

Beverages

―――― ❖ ――――

NAPITKI

*They brought me into their cellars and made me taste of
diverse kinds of drink, both wine and beer, mead and quassia, of sundry colours
and kinds. Such abundance of drink as they have in their cellars,
I do suppose few princes have more, or so much at once.
— Richard Chanceler, 1553
Emissary to Muscovy from King Edward VI of England*

Judging by this report from Muscovy in the mid-sixteenth century, and from a host of others besides, drinks of all kinds have long occupied the very center of the Russian imagination and the Russian lifestyle. According to historical legend, representatives of the different religions approached Prince Vladimir in the tenth century in order to persuade him to convert the young nation to their particular faith. Catholicism apparently did not appeal to Vladimir on account of its elaborate Latin-language services, and Judaism was rejected because of its complicated kosher laws. So the choice fell between Islam and the Byzantine Eastern Orthodox church. Although Vladimir found the Islamic faith both appealing and strategically sound, he in no way could tolerate the restrictions on alcohol it imposed. In A.D. 988, therefore, Vladimir officially converted pagan "Rus" to Orthodoxy, and happily proclaimed that "drinking is the joy of Rus." His founding toast to drink rings as true today as it did a millenium ago; and even the Islamic regions of the USSR are now partly converted to vodka.

But as we can tell from Richard Chanceler, vodka was not the preferred drink of the Russians in olden times. At the huge celebration of the conversion to Orthodoxy, Vladimir in fact ordered barrels of the two ancient Russian drinks, mead and *kvass*, to be ladeled out to the people on the streets — his way of publicizing the new religion no doubt. Mead is an alcoholic drink made from honey and hops, while *kvass* (from the Russian verb *kvasit*, meaning "to sour or to ferment") is a lightly fermented beer-like drink usually made from bread and yeast. While mead is now found only in fairy tales (*skazki*), *kvass* is still a much-loved national drink that, beside being made in the home, is also sold on the streets, in vending machines, and in special ships to which the customer brings his own bottles. *Kvass* is also commonly used in the kitchen to make cold soups such as *okroshka* and for stews and braising meats.

While I'm very partial to *kvass*, I find that making it at home is rather cumbersome as well as somewhat dangerous, as the bottling cork often pops out during fermentation. It's best to use the perfectly good concentrate available in Russian grocery stores (found in bigger cities). This is safer, and easier, and the results are usually better.

Around the Union

Each of the republics in the USSR has something special to offer in the way of drinks and drinking rituals. Georgia is famous for its fruity demi-sec wines, the best made from the outstanding Izabella (Concord-type) grape. And the red wines are a real discovery. Akhasheni red wine is semi-dry and powerfully rich in taste; Mukuzani, another red, similar to good Bordeaux, is drier, but still full-bodied. Made according to time-honored traditions and stored in huge underground jars (*kvevri*) that you can still see everywhere in the Georgian countryside, red wines are enjoyed at their best "nouveau style" in late September and October. The white

✿ Down the Hatch ✿

Throughout Russian history, feasts and raucous drinking bouts have often occupied center stage in the national drama. The feasts of Ivan the Terrible were notorious for their sheer scale and excess. It was customary for the Czar with his own hands to offer his guests silver vessels filled with drink. Sometimes, as one historical novel reliably informs us, these would contain poison so Ivan could get rid of troublesome boyars (nobles).

Peter the Great (late seventeenth to early eighteenth centuries), on the other hand, was a promoter of imported wines and spirits, including Madeira, Malaga, Tokay, brandy, and rum, as well as of coffee and hot chocolate, So, while the old-fashioned nobility stuck to the traditional vodka, mead, and *kvass*, Peter was busy innovating here and there, opening the first coffee house in 1704 and almost marching his recalcitrant boyars into the establishment with the threat that if they didn't consume the new-fangled dark, bitter drink they would be ostracized from the court and its privileges.

Coffee was also a passion of Catherine the Great (mid to late eighteenth century), who, according to one account, preferred it incredibly strong. But it didn't really catch on as a social institution until after the 1812 Napoleonic war, from which time on, until the Revolution, the coffee shops became important cultural havens for writers, artists, and politicians.

wines, on the other hand, are rather forgettable.

Armenia boasts a range of world-class brandies that have brought praise from connoisseurs as knowing as Chekhov and Winston Churchill. Unlike the passion of the West for after-dinner tipples, in Armenia brandy is drunk with the meal, the Armenians maintaining that this way the taste of food and drink alike is enhanced. If you try drinking brandy with one of our Armenian dishes, you might well be pleasantly surprised. A good Armenian brandy called Ararat is available at some bigger United States liquor stores.

In predominantly Muslim Central Asia, alcoholic drinks are not common, though vodka still has quite a following. Instead, there is a wide variety of refreshing soft drinks such as the yogurt-based *ayran*, exotic icy drinks called sherbets from Tadzikistan and Azerbaijan, and *kumiss*, a drink made from fermented mare's milk that generations of mothers and midwives from the region swear is the most healthful beverage on earth.

The Baltic republics enjoy drinks that are in many respects similar to those of Russia, Scandinavia, and Eastern Europe, but they have also developed their own unique concoctions, including a very interesting pine-needle liqueur called *balzam*, which is sold in distinctive opaque brown bottles.

Softer Drinks

Apart from their prolific varieties of flavored vodka, Russians consume gallons of tea and coffee and are specially partial to sour milk and buttermilk-based drinks. Almost everywhere you can find *sok* (juice) for sale in street corner groceries, where it is ritually dispensed by white-capped women juice vendors from precarious cone-shaped glass containers. They cost just a few kopeks, and the *sok* counters are haunted by throngs of children and commuting workers. The flavors can be quite unusual, including pomegranate and birch-tree juice. Sometimes they're very watery (like apple and orange *sok*), sometimes they're more like syrups (apricot for example) — although these will be generously diluted by the saleswoman who will want to have some to spare at the end of the day to set up a barter for other scarce and much-needed foodstuffs.

Even cheaper and even more ubiquitous are the street-side vending machines that offer up a glass of soda water for a kopek and a glass of soda water and syrup for three kopeks (about 1 to 2 cents) — prices that in my memory have never changed. While these new-age water fountains ensure that visitors to Soviet cities need never go thirsty, they best remember to bring their own plastic cup or they'll be doomed to sharing the communal vessel that dangles on a wire next to every machine.

In recent years Western sodas have made great inroads into the Soviet market, especially Pepsi (which is bartered for Stolichnaya vodka) and Fanta. While these soft drinks are much more expensive and much less refreshing than any of their Soviet counterparts, they have caught on like wildfire as a "taste of-the West." It's more than likely you will be proudly offered a bottle of soda at a private home; and, to make matters worse, such are the selling conditions in Russia that Pepsi is most often bought warm and flat from pre-opened bottles in the under-supplied street kiosks!

Now you can get your revenge on bad taste, however, by bringing a delicious taste of the Soviet Union into your own home.

Russian Tea

Russkiy Chay

Loose tea leaves, preferably
 Ceylonese or Indian
Very thin lemon slices
Sugar cubes

Assorted fruit preserves, preferably
 Swedish or Eastern European
 raspberry, black currant,
 cherry, or lingonberry

1 Bring a kettle of fresh cold water to a boil. Remove it from the heat and allow it to stand for 2 minutes. Rinse out a small teapot with a little of the boiling water just to heat it.

2 Add 2 teaspoons of loose tea leaves per cup of water, then fill the pot with the desired amount of water, making sure that there is enough water left in the kettle to dilute the *zavarka*. Stir the tea quickly and let it brew under a tea cozy for 4 to 5 minutes.

3 Pour the desired amount of *zavarka* through a strainer into each cup or glass (this should be done in front of the guest) and dilute with hot water. Serve the tea, accompanied by thinly sliced lemon, sugar cubes, and preserves.

Tea
Chay

The best tea is drunk in St. Petersburg and generally throughout Russia. Since China has a common border with Siberia, tea need not be transported by water to reach Moscow or St. Petersburg. Sea voyages are very bad for tea.

— Alexander Dumas
Dictionary of Cuisine

Everyday life in Russia would be simply unimaginable without the perennial accompaniment of tea. Like coffee in the United States, tea is the number one social drink. It is offered to you in homes as soon as you walk in the door. And it takes its place as the quintessence of the kitchen ritual. The compact kitchen table is the great gathering place of the Russian people, the scene of endless conversations about politics, art, and religion, during which the kettle never gets a minute off. The Russians actually give this domestic ceremony a name, *goniat' chay*, which literally means "chasing tea around."

Like other favored drinks, however, tea is a relative newcomer, reaching something like its present popularity only in the nineteenth century, when it replaced such Old Russian drinks as *sbityen*, a spiced honey drink, or herb and dried-berry teas that were staples of the peasantry. In 1638 a Russian ambassador brought around sixty kilos of tea from the Mongolian Khan as a present to Czar Mikhail Fyodorovich. Reports reveal that the Czar was furious to receive a few packages of dried leaves rather than the usual exotic furs and precious stones. Even when used for making tea, the Czar and his noblemen thought it too bitter and odd tasting. So it was only when a rumor spread that tea helped prevent drowsiness during the interminable church services (and that it might be a remedy for certain ailments) that a real use was

found for the substance. It took fifty years more before a treaty was signed with the East to supply Russia with a regular stock of the "Chinese herb," which was imported via Siberia. The middle classes and the peasantry were at first as suspicious as Mikhail Fyodorovich, especially the latter, who preferred to stick to their tried and tested drinks made from the herbs and berries that grew abundantly in the local forests. Most of them couldn't afford such a luxury import anyway. But by the middle of the nineteenth century, tea had become not only a preferred drink but had taken its place at the very center of family and social life.

The Samovar

The samovar is probably the most powerful symbol of Russian hospitality, and like the tea it serves, it comes from the east (Mongolia). The word itself means "self-boiler," and that's exactly what it does. The samovar in one form or another actually arrived in Russia before tea was yet popular, and it was used at first to make *sbityen*.

To use a traditional samovar, you first prime the central tube of the urn with coals, which heat the water. The samovar is only used to boil water, the tea being brewed separately to make the *zavarka*, or "essence." A dose of *zavarka* is poured into each cup and then diluted with boiling hot water taken by the hostess from the samovar's tap. The teapot is then rested in its niche on top of the samovar to keep warm.

The sound of the samovar became such a symbol of home and well-being that in the last century special "musical" samovars were made producing cozy peeps and whistles driven by the steam of the boiling water. These days, older samovars have become precious collector's item. My friend, the architectural historian Boris Brodsky, has an extraordinary collection in all shapes and sizes. The largest is over four feet tall and looks like it could serve an army. The best-quality samovars come from Tula, which is also famous for its traditional spice cakes. In fact, "taking your own samovar to Tula" is an equivalent expression for redundancy in Russia as "carrying coals to Newcastle" is in England.

A Glass of Tea

Tea is served in every imaginable context in Russia. On overnight trains the conductor will bring each passenger a glass of tea in a Soviet *podstakannik*—which gets just about as hot as the glass, so watch out! the Russians filter the tea through a tiny strainer called *sitechko*, which in the past was often silver.

At home tea is taken quite weak, and is served accompanied by sugar cubes which you bite and mix with tea in your mouth. This is called *vprikusku* ("tea with a bite"). There will invariably be small cut-glass plates of homemade preserves—gooseberry was the great nineteenth-century favorite. For colds a homemade raspberry preserve or honey is added to the tea, which is supposed to help sweat the symptoms out. Milk used to be a popular additive, but these days Russians will often smile at the Englishman who puts milk in his tea and claims it tastes better that way. Similarly, drinking from the saucer used to be customary, especially among the peasants; but now only old women and children cool their tea this way (children are sternly cautioned not to blow in their saucers to cool their tea even further).

Around the Soviet Union

Tea drinking is also popular in the other republics. In Central Asia there are tea parlors (*chaikana*) on almost every street corner, filled for the most part with men sipping, chatting, and playing backgammon. In this region green tea (*kuk cha*) always accompanies the meal and is the first thing offered to a visiting guest. In the Caucasus, the Russian way with tea is predominant. In Azerbaijan, as in neighboring Turkey and Iran, tea is drunk from small glasses about three times as big as a thimble. I was surprised to find out from an Iranian friend that these glasses are called *istakan* from the Russian *stakan*, and that the tradition of samovar and tea has also migrated to Turkey and the Middle East. There are even collections of old copper samovars on display in Turkish museums.

In Russia a custom startling to strangers is that men drink tea in glasses and women in china cups. Here is the legend behind this custom. It seems that teacups were first made in Krondstadt, and the bottom was decorated with a view of that city. When a teahouse proprietor stinted on the tea, this picture could be seen clearly, and the customer would say to him "I can see Krondstadt." Since the proprietor could not deny this, he was caught *in flagrante delicto*. It became customary, then, for tea to be served in teahouses in glasses, at the bottom of which there was nothing to see, let alone Krondstadt!

—Alexander Dumas
Dictionary of Cuisine

Turkish Coffee

Kofe po Turetsky

Turkish coffee is enjoyed not only in the Caucasus, where it is the preferred after-dinner and afternoon drink, but also in the western parts of the USSR, where it is served in homes, restaurants, and cafés in regular coffee cups, rather than demitasse. Every Russian family owns a *jezve* or *turka* (from "Turk"), as it's sometimes called; this is an elegant, long-handled copper or brass coffee pot. When we emigrated, my mother didn't hesitate to include a *jezve* among the few domestic items we were able to take with us. In today's Soviet café, coffee is still prepared in a *jezve*, nestled in hot sand — the heat being supplied by electric devices below. This adaption of the time-honored Middle-Eastern preparation ensures that the coffee is slowly and evenly heated, and brought to a boil without scorching the mixture.

Everywhere you look in Armenia, there always seems to be a woman meticulously grinding coffee in small, long-handled grinders that resemble pepper mills. For the Armenians this is a common social ritual. And if the coffee ritual in this part of the USSR has elaborate beginnings, then its endings are even more suggestive: The minute the empty coffee cup is put down, most likely someone will invert the cup and tell your fortune from the grounds.

---

1 full cup fresh, cold water

4 teaspoons sugar for regular,
*   2 tablespoons for very sweet*

2 tablespoons Turkish coffee
*   (very finely ground dark roast*
*   coffee)*

⅛ teaspoon ground cardamom

1 Combine the water and sugar in a Turkish coffee pot or a small saucepan with a long handle. Over high heat, bring the

> Coffee should be as black as night, as hot as fire and as sweet as love.
>
> —*Persian saying*
>
>

mixture to a boil, stirring to dissolve the sugar. Add the coffee and cardamom, then reduce the heat to low and heat, stirring constantly, until a thick foam rises to the surface. Remove from the heat and spoon the foam into three demitasse cups.

2 Return the coffee to the heat and bring to a boil once more. Again, spoon the foam into the cups, then allow the coffee to stand for 1 minute before pouring into the cups.

Serves 3

Coffee with Ice Cream

Kafe Gliase

This is one of the most popular after-dinner drinks in Russia, widely served in restaurants, homes, and ice cream parlors (*kafe morozhennoye*). Although it's better when made with iced coffee, it's not unusual in Moscow to see people dropping a scoop of ice cream into a cup of hot coffee.

3 cups hot, very strong black coffee or espresso
¼ cup heavy or whipping cream
1 tablespoon sugar

4 scoops vanilla or coffee ice cream
Whipped cream and chocolate shavings for garnish

1 Combine the coffee, heavy cream and sugar in a heatproof container. Stir, then cool and refrigerate.

2 Divide the coffee among four large cups. Place a scoop of ice cream into each cup. Pipe out some whipped cream from a pastry bag and sprinkle with chocolate shavings.

Serves 4

Chilled Yogurt Drink

Ayran

Enjoyed throughout the Caucasus and Central Asia and known by a dozen different names, *ayran* is sworn by in these regions as the best thirst quencher to combat the often overwhelming summer heat. I can personally vouch for the effectiveness of *ayran* on a sizzling afternoon.

3 cups plain low-fat yogurt
1 quart spring water
Salt, to taste
Ice cubes

½ cup club soda or other sparkling
    water (optional)
Mint leaves for garnish

1 In a blender, blend the yogurt and water in batches until smooth. Add salt.

2 Pour into a pitcher over ice cubes. Add the club soda and stir.

3 Serve in tall glasses over additional ice, decorated with a few mint leaves.

Serves 6

Old Russian Spiced Honey Drink

Sbityen

The many foreigners who traveled or lived in Russia during the time of Peter the Great often praised this five-hundred-year-old drink, calling it the Russian *Glühwein*. In the eighteenth and nineteenth centuries it was the most popular "street drink" — before the rise to everyday glory of tea, that is. Street vendors would haul enormous samovar-shaped copper pots of *sbityen* on their backs, covering them with decorative cloths to preserve the heat. And the figure of the *sbityenshik* (the vendor) was one of the most enduring emblems of authentic street life in the Russia of the bygone days.

½ cup honey

6 cups water

Spices: 1 piece (1 inch) fresh ginger, 8 cloves, 1 piece (1 inch) cinnamon stick, small piece of bay leaf, rind of ½ lemon, and 3 peppercorns tied in a cheesecloth bag

½ to ¾ cup brandy or vodka

1 In a medium-size pot, combine all the ingredients except the brandy or vodka. Bring to a boil over low heat, stirring to dissolve the honey and sugar. Simmer for 15 minutes.

2 Remove the spice bag, add the brandy or vodka, and heat for another 2 minutes.

3 Pour into mugs and serve at once.

Serves 6 to 8

Cranberry Drink

Mors

This is probably the most popular of all the Russian summer drinks. In the USSR it's made with much-beloved lingonberries, *kliukva*, but cranberries will do nicely. Try it for brunch or mix with Stolichnaya vodka for an "original" Cape Codder.

2 pounds fresh cranberries, picked over and rinsed

9 cups water

¾ cup sugar (to make a slightly tart drink), or more to taste

1 In a 2-quart nonreactive pot, combine the cranberries with 6 cups of water. Bring to a boil, then reduce the heat to medium-low and simmer, uncovered, until the berries soften, about 10 minutes.

2 Strain the liquid through a fine sieve, pressing the cranberries with the back of a spoon to extract as much juice as possible.

3 Return the liquid to the pot and add the sugar and the remaining water. Bring to a boil, then reduce the heat and simmer for 5 minutes. Adjust the amount of sugar, as desired. Although *mors* is not supposed to be perfectly clear, you can strain it through a sieve lined with cheesecloth, if desired. Chill.

4 Serve over ice.

Makes just over 2 quarts

Fruit and Berry Compote

Kompot

When I visit Russia during the summer, I always look forward to my father's *kompot*, made from apples, tart plums, and mixed berries — gooseberries, red currants, and black currants, which add a special flavor. This treat invariably awaits me as I walk into his apartment hot and tired after a long flight. You can use unsweetened canned black currants imported from Germany or Eastern Europe. Try serving Russian *kompot* as a nonalcoholic punch for your next garden party. You can also spike it up with a few tablespoons of crème de cassis if serving to adults.

11 cups water

1 cup sugar, or more to taste

½ to 1 teaspoon grated lemon zest

3 medium-size tart apples (such as Granny Smith), cored, peeled, and cut into wedges

12 to 15 small fresh prunes (see Note)

2 cups blackberries or raspberries

1½ cups fresh or canned black currants

Fresh lemon juice (optional)

Crème de cassis (optional)

In Russia compotes are made in huge quantities throughout both the summer and the winter (when they're made with dried fruit). Due to the large amount of liquid, they are considered more a refreshing drink than a dessert, as they are in the West. Served in glasses both at home and in every imaginable type of restaurant and snack bar, *kompot* will usually accompany a meal; and the fruit on the bottom will be scooped up with a spoon at its conclusion. (Children are repeatedly instructed not to make loud noises sucking up their fruit during the meal itself.)

1 In a large kettle, combine the water, 1 cup sugar, and lemon zest and bring to a boil over high heat, stirring to dissolve the sugar.

2 Add the apples and prunes and reduce the heat to medium-low. Simmer until the prunes are soft, 15 minutes.

3 Add the berries and simmer for another 5 to 7 minutes. Taste and add more sugar, if desired, or some lemon juice for a tarter taste. Cool and refrigerate.

4 Add some crème de cassis before serving if you wish.

Serves 12

Note: You can pit the prunes, but I find that the pits improve the taste of the *kompot.*

Rose Sherbet

Ovshala

This is supposed, of course, to be made from real rose petals. But even if you had the time, the know-how, and the money to make a cup of syrup from more than two dozen roses, the fact that roses with the same aroma and flavor as those of the Middle East are rarely found in the United States should give you pause. Better keep them for Valentine's Day or the vase.

3 cups sugar
1¾ cups spring water
2 teaspoons fresh lemon juice

⅓ cup rosewater
½ teaspoon red food coloring
Iced spring water

1 In a small nonreactive pan, stir the sugar, water, and lemon juice together over medium heat, until the sugar dissolves and the syrup is thick enough to coat the back of a spoon, 3 to 5 minutes.

2 Add the rosewater and food coloring and stir well for another 2 to 3 minutes. Pour the syrup into a bottle with a cap and

allow to cool to room temperature.

3 To serve, mix the desired amount of syrup with ice-cold spring water (it is usually about one-third syrup to two-thirds water, but you should decide for yourself) in a pitcher. Serve in tall glasses over ice.

Makes about 2½ cups syrup

Lemon Sherbet

Limon Sherbeti

Azerbaijanis often add a few coriander seeds for a special flavor and some saffron for color to this fine tart syrup. I think yellow food coloring works better; and as for the coriander seeds, they have a rather curious aroma. Try it and see.

Zest of 2 lemons
⅓ cup boiling water
3 to 4 coriander seeds, slightly
    crushed (optional)

1½ cups fresh lemon juice
2 cups sugar
½ teaspoon yellow food coloring
Iced spring water

Sherbet

Sherbet is a renowned cooling drink that is taken with the meal in Azerbaijan, Tadzhikistan, and some Middle Eastern countries. Though outstanding in taste and "refreshment value," sherbets are, in fact, nothing more than homemade fruit syrups diluted with ice-cold water. An Azerbaijani friend recently confessed to me that these days it's often considered "uncool" and old-fashioned to serve sherbet at parties, especially in the villages, where people will go out of their way to procure for their guests some commercial soft drink such as Pepsi or Fanta, which are considered prestigious in the USSR. Consequently, the recipes for traditional sherbets using coriander, saffron, basil, or sumakh for flavors are sadly being forgotten and lost.

Thankfully, though, there are still many families in which a beautiful glass pitcher of

sherbet will be brought to the table, adding a splendid, decorative touch to an exotic pilaf feast. Try though I might, however, I couldn't get hold of workable recipes for the most traditional of sherbets (such as those listed above), possibly because commercial syrups are now available everywhere. As sherbets are supposed to have a particularly intense color, many cooks add food coloring. It's certainly nice to have a couple of deeply colored sherbets to go with the meal. Some Persian housewives I know use Italian syrups to make sherbet. Of these, mint, lemon, orange, or grenadine are the most authentic flavors.

1 Blanch the lemon zest in boiling water for 1 minute. Drain, then chop the zest and place in a small bowl. Add the ⅓ cup boiling water and coriander seeds if desired. Let stand for 3 hours. Strain the liquid into a bowl and discard the lemon zest and coriander. Set aside.

2 In a small nonreactive saucepan, combine the lemon juice, sugar, and the reserved liquid. Stir over medium heat until the sugar dissolves and the syrup is thick enough to coat the back of a spoon, 3 to 5 minutes. Add the food coloring and stir for another minute. Pour into a clean bottle with a cap and let cool to room temperature.

3 Mix the desired amount of syrup with ice-cold water (usually one-third syrup to two-thirds water) and serve in a glass pitcher over ice.

Makes about 2 cups syrup

Vodka

Vodka is one of the most essential components of everyday life in Russia. And after World War II, it became the center of popular anecdotes and humorous rituals. Today vodka is sold in half-liter (*pollitra*) and quarter-liter (*chetvertinka*) bottles. My grandmother (no alcoholic, I might add) once complained that at some Moscow party a while ago there were only four *pollitras* to serve eight people: "They should have asked us to buy drinks instead of presents," she said out loud. But if they buy by the liter, Russians drink by the gram, 100 grams (about 3 ounces) being the smallest shot, taken before dinner.

There are three cardinal rules of drinking in Russia. The first is that you *never* drink alone. To sit by yourself in front of an open bottle is considered abnormal and antisocial. Even self-professed drunkards abide by the rule, coming together as a small group (*na troikh* — "for three") and chipping in for half a liter and some local sausage or a bite of herring to chase it down. In pre-Gorbachev days, when people still drank on the streets, they would form into random groups to pass the bottle round on a stoop or at the end of an alley. Our friend Ada tells the story of how she was once followed all over Moscow by a couple of drifters. When they finally caught up with her, they said "Grandma" — she was in her thirties — don't be scared, how about *na troikh*?" In more normal threesomes and drinking groups, conversation is always intense and personal. This is the place where real opinions are offered, hearts are poured out, novels are planned.

The second cardinal rule of Russian drinking is to *never* drink without eating something immediately after. In this context, the *zakuska* or "little bite" takes on its literal meaning. Around the vodka bottle the little bite should be salty — pickles, olives, herring. The Russians are convinced that pickle juice is a panacea for alcoholic overindulgence.

The third rule is to *never* sip your vodka, and never add ice or tonic.

Flavored Vodkas

Although you can easily purchase one of the readily-available, commercial, flavored vodkas, it's more fun to prepare your own, which you can do in just a few hours. Of course I prefer to use a real Russian vodka, such as Stolichnaya. Make at least two or three flavors and serve in cut crystal or glass decanters. Each 750 ml bottle makes about sixteen 1½ ounce drinks.

Lemon

Limonnaya

Grated zest of 1½ lemons (make sure no white is left on the rind, as it will make the taste bitter)
1 bottle (750 ml) Stolichnaya vodka

Add the zest to the vodka and infuse for at least 4 hours, but no more than 12 at room temperature. Strain and chill.

Buffalo Grass

Zubrovka

6 to 8 blades buffalo grass (available at herb stores)
1 bottle (750 ml) Stolichnaya vodka

Add the buffalo grass to the vodka and infuse for at least 8 hours. Remove all but two blades of the buffalo grass. Chill.

Pepper

Pertzovka

4 teaspoons pink peppercorns
1 bottle (750 ml) Stolichnaya vodka

Add the peppercorns to the vodka and infuse for at least 8 hours, 3 days maximum. Strain and chill.

Yes. Bison (buffalo) grass it was. And then, at Kalyaev Station, I had another glass, only this time it was coriander vodka. A man I knew used to say that coriander vodka does not have a humanizing effect, for, while it refreshes all the bodily parts it weakens the soul. For some strange reason the opposite happened to me, that is, my soul was wonderfully refreshed but my limbs weakened.

— Benedict Erofeev
Moscow Circles

Coriander
Koriandrovaya

1 tablespoon coriander seeds, lightly crushed
1 bottle (750 ml) Stolichnaya vodka

Add the coriander seeds to the vodka and infuse for at least 6 hours, maximum 24 hours. Strain and chill.

Anise
Anisovaya

1 tablespoon aniseed
1 bottle (750 ml) Stolichnaya vodka

Add the aniseed to the vodka and infuse for 3 to 5 hours. Strain and chill.

Fruit Vodka "Samovar"
Fruktovoay Vodka "Samovar"

Samovar is a wonderful Russian restaurant in Manhattan's theater district. Diners come to sample its outstanding food, enjoy the traditional Russian songs performed by talented musicians, and to watch the Soviet and emigré celebrities who frequent the restaurant. The bar area is especially friendly and filled with people chatting with the hospitable owners, and enjoying a whole range of flavored vodkas. The most special of these is the house vodka, infused with a half dozen exotic fruits and beautifully displayed in a large glass crock. Roman Kaplan, one of the owners, kindly shared his recipe with me and recommends serving fruit vodka at room temperature in order to taste all the fruits better. The selection of fruit in this vodka certainly satisfies Roman's taste for the exotic, but if some of these are not available, substitute other fruits or berries of your choice. Display this drink in its crock before serving it — it looks beautiful.

1 cup strawberries, hulled and sliced

3 kiwis, peeled and sliced

1 cup raspberries

1 cup lingonberries

1 cup sour cherries

2 passion fruit, pricked all over with the tip of a knife

2 cactus pears, pricked all over with the tip of a knife

3 large peaches, halved and pitted

12 sprigs fresh mint

1 tablespoon honey

2 bottles (750 ml each) Stolichnaya vodka

Combine the fruits, mint, honey, and vodka in a large glass crock or a punch bowl. Let stand at room temperature, covered, for at least 5 days. Serve in shot-size glasses, without the fruit.

Makes about 1½ quarts (serves about thirty-two 1½ ounce drinks)

Ukrainian Hot Spiced Vodka

Varenukha

Unlike the Russians, who insist on chilled vodkas, the Ukrainians prefer warm brandies and vodkas, which as they so quaintly put it "make a carnation bloom right inside your stomach." For centuries *varenukha*" — which means "boiled" — was the favored tipple of the fearsome Cossacks, fueling their warrior bodies by day and making them merry by night. It should be served warm.

3 tablespoon honey

1 liter vodka (4 cups)

3 ounces dried pears

3 ounces dried apples

3 ounces dried prunes

1 piece (1 inch) cinnamon stick

1 piece (½ inch) fresh ginger

4 white peppercorns

1 In an nonreactive saucepan, combine the vodka and honey and bring to a boil over medium-low heat, stirring to dissolve the honey.

2 Preheat the oven to 125°F.

3 Select an ovenproof pot with a very tight-fitting lid. Pour the vodka in it and add the dried fruit and the spices. Bake for about 5 hours.

4 Strain thoroughly and transfer to a bottle. Serve slightly warm.

Makes 1 quart

A Shot of Vodka the Proper Russian Way

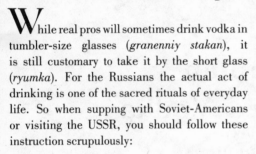

While real pros will sometimes drink vodka in tumbler-size glasses (*granenniy stakan*), it is still customary to take it by the short glass (*ryumka*). For the Russians the actual act of drinking is one of the sacred rituals of everyday life. So when supping with Soviet-Americans or visiting the USSR, you should follow these instruction scrupulously:

1. Pour a shot of ice-cold vodka nearly to the rim. Have ready a bite-size morsel of food.
2. Say a brief toast. Not "*Na Zdorovie.*" This is used to accompany food and will instantly betray you as a foreigner (if this hasn't already happened). Better, "*vashe zdorovie*" ("Your health"). Be patient during the inevitable torrent of toasts and witticisms and off-color humor that will be traded by your fellow drinkers.
3. Say "*Nu.*" Take a deep breath. Tilt your head right back, and down the entire shot, aiming it at your tonsils if you have them or straight at your stomach if you don't.
4. Breathe out loudly, producing a sound just short of a full whistle. (Some people smell their sleeves or their slice of bread in a quick ritual gesture. This is optional.)
5. Eat your chaser purposefully but quickly.
6. Say "*Oh khoroshooo*" ("It feels good"), or "*Khorosho poshla*" ("It went down well").
7. Repeat at 10- to 15-minute intervals. Desist and retire as soon as your performance becomes in any way flawed, or when it becomes significantly more flawed than that of your company.

Armenian Cuisine

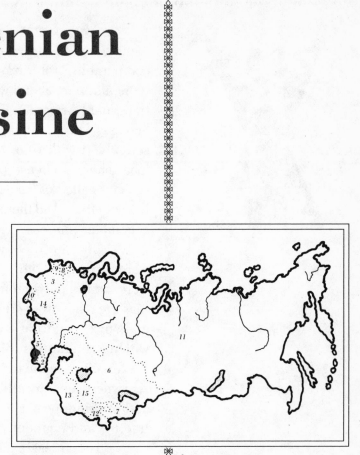

On a recent visit to the Soviet Union, John and I traveled from Georgia to the Armenian capital, Yerevan, by train along the present-day border with Turkey, which bisects the richly fertile Armenian plateau. Our constant companion was the great, enduring symbol of the Armenian people, Mount Ararat. Resonant with history and myth, Ararat raised its shoulders out of the morning mist, soared under the even glare of the midday sun, and glowed suggestively in the dim eastern moonlight. Few peoples have such a powerful natural monument around which their whole cultural tradition has been founded. The legendary resting place of Noah's Ark, Ararat is named for the ancient people of the region, the mysterious Urartu, one of whose citadels at Erebuni is still tucked under the wing of the modern capital.

Eventually the train reached the new city of Yerevan, where we were met by our musician friends and whisked away to a comfortable apart-

1. ARMENIA
2. AZERBAIJAN
3. BYELORUSSIA
4. ESTONIA
5. GEORGIA
6. KAZAKHSTAN
7. KIRGHIZIA
8. LATVIA
9. LITHUANIA
10. MOLDAVIA
11. RUSSIA
12. TADZHIKISTAN
13. TURKMENIA
14. UKRAINE
15. UZBEKISTAN

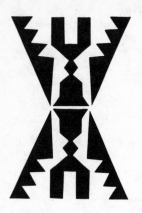

ment a stone's throw from Lenin Square. If the incomparable Ararat provided our first impression of Armenia, our second was the welcoming aroma of a traditional Armenian breakfast that wafted from our hostess, Suzy's, kitchen. We were greeted with eggs scrambled with ripe tomatoes and green peppers, local sheep's cheese (*chanakh*), a delicious spicy sausage called *sudjuk*, and generous cupfuls of strong black coffee. And there were freshly prepared stuffed vegetables (*dolma*) awaiting us for later.

Once fortified, we left to explore the city, and were struck by the sheer vivacity of the capital. Yerevan is a polychrome fantasy in stone; its buildings are made from ornate local marble, from basalt and onyx, and from a wonderful pink volcanic tufa with a granular texture like hard sponge. It's one of the few cities in the USSR, or anywhere for that matter, where a happy alliance between modern design and striking local materials results in a highly attractive and eminently livable urban environment.

The finest example of this well-fashioned modernity is found in Yerevan's chicly designed central market. Its huge barrel vaulted roof encloses an acre of fabulously tempting produce, neatly arranged on even ranks of white slab tables, and picturesquely backlit by sunbeams that dart and scatter through an ornate iron grille fronting onto the main street. A rumbling mercantile hubub hovers above the vendors, blending in with the headily scented air.

As soon as we entered the market, we came upon dozens of wise-looking old women, each carrying a basket of breads. There were sheets of Armenian flat bread (*lavash*), which is used to wrap around cheese, herbs, or grilled meats, much like the Mexican tortilla; and hot, puffy, round loaves of *churek*, sprinkled with sesame seeds. We had arrived at the peak of the fruit season, and were seduced by the rich aroma of the late summer harvest. Perfectly mounded grapes: tiny green ones with a thin translucent skin ("sweet as honey," the vendor told us when he saw us staring); huge purple ones swollen like plums; ripe muscats with enough fragrance to perfume a whole house. Nearby were displays of golden peaches looking as if they were about to burst with juiciness, tart plums, sweet crimson plums, and cherry-size red and yellow *alicha*, plums which are used widely in Armenia for cooking and preserves.

Even after a filling breakfast, it was impossible to resist such a glorious selection of food, so we purchased several bags of fruit and a loaf of *churek*. While washing the fruit at a public water fountain, John cupped his hands, took a long sip, and instantly proclaimed it some of the best he had ever tasted. I was quick to agree. We joked that we were eating luscious grapes in a syrup of pure Armenian water.

A Step Back in Time

For all the sense of modernity on the surface of Yerevan, the heartbeat of the capital and the nation alike is best in its historic older buildings. On Sunday we visited the romantically situated monastery of the Holy Lance (Gehard), and had a chance to witness the ritual sacrifice of the lamb. Armenia is the only Christian country that carries on this tradition, and even here it happens rather irregularly. Christian piety, local lore, and rank superstition are all combined in the brief ceremony. Often the animal (either a lamb or a rooster) will be provided

> "If you eat burned bread, you will be brave and the bears will not attack you."
>
> —Old Armenian saying

by a rich family in order to publicly give thanks for some good fortune, whether its a near-miss accident or their son's acceptance into medical school (though lamb alone is not sufficient for the latter — the family will probably have had to dig deep into their pockets to find a colossal ruble bribe.)

The lamb and some salt are first blessed in the church. Then the lamb is divided into seven pieces and boiled in a cauldron with the blessed salt (no other cooking preparation is permitted) to make a dish called *hashlama*. Of the many further rituals associated with the consumption of the lamb, the most sacred is the offering of a choice piece of meat to a passing stranger.

As evening fell, we wandered around the extraordinary cavernous, grotto-like chapels, scooped and chiseled out of the bare rock that make up the Gehard complex. Outside the church walls, we crossed over the nearby mountain stream and entered an eerie bankside copse in which almost every branch and twig was festooned with rags and handkerchiefs. These votive offerings and personal mementos flapped suggestively in the darkening air, and somehow combined with the haunting cave-church, left us with a bold and indelible impression of Armenia's passionate religious past.

An Ancient Cuisine

Fine food and good cheer have a long and dignified history in Armenia. Five-thousand-year-old carbonized grains of wheat and barley have been found in the vicinity of Lake Van, testifying to one of the oldest grain-bearing cultures in the world.

In the fourth century B.C., Xenophon described the fine wines and elaborate luncheons served at the court of the Persian governor. Armenia's fate since becoming, it is believed, the first state formally to adopt the Christian religion in the third century A.D., has been one of the most valiant and checkered of any smaller, independent nation. At one point in the Middle Ages, its territory stretched right down to the Mediterranean, but Armenia has often been overrun and abused by its more powerful neighbors — the Tatars, Persians, Russians (who acquired Armenia in 1828), and Turks. Yet throughout this adversity, and into the present century, the isolated valley communities have preserved much of their traditional culture and many of their ancestral recipes and preparations.

Armenian cuisine is, in fact, one of the most familiar in the West of any of the Soviet cuisines. This is because the Armenians have been scattered all over the world, including a large and vibrant community in Los Angeles known for its excellent bakeries, groceries, and restaurants. Chatting with the vendors at the market, I was persuaded at almost every step to take their news and gossip to relatives in New York, Paris, Istanbul, Syria, Athens, and Los Angeles (to anyone with friends and relatives in the central market, they send you greetings)! Yet Armenian cooking always makes distinct alliances with its neighboring cuisines, and there is great variety among Armenian preparations found in Lebanon, Syria, Greece, Turkey, and California. Likewise, while there are many similarities

In Yerevan, Armenia's modern capital, outdoor cafés are as popular as they are in Paris.

"If you leave a bit of food on your plate, you will marry someone with a scarred face, but if you lick your plate clean, you will get a handsome financier."

—Old Armenian saying

with Georgian cooking, each republic shades and colors its dishes differently: where the Georgians use walnuts, the Armenians use pine nuts and almonds; where the Georgians cook with beans, the Armenians prefer chick-peas; the Georgians eat rice and the Armenians enjoy bulgur. The use of spices is also subtly different, Armenian dishes tending to be milder and sweeter, using ground allspice, a little cumin, and cinnamon to flavor rice dishes and meat stews.

My favorite Armenian dishes are the appetizers (*meza*) and as with Russian *zakuski* their range is enormous. One day you might be offered a few slices of local cheese, a pile of fresh herbs, and a couple of bowls of olives and nuts; the next it might be a lavish production including cold stuffed vegetables, *sudjuk* (the spicy sausage), *basturma* (dried, spicy meat, usually homemade), *bourek* (a filled pastry), and superb cocktail meatballs. And the grilled kebabs, incredible variety of stuffed vegetables (*dolma*), delicately flavored bulgur and rice pilafs, stuffed wheat- and meatballs, called *keufteh*, and rice desserts made with honey and nuts, will delight even the most discerning food critic.

For those who have already fallen in love with Mediterranean and Middle Eastern cooking, Armenian dishes add a vivid new chapter to one of the world's great culinary stories. But whether sweet or savory, hot or cold, spicy or mellow, the taste of Armenian cooking is truly unique. Flavor is subtly layered over flavor with wonderful, palate-pleasing finesse. Throw an Armenian supper party, gather your friends around the *meza* table, or delight the whole family with a spicy, healthful home-style stew.

Desserts

❖

SLADKIYE BLYUDA

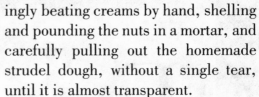

No matter how plentiful and filling a Russian meal might be, any initiated guest always knows how to save room for dessert, which the Russians call *tretye*, the "third course." The tea is brewed and poured into ornate porcelain cups, and the hostess proudly emerges with a tray full of tempting sweets. There are very few bad cooks and fewer noncooks in the Soviet Union, but even women who don't cook on principle always have a dessert recipe or two up their sleeves, inherited from their grandmother or their great-aunt—perhaps an airy sponge cake with cream, or a specially flavorful yeast dough, or a luscious cheesecake. But when the *babushka* herself goes to work, filling the house with the unbearably seductive aroma of fresh baking, it is to whip up a ten-layer cake filled with luxurious custard cream, a dream of meringues, butter-cream, and chocolate icing, or a comforting pie filled with cottage cheese and berries.

Nineteenth-century Russian cookbooks often suggest beating egg yolks and kneading dough for hours on end. Then they issue a solemn warning in small print at the bottom of the page: "This cake is extremely delicious when it comes out, but it almost never does." Older generations, however, take these instructions very seriously, painstak-ingly beating creams by hand, shelling and pounding the nuts in a mortar, and carefully pulling out the homemade strudel dough, without a single tear, until it is almost transparent.

The younger generation, on the other hand, though still committed to great results, is also willing to use a little modern ingenuity when they lack the time or ingredients. Margarine might be substituted for butter, and sour cream for fresh cream. Small wonders of the world are conjured from cans of sweetened condensed milk, or instant custard cream. We have learned to measure by the eye and to flavor according to taste; and I must admit that more often than not our grandmothers are proud of our apple charlottes (ready in just 20 minutes), meringue-topped pies filled with sour cherries, comforting puddings made from leftover bread, or our creamy cranberry mousses that go down easily after a filling meal.

The native Slavic dessert table was not always as rich and varied as it is today. But it was impressive, nevertheless. In the seventeenth century, to celebrate the birth of Peter the Great, his father, Czar Alexei Mikhail-ovich, was served a sugar cake in the shape of the Russian code of honor. It weighed 70 pounds, and featured exotic birds carved out of sugar, no less than 120 various confections, and to top it all (literally) there was an extraordinary replica of the Kremlin, complete in every detail down to people and horses, yet sculpted entirely from sugar. At less formal occasions, desserts might include a dried fruit compote, or a custard called *kissel*, both of which are Slavic ritual dishes; a sweetened porridge (*kasha*); fragrant spiced honey cake (*pryanik*), a dish as old as Russia itself; *pastilla*, a marshmallow-like confection made of apples; and a prodigious variety of dried fruits.

When Peter became Czar and "carved out a window onto Europe," he introduced the Russians to coffee, chocolate, and all types of European sweets. From then on, lavish cream cakes, puff pastry creations like Napoleans and strudels, sweet roulades, cream puffs and eclairs, sponge cakes, mousses, jellies, and charlottes were busy conquering the taste buds of Russia, and soon made a perfect marriage into even the most traditional households. Many of the European-originated desserts were elevated to the highest levels of culinary art as they were passed from generation to generation among the Russian aristocracy and lesser nobles in the nineteenth century. And you should remember that one mark of the excellence of Russian sweets is that they are always eaten, not with a fork, but with a spoon.

Lavish Chocolate Meringue Cake

Imposantniy Chokoliadovo Bilkoviy Tort

There is a touch of the old Austro-Hungarian decadence in desserts from the western Ukraine, the origin of this wonderful cake. This and several other recipes in the section were given to me by Christina Nawrocky, a distinguished cook who runs a food column in the Ukrainian woman's weekly in New York. Many of her splendid ideas come, in turn, from her mother, who left behind a beautiful, handwritten notebook of recipes, which is Christina's most prized family treasure, and which offers us perfect access to a rich and authentic regional cuisine.

MERINGUE LAYER

5 large egg whites, at room
    temperature
½ teaspoon cream of tartar

½ teaspoon white vinegar
½ cup superfine sugar

WALNUT-CHOCOLATE LAYER

8 large eggs, separated
½ cup granulated sugar
4 ounces bittersweet chocolate,
    grated
1¼ cups ground walnuts

¼ cup unflavored fine, dry bread
    crumbs
1 tablespoon finely ground coffee
    (not instant)
1 tablespoon fresh lemon juice

FILLINGS

1 cup heavy or whipping cream
3 tablespoons confectioners'
    sugar

1 tablespoon instant coffee powder
1 tablespoon rum extract
1 cup red currant preserves

CHOCOLATE ICING

8 ounces bittersweet chocolate
2 tablespoons solid vegetable
    shortening

2 tablespoons water

1 The day before assembling the cake, make the meringue layers. Cut out two 11-inch circles from parchment or freezer paper; grease well with butter and sprinkle lightly with flour.

2 Preheat the oven to 250°F. Fold the rim of the baking circles slightly upward.

3 In a large bowl, beat the egg whites, cream of tartar, and vinegar together until the whites hold a stiff peak. Add the superfine sugar, a few tablespoons at a time, beating until the mixture is stiff and glossy.

4 Gently fill each circle with half the meringue mixture, spreading evenly with a rubber spatula. Bake until the meringues are light golden and dry, 1 hour.

5 Invert the meringues onto a plate and

peel off the parchment paper. Leave in a dry spot overnight.

6 The next day, preheat the oven to 350°F. Line the bottom of a 10-inch spring-form pan with parchment or freezer paper. Lightly butter the paper and sprinkle lightly with flour.

7 To make the walnut-chocolate layer, in a large bowl, beat the egg yolks with the sugar until the mixture is pale yellow and forms a ribbon when the beaters are lifted.

8 With clean, dry beaters, beat the egg whites in a separate bowl until soft peaks form. Gently fold one-third of the whites into the beaten yolks, then fold in the rest, alternating with the grated chocolate and walnuts.

9 Fold in the bread crumbs, coffee, and lemon juice.

10 Pour the batter into the prepared pan. Bake for 20 minutes. Reduce the oven temperature to 300°F and bake until a cake tester comes out clean, another 20 to 25 minutes.

11 When the cake cools off a little, remove the sides of the pan. Invert the cake and peel off the paper. Using a serrated knife, cut it horizontally into two layers.

12 Whip the cream with the sugar, instant coffee, and rum extract until it holds stiff peaks.

13 Place one of the walnut-chocolate layers, cut side up, on a cake platter and

After Dinner

After the roast, man becomes full and falls into a delightful blankness . . . At that point the body feels good and the soul is filled with tender emotion. For a treat you could drink two or three glasses of a nice little spiced brandy [which is] better than any champagne. After the first glass, your whole soul is enveloped by a fragrance, such a mirage, and you imagine that you aren't sitting at home in an armchair, but somewhere in Australia, on some sort of softest possible ostrich . . .

— Anton Chekhov
The Siren

spread it with ½ cup of the red currant preserves and then with one-third of the coffee-flavored cream. Top with one meringue layer. Spread another one-third of the cream on the meringue layer and top with the second meringue layer. Spread the rest of the cream filling on the meringue. Spread the remaining preserves over the remaining walnut-chocolate layer. Place the walnut-chocolate layer, preserves side down, on top of the cream filling. You should have the following layers, starting at the bottom: walnut-chocolate, preserves, cream, meringue, cream, meringue, cream, preserves, walnut-chocolate.

14 For the icing, melt the chocolate and shortening in the water in the top of a double boiler, over barely simmering water.

15 Spread the top and sides of the cake with warm chocolate icing. Refrigerate the cake for at least 1 hour before serving.

Serves 12

Apple Baba

Yablochnaya Baba

Babas, not babkas, are the real pride and joy of eastern European and western Russian cooking. This recipe and the Rum Baba that follows are from Christina Nawrocky, and have quickly become my favorites.

4 tart apples (such as Granny
    Smith), peeled, cored, quartered
    and thinly sliced crosswise
2¼ cups granulated
    sugar
1 teaspoon ground cinnamon
4 large eggs
1 cup vegetable oil

½ cup fresh orange juice
2 teaspoons vanilla extract
4 cups unbleached all-purpose
    flour
1 teaspoon baking powder
Confectioners' sugar for
    sprinkling

1 Preheat the oven to 350°F. Grease a 10-inch tube pan.

2 Place the apples in a large bowl, sprinkle with ¼ cup of the sugar and the cinnamon and set aside.

3 In a large bowl, beat the eggs and the remaining 2 cups sugar with an electric mixer until pale yellow and thick. Gradually beat in the oil, orange juice, and vanilla extract.

4 Sift together the flour and baking powder. Gradually add it to the egg mixture, stirring with a large wooden spoon.

You will have a batter the consistency of thick honey.

5 Fold the apples into the batter, making sure they are well distributed.

6 Pour the apple batter into the prepared pan and smooth the top with a rubber spatula. Bake until the top is well browned and splitting, about 1¼ hours.

7 Invert the baba onto a rack and cool. Sprinkle with confectioners' sugar just before serving.

Serves 8 to 10

Rum Baba

Romovaya Baba

This is the homemade eastern European version for those who have only tasted *baba au rhum* (the fancy way of putting it) in restaurants or from Italian or French bakeries throughout the United States. Serve with whipped cream or ice cream, particularly rum raisin.

2 envelopes active dry yeast
¼ cup plus 1 teaspoon sugar
¾ cup lukewarm water (105° to 115°F)
6 eggs
Grated zest of 1 orange

12 tablespoons (1½ sticks) unsalted butter, cut into pieces, then brought to room temperature
3¾ cups unbleached all-purpose flour

SYRUP
2½ cups sugar
1¼ cups water

1⅓ cups rum

1 In a large bowl, combine the yeast, 1 teaspoon sugar, and ¼ cup water. Let stand until foamy, about 5 minutes.

2 Add the remaining ½ cup water, the ¼ cup sugar, and the eggs and beat with an electric mixer at medium-high speed until smooth, 3 to 4 minutes. Add the orange zest and butter and beat for another 2 minutes.

3 Turn the mixer off and add 3½ cups of the flour, 1 cup at a time, stirring well after each addition with a wooden spoon. Transfer the dough to a floured surface and knead until smooth and elastic, 5 to 7 minutes, adding more flour if necessary to prevent sticking. The dough will be rather soft.

4 Transfer the dough to a well-buttered 12-cup kugelhopf pan or tube pan. Cover with a linen or cotton (not terry cloth) kitchen towel and let rise in a warm, draft-free place until the dough almost fills the pan, leaving approximately ½ inch of rim showing, about 1 hour.

5 Meanwhile, preheat the oven to 375°F.

6 Bake the baba until golden and a cake tester comes out clean, about 45 minutes. Invert on a rack and let cool for at least 15 minutes. Transfer to a plate.

7 To prepare the syrup, combine the water and sugar in a small saucepan and simmer until the sugar is completely dissolved, about 10 minutes. Cool for a little while, then stir in the rum.

8 Transfer the baba to a serving platter. Prick it all over with a skewer. Pour the syrup evenly over the baba. Cool entirely.

Serves 8 to 10

> **The baba is a cake of Polish origin which should always be served in a size large enough to act as a "grosse piece"…, and remain for several days on the sideboard as a standby.**
>
> *—Alexandre Dumas*

Cherry Sour Cream Cake

Biskvit so Smetanoy i Vishney

In the west of the Soviet Union, sour cream is used in huge quantities, especially for baking, when it is often added to the pastry itself, as well as for creams and frostings. In this gorgeously moist cake the buttermilk-based sponge is soaked in a tangy sour cream and sour cherry mixture. The recipe comes from Alevtina Vasilievna, a good friend and a baking genius. The cake should be made at least 8 hours before serving.

¾ cup canned sour cherries, well
*   drained*
1 cup buttermilk
1¼ cups sugar
2 large eggs, beaten

2½ cups unbleached all-purpose
*   flour*
1½ teaspoons baking soda
Pinch of salt

CREAM

2 cups sour cream
2 tablespoons sugar, or more to taste
½ cup canned sour cherries, well
*   drained and mashed with a fork*

½ cup chopped walnuts
3 tablespoons cherry
*   liqueur*

GARNISHES

Whole fresh or canned sour cherries

Walnut halves

1 To make the cake process the cherries in a food processor for 1 to 2 pulses.

2 Transfer the cherries to a large bowl. Add the buttermilk, sugar, and eggs and beat for about 1 minute.

3 Sift the dry ingredients together. Fold into the cherry mixture and beat until well blended.

4 Preheat the oven to 375°F and butter a 9-inch springform pan.

5 Pour the batter into the pan and bake until a cake tester comes out clean, 40 minutes. Cool the cake completely on a rack.

6 To make the cream, whisk the sour cream and sugar together in a medium-size bowl, for 1 to 2 minutes. Add the cherries, walnuts and liqueur and beat until well blended.

7 Remove the sides of the pan from the cooled cake. Using a serrated knife, carefully cut the cake crosswise into three layers. Set one cake layer, cut side up, on a platter and brush with one-fourth of the cream. Top with the second layer and repeat the procedure. Top with the third layer, cut side up. Spread the remaining cream on the top and sides of the cake. Decorate the top with cherries and walnuts and refrigerate for 8 hours or overnight.

Serves 8

Orange Buttercream Torte

Pomiranchiviy Tort

An absolutely exquisite torte filled with hazelnut buttercream and topped with glazed orange slices. Serve it as a grand finale to an important meal or as a special birthday party treat.

2 large seedless oranges (not too
    thick skinned)

8 large eggs, separated

1¼ cups granulated sugar

¾ cup cake flour

1 cup ground blanched almonds

¼ cup water

¼ cup Grand Marnier, or other
    orange liqueur

1½ cups good-quality apricot jam

8 tablespoons (1 stick) unsalted
    butter, at room temperature

½ cup superfine sugar

1 teaspoon vanilla extract

1 cup shelled hazelnuts, toasted,
    skinned, and ground (see page
    5, Steps 1 and 2)

¼ cup heavy or whipping cream

1 large orange, peeled and thinly
    sliced

1 small orange, peeled and thinly
    sliced

1½ teaspoons unflavored gelatin

2½ tablespoons orange juice

½ tablespoon Cognac

1 Preheat the oven to 350°F. Cut out two 10-inch circles from parchment or freezer paper and line two 10-inch springform pans with them. Lightly butter the paper and the sides of the pan and sprinkle very lightly with flour.

2 Wash the seedless oranges thoroughly and dry with paper towels. Cut into quarters. Purée the oranges together with their skin, in a food processor. Set aside.

3 In a large bowl, beat the egg yolks and 1 cup of the granulated sugar until the mixture is pale yellow and forms a ribbon when the beaters are lifted. Beat in the orange purée.

4 With a clean dry beater, beat the egg whites in a separate bowl until soft peaks form. Gently fold one-third of the whites into the yolk mixture, then fold in the rest, alternating with the flour and almonds.

5 Divide the batter evenly between both pans and bake for 20 minutes. Lower the temperature to 325°F and bake until a cake tester comes out clean, another 15 to 20 minutes.

6 Cool the cakes slightly, then remove the sides of the pans. Allow them to cool completely on a rack before peeling off the parchment paper.

7 In a small saucepan combine the remaining ¼ cup granulated sugar and the water and bring to a boil, stirring to dissolve the sugar, 1 minute. Remove from heat, add the Grand Marnier and cool slightly.

8 Cut each cooled cake horizontally into two layers. Spread one cut side of two of the layers with ½ cup apricot jam each and brush with the Grand Marnier syrup. Top each prepared layer with another layer. You should now have two thick layers with jam in the middle.

9 In a medium-size bowl, beat the butter with the superfine sugar until light and fluffy. Add the vanilla extract, hazelnuts, and cream and beat until smooth.

10 Spread the hazelnut cream generously over one of the two layers. Place the second layer on top and press gently. Place on a cake platter.

11 Arrange the orange slices in a circular pattern over the top of the cake.

12 Sprinkle the gelatin over the orange juice and let stand to soften for 5 minutes.

13 Heat the remaining ½ cup apricot jam and the Cognac in a small saucepan until dissolved, about 5 minutes. Combine with the gelatin and stir well.

14 Brush the mixture over the top and the sides of the cake. Refrigerate until set, at least 2 hours.

Serves 12

Birthday Dessert Table

Orange Buttercream Torte

Chocolate Covered Cheese Confections

Meringue Delights

Alexandertorte

•

Coffee with Ice Cream

• • •

Ukrainian Farmer's Cheese Cake

Syrnik

I wouldn't trade the simplicity of this Ukrainian cheesecake even for the most temptingly decadent American version. If you like, you can decorate the top with sliced strawberries and kiwis. An excellent dessert for a large family gathering.

6 large eggs, separated
1½ cups sugar
1 cup (2 sticks) unsalted butter,
*   at room temperature*
⅓ cup uncooked cream of wheat
*   (not instant)*
1 teaspoon baking powder
2 pounds farmer's cheese (4 cups),
*   strained through a fine sieve*

Grated zest of 2 lemons
Juice of 1½ lemons
6 tablespoons raisins
Unflavored fine, dry bread crumbs
*   for sprinkling the mold*
Confectioners' sugar
Sliced strawberries and kiwis for
*   decoration (optional)*

1 In a large bowl, with an electric mixer, beat together the egg yolks with the sugar until the mixture is pale yellow and forms a ribbon when the beaters are lifted. Beat in the butter.

2 Sift together the cream of wheat and baking powder, and add to the mixture. Add the farmer's cheese and beat until completely smooth. Add the lemon zest, lemon juice, and beat some more. Stir in the raisins.

3 In a clean, dry bowl, beat the egg whites with clean, dry beaters until soft peaks form, and gently fold them, a little at a time, into the mixture.

4 Preheat the oven to 350°F.

5 Butter a 10-inch springform pan and sprinkle generously with bread crumbs. Pour the cheese mixture into the pan and bake until the cake pulls away from the side of the pan, 1 hour. Cool and refrigerate for at least 2 hours before serving. Sprinkle with confectioners' sugar and decorate, if desired, with sliced strawberries and kiwis.

Serves 12 to 14

"Guest-at-the-Doorstep" Apple Charlotte

Sharlotka "Gost' na Poroge"

As the nickname of this delicious dessert suggests, "Guest-at-the-Doorstep" Apple Charlotte takes almost no time to prepare and uses the kind of very basic ingredients that you might have readily on hand. As it's customary, indeed almost habitual, in Russia to drop in without notice on friends for tea (*chai*), you can just imagine how valuable this recipe has been, and how many friendships it has kept going — and even improved — over the years. Although we tend not to drop in on friends unexpectedly in the United States, this dessert can still add a special touch to a family meal, or provide a money-saving conclusion to a formal dinner. It's also perfect to have around in case of after-school invasions.

You should either commit the recipe to memory or make plenty of copies, as you will unfailingly receive dozens of requests for it. Whipped cream or vanilla ice cream make welcome additions, though they're not essential for the success of the dish.

Butter for greasing the form
Unflavored fine, dry bread
    crumbs for sprinkling
    the form
6 large tart apples (such as Granny
    Smith), cored, peeled, quar-
    tered, and sliced crosswise

1 teaspoon ground cinnamon
    (optional)
3 large eggs
1 cup less 1 tablespoon sugar
1 teaspoon vanilla extract
1½ cups sifted unbleached all-
    purpose flour

1 Butter a 9-inch springform pan and sprinkle with bread crumbs. Add the apples; they should fill the pan completely. Toss with cinnamon, if desired.

2 Preheat the oven to 350°F.

3 In a large bowl, using an electric mixer or a wire whisk, beat the eggs with the sugar until the mixture is pale yellow and forms a ribbon when the beaters are lifted. Beat in the vanilla extract.

4 Gradually beat in the flour. You will have a rather thick batter. Pour the batter evenly into the pan over the apples. The batter and apples should be level.

5 Bake until the top of the charlotte is puffy and golden, 50 to 55 minutes. Serve at room temperature.

Serves 8

Charlotte Russe

Sharlotka

A truly regal dessert — a ladyfinger mold, filled with a luscious Bavarian cream, and topped with a fruit purée — created by the incomparable Antoine Carême for the Russian Czar Alexander I. Although today it is virtually unheard of in the Soviet Union, I wanted to include it as an homage to the great chef whose name is synonymous with *haute cuisine en russie*.

Light vegetable oil for greasing the
 mold
24 to 26 single ladyfingers
1/3 cup Grand Marnier
2 cups fresh raspberries, plus additional for decoration, lightly
 rinsed and well drained

Bavarian Cream (recipe
 follows)
1 cup heavy or whipping cream
Raspberry Sauce (recipe
 follows)

1 Lightly grease a 2-quart charlotte mold with light vegetable oil.

2 Brush the ladyfingers with Grand Marnier. Line the bottom and the sides of the mold with the ladyfingers, arranging them flat side inward and tapering the sides, if necessary, to fit the bottom of the mold.

3 Fold the 2 cups raspberries into the Bavarian cream. Fill the charlotte mold with the cream. Chill, uncovered, until the cream is firmly set, at least 3 hours.

4 To serve, run a knife around the inside of the mold. Place a serving dish over the mold and invert, shaking lightly to loosen.

5 Whip the cream until it holds stiff peaks. Spoon the cream into a pastry bag

fitted with a decorating tip. Pipe over the top and sides of the charlotte decoratively.

6 Decorate with additional raspberries and serve with raspberry sauce.

Serves 8 to 10

Bavarian Cream

Bavarskiy Krem

2 envelopes unflavored gelatin
¼ cup Cognac
¾ cup milk
4 large eggs, separated

½ cup granulated sugar
1 cup heavy or whipping cream
¼ cup superfine sugar

1 In a small bowl, sprinkle the gelatin over the Cognac and let soak while preparing the next steps.

2 In a medium-size saucepan, bring the milk to a slow boil. Remove from the heat.

3 In a large bowl with an electric mixer, beat the egg yolks and granulated sugar until the mixture is pale yellow and forms a ribbon when the beaters are lifted. Gradually whisk in the hot milk.

4 Return the mixture to the saucepan and cook over low heat, stirring, until the mixture thickens, about 10 minutes; do not allow to boil. Add the gelatin mixture and stir to dissolve for 1 minute. Set the

saucepan in a large bowl filled with ice and chill, stirring frequently, until thickened, 20 to 25 minutes.

5 Beat the cream until it forms stiff peaks.

6 In a separate bowl, with clean, dry beaters, beat the egg whites until soft peaks form. Beat in the superfine sugar, 1 tablespoon at a time, then beat until the whites are stiff and glossy, but not dry.

7 Fold the cream and the egg whites into the egg yolk mixture gently but thoroughly, until well blended.

Makes about 6½ cups

Raspberry Sauce

Sous iz Malini

2 cups fresh raspberries, lightly
   rinsed and well drained
2 tablespoons superfine sugar, or
   to taste

2 teaspoons fresh lemon
   juice
1 tablespoon Cognac

1 Strain the raspberries through a fine sieve set over a bowl, pushing them through with the back of a wooden spoon.

2 Add the sugar, lemon juice, and Co-gnac and mix well. Taste and adjust the sugar, if desired.

Makes about 1½ cups

Sweet Strudels

Shtrudel

Although strudel can be successfully made with frozen phyllo dough or puff pastry, it's truly worthwhile to master the old-fashioned technique for making strudel dough. In Russian the dough is called "pull out" (*vityazhnoye*) dough because it is by pulling and pulling from all sides until the dough is almost transparent that one makes this paper-thin wonder. I find it great fun to make — though you will, at the same time, feel like a very serious cook. Once I've made plenty of dough, I always prepare two different fillings, since everyone always asks for seconds.

If you are going to use phyllo dough, follow the instructions for Savory Strudel (see Index).

2 cups sifted unbleached all-purpose
   flour
¼ teaspoon salt
1 large egg yolk, lightly beaten
1 tablespoon vegetable oil
1½ teaspoons white vinegar
½ cup lukewarm water (105° to 115°F)
1 cup (2 sticks) unsalted butter, melted

6 tablespoons unflavored fine, dry
   bread crumbs (see Note)
A double recipe Walnut, Rhubarb,
   or Cheese Filling (recipes
   follow)
Confectioners' sugar for sprinkling

1 Sift together the flour and the salt, mound on a pastry board, and make a well in the middle. Place the egg yolk, oil, vinegar, and water in the well and mix quickly with a pastry blender or broad knife. Knead with your hands until you have soft and smooth dough, 10 minutes. Slap the dough against the pastry board until bubbles begin to show. Shape into a ball on the board.

2 Rinse a medium-size metal bowl with hot water and dry quickly. Place the heated bowl over the dough and let stand for 30 minutes.

3 Spread a sheet of waxed paper or parchment paper at least 2 and up to 4 feet in length on a work surface. Dust with flour.

4 Divide the dough into two equal balls. Keeping the remaining ball covered, place one ball in the middle of the waxed paper and roll out with a floured rolling pin to a thickness of ½ inch.

5 Brush the dough with ¼ cup of melted butter. With your hands, knuckles placed under the edge of the dough, stretch it carefully in all directions until it is paper thin. The dough should be approximately 18 × 16 inches in area.

6 With a sharp knife, cut off the thick edges. Let the dough dry for about 15 minutes.

7 Preheat the oven to 375°F.

8 Sprinkle the dough lightly but thoroughly with half the bread crumbs. Thinly spread the desired filling lengthwise over two-thirds of the dough, leaving the other third empty. Brush the empty part with 2 tablespoons melted butter. Roll, starting with the filled side, by lifting the paper and letting the dough and filling roll over itself. Avoid handling the dough with your hands as much as possible, otherwise it might break. Trim the edges neatly and press to seal.

9 Repeat with the rest of the dough, using a different filling, if desired.

10 Place the strudels on an 15 × 11 × 1-inch jelly-roll pan and brush each with 2 tablespoons of the remaining butter. Bake until crisp and brown, 35 to 45 minutes.

Sprinkle with confectioners' sugar before serving.

Makes 2 strudels

Note: If using the Rhubarb Filling, increase bread crumbs to ½ cup.

Walnut Filling

Nachinka iz Gretskikh Orekhov

2½ *cups ground walnuts*
½ *cup confectioners' sugar*
2 *large egg yolks*
6 *tablespoons raisins*
¼ *cup dark rum*
¼ *cup milk*

In a large bowl, combine all the ingredients and stir until well blended.

Makes enough filling for 1 strudel

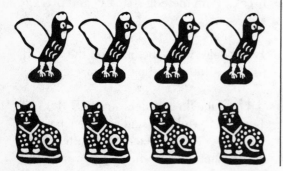

Rhubarb Filling

Nachinka iz Revenya

1½ *pounds fresh rhubarb stalks,*
    trimmed, rinsed, and dried
¾ *cup sugar*
2 *tablespoons raisins*
2 *tablespoons chopped walnuts*
3 *tablespoons Cognac*

1 Cut the rhubarb stalks into ½-inch pieces. Blanch in a large pot of boiling water for 1 minute. Drain well and pat dry.

2 In a large bowl, combine with the remaining ingredients.

Makes enough filling for 1 strudel

Cheese Filling

Nachinka iz Tvoroga

4 *tablespoons (½ stick) unsalted*
    butter, at room temperature
½ *cup sugar, or more to taste*
2 *large egg yolks*
1½ *pounds farmer's cheese (3 cups)*
¼ *cup sour cream*
3 *tablespoons golden raisins*
¾ *teaspoon grated lemon zest*

1 In a food processor, process the butter, sugar, and the egg yolks to blend. Add the farmer's cheese and sour cream and continue to process until the mixture is smooth.

2 Stir in the raisins and lemon zest and mix well.

Makes enough filling for 1 strudel

Birch Tree Log

Béržo Sakà

An exquisite jelly roll from the Baltic, this dessert is filled with luscious apricot mousse. If you prefer, you can use fresh raspberries or strawberries or your favorite butter cream for the filling.

FILLING
1½ cups canned apricots, drained but 2 tablespoons of syrup reserved
2 packages unflavored gelatin
¼ cup apricot brandy

1 tablespoon granulated sugar, or more to taste
2 tablespoons grated lemon zest
1 cup heavy or whipping cream, chilled

CAKE
4 large eggs, separated, whites at room temperature
¼ cup granulated sugar
1 teaspoon grated lemon zest

⅓ cup unbleached all-purpose flour
2 tablespoons potato starch
Confectioners' sugar

1 To make the filling, purée the apricots and reserved syrup in a food processor.

2 In a small bowl, sprinkle the gelatin over the brandy and let the gelatin soften for a few minutes.

3 Combine the puréed apricots, granulated sugar, and lemon zest in a large saucepan and bring to a simmer without letting the mixture boil.

4 Stir in the gelatin mixture and cook

over low heat, stirring constantly until the gelatin is completely dissolved, about 1 minute. Cool over a bowl of ice to room temperature.

5 Whip the cream until soft peaks begin to form and gently fold into the apricot mixture. Refrigerate for several hours, or until ready to use.

6 Line a 15 × 11 × 1-inch jelly-roll pan with waxed paper or parchment. Butter the paper and dust lightly with flour. Preheat the oven to 375°F.

7 In a large bowl, beat the egg yolks with the sugar and lemon zest until pale yellow and the mixture forms a ribbon when the beaters are lifted. Gradually add the flour and potato starch and beat until blended.

8 In another large bowl, beat the egg whites with clean, dry beaters until they hold stiff peaks. Gently fold one-third of the beaten whites into the yolks and then, gently, fold in the rest.

9 Spread the batter evenly in the prepared pan and bake, without disturbing, until lightly colored and the top springs back when touched with a finger, 12 to 15 minutes.

10 Let cool for several minutes and invert onto a large linen or cotton (not terry cloth) kitchen towel sprinkled generously with confectioners' sugar. Carefully peel off the paper, then roll up the cake in the towel, starting from one long side. Let the cake cool on a rack for at least 1 hour.

11 Unroll the cake gently and spread all but ¾ cups of the filling over it. Re-roll the cake carefully, this time without the towel, and transfer to a cake board. Trim the edges neatly. Sprinkle with confectioners' sugar. Place the reserved filling in a pastry bag with a decorative tip. Pipe in an attractive pattern along the length of the roll.

Serves 6

> She hears the serving maids at song
> While picking berries in the close.
> By cunning masters they were bidden
> To sing at work (lest they should try),
> However berries might abound,
> To eat a few upon the sly, —
> A rural shrewd device to stop
> Them plundering the berry-crop.
>
> — Alexander Pushkin
> *Eugene Onegin*

Sour Cherry Meringue Pie

Pirog iz Vishni s Beze

The delicate meringue topping beautifully complements the refreshing sour cherry filling in this elegant Russian pie. By all means use fresh sour cherries when available.

CRUST

1½ cups unbleached all-purpose flour

¼ cup sugar

1 tablespoon vanilla sugar (see Index)

7 tablespoons unsalted butter, chilled and cut into pieces

2 large egg yolks

1 heaping tablespoon sour cream

Ice water (optional)

FILLING

3 cups canned sour or Morello cherries, well drained

¼ cup sugar

¼ cup unflavored, fine, dry bread crumbs

1 teaspoon grated lemon zest

3 tablespoons cherry liqueur

MERINGUE

2 large egg whites, at room temperature

¼ teaspoon cream of tartar

3½ tablespoons sugar

1 To make the crust, sift the dry ingredients into a large bowl. Add the butter, and using a pastry blender, two knives, or your fingertips, cut it into the flour until the mixture resembles coarse crumbs.

2 Add the egg yolks and sour cream and quickly blend them into the dough, using your fingertips. I don't add water, but if you find that your dough doesn't hold together, add just a few drops of ice water. Shape the dough into a ball, wrap in plastic, and refrigerate for 2 hours.

3 Preheat the oven to 400°F.

4 On a well-floured surface with a floured rolling pin, roll out the dough to a thickness of ¼ inch. Fit into a 9-inch tart pan with a removable bottom, trim the edges and crimp them decoratively. Prick the bottom all over with a fork, line with aluminum foil, and fill with pie weights, rice, or dried beans.

5 Bake the crust until light golden, about 15 minutes. Remove from the oven and remove the foil and weights. Reduce the oven temperature to 350°F.

6 In a large bowl, mix together the cherries, sugar, bread crumbs, lemon zest, and liqueur. Pour the cherry filling into the crust and bake for 15 minutes. Remove the pie from the oven and set it aside. Reduce the oven temperature to 275°F.

7 To make the meringue, beat the egg whites until frothy in a clean, dry bowl. Add the cream of tartar, and continue beating until they hold stiff peaks. Add the sugar, a little at a time, and beat for 1 to 2 minutes more.

8 Place the meringue in a pastry bag fitted with a decorative tip. Pipe onto the pie and bake until the meringue is lightly colored, about 12 minutes more. Cool to room temperature and serve.

Serves 8

Cranberry Apple Pie

Pirog s Klyukvoy i Yablokami

A delicately tart filling enclosed in a delicious cream cheese and butter pastry. When cranberries are out of season, try a filling of apples and strawberries (use about 1 pint berries and reduce the amount of sugar to ½ cup). Serve with vanilla ice cream or whipped cream, if you wish.

PASTRY

2 cups unbleached all-purpose flour
⅓ cup sugar
⅛ teaspoon salt
12 tablespoons (1½ sticks) unsalted butter, chilled, cut into bits

6 ounces cream cheese, at room temperature, cut into bits
½ teaspoon vanilla extract

◆◆◆

FILLING

2 large sweet apples (such as
Rome Beauty), peeled,
cored, quartered, and
sliced crosswise

2 cups fresh cranberries, picked
over, rinsed, and well drained

⅔ cups granulated sugar

¼ teaspoon ground cinnamon

2 tablespoons unflavored fine, dry
bread crumbs

Confectioners' sugar

1 To make the pastry, sift the dry ingredients into a large bowl. Add the butter and cream cheese, and using a pastry blender, two knives, or your fingertips, cut them into the flour, sprinkling in the vanilla extract as you work, until the mixture resembles coarse crumbs. Transfer to a cool pastry board and knead very briefly, about 15 seconds. Shape into two balls, wrap in plastic, and refrigerate for 1 hour.

2 Meanwhile, combine the apples, cranberries, granulated sugar, and cinnamon in a large bowl.

3 Preheat the oven to 350°F.

4 On a lightly floured surface with a floured rolling pin, roll out 1 piece of the pastry into a 12-inch round. Fit into a 10-inch tart pan with a removable bottom. Trim the dough, leaving a 1-inch overhang.

5 Roll out the remaining dough into a

Leftover Dough

D o as the Russians do with leftover pie crust or puff pastry: wrap it around whole apples, or purple plums, bake at 375°F for 30 minutes for apples and 350°F for 25 to 30 minutes for plums. Enjoy while it is still warm, generously sprinkled with confectioners' sugar.

slightly smaller and thicker round.

6 Sprinkle the bottom of the crust evenly with the bread crumbs and fill with the apple-cranberry mixture. Drape the top crust over the rolling pin and unroll it over the filling, centering it. Fold the bottom crust overhang over the top crust and press gently to seal. (Don't worry about the look of the top crust, as the pie will be inverted after baking.) Make a few slits in the top crust to allow the steam to escape.

7 Bake the pie until the crust is golden and the filling is bubbling, about 50 minutes. Remove from the oven and let cool in the pan.

8 To serve, remove the sides of the pan and invert the pie onto a serving platter.

Sprinkle generously with confectioners' sugar right before serving, at room temperature.

Serves 8

Cheese and Blueberry Pie

Pirog s Chernikoy i Tvorogom

A quintessentially northern Slavic pie, just perfect with milk or tea on a cool autumn afternoon. Unlike American and European pies that use flaky pie pastry, this one is made with brioche-like yeast dough. Serve it just slightly warm.

1¼ cups farmer's cheese, sieved

6 tablespoons sugar

1 tablespoon sour cream

Grated zest of 1 lemon

½ teaspoon vanilla extract

2 large egg yolks

2½ cups fresh blueberries,
 picked over, rinsed,
 and dried

½ recipe Sweet Yeast Dough (see
 Index)

1 teaspoon milk

1 In a medium-size bowl, combine the farmer's cheese, 2 tablespoons of the sugar, sour cream, lemon zest, vanilla extract, and 1 egg yolk. Beat with an electric mixer until the ingredients are just blended, about 30 seconds.

2 In another bowl, toss the blueberries with the remaining 4 tablespoons sugar.

3 On a floured surface with a floured rolling pin, roll out three-fourths of the dough to a round about 13 inches in diameter.

4 Fit the dough into a 10-inch pie plate, letting the excess hang over the rim. Spread the cheese mixture over the bottom. Place an even layer of blueberries over the cheese.

5 Roll the remaining pastry into a round about 10 inches in diameter. Cut into strips no more than ¼ inch wide (the yeast dough expands during baking). Weave the strips in a lattice fashion over the top of the pie and fold the ends in at the edge of the bottom crust. Pinch tightly to seal. Press decoratively around the edge with the tines of a fork. Let the pie rest, covered, for 30 minutes.

6 Preheat the oven to 375°F.

7 Beat the remaining egg yolk with the milk. Brush the top of the pie with the egg wash and bake in the middle of the oven until deep golden, about 40 minutes. Cover with a linen or cotton (not terry cloth) kitchen towel and cool on a rack. Serve warm.

Serves 8

Chocolate-Covered Cheese Confections

Glazirovanniye Sirki

These rich chocolate-covered cheese confections, sold in the dairy departments in Soviet grocery shops, used to be a favorite childhood treat. It took a little trial and error to come up with a homemade version, but it was worth it just to get the happy smile of recognition from my Russian friends and compliments from my American guests. Decorate the confections with melted white chocolate for an extra effect.

12 ounces farmer's cheese
4 ounces cream cheese
7 tablespoons sugar
2 large egg yolks, lightly beaten
Grated zest of 2 lemons

1½ teaspoons lemon extract
1 tablespoon fresh lemon juice
12 ounces bittersweet chocolate
3 tablespoons solid vegetable shortening

1 In a food processor, combine the cheeses, sugar, and egg yolks and process until completely smooth. Transfer to a bowl and stir in the lemon zest, lemon extract, and lemon juice.

2 Wrap the mixture in a double thickness of damp cheesecloth and place in a colander set over a bowl. Fold the ends of the cheesecloth over the top. Place a small plate on the cheesecloth and put a 2-pound weight, such as a can, on the plate. Refrigerate overnight.

3 Unwrap the cheese mixture and form into 1½-inch balls with your hands. Place the balls on a plate and freeze to firm up, 30 minutes.

4 Melt the chocolate and shortening in a heavy saucepan over low heat, stirring constantly. Allow the chocolate to cool to lukewarm.

5 Remove the cheese balls from the freezer. Insert a toothpick into the center of one ball and dip it into the chocolate, coating it completely and allowing the excess to drip back into the pan. Place on a waxed-paper covered plate and remove the toothpick. Dab a small amount of chocolate over the toothpick hole. Repeat with the rest of the cheese balls. Refrigerate until the chocolate is set.

Makes about 25 confections

Alexandertort

Aleksandertort

A delicate cookie-like pastry from the Baltic, Alexandertort is filled with tart lingonberry preserves. An alternate way to make it is to trim off a small portion of both pastry sheets and crumble. Spread both pastry layers with preserves, stack, and sprinkle the top with the pastry crumbs.

3 cups unbleached all-purpose flour

2¼ cups confectioners' sugar

1 cup (2 sticks) unsalted butter, chilled, cut into pieces

3½ tablespoons sour cream

1⅔ cups imported lingonberry preserves

2 tablespoons fresh lemon juice

Cold water, as needed

1 In a large bowl, combine the flour and ¼ cup of the sugar. Add the butter, and working quickly and using a pastry blender, two knives, or your fingertips, cut the butter into the flour until the mixture resembles coarse crumbs.

2 Add the sour cream, a little at a time, and quickly work into the mixture. On a cool, lightly floured surface, knead the pastry very briefly with the heels of your hands. Shape into a ball, wrap in plastic, and refrigerate for 1 hour.

3 Preheat the oven to 300°F.

4 Divide the pastry in half. Roll out each half between two sheets of waxed paper to form a 15 × 10-inch rectangle. Remove the top piece of waxed paper from each pastry and carefully flip each onto an ungreased baking sheet.

5 Remove the remaining waxed paper. Prick the pastry all over with a fork and bake until just golden, about 30 minutes.

6 Allow to cool for about 5 minutes, then spread one of the pastry sheets evenly with the preserves. Carefully cover with the second pastry sheet.

7 Whisk together the remaining 2 cups confectioners' sugar and the lemon juice. With a teaspoon, add just enough cold water to make a spreadable glaze.

8 Spread the glaze over the pastry with a spatula as evenly as you can. Allow the glaze to set.

9 With a sharp knife, cut the pastry into neat 2-inch diamond shapes.

Makes 35 to 40 pastries

Meringue Delights

Beze

We call meringues *beze*, which derives from the French *baiser*, meaning "to kiss"; and they are great favorites with the Russians. This particular recipe for meringues topped with pink whipped cream was given to me by a well-known Russian psychologist, Maria Neimark, who like many Russian women in the United States combines a successful career with a beautiful and hospitable home. Wait for your friends' reactions when you tell them that you made these meringues yourself!

*5 large egg whites, at room
   temperature*
*1¾ cups superfine sugar, or as
   needed*
¼ teaspoon cream of tartar
1 cup heavy or whipping cream

1 tablespoon sloe gin
1 tablespoon vodka
*1½ tablespoons granulated sugar,
   or more to taste*
*Raspberries or canned, pitted
   Morello cherries for decoration*

1 Place the egg whites in a measuring cup used for liquid measures. In a measuring cup used for dry measures, measure the superfine sugar to exactly 3 times the volume of the whites.

2 Preheat the oven to 250° degrees. Line two baking sheets with aluminum foil or parchment.

3 In a large, dry bowl, beat the egg whites with an electric mixer until frothy. Add the cream of tartar and beat at high speed until stiff peaks begin to form. Continuing to beat at lower speed, gradually add the sugar, 3 to 4 tablespoons at a time. Beat until very stiff and glossy, 7 to 8 minutes more.

4 With a large spoon, scoop up the meringue mixture and place it on the prepared baking sheet, forming rounds about 2 inches in diameter. Flatten the tops slightly.

5 Bake until the meringues are completely dry and slightly golden, about 35 minutes. Cool completely on wire racks.

6 To make the topping, whip the cream until almost thick. Add the sloe gin, vodka, and granulated sugar and continue to whip for a few seconds more. The cream should not be very stiff.

7 Place the cream in a pastry bag with a decorative tip or on a tablespoon. Top each meringue with a scant tablespoon of the cream. As you do this, transfer the meringues to a serving platter. Refrigerate for at least 2 hours.

8 Place a berry on each meringue before serving.

Makes about 12 to 14 meringues

Russian Cranberry Mousse

Klyukvenniy Muss

This mousse is one of my fondest memories from early childhood. I can remember tasting it at someone's *dacha*; I can even remember the faces and the voices of the people around me; but I have no idea who they were or whose place we were at. I searched for this taste for a long, long time, and had almost given up when I tried making a traditional Russian mousse with cream of wheat (which up until then I hadn't thought was such a good idea). And there it was again, a much-cherished taste that like Proust's madeleines brought back all my memories and turned me into a four-year-old once again. I obviously can't be objective about this recipe, but my friends tell me that even for them it offers an extraordinarily comforting, home-like taste.

1½ cups fresh cranberries, picked
over and rinsed
2½ cups plus ⅓ cup water
¼ cup uncooked cream of wheat
(not instant)

½ cup sugar
Imported lingonberry preserves for
topping
Whipped cream for topping

1 Place the cranberries in a medium-size saucepan, add the ⅓ cup of water, and bring to a gentle boil. Reduce the heat to low and simmer until the cranberries pop open, 8 to 10 minutes.

2 Remove from the heat, let cool until manageable, then mash the cranberries thoroughly with a wooden spoon or a potato masher. Pass the cranberries through a fine sieve into a clean saucepan. Add the

2½ cups water and bring to a boil.

3 Reduce the heat to low and gradually add the cream of wheat and sugar, stirring constantly. Simmer, stirring, until the sugar is completely dissolved and the mixture has thickened, 10 to 15 minutes. Remove from the heat and cool to room temperature.

4 Transfer the mixture to a large bowl

and beat with an electric mixer set on the highest speed until the mousse doubles in size, 7 to 10 minutes. Transfer to individual serving bowls and refrigerate until thoroughly chilled. Served topped with lingonberry preserves and whipped cream.

Serves 8 to 10

Apricot Mousse

Abrikosoviy Muss

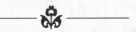

I tasted this refreshing dessert consisting of yogurt and apricots in an Armenian home in Moscow. Unfortunately, that was before I began working on this book, and it didn't occur to me to get a recipe from my hosts. I have devised a recipe that tastes similar, although I've got a suspicion that they prepared it differently. In any case, it makes a light and lovely conclusion to a summer meal.

1½ cups dried apricots, preferably
   Californian
¾ cup water
¾ cup sugar
1 tablespoon grated lemon zest
1 envelope unflavored gelatin
3 tablespoons fresh lemon juice

4 fresh, ripe apricots, pitted and
   quartered
1 cup heavy or whipping cream
1¼ cups plain low-fat yogurt
Chopped natural pistachio nuts
   for decoration

1 Combine the dried apricots, water, sugar, and lemon zest in a medium-size saucepan. Bring to a gentle boil over medium heat, then reduce the heat to low and simmer, covered, until the apricots are soft, 25 to 30 minutes. Cool a little.

2 Meanwhile, sprinkle the gelatin over the lemon juice and let stand for 5 minutes.

3 In a food processor, combine the dried apricots, their cooking liquid, and the fresh apricots. Purée until smooth. Return to the saucepan.

4 Stir the gelatin mixture into the apricot

mixture and heat for 1 minute over low heat, stirring. Allow to cool completely.

5 Whip the cream with an electric mixer until soft peaks form. Fold the cream and yogurt into the apricot mixture gently but thoroughly. Spoon the mousse into a glass bowl or wineglasses and refrigerate until set, at least 2 hours. Serve sprinkled with pistachios.

Serves 8

Russian Berry Custard

Kissel

One of the oldest ritual foods known to the Slavs is *kissel*, a fruit-gelatin-like custard. Today it is still a widely enjoyed home-style desserts. For a more sophisticated flavor, add a few tablespoons of grenadine to the cranberries, or if you're using strawberries or raspberries, a few tablespoons of your favorite berry liqueur. Serve the *kissel* topped with whipped cream.

2 cups fresh cranberries, straw-
berries, or raspberries, hulled
and washed
5 cups water

6 tablespoons sugar for cranberries,
3 to 4 for strawberries or
raspberries
¼ cup potato starch

1 Place the berries and 4 cups of the water in a medium-size saucepan over medium-high heat. Bring to a boil, then reduce the heat to medium-low and cook until the cranberries pop open or the strawberries or raspberries get somewhat mushy, 10 to 15 minutes.

2 Allow to cool slightly, then with the back of a spoon, press the berries through a fine-mesh sieve set over a bowl. Be sure to extract as much juice as possible.

3 Return the sieved berries and liquid to the saucepan. Add the sugar and bring to a boil, stirring over medium heat. Reduce the heat to low and simmer until the sugar is completely dissolved, 2 to 3 minutes.

4 In a small bowl, dilute the potato

starch with the remaining 1 cup water, stirring carefully until there are no lumps. Whisk the mixture into the simmering berry mixture and bring to a boil, stirring vigorously until the mixture thickens.

5 Remove from the heat and cool, stirring from time to time. Spoon into serving glasses or bowls and refrigerate.

Serves 6

Crème Brûlée Ice Cream

Morozhennoye Krem Bryule

1¾ cups granulated sugar
3 tablespoons water
3 cups heavy or whipping cream
1½ cups milk

6 large egg yolks
3 tablespoons vanilla sugar
   (see Index)

1 In a medium-size heavy skillet, combine 6 tablespoons of the granulated sugar and the water. Over medium-high heat stir the sugar until it dissolves and becomes golden in color.

2 Add ¼ cup of the cream and continue to stir over high heat until you have a thickish, light brown mixture, about 3 to 4 minutes. Remove from the heat and set aside. The mixture will harden to a candy-like consistency.

3 In a medium-size saucepan, scald the remaining 2¾ cups cream and the milk over medium heat. Set aside.

4 In the top of a double boiler set over hot but not boiling water, whisk the egg yolks, remaining granulated sugar, and vanilla sugar until fluffy and light yellow in color.

5 Gradually add the hot cream, stirring constantly. Cook, without allowing the mixture to boil, until rather thick, about 20 minutes.

6 Break the caramel mixture into small pieces and add it to the custard, mixing it in well. Cool to room temperature, stirring from time to time. Refrigerate, covered, for 1½ hours.

7 Transfer the custard to an ice-cream maker and freeze according to the manufacturer's instructions.

Makes 1½ quarts

🌼 Ice Cream 🌼

Many years ago, soon after my mother and I came to the United States, a saleswoman in a department store, who had just encountered her very first Russians, sympathetically asked my mother if she missed the wonderful ice cream of her homeland. My polite but terribly homesick mother remarked that after she had left her family and her country, she could hardly be worried about such trivialities as ice cream. I, on the other hand, admitted that waffle cups filled with probably the richest and creamiest ice cream in the world, were

not easily forgotten.

The reason Russian ice cream (which is called *morozhennoye*, literally "frozen stuff") is world famous is because it uses the best and purest ingredients — unadulterated thick cream, which accounts for the richness, sugar, and all-natural flavorings. This is undoubtedly one case when old-fashioned equipment and lack of preservatives come into their own.

Strawberry Ice Cream

Klubnichnoye Morozhennoye

In nineteenth-century Russia, this ice cream was made with beautifully fragrant wild strawberries. If you're lucky enough to have wild strawberries available to you, definitely use them in this recipe.

1¾ pints fresh strawberries, rinsed
    and stemmed
2 cups heavy or whipping cream

4 large egg yolks
1 cup sugar
Pinch of salt

1 In a food processor, purée the strawberries. Press the puréed berries through a fine sieve to remove the seeds. You should have about 2 cups of purée. Set aside.

2 In a medium-size saucepan, scald the cream over medium heat. Set aside.

3 In the top of a double boiler set over hot but not boiling water, whisk the egg yolks, sugar, and salt until fluffy and light yellow in color.

4 Gradually add the hot cream, stirring frequently. Cook, without allowing the mixture to boil, until rather thick, about 20 minutes.

5 Transfer the mixture to a bowl. Add the strawberry purée and mix until well blended.

6 Cool to room temperature, stirring from time to time. Refrigerate, covered, for 1½ hours.

7 Transfer the custard to an ice-cream maker and freeze according to the manufacturer's instructions.

Makes about 1½ quarts

Almond and Pistachio Paklava

Paklava

Although making *paklava* (or *baklava*) might seem a very difficult task, I find that it takes about the same time to make my own as it does to search out a good Greek, Armenian, or Middle Eastern store in which to buy it — and not every city has such stores anyway. The homemade effort is well worth the trouble, resulting as it does in a beautiful confection, moist from a not-too-sweet syrup. This recipe is from Azerbaijan where the filling is made from almond and pistachio nuts rather than the usual walnuts.

FILLING

2 cups blanched almonds, coarsely
    ground
2 cups shelled pistachio nuts,
    coarsely ground
1/3 cup sugar
1 teaspoon ground cinnamon
1 teaspoon ground cardamom

SUGAR SYRUP

2 cups sugar
1/2 cup honey
1 1/2 cups water
2 slices lemon
1 piece (1 inch) cinnamon
    stick

PASTRY

1 cup (2 sticks) unsalted butter,
    melted
1/4 teaspoon saffron threads, crushed
    in a mortar
24 sheets phyllo pastry
    (about 1 pound), thawed
    if frozen

Whole almonds or pistachios for
    decoration

1 In a small bowl, mix together the filling ingredients. Set aside.

2 Combine the syrup ingredients in a small saucepan. Bring to a boil over medium-low heat, stirring constantly, until the sugar dissolves, about 5 minutes.

Remove from the heat, and remove the lemon slice and cinnamon stick. Set aside to cool.

3 Preheat the oven to 350°F. Butter a 13 × 9-inch baking pan.

4 Heat 3 tablespoons of the melted butter over low heat in a small saucepan. Remove from the heat, add the saffron, and steep while preparing the *paklava*.

5 Keeping the unused pastry sheets covered to prevent them from drying out, lay eight sheets of pastry in the prepared pan, brushing each one carefully with melted butter as you lay it in. (You might have to trim the sheets to fit the pan dimensions.) Sprinkle half the filling over the eight-sheet stack of pastry. Then layer another eight sheets of pastry over the filling, brushing each sheet with some of the melted butter. Spread the remainder of the filling over the pastry, and layer on the remaining eight sheets of pastry, brushing each with the remaining melted butter. Brush the top sheet of pastry especially well with the reserved saffron butter.

6 With a very sharp knife, cut the pastry into 2 to 2 1/2-inch diamonds or squares, cutting only halfway through. This facilitates cutting the *paklava* later.

7 Bake for 20 minutes. Reduce the oven temperature to 300°F and bake until the top is light brown, about 15 minutes longer.

8 Remove the *paklava* from the oven and cool completely. Pour the syrup evenly over it. Let stand overnight.

9 Cut into portions, garnish each piece with a nut, and serve.

Serves 12

Hazelnut Cake in Honey Syrup

Revani

T his is an Armenian rendition of a popular Middle Eastern dessert. A hazelnut sponge cake is soaked overnight in the traditional honey syrup, producing a deliciously moist cake. Try making it with almonds or pecans. Serve with thickly whipped cream, vanilla or cinnamon ice cream, or a tart sorbet.

HONEY SYRUP

1 cup water

¾ cup sugar

2 tablespoons honey

1 piece (2 inches) cinnamon stick

2 lemon slices

1½ tablespoons brandy

CAKE AND DECORATION

4 large eggs, separated

½ cup sugar

3 tablespoons vegetable oil

¼ cup plain low-fat yogurt

1 cup unbleached all-purpose flour

1½ cups hazelnuts, toasted, skinned, and ground (see page 5, Steps 1 and 2)

½ cup ground walnuts

1½ teaspoons baking powder

¾ teaspoon ground cinnamon

Grated zest of 1 orange

Grated zest of 1 lemon

Blanched almond halves for decoration

Eastern Delights

Shops with an inviting sign proclaiming "Oriental Sweets" are scattered all over the big cities of the Soviet Union. Even before I made my first trips to the Caucasus and Central Asia, my school friends and I would scrupulously save up our lunch-money *kopeks* to buy some exotic morsel: 100 grams of richly sweet *halvah*; some chewy nougat studded with pistachios; a few cookies, called *koorabie*, that are so buttery they crumble at the lightest touch; a box of nut-filled *paklava* (or *baklava*); or a translucent *rakhat lokum* (Turkish delight), exotically flavored with rosewater. We would lounge on park benches, triumphantly indulging in these furtive sweets, and eventually go back home so stuffed we'd have to make up stories about having had dinner at a friend's house.

The Soviet Caucasus, and to some extent, Central Asia both share in the great tradition of sweets that we associate with the Middle East. You can find sweets based on honey and nuts — often steeped in a flavored sugar syrup — and a dozen other mouthwatering delights.

But this enticing array is not usually served as an after-dinner dessert. People in this part of the world know full well that the best thing to do after a filling meal is to enjoy a luscious piece of fresh fruit; or at

most, to indulge in a creamy custard, slightly thickened with semolina or rice flour, or a quince poached in syrup. During afternoon coffee, and especially on special holidays, however, everyone indulges their sweet tooth to the full. Near-transparent phyllo leaves are painstakingly made at home and turned into a *paklava* or a "bird's nest"; rich coffee cakes are produced, laden with nuts; golden fritters are served drenched in syrup; and accompanied by thick, clotted cream, called *kaimak*.

Although some of these sweets can be purchased in this country at Greek and Arabic pastry shops, many people find them heavy and almost unbearably sweet. Learning to make the sweets for yourself, though, will open a new door into a rich and exotic, yet surprisingly accessible, tradition. Make a tray of them for your next coffee party.

1 To make the syrup, combine the water, sugar, honey, cinnamon stick, and lemon in a small saucepan. Bring to a boil, stirring to dissolve the honey, then reduce the heat to low and simmer for 5 minutes. Remove from the heat. Discard the cinnamon stick and lemon slices, then add the brandy and let the syrup cool completely.

2 Preheat the oven to 325°F. Oil a 12 × 9-inch baking pan.

3 To make the cake, beat the egg yolks and sugar in a large bowl with an electric mixer until the mixture is pale yellow and forms ribbons when the beaters are lifted. Add the oil, yogurt, flour, hazelnuts, walnuts, baking powder, cinnamon, and orange and lemon zest. Beat for 1 minute.

4 In a clean, dry bowl, beat the egg whites with clean beaters until they hold stiff but not dry peaks. Fold into the batter.

5 Pour the batter into the prepared pan and bake until a cake tester comes out clean, 30 to 35 minutes. Cool slightly.

6 Lightly pierce the cake all over with a tip of a knife and pour the syrup over the cake, adding only as much as it can absorb at one time. Repeat until all the syrup is absorbed. Cool the cake completely, then cover with plastic wrap and refrigerate overnight.

7 Cut the cake into 3-inch diamonds or squares and decorate each piece with an almond half.

Serves 6 to 8

Poached Quinces
with
Whipped Cream

Kompot iz Aivi so Vsbitimi Slivkami

This is a truly exquisite dessert, which will seem very exotic to those unfamiliar with the taste of quince. In the short time when quinces are in season, I serve them at nearly every dinner party and they are always a hit. In the Caucasus and Central Asia, they are topped with very thick clotted cream, called *kaimak*. I serve these quinces with thickly whipped cream or vanilla ice cream.

1½ cups sugar

2 cups water

2 lemon slices

3 cloves

3 large quinces, peeled but
    with skins reserved, cored,
    and halved

2 teaspoons rosewater

1½ cups thickly whipped cream

1 Place the sugar and water in a large heavy pot and bring to a boil over high heat. Stir constantly until the sugar completely dissolves, 2 to 3 minutes.

2 Add the lemon slices, cloves, the reserved quince skins, and the quinces, turning them to coat with the syrup. Reduce the heat to low and simmer, covered, turning the quinces occasionally, until they are tender, 35 to 40 minutes.

3 Remove the lemon slices, cloves, and quince skins. Stir in the rosewater and allow the quinces to cool to room temperature in the syrup.

4 To serve, place a quince half on each of six dessert plates. Spoon some syrup over each quince half and top with whipped cream. If you are serving the quinces the next day and find that the syrup thickens too much, just reheat the fruit and syrup slowly and let cool.

Serves 6

Quince
Aiva

A sick man was dying, and even the wise man (*tabib*) could not help him. The man happened to be lying under a quince tree, and juice was dripping from the golden fruit. Little by little the sick man regained his strength, until finally he had fully recovered. When the *tabib* found out the circumstances of the recovery, he grew angry with the quince: "You have accomplished what I have failed, and I am going to punish you," he said. The *tabib* squeezed the quince for as long and as hard as he could until he had squeezed it dry; and since that time the quince has had no juice.

So runs the legend from Uzbekistan, where the fruit is still especially revered for its fragrance, taste, and medicinal qualities—all of which were also described by medieval philosophers and doctors. In fact, quinces were cultivated in Asia Minor as early as the seventh century B.C. and were well known to the ancient Greeks who called them *melon kidonian*. Throughout Central Asia, quinces, or their dried peel, are kept in closets and on kitchen shelves as a deodorizer. They are also used in pilaf and meat dishes, and made into tempting preserves, syrups, and compotes.

Saffron Pudding

Zerde

S affron features prominently in Azerbaijani cuisine, where this silky, refreshing pudding originates. Blending beautifully with the almonds, cinnamon, and a dash of rosewater, it adds a pleasing yellow color, and a faint, almost unrecognizable, aroma.

1¼ cups ground blanched almonds

5 cups milk

¼ to ⅓ cup sugar

1 tablespoon unsalted butter

¼ cup semolina

¼ cup slivered almonds

*½ teaspoon ground cinnamon, plus
    additional for decoration*

2 teaspoons rosewater

*¼ teaspoon saffron threads, crushed
    in a mortar and diluted in 1
    tablespoon warm water*

1 Combine the ground almonds, milk, and sugar to taste in a medium-size saucepan and bring to a boil. Remove from the heat and let cool just until slightly warm.

2 In another saucepan, melt the butter over low heat. Add the semolina and brown gently, stirring constantly, for 3 to 4 minutes. Pour the milk-almond mixture into the saucepan and bring to a gentle boil, stirring constantly. Cook, uncovered, stir-ring occasionally until the mixture begins to thicken, 15 to 20 minutes.

3 Off the heat, stir in the slivered almonds, cinnamon, rosewater, and the diluted saffron, and stir to blend. Spoon into individual dessert bowls and refrigerate for at least 2 hours. Sprinkle with cinnamon before serving.

Serves 8

Basics

·

OSNOVNIYE RETSEPTI

My basics includes some of the recipes that are called for time and again on the pages of this book. Many, such as stocks, béchamel sauce, and mayonnaise, are quite familiar — but setting out my own preparations is still useful, I think, even though the Russians have adopted French basics pretty much as they found them in the nineteenth century. Russian have not been particularly inventive with stock, for example, as for them a stock is the product of a soup and is made when soup is made. Having a stock on hand, though, can shorten the long simmering time soups require. Doughs and pastries, on the other hand, are an integral part of Russian cuisine and recipes for the most basic of them I offer here.

Sweet Yeast Dough

Sdobnoye Drozhzhevoye Testo

This dough is wonderful for Russian-style fruit pies, filled tea rolls, or simple breakfast buns. Most of the recipes in this book that call for this dough require half of the amount given here, so make the rest into a delicious loaf of sweet bread. This recipe, from Mrs. Irina Rusnak, was first published in a Ukrainian weekly journal.

1½ cups warm milk (105° to 115°F)

2 packages active dry yeast

¾ cup plus 1 teaspoon sugar

½ teaspoon salt

4 large egg yolks, beaten

8 tablespoons (1 stick) unsalted
   butter, melted and cooled to warm

Grated zest of 1 lemon

4½ to 5 cups unbleached
   all-purpose flour

1 In a large bowl, combine the milk, yeast, and the 1 tablespoon sugar. Let stand until foamy, about 5 minutes.

2 Add the egg yolks, butter, lemon zest, and ¾ cup sugar and mix well with an electric mixer. Add 4 to 4½ cups flour, 1 cup at a time, stirring well after each addition. The dough shouldn't be too thick, but it also shouldn't stick to your hands.

3 Transfer the dough to a floured surface and knead until smooth and elastic, about 7 minutes, adding the remaining flour as necessary to prevent sticking.

4 Shape the dough into a ball. Place in a buttered bowl and turn to coat. Cover with a linen or cotton (not terry cloth) kitchen towel and let rise in a warm, draft-free spot until doubled in bulk, about 1¼ hours. Punch down the dough; it is now ready to use or it will keep, covered, in the refrigerator for up to 24 hours.

Makes enough for 2 pies, 2 Poppy Seed Rolls, or 30 vatrushkas

Yeast Dough

Drozhzhevoye Testo

If I was asked what are the first three things that come to my mind when I think of Russian cooking, I would probably name wild mushrooms, sour cream, and this plump raised dough (probably enclosing a filling of some sort). Use the leftover dough to make delicious buns for breakfast.

¾ cup milk
5 tablespoons unsalted butter
1 package active dry yeast
1½ tablespoons sugar
¼ cup lukewarm water (105° to 115°F)

1 large egg plus 2 large egg yolks, well beaten
¾ teaspoon salt
4 cups unbleached all-purpose flour

1 Combine the milk and butter in medium-size saucepan and bring to a boil. Remove from the heat and cool to lukewarm (105° to 115°F).

2 In a large bowl, stir together the yeast, sugar, and water. Let stand until foamy, about 5 minutes.

3 Add the milk mixture, egg and egg yolks, and salt to the yeast mixture and mix well with a wooden spoon.

4 Stir in 3½ cups of the flour, 1 cup at a time, stirring well after each addition.

5 Transfer the dough to a floured surface and knead, until smooth and elastic, about 10 minutes, adding as much of the remain-ing flour as needed to prevent sticking. Place the dough in a buttered bowl and turn to coat. Cover with a linen or cotton (not terry cloth) kitchen towel and let rise in a warm, draft-free spot until doubled in bulk, about 1½ hours.

6 Punch the dough down and knead very briefly before using.

Makes enough dough for 1 large pirog *or* kulebiaka, *2 Tatar Wedding Pies, or 48 Estonian Ham and Cheese Rolls*

Quick Yeast Dough

Drozhzhevoye Testo na Skoruyu Ruku

This is a great, easy, nonrising yeast dough that produces something between yeast dough and short pastry. The recipe is well known to every working Russian woman.

1 package active dry yeast
2 teaspoons sugar
⅔ cup lukewarm milk (105° to 115°F)
1 cup (2 sticks) unsalted butter, melted, and cooled to lukewarm

1 large egg, lightly beaten
½ teaspoon salt
3¼ to 3¾ cups unbleached all-purpose flour

1 In a large bowl, combine the yeast, sugar, and milk and let stand until foamy, about 5 minutes.

2 Add the butter, egg, and salt to the yeast mixture and mix well with a wooden spoon.

3 Stir in 3¼ cups flour, 1 cup at a time, stirring well after each addition.

4 Transfer the dough to a floured surface and knead gently until you have smooth, rather loose dough, about 3 minutes, adding just enough of the remaining flour to prevent sticking. Shape into a ball, cover with a linen or cotton (not terry cloth) kitchen towel and let stand for 10 minutes.

The dough is now ready to use. You can refrigerate it for up to 24 hours.

Makes enough dough for 50 pirozhki *or 1 large* pirog

Sour Cream Pastry

Rassipchatoye Testo so Smetanoy

Sour cream makes this great flaky short pastry pleasantly tart. Use it for *pirozhki, piroghi,* or *kulebiaka,* or any other favorite savory tart. For a sweet pie crust, add 2 tablespoons of sugar.

3 cups all-purpose unbleached flour
¾ teaspoon salt
½ teaspoon baking powder
14 tablespoons (1¾ sticks) unsalted
    butter, chilled and cut into bits

2 large egg yolks, lightly beaten
⅔ cup sour cream

1 In a large bowl, combine the flour, salt, and baking powder. Add the butter, and using a pastry blender, two knives, or your fingertips, cut it into the flour until it resembles coarse crumbs.

2 Mix the egg yolks and sour cream to-gether and add to the flour mixture a little at a time, quickly working it into the mix-ture with your hands.

3 Transfer the pastry to a cool, lightly floured surface and knead very briefly, no more than 30 seconds. Divide the pastry into two balls, wrap them in plastic wrap, and refrigerate for 1 hour.

Makes enough dough for about 50 pirozhki, 1 pirog, or 1 kulebiaka

Beef Stock

Miasnoy Bulyon

T his is a white beef stock, so called because the meat and vegetables are not roasted before they are simmered in liquid. I find it more suitable for adding to Russian soups and stews than the French brown stock. Since Russians rarely make stock just for the sake of it, this recipe includes a beef brisket, which will make a great meal in itself.

2 pounds beef marrow bones
3 pounds first-cut beef brisket,
    trimmed of all fat
3 quarts water
Salt, to taste
2 leeks, well rinsed and halved
    lengthwise
1 rib celery with its top, halved

2 carrots, peeled and halved
2 parsnips, peeled and halved
12 sprigs fresh parsley
3 sprigs fresh dill
12 black peppercorns
2 small bay leaves

1 Place the marrow bones and water in a large soup pot and bring to a boil. Skim off the foam as it rises to the surface.

2 Add the remaining ingredients. Reduce the heat to low, cover, and simmer, skimming occasionally, until the brisket

is tender, about 3 hours.

3 Strain the stock, reserving the brisket. Cool and refrigerate, degreasing the stock before using. Freeze for longer storage.

Makes about 2 quarts

Lamb Stock

Bulyon iz Baranini

Lamb stock is not really a mandatory kitchen basic, but since I often find myself stuck with lamb bones, I use them for stock to enhance the flavor of lamb stews or soups.

2 pounds lamb bones
2 quarts water
2 large onions, halved
2 carrots, peeled and halved
1 parsnip, peeled
3 large cloves garlic, sliced

2 bay leaves
6 coriander seeds, crushed
10 sprigs fresh parsley
6 sprigs fresh cilantro
10 black peppercorns
Salt, to taste

1 Place the lamb bones and water in a large soup pot and bring to a boil. Skim off the foam as it rises to the surface.

2 Add the remaining ingredients. Reduce the heat to low, cover, and simmer, skimming occasionally, for 2 hours.

3 Strain the stock. Cool and refrigerate, degreasing the stock before using. Freeze for longer storage.

Makes about 6 cups

Chicken Stock

Kuriniy Bulyon

Add this light chicken stock to your soups or stews. For a quick soup, add some cooked rice, sliced celery and carrots, and cook until the vegetables are just tender. Serve with *pirozhki*.

3 pounds chicken backs, necks, and
    wings, well rinsed
3 quarts water
Salt, to taste
1 large carrot, peeled and halved
2 medium-size onions, sliced
2 ribs celery with their tops, halved

2 medium-size parsnips, peeled and
    halved
5 sprigs fresh parsley
3 sprigs fresh dill
10 black peppercorns
2 small bay leaves

1 Place the chicken pieces and water in a large soup pot and bring to a boil. Skim off the foam as it rises to the surface.

2 Add the remaining ingredients. Reduce the heat to low, cover, and simmer, skimming occasionally, for 1½ hours.

3 Strain the stock. Cool and refrigerate, degreasing the stock before using. Freeze for longer storage.

Makes about 2 quarts

Vegetable Stock

Ovoshchnoy Bulyon

Although Russians hardly ever make vegetable stock, I find it useful to have some at hand to add to vegetable soups or vegetarian versions of borscht or *shchi.*

4½ tablespoons unsalted butter
2 cups chopped onions
1 cup chopped carrots
2 ribs celery, chopped
2 leeks, white part only, well rinsed
    and chopped
2 large parsnips, peeled and
    chopped

9 cups water
6 to 8 imported dried mushrooms,
    well rinsed
12 sprigs parsley
5 sprigs fresh dill
1 bay leaf
8 black peppercorns
Salt, to taste

1 Melt the butter in a large heavy soup pot over medium heat. Add the onions, carrots, celery, leeks, and parsnips and sauté, stirring occasionally, until the vegetables are softened but not browned, about 10 minutes.

2 Add the remaining ingredients and bring to a boil. Reduce the heat to low and simmer the stock, uncovered, until the liquid is reduced to about 6 cups, about 1 hour.

3 Strain through a fine sieve, pressing on the vegetables with the back of a wooden spoon to extract as much liquid as possible. Cool and refrigerate the stock until ready to use. Freeze for longer storage.

Makes about 1½ quarts

Fish Stock

Ribniy Bulyon

I t is traditional in classic Russian cuisine to prepare fish stock from several varieties of whole freshwater fish. Lacking a country estate with a fish pond, and reluctant to buy 4 pounds of fresh fish to make 6 cups of stock, I use fish trimmings for my stock.

2 tablespoons unsalted butter
1 cup chopped onions
1 carrot, peeled and chopped
1 parsnip, peeled and chopped
1 small rib celery, chopped
1 pound fish trimmings, such as
*   heads, tails, and carcasses, well*
*   rinsed*
4 cups water
½ cup dry white wine
2 tablespoons fresh lemon juice
8 sprigs fresh parsley
4 sprigs fresh dill
2 bay leaves
Salt, to taste

1 Melt the butter in a heavy soup pot over medium-low heat. Add the onions, carrot, parsnip, and celery and sauté until the vegetables are softened but not brown; about 10 minutes.

2 Add the remaining ingredients and bring to a boil. Skim off the foam as it rises to the top. Reduce the heat to low, cover, and simmer for 40 minutes.

3 Taste, and if a stronger stock is desired, reduce the liquid to about 3 cups, about 7 minutes. Strain through a fine sieve, pressing on the solids with the back of a wooden spoon to extract as much liquid as possible. Cool and refrigerate the stock until ready to use. Freeze for longer storage.

Makes 3 to 4 cups

Homemade Mayonnaise

Mayonez Domashnego Izgotovleniya

The Russians love to dress their food with mayonnaise, and in fact, this French sauce became a trademark of Russian nineteenth-century cooking. Dishes such as *Homard à la Russe, Oeufs à la Russe,* and the Russian Salad are all dishes prepared with mayonnaise. Needless to say these Russian classics didn't earn their international reputation by using commercial mayonnaise. Here is the Russian homemade version for your *à la Russe* dishes.

1 large egg, at room temperature
1 hard-cooked egg yolk
1 teaspoon Dijon mustard
2 tablespoons fresh lemon juice, or
  more to taste

Pinch of salt and freshly ground
  white pepper
1 cup vegetable oil

1 Combine the egg, egg yolk, mustard, lemon juice, and salt and pepper in a food processor and process until blended.

2 With the motor running, gradually add the oil through the feed tube in a slow steady stream. Taste and correct the seasoning.

3 Transfer the mayonnaise into a container and refrigerate. It will keep in the refrigerator for up to 5 days.

Makes about 1⅓ cups

Yogurt and Garlic Sauce

Sikhdorov Madzoon

A bowl of yogurt accompanies almost every family meal in the Caucasus or Central Asia, and is spooned over stews, rice dishes, dumplings, and stuffed vegetables. This yogurt and garlic sauce is called for in a good many of the recipes in this book.

1 cup plain low-fat yogurt
2 medium-size cloves garlic, crushed
*   in a garlic press*
Salt, to taste

3 tablespoons finely chopped fresh
*   cilantro or mint, plus a sprig of*
*   either as garnish*

In a small bowl, stir all the ingredients to mix well. Refrigerate, covered, for at least 12 hours. Garnish with the herb sprig and serve.

Makes about 1½ cups

Béchamel Sauce

Sous Beshamel

This basic white sauce, which comes from Turkey, of all places, is indispensable for many Russian dishes. If you wish to make the sauce thinner, just add more liquid, a tablespoon at a time, until it reaches the desired consistency.

3 tablespoons unsalted butter

3 tablespoons all-purpose flour

1½ cups milk, hot

*Salt and freshly ground white
pepper, to taste*

Pinch of freshly grated nutmeg

1 Melt the butter in a heavy saucepan over low heat. Add the flour and cook, stirring, for 3 minutes.

2 Remove the pan from the heat and add the milk in a steady stream, whisking vigorously until the mixture is thick and smooth.

3 Return the pan to the heat and simmer the sauce until thickened, about 10

minutes. Season with salt, pepper, and nutmeg. If you are not going to use it right away, keep the sauce covered with buttered waxed paper to prevent a skin from forming.

Makes about 1¾ cups

Crème Fraîche

While crème fraîche is certainly not a Russian ingredient, it often provides just the perfect answer when sour cream seems a touch too heavy and whipped cream too bland.

2 cups heavy whipping cream

¼ cup buttermilk

In a saucepan, heat the cream to lukewarm (about 100°F) over medium heat. Transfer the mixture to a large container with a lid. Stir in the buttermilk and let stand at room temperature, uncovered, until thickened, about 12 hours. Cover and refrigerate for

another 24 hours. This will keep in the refrigerator for up to 3 days.

Makes about 2¼ cups

Quick Tomato Sauce

Tomatniy Sous na Skoruyu Ruku

This is a very simple recipe that resembles the Soviet commercial equivalent of ketchup, called "Southern Sauce." The home-style version is spicy and tangy, with lots of garlic and plenty of fresh herbs. It is one of the traditional accompaniments to kebabs or small meatballs.

2 tablespoons olive oil

¾ cup finely chopped onion

1 can (6 ounces) tomato paste

1¼ cups Chicken Stock (see page 613) or canned broth

6 cloves garlic, crushed in a press

1 teaspoon sweet Hungarian paprika

¼ to ½ teaspoon dried red pepper flakes

1 tablespoon red wine vinegar

⅛ teaspoon sugar, or more to taste

Salt, to taste

¼ cup chopped fresh Italian (flat-leaf) parsley

¼ cup chopped fresh cilantro

1 Heat the oil in a heavy skillet over medium heat. Add the onion and sauté until lightly colored, about 10 minutes.

2 Add the tomato paste and stock, and stir with a wooden spoon until well blended. Bring to a boil, then reduce the heat to low. Add the garlic, paprika, ¼ teaspoon pepper flakes, vinegar, sugar, and salt and simmer for 3 to 4 minutes.

Taste and add more pepper flakes and sugar, if needed.

3 Remove from the heat and stir in the herbs. Let cool to room temperature. The sauce will keep in the refrigerator for about 5 days.

Makes about 2 cups

Notes on Ingredients

Apples

A very tart, juicy, and aromatic apple, called *antonovka*, is considered by Russians the apple of choice for cooking and eating. It is used for pies and strudels, chopped raw into salads, added to sauerkraut, and pickled for the winter. Granny Smith, although not nearly as aromatic and crisp as *antonovka*, makes a good substitute and should be used in the recipes that call for tart apples.

Basmati rice

Basmati rice is the very long-grained, aromatic rice used in Persian, Indian, Thai, and Azerbaijani cooking. It is now widely available in health-food stores and specialty grocery stores and comes packaged or loose. (A far superior basmati rice, however, can be purchased in Indian and Middle Eastern groceries. There are many varieties of basmati rice imported from India. Pari, White Elephant, and Super Sadhu brands are considered the best. They usually come in 5- and 11-pound bags.

Cheese

Imported cheeses, especially Parmesan, Swiss, Gruyère, Gouda, and Havarti, have been used in Russian cooking for centuries, becoming an integral part of many "authentic" Russian dishes. However, cottage cheese, so essential to Slavic cooking, is very different in the Soviet Union.

It has a higher fat content, is much tarter than American cottage cheese and has very small curds. I find that Friendship brand farmer's cheese, available at many supermarkets throughout the country, is the closest available substitute. For best results, it should be passed through a sieve and mixed with some sour cream for a tarter flavor and smoother consistency. American cottage cheese, used as is, generally is not suitable for most Russian dishes.

In the Caucasus and Moldavia, most cheeses are made from goat's or sheep's milk and are often more difficult to approximate. Suitable substitutes are specified in the individual recipes throughout this book. In the recipes calling for feta, try to use Bulgarian or French feta as it is much creamier and less salty than the Greek, Syrian, and American varieties. Other cheeses to look out for are the Greek kasseri and kefalotyri, and the Balkan kaskaval.

Cherries

Sour cherries are considered the true cherries in the Soviet Union. (Sweet cherries are called by another name and are almost never used in cooking.) Fortunately, fresh sour cherries are catching on in this country and are available at farmers' markets in most big cities in the mid-summer. As the fresh cherry season is short, canned sour cherries in light syrup, available at some supermarkets, gourmet groceries, and

Eastern European and German groceries, can be used instead. I like the Adriatic brand, imported from Yugoslavia.

Coriander/Cilantro

Coriander is an aromatic sweet-smelling seed, and cilantro, which grows from the coriander seed, is the gutsy herb that has finally become popular in the United States via Mexican and Thai cooking. Both are adored by the Russians and used extensively by Georgians and Central Asians. The coriander seed can be used whole (mainly for pickling), ground, or crushed like peppercorns. I prefer grinding coriander myself in a spice mill, as the delicate aroma of ground coriander quickly fades. Cilantro is munched raw by the Georgians and added to salads and stews in great profusion.

Dried Herbs

Packaged dried herbs are not usually available in the Soviet Union; therefore, people either dry them themselves or make do without them. I recommend using the whole dried herb sprigs found in specialty food shops and some supermarkets whenever possible.

Fenugreek

Fenugreek is a pleasantly pungent spice used extensively in Indian, Middle Eastern, and Georgian cooking. Dried fenugreek, made from the fenugreek seeds, is readily available at specialty groceries. Dried fenugreek leaves, called for in some Azerbaijani recipes in this book, are harder to come by. They can be bought or mail-ordered from Middle Eastern and Indian groceries.

Herring

Plump, salty herring is one of the most beloved items in Russian cuisine. Schmaltz, or salt herring, available at Jewish, German, and Eastern European delis and specialty groceries, is the choice for recipes that call for herring. Matjes herring fillets can also be used. I don't recommend using marinated herring sold in jars. It tastes far too sweet and vinegary and has nothing in common with the herring used in the Soviet Union. If you have to use jarred herring, use the one packed in wine sauce, available at most supermarkets.

Kvass

The old Russian favorite, *kvass*, a fermented drink made from rye bread or fruit and sugar, is still very much enjoyed by the Russians today. Although it is possible to make *kvass* at home, the results are not always consistent and there is a slight danger that the pressure of fermentation could cause the container to explode. If you would like to make *kvass* at home, use *kvass* concentrate imported from the Soviet Union. It can be purchased at Russian grocery shops.

Mushrooms

Strictly speaking, all of the recipes in this book that call for mushrooms should be made with wild mushrooms because cultivated mushrooms are not available in the Soviet Union. But since wild mushrooms are costly and not always available in the United States, cultivated will do for many recipes in which fresh mushrooms are used. Dried wild mushrooms, with their deep woodsy taste, are an absolutely essential ingredient in the Russian kitchen. Italian dried porcini, French cèpes, or Polish dried mushrooms, available at Eastern European groceries, are the best. Much cheaper and more than adequate are the dried mushrooms imported from South America. They come from several distributors, but the most widely available are the ones imported by the Kirsch Mushroom Company. They come in ½-ounce round plastic jars and can be purchased in many supermarkets and Jewish-style delis.

Pickles

Pickled fruit and vegetables are as basic to Slavic cuisines as soy sauce is to the Chinese. Crunchy tart pickled cucumbers are invariably served as accompaniments to Russian home meals, chopped into soups or composed salads, and cooked in sauces to provide a piquant accent. The best thing, of course, is to pickle cucumbers yourself, but if you have to buy them, avoid the ones that taste sweet and vinegary. For cooking I would recommend deli-style dill pickles or the ones imported from Hungary or Poland, available at Eastern European groceries and some specialty groceries.

Pomegranate Juice

For those who have never cooked with or drunk pomegranate juice, its tart and refreshing taste will be a true discovery. A favorite staple in the Caucasus and the Middle East, it is used for marinating meats and making delicately tart and sweet sauces and stews. Bottled pomegranate juice is available at most health-food stores and some specialty groceries, although I always keep a bottle of pomegranate concentrate — or grenadine molasses, as it is sometimes called — handy in case of an emergency. Diluted with water, it provides a good substitute for pomegranate juice. It can be purchased or mail-ordered from Middle Eastern groceries.

Sauerkraut

The delightfully tart taste and crispy texture of Russian homemade sauerkraut is dramatically different from the canned or jarred sauerkraut sold in this country. However, commercial sauerkraut can be quite adequate for the recipes that require slow cooking. I use jarred sauerkraut imported from Germany and available at German and Jewish delis. You can also use domestic sauerkraut that comes in plastic bags, but avoid the canned varieties.

Sour Plums

Small very tart plums, called *tkemali*, are the pride and joy of Georgian cooks. As big as cherry tomatoes, and almost as tart as lemons but with a touch of sweetness, they are considered the best accompaniment to grills and roasts — that is, of course, when they are cooked with garlic and spices to make *tkemali* sauce, a trademark of Georgian cuisine. For winter, the plums are mashed, dried in the sun, and rolled into a sheet, called *tklapi*, which is used to give a tartness to soups and stews. Although the unique flavor of the *tkemali* plum cannot really be approximated, slightly underripe fresh prunes can be used to make the *tkemali* sauce. Tamarind, although an entirely different species, has a similar tart taste and is often used by the Georgian emigrés instead of the *tkemali* plums. (See Tamarind Concentrate).

Sumakh

Sumakh, or sumac, is a tart purple powder that comes from a tiny berry indigenous to the Caucasus and the Middle East. A container of sumakh is always placed on the table in Azerbaijan so it can be sprinkled on kebabs, soups, and salads, providing a lively accent and some unusual color to the dishes. I like sprinkling sumakh on feta slices or light-colored dips for a striking presentation. Sumakh is available in quality spice shops and Middle Eastern groceries.

Tamarind Concentrate

Tamarind concentrate, available at Indian and Thai groceries, is sometimes used by Georgian emigrés instead of their native sour plums. They add it in small quantities to winter soups and stews to add a bit of tang. Once I discovered it, I began adding it to winter dishes in place of lemon juice. The concentrate is rather dense and has to be softened and diluted in a little hot water.

Mail-Order Sources

Specialty Food Stores

Spice and specialty stores that carry a large selection of spices and herbs frequently used in Soviet cooking are:

Pete's Spice
174 First Avenue
New York, NY 10009
(212) 254-8773

Dean & Deluca
560 Broadway
New York, NY 10012
(212) 431-8230

The Spice House
1048 North Third Street
Milwaukee, WI 53203
(414) 272-0977

Middle Eastern Stores

Middle Eastern stores that carry sumakh, ground fenugreek, saffron, rose water, pomegranate concentrate, and which will sometimes accept orders for *lavash* are:

K. Kalustyan
123 Lexington Avenue
New York, NY 10016
(212) 683-8458

Kalpana Groceries and Spices
2528 Broadway
New York, NY 10025
(212) 663-4190

Middle East Market
2054 San Pablo
Berkeley, CA 94702
(415) 548-2213

Westwood Grocery
2091 Westwood Boulevard
Westwood, CA 90025
(213) 475-9804

Indian Stores

Indian stores that carry Basmati rice, tamarind concentrate, dried fenugreek leaves, ground turmeric, saffron, and cumin seeds are:

Foods of India
121 Lexington Avenue
New York, NY 10016
(212) 683-4419

House of Spices
76-17 Broadway
Jackson Heights, NY 11373
(718) 476-1577

Indian Grocery Store
2342 Douglas Road
Coral Gables, FL 33134
(305) 448-5869

Seema Enterprises
10616 Page Avenue
St. Louis, MO 63132
(314) 423-9990

Bazaar of India
1331 University Avenue
Berkeley, CA 94702
(415) 586-4110

Index

C

H

I

J

Q

R